COUNCIL OF LITERARY MAGAZINES AND PRESSES

THE LITERARY PRESS AND MAGAZINE DIRECTORY 2008/2009

COUNCIL OF LITERARY MAGAZINES AND PRESSES

THE LITERARY PRESS AND MAGAZINE DIRECTORY 2008/2009

Soft Skull Press, Brooklyn NY

978-1-59376-190-5

Library of Congress Cataloging-in-Publication Data for this title is available from the Library of Congress

Directory Editor: Jay Baron Nicorvo
Cover Design by Luke Gerwe
Interior design by Nick Stone Design
Editorial Production: Matthew Schwartz, Anne Horowitz, Megan Gannon, Elaine Chan, Robert Calero
Printed in the United States of America

Soft Skull Press
An Imprint of Counterpoint LLC
2117 Fourth St
Berkeley CA 94710

www.softskull.com
www.counterpointpress.com

Distributed by Publishers Group West

10 9 8 7 6 5 4 3 2 1

Profiles

Directory Note

All publishers in this Directory are listed in alphabetical order (additional indices appear in the back). The Directory includes print magazines, online publishers, and small presses in the United States, Canada, and England. Publishers who fit into more than one of these categories may have multiple listings—be sure to check under "Publisher Type." For writers, here are a few tips to keep in mind:

- Support independent publishing by buying literary magazines and books.
- Read a publication and learn about its editorial viewpoint and specific areas of interest before sending work.
- Follow all the submission guidelines provided by each publisher.
- Always include a self-addressed stamped envelope with enough postage for return of your work and/or a reply. Make clear to the editors whether or not your manuscript should be returned.
- Check your manuscript carefully for spelling and grammatical errors; if possible, have someone else proofread the work as well.
- Include a brief cover letter about who you are, and mention if you've read the publication.
- Include contact information on every page (including phone number and e-mail address) unless otherwise stated in the publisher's guidelines. Never send the only copy of your work.
- Check policies on simultaneous submissions and whether submissions via e-mail or fax are acceptable.
- Keep a log of where you have submitted. Be sure to notify any publishers if a simultaneously submitted work sent to them has subsequently been accepted for publication.

We hope you are well served by this edition of *The Literary Press and Magazine Directory*. For more information about the Council of Literary Magazines and Presses, visit http://www.clmp.org.

Foreword
by Steve Almond

Young writers often ask me how I made it in a dying concern like literature, by which they really mean, "How am I going to make it in a dying concern like literature?" Any ideas I have in this regard are completely worn out. Fuck style. Tell the truth. Fail better. And so on. It's too early to tell these whippersnappers that no one makes it in literature. They don't need my exhaust fumes stinking up their hopes.

For those few unfortunates genuinely interested in my literary evolution, a decent university library will tell you everything. Want to read the first story I ever published? Track down *The Rio Grande Review*, Summer 1996. Want to find the crappiest story I ever published—and you kind of have to trust me, don't you?—peruse the Spring 1998 issue of *City Primeval*, which includes my mawkish saga of an NBA Oedipus, "Jimmybug to the Hole." It's all a matter of record, is my point.

Most authors leave behind a similar record of their young selves, and they do so via the independent press, in the little magazines and publishing houses who haven't the money to screw their adherents up by confusing financial success with literary achievement.

I speak here from painful experience—my own idiot decision, for instance, a few years after these earliest stories appeared, to place my trust in a scumbag who pretended to love art, but kept score with money. The technical term is agent. This woman got a kick out of torturing her writers. She probably wanted to write herself, but lacked the courage. That's how it is with most agents, frankly. They lack the inner resources for private struggle and settle for fancy lunches instead. The worst editors at the big money houses are the same way. Books are a dying business, after all, so they spend their hours watching cable TV and trying to figure out what the next bestseller is going to be. And not returning your phone calls. This is nothing new. It's just commerce showing creativity the ass-end of the capitalist arrangement.

But it's also why you might want to stop worshipping all those fancy New York agents and editors—trust me folks, they don't need any more eggs—and to place your faith instead in those who do the lonely work of writing and editing without regard to extrinsic reward. Such people still exist. You, in fact, still exist. As do the editors assembled for your convenience in this volume. They will not make you much money, if they're doing their jobs properly. They will only gratify those precincts of the soul beyond the reach of vanity and greed. You are one lucky bastard to need this book, in other words. You're still free of the goons. The brain eaters. The idolaters. The zombie swells. May you go forth now and behave like an artist.

Introduction

The Council of Literary Magazines and Presses has provided technical assistance to and advocated on the behalf of the diverse, essential community of independent literary publishers since 1967. I invite you to use the CLMP *Directory of Literary Magazines and Presses* to explore this world. Whether participating as a reader or a writer, please support this vital community by purchasing literary magazines and small press books.

Placing the cause and calling of literature ahead of the financial bottom line, independent literary publishers serve as a primary link between readers and writers—particularly those representing emerging voices, culturally specific communities, and literary art forms not fostered by mainstream publishers. Independent literary publications create an enduring record of cultural activity, and provide an indispensable alternative to the work presented by large-scale commercial publishing. Hundreds of literary magazines, presses, and online publishers can be found across the country, in every state, serving an amalgam of unique audiences. Ultimately, they connect diverse communities of readers who would otherwise remain isolated from their living literary heritage.

What makes a publisher an "independent literary publisher"? Independent literary publishers focus on publishing poetry, fiction, and creative nonfiction—they are mission-driven, free to publish works that may or may not meet the demands of the larger marketplace. They operate as either not-for-profit organizations or traditional small businesses. By virtue of being smaller they often establish long-term, nurturing relationships with their authors and make special efforts to reach niche markets hungry for quality writing. Literature today lives through these publishers.

—Jeffrey Lependorf, Executive Director, CLMP

Organization: 13th Moon

Type: magazine
CLMP member: no
Primary Editor/Contact Person: Judith Johnson
Address: Department Of English, HU 378
SUNY Albany
Albany, NY 12222
Web Site Address:
http://www.albany.edu/13thMoon/index.html
Publishes: fiction, poetry, art, and translation
Editorial Focus: 13th Moon's wide array of contributors creates a dynamic journal that constantly evolves to meet the needs of literature.
Representative Authors: Ursula Le Guin, Carolee Schneeman, and Ethal Schwabacher
Submissions Policy: We welcome submissions from all women, as well as men who write about women or translate women's writings.
Simultaneous Submissions: no
Reading Period: 9/1 to 5/31
Reporting Time: five to six months
Author Payment: none
Founded: 1973
Non Profit: yes
Paid Staff: zero
Unpaid Staff: four
Distributors: EBSCO, Swets Blackwell
ISSN Number/ISBN Number: ISSN 0094-3320
Total Circulation: 1,200

Organization: 1913 a journal of forms

Type: magazine
CLMP member: yes
Primary Editor/Contact Person: l'editrice
Address: Markstein Hall 137, LTWR Department
Cal State San Marcos, 333 Twin Oaks Blvd
San Marcos, CA 92096
Web Site Address: www.journal1913.org
Publishes: essays, fiction, nonfiction, poetry, reviews, art, translation, audio, and video
Editorial Focus: Intersections between art forms
Submissions Policy: Accepts only electronic submissions for the mag year-round (pdf, doc, rtf, jpeg, mp3, tif). Reading periods for 1913 Press.
Simultaneous Submissions: yes
Reading Period: year-round
Reporting Time: three to nine months
Author Payment: royalties, copies, and subscription.
Contests: The 1913 Prize + The Rozanova Prize; see web site for contest guidelines

Founded: 2003
Non Profit: yes
Paid Staff: zero
Unpaid Staff: two
Distributors: Small Press Distributors
ISSN Number/ISBN Number: ISSN 1548-9914
Total Circulation: 750
Average Print Run: 1,000
Subscription Rate: individual $13/institution $25
Single Copy Price: $13
Current Volume/Issue: issue two
Frequency per year: annual
Backfile Available: no
Unsolicited MSS Received: yes
Format: perfect
Average Pages: 200
Ads: yes
Ad Rates: $500—please contact l'editrice

Organization: 1913 Press

Type: press
CLMP member: yes
Primary Editor/Contact Person: l'editrice
Address: PO Box 9654
Hollins University
Roanoke, VA 24020
Web Site Address: www.1913press.org
Publishes: essays, fiction, nonfiction, poetry, reviews, art, translation, audio, and video
Editorial Focus: Intersections between art forms
Submissions Policy: Not accepting unsolicited submissions, except via 1913's contests
Simultaneous Submissions: yes
Reading Period: year-round
Reporting Time: three to nine months
Author Payment: none
Contests: The Rozanova Prize, for a visual and/or collaborative book; see website for contest guidelines
Founded: 2003
Non Profit: yes
Paid Staff: zero
Unpaid Staff: two
Distributors: SPD
Wholesalers: Baker & Taylor
ISSN Number/ISBN Number: ISBN 0-9779351-0-8
Number of Books Published per year: 1-5
Titles in Print: one
Average Print Run: 1,500
Average Percentage Printed: paperback 80%,

chapbook 10%, other 10%
Average Price: $15

Organization: 2River

Type: online
CLMP member: no
Primary Editor/Contact Person: Richard Long
Address: 7474 Drexel Dr.
University City, MO 63130
Web Site Address: http://www.2River.org
Publishes: poetry and art
Editorial Focus: 2River publishes The 2River View and the 2River Chapbook Series, and podcasts poems from Muddy Bank.
Representative Authors: Wendy Taylor Carlisle, Robert Creeley, and Ann Politte
Submissions Policy: Submit no more than four poems, along with a brief bio. Paste poems and bio into e-mail or use Word or RTF attachments.
Simultaneous Subs: no
Reading Period: Year-round
Reporting Time: one to three months
Author Payment: copies
Founded: 1996
Non Profit: yes
ISSN Number/ISBN Number: 15636-2280/1536-2086
Average Page Views per Month: 2,500
Average Unique Visitors per Month: 1,800
Frequency per Year: quarterly
Publish Print Anthology: no
Average Percentage of Pages per Category: Poetry 95%, Art 5%
Ads: no

Organization: 32 Poems

Type: magazine
CLMP member: no
Primary Editor/Contact Person: Deborah Ager
Address: P.O. Box 5824
Hyattsville, MD 20782
Web Site Address: http://www.32poems.com
Publishes: poetry
Editorial Focus: 32 Poems is a semiannual. Each issue contains only 32 poems so that readers may give an intimate, unhurried attention to each.
Representative Authors: Medbh McGuckian, B.H. Fairchild, and Brigit Pegeen Kelly
Submissions Policy: Please visit

http://www.32poems.com/submit.html for latest guidelines
Simultaneous Subs: no
Reading Period: 9/1 to 5/31
Reporting Time: two to four months
Author Payment: copies
Contests: See web site for contest guidelines
Founded: 2003
Non Profit: yes
Paid Staff: zero
Unpaid Staff: three
Distributors: available exclusively via subscription
ISSN Number/ISBN Number: ISSN pending
Total Circulation: 300
Paid Circulation: 200
Subscription Rate: Individual $12/Institution $12
Single Copy Price: $6
Current Volume/Issue: 1/2
Frequency per Year: biannual
Backfile Available: yes
Unsolicited Ms. Received: yes
% of Unsolicited Ms. Published per Year: 50%
Format: stapled
Size: H 5" W 7"
Ads: yes
Ad Rates: See web site for details.

Organization: 580 Split

Type: magazine
CLMP member: no
Primary Editor/Contact Person: Michell Simotas
Address: P.O. Box 9982
Mills College
Oakland, CA 94613-0982
Web Site Address: http://www.mills.edu/580Split/
Publishes: fiction, poetry, and art
Editorial Focus: Innovative prose, poetry, and art
Representative Authors: Victo LaValle, Lisa Jarnot, and Cecile Pineda
Submissions Policy: see web site
Simultaneous Subs: no
Reading Period: 7/1 to 11/1
Reporting Time: three to six months
Author Payment: copies
Founded: 1998
Non Profit: yes
Paid Staff: zero
Unpaid Staff: 12
Distributors: Ingram
ISSN Number/ISBN Number: ISSN 1523-4762

Total Circulation: 650
Average Print Run: 750
Subscription Rate: Individual $14/2 yrs./Institution $12/2 yrs.
Single Copy Price: $7.50
Current Volume/Issue: Issue eight
Frequency per Year: annual
Backfile Available: yes
Unsolicited Ms. Received: yes
% of Unsolicited Ms. Published per Year: 5%
Format: perfect
Size: H 8.5" W 5.5"
Average Pages: 110
Ads: yes
Ad Rates: $25 1/4 page, $50 1/2 page, $100 full page; see web site for details.

Organization: 6x6

Type: magazine
CLMP member: yes
Primary Editor/Contact Person: Matvei Yankelevich
Address: 232 Third Street, #E-002
Brooklyn, NY 11215
Web Site Address:
http://www.uglyducklingpresse.org
Publishes: poetry
Editorial Focus: 6x6 publishes six poets with six pages each in every issue. Our tastes change and so do our editors. We also do translations.
Representative Authors: Keith Waldrop, Jacqueline Waters, and Novica Tadic
Submissions Policy: Send enough for six pages. Series, longer work, especially made to fit the format. Open to all. Please read before sending.
Simultaneous Submissions: yes
Reading Period: year-round
Reporting Time: two to four months
Author Payment: copies
Founded: 2000
Non Profit: yes
Paid Staff: zero
Unpaid Staff: five
Distributors: Ugly Duckling Presse
ISSN Number/ISBN Number: ISSN 1533-9459
Total Circulation: 600
Paid Circulation: 50
Subscription Rate: Individual $10/Institution $20
Single Copy Price: $3
Current Volume/Issue: issue fourteen
Frequency per Year: triquarterly

Backfile Available: yes
Unsolicited Ms. Received: yes
% of Unsolicited Ms. Published per Year: 30%
Format: Industrial Rubber Band Binding
Size: H 7" W 7"
Average Pages: 56
Ads: no

Organization: A Gathering of the Tribes

Type: magazine
CLMP member: yes
Primary Editor/Contact Person: Steve Cannon
Address: P.O. Box 20693
Tompkins Square Station
New York, NY 10009
Web Site Address: http://www.tribes.org/
Publishes: essays, fiction, poetry, and art
Simultaneous Submissions: yes
Reading Period: Year-round
Reporting Time: one to two months
Author Payment: copies
Founded: 1991
Non Profit: yes
Paid Staff: zero
Unpaid Staff: 15
Distributors: Ubiquity, DeBoer, Blue Moon
ISSN Number/ISBN Number: 7447088604
Total Circulation: 2,500
Paid Circulation: 200
Subscription Rate: Individual $12.50/Institution $30
Single Copy Price: $12.50
Current Volume/Issue: Issue 13
Frequency per Year: bianual
Backfile Available: yes
Unsolicited Ms. Received: yes
% of Unsolicited Ms. Published per Year: 10%
Format: perfect
Average Pages: 120
Ads: yes
Ad Rates: $100-$495

Organization: A Public Space

Type: magazine
CLMP member: yes
Primary Editor/Contact Person: Brigid Hughes
Address: 323 Dean Street
Brooklyn, NY 11217
Web Site Address: http://www.apublicspace.org/
Publishes: essays, fiction, poetry, and art

Editorical Focus: contemporary fiction and poetry, including translations. Cultural criticism.
Representative Authors: Kelly Link, Charles D'Ambrosio, and Matthea Harvey
Submissions Policy: submit via website or regular mail
Simultaneous Submissions: yes
Reading Period: 9/1 to 7/1
Reporting Time: three to four months
Author Payment: cash, copies, and subscription
Founded: 2005
Non Profit: yes
Paid Staff: two
Unpaid Staff: five
Distributors: Ubiquity, Kent News, Small Changes, Ingram, and DeBoer
ISSN Number/ISBN Number: 74470-28823
Total Circulation: 7,000
Paid Circulation: 2,000
Average Print Run: 7,000
Subscription Rate: Individual $36/Institution $36
Single Copy Price: $12
Current Volume/Issue: Issue 5
Frequency per Year: quarterly
Backfile Available: yes
Unsolicited Ms. Received: yes
% of Unsolicited Ms. Published per Year: 1-2%
Format: perfect
Size: H 8.5" W 6.5"
Average Pages: 224
Ads: yes
Ad Rates: full-page: $1,000

Organization: Abraxas Press, Inc.

Type: press
CLMP member: yes
Primary Editor/Contact Person: Ingrid Swanberg
Address: P.O. Box 260113
Madison, WI 53726-0113
Web Site Address: http://www.geocities.com/abraxaspress
Publishes: essays, poetry, reviews, art, and translation
Editorial Focus: Abraxas Magazine is interested in lyrical and experimental poetry, translations of poetry, and essays on contemporary poetry.
Representative Authors: D.A.levy, Prospero Saiz, and Andrea Moorhead
Submissions Policy: No unsolicited manuscripts except as announced when projects arise. Please see

our website.
Simultaneous Subs: no
Reading Period: 9/01 to 11/30
Reporting Time: up to one month
Author Payment: copies
Founded: 1968
Non Profit: yes
Paid Staff: zero
Unpaid Staff: four
Distributors: none currently
Titles in Print: nine
Average Print Run: 700
Average Percentage Printed: Paperback 60%, Chapbook 40%
Average Pice: $4

Organization: The Absinthe Literary Review

Type: online
CLMP member: yes
Primary Editor/Contact Person: Charles Allen Wyman
Address: P.O. Box 328
Spring Green, WI 53588
Web Site Address: http://www.absinthe-literary-review.com
Publishes: essays, fiction, poetry, reviews, and art
Editorial Focus: ALR publishes work of high literary caliber dealing with excess, sex, death, disease, philosophy, experiment, and language.
Recent Awards Received: Voted most important online journal by LOCKSS program. Lit Rep panel judges from Stanford, IU, Harvard, FSU, UW, UM, Penn
Representative Authors: Norman Lock, Virgil Suarez, and Davis Schneiderman
Submissions Policy: See detailed guidelines at http://www.absinthe-literary-review.com/submit.htm. Failure to do so generally results in sub dismissal.
Simultaneous Submissions: yes
Reading Period: Year-round
Reporting Time: one to five months
Author Payment: cash
Founded: 1998
Non Profit: yes
Paid Staff: one
Unpaid Staff: six
Distributors: Online only (print version expected eventually))
Wholesalers: Online only
ISSN Number/ISBN Number: ISSN pending

Average Page Views per Month: 1,000,000
Average Unique Visitors per Month: 250-300K
Frequency per Year: quarterly
Publish Print Anthology: no
Average Percentage of Pages per Category: Fiction 24%, Poetry 24%, Reviews 24%, Essays 4%, Art 24%
Ads: no

Organization: Absinthe: New European Writing

Type: magazine
CLMP member: yes
Primary Editor/Contact Person: Dwayne D. Hayes
Address: Absinthe Arts 21
P.O. Box 11445
Detroit, MI 48211-1445
Web Site Address: http://www.absinthenew.com
Publishes: essays, fiction, nonfiction, poetry, reviews, art, and translation
Editorial Focus: Poetry and prose by contemporary European writers.
Representative Authors: Christa Wolf, Herberto Helder, and Ulrike Draesner
Submissions Policy: See web site
Simultaneous Subs: yes
Reading Period: 09/01 to 04/30
Reporting Time: two to three months
Author Payment: copies and subscription
Founded: 2003
Non Profit: yes
Paid Staff: zero
Unpaid Staff: six
Distributors: DeBoer
ISSN Number/ISBN Number: ISSN 1543-8449
Total Circulation: 500
Paid Circulation: 200
Average Print Run: 750
Subscription Rate: Individual $12/Institution $25
Single Copy Price: $7
Current Volume/Issue: Issue 7
Frequency per Year: biannual
Backfile Available: yes
Unsolicited Ms. Received: yes
Format: perfect
Size: H 9" W 6"
Average Pages: 104
Ads: yes

Organization: The Adirondack Review

Type: online
CLMP member: no
Primary Editor/Contact Person: Colleen Marie Ryor
Address: P.O. Box 46
Watertown, NY 13601
Web Site Address: http://www.adirondackreview.com
Publishes: essays, fiction, nonfiction, poetry, reviews, and art
Representative Authors: Lee Upton, D.C. Berry, and Ilya Kaminsky
Submissions Policy: See web site for guidelines.
Simultaneous Submissionns: yes
Reading Period: Year-round
Reporting Time: 1 to 12 weeks
Author Payment: none
Contests: The St. Lawrence Book Award for a first collection: $1,000 and publication. The 46er Prize for Short Fiction: $500; see web site for guidelines.
Founded: 2000
Non Profit: yes
Paid Staff: zero
Unpaid Staff: nine
ISSN Number/ISBN Number: ISSN 1533-2063
Average Page Views per Month: 18,000
Average Unique Visitors per Month: 5,000
Frequency per Year: quarterly
Publish Print Anthology: no
Average Percentage of Pages per Category: Fiction 25%, Nonfiction 10%, Poetry 45%, Reviews 10%, Essays 2%, Art 3%, Translation 5%
Ad Rates: $40/classified ad with graphic (three months), discounts; see web site for details.

Organization: Aethlon

Type: magazine
CLMP member: yes
Primary Editor/Contact Person: Joyce Duncan
Address: PO Box 70270
ETSU
Johnson City, TN 37614
Web Site Address: www.uta.edu/english/sla
Publishes: essays, fiction, poetry, and reviews
Editorial Focus: Aethlon is a print journal designed to celebrate the intersection of literature with the world of play, games, and sport.
Representative Authors: Cris Mazza, Joseph Stanton, and John B. Lee
Submissions Policy: All submissions must relate to sport in some way. Please see our Web site to direct

your submissions to the proper editor.
Simultaneous Submissions: yes
Reading Period: year-round
Reporting Time: two to four months
Author Payment: copies
Contests: poetry and fiction contests. See web site for contest guidelines
Founded: 1983
Non Profit: yes
Paid Staff: zero
Unpaid Staff: six
Total Circulation: 600
Paid Circulation: 600
Average Print Run: 750
Subscription Rate: individual $50/institution $75
Single Copy Price: $20
Current Volume/Issue: 25/1
Frequency per year: biannual
Backfile Available: yes
Unsolicited MSS Received: yes
% of Unsolicited MSS Published per year: 15%
Format: perfect
Size: H 9" W 6"
Average Pages: 225
Ads: yes
Ad Rates: see web site for details

Organization: African American Review

Type: magazine
CLMP member: yes
Primary Editor/Contact Person: Joycelyn Moody/Aileen Keenan
Address: 3800 Lindell Blvd.
St. Louis, MO 63108
Web Site Address: aar.slu.edu
Publishes: essays, fiction, poetry, and reviews
Editorial Focus: African American Review promotes a lively exchange among writers and scholars in the arts, humanities, and social sciences who hold diverse perspectives on African American literature and culture. AAR publishes essays on African American literature, theatre, film, art, and culture generally; interviews; poetry; fiction; and book reviews.
Recent Awards Received: 2005 CELJ Distinguished Editor of the Year
Representative Authors: Farah Jasmine Griffin, Kalamu ya Salaam, and Sandra Shannon
Submissions Policy: http://aar.slu.edu/submsinf.html
Simultaneous Submissions: no

Reading Period: year-round
Reporting Time: six to seven months
Author Payment: cash and copies
Founded: 1967
Non Profit: yes
Paid Staff: two
Unpaid Staff: zero
ISSN Number/ISBN Number: ISSN 1062-4783
Paid Circulation: 1,800
Average Print Run: 2,400
Subscription Rate: individual $40/institution $80
Single Copy Price: $12
Current Volume/Issue: 40/1-4
Frequency per year: quarterly
Backfile Available: yes
Unsolicited MSS Received: yes
% of Unsolicited MSS Published per year: 15%
Format: perfect
Size: H 10" W 7"
Average Pages: 176
Ads: yes
Ad Rates: $120 1/2 page, $200 full page; see web site for details

Organization: African Heritage Press

Type: press
CLMP member: no
Primary Editor/Contact Person: Basil Njoku
Address: P.O. Box 1433
New Rochelle, NY 10802
Web Site Address: http://www.africanheritagepress.com
Publishes: essays, fiction, nonfiction, and poetry
Editorial Focus: We are committed to publishing original poetry, prose fiction and drama that uniquely inform, reveal and project the rich socio-cultural experiences and worlds of the diverse peoples of African descent, beyond borders.
Recent Awards Received: ANA Best Poetry Prize, 2003 BBC Drama Documentary, Radio Drama.
Representative Authors: Tess Onwueme, Tanure Ojaide, and Ernest Emenyonu
Submissions Policy: Include a hard copy printed on one side only and double-spaced. Pages should be numbered, and manuscripts bound or securely clipped without rubber bands, staples, paper clips, or loose pages. An author's bio must include address, phone number, and e-mail. Include a one-page description of the subject and purpose of the book, and a disk or CD copy developed in Microsoft Word.

Simultaneous Submissions: yes
Reading Period: Year-round
Reporting Time: one to two months
Author Payment: royalties and copies
Founded: 2000
Non Profit: yes
Paid Staff: four
Unpaid Staff: three
Distributors: http://www.africanbookscollective.com
Wholesalers: African books collective/Michigan State University
Number of Books Published per Year: five
Titles in Print: eight
Average Percentage Printed: Paperback 100%
Average Price: $14.95

Organization: African Voices Communications

Type: magazine
CLMP member: yes
Primary Editor/Contact Person: Carolyn A. Butts
Address: 270 West 96th St.
New York, NY 10025
Web Site Address: http://www.africanvoices.com/
Publishes: essays, fiction, nonfiction, poetry, reviews, art, and translation
Editorial Focus: African Voices publishes compelling short stories, poetry and art by people of color.
Representative Authors: Willie Perdomo, Nalo Hopkinson, and Ngugi wa Thiong'o
Submissions Policy: Please submit no more than three poems at a time. Fiction stories between 300 to 2,500 words are considered for publication.
Simultaneous Submissions: yes
Reading Period: Year-round
Reporting Time: one to three months
Author Payment: copies
Contests: Periodic fiction and poetry contests are announced.
Founded: 1992
Non Profit: yes
Unpaid Staff: seven
Distributors: Ingram and Ubiquity
ISSN Number/ISBN Number: ISSN 1530-0668
Total Circulation: 20,000
Paid Circulation: 95%
Subscription Rate: Individual $12/Institution $12
Single Copy Price: $4
Current Volume/Issue: 10/17
Frequency per Year: quarterly

Backfile Available: yes
Unsolicited Ms. Received: yes
% of Unsolicited Ms. Published per Year: 80%
Format: saddle stitched
Size: H 11" W 8.5"
Average Pages: 44
Ads: yes
Ad Rates: Full page $1,200; see web site for details.

Organization: AGNI

Type: magazine
CLMP member: yes
Primary Editor/Contact Person: Sven Birkerts, Editor
Address: Boston University
236 Bay State Road
Boston, MA 02215
Web Site Address: http://www.agnimagazine.org
Publishes: essays, fiction, nonfiction, poetry, art, and translation
Editorial Focus: Following Ezra Pound's dictum that "artists are the antennae of the race," we publish the best, most provocative "signals."
Recent Awards Received: Two Pushcart Prizes for 2006. Stories published at AGNI Online were named Top Ten Online Stories in 2004 and 2005.
Representative Authors: Seamus Heaney, David Foster Wallace, and Alden Jones
Submissions Policy: Mail one story, essay, or one to five poems per submission, with SASE, addressed to Fiction, Poetry, or Nonfiction Editor. No e-mail.
Simultaneous Submissions: yes
Reading Period: 9/1 to 5/31
Reporting Time: two to four months
Author Payment: cash, copies, and subscription
Founded: 1972
Non Profit: yes
Paid Staff: six
Unpaid Staff: three- four
Distributors: Ingram, DeBoer, Kent News Service
ISSN Number/ISBN Number: ISSN 0191-3352
Total Circulation: 3,400
Paid Circulation: 1,200
Average Print Run: 3,500
Subscription Rate: Individual $17/Institution $20
Single Copy Price: $10
Current Volume/Issue: Issue 66
Frequency per Year: biannual
Backfile Available: yes
Unsolicited Ms. Received: yes
% of Unsolicited Ms. Published per Year: 1%

Format: perfect
Size: H 8.5" W 5-3/8"
Average Pages: 240
Ads: yes
Ad Rates: $500 full page; $350 half, sold with Harvard Review; see web site for Details.

Organization: Ahsahta Press

Type: press
CLMP member: yes
Primary Editor/Contact Person: Janet Holmes
Address: Boise State University
1910 University Dr.
Boise, ID 83725-1525
Web Site Address: http://ahsahtapress.boisestate.edu
Publishes: poetry
Editorial Focus: We publish full-length collections and seek out work that surprises and innovates. Annual Sawtooth Prize honors new poetry.
Representative Authors: Brian Henry, Kate Greenstreet, and LIsa Fishman
Submissions Policy: 48-80 pages. Cover letter with bio info, description of manuscript, list of publications (if applicable). SASE.
Simultaneous Submissions: yes
Reading Period: 3/1 to 5/1
Reporting Time: one to two months
Author Payment: royalties and copies
Contests: See Web Site for guidelines.
Founded: 1974
Non Profit: yes
Paid Staff: zero
Unpaid Staff: seven
Distributors: SPD
Wholesalers: Baker & Taylor
ISSN Number/ISBN Number: ISBN 0-916272-
Number of Books Published per Year: 5-6
Titles in Print: 75
Average Print Run: 1,000
Average Percentage Printed: Paperback 100%
Average Price: $16

Organization: Akashic Books

Type: press
CLMP member: yes
Primary Editor/Contact Person: Johnny Temple
Address: P.O. Box 1456
New York, NY 10009
Web Site Address: http://www.akashicbooks.com
Publishes: fiction and nonfiction
Editorial Focus: Brooklyn-based independent company dedicated to publishing urban literary fiction and political nonfiction.
Recent Awards Received: Edgar, Miriam Bass, Anthony
Representative Authors: Amiri Baraka, MIke Farrell, and Chris Abani
Submissions Policy: Currently not accepting new submissions, but okay to e-mail or mail inquiry and short synopsis.
Simultaneous Submissions: yes
Reading Period: Year-round
Reporting Time: one to eight months
Author Payment: royalties
Founded: 1997
Non Profit: no
Paid Staff: three
Unpaid Staff: two
Distributors: Consortium
Wholesalers: Ingram, Koen, Baker & Taylor, SPD, Turnaround-UK
ISSN Number/ISBN Number: ISBN 978-1-933354
Number of Books Published per Year: 24
Titles in Print: 90
Average Print Run: 5,000
Average Percentage Printed: Hardcover 20%, Paperback 80%
Average Price: $14.95

Organization: Alaska Quarterly Review

Type: magazine
CLMP member: yes
Primary Editor/Contact Person: Ronald Spatz
Address: University of Alaska Anchorage
3211 Providence Dr.
Anchorage, AK 99508
Web Site Address: http://aqr.uaa.alaska.edu
Publishes: essays, fiction, nonfiction, poetry, and translation
Editorial Focus: publishing fiction, short plays, poetry and literary nonfiction in traditional and experimental styles.
Representative Authors: Jane Hirshfield, Deborah A. Lott, and Ann Stapleton
Submissions Policy: Alaska Quarterly Review is a literary journal devoted to literary art, publishing fiction, short plays, poetry and literary nonfiction in traditional and experimental styles. The editors encourage new

and emerging writers, while continuing to publish award-winning and established writers.
Simultaneous Submissions: yes
Reading Period: 8/15 to 5/15
Reporting Time: one to six months
Author Payment: copies and subscription
Founded: 1981
Non Profit: yes
Paid Staff: one
Unpaid Staff: six
Distributors: Ingram, Source Interlink, DeBoer
ISSN Number/ISBN Number: ISSN 0737-268X
Total Circulation: 2,700
Paid Circulation: 160
Average Print Run: 3,000
Subscription Rate: Individual $18/Institution $18
Single Copy Price: $6.95
Current Volume/Issue: V24/3-4
Frequency per Year: biannual
Backfile Available: yes
Unsolicited Ms. Received: yes
% of Unsolicited Ms. Published per Year: 1/2%
Format: perfect
Size: H 9" W 6"
Average Pages: 250
Ads: no

Organization: Alehouse

Type: magazine
CLMP member: yes
Primary Editor/Contact Person: Jay Rubin
Address: PO Box 31655
San Francisco, CA 94131
Web Site Address: http://www.alehousepress.com
Publishes: essays, nonfiction, poetry, reviews, and art
Editorial Focus: Prose about poetry, poetry about everything
Representative Authors: Allison Joseph, Michael Waters, and Margaret J. Hoehn
Submissions Policy: We read prose all year long, poetry during July. Please visit our website for more details.
Simultaneous Submissions: yes
Reading Period: year-round
Reporting Time: two to six months
Author Payment: subscription
Founded: 2006
Non Profit: yes
Paid Staff: zero
Unpaid Staff: two

Total Circulation: 900
Paid Circulation: 500
Average Print Run: 900
Subscription Rate: Individual $10/Institution $12
Single Copy Price: $10
Current Volume/Issue: 1/2
Frequency per Year: one
Backfile Available: yes
Unsolicited Ms. Received: yes
% of Unsolicited Ms. Published per Year: 50%
Format: perfect
Size: H 8.5" W 5.5"
Average Pages: 150
Ads: yes
Ad Rates: contact editor

Organization: Alehouse Press

Type: press
CLMP member: yes
Primary Editor/Contact Person: Jay Rubin
Address: PO Box 31655
San Francisco, CA 94131
Web Site Address: http://www.alehousepress.com
Publishes: essays, nonfiction, poetry, reviews, and art
Editorial Focus: Prose about poetry, poetry about everything
Representative Authors: Allison Joseph, Michael Waters, and Margaret J. Hoehn
Submissions Policy: We read prose all year long, poetry during July. Please visit our website for more details.
Simultaneous Submissions: yes
Reading Period: year-round
Reporting Time: two to six months
Author Payment: cash, copies, and subscription
Founded: 2006
Non Profit: yes
Paid Staff: zero
Unpaid Staff: two
Numer of Books Published Per Year: two
Titles in Print: two
Average Print Run: 900
Average Percentage Printed: Paperback 50%, Chapbook 50%
Average Price: $10

Organization: Alice James Books

Type: press
CLMP member: yes
Primary Editor/Contact Person: April Ossmann

Address: 238 Main St.
Farmington, ME 04938
Web Site Address: http://www.alicejamesbooks.org
Publishes: poetry
Editorial Focus: Publishes poetry by established and beginning poets, both national and regional; emphasizes involving poets in publishing process.
Representative Authors: B.H. Fairchild, Matthea Harvey, and Cole Swensen
Submissions Policy: The cooperative board selects manuscripts through annual regional and national competitions; see web site for guidelines.
Simultaneous Subs: yes
Reading Period: 7/1 to 12/1
Reporting Time: three to four months
Author Payment: cash
Contests: The Beatrice Hawley Award and The Kinereth Gensler Awards; see website for guidelines
Founded: 1973
Non Profit: yes
Paid Staff: four
Unpaid Staff: five
Distributors: Consortium, SPD
Wholesalers: Ingram, Baker & Taylor
ISSN Number/ISBN Number: ISBN 0-914086, 1-882295, 0-914086
Number of Books Published per Year: five
Titles in Print: 120
Average Print Run: 1,500
Average Percentage Printed: Paperback 100%
Average Price: $14.95

Organization: All Info-About Poetry

Type: online
CLMP member: no
Primary Editor/Contact Person: Paula Bardell
Address: Pussy Willow
2 Singrett Hill
Llay, Wr LL12 0NS, United Kingdom
Web Site Address: http://allinfoaboutpoetry.com
Publishes: essays, nonfiction, poetry, reviews, and translation
Editorial Focus: We are pleased to accept well-crafted poetry and verse; book, film and performance reviews; essays and articles concerning poets and poetry; and any other appropriate contribution.
Representative Authors: Ruth Daigon, Liam Wilkinson, and Karen Alkalay-Gut
Submissions Policy: see website for guidelines
Simultaneous Subs: yes

Reading Period: year-round
Reporting Time: four to six weeks
Author Payment: none
Contests: see web site for guidelines.
Founded: 2001
Non Profit: yes
Paid Staff: zero
Unpaid Staff: one
ISSN Number/ISBN Number: ISSN 1740-4428
Average Page Views per Month: 10,000
Average Unique Visitors per Month: 8,000
Publish Print Anthology: no
Average Percentage of Pages per Category: Fiction 10%, Nonfiction 10%, Poetry 50%, Reviews 20%, Essays 20%
Ad Rates: see web site for details.

Organization: Allbook Books

Type: press
CLMP member: no
Primary Editor/Contact Person: Walter E. Harris III (Mankh)
Address: PO Box 562
Selden, NY 11784
Web Site Address: http://www.allbook-books.com
Publishes: essays, nonfiction, and poetry
Editorial Focus: Educational, informational, enlightening, uplifting, esoteric, ,metaphysical, inspiring, imaginative, realistic
Representative Authors: Edgar Carlson, Mira McEwan, and Richard Savadsky
Submissions Policy: E-mail/snail-mail inquiry
Simultaneous Subs: yes
Reading Period: year-round
Reporting Time: one to four weeks
Author Payment: copies
Founded: 2002
Non Profit: no
Paid Staff: zero
Unpaid Staff: one
Number of Books Published per Year: two-three
Titles in Print: 11
Average Print Run: 400
Average Percentage Printed: Paperback 65%, Chapbook 35%
Average Price: $10

Organization: Alligator Juniper

Type: magazine
CLMP member: yes

Primary Editor/Contact Person: Rachel Yoder
Address: 220 Grove Ave.
Prescott College
Prescott, AZ 86301
Web Site Address: http://www.prescott.edu/high-lights/alligator_juniper
Publishes: fiction, nonfiction, and poetry
Editorial Focus: Literary fiction, poetry, nonfiction, and black and white photography.
Recent Awards Received: AWP Director's Prize for Content in 2001 and 2004.
Representative Authors: Wendy Bishop, Kurt Brown, and Fatima Lim-Wilson
Submissions Policy: The majority of our material comes from contest submissions. Please read our guidelines before entering.
Simultaneous Submissions: yes
Reading Period: 5/1 to 10/1
Reporting Time: three to five months
Author Payment: cash and copies
Contests: see web site for guidelines.
Founded: 1994
Non Profit: yes
Paid Staff: three
Unpaid Staff: 24
Distributors: Ingram
ISSN Number/ISBN Number: ISSN 1547-187X
Total Circulation: 1,200
Paid Circulation: 150
Average Print Run: 1,500
Subscription Rate: Individual $15/2 years/Institution $15/2 years
Single Copy Price: $10
Current Volume/Issue: 12/2007
Frequency per Year: annual
Backfile Available: yes
Unsolicited Ms. Received: yes
% of Unsolicited Ms. Published per Year: 90%
Format: perfect
Size: H 9" W 6"
Average Pages: 180
Ads: no

Organization: American Book Review

Type: magazine
CLMP member: yes
Primary Editor/Contact Person: Rebecca Kaiser
Address: ISU Campus Box 4241
Normal, IL 61790-4241
Web Site Address: http://www.litline.org/abr

Publishes: essays and reviews
Editorial Focus: reviews of literary books.
Submissions Policy: contact for guidelines
Simultaneous Submissions: yes
Reading Period: year-round
Reporting Time: two to six weeks
Author Payment: cash, copies, and subscription
Founded: 1977
Non Profit: yes
Paid Staff: three
Unpaid Staff: 16
Distributors: Ingram, Interstate
ISSN Number/ISBN Number: ISSN 0149-9408
Total Circulation: 5,000
Paid Circulation: 2,000
Subscription Rate: Individual $24/Institution $30
Single Copy Price: $4
Current Volume/Issue: 25/1
Frequency per Year: bimonthly
Backfile Available: yes
Unsolicited Ms. Received: yes
% of Unsolicited Ms. Published per Year: 15%
Format: tabloid
Size: H 17" W 11"
Average Pages: 32
Ads: yes
Ad Rates: full page $1,050, half page $750, 2 half-columns $300

Organization: American Letters & Commentary

Type: magazine
CLMP member: yes
Primary Editor/Contact Person: David Ray Vance and Catherine Kasper
Address: PO Box 830365
San Antonio, TX 78283
Web Site Address: http://www.amletters.org
Publishes: essays, fiction, nonfiction, poetry, reviews, art, and translation
Editorial Focus: Challenging, innovative work in all genres
Representative Authors: Ann Lauterbach, Charles Bernstein, and Marjorie Perloff
Submissions Policy: Only unpublished work, simultaneous submissions accepted if notified
Simultaneous Submissions: yes
Reading Period: 10/1 to 3/1
Reporting Time: one to four months
Author Payment: copies

Founded: 1987
Non Profit: yes
Paid Staff: zero
Unpaid Staff: three
Distributors: Ingram, DeBoer, SPD, Ubiquity
ISSN Number/ISBN Number: ISSN 1049-7153
Total Circulation: 1,500
Paid Circulation: 200
Average Print Run: 1,600
Subscription Rate: Individual $8/Institution $8
Single Copy Price: $8
Current Volume/Issue: 17/.0
Frequency per Year: annual
Backfile Available: yes
Unsolicited Ms. Received: yes
% of Unsolicited Ms. Published per Year: 5%
Format: perfect
Size: H 7" W 8"
Average Pages: 200
Ads: yes
Ad Rates: $35 half page, $50 whole page; see Web Site for Details.

Organization: The American Poetry Review

Type: magazine
CLMP member: yes
Primary Editor/Contact Person: David Bonanno
Address: 117 S. 17th St. #910
Philadelphia, PA 19103
Web Site Address: http://www.aprweb.org
Publishes: essays, fiction, nonfiction, poetry, reviews, and translation
Editorial Focus: Broad range of poetry, translations, criticism, reviews, interviews, and columns.
Representative Authors: Louise Gluck, Dana Levin, and W.S. Merwin
Submissions Policy: Send one to five poems with SASE
Simultaneous Submissions: no
Reading Period: year-round
Reporting Time: 8 to 12 weeks
Author Payment: cash, copies, and subscription
Contests: See web site for contest guidelines.
Founded: 1972
Non Profit: yes
Paid Staff: six
Unpaid Staff: four
Distributors: Ingram, DeBoer, Ubiquity, Media Solutions, Armadillo

ISSN Number/ISBN Number: ISSN 0360-3709
Total Circulation: 16,000
Paid Circulation: 11,000
Average Print Run: 17,500
Subscription Rate: Individual $22/Institution $22
Single Copy Price: $4.25
Current Volume/Issue: 36/208
Frequency per Year: bimonthly
Backfile Available: yes
Unsolicited Ms. Received: yes
% of Unsolicited Ms. Published per Year: .6%
Format: tabloid
Size: H 13" W 9 1/2"
Average Pages: 56
Ads: yes
Ad Rates: see web site for details.

Organization: American Short Fiction

Type: magazine
CLMP member: yes
Primary Editor/Contact Person: Stacey Swann
Address: PO Box 301209
Austin, TX 78703
Web Site Address: www.americanshortfiction.org
Publishes: essays, fiction, art, and translation
Simultaneous Submissions: yes
Reading Period: year-round
Reporting Time: four to five months
Author Payment: cash and subscription
Contests: We have a yearly fall contest with a prize of $1000 and publication; see web site for guidelines
Founded: 1991
Non Profit: yes
Paid Staff: three
Unpaid Staff: eight
Distributors: Ingram, Source Interlink, Ubiquity
ISSN Number/ISBN Number: ISSN 1051-4813
Total Circulation: 1,500
Paid Circulation: <500
Average Print Run: 1,775
Subscription Rate: individual $30/institution $40
Single Copy Price: $10
Current Volume/Issue: 10/38
Frequency per year: quarterly
Backfile Available: yes
Unsolicited MSS Received: yes
% of Unsolicited MSS Published per Year: 50%
Format: perfect
Size: H 9" W 6.75"
Average Pages: 120

Ads: yes
Ad Rates: from $250 to $750, depending on size and placement

Organization: Amherst Writers & Artists Press

Type: press
CLMP member: no
Primary Editor/Contact Person: Nancy Rose
Address: 190 University Drive
Amherst, MA 01002
Web Site Address: www.amherstwriters.com
Publishes: fiction and poetry
Editorial Focus: AWA Press is committed to finding exceptional work by new as well as established writers
Representative Authors: Virgil Suarez, Jane Yolen, and Gina Ochsner
Submissions Policy: No electronic or chapbook submissions now. For Peregrine: prose, 3,000 words; poetry 50 lines. Include SASE for response.
Simultaneous Submissions: yes
Reading Period: 1/1 to 6/1
Reporting Time: six to nine months
Author Payment: copies
Contests: no contest
Founded: 1983
Non Profit: yes
Paid Staff: zero
Unpaid Staff: three
Distributors: Amherst Writers & Artists Press
ISSN Number/ISBN Number: ISSN 0890-622x
Number of Books Published per Year: five
Titles in Print: 42
Average Print Run: 1,500
Average Percentage Printed: paperback 40%, chapbook 60%
Average Price: $16

Organization: anderbo.com

Type: online
CLMP member: yes
Primary Editor/Contact Person: Rick Rofihe
Address: 341 Lafayette St. #974
New York, NY 10012
Web Site Address: http://www.anderbo.com
Publishes: fiction, nonfiction, and poetry
Editorial Focus: Look at our website
Representative Authors: Martha Wilson, Lisa

Margonelli, and Susan Breen
Submissions Policy: fiction up to 3,500 words; nonfiction up to 750 words; up to six poems
Simultaneous Submissions: yes
Reading Period: year-round
Reporting Time: zero to four weeks
Author Payment: none
Contests: Anderbo Poetry Prize
Founded: 2005
Non Profit: no
Paid Staff: zero
Unpaid Staff: 14
Average Page Views per Month: 12,000
Average Unique Visitors per Month: 4,000
Frequency: 12
Publish Print Anthology: no
Average Percentage of Pages per Category: Fiction 50%, Nonfiction 20%, Poetry 30%
Ads: yes
Ad Rates: sliding scale

Organization: Anhinga Press

Type: press
CLMP member: yes
Primary Editor/Contact Person: Rick Campbell
Address: P.O. Box
Tallahassee, FL 32302
Web Site Address: http://www.anhinga.org
Publishes: poetry
Editorial Focus: We are looking for good poetry—it's that simple.
Representative Authors: Naomi Shihab Nye, Robert Dana, and Frank X. Gaspar
Submissions Policy: Send submissions to our post office address; we don't accept electronic submissions.
Simultaneous Submissions: yes
Reading Period: year-round
Reporting Time: six to ten weeks
Author Payment: royalties, cash, and copies
Contests: Anhinga Prize for Poetry. For 1st or 2nd books. Reading period 2/15-5/1. Fee: $25. See web site for contest guidelines.
Founded: 1973
Non Profit: yes
Paid Staff: two
Unpaid Staff: six
Distributors: SPD
ISSN Number/ISBN Number: ISBN 0938078
Number of Books Published per Year: five

Titles in Print: 54
Average Print Run: 1,200
Average Percentage Printed: Hardcover 5%, Paperback 95%
Average Price: $14

Organization: Another Chicago Magazine/Left Field Press

Type: magazine
CLMP Member: no
Address: 3709 N. Kenmore
Chicago, IL 60613-2905
Web Site Address:
http://www.anotherchicagomag.com
Publishes: essays, fiction, nonfiction, poetry, reviews, and translation
Reading Period: year-round
Reporting Time: one to two months
Author Payment: none
Founded: 1977
Non Profit: no
Frequency per Year: biannual
Price: $8

Organization: Antioch Review

Type: magazine
CLMP member: yes
Primary Editor/Contact Person: Robert Fogarty
Address: P.O. Box 148
Yellow Springs, OH 45387
Web Site Address: http://www.review.antioch.edu
Publishes: essays, fiction, nonfiction, poetry, and translation
Editorial Focus: A quarterly of critical and creative thought printing fiction, poetry and essays. We print the best words in the best order.
Representative Authors: Jeffrey Meyers, Rick Demarinis, and Nathan Oates
Submissions Policy: Send only one story at a time. Do not mix poetry and prose. Rarely do we publish anything over 8,000 words.
Simultaneous Submissions: no
Reading Period: 9/1 to 6/1
Reporting Time: four to six months
Author Payment: cash and copies
Founded: 1941
Non Profit: yes
Paid Staff: 1.5
Unpaid Staff: zero

Distributors: Ingram, Media Solutions, Ubiquity, Central Bks.-UK
ISSN Number/ISBN Number: ISSN 0003-5769
Total Circulation: 2,850
Paid Circulation: 1,000
Average Print Run: 3,000
Subscription Rate: Individual $40/Institution $80
Single Copy Price: $9.50
Current Volume/Issue: 65/1
Frequency per Year: quarterly
Backfile Available: yes
Unsolicited Ms. Received: yes
% of Unsolicited Ms. Published per Year: 1%
Format: perfect
Size: H 9" W 6"
Average Pages: 200
Ads: yes
Ad Rates: $250 full page, $150 1/2 page, $100 1/4 page; see web site for details

Organization: Antrim House

Type: press
CLMP member: no
Primary Editor/Contact Person: Robert R. McQuilkin
Address: PO Box 111
Tariffville, CT 06081
Web Site Address: www.antrimhousebooks.com
Publishes: poetry
Editorial Focus: We publish New England poets
Recent Awards Received: Center for the Books Award for Advocacy of the Arts in CT
Representative Authors: Joan Joffe Hall, Edwina Trentham, and Norah Pollard
Submissions Policy: three to five poems
Simultaneous Submissions: yes
Reading Period: year-round
Reporting Time: one to three weeks
Author Payment: none
Founded: 1990
Non Profit: no
Paid Staff: one
Unpaid Staff: zero
ISSN Number/ISBN Number: ISSN 978-0-9770633-3-8
Number of Books Published per year: eight
Titles in Print: 28
Average Print Run: 500
Average Percentage Printed: hardcover 5%, paperback 90%, chapbook 5%
Average Price: $17

Organization: Anvil Press

Type: press
CLMP member: no
Primary Editor/Contact Person: Brian Kaufman
Address: 278 East First Ave.
Vancouver, BC V5T1A6
Web Site Address: http://www.anvilpress.com
Publishes: fiction, nonfiction, and poetry
Editorial Focus: Anvil Press publishes contemporary and exciting work by Canadian writers. We look for work that is fresh, edgy and unique.
Representative Authors: Annette Lapointe, Stuart Ross, and Mark Anthony Jarman
Submissions Policy: Only Canadian authors. No genre fiction, self-help, cookbooks, etc. Enclose SASE for reply or sufficient postage for return of ms.
Simultaneous Submissions: yes
Reading Period: year-round
Reporting Time: four to six months
Author Payment: royalties and cash
Founded: 1988
Non Profit: no
Paid Staff: two
Unpaid Staff: one
Distributors: University of Toronto Press
Number of Books Published per Year: ten
Titles in Print: 66
Average Print Run: 1,500
Average Percentage Printed: Paperback 100%
Average Price: $18

Organization: Apalachee Review

Type: magazine
CLMP member: yes
Primary Editor/Contact Person: Michael Trammell
Address: P.O. Box 10469
Tallahassee, FL 32302
Web Site Address: http://www.apalacheereview.org
Publishes: essays, fiction, poetry, reviews, art, and translation
Editorial Focus: The best writing we can get our hands on.
Representative Authors: Rita Mae Reese, Lu Vickers, and Marlin Barton
Simultaneous Submissions: yes
Reading Period: year-round
Reporting Time: three to eight months
Author Payment: copies
Contests: no
Founded: 1978

Non Profit: yes
Paid Staff: zero
Unpaid Staff: 15
Distributors: DeBoer
ISSN Number/ISBN Number: ISSN 0890-6408
Total Circulation: 500
Paid Circulation: 200
Average Print Run: 600
Subscription Rate: Individual $15/Institution $20
Single Copy Price: $8
Current Volume/Issue: Issue 57
Frequency: one
Backfile Available: yes
Unsolicited Ms. Received: yes
% of Unsolicited Ms. Published per Year: 10%
Format: perfect
Size: H 8 1/2" W 5 1/2"
Average Pages: 100
Ads: no

Organization: Apogee Press

Type: press
CLMP member: yes
Primary Editor/Contact Person: Editor
Address: P.O. Box 8177
Berkeley, CA 94707-8177
Web Site Address: http://www.apogeepress.com
Publishes: poetry
Editorial Focus: innovative poetry
Simultaneous Submissions: yes
Reading Period: year-round
Reporting Time: two to four months
Author Payment: royalties and copies
Founded: 1998
Non Profit: yes
Paid Staff: zero
Unpaid Staff: one
Distributors: SPD
Number of Books Published per Year: three to four
Titles in Print: 18
Average Print Run: 1,000
Average Percentage Printed: Paperback 100%
Average Price: $14.95

Organization: Appalachian Heritage

Type: magazine
CLMP member: yes
Primary Editor/Contact Person: George Brosi
Address: CPO 2166, Berea, Kentucky 40404

Web Site Address: www.berea.edu/appalachianheritage
Publishes: poetry and art
Editorial Focus: The Literature of the Appalachian South
Representative Authors: Charles Wright, Wendell Berry, Fred Chappell,
Submissions Policy: Submit via snail mail
Simultaneous Submissions: No
Reading Period: year-round
Reporting Time: three to six months
Author Payment: copies
Founded: 1973
Non Profit: yes
Paid Staff: three
Unpaid Staff: zero
Distributors: Ingram, DeBoer, SPD
ISSN Number: 03632318
Total Circulation: 600 +
Paid Circulation: 600 +
Average Print Run: 1100
Subscription Rate: Individual $20/Institution $20
Single Copy Price: $6
Current Volume/Issue: Volume 35/Number 2
Frequency per year: quarterly
Backfile Available: almost all issues
Unsolicited MSS Received: yes
% of Unsolicited MSS Published per year: 90+%
Format: perfect
Average Pages: 116
Ads: no

Organization: Apple Valley Review

Type: online
CLMP member: yes
Primary Editor/Contact Person: Leah Browning
Address: c/o Queen's Postal Outlet
Box 12
Kingston, ON K7L 3R9
Web Site Address: www.applevalleyreview.com/
Publishes: essays, fiction, and poetry
Editorial Focus: We prefer work that has both mainstream and literary appeal. No genre fiction, explicit or scholarly work, or violence.
Representative Authors: Jenny Steele, Anna Evans, and Patricia Gosling
Submissions Policy: Please submit one prose piece or two to six poems in the body of an email message. Include a cover letter with contact info and bio.
Simultaneous Submissions: no

Reading Period: year-round
Reporting Time: 1 to 12 weeks
Author Payment: none
Founded: 2005
Non Profit: no
Paid Staff: zero
Unpaid Staff: one
ISSN Number/ISBN Number: ISSN 1931-3888
Average Page Views per Month: 1,200+
Average Unique Visitors per Month: 800+
Frequency per year: biannual
Publish Print Anthology: no
Average Percentage of Pages per Category: fiction 10%, poetry 75%, essays 10%, art 5%
Ads: no

Organization: Archipelago Books

Type: press
CLMP member: yes
Primary Editor/Contact Person: Zoe Ward
Address: 232 Third St. #A111
Brooklyn, NY 11215
Web Site Address: http://www.archipelagobooks.org
Publishes: fiction, poetry, art, and translation
Editorial Focus: Archipelago Books focuses on bringing classic and contemporary works of literature to an American audience.
Representative Authors: Witold Gombrowicz, Ahmed Hamdi Tanpinar, and Elias Khoury
Submissions Policy: We are not accepting submissions at this time.
Simultaneous Submissions: no
Reading Period: n/a
Reporting Time: n/a
Author Payment: royalties, cash, and copies
Founded: 2003
Non Profit: yes
Paid Staff: three
Unpaid Staff: two
Distributors: Consortium
ISSN Number/ISBN Number: ISBN 0-9728692, 0-9749680, 0-9778576
Number of Books Published per Year: eight to ten
Titles in Print: 32
Average Print Run: 2,500
Average Percentage Printed: Hardcover 25%, Paperback 75%
Average Price: $14/$24

Organization: Archipelago

Type: online
CLMP member: yes
Primary Editor/Contact Person: Katherine McNamara, Editor
Address: PO Box 2485
Charlottesville, VA 22902-2485
Web Site Adress: http://www.archipelago.org
Publishes: essays, fiction, nonfiction, poetry, reviews, art, translation, and audio
Editorial Focus: Intelligent writing for educated readers formed by more than one culture, knowing the world is larger than the US.
Submissions Policy: Query required first for electronic submission. Paper with SASE.
Simultaneous Subs: no
Reading Period: Year-round
Reporting Time: one to six months
Author Payment: none
Founded: 1997
Non Profit: yes
Paid Staff: one
Average Page Views per Month: 44,000
Average Unique Visitors per Month: 12,000
Frequency per Year: quarterly
Average Percentage of Pages per Category: Audio 100%

Organization: Arctos Press

Type: press
CLMP member: yes
Primary Editor/Contact Person: C.B. Follett
Address: P.O. Box 401
Sausalito, CA 94966
Web Site Address: http://members.aol.com/Runes
Publishes: poetry
Editorial Focus: Submit only when our call is out for an anthology. We do not consider unsolicited work
Representative Authors: David St. John, Lucille Clifton, and Li-Young Lee
Submissions Policy: Watch for announcements in Poets & Writers, etc. Then send up to five poems on theme
Simultaneous Submissions: yes
Reading Period: year-round
Reporting Time: two to four months
Author Payment: copies
Contests: see web site for guidelines.
Founded: 1996
Non Profit: yes

Paid Staff: zero
Unpaid Staff: four
Distributors: SPD
Wholesalers: Baker & Taylor
ISSN Number/ISBN Number: ISBN 0-9725384-
Number of Books Published per Year: one to three
Titles in Print: 16
Average Print Run: 1,200
Average Percentage Printed: Paperback 100%
Average Price: $14

Organization: Argonne House Press

Type: press
CLMP member: no
Primary Editor/Contact Person: R.D. Baker
Address: 1620 Argonne Place NW
Washington, DC 20009
Web Site Address: http://www.wordwrights.com
Publishes: essays, fiction, nonfiction, and poetry
Editorial Focus: We publish books by authors previously published in Wordwrights Magazine.
Representative Authors: Judith Podell, Grace Cavalieri, and Richard Peabody
Submissions Policy: We publish books by authors previously published in Wordwrights Magazine.
Simultaneous Submissions: yes
Reading Period: year-round
Reporting Time: three to six months
Author Payment: royalties
Founded: 1993
Non Profit: no
Paid Staff: zero
Unpaid Staff: 25
Distributors: Argonne House Press
Wholesalers: Argonne House Press
Number of Books Published per Year: 12
Titles in Print: 48
Average Percentage Printed: Paperback 10%, Chapbook 90%

Organization: Arkansas Review: A Journal of Delta Studies

Type: magazine
CLMP member: yes
Primary Editor/Contact Person: Tom Williams
Address: P.O. Box 1890
Arkansas State University
State University, AR 72467
Web Site Address: http://www.clt.astate.edu/arkre-

view
Publishes: essays, fiction, nonfiction, poetry, reviews, and art
Editorial Focus: Material that evokes or responds to the Mississippi River Delta region.
Representative Authors: Sterling Plumpp, Pia Erhardt, and George Singleton
Submissions Policy: All submissions must address the journal's regional focus.
Simultaneous Subs: yes
Reading Period: year-round
Reporting Time: one to four months
Author Payment: copies
Founded: 1996
Non Profit: yes
Paid Staff: five
Unpaid Staff: zero
ISSN Number/ISBN Number: ISSN 0022-8745
Total Circulation: 500
Paid Circulation: 250
Average Print Run: 550
Subscription Rate: Individual $20/Institution $20
Single Copy Price: $7.50
Current Volume/Issue: 34/3
Frequency per Year: triquarterly
Backfile Available: yes
Unsolicited Ms. Received: yes
% of Unsolicited Ms. Published per Year: 8%
Format: stapled
Size: H 11" W 8 1/2"
Average Pages: 88
Ads: yes

Organization: Arsenal Pulp Press

Type: press
CLMP member: yes
Primary Editor/Contact Person: Blaine Kyllo
Address: 341 Water Street, Suite 200
Vancouver, BC V6B 1B8
Web Site Address: http://www.arsenalpulp.com
Publishes: fiction, nonfiction, and art
Editorial Focus: Arsenal Pulp Press books subvert genres and speak with authority from the fringes of society.
Representative Authors: Hiromi Goto, Ivan Coyote, and Nalo Hopkinson
Submissions Policy: Query with sample and SASE (IRCs from outside Canada). Non-Canadians only in anthologies.
Simultaneous Submissions: yes

Reading Period: year-round
Reporting Time: three to four months
Author Payment: royalties and copies
Founded: 1971
Non Profit: no
Paid Staff: four
Unpaid Staff: zero
Distributors: US: Consortium, Canada: Jaguar, UK: Turnaround, Australia: Wakefield
Wholesalers: Ingram, Baker/Taylor, Koen, Bookazine et. al.
ISSN Number/ISBN Number: ISBN 0-888978; 1-55152
Number of Books Published per Year: 20
Titles in Print: 165
Average Percentage Printed: Paperback 100%

Organization: Arte Público Press

Type: press
CLMP member: yes
Primary Editor/Contact Person: Nicolas Kanellos
Address: University of Houston
452 Cullen Performance
Houston, TX 77204-2004
Web Site Address: http://www.artepublicopress.com
Publishes: fiction, nonfiction, poetry, and translation
Editorial Focus: To broaden America's vision of itself by increasing awareness and appreciation of Hispanic Culture.
Representative Authors: Pat Mora, Victor Villaseõor, and Diane Gonzales Betrand
Submissions Policy: available on our web site
Simultaneous Submissions: no
Reading Period: year-round
Reporting Time: three to six months
Author Payment: royalties, cash, and copies
Founded: 1979
Non Profit: yes
Paid Staff: 30
Unpaid Staff: two
Distributors: all the major book distributors
Wholesalers: all the major book wholesalers
ISSN Number/ISBN Number: ISBN 0-934770 and 1-55885
Number of Books Published per Year: 30
Titles in Print: 500
Average Print Run: 3,000
Average Percentage Printed: Hardcover 25%, Paperback 75%
Average Price: $10

Organization: Artful Dodge

Type: magazine
CLMP member: no
Primary Editor/Contact Person: Daniel Bourne
Address: Department of English
The College of Wooster
Wooster, OH 44691
Web Site Address: http://www.wooster.edu/artful-dodge
Publishes: essays, fiction, nonfiction, poetry, reviews, art, and translation
Editorial Focus: Along with the best new American work we can find, we're also open to literature in translation from all over the world.
Representative Authors: Dan Chaon, Tess Gallagher, and Charles Simic
Submissions Policy: SASE; no previously published work; no more than six poems or 30 pages of prose, though long poems are encouraged.
Simultaneous Submissions: yes
Reading Period: Year-round
Reporting Time: 3 to 12 months
Author Payment: cash and copies
Founded: 1979
Non Profit: yes
Paid Staff: one
Unpaid Staff: six
Distributors: DeBoer, Ubiquity
ISSN Number/ISBN Number: ISSN 0196-091X
Total Circulation: 900
Paid Circulation: 100
Average Print Run: 1,000
Subscription Rate: Individual $7/Institution $10
Single Copy Price: $7
Current Volume/Issue: Issue 44/5
Frequency per Year: 1
Backfile Available: yes
Unsolicited Ms. Received: yes
% of Unsolicited Ms. Published per Year: 2%
Format: perfect
Size: H 9" W 6"
Average Pages: 170
Ads: yes
Ad Rates: See web site for details.

Organization: Arts & Letters

Type: magazine
CLMP member: no
Primary Editor/Contact Person: Martin Lammon
Address: Campus Box 89
Georgia College & State University
Milledgeville, GA 31061
Web Site Address: http://al.gcsu.edu
Publishes: essays, fiction, nonfiction, poetry, reviews, art, and translation
Editorial Focus: The best contemporary literature available.
Representative Authors: Margaret Gibson, Dinty W. Moore, and Daniel Wallace
Submissions Policy: Poetry, fiction, creative nonfiction. Query first for other kinds of work. No electronic submissions. Include SASE.
Simultaneous Submissions: yes
Reading Period: 9/1 to 4/1
Reporting Time: three to six weeks
Author Payment: cash, copies, and subscription
Contests: Annual Arts & Letters prizes in fiction, poetry, and drama. $1,000 prize to each winner, publication, and visit to campus.
See web site for contest guidelines.
Founded: 1999
Non Profit: yes
Paid Staff: 18
Unpaid Staff: zero
ISSN Number/ISBN Number: ISSN 1523-4592
Total Circulation: 1,200
Paid Circulation: 900
Subscription Rate: Individual $15/Institution $15
Single Copy Price: $8
Current Volume/Issue: Issue 10
Frequency per Year: biannual
Backfile Available: yes
Unsolicited Ms. Received: yes
% of Unsolicited Ms. Published per Year: .5%
Format: perfect
Size: H 10" W 7"
Average Pages: 184
Ads: yes
Ad Rates: $50 for 6" x 9" full-page ad; contact al@gcsu.edu

Organization: ArtsEditor

Type: online
CLMP member: no
Primary Editor/Contact Person: S. Edward Burns
Address: Postal Box 381921
Cambridge, MA 02238
Web Site Address: http://www.ArtsEditor.com

Publishes: essays, nonfiction, poetry, reviews, and art

Editorial Focus: ArtsEditor develops and publishes articles in the areas of visual, performing, literary, film, and musical arts.

Representative Authors: Jeremy Perkins, Scott Ruescher, and Paul Jump

Submissions Policy: Send via the postal mail, a letter of introduction including a current resume, two writing samples, and three references.

Simultaneous Submissions: yes

Reading Period: Year-round

Reporting Time: two to three weeks

Author Payment: cash

Founded: 1999

Non Profit: no

Paid Staff: one

Unpaid Staff: seven

Average Page Views per Month: 32,000

Average Unique Visitors per Month: 6,000

Frequency per Year: annual 12

Publish Print Anthology: no

Average Percentage of Pages per Category: Fiction 15%, Nonfiction 10%,Poetry 5%, Reviews 45%, Essays 15%, Art 10%

Ad Rates: $475

See web site for details

Organization: Ascent

Type: magazine

CLMP member: yes

Primary Editor/Contact Person: W. Scott Olsen

Address: Dept. of English/Concordia College

901 8th St. S.

Moorhead, MN 56562

Web Site Address: http://www.cord.edu/dept/english/ascent/

Publishes: essays, fiction, nonfiction, and poetry

Editorial Focus: We are open to all styles and lengths.

Representative Authors: Peter Chilson, Edith Pearlman, and Kate Coles

Simultaneous Submissions: yes

Reading Period: Year-round

Reporting Time: one to four months

Author Payment: none, copies, and subscription

Founded: 1975

Non Profit: yes

Paid Staff: zero

Unpaid Staff: one

ISSN Number/ISBN Number: ISSN 0098-9363

Total Circulation: 750

Paid Circulation: 700

Subscription Rate: Individual $12/Institution $12

Single Copy Price: $5

Current Volume/Issue: 28/3

Frequency per Year: triquarterly

Backfile Available: yes

Unsolicited Ms. Received: yes

Format: perfect

Size: H 9" W 6"

Average Pages: 115

Ads: no

Organization: The Asian American Writers' Workshop

Type: press

CLMP member: no

Primary Editor/Contact Person: Noel Shaw

Address: 16 West 32nd St. #10A

New York, NY 10001

Web Site Address: http://www.aaww.org

Publishes: essays, fiction, nonfiction, poetry, reviews, art, and translation

Editorial Focus: We publish literature that focuses on underrepresented Asian American ethnic groups and topics absent from the mainstream.

Representative Authors: Ishle Yi Park, Ed Lin, and Eric Gamalinda

Submissions Policy: For submissions guidelines please go to http://www.aaww.org/publications/submissions.html

Simultaneous Submissions: yes

Reading Period: Year-round

Reporting Time: thee to four months

Author Payment: copies and subscription

Contests: See web site for Contest Guidelines.

Founded: 1991

Non Profit: yes

Paid Staff: six

Unpaid Staff: zero

Distributors: Temple University Press

Number of Books Published per Year: 1

Titles in Print: 9

Average Percentage Printed: Hardcover 10%, Paperback 90%

Organization: Asphodel Press

Type: press

CLMP member: no

Address: Master of Arts in Writing Program, Rowan

University
Glassboro, NJ 8028
Web Site Address:
http://www.rowan.edu/colleges/communication/current_students/student_orgs.htm
Publishes: essays, fiction, nonfiction, poetry, and art
Reading Period: Year-round
Reporting Time: one to two months
Author Payment: none
Founded: 1990
Non Profit: no
Average Percentage Printed: Hardcover 100%

Organization: Atlanta Review

Type: magazine
CLMP member: no
Primary Editor/Contact Person: Dan Veach
Address: Poetry Atlanta
P.O. Box 8248
Atlanta, GA 31106
Web Site Address: http://www.atlantareview.com/
Publishes: fiction and poetry
Editorial Focus: Quality poetry of genuine human appeal.
Representative Authors: Seamus Heaney, Derek Walcott, and Maxine Kumin
Submissions Policy: Up to five poems. SASE for reply.
Simultaneous Submissions: yes
Reading Period: Year-round
Reporting Time: two to six weeks
Author Payment: copies
Contests: International Poetry Competition; see website for guidelines.
Founded: 1994
Non Profit: yes
Paid Staff: zero
Unpaid Staff: four
Distributors: Ingram, Media Solutions, EBSCO, Blackwell
ISSN Number/ISBN Number: ISSN 1073-9696
Total Circulation: 2,000
Paid Circulation: 1,000
Subscription Rate: Individual $10/Institution $12
Single Copy Price: $6
Current Volume/Issue: 10/1
Frequency per Year: biannual
Backfile Available: yes
Unsolicited Ms. Received: yes
% of Unsolicited Ms. Published per Year: 1%

Format: perfect
Size: H 9" W 6"
Average Pages: 128
Ads: yes
Ad Rates: 500/250/125

Organization: Atomic Quill Press

Type: press
CLMP member: yes
Primary Editor/Contact Person: Timothy Dugdale
Address: P.O. Box 39859
Detroit, MI 48240
Web Site Address: http://press.atomicquill.com
Publishes: essays, fiction, nonfiction, and audio
Editorial Focus: We are interested in compelling fiction and nonfiction. We have an academic imprint and a spirituality imprint as well.
Representative Authors: Isaiah McKinnon, Lincoln Swain, and Bruce Henricksen
Submissions Policy: Previously published authors only. Please send a proposal and two sample chapters. No electronic submissions, please.
Simultaneous Submissions: yes
Reading Period: Year-round
Reporting Time: one to two months
Author Payment: royalties and copies
Founded: 2004
Non Profit: no
Paid Staff: one
Unpaid Staff: zero
Distributors: Ingram via Pathway Book Service
ISSN Number/ISBN Number: ISBN 09760535
Number of Books Published per Year: 4
Titles in Print: four
Average Print Run: 1,000
Average Percentage Printed: Paperback 100%
Average Price: $14.95

Organization: Aufgabe

Type: magazine
CLMP member: yes
Primary Editor/Contact Person: E. Tracy Grinnell
Address: Litmus Press
P.O. Box 25526
Brooklyn, NY 11202-5526
Web Site Address: http://www.litmuspress.org
Publishes: essays, fiction, poetry, reviews, art, and translation
Editorial Focus: Emerging and established American

writers working in the experimental tradition and writing/poetry in translation.

Representative Authors: Rosmarie Waldrop, Xue Di, and Jen Hofer

Submissions Policy: Submission via regular mail should be accompanied by cover letter and current contact information.

Simultaneous Submissions: yes

Reading Period: 1/1 to 3/1

Reporting Time: one to three months

Author Payment: copies

Founded: 2000

Non Profit: yes

Paid Staff: 0

Unpaid Staff: six

Distributors: SPD

ISSN Number/ISBN Number: ISSN 1532-5539

Total Circulation: 500

Paid Circulation: 50

Average Print Run: 500

Subscription Rate: Individual $20/Institution $30

Single Copy Price: $12

Current Volume/Issue: Issue 5

Frequency per Year: annual

Backfile Available: yes

Unsolicited Ms. Received: yes

% of Unsolicited Ms. Published per Year: 60%

Format: perfect

Size: H 9" W 6"

Average Pages: 250

Ads: no

Organization: Aunt Lute Books

Type: press

CLMP member: no

Primary Editor/Contact Person: Joan Pinkvoss, Exec. Director

Address: PO Box 410687

San Francisco, CA 94141

Web Site Address: www.auntlute.com

Publishes: fiction, nonfiction, and translation

Editorial Focus: Aunt Lute Books publishes writing by women whose voices are underrepresented (or not represented at all) in mainstream media.

Recent Awards Received: Silver Medal for Anthologies from ForeWord Magazine (2005), American Book Award (2002).

Representative Authors: Gloria Anzaldua, LeAnne Howe, and Audre Lorde

Submissions Policy: Submissions accepted by mail.

Please check web site or call for details.

Simultaneous Submissions: yes

Reading Period: year-round

Reporting Time: one to three months

Author Payment: royalties, cash, and copies

Founded: 1982

Non Profit: yes

Paid Staff: five

Unpaid Staff: two

Distributors: SPD, Consortium

ISSN Number/ISBN Number: ISBN 1-879960-

Number of Books Published per year: two to four

Titles in Print: 42

Average Print Run: varies

Average Percentage Printed: paperback 100%

Average Price: $11.95

Organization: Ausable Press

Type: press

CLMP member: yes

Primary Editor/Contact Person: Chase Twichell

Address: 1026 Hurricane Rd.

Keene, NY 12942

Web Site Address: http://www.ausablepress.org

Publishes: poetry

Editorial Focus: full-length collections of poetry

Recent Awards Received: Kate Tufts Discovery Award Finalist, National Book Critics Circle Award

Representative Authors: Laura Kasischke, Eric Pankey, and James Richardson

Submissions Policy: We accept unsolicited submissions during the month of June. Please see guidelines for details.

Simultaneous Submissions: yes

Reading Period: 6/1 to 6/30

Reporting Time: two to four months

Author Payment: royalties, cash, and copies

Founded: 1999

Non Profit: yes

Paid Staff: four

Unpaid Staff: one

Distributors: Consortium; SPD

Wholesalers: Amazon.com

ISSN Number/ISBN Number: ISBN 1-931337

Number of Books Published per Year: four

Titles in Print: 24

Average Print Run: 1,500

Average Percentage Printed: Paperback 100%

Average Price: $14

Organization: Authorlink.com

Type: online
CLMP member: no
Primary Editor/Contact Person: Doris Booth
Address: 3720 Millswood Dr.
Irving, TX 75062
Web Site Address: www.authorlink.com
Publishes: fiction, nonfiction, reviews, and audio
Editorial Focus: News, information, marketing for editors, agents, writers, readers
Simultaneous Submissions: yes
Reading Period: year-round
Reporting Time: one to six months
Author Payment: royalties
Founded: 1996
Non Profit: no
Paid Staff: five
Unpaid Staff: five
Distributors: LightningSource, Amazon.com
ISSN Number/ISBN Number: ISSN 1928704
Average Page Views per Month: 500,000
Average Unique Visitors per Month: 80,000
Frequency per year: weekly
Publish Print Anthology: no
Average Percentage of Pages per Category:
reviews 40%, essays 40%, Audio 20%
Ad Rates: see web site for details

Organization: Autumn House Press

Type: press
CLMP member: yes
Primary Editor/Contact Person: Michael Simms
Address: 87 1/2 Westwood St.
Pittsburgh, PA 15211
Web Site Address: http://autumnhouse.org
Publishes: fiction and poetry
Recent Awards Received: Maurice English Poetry Award (selected by Naomi Shihab Nye), Brockman-Campbell Award (Selected by Colette Inez)
Representative Authors: Ed Ochester, Gerald Stern, and Sue Ellen Thompson
Submissions Policy: We ask that all submissions come through our annual contest. Please see our web site for guidelines
Simultaneous Submissions: yes
Reading Period: year-round
Reporting Time: one to four months
Author Payment: royalties, cash, and copies
Contests: see web site for contest guidelines
Founded: 1998

Non Profit: yes
Paid Staff: three
Unpaid Staff: six
Wholesalers: Baker & Taylor, Book House, Coates, etc.
Number of Books Published per year: eight to ten
Titles in Print: 4
Average Print Run: 1,500
Average Percentage Printed: hardcover 10%, paperback 90%
Average Price: $14-$30

Organization: Avenue B

Type: press
CLMP member: no
Primary Editor/Contact Person: Stephen Ratcliffe
Address: P.O. Box 714
Bolinas, CA 94924
Web Site Address: http://durationpress.com
Publishes: poetry
Editorial Focus: contemporary poetry in "experimental/innovative" forms
Representative Authors: Clark Coolidge, Jackson Mac Low, and Ron Padgett
Submissions Policy: no unsolicited manuscripts
Simultaneous Submissions: no
Reading Period: Year-round
Reporting Time: two to three months
Author Payment: copies
Contests: no
Founded: 1986
Non Profit: yes
Distributors: SPD
ISSN Number/ISBN Number: none/0-939691-xx-x
Number of Books Published per Year: zero to one
Titles in Print: 14
Average Percentage Printed: Paperback 100%

Organization: Backwards City Review

Type: magazine
CLMP member: yes
Primary Editor/Contact Person: Gerry Canavan
Address: P.O. Box 41317
Greensboro, NC 27404-1317
Web Site Address: http://www.backwardscity.net
Publishes: fiction, nonfiction, poetry, and art
Editorial Focus: Prose, poetry, and comics. We favor literary and experimental work.
Recent Awards Received: One of Library Journal's

top ten new journals of 2004.
Representative Authors: Kurt Vonnegut, Chris Bachelder, and Kenneth Koch
Submissions Policy: See web site for full guidelines and contest details.
Simultaneous Submissions: yes
Reading Period: 09/06 to 05/07
Reporting Time: one to two months
Author Payment: copies
Contests: We have an annual literary contest and a chapbook contest with deadlines in March. Check the web site for details.
See web site for contest guidelines.
Founded: 2004
Non Profit: yes
Paid Staff: zero
Unpaid Staff: five
Total Circulation: 550
Paid Circulation: 300
Average Print Run: 750
Subscription Rate: Individual $12/Institution $20
Single Copy Price: $7
Current Volume/Issue: 4
Frequency per Year: two
Backfile Available: yes
Unsolicited Ms. Received: yes
% of Unsolicited Ms. Published per Year: 50%
Format: perfect
Size: H 9" W 6"
Average Pages: 128
Ads: yes
Ad Rates: E-mail ads@backwardscity.net for rates. Open to ad swaps.

Organization: The Backwaters Press

Type: press
CLMP member: yes
Primary Editor/Contact Person: Greg Kosmicki
Address: 3502 N. 52nd St.
Omaha, NE 68104-3506
Web Site Address:
http://www.thebackwaterspress.homestead.com
Publishes: poetry
Editorial Focus: Regional, Great Plains, Nebraska, women, poets submitted through open submissions.
Representative Authors: David Ray, John McKernan, and Susan Eisenberg
Submissions Policy: No longer running contests. Open to all submissions. Please see web site for guidelines or e-mail for guidelines.

Simultaneous Submissions: yes
Reading Period: Year-round
Reporting Time: one to two months
Author Payment: copies
Contests: None.
Founded: 1997
Non Profit: no
Paid Staff: zero
Unpaid Staff: two to six
Distributors: Amazon.com, Ingram, Baker & Taylor, Barnes and Noble
Wholesalers: Ingram, Baker & Taylor
Number of Books Published per Year: 10
Titles in Print: 40
Average Print Run: 300
Average Percentage Printed: Paperback 100%
Average Price: $14-$16

Organization: Ballista

Type: magazine
CLMP member: no
Primary Editor/Contact Person: Paul Neads
Address: Mucusart Publications, 6 Chiffon Way
Trinity Riverside
Gtr Manchester UK, UK M36AB
Web Site Address: www.mucusart.co.uk/ballista.htm
Publishes: fiction
Editorial Focus: short supernatural fiction; paranormal, horror, occult, psychological, macabre, Gothick -- even SF & dark fantasy considered
Representative Authors: H. Ann Dyess, Andrew Myers, and Rosie Lugosi
Submissions Policy: Email subs preferred up to 4,000 words. Flash fiction also considered.
Simultaneous Submissions: yes
Reading Period: year-round
Reporting Time: two to six weeks
Author Payment: cash and copies
Contests: Under consideration for 2007
See web site for contest guidelines
Founded: 2006
Non Profit: yes
Paid Staff: zero
Unpaid Staff: two
ISSN Number/ISBN Number: ISSN 1750-6646
Total Circulation: 100
Paid Circulation: 35
Average Print Run: 100
Subscription Rate: individual $16/institution $16
Single Copy Price: $5.50

Current Volume/Issue: 1/2
Frequency per year: biannual
Backfile Available: yes
Unsolicited MSS Received: yes
% of Unsolicited MSS Published per Year: 80%
Format: stapled
Size: H 8" W 5.5"
Average Pages: 52
Ads: no

Organization: Ballyhoo Stories

Type: magazine
CLMP member: yes
Primary Editor/Contact Person: Joshua Mandelbaum
Address: 18 Willoughby Ave., #3
Brooklyn, NY 11205
Web Site Address: http://www.ballyhoostories.com
Publishes: essays, fiction, and nonfiction
Submissions Policy: Visit http://www.ballyhoostories.com
Simultaneous Submissions: yes
Reading Period: Year-round
Reporting Time: two to three months
Author Payment: copies
Founded: 2005
Non Profit: no
Paid Staff: zero
Unpaid Staff: three
Distributors: Ingram
ISSN Number/ISBN Number: ISSN 1554-6950
Total Circulation: 400
Paid Circulation: 16
Average Print Run: 1,000
Subscription Rate: Individual $16/Institution $16
Single Copy Price: $8
Current Volume/Issue: 1/2
Frequency per Year: biannual
Backfile Available: yes
Unsolicited Ms. Received: yes
% of Unsolicited Ms. Published per Year: 100%
Format: perfect
Average Pages: 88
Ads: yes
Ad Rates: exchange

Organization: The Baltimore Review

Type: magazine
CLMP member: yes
Primary Editor/Contact Person: Barbara Diehl/Lalita Noronha
Address: P.O. Box 410
Riderwood, MD 21286
Web Site Address: http://www.baltimorewriters.org
Publishes: fiction and poetry
Editorial Focus: Literary fiction and poetry
Submissions Policy: Traditional and experimental prose and poetry. No themes, or previously published work.
Simultaneous Submissions: yes
Reading Period: Year-round
Reporting Time: two to four months
Author Payment: copies
Contests: See web site for contest guidelines.
Founded: 1980
Non Profit: yes
Paid Staff: no
Unpaid Staff: 10
Distributors: Ingram
ISSN Number/ISBN Number: ISSN 1092-5716
Total Circulation: 600
Paid Circulation: 100
Subscription Rate: Individual $14.75/Institution $14.75
Single Copy Price: $7.95
Current Volume/Issue: VII/2
Frequency per Year: biannual
Backfile Available: yes
Unsolicited Ms. Received: yes
% of Unsolicited Ms. Published per Year: 95%
Format: perfect
Size: H 9" W 6"
Average Pages: 128
Ads: no

Organization: Bamboo Ridge

Type: magazine
CLMP member: yes
Primary Editor/Contact Person: Eric Chock
Address: P.O. Box 61781
Honolulu, HI 96839-1781
Web Site Address: http://www.bambooridge.com
Publishes: essays, fiction, poetry, art, and audio
Editorial Focus: Literature by, for, and about the people of Hawaii.
Recent Awards Received: Pushcart Prize, O. Henry
Representative Authors: Juliet S. Kono, Lee Cataluna, and Ian MacMillan
Submissions Policy: 10 pages poetry, 20 pages

prose, double-spaced. SASE required.
Simultaneous Submissions: no
Reading Period: Year-round
Reporting Time: up to one year
Author Payment: cash, copies, and submission
Contests: Submissions selected for publication are automatically entered in the Bamboo Ridge Writing Contest. Cash awards.
Founded: 1978
Non Profit: yes
Paid Staff: four
Distributors: Booklines Hawaii, SPD
Wholesalers: Booklines Hawaii, SPD
ISSN Number/ISBN Number: 0733-0308/0-910043-XX-X
Total Circulation: 1,500
Paid Circulation: 500
Average Print Run: 2,000
Subscription Rate: Individual $25/2 issue/Institution $35/2-issue
Single Copy Price: $15
Current Volume/Issue: Issue #84
Frequency per Year: Biannual
Backfile Available: yes
Unsolicited Ms. Received: yes
Format: perfect
Size: H 9" W 6"
Average Pages: 300
Ads: yes
Ad Rates: $150 full page, $100 half page

Organization: The Barnwood Press

Type: press
CLMP member: yes
Primary Editor/Contact Person: Tom Koontz
Address: 4604 47th Ave S
Seattle, WA 98118-1824
Web Site Address: http://www.barnwoodpress.org
Publishes: poetry
Editorial Focus: books, chapbooks, and magazine of contemporary poetry
Representative Authors: Robert Bly, Martha Collins, and Peter Davis
Submissions Policy: Ten poems from a manuscript or one to three for the magazine. SASE and cover letter with brief bio.
Simultaneous Submissions: yes
Reading Period: Year-round
Reporting Time: one to three weeks
Author Payment: cash and copies

Founded: 1975
Non Profit: yes
Paid Staff: zero
Unpaid Staff: one
ISSN Number/ISBN Number: 1063-0929/935306
Number of Books Published per Year: 2
Titles in Print: 48
Average Print Run: 1,000
Average Percentage Printed: Paperback 50%, Chapbook 50%
Average Price: $12

Organization: Barnwood

Type: online
CLMP member: yes
Primary Editor/Contact Person: Tom Koontz
Address: 4604 47th Ave S
Seattle, WA 98118-1824
Web Site Address: http://www.barnwoodpress.org
Publishes: poetry
Editorial Focus: international contemporary poetry
Representative Authors: Luis Benitez, Joshua Cushing, and Marge Piercy
Submissions Policy: 1-3 poems with brief bio and SASE
Simultaneous Submissions: twa
Reading Period: Year-round
Reporting Time: one to three weeks
Author Payment: cash
Founded: 2002
Non Profit: yes
Paid Staff: zero
Unpaid Staff: one
ISSN Number/ISBN Number: ISSN 1063-0929
Number of Books Published per Year: 2
Average Page Views per Month: 1,600
Average Unique Visitors per Month: 350
Frequency: 52
Publish Print Anthology: No
Average Percentage of Pages per Category: Poetry 95%, Essays 4%, Art 1%
Ads: No

Organization: Barrelhouse Journal

Type: magazine
CLMP member: yes
Primary Editor/ Contact Person: Barelhouse Man
Address: 3500 Woodridge Ave.
Wheaton, MD 20902

Web Site Address: http://www.barrelhousemag.com
Publishes: fiction, nonfiction, poetry, and art.
Editorial Focus: Bridging the gap between serious art and popular culture.
Representative Authors: Steve Almond and Dave Barringer
Simultaneous Submissions: yes
Reading Period: Year-round
Reporting Time: three to four months
Author Payment: none
Contests: 1st Annual Barrelhouse nonfiction Essay Contest (over), winner featured in issue three.
Founded: 2004
Non Profit: yes
Paid Staff: zero
Unpaid Staff: five to eight
Total Circulation: 1 to 500
Paid Circulation:1 to 500.
Average Print Run: 500
Subscription Rate: individual $15/ institution same.
Single Copy Price: $9
Current Volume/ Issue: issue three
Frequency per year: biannual
Backfile Available: no
Unsolicited MSS Recieved: yes
% of Unsolicited MSS published per Year: 95%
Format: perfect

Organization: Barrow Street

Type: magazine
CLMP member: yes
Primary Editor/Contact Person: Patricia Carlin
Address: P.O. Box 1831
New York, NY 10156-1831
Web Site Address: http://barrowstreet.org
Publishes: essays, poetry, and reviews
Editorial Focus: To publish a literary journal dedicated to giving new and established authors a forum and to publish their highest quality work
Recent Awards Received: Work selected for inclusion in The Best American Poetry 2005
Representative Authors: Donald Revell, Lyn Hejinian, and Tony Hoagland
Submissions Policy: Submit up to five of your best, unpublished poems. Include a SASE and a short bio, please. We accept reviews/essays as well.
Simultaneous Submissions: yes
Reading Period: Year-round
Reporting Time: three to six months
Author Payment: copies

Contests: Barrow Street Annual Book Prize, deadline on or about July 1, for an unpublished manuscript of 48-70 pages of poetry.
See web site for contest guidelines.
Founded: 1998
Non Profit: yes
Paid Staff: one
Unpaid Staff: 30
Distributors: Ingram, Armadillo, DeBoer
ISSN Number/ISBN Number: 0-9728302/1522-2160
Total Circulation: 2,000
Paid Circulation: 350
Subscription Rate: Individual $15/Institution $8
Single Copy Price: $8
Current Volume/Issue: 8/16
Frequency per Year: biannual
Backfile Available: no
Unsolicited Ms. Received: yes
% of Unsolicited Ms. Published per Year: 10%
Format: perfect
Size: H 9" W 6"
Average Pages: 110
Ads: no

Organization: Barrytown/Station Hill Press

Type: press
CLMP member: no
Primary Editor/Contact Person: George Quasha or Jenny Fox
Address: 120 Station Hill Road
Barrytown, NY 12507
Web Site Address: http://www.stationhill.org
Publishes: essays, fiction, nonfiction, poetry, art, translation, and video
Editorial Focus: The focus is open and variable; unique or innovative contribution to language, poetics, art, thinking; bodywork; maybe other.
Representative Authors: Maurice Blanchot, Deane Juhan, and Rosmarie Waldrop
Submissions Policy: Letter of inquiry must precede submission. E-mail preferred: publishers@stationhill.org.
Simultaneous Submissions: yes
Reading Period: Year-round
Reporting Time:one to six months
Author Payment: royalties and copies
Founded: 1977
Non Profit: yes
Paid Staff: two

Unpaid Staff: two
Distributors: Midpoint
Wholesalers: Ingram, Baker & Taylor, SPD, etc.
ISSN Number/ISBN Number: ISBN 1-58177-/0-88268-
Number of Books Published per Year: 5+/-
Titles in Print: 300+/-
Average Print Run: 1,000
Average Percentage Printed: Paperback 100%
Average Price: $19.95

Organization: Bat City Review

Type: magazine
CLMP member: no
Primary Editor/Contact Person: Nathan Rostron
Address: U. of Texas at Austin, Dept. of English
1 University Station B50000
Austin, TX 78712
Web Site Address: www.batcityreview.com
Publishes: fiction, poetry, and art
Editorial Focus: Bat City Review publishes new poetry and prose that ranges from the elegantly formal to the brashly experimental.
Representative Authors: George Saunders, James Tate, and Dean Young
Submissions Policy: Send up to 6 poems or 25 pages of prose. Address submissions to appropriate genre editor and include a SASE for response.
Simultaneous Submissions: yes
Reading Period: 05/01 to 11/15
Reporting Time: three to six month
Author Payment: none
Founded: 2005
Non Profit: yes
Paid Staff: zero
Unpaid Staff: 25
Distributors: Ingram and DeBoer
ISSN Number/ISBN Number: ISSN 1555-7952
Total Circulation: 800
Paid Circulation: 80
Average Print Run: 1250
Subscription Rate: Individual $14/2 years/Institution $14
Single Copy Price: $8
Current Volume/Issue: 3/1
Frequency per Year: 1
Backfile Available: yes
Unsolicited Ms. Received: yes
% of Unsolicited Ms. Published per Year: 5%
Format: perfect

Size: H 9" W 6"
Average Pages: 190
Ads: yes
Ad Rates: $50-$100

Organization: Bathtub Gin

Type: magazine
CLMP member: no
Primary Editor/Contact Person: Christopher Harter
Address: P.O. Box 178
Erie, PA 16512
Web Site Address: http://www.pathwisepress.com
Publishes: essays, fiction, nonfiction, poetry, reviews, art, and translation
Editorial Focus: Publishes work not found in overly academic or post-Beat journals. Strong emphasis on imagery.
Representative Authors: Mark Terrill, Kell Robertson, and Mike James
Submissions Policy: four to five poems. Prose not over 3,000 words. Eclectic in the styles and works accepted.
Simultaneous Submissions: yes
Reading Period: 6/1 to 9/15
Reporting Time: four to six weeks
Author Payment: copies
Founded: 1997
Non Profit: yes
Paid Staff: zero
Unpaid Staff: one
Distributors: Via web site and catalogs
Wholesalers: Baker & Taylor
ISSN Number/ISBN Number: ISSN 1094-7965
Total Circulation: 300
Paid Circulation: 60
Average Print Run: 400
Subscription Rate: Individual $8/Institution $8
Single Copy Price: $5
Current Volume/Issue: Issue 18
Frequency per Year: biannual
Backfile Available: yes
Unsolicited Ms. Received: yes
% of Unsolicited Ms. Published per Year: 1%
Format: stapled
Size: H 8.5" W 5.5"
Average Pages: 52
Ads: yes
Ad Rates: See web site for details.

Organization: Bayou Magazine

Type: magazine
CLMP member: yes
Primary Editor/Contact Person: Joanna Leake, Editor
Address: University of New Orleans
Dept. of English/Lakefront
New Orleans, LA 70148
Web Site Address:
http://www.cola.uno.edu/cww/bayou.htm
Publishes: essays, fiction, nonfiction, poetry, reviews, and translation
Representative Authors: Virgil Suarez, Lyn Lifshin, and Tom Whalen
Submissions Policy: three to five poems. Fiction/nonfiction up to 7500 words. Short-shorts welcome. Cover letter, SASE. Always include email and phone.
Simultaneous Submissions: yes
Reading Period: year-round
Reporting Time: one to four months
Author Payment: copies
Contests: Nonfiction Bonanza. Runs from September 1-March 31. $10 fee/$250 prize. Details at http://www.cola.uno.edu/cww/bayou
Founded: 2000
Non Profit: yes
Paid Staff: zero
Unpaid Staff: 30
Total Circulation: 500
Paid Circulation: varies
Subscription Rate: Individual $15/Institution $15
Single Copy Price: $8
Current Volume/Issue: Issue #47
Frequency per Year: biannual
Backfile Available: yes
Unsolicited Ms. Received: yes
Format: perfect
Size: H 9" W 6"
Average Pages: 128

Organization: Beach Holme Publishing

Type: press
CLMP member: no
Primary Editor/Contact Person: Michael Carroll
Address: 1010-409 Granville St.
Vancouver, BC V6C 1T2
Web Site Address: http://www.beachholme.bc.ca
Publishes: fiction, nonfiction, and poetry
Editorial Focus: Adult literary fiction, nonfiction, and
poetry. Also publishes historical young adult fiction and juvenile books.
Representative Authors: Eric Walters, Marilyn Bowering, and David Watmough
Submissions Policy: Please submit with a SASE, first three chapters, synopsis, and author bio.
Simultaneous Submissions: yes
Reading Period: Year-round
Reporting Time: four to six months
Author Payment: royalties
Contests: none
See web site for contest guidelines.
Founded: 1971
Non Profit: no
Paid Staff: two
Unpaid Staff: zero
Distributors: LitDistCo
Wholesalers: LitDistCo
ISSN Number/ISBN Number: ISBN 088878
Number of Books Published per Year: 13
Titles in Print: 91
Average Percentage Printed: Paperback 100%

Organization: Beacon Press

Type: press
CLMP member: yes
Primary Editor/Contact Person: Hilary Jaccqmin
Address: 25 Beacon St.
Boston, MA 02108
Web Site Address: http://www.beacon.org
Publishes: essays, fiction, and nonfiction
Editorial Focus: Beacon Press, the non-profit publisher owned by the Unitarian Universalist Association, publishes scholarly works for the general reader.
Submissions Policy: If you would like Beacon Press to consider publishing your work, please submit a letter of inquiry, proposal, and current CV.
Simultaneous Submissions: yes
Reading Period: Year-round
Reporting Time: 8 to 12 weeks
Author Payment: royalties and copies
Founded: 1854
Non Profit: yes
Paid Staff: 26
Unpaid Staff: five
Distributors: Houghton Mifflin Co.
Number of Books Published per Year: 65
Titles in Print: 500
Average Print Run: Varies
Average Percentage Printed: Hardcover 60%,

Paperback 40%
Average Price: Varies

Organization: The Bear Deluxe Magazine

Type: magazine
CLMP member: no
Primary Editor/Contact Person: Tom Webb
Address: P.O. Box 10342
Portland, OR 97296
Web Site Address: http://www.orlo.org
Publishes: essays, fiction, nonfiction, poetry, reviews, and art
Editorial Focus: We take a pretty open-minded, creative look at environmental/landscape issues and how those often overlap with culture.
Recent Awards Received: Oregon arts Comission, Print Magazine Literary Arts, Inc. Portland Monthly Regional Arts and Culture Council
Representative Authors: Gina Ochsner, David James Duncan, and Amy Roe
Submissions Policy: See guides at http://www.orlo.org. 4,000 word max for fiction and essay. 50 line max on poetry. Best to query on nonfiction.
Simultaneous Submissions: yes
Reading Period: Year-round
Reporting Time: two to six months
Author Payment: cash and subscription
Founded: 1993
Non Profit: yes
Paid Staff: .five
Unpaid Staff: eight
Distributors: in house
ISSN Number/ISBN Number: ISSN 1074-2700
Total Circulation: 44,000
Paid Circulation: 500
Average Print Run: 20,000
Subscription Rate: Individual $16/Institution $16
Single Copy Price: $3
Current Volume/Issue: Issue 22
Frequency per Year: four
Backfile Available: yes
Unsolicited Ms. Received: yes
% of Unsolicited Ms. Published per Year: 10%
Format: magazine format, saddle stitched
Size: H 11" W 9"
Average Pages: 48
Ads: yes
Ad Rates: $800 full-page, black and white, color

available
See web site for details

Organization: Bear Parade

Type: press
CLMP member: yes
Primary Editor/Contact Person: Gene Morgan
Address: 2700 Albany St. #1E
Houston, TX 77006
Web Site Address: http://bearparade.com
Publishes: fiction and poetry
Editorial Focus: internet specific books of poetry and fiction.
Representative Authors: Tao Lin, Ellen Kennedy, and Matthew Rohrer
Submissions Policy: 10-15 short works.
Simultaneous Submissions: yes
Reading Period: year-round
Reporting Time: one to three weeks
Author Payment: cash
Founded: 2006
Non Profit: yes
Paid Staff: zero
Unpaid Staff: four
Number of Books Published per year: one to two
Titles in Print: five
Average Print Run: 40,000
Average Percentage Printed: other 100%

Organization: Bear Star Press

Type: press
CLMP member: yes
Primary Editor/Contact Person: Beth Spencer
Address: 185 Hollow Oak Dr.
Cohasset, CA 95973
Web Site Address: http://www.bearstarpress.com
Publishes: poetry
Editorial Focus: We publish the best poetry (& occasional short fiction) we can attract from US writers living west of the central time zone.
Representative Authors: Lynne Knight, Arlitia Jones, and Manuel Paul; Lopez.
Submissions Policy: Send 50-65 pages of poems, not counting sec seps, front matter, etc. Any theme, subject. New writers especially welcome!
Simultaneous Submissions: yes
Reading Period: 9/1 to 11/30
Reporting Time: one to four months
Author Payment: cash and copies

Contests: See web site for contest guidelines.
Founded: 1996
Non Profit: no
Paid Staff: zero
Unpaid Staff: three
Distributors: SPD
ISSN Number/ISBN Number: ISBN 0-9179607...
Number of Books Published per Year: two
Titles in Print: 18
Average Print Run: 750
Average Percentage Printed: Paperback 80%,
Chapbook 20%
Average Price: $12-$18

Organization: Beginnings Publishing

Type: magazine
CLMP member: no
Primary Editor/Contact Person: Jenine Boisits,
Editor/Publisher
Address: P.O. Box 92
Shirley, NY 11967
Web Site Address: http://www.scbeginnings.com
Publishes: fiction and poetry
Editorial Focus: We cater strictly to the novice writer.
We believe in giving the new writer a chance to be
heard.
Representative Authors: Ben Ogle, Beverly Jo
Dittmer, and Johnathon Madden
Submissions Policy: Only one submission at a time,
please. Cover letters are appreciated but not
required.
Simultaneous Submissions: yes
Reading Period: Year-round
Reporting Time: 6 to 12 weeks
Author Payment: copies
Contests: Four contests per year with substantial
cash prizes for fiction and poetry.
See web site for contest guidelines.
Founded: 1999
Non Profit: yes
Paid Staff: five
Unpaid Staff: 10
Distributors: Ingram
Total Circulation: 2,000
Paid Circulation: 400
Subscription Rate: $14
Single Copy Price: $5.50
Current Volume/Issue: Fall
Frequency per Year: three
Backfile Available: yes

Unsolicited Ms. Received: yes
% of Unsolicited Ms. Published per Year: 100%
Format: perfect
Size: H 8" W 11"
Average Pages: 48
Ads: yes
Ad Rates: $200 full page, $50 business card
See web site for details.

Organization: Belladonna Books

Type: press
CLMP member: yes
Primary Editor/Contact Person: Erica
Kaufman/Rachel Levitsky
Address: 925 Bergen Street, Ste. 405
Brooklyn, NY 11238
Web Site Address:
http://www.belladonabooks.blogspot.com
Publishes: poetry, and translation
Editorial Focus: Belladonna promotes the work of
avant garde women writers of diverse backgrounds
and cultures.
Representative Authors: Alice Notley, Renee
Gladman, and Mei-Mei Berssenbrugge
Simultaneous Submissions: no
Reading Period: year-round
Reporting Time: six to twelvemonths
Author Payment: cash and copies
Founded: 1999
Non Profit: yes
Paid Staff: zero
Unpaid Staff: three
Number of Books Published per Year: 20
Titles in Print: 50
Average Print Run: 126
Average Percentage Printed: Paperback 20%,
Chapbook 75%, Other 5%
Average Price: $4, $12

Organization: Bellevue Literary Press

Type: press
CLMP member: yes
Primary Editor/Contact Person: Erika Goldman
Address: Department of Medicine
NYU School of Medicine
550 First Avenue, OBV A640
New York, NY 10016
Web Site Address:
Publishes: fiction and nonfiction

Editorial Focus: Literary and authoritative works that range the intersection of the sciences and the arts
Submissions Policy: Solicited and unsolicited manuscripts
Simultaneous Submissions: yes
Reading Period: year-round
Reporting Time: one to six weeks
Author Payment: royalties
Founded: 2006
Non Profit: yes
Paid Staff: one
Unpaid Staff: one
Distributors: CBSD (Consortium)
Number of Books Published per year: eight
Titles in Print: four
Average Print Run: 3,000
Average Percentage Printed: hardcover 50%, paperback %50
Average Price: $25

Organization: The Bellevue Literary Review

Type:: magazine
CLMP member: yes
Primary Editor/Contact Person: Danielle Ofri
Address: NYU School of Medicine, Dept. of Medicine
550 First Ave.-OBV-612
New York, NY 10016
Web Site Address: http://www.BLReview.org
Publishes: essays, fiction, nonfiction, and poetry
Editorial Focus: The BLR examines the human condition through the prism of health, healing, illness, disease, the mind and body.
Recent Awards Received: Grants from NYSCA, NY Council for the Humanities, CLMP, private foundations.
Representative Authors: Abraham Verghese, Sheila Kohler, and Rafael Campo
Submissions Policy: three poems, prose up to 5,000 words. Submit online at http://www.BLReview.org
Simultaneous Submissions: yes
Reading Period: year-round
Reporting Time: two to five months
Author Payment: copies and submission
Contests: Annual contest for superlative writing related to health, healing, illness, disease, mind and body; see Web Site for Contest Guidelines.
Founded: 2000
Non Profit: yes
Paid Staff: one
Unpaid Staff: six

Distributors: Ingram, DeBoer, Ubiquity
ISSN Number/ISBN Number: 1537-5048/with each issue
Total Circulation: 3,500
Paid Circulation: 2,000
Average Print Run: 5,000
Subscription Rate: Individual $12/Institution $18
Single Copy Price: $7
Current Volume/Issue: 6/2
Frequency per Year: biannual
Backfile Available: yes
Unsolicited Ms. Received: yes
% of Unsolicited Ms. Published per Year: 3%
Format: perfect
Size: H 9" W 6"
Average Pages: 160-200
Ads: yes
Ad Rates: exchange ads and paid ads; see web site for details.

Organization: Bellingham Review

Type: magazine
CLMP member: yes
Primary Editor/Contact Person: Brenda Miller, Editor-in-Chief
Address: Mail Stop 9053
Western Washington U.
Bellingham, WA 98225
Web Site Address: http://www.wwu.edu/~bhreview/
Publishes: essays, fiction, nonfiction, and poetry
Representative Authors: Albert Goldbarth, Patricia Vigderman, and Meghan Daum
Submissions Policy: Prose under 9,000 words, three to five poems. Must be previously unpublished in North America. We do not accept e-submissions.
Simultaneous Submissions: yes
Reading Period: 9/15 to 2/1
Reporting Time: one to six months
Author Payment: cash, copies, and subscription
Contests: See web site for contest guidelines.
Founded: 1977
Non Profit: yes
Paid Staff: two
Unpaid Staff: one to six
ISSN Number/ISBN Number: ISSN 0734-2934
Total Circulation: 2,000
Paid Circulation: 1,480
Average Print Run: 2,000
Subscription Rate: Individual $14/Institution $28
Single Copy Price: $7

Current Volume/Issue: 30/59
Frequency per Year: biannual
Backfile Available: yes
Unsolicited Ms. Received: yes
Format: perfect
Size: H 8 3/4"W 6"
Average Pages: 150-200
Ads: yes

Organization: Beloit Poetry Journal
Type: magazine
CLMP member: yes
Primary Editor/Contact Person: John Rosenwald
and Lee Sharkey
Address: P.O. Box 151
Farmington, ME 04938
Web Site Address: http://www.bpj.org
Publishes: poetry and reviews
Editorial Focus: We publish poets without regard to
their reputation. Our tastes are eclectic, but we're
looking for quickened language.
Recent Awards Received: 5 BPJ poems in Best
American Poetry 2007, 7 in Poetry Daily anthology, 1
in Best New Poets
Representative Authors: Susan Tichy, Karl Elder, and
Albert Goldbarth
Submissions Policy: Five pages or so of poetry,
unless it's a long poem. No cover letter required.
Simultaneous Submissions: no
Reading Period: Year-round
Reporting Time: 1 to 14 weeks
Author Payment: copies
Contests: No contests, but we award annual $3,000
Chad Walsh Prize to the strongest poem we've published.
Founded: 1950
Non Profit: yes
Paid Staff: zero
Unpaid Staff: seven
Distributors: DeBoer, Ubiquity, Media Solutions
Wholesalers: Subscription services: EBSCO, Swets,
Harrassowitz
ISSN Number/ISBN Number: ISSN 0005-8661
Total Circulation: 1,100
Paid Circulation: 623
Average Print Run: 1,300
Subscription Rate: Individual $18/Institution $23
Single Copy Price: $5
Current Volume/Issue: 56/1
Frequency per Year: quarterly
Backfile Available: yes

Unsolicited Ms. Received: yes
% of Unsolicited Ms. Published per Year: 0.5%
Format: stapled
Size: H 9" W 6"
Average Pages: 48
Ads: no

Organization: The Berkeley Fiction Review
Type: magazine
CLMP member: yes
Primary Editor/Contact Person: Rhoda Piland
Address: 10 B Eshleman Hall
University of California
Berkeley, CA 94720
Web Site Address::
http://www.ocf.berkeley.edu/~bfr/
Publishes: fiction
Editorial Focus: Short (less than 10,000 words) fic-
tion, particularly experimental work
Submissions Policy: No e-mail submissions accept-
ed. Please do not send submissions in standard busi-
ness size envelopes. 9x12 envelopes preferred.
Simultaneous Submissions: yes
Reading Period: Year-round
Reporting Time: 1 to 6 months
Author Payment: copies
Contests: Sudden Fiction Contest (1,000 words or
less)
See Web Site for Contest Guidelines.
Founded: 1983
Non Profit: yes
Paid Staff: zero
Unpaid Staff: 30
Distributors: Ubiquity Publishing
ISSN Number/ISBN Number: ISSN 1087-7053
Total Circulation: 300
Paid Circulation: none
Average Print Run: 300
Subscription Rate: Individual $8.50/Institution $8.50
Single Copy Price: $8.50
Current Volume/Issue: Issue 28
Frequency per Year: annual
Backfile Available: yes
Unsolicited Ms. Received: yes
% of Unsolicited Ms. Published per Year: 2%
Format: perfect
Ads: yes
Ad Rates: e-mail if interested

Organization: Big Bridge

Type: online
CLMP member: no
Primary Editor/Contact Person: Michael Rothenberg
Address: 16083 Fern Way
Guerneville, CA 95446
Web Site Address: http://www.bigbridge.org
Publishes: essays, fiction, nonfiction, poetry, reviews, art, translation, and audio
Editorial Focus: Language, sonnets, haiku, spoken word, experimental, workshop agit-smut poetry. We want art of whimsy, passion, and urgency.
Representative Authors: Philip Whalen, Joanne Kyger, and David Meltzer
Submissions Policy: We only accept online submission to walterblue@bigbridge.org. Paste work into body of e-mail and include word doc attachment.
Simultaneous Submissions: yes
Reading Period: Year-round
Reporting Time: one to six weeks
Author Payment: none
Founded: 1997
Non Profit: no
Paid Staff: zero
Unpaid Staff: two
Distributors: online
Average Page Views per Month: 40,000
Average Unique Visitors per Month: 800
Publish Print Anthology: no
Average Percentage of Pages per Category: Fiction 15%, Nonfiction 5%, Poetry 40%, Reviews 3%, Essays 5%, Art 30%, Translation 1%, Audio 1%
Ads: no

Organization: Big Muddy: Journal of the Mississippi River Valley

Type: magazine
CLMP member: yes
Primary Editor/Contact Person: Dr. Susan Swartwout
Address: MS 2650, One University Plaza
Cape Girardeau, MO 63701
Web Site Address: www6.semo.edu/university-press/bigmuddy/index.htm
Publishes: essays, fiction, nonfiction, poetry, reviews, art, and translation.
Recent Awards Received: Small Press Review Pic
Representative Authors: Colleen McElroy, Stephen Graham Jones, and Kevin Stein

Submissions Policy: high-quality, previously unpublished mss.; SASE if you wish your manuscript to be returned
Simultaneous Submissions: yes
Reading Period: year-round
Reporting Time: 8 to 10 weeks
Author Payment: copies
Contests: Mighty River Short-story Contest, Wilda Hearne Flash Fiction Contest; see website for guidelines
Founded: 2000
Non Profit: yes
Paid Staff: 2
Unpaid Staff: 3
ISSN Number/ISBN Number: ISSN 1532-9860
Total Circulation: 300
Paid Circulation: 150
Average Print Run: 400
Subscription Rate: Individual $20/Institution $20
Single Copy Price: $8+ship
Current Volume/Issue: 7/1
Frequency: 2
Backfile Available: yes
Unsolicited Ms. Received: yes
% of Unsolicited Ms. Published per Year: 7%
Format: perfect
Size: H 8.5" W 5.5"
Average Pages: 150
Ads: yes
Ad Rates: contact us

Organization: Bilingual Review Press

Type: press
CLMP member: no
Primary Editor/Contact Person: Karen Van Hooft
Address: Hispanic Research Center
Arizona State University, Box 875303
Tempe, AZ 85287-5303
Web Site Address: http://www.asu.edu/brp
Publishes: fiction, nonfiction, poetry, art, and translation
Editorial Focus: Literary works, criticism, and art books by or about US Hispanics. English, Spanish, and bilingual editions.
Representative Authors: Ana Castillo, Lourdes Vazquez, and Stella Pope Duarte
Submissions Policy: See web site for details.
Simultaneous Submissions: no
Reading Period: Year-round
Reporting Time: one to two months

Author Payment: royalties and copies
Founded: 1973
Non Profit: yes
Paid Staff: six
Unpaid Staff: zero
Distributors: Ingram, Baker & Taylor, SPD
Titles in Print: 150
Average Print Run: 5,000
Average Percentage Printed: Hardcover 5%, Paperback 95%
Average Price: $16

Organization: Bilingual Review

Type: magazine
CLMP member: no
Primary Editor/Contact Person: Karen Van Hooft
Address: Hispanic Research Center
Arizona State University, Box 872702
Tempe, AZ 85287-2702
Web Site Address: http://www.asu.edu/brp
Publishes: essays, fiction, poetry, and translation
Editorial Focus: Bilingual Review focuses on bilingualism, bilingual education and ethnic scholarship, and features Hispanic creative writing.
Submissions Policy: see our web site.
Simultaneous Submissions: no
Reading Period: year-round
Reporting Time: one to two months
Author Payment: copies
Founded: 1973
Non Profit: yes
Paid Staff: six
Unpaid Staff: zero
Distributors: Distributed directly by publisher.
ISSN Number/ISBN Number: ISSN 0094-5366
Total Circulation: 1,000
Paid Circulation: 500
Subscription Rate: Individual $25/Institution $25
Single Copy Price: $12-28
Current Volume/Issue: 26/1
Frequency per Year: triquarterly
Backfile Available: yes
Unsolicited Ms. Received: yes
Format: perfect
Size: H 7" W 10"
Average Pages: 90
Ads: yes

Organization: The Bitter Oleander

Type: magazine
CLMP member: yes
Primary Editor/Contact Person: Paul B. Roth
Address: 4983 Tall Oaks Dr.
Fayetteville, NY 13066-9776
Web Site Address: http://www.bitteroleander.com
Publishes: essays, fiction, poetry, and translation
Editorial Focus: TBO publishes poetry and fiction in pursuit of the imagination unfolding specific aspects of the concrete particular.
Recent Awards Received: Recognized as "Best Literary Journal" by Public Radio's Tenth Annual "Excellence in Print" Award
Representative Authors: Anthony Seidman, Christine Boyka Kluge, and George Kalamaras.
Submissions Policy: e-mail submissions allowed only from outside the U.S. All others use SASE. No response without a SASE.
Simultaneous Submissions: yes
Reading Period: 8/1 to 6/30
Reporting Time: one to two months
Author Payment: copies
Contests: The Frances Locke Memorial Poetry Award See web site for Contest Guidelines.
Founded: 1974
Non Profit: no
Paid Staff: zero
Unpaid Staff: one
Distributors: Ingram, SPD
ISSN Number/ISBN Number: ISSN 1087-8483
Total Circulation: 1,500
Paid Circulation: 200
Average Print Run: 2,000
Subscription Rate: Individual $15/Institution $12
Single Copy Price: $8
Current Volume/Issue: 12/1
Frequency per Year: biannual
Backfile Available: yes
Unsolicited Ms. Received: yes
% of Unsolicited Ms. Published per Year: .1%
Format: perfect
Size: H 9" W 6"
Average Pages: 128
Ads: yes
Ad Rates: whole: $200 half: $125; See web site for details.

Organization: The Bitter Oleander Press

Type: press
CLMP member: yes
Primary Editor/Contact Person: Paul B. Roth
Address: 4983 Tall Oaks Dr.
Fayetteville, NY 13066-9776
Web Site Address: http://www.bitteroleander.com
Publishes: poetry
Editorial Focus: Aside from our journal, our books represent the total imaginative work of a single poet.
Representative Authors: Anthony Seidman, George Kalamaras, and Christine Boyka Kluge
Submissions Policy: Ask with a SASE or via e-mail whether we are looking for manuscripts.
Simultaneous Submissions: yes
Reading Period: Year-round
Reporting Time: one to two months
Author Payment: copies
Founded: 1974
Non Profit: no
Paid Staff: one
Unpaid Staff: zero
Distributors: Ingram
ISSN Number/ISBN Number: ISBN 0-9664358
Number of Books Published per Year: 2
Titles in Print: 12
Average Print Run: 500
Average Percentage Printed: Paperback 100%
Average Price: $16

Organization: BkMk Press

Type: press
CLMP member: yes
Primary Editor/Contact Person: Ben Furnish, Managing Editor
Address: University of Missouri-Kansas City
5101 Rockhill Road
Kansas City, MO 64110
Web Site Address: http://www.umkc.edu/bkmk
Publishes: essays, fiction, and poetry
Editorial Focus: Contemporary writers
Recent Awards Received: William Rockhill Nelson Award/poetry, recent finalists: ForeWord BOTY, Paterson Poetry Prize, Society of Midland Authors
Representative Authors: Marilyn Kallet, Rane Arroyo, and Billy Lombardo
Submissions Policy: Poetry, short fiction, creative nonfiction
Simultaneous Submissions: yes

Reading Period: 1/1 to 6/30
Reporting Time: six to eight months
Author Payment: royalties
Contests: see web site for contest guidelines.
Founded: 1971
Non Profit: yes
Paid Staff: two
Unpaid Staff: four
Distributors: SPD
Wholesalers: Baker & Taylor
ISSN Number/ISBN Number: ISBN 0-933532, 1-886157
Number of Books Published per Year: 4
Titles in Print: 100
Average Print Run: 800
Average Percentage Printed: Paperback 100%
Average Price: $13.95

Organization: Black Clock

Type: magazine
CLMP member: no
Primary Editor/Contact Person: Steve Erickson/Dwayne Moser
Address: CalArts
24700 McBean Parkway
Valencia, CA 91355
Web Site Address: http://www.blackclock.org
Publishes: essays, fiction, nonfiction, and poetry
Editorial Focus: Featuring works by some of the most prominent writers of our time, talented regional authors, and selected CalArts students.
Representative Authors: David Foster Wallace, Joanna Scott, and Jonathan Lethem
Submissions Policy: At this point we are not accepting unsolicited submissions.
Author Payment: cash
Founded: 2004
Non Profit: yes
Paid Staff: three
Unpaid Staff: three
Wholesalers: BigTop Newsstand Services
ISSN Number/ISBN Number: ISSN 7447058384
Total Circulation: 2,500
Paid Circulation: 120
Subscription Rate: Individual $20/Institution $20
Single Copy Price: $12
Current Volume/Issue: Issue one
Frequency per Year: biannual
Backfile Available: no
Unsolicited Ms. Received: no

Format: Smythe sewn, very nice
Size: H 12" W 9"
Average Pages: 160
Ads: yes
Ad Rates: See web site for details.

Organization: Black Issues Book Review

Type: magazine
CLMP member: no
Primary Editor/Contact Person: Angela P. Dodson
Address: Empire State Building
350 Fifth Ave., Ste. 1522
New York, NY 10118-0165
Web Site Address: http://www.bibookreview.com
Publishes: reviews
Simultaneous Submissions: no
Reading Period: Year-round
Reporting Time: one to two months
Author Payment: none
Founded: 1999
Non Profit: no
Paid Staff: 14
Unpaid Staff: three
ISSN Number/ISBN Number: ISSN 1522-0524
Paid Circulation: 18,000
Average Print Run: 75,000
Subscription Rate: Individual $14.95/Institution $14.95
Single Copy Price: $4.95
Current Volume/Issue: S/O/5
Frequency: bimonthly
Backfile Available: yes
Unsolicited Ms. Received: no
Format: stapled
Size: H 11" W 8"
Average Pages: 64
Ads: yes

Organization: Black Lawrence Press

Type: press
CLMP member: no
Primary Editor/Contact Person: Colleen Ryor
Address: P.O. Box 46
Watertown, NY 13601
Web Site Address:
http://www.blacklawrencepress.com
Publishes: fiction, nonfiction, poetry, and translation
Editorial Focus: Contemporary fiction, poetry, politics, culture, and some translation (German and French

only).
Representative Authors: D.C. Berry, Frank Matagrano, and James Owens
Submissions Policy: see web site for guidelines.
Simultaneous Submissions: yes
Reading Period: year-round
Reporting Time: one to four months
Author Payment: royalties and copies
Contests: The St. Lawrence Book Award for a first collection: $1,000 prize and publication. The 46er Prize for Short Fiction: $500; see web site for contest guidelines.
Founded: 2003
Non Profit: yes
Paid Staff: one
Unpaid Staff: one
Number of Books Published per Year: two to four
Average Percentage Printed: Paperback 100%

Organization: Black Ocean

Type: press
CLMP member: yes
Primary Editor/Contact Person: Janaka Stucky
Address: P.O. Box 990962
Boston, MA 02199
Web Site Address: www.blackocean.org
Publishes: essays, fiction, nonfiction, and poetry
Editorial Focus: Writing that instantly grabs the reader, is compelling, exhibits originality and skill and contains powerful imagery.
Representative Authors: Zachary Schomburg, Paula Cisewski, and Carrie O. Adams
Submissions Policy: Black Ocean does not accept unsolicited submissions except during the open reading period during the months of May and June.
Simultaneous Submissions: yes
Reading Period: 5/1 tp 6/30
Reporting Time: two to three months
Author Payment: royalties and copies
Founded: 2004
Non Profit: no
Paid Staff: one
Unpaid Staff: four
Distributors: Small Press Districbution
Number of Books Published per Year: one to three
Titles in Print: 9
Average Print Run: 1,200
Average Percentage Printed: Paperback 75%, Chapbook 25%
Average Price: $11.95

Organization: Black Square Editions/Hammer Books

Type: press
CLMP member:no
Primary Editor/Contact Person: John Yau
Address: 1200 Broadway (3C)
New York, NY 10001
Web Site Address: http://blacksquareeditions.com
Publishes: essays, fiction, nonfiction, poetry, art, and translation
Editorial Focus: Innovative poetry and fiction, essays about postwar and contemporary art, translations of the above.
Representative Authors: Gary Lutz, Jacques Dupin, and Albert Mobilio
Submissions Policy: queries preferred.
Simultaneous Submissions: yes
Reading Period: Year-round
Reporting Time: four to six months
Author Payment: copies
Contests: no
Founded: 1999
Non Profit: yes
Paid Staff: zero
Unpaid Staff: three
Distributors: SPD and PGW
ISSN Number/ISBN Number: ISBN 0-9744065, 0-9712485
Number of Books Published per Year: two to five
Titles in Print: 17
Average Percentage Printed: Paperback 75%, Chapbook 20%, Other 5%
Backfile Available: yes

Organization: Black Warrior Review

Type: magazine
CLMP member: yes
Primary Editor/Contact Person: Alissa Nutting, Editor
Address: Box 862936
Tuscaloosa, AL 35486-0027
Web Site Address: http://webdelsol.com/bwr
Publishes: essays, fiction, nonfiction, poetry, art, and translation
Editorial Focus: The freshest work out there, by new and established writers.
Representative Authors: Bob Hicok, Rachel Zucker, and Gary Fincke
Submissions Policy: Send five to seven poems. Fiction up to 7,500 words; short-shorts welcome.

Address to appropriate genre editor. No e-mail submissions.
Simultaneous Submissions: yes
Reading Period: year-round
Reporting Time: one to five months
Author Payment: cash and subscription
Contests: annual fiction and poetry contests-deadline Oct. 1st; three poems or one story per entry; fee $15 includes 1-yr subscription
Founded: 1974
Non Profit: yes
Paid Staff: eight
Unpaid Staff: 30
Distributors: Ingram
Wholesalers: Ingram
ISSN Number/ISBN Number: ISSN 0193-6301
Total Circulation: 2,000
Paid Circulation: 500
Average Print Run: 2,500
Subscription Rate: Individual $16/Institution $20
Single Copy Price: $10
Current Volume/Issue: 32/2
Frequency: biannual
Backfile Available: yes
Unsolicited Ms. Received: yes
% of Unsolicited Ms. Published per Year: 1%
Format: perfect
Size: H 9" W 6"
Average Pages: 168
Ads: yes
Ad Rates: contact bwr@ua.edu for details

Organization: Black Widow Press

Type: press
CLMP member:no
Primary Editor/Contact Person: Joe Phillips
Address: 134 Boylston Street
Boston, MA 02116
Web Site Address: www.blackwidowpress.com
Publishes: fiction, poetry, and translation
Editorial Focus: Modern poetry and translation, primarily from the French. Especially late 19th century through the Dadaists and Surrealists.
Representative Authors: Paul Eluard, Tristan Tzara, and Clayton Eshleman
Submissions Policy: None. Only referrals and publishers program.
Simultaneous Submissions: no
Reading Period: year-round
Reporting Time: six to eight weeks

Author Payment: royalties, cash, and copies
Founded: 2005
Non Profit: no
Paid Staff: three
Unpaid Staff: two
Distributors: biblio/MBN
Wholesalers: All
Number of Books Published per Year: six to eight
Titles in Print: 8
Average Print Run: 2,000
Average Percentage Printed: Paperback 100%
Average Price: $18.95

Organization: Blackbird

Type: online
CLMP member: no
Primary Editor/Contact Person: Kate Beles, Associate Editor
Address: P.O. Box 843082
Richmond, VA 23284-3082
Web Site Address: http://www.blackbird.vcu.edu
Publishes: essays, fiction, nonfiction, poetry, reviews, art, translation, and audio
Representative Authors: Gerald Stern, Norman Dubie, and Lily Tuck
Submissions Policy: We accept submissions in fiction and poetry only. All other material is solicited.
Simultaneous Submissions: yes
Reading Period: 9/15 to 4/15
Reporting Time: three to six months
Author Payment: cash
Founded: 2001
Non Profit: yes
Paid Staff: three
Unpaid Staff: eight
ISSN Number/ISBN Number: ISSN 1540-3068
Average Page Views per Month: 400,000
Average Unique Visitors per Month: 40,000
Frequency: biannual
Publish Print Anthology: no
Average Percentage of Pages per Category: Fiction 25%, Nonfiction 5%, Poetry 25%, Reviews 5%, Essays 5%, Art 15%, Translation 5%, Audio 15%
Ads: no

Organization: Blithe House Quarterly

Type: online
CLMP member: no
Primary Editor/Contact Person: Aldo Alvarez
Address: 5100 N. Winchester #3
Chicago, IL 60640
Web Site Address: http://www.blithe.com
Publishes: fiction and translation
Editorial Focus: BHQ features a diversity of new short stories by emerging and established gay, lesbian, bisexual, and transgendered authors.
Submissions Policy: Stories should be between 1,500 and 7,500 words in length. We ask for First Serial Rights—all rights return to the author on publication. We do not consider previously published material. We only accept submissions via e-mail. For more details, submission guidelines are available on site.
Simultaneous Submissions: yes
Reading Period: 9/1 to 12/1
Reporting Time: two to four months
Author Payment: none
Founded: 1997
Non Profit: yes
Paid Staff: zero
Unpaid Staff: six
Average Page Views per Month: 50,000
Average Unique Visitors per Month: 8,000
Frequency per Year: four
Average Percentage of Pages per Category: Fiction 98%, Translation 2%
Ads: no

Organization: Blood and Thunder

Type: magazine
CLMP member: no
Address: 941 Stanton L Young Blvd.
BSEB Room 100
Oklahoma City, OK 73190
Web Site Address: http://www.bloodandthunder.org
Publishes: essays, fiction, poetry, and art
Reading Period: year-round
Reporting Time: one to two months
Author Payment: none
Founded: 2000
Non Profit: no
Backfile Available: yes

Organization: The Blood Moon Productions

Type: press
CLMP member: no
Primary Editor/Contact Person: Danforth Prince
Address: 75 Saint Marks Place
Staten Island, NY 10301
Web Site Address:
http://www.BloodMoonProductions.com
Publishes: fiction and nonfiction
Editorial Focus: Controversial but carefully researched Hollywood biographies. Potboiling novels for sexually sophisticated adults.
Representative Authors: Darwin Porter and Danforth Prince
Submissions Policy: Author's contact info, a plot synopsis, two to three sample chapters.
Simultaneous Submissions: yes
Reading Period: Year-round
Reporting Time: one to three months
Author Payment: royalties and cash
Founded: 1997
Non Profit: no
Paid Staff: four
Unpaid Staff: two
Distributors: Bookazine, Ingram, Baker & Taylor, Turnaround
ISSN Number/ISBN Number: ISBN 09668030 and 9748118
Number of Books Published per Year: three
Titles in Print: eight
Average Percentage Printed: Hardcover 20%, Paperback 80%

Organization: Bloom: Queer Fiction, Art, Poetry and More

Type: magazine
CLMP member: yes
Primary Editor/Contact Person: Charles Flowers
Address: P.O. Box 1231
Old Chelsea Station
New York, NY 10013
Web Site Address: http://www.bloommagazine.org
Publishes: essays, fiction, nonfiction, poetry, art, and translation
Editorial Focus: Authors must identify as queer, but Bloom does not discriminate against the imagination.
Representative Authors: Adrienne Rich, Andrew Holleran, and Carl Phillips
Submissions Policy: Send as attachments to:

asklambda@earthlink.net
Simultaneous Submissions: yes
Reading Period: Year-round
Reporting Time: five to six months
Author Payment: copies and subscription
Founded: 2003
Non Profit: yes
Paid Staff: 0
Unpaid Staff: four
Distributors: Bookazine
ISSN Number/ISBN Number: ISSN 1550-3291
Total Circulation: 1,000
Paid Circulation: 300
Average Print Run: 1,000
Subscription Rate: Individual $16/Institution $40
Single Copy Price: $10
Current Volume/Issue: 3/1
Frequency per Year: biannual
Backfile Available: yes
Unsolicited Ms. Received: yes
% of Unsolicited Ms. Published per Year: 20%
Format: perfect
Size: H 8" W 5"
Average Pages: 200
Ads: yes
Ad Rates: $100 1/2 page, $175 full page, $250 bookmark flap

Organization: The Blotter Magazine, Inc.

Type: magazine
CLMP member: yes
Primary Editor/Contact Person: John Pence, editor
Address: 1010 Hale St.
Durham, NC 27705
Web Site Address: www.blotterrag.com
Publishes: essays, fiction, nonfiction, poetry, and art
Editorial Focus: The Blotter Magazine exists to nurture underground, outsider literature and art and to provide it to a wide audience.
Representative Authors: Ron Cooper, Denver Hill, and mckenzee
Submissions Policy: submissions? open. bring it on. mermaid@blotterrag.com
Simultaneous Submissions: yes
Reading Period: year-round
Reporting Time: three to four weeks
Author Payment: copies
Founded: 2003
Non Profit: yes

Paid Staff: zero
Unpaid Staff: six
ISSN Number/ISBN Number: ISSN 1549-0351
Total Circulation: 6,400
Paid Circulation: 100
Average Print Run: 6,500
Subscription Rate: individual $25/institution $25
Single Copy Price: $1
Current Volume/Issue: issue 50
Frequency per year: 12
Backfile Available: yes
Unsolicited MSS Received: yes
% of Unsolicited MSS Published per Year: 30%
Format: stapled
Size: H 8.5" W 12"
Average Pages: 16
Ads: yes
Ad Rates: see web site for details.

Organization: Blue Collar Review

Type: magazine
CLMP member: no
Primary Editor/Contact Person: Al Markowitz
Address: P.O. Box 11417
Norfolk, VA 23517
Web Site Address: http://partisanpress.org
Publishes: essays, poetry, and reviews
Editorial Focus: Our mission is the preservation, expansion, and promotion of the literature of our working class, primarily poetry, which might not find a place in profit-driven publishing channels.
Representative Authors: Marge Piercy, Robert Edwards, and Jim Daniels
Submissions Policy: Submissions should have name and address on each page. SASE for response. Prose limit 2,500 words. Send no more than four poems
Simultaneous Submissions: no
Reading Period: year-round
Reporting Time: four to six weeks
Author Payment: copies
Contests: see web site for contest guidelines.
Founded: 1997
Non Profit: yes
Paid Staff: zero
Unpaid Staff: four
ISSN Number/ISBN Number: ISSN 1535-136X
Total Circulation: 520
Paid Circulation: 350
Average Print Run: 650
Subscription Rate: Individual $15/Institution $15

Single Copy Price: $5
Current Volume/Issue: 6/4
Frequency per Year: quarterly
Backfile Available: yes
Unsolicited Ms. Received: yes
% of Unsolicited Ms. Published per Year: 5%
Format: stapled
Size: H 8.5" W 5.5"
Average Pages: 60
Ads: yes
Ad Rates: $40 half page $70 full page

Organization: Blue Cubicle Press

Type: press
CLMP member: no
Primary Editor/Contact Person: David LaBounty
Address: PO Box 250382
Plano, Tx 75025-0382
Web Site Address: www.bluecubiclepress.com
Publishes: fiction
Editorial Focus: Supporting writers trapped in the daily grind.
Submissions Policy: We are looking for novelettes, 8,000 to 12,000 word stories, and novels about the workplace.
Simultaneous Submissions: yes
Reading Period: year-round
Reporting Time: four to six weeks
Author Payment: royalties, cash, and copies
Founded: 2004
Non Profit: no
Paid Staff: one
Unpaid Staff: zero
ISSN Number/ISBN Number: ISBN 0-9745900
Number of Books Published per year: two
Titles in Print: five
Average Print Run: 1,000
Average Percentage Printed: paperback 100%
Average Price: $8

Organization: blue lion books

Type: press
CLMP member: no
Primary Editor/Contact Person: Peter Ganick
Address: 181 Edgemont Ave.
West Hartford, CT 06110-1005
Web Site Address: www.cafepress.com/bluelion-books66
Publishes: fiction and poetry

Editorial Focus: experimental poetry and fiction. manuscripts 250pp+ from new or established writers. print-on-demandproduction.
Recent Awards Received: none yet.
Representative Authors: Jukka-Pekka Kervinen, Jim Leftwich, and J Hayes Hurley
Submissions Policy: mss. 250+. send poetry to Peter Ganick, address above. Send fiction to J Hayes Hurley, 367 Waterville Rd, Avon CT 06001.
Simultaneous Submissions: yes
Reading Period: year-round
Reporting Time: four to six weeks
Author Payment: none
Contests: none at the moment.
Founded: 2005
Non Profit: yes
Paid Staff: zero
Unpaid Staff: three
Distributors: www.cafepress.com/bluelionbooks66
ISSN Number/ISBN Number: ISSN 952-5645
Number of Books Published per year: 15
Titles in Print: 15
Average Print Run: varies
Average Percentage Printed: paperback 100%
Average Price: $22

Organization: Blue Mesa Review

Type: magazine
CLMP member: no
Primary Editor/Contact Person: Julie Shigekuni
Address: Dept. of English, Humanities Bldg. University of New Mexico Albuquerque, NM 87131-1106
Web Site Address: http://www.unm.edu/~bluemesa/
Publishes: essays, fiction, nonfiction, poetry, and reviews
Submissions Policy: Four poems or six pages of poetry, or one story fewer than 7,500 words, or one work of creative nonfiction
Simultaneous Submissions: yes
Reading Period: 7/1 to 10/1
Reporting Time: three to six months
Author Payment: copies
Founded: 1989
Non Profit: yes
Paid Staff: five
Unpaid Staff: 15
Distributors: University of New Mexico Press
ISSN Number/ISBN Number: ISBN 1-885290-15-2
Total Circulation: 1,000

Paid Circulation: 100
Subscription Rate: Individual $12/Institution $12
Single Copy Price: $12
Current Volume/Issue: Issue 16
Frequency per Year: annual
Backfile Available: yes
Unsolicited Ms. Received: yes
% of Unsolicited Ms. Published per Year: 90%
Format: perfect
Size: H 9" W 6"
Average Pages: 250
Ads: yes

Organization: The Blue Moon Review

Type: online
CLMP member: no
Primary Editor/Contact Person: Doug Lawson, Executive Editor
Address: 14313 Winter Ridge Ln. Midlothian, VA 23113
Web Site Address: http://thebluemoon.com
Publishes: fiction
Editorial Focus: Narrative fiction up to 4,500 words.
Submissions Policy: We only accept submissions via e-mail. Please review web site for all guidelines, current needs, and submission addresses.
Simultaneous Submissions: no
Reading Period: year-round
Reporting Time: one to four months
Author Payment: none
Founded: 1994
Non Profit: yes
Paid Staff: zero
Unpaid Staff: one
ISSN Number/ISBN Number: ISSN 1079-042x
Average Page Views per Month: 34,000
Average Unique Visitors per Month: 17,500
Frequency: biannual
Publish Print Anthology: no
Average Percentage of Pages per Category: Fiction 100%
Ads: no

Organization: Blueline

Type: magazine
CLMP member: yes
Primary Editor/Contact Person: Rick Henry
Address: 122 Morey Hall, Dept. of English 125 Morey Hall

Potsdam, NY 13676
Web Site Address:
http://www.potsdam.edu/ENGL/Blueline/default
Publishes: essays, fiction, nonfiction, poetry, reviews, and art
Editorial Focus: Literary work relating to the Adirondacks and regions similar in geography and spirit, or on the shaping influence of nature.
Representative Authors: M.J. Iuppa, Susan J. Newell, and Elizabeth Biller Chapman
Submissions Policy: Submissions must not have been previously published. Simultaneous submissions as long as they are announced as such.
Simultaneous Submissions: yes
Reading Period: 9/1 to 11/30
Reporting Time: two to three months
Author Payment: copies
Founded: 1979
Non Profit: yes
Paid Staff: zero
Unpaid Staff: six
Distributors: EBSCO
Total Circulation: 400
Paid Circulation: 250
Average Print Run: 400
Subscription Rate: Individual $10/Institution $10
Single Copy Price: $10
Current Volume/Issue: 27/XXVI
Frequency per Year: annual
Backfile Available: yes
Unsolicited Ms. Received: yes
% of Unsolicited Ms. Published per Year: 100%
Format: perfect
Size: H 9" W 6"
Average Pages: 200
Ads: no

Organization: BOA Editions, Ltd.

Type: press
CLMP member: yes
Primary Editor/Contact Person: Thom Ward
Address: 250 North Goodman Street
Suite 306
Rochester, NY 14607
Web Site Address: http://www.boaeditions.org
Publishes: fiction, poetry, and translation
Editorial Focus: Contemporary American poetry and poetry in translation and prose on poetry and poetics, as well as literary fiction.
Recent Awards Received: National Book Award for

Poetry
Representative Authors: Lucille Clifton, Li-Young Lee, and Naomi Shihab Nye
Submissions Policy: look at our submissions policies on our web site
Simultaneous Submissions: yes
Reading Period: 01/1 to 03/31
Reporting Time: three to four months
Author Payment: royalties and copies
Contests: see web site for guidelines.
Founded: 1976
Non Profit: yes
Paid Staff: three
Unpaid Staff: one
Distributors: Consortium
ISSN Number/ISBN Number: ISBN 1-929918
Number of Books Published per Year: 11
Titles in Print: 160
Average Print Run: 1,500
Average Percentage Printed: Hardcover 30%, Paperback 70%
Average Price: $15.50

Organization: Bogg: A Journal of Contemporary Writing

Type: magazine
CLMP member: yes
Primary Editor/Contact Person: John Elsberg
Address: 422 N. Cleveland St.
Arlington, VA 22201
Publishes: essays, fiction, poetry, reviews, and art
Editorial Focus: Bogg tries to capture current trends, combining innovative US work with a leavening of British and Commonwealth writing
Representative Authors: Ann Menebroker, Gary Blankenburg, and Kathy Ernst
Submissions Policy: Poems can be single-spaced; double-spaced copy for fiction, interviews, reviews. Stamped return envelope required.
Simultaneous Submissions: no
Reading Period: year-round
Reporting Time: one to two weeks
Author Payment: copies
Founded: 1968
Non Profit: no
Paid Staff: zero
Unpaid Staff: three
ISSN Number/ISBN Number: ISSN 0882-648X
Total Circulation: 800
Paid Circulation: 350

Average Print Run: 850
Subscription Rate: Individual $15/Institution $20
Single Copy Price: $6
Current Volume/Issue: Issue 73/4
Frequency per Year: 2
Backfile Available: yes
Unsolicited Ms. Received: yes
% of Unsolicited Ms. Published per Year: 1%
Format: stapled
Size: H 9" W 6"
Average Pages: 56
Ads: no

Organization: BOMB Magazine

Type: magazine
CLMP member: yes
Primary Editor/Contact Person: Nell McClister
Address: 594 Broadway, Ste. 905
80 Hanson Place #703
New York, NY 11217
Web Site Address: http://www.bombsite.com/
Publishes: essays, fiction, nonfiction, poetry, reviews, art, and translation
Editorial Focus: Peer-to-Peer interviews with artists, writers, musicians, architects, playwrights, filmmakers, and actors.
Representative Authors: Eric Bogosian, Peter Carey, and Laurie Anderson
Simultaneous Submissions: yes
Reading Period: year-round
Reporting Time: four to six months
Author Payment: subscription
Founded: 1981
Non Profit: yes
Paid Staff: six
Unpaid Staff: three
Distributors: BigTop Newsstands, a division of the IPA
ISSN Number/ISBN Number: ISSN 0743-3204
Total Circulation: >55,000
Subscription Rate: Individual $18/Institution $24
Single Copy Price: $4.95
Current Volume/Issue: Issue 85
Frequency per Year: quarterly
Backfile Available: yes
Unsolicited Ms. Received: yes
Format: perfect
Size: H 10.75" W 8.25"
Average Pages: 112
Ads: yes
Ad Rates: See web site for details.

Organization: Bombay Gin

Type: magazine
CLMP member: yes
Primary Editor/Contact Person: Amy Catanzano
Address: Naropa University/Writing and Poetics
2130 Arapahoe Avenue
Boulder, CO 80302
Web Site Address:
www.naropa.edu/academics/graduate/writingpoetics/mfa
Publishes: essays, fiction, nonfiction, poetry, reviews, art, translation, and audio
Editorial Focus: Bombay Gin, literary journal of The Jack Kerouac School of Disembodied Poetics, publishes experimental and hybrid texts.
Representative Authors: Anne Waldman, Amiri Baraka, and Brian Evenson
Submissions Policy: Submission guidelines are out in September of each year and can be found on the website.
Simultaneous Submissions: yes
Reading Period: 9/07 to 5/08
Reporting Time: two to three months
Author Payment: copies
Contests: see website for guidelines
Founded: 1974
Non Profit: yes
Paid Staff: two
Unpaid Staff: ten
Total Circulation: 500
Paid Circulation: 10
Subscription Rate: Individual $31/Institution $31
Single Copy Price: $12
Current Volume/Issue: Issue 33
Frequency per Year: one
Backfile Available: yes
Unsolicited Ms. Received: yes
% of Unsolicited Ms. Published per Year: 10%
Format: perfect
Average Pages: 200
Ads: yes
Ad Rates: see web site for details.

Organization: Book/Mark Small Press Quarterly Review

Type: magazine
CLMP member: yes
Primary Editor/Contact Person: Mindy Kronenberg
Address: P.O. Box 516
Miller Place, NY 11764

Publishes: essays and reviews
Editorial Focus: To bring attention to
the variety of books by small press publishers. We are
eclectic and include the arts and popular culture.
Representative Authors: Richard Kostelanetz,
Thaddeus Rutkowski, and Jodee Stanley
Submissions Policy: We accept freelance submissions and prefer reviews that are empathetic to the genre or subject of the book, citing excerpts.
Simultaneous Submissions: yes
Reading Period: year-round
Reporting Time: two to six weeks
Author Payment: copies and subscription
Founded: 1994
Non Profit: yes
Paid Staff: zero
Unpaid Staff: 15
Distributors: Suffolk Cooperative Library System
ISSN Number/ISBN Number: ISSN 1081-3209
Total Circulation: 850
Paid Circulation: 125
Average Print Run: 1,000
Subscription Rate: Individual $12/Institution $15
Single Copy Price: $3
Current Volume/Issue: 11/3
Frequency per Year: quarterly
Backfile Available: yes
Unsolicited Ms. Received: yes
% of Unsolicited Ms. Published per Year: 50%
Format: stapled
Size: H 11" W 8 1/2"
Average Pages: 12
Ads: yes
Ad Rates: $75/quarter page, $135/column

Organization: Born Magazine

Type: online
CLMP member: no
Primary Editor/Contact Person: Anmarie Trimble
Address: P.O. Box 1313
Portland, OR 97215
Web Site Address: http://www.bornmagazine.org
Publishes: essays, fiction, nonfiction, poetry, art, translation, and audio
Editorial Focus: Experimental collaborations between writers and interactive artists.
Representative Authors: Michele Glazer, Major Jackson, and Joyelle McSweeney
Submissions Policy: three to five poems or one to two short prose works (e-mailed MS Word documents preferred). Accepts both new and previously published works.
Simultaneous Submissions: no
Reading Period: year-round
Reporting Time: three to five months
Author Payment: none
Founded: 1997
Non Profit: yes
Paid Staff: zero
Unpaid Staff: 11
Average Page Views per Month: 300,000
Average Unique Visitors per Month: 35,000
Frequency per Year: quarterly
Publish Print Anthology: no
Average Percentage of Pages per Category: Fiction 8%, Poetry 40%, Essays 1%, Art 50%, Translation 1%
Ads: no

Organization: Boston Review

Type: magazine
CLMP member: yes
Primary Editor/Contact Person: Deborah Chasman
Address: 35 Medford St. Ste. 302
Somerville, MA 02143
Web Site Address: http://bostonreview.net
Publishes: essays, fiction, nonfiction, poetry, and reviews
Editorial Focus: Public policy, progressive politics and political science, culture, art, poetry, writing, film, mind/brain, book reviews
Representative Authors: Susie Linfield, Elaine Scarry, and Bin Ramke
Simultaneous Submissions: yes
Reading Period: year-round
Reporting Time: one to three months
Author Payment: cash and copies
Contests: Annual poetry and short story contests. Winners of each receive publication in Boston Review plus $1,000 prize; see website for guidelines
Founded: 1975
Non Profit: yes
Paid Staff: four
Unpaid Staff: one to three
Distributors: IPA/Disticor
ISSN Number/ISBN Number: ISSN 0734-2306
Total Circulation: 10,000
Paid Circulation: 7,000
Average Print Run: 10,000
Subscription Rate: Individual $20/Institution $40
Single Copy Price: $5

Current Volume/Issue: 31/3
Frequency: bimonthly
Backfile Available: yes
Unsolicited Ms. Received: yes
% of Unsolicited Ms. Published per Year: 1%
Format: tabloid
Size: H 14" W 10"
Average Pages: 60
Ads: yes
Ad Rates: see web site for details.

Organization: bottle rockets: a collection of short verse

Type: magazine
CLMP member: no
Primary Editor/Contact Person: Stanford M. Forrester
Address: P.O. Box 189
Windsor, CT 06095
Web Site Address: http://www.geocities.com/bottle-rockets_99
Publishes: poetry
Editorial Focus: We are primarily a haiku magazine that publishes non 5-7-5 and related haiku forms
Representative Authors: Lawrence Ferlinghetti, Cid Corman, and Vincent Tripi
Submissions Policy: please visit website for the complete list of policies.
Simultaneous Submissions: no
Reading Period: year-round
Reporting Time: two to four weeks
Author Payment: cash
Founded: 1998
Non Profit: yes
Paid Staff: zero
Unpaid Staff: four
Distributors: bottle rockets press
ISSN Number/ISBN Number: ISSN 1930-9406
Total Circulation: 300
Paid Circulation: 275
Average Print Run: 300
Subscription Rate: Individual $16/Institution $16
Single Copy Price: $8
Current Volume/Issue: 9/2
Frequency: 2
Backfile Available: no
Unsolicited Ms. Received: yes
% of Unsolicited Ms. Published per Year: 95%
Format: perfect
Size: H 11" W 5.5"

Average Pages: 90
Ads: no

Organization: Bottom Dog Press

Type: press
CLMP member: yes
Primary Editor/Contact Person: Larry Smith
Address: P.O. Box 425
Huron, OH 44839
Web Site Address: http://members.aol.com/lsmith-dog/bottomdog
Publishes: essays, fiction, nonfiction, and poetry
Editorial Focus: Midwest-Working Class-Buddhist-Performance Poets
Representative Authors: Jim Ray Daniels, Ray McNiece, and Richard Hague
Simultaneous Submissions: yes
Reading Period: year-round
Reporting Time: one to three months
Author Payment: royalties and copies
Founded: 1985
Non Profit: yes
Paid Staff: one
Unpaid Staff: one
Distributors: SPD, Baker & Taylor, direct from publisher
ISSN Number/ISBN Number: ISBN 978-1-933964
Number of Books Published per Year: 5
Titles in Print: 105
Average Print Run: 1,000
Average Percentage Printed: Hardcover 10%, Paperback 85%, Other 5%
Average Price: $14

Organization: Bound Off

Type: online
CLMP member: yes
Primary Editor/Contact Person: Kelly Shriver
Address: 3900 Cottage Grove Ave.
Cedar Rapids, IA 52403
Web Site Address: http://boundoff.com
Publishes: fiction
Editorial Focus: Short literary fiction in audio format. Distributed as podcast via web site, iTunes and RSS feeds.
Representative Authors: Mark Budman, Steven Gullion, and Vincent Louis Carrella
Submissions Policy: 250-2,500 words; please read guidelines available on web site.
Simultaneous Submissions: yes

Reading Period: year-round
Reporting Time: one to two months
Author Payment: cash
Founded: 2006
Non Profit: no
Paid Staff: zero
Unpaid Staff: four
Average Page Views per Month: 1,400
Average Unique Visitors per Month: 1,000
Frequency per year: monthly
Publish Print Anthology: no
Average Percentage of Pages per Category: Fiction 100%
Ads: no

Organization: The Briar Cliff Review

Type: magazine
CLMP member: yes
Primary Editor/Contact Person: Tricia Currans-Sheehan
Address: Briar Cliff University
3303 Rebecca St.
Sioux City, IA 51104-0100
Web Site Address: http://briarcliff.edu/bcreview
Publishes: essays, fiction, nonfiction, poetry, reviews, and art
Editorial Focus: The Briar Cliff Review is an eclectic literary/cultural magazine focusing on, but not limited to, Siouxland writers/subjects
Representative Authors: Josip Novakovich, Lee Ann Roripaugh, and Brian Bedard
Submissions Policy: Unpublished work. No e-mail submissions. Send cover letter with SASE.
Simultaneous Submissions: yes
Reading Period: 8/1 to 11/1
Reporting Time: three to five months
Author Payment: copies
Contests: see web site for guidelines.
Founded: 1989
Non Profit: yes
Paid Staff: 0
Unpaid Staff: 7-12
Distributors: Tricia Currans-Sheehan and Briar Cliff Bookstore
ISSN Number/ISBN Number: 1550-0926/0
Total Circulation: 750
Paid Circulation: 100
Average Print Run: 750
Subscription Rate: Individual $12/Institution $12
Single Copy Price: $12

Current Volume/Issue: Issue 18
Frequency per Year: 1
Backfile Available: yes
Unsolicited Ms. Received: yes
% of Unsolicited Ms. Published per Year: 10%
Format: perfect
Size: H 11" W 81/2"
Average Pages: 120
Ads: no

Organization: Brick Books

Type: press
CLMP member: no
Primary Editor/Contact Person: Kitty Lewis
Address: PO Box 20081, 431 Boler Road
London, ON N6K4G6
Web Site Address: http://www.brickbooks.ca
Publishes: poetry
Editorial Focus: Brick Books was founded in 1975 and publishes books by emerging and established Canadian authors
Recent Awards Received: Winner of Griffin Poetry Prize by Margaret Avison in 2002; Karen Solie nominated in 2001 and Phil Hall in 2006
Representative Authors: Jan Zwicky, Margaret Avison, and Helen Humphreys
Submissions Policy: Canadian authors only; check guidelines at www.brickbooks.ca
Simultaneous Submissions: no
Reading Period: 1/1 to 4/30
Reporting Time: two to three months
Author Payment: copies
Founded: 1975
Non Profit: no
Paid Staff: 1.5
Unpaid Staff: seven
Distributors: LitDistCo
ISSN Number/ISBN Number: ISSN 1894078, 0919626
Number of Books Published per Year: seven
Titles in Print: 115
Average Print Run: 750
Average Percentage Printed: Paperback 100%
Average Price: $18 Cdn

Organization: Brick, A Literary Journal

Type: magazine
CLMP member: no

Primary Editor/Contact Person: Nadia Szilvassy
Address: PO Box 537, Stn. Q
Toronto, ON M4T 2M5
Web Site Address: http://www.brickmag.com
Publishes: essays, fiction, nonfiction, poetry, reviews, art, and translation
Editorial Focus: We are interested in literary nonfiction essays on the writing life and the arts in general
Simultaneous Submissions: yes
Reading Period: year-round
Reporting Time: one to nine months
Author Payment: cash and copies
Founded: 1977
Non Profit: no
Paid Staff: three
Unpaid Staff: five plus
Distributors: CMPA, Ingram, Pan Macmillan (Australia)
ISSN Number/ISBN Number: ISSN 0382-8565
Total Circulation: 4,500
Paid Circulation: 1,000
Average Print Run: 5,000
Subscription Rate: Individual $41 USD/Institution $28 USD
Single Copy Price: $14
Current Volume/Issue: Issue 79
Frequency: biannual
Backfile Available: yes
Unsolicited Ms. Received: yes
% of Unsolicited Ms. Published per Year: 5%
Format: perfect
Average Pages: 150
Ads: yes
Ad Rates: see website for details

Organization: BrickHouse Books, Inc.

Type: press
CLMP member: no
Primary Editor/Contact Person: Clarinda Harriss
Address: 306 suffolk Rd.
Baltimore, MD 21218
Web Site Address: http://www.towson.edu/~harriss/!bhbwebs.ite/bhb.htm
Publishes: fiction, nonfiction, and poetry
Editorial Focus: excellent, literate, original poetry: any form, any subject
Recent Awards Received: Outstanding Small Press (Dustbooks); Richard Fein won Maurice English Award; Jan-Mitchell Sherrill nominated for National Book Award
Representative Authors: Richard Fein, Jan-Mitchell Sherrill, and Joyce Brown

Submissions Policy: Submit complete ms bet. 48-96 pp.; no electronic submissions; $10 reading fee
Simultaneous Submissions: yes
Reading Period: year-round
Reporting Time: six to twelve months
Author Payment: copies
Contests: Stonewall Chapbook Competition-every two years-$25 entry fee; 30 pages max, gay/lesbian bisexual themes; deadline Aug 15
Founded: 1970
Non Profit: yes
Paid Staff: zero
Unpaid Staff: four
Distributors: Itascabooks.com
ISSN Number/ISBN Number: ISSN 0 932616
Number of Books Published per year: four
Titles in Print: 70+
Average Print Run: 500
Average Percentage Printed: paperback 100%
Average Price: $15

Organization: Bright Hill Press

Type: press
CLMP member: yes
Primary Editor/Contact Person: Bertha Rogers
Address: P.O. Box 193
94 Church St.
Treadwell, NY 13846-0193
Web Site Address: http://www.brighthillpress.org
Publishes: essays, fiction, nonfiction, poetry, and art
Editorial Focus: Finely crafted poetry by accomplished poets; no memoiristic poems or poetry that sounds more like prose.
Recent Awards Received: Best Book of Poetry Published by a North Carolina poet, 2004 (Possum by Shelby Stephenson)
Representative Authors: Shelby Stephenson, Victoria Hallerman, and Nicholas Johnson
Submissions Policy: Query letter only, with ten-poem sample. Reading January-March only.
Simultaneous Submissions: yes
Reading Period: 1/3 to 1/31
Reporting Time: up to four months
Author Payment: cash and copies
Contests: see web site for contest guidelines
Founded: 1992
Non Profit: yes
Paid Staff: two to four
Unpaid Staff: two
Distributors: North Country Books, SPD

Wholesalers: Baker & Taylor
ISSN Number/ISBN Number: ISBN 1-892471
Number of Books Published per Year: 7-10
Titles in Print: 35
Average Print Run: 1,000
Average Percentage Printed: Paperback 50%, Chapbook 50%
Average Price: $10

Organization: Brilliant Corners

Type: magazine
CLMP member: no
Primary Editor/Contact Person: Sascha Feinstein
Address: Lycoming College
Williamsport, PA 17701
Web Site Address:
http://www.lycoming.edu/BrilliantCorners
Publishes: essays, fiction, poetry, reviews, and art
Editorial Focus: Exclusively publishes jazz-related literature.
Representative Authors: Yusef Komunyakaa, Jayne Cortez, and Philip Levine
Submissions Policy: Nothing electronic. SASE a must. Bio preferable but not essential.
Simultaneous Submissions: no
Reading Period: 9/15 to 5/1
Reporting Time: one to three months
Author Payment: copies
Founded: 1996
Non Profit: yes
Paid Staff: one
Unpaid Staff: three
Distributors: Ingram
ISSN Number/ISBN Number: ISSN 1091-1197
Total Circulation: 600
Paid Circulation: 150
Average Print Run: 900
Subscription Rate: Individual $12/Institution $12
Single Copy Price: $7
Current Volume/Issue: IX/2
Frequency: biannual
Backfile Available: yes
Unsolicited Ms. Received: yes
% of Unsolicited Ms. Published per Year: 95%
Format: perfect
Size: H 9" W 6"
Average Pages: 90
Ads: yes
Ad Rates: $125 per page

Organization: Brindle & Glass Publishing

Type: press
CLMP member: no
Primary Editor/Contact Person: Ruth Linka
Address: 6, 356 Simcoe Street
Victoria, BC V8V 1L1
Web Site Address: http://www.brindleandglass.com
Publishes: fiction and nonfiction
Editorial Focus: Fiction, creative nonfiction, and drama by leading and emerging Canadian writers.
Representative Authors: Keith Maillard, Curtis Gillespie, and Max Foran
Submissions Policy: Prospective authors should query via e-mail before submitting. We only publish Canadian citizens or landed immigrants.
Simultaneous Submissions: yes
Reading Period: Year-round
Reporting Time: two to six months
Author Payment: royalties
Founded: 2001
Non Profit: no
Paid Staff: 2
Unpaid Staff: 0
Distributors: BCLitDistCo, Heritage Distribution ISBN
ISSN Number/ISBN Number: 0-9732481, 1-897142, 1-894739
Number of Books Published per Year: 12
Titles in Print: 45
Average Percentage Printed: Hardcover 10%, Paperback 90%

Organization: Bristol Banner Books

Type: press
CLMP member: no
Primary Editor/Contact Person: Melody Myers
Address: 14041 C.R. 8
Middlebury, IN 46540
Publishes: fiction, nonfiction, and poetry
Simultaneous Submissions: yes
Reading Period: Year-round
Reporting Time: up to 1month
Author Payment: none
Founded: 1877
Non Profit: no
Paid Staff: zero
Unpaid Staff: one
ISSN Number/ISBN Number: ISSN 1-879183
Number of Books Published per Year: 4
Titles in Print: 20

Average Print Run: five
Average Percentage Printed: Paperback 100%
Average Price: $24.95

Organization: Broken Bridge Review

Type: magazine
CLMP member: yes
Primary Editor/Contact Person: Brad Davis
Address: 398 Pomfret Street
Pomfret School
Pomfret, CT 06258
Web Site Address: www.brokenbridge.us
Publishes: fiction, poetry, and reviews
Editorial Focus: emerging adult poets and short fiction writers; publishes reviews of first books of poems
Representative Authors: Paul Hostovsky, Stephen Morison Jr., and A. M. Heny
Submissions Policy: one submission per year: no more than two short stories (4000 words) or up to 5 poems
Simultaneous Submissions: no
Reading Period: 09/01 to 11/30
Reporting Time: two to three months
Author Payment: copies
Contests: Broken Bridge Poetry Prize (for private school students, grades 9-12: submit Sept. 1-Nov. 30); see website for guidelines
Founded: 2005
Non Profit: yes
Paid Staff: four
Unpaid Staff: zero
Total Circulation: 400
Paid Circulation: 27
Average Print Run: 500
Subscription Rate: Individual $12/Institution $12
Single Copy Price: $12
Current Volume/Issue: 2/1
Frequency: 1
Backfile Available: yes
Unsolicited Ms. Received: yes
% of Unsolicited Ms. Published per Year: 99%
Format: perfect
Size: H 8" W 7"
Average Pages: 150
Ads: no

Organization: Broken Jaw Press

Type: press
CLMP member: yes

Primary Editor/Contact Person: Joe Blades
Address: PO Box 596 Stn A
Fredericton, NB E3B 5A6
Web Site Address: www.brokenjaw.com
Publishes: essays, fiction, nonfiction, poetry, art, translation, audio
Editorial Focus: Mostly Canadian authored, non-mainstream poetry and fiction, including translation& multilingual, with some art & creative non-fiction
Recent Awards Received: Three BJP authors appointed to Poet Laureatships in Halifax, Edmonton & Parliament/Canada
Representative Authors: Nela Rio, rob mclennan and Pauline Michel
Simultaneous Submissions: no
Reading Period: Year-round
Reporting Time: up to 2 months
Author Payment: royalties and copies
Contests: Poets' Corner Award [www.brokenjaw.com/poetscorner.htm] for book-length poetry MS, see website for guidelines
Founded: 1983
Non Profit: no
Paid Staff: zero
Unpaid Staff: one
Distributors: LitDistCo, Ingram, Baker & Taylo
ISSN Number/ISBN Number: ISBN 0-921411, 1-55391, 1-896647
Titles in Print: 150
Average Print Run: 500
Average Percentage Printed: Paperback 90%, Chapbook 6%, Other 4%
Average Price: $18

Organization: Broken Pencil

Type: magazine
CLMP member: no
Address: P.O. Box 203
Station P
Toronto, Ontario M5S2S7, Canada
Web Site Address: http://www.brokenpencil.com
Publishes: essays, fiction, nonfiction, and reviews
Reading Period: Year-round
Reporting Time: one to two months
Author Payment: none
Founded: 1995
Non Profit: yes

Brunswick Publishing Corp.

Type: press
CLMP member: no
Primary Editor/Contact Person: M. S. Raymond
Address: 1386 Lawrenceville Plank Rd
Web Site Address: www.brunswickbooks.com
Publishes: essays, fiction, nonfiction, poetry, and translation
Editorial Focus: New authors and/or esoteric subject matter which is not very attractive to bottom-line oriented big publishers
Recent Awards Received: Nominated for Literary Award by Library of Virginia for Izzy's Fire as well as the People's Choice Award
Representative Authors: Nancy Wright Beasley, J. Chester Johnson, and Richard Heim
Submissions Policy: Email query. Send hard copy manuscript double-spaced for easier reading, if invited.
Simultaneous Submissions: yes
Reading Period: Year-round
Reporting Time: two to six weeks
Author Payment: none, royalties, and copies
Founded: 1972
Non Profit: no
Paid Staff: one
Unpaid Staff: two
Distributors: Baker & Taylor, Bookazine
Wholesalers: Baker & Taylor, Midwest Library, Coutts, etc.
ISSN Number/ISBN Number: 1-55618/0-931494
Number of Books Published per Year: 6-8
Titles in Print: 16
Average Print Run: 2,000
Average Percentage Printed: Hardcover 45%, Paperback 55%
Average Price: $24.50

Organization: Bullfight Media

Type: magazine
CLMP member: no
Address: P.O. Box 362
Walnut Creek, CA 94597-4512
Web Site Address: http://www.bullfightreview.com
Publishes: fiction, poetry, and reviews
Reading Period: Year-round
Reporting Time: one to two months
Author Payment: none
Non Profit: yes
Backfile Available: yes

Organization: Bureau of Public Secrets

Type: press
CLMP member: no
Primary Editor/Contact Person: Ken Knabb
Address: P.O. Box 1044
Berkeley, CA 94701
Web Site Address: http://www.bopsecrets.org
Publishes: essays, fiction, nonfiction, reviews, and translation
Editorial Focus: Radical political and cultural critique.
Representative Authors: Guy Debord, Kenneth Rexroth, and Raoul Vaneigem, Situationist International
Simultaneous Submissions: no
Reading Period: Year-round
Reporting Time: one to six weeks
Author Payment: none
Founded: 1973
Non Profit: yes
Paid Staff: zero
Unpaid Staff: one
Distributors: AK Distribution, Small Press Dist., Koen Dist.
ISSN Number/ISBN Number: ISSN 0-939682
Number of Books Published per Year: one
Titles in Print: three
Average Percentage Printed: Paperback 100%

Organization: Burning Bush Publications

Type: online
CLMP member: no
Primary Editor/Contact Person: Amanda Majestie
Address: P.O. Box 4658
Santa Rosa, CA 95402
Web Site Address: http://www.bbbooks.com
Publishes: essays, fiction, nonfiction, and poetry
Editorial Focus: Social and economic justice, love, romance, beauty.
Representative Authors: Lyn Lifshin, Abby Bogomolny, and Abdul Jabbar
Submissions Policy: Send paper copy to US mail address. No e-mail submissions.
Simultaneous Submissions: yes
Reading Period: 4/1 to 8/1
Reporting Time: two to five months
Author Payment: none
Contests: People Before Profits Poetry Prize. See www.bbbooks.com/contest.html for guidelines.

Founded: 1996
Non Profit: yes
Paid Staff: none
Unpaid Staff: two
ISSN Number/ISBN Number: ISSN 0965066592
Average Page Views per Month: 160,000
Frequency per Year: annual
Average Percentage of Pages per Category: Fiction 10%, Nonfiction 10%, Poetry 70%, Essays 10%

Organization: Cabinet

Type: magazine
CLMP member: no
Primary Editor/Contact Person: Sina Najafi
Address: 181 Wyckoff St.
Brooklyn, NY 11217
Web Site Address: http://www.cabinetmagazine.org/
Publishes: essays, nonfiction, and art
Editorial Focus: nonfiction essays and art projects
Representative Authors: Marina Warner, Brian Dillon, and Slavoj Zizek
Submissions Policy: we will only accept full manuscripts for consideration.
Simultaneous Submissions: yes
Reading Period: Year-round
Reporting Time: one to two months
Author Payment: cash and copies
Founded: 2000
Non Profit: yes
Paid Staff: two
Unpaid Staff: seven
Distributors: Disticor, Ingram, IPD, Central Books, etc.
ISSN Number/ISBN Number: ISSN 1531-1430
Total Circulation: 11,000
Paid Circulation: 3,600
Average Print Run: 12,000
Subscription Rate: Individual $28/Institution $34
Single Copy Price: $10
Current Volume/Issue: Issue 26
Frequency per Year: quarterly
Backfile Available: yes
Unsolicited Ms. Received: yes
% of Unsolicited Ms. Published per Year: 5%
Format: perfect
Size: H 10" W 8"
Average Pages: 112
Ads: yes
Ad Rates: see website for details

Organization: Cadillac Cicatrix

Type: online and print magazine
CLMP member: yes
Primary Editor/Contact Person: B. Spencer
Address: 21800 Parrot Ranch Road
Carmel Valley, CA 93924
Web Site Address: http://www.CadillacCicatrix.com
Publishes: fiction, poetry, prose, interviews, reviews, art.
Editorial Focus: Innovative emerging and established writers and artists.
Representative Authors: Sam Abrams, Peter Orner, and Erin Ergenbright.
Submissions Policy: All submissions should arrive with a cover letter that includes contact information, a brief description of the work, a professional/personal biography, and a self-addressed, stamped envelope (SASE): see website fo details.
Simultaneous Submissions: yes
Reading Period: Year-round
Reporting Time: one to four months
Author Payment: contributor copies
Founded: 2006
Non Profit: no
Paid Staff: zero
Unpaid Staff: nine
Average Page Views per Month: 6,000
Average Unique Visitors per Month: 5,000
Frequency per Year: two print issues and multiple online serials, features
Publish Print Anthology: no
Average Percentage of Pages per Category: Prose 50%, Poetry 25%, Interviews/Reviews 10%, Art 5%, Translation 5%.
Ads: yes

Organization: The Cafe Irreal

Type: online
CLMP member: no
Primary Editor/Contact Person: G.S. Evans
Address: editors@cafeirreal.com
Tucson, AZ 85754
Web Site Address: http://www.cafeirreal.com
Publishes: essays, fiction, and translation
Editorial Focus: We present a kind of fantastic fiction infrequently published in English, resembling the work of Kafka, Borges, or Barthelme.
Representative Authors: Ignacio Padilla, Ana Maria Shua, Charles Simic.
Submissions Policy: We accept unsolicited fiction up to 2,000 words in length. There is no minimum length. Electronic submissions only.
Simultaneous Submissions: no

Reading Period: Year-round
Reporting Time: four to ten weeks
Author Payment: cash
Founded: 1998
Non Profit: yes
Paid Staff: zero
Unpaid Staff: two
Average Page Views per Month: 22,000
Average Unique Visitors per Month: 12,000
Frequency per Year: quarterly
Average Percentage of Pages per Category: Fiction 75%, Essays 5%, Art 5%, Translation 15%
Ads: no

Organization: Cairn

Type: magazine
CLMP member: no
Primary Editor/Contact Person: Tom Heffernan/Lindsay Hess
Address: 1700 Dogwood Mile
Laurinburg, NC 28352
Web Site Address: http://www.sapc.edu/sapress
Publishes: fiction, nonfiction, and poetry
Editorial Focus: We look for excellent literary prose and poetry. Our name means marking the way. New writers are our mission.
Representative Authors: Robert Creeley, Dana Levin, and Ilya Kaminsky
Submissions Policy: SASE, manuscripts not returned, electronic submissions okay, up to 20 pages of fiction/nonfiction, 10 pages of poetry
Simultaneous Submissions: yes
Reading Period: 9/1 to 12/15
Reporting Time: 8 to 12 weeks
Author Payment: copies and subscription
Contests: See Web Site for Contest Guidelines.
Founded: 1969
Non Profit: yes
Paid Staff: three
Unpaid Staff: four
Total Circulation: 500
Paid Circulation: 100
Average Print Run: 1,000
Subscription Rate: Individual $6/Institution $6
Single Copy Price: $8
Current Volume/Issue: Issue 37
Frequency per Year: annual
Backfile Available: yes
Unsolicited Ms. Received: yes
% of Unsolicited Ms. Published per Year: 5%

Format: perfect
Size: H 8.5" W 5.5"
Average Pages: 150
Ads: no

Organization: Calaca Press

Type: press
CLMP member: no
Primary Editor/Contact Person: Brent E. Beltran
Address: P.O. Box 2309
National City, CA 91951
Web Site Address: http://calacapress.com
Publishes: fiction
Editorial Focus: Calaca Press is dedicated to publishing and producing works by progressive Chicano and Latino voices.
Representative Authors: Raul R. Salinas, Alurista, and Tatiana de la Tierra
Submissions Policy: Calaca only accepts submissions when we make a call. No unsolicited manuscripts.
Simultaneous Submissions: yes
Reading Period: 11/11 to 2/2
Reporting Time: up to one month
Author Payment: copies
Founded: 1997
Non Profit: no
Unpaid Staff: two
Distributors: SPD and Baker & Taylor
Number of Books Published per Year: 2.333
Titles in Print: 15
Average Percentage Printed: Paperback 50%, Chapbook 25%, Other 25%

Organization: Call: Review

Type: magazine
CLMP member: yes
Primary Editor/Contact Person: J. D. Kilpatrick
Address: 179 Azalea Drive
Afton, VA 22920
Web Site Address: www.callreview.net
Publishes: essays, fiction, and poetry
Simultaneous Submissions: yes
Reading Period: year-round
Reporting Time: 1 to 16 weeks
Author Payment: none
Founded: 2003
Non Profit: yes
Paid Staff: zero

Unpaid Staff: 10
ISSN Number/ISBN Number: ISSN 1546-6388
Total Circulation: 1,000
Paid Circulation: 150
Average Print Run: 1,000
Subscription Rate: individual $35/institution $35
Single Copy Price: $10
Current Volume/Issue: issue three
Frequency per year: annual
Backfile Available: yes
Unsolicited MSS Received: yes
Format: perfect
Ads: no

Organization: Callaloo

Type: magazine
CLMP member: yes
Primary Editor/Contact Person: Charles H. Rowell
Address: Department of English
Texas A&M University 4227 TAMU
College Station, TX 77843-4227
Publishes: essays, fiction, nonfiction, poetry, reviews, art, and translation
Editorial Focus: Publishes orignal works by. and studies of, writers throughout the African Diaspora.
Representative Authors: Edwidge Danticat, Terrance Hayes, and Suzan Lori-Parks.
Submissions Policy: All manuscripts should be submitted in triplicate, with name/address on one page and SASE. Documented articles in MLA format.
Simultaneous Submissions: no
Reading Period: Year-round
Reporting Time: three to six months
Author Payment: copies
Founded: 1976
Non Profit: yes
Paid Staff: three
Unpaid Staff: nine
Distributors: Johns Hopkins Press
ISSN Number/ISBN Number: ISSN 0161-2492
Total Circulation: 1,110
Paid Circulation: 1,003
Average Print Run: 1,200
Subscription Rate: Individual $45/Institution $133
Single Copy Price: $15
Current Volume/Issue: 30/1
Frequency per Year: quarterly
Backfile Available: yes
Unsolicited Ms. Received: yes
% of Unsolicited Ms. Published per Year: 70%
Format: perfect

Average Pages: 300+
Ads: yes.
Ad Rates: see website for details

Organization: Calyx, A Journal of Art and Lit by Women

Type: magazine
CLMP member: yes
Primary Editor/Contact Person: Margarita Donnelly, Director
Address: P.O. Box B
216 SW Madison Ave. E#7
Corvallis, OR 97339

Web Site Address: www.proaxis.com/~calyx/journal.html
Publishes: essays, fiction, nonfiction, poetry, reviews, art, and translation
Editorial Focus: Publish fine art and literature by women in an elegant format.
Representative Authors: Marianne Villanueva, Susan Elbe, and Ingrid Wendt
Submissions Policy: Submit up to six poems, prose 5,000 words, reviews 500-1,000 words, art six slides or black and white photos-all with bio and SASE.
Simultaneous Submissions: yes
Reading Period: 10/1 to 12/31
Reporting Time: six to eight months
Author Payment: copies and subscription
Contests: Lois Cranston Memorial Poetry Prize, three poems, March 1-May 31, $15 submission fee per entry. See website for guidelines.
Founded: 1976
Non Profit: yes
Paid Staff: four
Unpaid Staff: 75
Distributors: Ingram, Periodicals, Armadillo, Small Changes
ISSN Number/ISBN Number: ISSN 0147-1627
Total Circulation: 2,500
Paid Circulation: 900
Average Print Run: 3,000
Subscription Rate: Individual $21/Institution $27
Single Copy Price: $9.50
Current Volume/Issue: 22/3
Frequency per Year: biannual
Backfile Available: yes
Unsolicited Ms. Received: yes
% of Unsolicited Ms. Published per Year: 100%
Format: perfect
Size: H 8" W 6"

Average Pages: 128
Ads: yes
Ad Rates: $550/full page, $285/half page, $150/quarter page

Organization: Canadian Literature

Type: magazine
CLMP member: no
Primary Editor/Contact Person: Margery Fee
Address: Buchanan E158
1866 Main Mall
Vancouver, BC V6T 1Z1
Web Site Address: http://www.canlit.ca
Publishes: essays, nonfiction, poetry, and reviews.
Editorial Focus: Previously unpublished English- or French-language articles, interviews, and commentaries on writers and writing in Canada.
Recent Awards Received: Former Editor Eva--Marie Kruller received the CELJ Distinguished Editor of 2004 award.
Representative Authors: George Elliott Clarke, Heather Milne, and M.G. Vassanji.
Submissions Policy: Articles should follow current MLA bibliographic format. Maximum word length for articles is 6,500 words.
Simultaneous Submissions: no
Reading Period: Year-round
Reporting Time: two to three months
Author Payment: none
Contests: None at current time.
Founded: 1959
Non Profit: yes
Paid Staff: four
Unpaid Staff: six
ISSN Number/ISBN Number: ISSN 0008-4360
Total Circulation: 900
Paid Circulation: 800
Average Print Run: 1,100
Subscription Rate: Individual $75 US/Institution $104 US
Single Copy Price: $19
Current Volume/Issue: Issue 2007/ 192
Frequency per Year: quarterly
Backfile Available: yes
Unsolicited Ms. Received: yes
% of Unsolicited Ms. Published per Year: 75%
Format: perfect
Size: H 9" W 6"
Average Pages: 208
Ads: yes

Ad Rates: $400 US; see website for details

Organization: Canadian Poetry: Studies, Documents, Reviews

Type: magazine
CLMP member: no
Primary Editor/Contact Person: D.M.R. Bentley
Address: Department of English
University of Western Ontario
London, ON N6A 3K7
Web Site Address: http://www.canadianpoetry.ca
Publishes: essays and reviews
Editorial Focus: Canadian Poetry publishes scholarly articles, documents and reviews on poetry from all periods and regions in Canada.
Representative Authors: Frank Davey, W.H. New, and Tracy Ware
Submissions Policy: Submissions should follow the MLA style, and be submitted in duplicate and with an accompanying stamped, addressed envelope.
Simultaneous Submissions: yes
Reading Period: Year-round
Reporting Time: three to six weeks
Author Payment: copies
Founded: 1977
Non Profit: yes
Paid Staff: zero
Unpaid Staff: two
Distributors: Canada Post, IUTS
ISSN Number/ISBN Number: ISSN 0704 5646
Total Circulation: 400
Paid Circulation: 400
Average Print Run: 400
Subscription Rate: Individual $15/Institution $18
Single Copy Price: $7.50
Current Volume/Issue: Issue 55
Frequency per Year: biannual
Backfile Available: yes
Unsolicited Ms. Received: yes
% of Unsolicited Ms. Published per Year: 40%
Format: perfect
Size: H 9" W 6"
Average Pages: 130
Ads: yes
Ad Rates: Exchange
See Web Site for Details.

Organization: The Canary

Type: magazine
CLMP member: yes
Primary Editor/Contact Person: Joshua Edwards

Address: 512 Clear Lake Road
Kemah, TX 77565
Web Site Address: http://www.thecanary.org
Publishes: poetry
Editorial Focus: The Canary publishes poems that, like the eponymous bird, venture into the labyrinthine mineshafts of mind and culture.
Recent Awards Received: Best American Poetry
Representative Authors: D.A. Powell, Rae Armantrout, and Fanny Howe
Submissions Policy: August 1-December 1. E-mail (as Word or RTF) up to six poems w/ a brief cover letter to: submissions@thecanary.org
Simultaneous Submissions: yes
Reading Period: 8/1 to 12/1
Reporting Time: two to four months
Author Payment: copies
Contests: See web site for contest guidelines.
Founded: 2002
Non Profit: no
Paid Staff: zero
Unpaid Staff: three
Distributors: DeBoer, Ingram
ISSN Number/ISBN Number: ISSN 1543-0030
Total Circulation: 700
Paid Circulation: 100
Average Print Run: 1,100
Subscription Rate: Individual $30/Institution $30
Single Copy Price: $10
Current Volume/Issue: Issue 5
Frequency per Year: annual
Backfile Available: yes
Unsolicited Ms. Received: yes
% of Unsolicited Ms. Published per Year: 2%
Format: perfect
Size: H 8" W 7"
Average Pages: 120
Ads: no

Organization: Cantaraville

Type: online
CLMP member: yes
Primary Editor/Contact Person: Michael Matheny
Address: 8721 Santa Monica Blvd. #129
Los Angeles, CA 90069
Web Site Address: www.cantaraville.com
Publishes: essays, fiction, nonfiction, poetry, reviews, and translation
Editorial Focus: General interest fiction, nonfiction and poetry of the highest quality

Representative Authors: Stephen Gyllenhaal, Gary Walkow, and Sandra Sanchez
Submissions Policy: PDF-only publication. Please read and follow guidelines at website. Email submissions only. Prev/sim published okay.
Simultaneous Submissions: yes
Reading Period: year-round
Reporting Time: one to eight weeks
Author Payment: copies
Contests: none
Founded: 2006
Non Profit: no
Paid Staff: zero
Unpaid Staff: two
ISSN Number/ISBN Number: ISSN 1933-6624
Average Page Views per Month: 1,000
Average Unique Visitors per Month: 1,000
Frequency per Year: biannual
Average Percentsge of Psges per Category: Fiction 40%, Nonfiction 10%, Poetry 20%, Reviews 10%, Essays 10%, Translations 10%
Publish Print Anthology: no
Ads: no

Organization: Cape Breton University Press

Type: press
CLMP member: no
Primary Editor/Contact Person: Mike R. Hunter
Address: PO Box 5300
Sydney, NS B1P 5300
Web Site Address: www.cbupress.ca
Publishes: fiction, nonfiction, and poetry
Editorial Focus: CBU Press publishes works with a primary focus on Cape Breton Island and works of a broader academic nature.
Recent Awards Received: "A Forest for Calum" short-listed for the 2006 Dartmouth Book Award and long-listed for the International IMPAC Dublin Award.
Representative Authors: A. J. B. Johnston, Carol Corbin, and Jim Lotz
Submissions Policy:
http://www.cbupress.ca/Submissions.html
Simultaneous Submissions: yes
Reading Period: year-round
Reporting Time: two to four months
Author Payment: royalties
Founded: 1974
Non Profit: yes
Paid Staff: three

Unpaid Staff: three
Unpaid Staff: zero
Distributors: Nimbus Publishing
ISSN Number/ISBN Number: ISBN0920336,1897009
Number of Books Published per Year: six to eight
Titles in Print: 75
Average Print Run: 1,500
Average Percentage Printed: Paperback 100%
Average Price: $24.95

Organization: The Caribbean Writer

Type: magazine
CLMP member: yes
Primary Editor/Contact Person: Marvin E. Williams
Address: University of the Virgin Islands
Kingshill, St. Croix, VI 00850
Web Site Address:
http://www.TheCaribbeanWriter.com
Publishes: essays, fiction, nonfiction, poetry, reviews, art, and translation
Editorial Focus: International literary anthology with Caribbean focus. Work should reflect Caribbean heritage, experience or perspective.
Recent Awards Received: Pushcart Prize (2000)
Representative Authors: Opal Palmer, Adisa, Edwidge Danticat, and Ian McDonald
Submissions Policy: Put name, address, and title of work on separate sheet. Title only on work. Include brief bio. Type (double-space) all work.
Simultaneous Submissions: yes
Reading Period: 8/1 to 1/30
Reporting Time: two to three months
Author Payment: copies
Contests: Prizes awarded for best poetry, short fiction, first-time publication, Caribbean author and Virgin Islands author.
See web site for contest guidelines.
Founded: 1987
Non Profit: yes
Paid Staff: two
Unpaid Staff: zero
Distributors: Ubiquity (US), Novelty Trading (Jam), Lexicon (Trinidad)
ISSN Number/ISBN Number: ISBN 0-9769273-1-4
Total Circulation: 1,000
Paid Circulation: 175
Average Print Run: 1,200
Subscription Rate: Individual $25/Institution $40
Single Copy Price: $15
Current Volume/Issue: Volume 20/0

Frequency per Year: annual
Backfile Available: yes
Unsolicited Ms. Received: yes
% of Unsolicited Ms. Published per Year: 80%
Format: perfect
Size: H 9" W 6"
Average Pages: 304
Ads: yes
Ad Rates: Full page $250, 1/2 page $150, 1/4 page $100
See web site for details.

Organization: The Carolina Quarterly

Type: magazine
CLMP member: no
Primary Editor/Contact Person: Tessa Joseph
Address: CB 3520, Greenlaw Hall
UNC-Chapel Hill
Chapel Hill, NC 27599
Web Site Address: http://www.unc.edu/depts/cqonline
Publishes: essays, fiction, nonfiction, poetry, reviews, and art
Representative Authors: Elizabeth Spencer, Ha Jin, and Richard Wilbur
Submissions Policy: No e-mail submissions. One clean copy addressed to appropriate genre editor, containing contact information.
Simultaneous Submissions: no
Reading Period: 8/3 to 4/4
Reporting Time: four to six months
Author Payment: copies
Founded: 1948
Non Profit: yes
Paid Staff: zero
Unpaid Staff: 50
Distributors: Ingram, EBSCO, Swets Blackwell
Total Circulation: 600
Paid Circulation: 400
Subscription Rate: Individual $18/Institution $21
Single Copy Price: $6
Current Volume/Issue: 56/55.3
Frequency per Year: triquarterly
Backfile Available: yes
Unsolicited Ms. Received: yes
Format: perfect
Average Pages: 100
Ads: yes

Organization: Carousel

Type: magazine
CLMP member: no
Primary Editor/Contact Person: Mark Laliberte, Managing Editor
Address: UC274
University of Guelph
Guelph, ON N1G 2W1
Web Site Address: http://www.carouselmagazine.ca
Publishes: fiction, poetry, and art
Editorial Focus: We are a hybrid literary and arts mag: from cover to cover, we act as a venue for those interested in "exploring the page."
Recent Awards Received: Honorable Mention for "Best Art Direction for an Entire Issue, 2004" by The National Magazine Awards Foundation (Canada)
Representative Authors: bill bissett, Emily Schultz, and Marc Ngui.
Submissions Policy: Please visit web site for our most current submission guidelines. E-mail submissions are accepted.
Simultaneous Submissions: yes
Reading Period: Year-round
Reporting Time: three to four months
Author Payment: cash, copies, and subscription
Contests: Occasional contests and special projects
Founded: 1983
Non Profit: yes
Paid Staff: zero
Unpaid Staff: one
Distributors: Magazines Canada, Ubiquity, DeBoer
ISSN Number/ISBN Number: ISSN 0835-7994
Total Circulation: 900
Paid Circulation: 300
Average Print Run: 1,200
Subscription Rate: Individual $25/2 years/Institution $34/2 years
Single Copy Price: $10
Current Volume/Issue: Issue 20
Frequency per Year: biannual
Backfile Available: yes
Unsolicited Ms. Received: yes
Format: perfect
Size: H 9.5" W 7.5"
Average Pages: 76
Ads: yes
Ad Rates: See Web Site for Details.

Organization: Carve Magazine

Type: online
CLMP member: no
Primary Editor/Contact Person: Matthew Limpede
Address: P.O. Box 701510
Dallas, Texas 75287
Web Site Address: http://www.carvezine.com
Publishes: fiction
Editorial Focus: We publish short stories only, literary fiction. Open to new authors but only strong, polished writing.
Representative Authors: Sallie Bingham, Lynn Stegner, and Kate Braverman
Submissions Policy: Mail-in only until further notice . Guidelines on website.
Simultaneous Submissions: yes
Reading Period: Year-round
Reporting Time: three to six months
Author Payment: none
Contests: See Web Site for Contest Guidelines.
Founded: 2000
Non Profit: no
Paid Staff: zero
Unpaid Staff: nine
ISSN Number/ISBN Number: ISSN 1529-272X
Average Page Views per Month: 8,556
Average Unique Visitors per Month: 3,136
Frequency per Year: 4
Publish Print Anthology: no
Average Percentage of Pages per Category: Fiction 100%
Ads: no

Organization: Casagrande Press

Type: press
CLMP member: yes
Primary Editor/Contact Person: Paul Diamond
Address: see www.casagrandepress.com
Solana Beach, CA 92057
Web Site Address: www.casagrandepress.com
Publishes: nonfiction and poetry
Editorial Focus: Outdoors/recreation/sports books including the "Greatest Misadventure" series. Occasionally we publish poetry books. Occasionally we publish poetry books.
Representative Authors: Surfing's Greatest Misadventures--LA Times best seller.
Representative Authors: Mary Ruefle, Robert Cording, and Howard Levy
Submissions Policy: Submit nonfiction stories for Golf's, Fishing's, Wedding's & other Greatest Misadventures books online at casagrandepress.com
Simultaneous Submissions: yes

Reading Period: year-round
Reporting Time: one to three months
Author Payment: royalties, cash, and copies
Contests: none.
Founded: 2004
Non Profit: no
Paid Staff: one
Unpaid Staff: one
Distributors: Wilderness Press, Lightning Source (poetry only)
ISSN Number/ISBN Number: ISBN 0-9769516
Number of Books Published per Year: three
Titles in Print: 4
Average Percentage Printed: Paperback 100%
Average Price: $16.00

Organization: CavanKerry Press, Ltd.

Type: press
CLMP member: yes
Primary Editor/Contact Person: Joan Cusack Handler
Address: 6 Horizon Rd #2901
Fort Lee, NJ 07024
Web Site Address: http://www.cavankerrypress.org
Publishes: poetry
Representative Authors: Mary Ruefle, Robert Cording, and Howard Levy
Simultaneous Submissions: yes
Reading Period: check
http://www.cavankerrypress.org
Reporting Time: up to six months
Author Payment: royalties
Contests: None.
Founded: 1999
Non Profit: yes
Paid Staff: five
Unpaid Staff: three
Distributors: University Press of New England
Number of Books Published per Year: three
Titles in Print: 28
Average Percentage Printed: Paperback 100%
Average Price: $16

Organization:Cave Wall

Type: magazine
CLMP member: yes
Primary Editor/Contact Person: Rhett Iseman Trull
Address: P.O. Box 29546
Greensboro, NC 27429-9546

Web Site Address: www.cavewallpress.com
Publishes: poetry and art
Editorial Focus: We publish black and white art, along with the best contemporary poetry by established and emerging writers.
Representative Authors: Claudia Emerson, Carl Phillips, and Robert Wrigley
Submissions Policy: We read unsolicited poetry twice a year. Previously unpublished work only. See website for full guidelines.
Simultaneous Submissions: yes
Reading Period: 8/1 to 10/31
Reporting Time: one to three months
Author Payment: copies
Founded: 2006
Non Profit: no
Paid Staff: zero
Unpaid Staff: two
ISSN Number/ISBN Number: ISSN 1937-2507
Total Circulation: 300
Paid Circulation: 64
Average Print Run: 500
Subscription Rate: Individual $10/Institution $10
Single Copy Price: $5
Current Volume/Issue: Issue 2
Frequency: 2
Backfile Available: yes
Unsolicited Ms. Received: yes
% of Unsolicited Ms. Published per Year: 75%
Format: perfect
Size: H 8.5" W 5"
Average Pages: 72
Ads: yes
Ads: exchange

Organization: The Center for Literary Publishing

Type: press
CLMP member: yes
Primary Editor/Contact Person: Stephanie G'Schwind
Address: Department of English
Colorado State University
Fort Collins, CO 80523
Web Site Address:
http://coloradoreview.colostate.edu
Publishes: essays, fiction, nonfiction, poetry, reviews, and translation
Editorial Focus: Publisher of Colorado Review, the Colorado Prize for Poetry, and the Series in

Contemporary Fiction.
Representative Authors: Rusty Morrison, Dean Young, and G.C. Waldrep
Submissions Policy: See guidelines for Colorado Prize for Poetry on our web site. Not currently accepting submissions to Series in Cont. Fiction.
Simultaneous Submissions: yes
Reading Period: 9/1 to 5/1
Reporting Time: one to three months
Author Payment: royalties, cash, and copies
Contests: Colorado Prize for Poetry and the Nelligan Prize for Short Fiction.
See Web Site for Contest Guidelines.
Founded: 1992
Non Profit: yes
Paid Staff: one
Unpaid Staff: 20
Distributors: Ingram, Kent News, UP of Colorado, U of Oklahoma P
ISSN Number/ISBN Number: 1046-3348/0-885635
Number of Books Published per Year: one
Titles in Print: 17
Average Print Run: 1000
Average Percentage Printed: Paperback 100%
Average Price: $14.95

Organization: Century Press

ype: press
CLMP member: no
Primary Editor/Contact Person: Robert W. Olmsted
Address: PO BOX 298
Thomaston, ME 04861
Web Site Address: http://www.americanletters.org
Publishes: fiction, nonfiction, and poetry
Editorial Focus: Anything!
Representative Authors: Diane Lau Cordrey, Steven Janasik, and Nora Hamilton
Submissions Policy: Send personal marketing plan first. No electronic submissions or queries.
Simultaneous Submissions: yes
Reading Period: Year-round
Reporting Time: one to six weeks
Author Payment: royalties
Founded: 1999
Non Profit: yes
Paid Staff: one
Unpaid Staff: one
Distributors: Baker & Taylor, Ingram, Barnes & Noble, amazon.com
ISSN Number/ISBN Number: ISBN 0-89754-xxx-x

Number of Books Published per Year: 2
Titles in Print: six
Average Percentage Printed: Hardcover 5%, Paperback 95%

Organization: Chapman Magazine

Type: magazine
CLMP member: no
Primary Editor/Contact Person: Joy Hendry
Address: 4 Broughton Place
Edinburgh, UK EH1 3RX
Web Site Address: http://www.chapman-pub.co.uk
Publishes: essays, fiction, nonfiction, and poetry
Editorial Focus: The best in Scottish and international poetry, short stories and critical essays. Scottish in location, international in outlook.
Representative Authors: Alasdair Reid, Louise Welsh, and Sorley MacLean
Submissions Policy: Covering letter w/ enough IRCs to cover reply. No IRCs means a reply is not likely. Guidelines on request.
Simultaneous Submissions: yes
Reading Period: Year-round
Reporting Time: up to four weeks
Author Payment: cash, copies, and subscription
Founded: 1970
Non Profit: yes
Paid Staff: two
Unpaid Staff: four
ISSN Number/ISBN Number: 0308-2695/1-903700
Total Circulation: 2,000
Paid Circulation: 1,000
Average Print Run: 2,000
Subscription Rate: Individual $48/Institution $58
Single Copy Price: $12.50
Current Volume/Issue: Issue 107
Frequency per Year: triquarterly
Backfile Available: yes
Unsolicited Ms. Received: yes
% of Unsolicited Ms. Published per Year: 0.5%
Format: perfect
Size: H 8.5" W 6"
Average Pages: 144
Ads: yes
Ad Rates: ad sheet on request (e-mail)

Organization: Chatoyant

Type: press
CLMP member: yes
Primary Editor/Contact Person: Suki Wessling

Address: P.O. Box 832
Aptos, CA 95001
Web Site Address: http://chatoyant.com
Publishes: poetry
Editorial Focus: Well-crafted poetry.
Representative Authors: Penny Cagan, Virginia Chase Sutton, and William Minor
Submissions Policy: No unsolicited submissions. All unsolicited mail and e-mail will not receive a reply.
Simultaneous Submissions: no
Reading Period: Year-round
Reporting Time: three to six months
Author Payment: royalties
Founded: 1997
Non Profit: no
Paid Staff: one
Unpaid Staff: one
Wholesalers: Baker & Taylor
ISSN Number/ISBN Number: ISBN 0-9661452
Number of Books Published per Year: one
Titles in Print: four
Average Percentage Printed: Paperback 90%, Chapbook 10%
Backfile Available: yes

Organization: The Chattahoochee Review

Type: magazine
CLMP member: yes
Primary Editor/Contact Person: Marc Fitten
Address: 2101 Womack Road
Dunwoody, GA 30338-4497
Web Site Address: http://www.chattahoochee-review.org
Publishes: essays, fiction, nonfiction, poetry, reviews, art, and translation
Editorial Focus: Literary quality in a variety of genres and subject matter. See web site for details,
Representative Authors: George Singleton, Ignacio Padilla, and William Gay
Submissions Policy: See web site for details
Simultaneous Submissions: yes
Reading Period: Year-round
Reporting Time: two to three months
Author Payment: cash and copies
Contests: See web site for contest guidelines.
Founded: 1980
Non Profit: yes
Paid Staff: three
Unpaid Staff: 10

ISSN Number/ISBN Number: ISSN 0741-9155
Total Circulation: 1,250
Paid Circulation: 800
Average Print Run: 1,250
Subscription Rate: Individual $20/Institution $20
Single Copy Price: $6
Current Volume/Issue: 26/1
Frequency per Year: quarterly
Backfile Available: yes
Unsolicited Ms. Received: yes
% of Unsolicited Ms. Published per Year: 1%
Format: perfect
Size: H 6" W 9"
Average Pages: 120
Ads: yes
Ad Rates: $200 for full page

Organization: Chelsea Editions

Type: press
CLMP member: yes
Primary Editor/Contact Person: Alfredo de Palchi
Address: c/o Alfredo de Palchi
33 Union Square West, 6R
New York, NY 10003
Publishes: poetry and translation
Editorial Focus: Translations of modern Italian poetry into English. Bilingual edition
Representative Authors: Carlo Betocchi, Giorgio Caproni, and Camillo Sbarbaro
Submissions Policy: Send 10-12 translations plus bio
Simultaneous Submissions: yes
Reading Period: 10/1 to 4/30
Reporting Time: two to four months
Author Payment: cash
Founded: 2002
Non Profit: yes
Paid Staff: zero
Unpaid Staff: one
ISSN Number/ISBN Number: 0009-2185/0-9725271
Number of Books Published per Year: two
Titles in Print: seven
Average Print Run: 500
Average Percentage Printed: Paperback 100%
Average Price: $15.00

Organization: The Chesapeake Reader: an online literary journal

Type: online

CLMP member: yes
Primary Editor/Contact Person: Holly T. Sneeringer
Address: PO Box 21151
Baltimore, MD 21228
Website Address: www.chesapeakereader.com
Publishes: essays, fiction, nonfiction, poetry, and reviews
Editorial Focus: The Chesapeake Reader is dedicated to publishing poetry, fiction, and nonfiction of the highest quality by both emerging and established writers. We have a special interest in the work of writers living in the Chesapeake Bay region and in literature that reflects the area's unique inspirations. Our mission is to publish our area's finest new literature and to provide an online publication for both readers and writers.
Representative Authors: Maribeth Fischer, Elizabeth Spires, and Christopher Corbett
Submissions Policy: We accept previously unpublished fiction, nonfiction, and poetry during two submission periods. See website for specifics.
Simultaneous Submissions: yes
Reading Period: 11/01 to 01/31
Reporting Time: 1 to 2 months
Author Payment: none
Founded: 2006
Non Profit: yes
Paid Staff: 0
Unpaid Staff: 4
Average Page Views per Month: 350
Average Unique Visitors per Month: 300
Frequency: 1
Average Percentage of Pages per Category: Fiction 25%, Nonfiction 25%, Poetry 25%, Essays 25%
Ads: no

Organization: Chicago Review

Type: magazine
CLMP member: yes
Primary Editor/Contact Person: Eirik Steinhoff
Address: 5801 S. Kenwood Ave.
Chicago, IL 60637
Web Site Address: humanities.uchicago.edu/review
Publishes: essays, fiction, nonfiction, poetry, reviews, art, and translation
Submissions Policy: read the magazine before submitting.
Simultaneous Submissions: yes
Reading Period: 9/30 to 5/31
Reporting Time: three to six months

Author Payment: copies
Founded: 1946
Non Profit: yes
Paid Staff: three
Unpaid Staff: 15
Total Circulation: 2,000`
Paid Circulation: 900
Subscription Rate: Individual $18/Institution $42
Single Copy Price: $6
Current Volume/Issue: 49/2
Frequency per Year: triquarterly
Backfile Available: yes
Unsolicited Ms. Received: yes
Format: perfect

Organization: Chicory Blue Press, Inc.

Type: press
CLMP member: yes
Primary Editor/Contact Person: Sondra Zeidenstein
Address: 795 East St. N.
Goshen, CT 06756
Web Site Address: http://www.chicorybluepress.com
Publishes: poetry
Editorial Focus: focuses on strong voices of women poets over 65
Representative Authors: Honor Moore, Betty Buchsbaum, and Nellie Wong
Submissions Policy: send ten poems and brief cover letter
Simultaneous Submissions: yes
Reading Period: Year-round
Reporting Time: three to four months
Author Payment: none, royalties, and copies
Founded: 1986
Non Profit: no
Distributors: SPD
Number of Books Published per Year: one to two
Titles in Print: 12
Average Print Run: 750
Average Percentage Printed: Paperback 100%
Average Price: $16

Organization: Cimarron Review

Type: magazine
CLMP member: yes
Primary Editor/Contact Person: E.P. Walkiewicz
Address: 205 Morrill
Oklahoma State University
Stillwater, OK 74078-0135

Web Site Address: http://cimarronreview.okstate.edu
Publishes: essays, fiction, nonfiction, poetry, reviews, art, and translation
Editorial Focus: Gritty realism with healthy doses of irony, humor (when possible), drama, intelligence and humanity.
Recent Awards Received: N/A
Representative Authors: Rick Moody, Kim Addonizio, and Gary Fincke
Submissions Policy: Send three to five poems, one short story or one nonfiction piece with an SASE. E-mail submissions accepted from foreign countries only.
Simultaneous Submissions: yes
Reading Period: Year-round
Reporting Time: two to six months
Author Payment: copies
Contests: none
Founded: 1967
Non Profit: yes
Paid Staff: three
Unpaid Staff: 17
Distributors: Ingram, Kent News
ISSN Number/ISBN Number: 0009-6849
Total Circulation: 600
Paid Circulation: 260
Average Print Run: 600
Subscription Rate: Individual $24/Institution $24
Single Copy Price: $7
Frequency per Year: quarterly
Backfile Available: yes
Unsolicited Ms. Received: yes
% of Unsolicited Ms. Published per Year: 3%
Format: perfect
Size: H 9" W 6"
Average Pages: 112
Ads: yes
Ad Rates: Contact us via e-mail: cimarronreview@yahoo.com

Organization: The Cincinnati Review
Type: magazine
CLMP member: yes
Primary Editor/Contact Person: Nicola Mason, Managing Editor
Address: University of Cincinnati
P.O. Box 210069
Cincinnati, OH 45221-0069
Web Site Address: http://cincinnatireview.com
Publishes: essays, fiction, nonfiction, poetry, reviews, art, and translation
Editorial Focus: We publish poetry and prose of any stripe provided there is great care given to craft.
Recent Awards Received: Poems and fiction appeared in Best American Poetry, Best American Essays and New Stories from the South
Representative Authors: Antonya Nelson, Caroline Knox, and George Singleton
Submissions Policy: Submit up to ten pages of poetry or up to forty pages of fiction. SASE required for response. No e-mail or fax submissions.
Simultaneous Submissions: yes
Reading Period: 9/1 to 5/31
Reporting Time: one to two months
Author Payment: cash, copies, and subscription
Founded: 2003
Non Profit: yes
Paid Staff: six
Unpaid Staff: eight
ISSN Number/ISBN Number: ISSN 1546-9034
Total Circulation: 500
Paid Circulation: 400
Average Print Run: 1,000
Subscription Rate: Individual $15/Institution $30
Single Copy Price: $9
Current Volume/Issue: 4/1
Frequency per Year: biannual
Backfile Available: yes
Unsolicited Ms. Received: yes
% of Unsolicited Ms. Published per Year: 2%
Format: perfect
Size: H 9" W 6"
Average Pages: 225
Ads: yes
Ad Rates: upon request
See web site for details.

Organization: Cinco Puntos Press
Type: press
CLMP member: no
Primary Editor/Contact Person: Lee or Bobby Byrd
Address: 701 Texas Ave.
El Paso, TX 79901
Web Site Address: http://www.cincopuntos.com
Publishes: fiction and nonfiction
Editorial Focus: Literatures of Southwest, the Border region, and Latin America. Known for bilingual children's books with political edge.
Recent Awards Received: Lannan Foundation 2005 Cultural Freedom Foundation

Representative Authors: Benjamin Alire Saenz, Luis Alberto Urrea, and Joe Hayes
Submissions Policy: Contact Lee Byrd before submitting. We do not accept unsolicited manuscripts. Please study our list before sending blindly.
Simultaneous Submissions: yes
Reading Period: Year-round
Reporting Time: two to three months
Author Payment: royalties
Contests: See web site for contest guidelines.
Founded: 1985
Non Profit: no
Paid Staff: seven
Unpaid Staff: zero
Distributors: Consortium
Wholesalers: All
ISSN Number/ISBN Number: ISBN 0-938317
Number of Books Published per Year: 6-8
Titles in Print: 70
Average Print Run: 7,000
Average Percentage Printed: Hardcover 40%, Paperback 60%
Average Price: $15.95

Organization: Circumference

Type: magazine
CLMP member: yes
Primary Editor/Contact Person: J. Kronovet, S. Heim
Address: P.O. Box 27
New York, NY 10159
Web Site Address:
http://www.circumferencemag.com
Publishes: poetry and translation
Editorial Focus: Circumference publishes new translations of poetry. We print original poems side-by-side with translations.
Submissions Policy: Mail 5-10 translations. Include originals.
Simultaneous Submissions: yes
Reading Period: Year-round
Reporting Time: one to five months
Author Payment: copies and subscription
Founded: 2002
Non Profit: yes
Paid Staff: zero
Unpaid Staff: three
Distributors: Ingram, DeBoer, Ubiquity
Total Circulation: 1,800
Paid Circulation: 400
Average Print Run: 2,000

Subscription Rate: Individual $15/Institution $40
Single Copy Price: $10
Current Volume/Issue: 2/2
Frequency per Year: biannual
Backfile Available: yes
Unsolicited Ms. Received: yes
Format: perfect
Ads: yes

Organization: City Lights Books

Type: press
CLMP member: no
Primary Editor/Contact Person: Editorial Staff/City Lights Books
Address: 261 Columbus Ave.
San Francisco, CA 94133
Web Site Address: http://www.citylights.com
Publishes: fiction, nonfiction, and poetry
Editorial Focus: Literary fiction, translations, poetry and books on radical politics, social and cultural history, and current events.
Representative Authors: Julio Cortázar, Rebecca Brown, and Michael Parenti
Submissions Policy: Please see our web site for submission guidelines.
Simultaneous Submissions: no
Reading Period: Year-round
Reporting Time: two to six months
Author Payment: royalties
Founded: 1955
Non Profit: no
Paid Staff: four
Unpaid Staff: two
Distributors: Consortium Books
Wholesalers: Ingram, Baker & Taylor, and all majors
ISSN Number/ISBN Number: ISBN 0-87286
Number of Books Published per Year: 12
Titles in Print: 200
Average Percentage Printed: Paperback 100%

Organization: Cleveland State University Poetry Center

Type: press
CLMP member: no
Primary Editor/Contact Person: Dr. Ted Lardner
Address: 2121 Euclid Ave.
Cleveland, OH 44115-2214
Web Site Address: http://www.csuohio.edu/poetrycenter

Publishes: poetry
Representative Authors: Tim Seibles and Jared Carter
Submissions Policy: Only through annual contests.
Simultaneous Submissions: yes
Reading Period: 11/1 to 6/15
Reporting Time: seven to eight months
Author Payment: cash and copies
Contests: Have offered first book and "open" competitions; See web site for contest guidelines.
Founded: 1971
Non Profit: yes
Paid Staff: one
Unpaid Staff: one
Distributors: Spring Church, Ingram
Wholesalers: Baker & Taylor, Coutts, Midwest Library Service
ISSN Number/ISBN Number: ISBN 1-880834-
Number of Books Published per Year: four
Titles in Print: 120
Average Percentage Printed: Hardcover 15%, Paperback 65%, Chapbook 20%

Organization: Coach House Books

Type: press
CLMP member: yes
Primary Editor/Contact Person: Christina Palassio
Address: 401 Huron St. (rear)
on bpNichol Lane
Toronto, ON M5S 2G5
Web Site Address: http://www.chbooks.com
Publishes: fiction and poetry
Editorial Focus: Innovative/experimental fiction and poetry by Canadian authors
Recent Awards Received: 2007 Lambda Literary Award for Sina Queyras' "Lemon Hound," 2006 Griffin Poetry Prize for "Nerve Squall" by Sylvia Legris
Representative Authors: Christian Bok, Nicole Brossard, and Sina Queyras
Submissions Policy: Query letter, CV and sample-from Canadian authors only
Simultaneous Submissions: yes
Reading Period: Year-round
Reporting Time: two to six months
Author Payment: royalties and cash
Founded: 1997
Non Profit: no
Paid Staff: three
Unpaid Staff: zero
Distributors: LitDistCo (Canada), Northwestern

University Press
Wholesalers: Ingram, Baker & Taylor
ISSN Number/ISBN Number: ISBN 1 55245
Number of Books Published per Year: 15
Titles in Print: 120
Average Print Run: 1,000
Average Percentage Printed: Paperback 100%
Average Price: $15

Organization: Codhill Press

Type: press
CLMP member: yes
Primary Editor/Contact Person: David Appelbaum
Address: 1 Arden Ln.
New Paltz, NY 12561
Web Site Address: http://codhill.com
Publishes: nonfiction and poetry
Editorial Focus: The union of philosophy, poetry, and spirit.
Representative Authors: Frederick Franck, Laura Simms, and Christopher Bamford
Submissions Policy: query first
Simultaneous Submissions: no
Reading Period: 9/1 to 6/30
Reporting Time: 1 to 12 weeks
Author Payment: none
Contests: Codhill annual chapbook contest
Founded: 2000
Non Profit: no
Paid Staff: zero
Unpaid Staff: one
Distributors: Faherty and Associates
ISSN Number/ISBN Number: ISBN 1930337
Number of Books Published per Year: seven
Titles in Print: 31
Average Print Run: 1,000
Average Percentage Printed: Paperback 80%, Chapbook 20%
Average Price: $14

Organization: Coffee House Press

Type: press
CLMP member: yes
Primary Editor/Contact Person: Allan Kornblum/Chris Fischbach
Address: 27 N. Fourth St, Ste. 400
Minneapolis, MN 55401
Web Site Address: http://www.coffeehousepress.org
Publishes: essays, fiction, and poetry

Editorial Focus: Experimental fiction, New York School poets, Minnesota Writers, African American and Asian American poetry and fiction
Representative Authors: Anne Waldman, Karen Tei Yamashita, and Quincy Troupe
Simultaneous Submissions: no
Reading Period: Year-round
Reporting Time: one to two months
Author Payment: royalties
Founded: 1984
Non Profit: yes
Paid Staff: six
Unpaid Staff: three
Distributors: Consortium/SPD
Wholesalers: Ingram, Baker & Taylor, other major wholesalers
ISSN Number/ISBN Number: ISBN 1-56689
Number of Books Published per Year: 13
Titles in Print: 225
Average Print Run: 3,000
Average Percentage Printed: Hardcover 10%, Paperback 90%
Backfile Available: yes
Average Price: $15

Organization: Cold Mountain Review

Type: magazine
CLMP member: yes
Address: Dept. of English, ASU
Boone, NC 28608
Web Site Address: http://www.coldmountain.appstate.edu
Publishes: poetry, reviews, and art
Reading Period: Year-round
Reporting Time: one to two months
Author Payment: none
Founded: 1972
Non Profit: no
Backfile Available: yes

Organization: College Literature

Type: magazine
CLMP member: yes
Primary Editor/Contact Person: Kostas Myrsiades
Address: 210 E. Rosedale Ave.
West Chester University
West Chester, PA 19383
Web Site Address: http://www.collegeliterature.org
Publishes: essays and reviews

Editorial Focus: College Literature features a wide variety of approaches to textual analysis and the teaching of literary texts.
Representative Authors: Henry Giroux, Mustapha Marrouchi, and Jeffrey Williams
Submissions Policy: 8,000-10,000 words on textual analysis, literary theory, and pedagogy for today's college English classroom.
Simultaneous Submissions: yes
Reading Period: Year-round
Reporting Time: one to four months
Author Payment: none
Founded: 1974
Non Profit: yes
Paid Staff: two
Unpaid Staff: zero
ISSN Number/ISBN Number: ISSN 0093-3139
Total Circulation: 800
Paid Circulation: 600
Average Print Run: 900
Subscription Rate: Individual $40/Institution $100
Single Copy Price: $10
Current Volume/Issue: 34/1
Frequency per Year: quarterly
Backfile Available: yes
Unsolicited Ms. Received: yes
% of Unsolicited Ms. Published per Year: 75%
Format: perfect
Size: H 9" W 6"
Average Pages: 220
Ads: yes
Ad Rates: $175 full page; discount for successive issues
See web site for details.

Organization: Colorado Review

Type: magazine
CLMP member: yes
Primary Editor/Contact Person: Stephanie G'Schwind
Address: Dept. of English
Colorado State University
Fort Collins, CO 80523
Web Site Address:
http://coloradoreview.colostate.edu
Publishes: essays, fiction, nonfiction, poetry, and translation
Representative Authors: Paul Mandelbaum, Charles Baxter and Rae Armantrout
Submissions Policy: Please submit no more than one

story or essay, and no more than five poems at a time.
Simultaneous Submissions: yes
Reading Period: 9/1 to 4/30
Reporting Time: two to three months
Author Payment: cash and copies
Contests: See Web Site for Contest Guidelines.
Founded: 1956
Non Profit: yes
Paid Staff: one
Unpaid Staff: 20
Distributors: Ingram, Kent
ISSN Number/ISBN Number: ISSN 1046-3348
Total Circulation: 1,100
Paid Circulation: 800
Average Print Run: 1,400
Subscription Rate: Individual $24/Institution $34
Single Copy Price: $9.50
Current Volume/Issue: 34/3
Frequency per Year: triquarterly
Backfile Available: yes
Unsolicited Ms. Received: yes
% of Unsolicited Ms. Published per Year: 50%
Format: perfect
Size: H 6" W 9"
Average Pages: 200
Ads: yes
Ad Rates: whole page $150, half page $75
See web site for details.

Organization: Columbia: A Journal of Literature & Art

Type: magazine
CLMP member: yes
Primary Editor/Contact Person: Kristin Vukovic
Address: 415 Dodge Hall, Columbia University
2960 Broadway
New York, NY 10027
Web Site Address: http://www.columbiajournal.org
Publishes: essays, fiction, nonfiction, poetry, art, and translation
Representative Authors: : Wayne Koestenbaum, Lydia Davis, and Heather McHugh
Submissions Policy: see web site for guidelines
Simultaneous Submissions: yes
Reading Period: 9/1 to 5/1
Reporting Time: two to four months
Author Payment: copies
Contests: See web site for contest guidelines.
Founded: 1977

Non Profit: yes
Paid Staff: zero
Unpaid Staff: 20
Distributors: Ingram, Ubiquity, DeBoer
Wholesalers: EBSCO
ISSN Number/ISBN Number: ISBN 7-4470867-6-4
Total Circulation: 2,000
Paid Circulation: 100
Average Print Run: 2,000
Subscription Rate: Individual $15/Institution $15
Single Copy Price: $10
Current Volume/Issue: Issue 45
Frequency per Year: biannual
Backfile Available: yes
Unsolicited Ms. Received: yes
% of Unsolicited Ms. Published per Year: 30%
Format: perfect
Size: H 9" W 6"
Average Pages: 180
Ads: yes
See web site for details.

Organization: COMBAT

Type: online
CLMP member: no
Primary Editor/Contact Person: Ed. staff
Address: P.O. Box 3
Circleville, WV 26804-0003
Web Site Address: http://www.combat.ws/
Publishes: essays, fiction, nonfiction, poetry, art, and translation
Editorial Focus: non-partisan analysis and depiction of war and its aftermath
Submissions Policy: electronic submissions only
Simultaneous Submissions: yes
Reading Period: Year-round
Reporting Time: up to two weeks
Author Payment: none
Founded: 2002
Non Profit: yes
Paid Staff: zero
Unpaid Staff: five
ISSN Number/ISBN Number: ISSN 1542-1546
Frequency per Year: quarterly
Publish Print Anthology: no
Average Percentage of Pages per Category: Fiction 25%, Nonfiction 25%, Poetry 25%, Essays 25%
Ads: no

Organization: The Common Review

Type: magazine
CLMP member: no
Primary Editor/Contact Person: J.A. Smith
Address: 35 E. Wacker Dr., Ste. 2300
Chicago, IL 60601
Web Site Address: http://www.thecommonreview.org
Publishes: essays, poetry, reviews, and art
Editorial Focus: We publish intelligent, but not only academic writing including book reviews, literary travel pieces, and author profiles.
Representative Authors: Phillip Lopate, Regina Barreca, and Michael Berube
Submissions Policy: Unsolicited manuscripts should be preceded by a query. All others via e-mail or disk in MS Word/RTF with works/quotes cited.
Simultaneous Submissions: yes
Reading Period: Year-round
Reporting Time: one to two months
Author Payment: cash
Founded: 2001
Non Profit: yes
Paid Staff: three
Unpaid Staff: two
Distributors: Ingram, DeBoer
ISSN Number/ISBN Number: ISSN 1535-4784
Total Circulation: 10,000
Paid Circulation: 1,100
Average Print Run: 10,000
Subscription Rate: Individual $17.95/Institution $17.95
Single Copy Price: $4.95
Current Volume/Issue: 4/3
Frequency per Year: quarterly
Backfile Available: yes
Unsolicited Ms. Received: yes
% of Unsolicited Ms. Published per Year: 10%
Format: perfect
Size: H 10" W 8"
Average Pages: 64
Ads: yes
Ad Rates: Negotiable/swap-ads

Organization: Conduit

Type: magazine
CLMP member: yes
Primary Editor/Contact Person: William Waltz
Address: 510 8th Ave. N.E.
Minneapolis, MN 55413
Web Site Address: http://www.conduit.org
Publishes: essays, fiction, nonfiction, poetry, art, and translation
Recent Awards Recieved: Best of the Twin Cities
Representative Authors: Sawako Nakayasu, Tomaz Salamun, and Dean Young
Submissions Policy: Send three to five poems or one to three prose pieces (3,500 word maximum) with SASE. No electronic submissions.
Simultaneous Submissions: no
Reading Period: Year-round
Reporting Time: one to nine months
Author Payment: copies and submission
Founded: 1992
Non Profit: yes
Paid Staff: zero
Unpaid Staff: six
Distributors: DeBoer, Don Olson Distribution
ISSN Number/ISBN Number: ISSN 1073-6182
Total Circulation: 1,000
Paid Circulation: 400
Average Print Run: 1,000
Subscription Rate: Individual $18/Institution $28
Single Copy Price: $10
Current Volume/Issue: Issue 18
Frequency per Year: biannual
Backfile Available: yes
Unsolicited Ms. Received: yes
% of Unsolicited Ms. Published per Year: 5%
Format: perfect
Size: H 11" W 5"
Average Pages: 96
Ads: no

Organization: Confrontation Magazine

Type: press
CLMP member: yes
Primary Editor/Contact Person: Martin Tucker
Address: English department, C.W. Post of L.I.U.
Brookville, NY 11548
Web Site Address: http://www.liu.edu
Publishes: essays, fiction, nonfiction, poetry, reviews, art, and translation
Editorial Focus: literary Journal open to all forms and style; merit of style is criterion.
Representative Authors: David Ray, Nadine Gordimer, and Cynthia Ozick
Submissions Policy: open to poetry and stories. Essays for special topic supplement usually assigned;

memoirs a regular feature.
Simultaneous Submissions: yes
Reading Period: 9/1 to 3/31
Reporting Time: up to six weeks
Author Payment: cash and copies
Founded: 1968
Non Profit: yes
Paid Staff: two
Unpaid Staff: eight
Distributors: Ubiquity, DeBoer
Wholesalers: Baker & Taylor
ISSN Number/ISBN Number: 0010-5716/many
Number of Books Published per Year: two
Titles in Print: 19
Average Percentage Printed: Hardcover 20%, Paperback 70%, Chapbook 10%

Organization: Confrontation

Type: magazine
CLMP member: yes
Primary Editor/Contact Person: Martin Tucker
Address: CW Post of Long Island University
720 Northern Blvd/English Department
Brookville, NY 11548-1300
Publishes: essays, fiction, nonfiction, poetry, reviews, art, and translation
Editorial Focus: open to all forms and styles; quality is our main concern. We are an eclectic mix.
Representative Authors: Cynthia Ozick, David Ray, and Ihab Hassan
Submissions Policy: We do not consider mss. during June, July, August. Stories in print version only, poetry may be in e-mail submission. SASE
Simultaneous Submissions: yes
Reading Period: Year-round
Reporting Time: one to two months
Author Payment: cash and copies
Founded: 1968
Non Profit: yes
Paid Staff: two
Unpaid Staff: six
Distributors: DeBoer, Ubiquity
ISSN Number/ISBN Number: ISSN 0010 5716
Total Circulation: 2,000
Paid Circulation: 500
Average Print Run: 2,000
Subscription Rate: Individual $10/Institution $10
Single Copy Price: $10
Current Volume/Issue: Issue 90
Frequency per Year: biannual

Backfile Available: yes
Unsolicited Ms. Received: yes
% of Unsolicited Ms. Published per Year: 80%
Format: perfect
Size: H 9" W 6"
Average Pages: 300
Ads: yes
Ad Rates: varies

Organization: Conjunctions

Type: magazine
CLMP member: yes
Primary Editor/Contact Person: Bradford Morrow
Address: Bard College
Annandale-on-Hudson, NY 12504
Web Site Address: http://www.conjunctions.com
Publishes: essays, fiction, nonfiction, poetry, art, and translation
Editorial Focus: Features previously unpublished innovative contemporary fiction, poetry, drama, art, essays, interviews, and translations.
Representative Authors: William H. Gass, Joyce Carol Oates, and Rick Moody
Submissions Policy: Accepts previously unpublished submissions only. No electronic submissions will be considered. Please include an SASE.
Simultaneous Submissions: no
Reading Period: Year-round
Reporting Time: one to two months
Author Payment: cash, and copies
Founded: 1981
Non Profit: yes
Unpaid Staff: zero
Distributors: DAP
ISSN Number/ISBN Number: ISSN 0278-2324
Total Circulation: 4,000
Paid Circulation: 1,000
Average Print Run: 5,000
Subscription Rate: Individual $18/Institution $25
Single Copy Price: $15
Current Volume/Issue: 46/46
Frequency per Year: biannual
Backfile Available: yes
Unsolicited Ms. Received: yes
% of Unsolicited Ms. Published per Year: 33%
Format: perfect
Size: H 9" W 5"
Average Pages: 400
Ads: yes
Ad Rates: $350 per full page

Organization: Connecticut Review

Type: magazine
CLMP member: yes
Address: 39 Woodland St.
Hartford, CT 06790
Web Site Address:
http://www.connecitcutreview.com
Publishes: essays, fiction, nonfiction, poetry, reviews, art and translation
Reading Period: Year-round
Reporting Time: one to two months
Author Payment: none
Founded: 1967
Non Profit: no
Backfile Available: yes

Organization: Contemporary Poetry Review

Type: online
CLMP member: yes
Primary Editor/Contact Person: Ernest Hilbert
Address: P.O. Box 5222
Arlington, VA 22205
Web Site Address: http://www.cprw.com
Publishes: reviews
Editorial Focus: The CPR is the largest archive of poetry criticism in the world.
Representative Authors: Adam Kirsch, Peter Campion, and William Logan
Submissions Policy: The CPR only publishes criticism on poets and poetry. It does not print poetry.
Simultaneous Submissions: no
Reading Period: Year-round
Reporting Time: one to four weeks
Author Payment: cash
Contests: Contributors are paid $100 per article.
Founded: 1998
Non Profit: yes
Paid Staff: 25
Unpaid Staff: zero
Average Page Views per Month: 30,000
Average Unique Visitors per Month: 15,000
Frequency per Year: 12
Publish Print Anthology: no
Average Percentage of Pages per Category: Reviews 100%
Ad Rates: See web site for details.

Organization: CONTEXT

Type: magazine
CLMP member: no
Primary Editor/Contact Person: Martin Riker
Address: Dalkey Archive Press
605 E. Springfield, MC-475
Champaign, IL 61820
Website Address:
http://www.dalkeyarchive.com/context
Publishes: essays, fiction, nonfiction, reviews, and translation
Editorial Focus: Creating a historical and cultural context in which to read modern and contemporary literature.
Representative Authors: Gilbert Sorrentino, Jaimy Gordon, and Robert Creeley
Submissions Policy: no unsolicited submissions
Simultaneous Submissions: no
Reading Period: year-round
Reporting Time: 1 to 3 months
Author Payment: cash
Founded: 1981
Non Profit: yes
Paid Staff: 15
Unpaid Staff: 2
Total Circulation: 10,000
Paid Circulation: 0
Average Print Run: 10,000
Subscription Rate: Individual $0/Institution $0
Single Copy Price: $0
Current Volume/Issue: Issue 20
Frequency: 2
Backfile Available: yes
Unsolicited Ms. Received: no
Format: tabloid
Average Pages: 32
Ads: yes

Organization: CONTEXT

Type: online
CLMP member: no
Primary Editor/Contact Person: Martin Riker
Address: Dalkey Archive Press
605 E. Springfield Ave, MC-475
Champaign, IL 61820
Web Site Address: : www.dalkeyarchive.com
Publishes: essays, nonfiction, reviews, and translation
Editorial Focus: Creating a historical and cultural context in which to read modern and contemporary

literature.

Representative Authors: Gilbert Sorrentino, Jaimy Gordon, and Robert Creeley

Submissions Policy: no unsolicited submissions

Simultaneous Submissions: no

Reading Period: Year-round

Reporting Time: one to three months

Author Payment: cash

Founded: 1981

Non Profit: yes

Paid Staff: 15

Unpaid Staff: two

Distributors: Dalkey Archive Press

Average Page Views per Month: 20,000

Average Unique Visitors per Month: 200

Frequency per Year: biannual

Publish Print Anthology: no

Average Percentage of Pages per Category: Fiction 10%, Nonfiction 35%, Reviews 5%, Essays 35%, Translation 15%

Ads: yes

Organization: Contrary

Type: online

CLMP member: yes

Primary Editor/Contact Person: Jeff McMahon

Address: 3114 S. Wallace St. Ste. 2

Chicago, IL 60616-3299

Web Site Address:

http://www.contrarymagazine.com

Publishes: essays, fiction, nonfiction, poetry, and art

Editorial Focus: We like poetic fiction, fictional commentary, commenting poetry, work that confronts the constraints of its genre.

Representative Authors: see Andrew Coburn, Patrick Loafman, and Edward Mc Whinney

Submissions Policy: We accept only electronic submissions though the submissions form at our website: www.contrarymagazine.com

Simultaneous Submissions: yes

Reading Period: Year-round

Reporting Time: one to three months

Author Payment: cash

Founded: 2003

Non Profit: yes

Paid Staff: zero

Unpaid Staff: nine

ISSN Number/ISBN Number: ISSN 1549-7038

Average Page Views per Month: 62,000

Average Unique Visitors per Month: 5,500

Frequency per Year: quarterly

Publish Print Anthology: yes

Average Percentage of Pages per Category: Fiction 33%, Nonfiction 20%, Poetry 33%, Essays 10%, Art 4%

Ads: no

Organization: conundrum press

Type: press

CLMP member: no

Primary Editor/Contact Person: Andy Brown

Address: PO Box 55003 CSP Fairmount

Montreal, PQ H2T 3E2

Web Site Address: www.conundrumpress.com

Publishes: fiction and art

Editorial Focus: We publish quirky or experimental fiction and graphic novels which are difficult to classify for bookstores.

Recent Awards Received: Winnipeg Book Award, shortlisted for ReLit Awards

Representative Authors: Corey Frost, Shary Boyle, and Catherine Kidd

Submissions Policy: No submissions

Author Payment: royalties

Contests: None

Founded: 1996

Non Profit: no

Distributors: Litdistco, Diamond, Bodega, Cold Cut

Wholesalers: Ingram, Baker and Taylor

Number of Books Published per Year: five

Titles in Print: 25

Average Print Run: 1,000

Average Percentage Printed: paperback 100%

Average Price: $17

Organization: Cool Grove Press

Type: press

CLMP member: yes

Primary Editor/Contact Person: Tej Hazarika

Address: 512 Argyle Road

Brooklyn, NY 11218

Web Site Address: http://www.coolgrove.com

Publishes: fiction, nonfiction, poetry, art, and translation

Editorial Focus: Social transformation and education through literature, art and culture.

Recent Awards Received: Council of Literary Magazines and Presses (CLMP) Face Out recipient,

2007-2008
Representative Authors: ihsan bracy, Kevin
Bartelme, and Louise Landes Levi
Submissions Policy: No unsolicited manuscripts.
Send one page or less letter to tej@coolgrove.com
with synopsis and reasons
Simultaneous Submissions: no
Reading Period: Year-round
Reporting Time: one to two months
Author Payment: royalties, cash, and copies
Founded: 1993
Non Profit: no
Paid Staff: one
Unpaid Staff: one
Distributors: no exclusive distributors
Wholesalers: Baker & Taylor Books, Small Press
Distribution
ISSN Number/ISBN Number: ISBN 1-887276-
Number of Books Published per Year: 2
Titles in Print: 17
Average Print Run: 1,000
Average Percentage Printed: Hardcover 25%,
Paperback 75%
Average Price: $17.95

Organization: Copper Canyon Press

Type: press
CLMP member: yes
Primary Editor/Contact Person: Michael Wiegers
Address: P.O. Box 271
Port Townsend, WA 98368
Web Site Address:
http://www.coppercanyonpress.org/
Publishes: poetry
Editorial Focus: CCP publishes contemporary
American poetry and poetry in translation.
Recent Awards Received: Pulitzer Prize, National
Book Award, Lenore Marshall Award, Lambda Literary
Award
Representative Authors: Ted Kooser, C. D. Wright,
and W. S. Merwin
Submissions Policy: We do not accept unsolicited
manuscripts.
Simultaneous Submissions: no
Reading Period: Year-round
Reporting Time: two to three months
Author Payment: royalties
Contests: none
Founded: 1972
Non Profit: yes

Paid Staff: seven
Unpaid Staff: two
Distributors: Consortium
Wholesalers: Ingram, Baker & Taylor, SPD
ISSN Number/ISBN Number: ISBN 1-55659
Number of Books Published per Year: 14-18
Titles in Print: 350
Average Print Run: 2,500
Average Percentage Printed: Hardcover 10%,
Paperback 90%
Average Price: $16

Organization: The Cortland Review

Type: online
CLMP member: no
Primary Editor/Contact Person: Guy Shahar
Address: 527 Third Ave. #279
New York, NY 10016
Web Site Address: http://www.cortlandreview.com
Publishes: essays, fiction, nonfiction, poetry, reviews,
art, translation, and audio
Representative Authors: R.T. Smith, John Kinsella,
and David Lehman
Submissions Policy: Varies, please see our submis-
sion page on web site.
Simultaneous Submissions: no
Reading Period: 9/1 to 5/31
Reporting Time: 6 to 12 months
Author Payment: none
Founded: 1997
Non Profit: yes
Paid Staff: zero
Unpaid Staff: 12
ISSN Number/ISBN Number: ISSN 1524-6744
Backfile Available: no
Average Page Views per Month: 250,000
Average Unique Visitors per Month: 30,000
Frequency per Year: eight times
Publish Print Anthology: no
Average Percentage of Pages per Category: Fiction
5%, Nonfiction 5%, Poetry 30%, Reviews 5%, Essays
5%, Audio 50%
Ads: no

Organization: Coteau Books

Type: press
CLMP member: no
Primary Editor/Contact Person: Nik L. Burton,
Managing Editor

Address: 2517 Victoria Ave.
Regina, SK S4P 0T2
Web Site Address: http://www.coteaubooks.com
Publishes: fiction, nonfiction, and poetry
Editorial Focus: Canadian works of literary art, with an emphasis on western Canada
Representative Authors: J. Jill Robinson, Linda Smith, and Terrence Heath
Submissions Policy: Canadian or "permanent residence" authors only. Complete manuscript, hard copy submissions only. No simultaneous.
Simultaneous Submissions: no
Reading Period: Year-round
Reporting Time: two to three months
Author Payment: royalties
Founded: 1975
Non Profit: yes
Paid Staff: six
Unpaid Staff: zero
Distributors: Fitzhenry & Whiteside
Wholesalers: As many as possible
ISSN Number/ISBN Number: ISBN 978-1-55050-
Number of Books Published per Year: 16
Titles in Print: 150
Average Print Run: 2,000
Average Percentage Printed: Paperback 100%
Average Price: $18.95

Organization: Cottonwood Magazine and Press

Type: magazine
CLMP member: yes
Primary Editor/Contact Person: Tom Lorenz, Editor
Address: 1301 Jayhawk Blvd. Rm. 400 Kansas Union
Kansas Union, Univ. of Kansas
Lawrence, KS 66045
Publishes: essays, fiction, poetry, and reviews
Editorial Focus: We publish fiction and poetry with clear images and interesting narratives. Submissions from throughout the US considered.
Representative Authors: Rita Dove, Virgil Suarez, and Cris Mazza
Submissions Policy: Submit 4-6 poems and 1 story (1,000 to 7,000 words); include SASE
Simultaneous Submissions: yes
Reading Period: Year-round
Reporting Time: three to six months
Author Payment: copies
Founded: 1965
Non Profit: yes

Paid Staff: zero
Unpaid Staff: 14
Total Circulation: 500
Paid Circulation: 150
Average Print Run: 600
Subscription Rate: Individual $15/Institution $10.50
Single Copy Price: $8.50
Current Volume/Issue: Issue 65/65
Frequency per Year: annual
Backfile Available: yes
Unsolicited Ms. Received: yes
% of Unsolicited Ms. Published per Year: 1%
Format: perfect
Size: H 9" W 6"
Average Pages: 104
Ads: no

Organization: Crab Creek Review

Type: magazine
CLMP member: yes
Primary Editor/Contact Person: Emily Bedard
Address: P.O. Box 85088
Seattle, WA 98145-1088
Web Site Address: http://www.crabcreekreview.org
Publishes: fiction, poetry, and art
Editorial Focus: Eclectic poetry and dynamic short fiction. Memorable voices and canny cover art.
Representative Authors: Martha Silano, Kathleen Flenniken, and Gregory Hischak
Submissions Policy: Up to five poems. Short shorts and stories up to 6,000 words.
Simultaneous Submissions: no
Reading Period: Year-round
Reporting Time: four to five months
Author Payment: copies
Contests: See web site for contest guidelines.
Founded: 1983
Non Profit: yes
Paid Staff: zero
Unpaid Staff: four
Distributors: Ubiquity, Small Changes
Wholesalers: EBSCO
ISSN Number/ISBN Number: ISSN 0738-7008
Total Circulation: 400
Paid Circulation: 200
Average Print Run: 600
Subscription Rate: Individual $12/Institution $20
Single Copy Price: $7
Current Volume/Issue: XIX/1
Frequency per Year: biannual

Backfile Available: yes
Unsolicited Ms. Received: yes
% of Unsolicited Ms. Published per Year: 5%
Format: perfect
Size: H 9" W 6"
Average Pages: 100
Ads: no

Organization: Crab Orchard Review

Type: magazine
CLMP member: yes
Primary Editor/Contact Person: Allison Joseph/Jon Tribble
Address: Department of English, Mail Code 4503 SIUC, 1000 Faner Dr.
Carbondale, IL 62901
Web Site Address: http://www.siu.edu/~crborchd/
Publishes: essays, fiction, nonfiction, and poetry
Editorial Focus: A biannual journal of new works by writers from across the nation and around the world.
Recent Awards Received: 2007 Illinois Arts Literary Awards
Representative Authors: Luisa A. Igloria, Kevin Stein, and Donna Hemans
Submissions Policy: Simultaneous submissions welcome with notice. No e-mail submissions. Check the web site for complete guidelines.
Simultaneous Submissions: yes
Reading Period: 9/06 to 4/07
Reporting Time: one to seven months
Author Payment: cash, copies, and subscription
Contests: See web site for contest guidelines.
Founded: 1995
Non Profit: yes
Paid Staff: nine
Unpaid Staff: 16
ISSN Number/ISBN Number: ISSN 1083-5571
Total Circulation: 2,700
Paid Circulation: 2,300
Average Print Run: 3,300
Subscription Rate: Individual $15/Institution $16
Single Copy Price: $10
Current Volume/Issue: 12/2
Frequency per Year: biannual
Backfile Available: yes
Unsolicited Ms. Received: yes
% of Unsolicited Ms. Published per Year: 1%
Format: perfect
Size: H 8 1/2" W 5 1/2"
Average Pages: 304

Ads: no

Organization: Cranky Literary Journal

Type: magazine
CLMP member: no
Primary Editor/Contact Person: Amber Curtis
Address: 322 10th Ave. E. C-5
Seattle, WA 98102
Web Site Address: http://www.failedpromise.org
Publishes: essays, fiction, poetry, and reviews
Editorial Focus: Cranky Literary Journal is like a kid let out for recess: small, but with a big shouting voice.
Representative Authors: Olena Kalytiak Davis, Kary Wayson, and Matthew Zapruder
Submissions Policy: We only accept submissions via e-mail. Your submission must be accompanied by a brief cover letter and a bio of less than 50 words. Send three to five poems or one to two prose pieces under 2,000 words each. Paste your submission into the body of an e-mail and send to submissions@failedpromise.org. Please write either Poetry Submission or Fiction Submission in the subject line. We do not accept attachments.
Simultaneous Submissions: yes
Reading Period: Year-round
Reporting Time: up to six weeks
Author Payment: copies
Contests: no contests.
Founded: 2003
Non Profit: yes
Paid Staff: zero
Unpaid Staff: five
ISSN Number/ISBN Number: ISSN 1550-0330
Total Circulation: 500
Paid Circulation: 100
Average Print Run: 500
Subscription Rate: Individual $20/Institution $20
Single Copy Price: $8
Current Volume/Issue: 1/6
Frequency per Year: triquarterly
Backfile Available: yes
Unsolicited Ms. Received: yes
% of Unsolicited Ms. Published per Year: 95%
Format: perfect
Size: H 9" W 6"
Average Pages: 110
Ads: no

Organization: Crazyhorse

Type: magazine

CLMP member: yes
Primary Editor/Contact Person: Garrett Doherty, Co-Editor
Address: English Dept., College of Charleston
66 George St.
Charleston, SC 29424
Web Site Address: http://crazyhorse.cofc.edu
Publishes: essays, fiction, nonfiction, poetry, art, and translation
Editorial Focus: Today's fiction, essays, and poetry: from the mainstream to the avant-garde, from the established to the undiscovered writer.
Recent Awards Received: Best American Poetry 2007, 2006, 2005; Pushcart Prize; reprinted in Harper's
Representative Authors: Dean Young, Michael Martone, and Nance Van Winckel
Submissions Policy: Send up to 25 pages of prose or three to five poems. Send with SASE.
Simultaneous Submissions: yes
Reading Period: Year-round
Reporting Time: three to four months
Author Payment: cash, copies, and subscription
Contests: See web site for contest guidelines.
Founded: 1960
Non Profit: yes
Paid Staff: three
Unpaid Staff: four
Distributors: Ingram, DeBoer
ISSN Number/ISBN Number: ISSN 0011-0841
Total Circulation: 2,500
Paid Circulation: 2,000
Average Print Run: 2,800
Subscription Rate: Individual $15/Institution $15
Single Copy Price: $8.50
Current Volume/Issue: Issue 71
Frequency per Year: biannual
Backfile Available: yes
Unsolicited Ms. Received: yes
% of Unsolicited Ms. Published per Year: 3%
Format: perfect
Size: H 8.75" W 8.25"
Average Pages: 160
Ads: yes
Ad Rates: $200/full page
See web site for details.

Organization: Creative Nonfiction

Type: magazine
CLMP member: yes
Primary Editor/Contact Person: Lee Gutkind
Address: 5501 Walnut St, Ste. 202
Pittsburgh, PA 15232-2329
Web Site Address: http://www.creativenonfiction.org
Publishes: essays and nonfiction
Editorial Focus: First journal devoted exclusively to literary nonfiction. Publishes personal essay, memoir, and literary journalism.
Representative Authors: Richard Rodriguez, Tracy Kidder, and Annie Dillard
Submissions Policy: Accepts hard copy only. SASE and cover letter required for reply. No queries. No reprints.
Simultaneous Submissions: yes
Reading Period: Year-round
Reporting Time: three to five months
Author Payment: cash and copies
Contests: See web site for contest guidelines.
Founded: 1993
Non Profit: yes
Paid Staff: three
Unpaid Staff: two
Distributors: Ingram, Media Solutions
ISSN Number/ISBN Number: ISSN 1070-0714
Total Circulation: 3,500
Paid Circulation: 2,100
Average Print Run: 4,500
Subscription Rate: Individual $29.95/Institution $40
Single Copy Price: $10
Current Volume/Issue: Issue 26
Frequency per Year: triquarterly
Backfile Available: yes
Unsolicited Ms. Received: yes
% of Unsolicited Ms. Published per Year: 10%
Format: perfect
Size: H 8" W 5.5"
Average Pages: 144
Ads: yes
Ad Rates: See Web Site for Details.

Organization: Creative Nonfiction

Type: press
CLMP member: yes
Primary Editor/Contact Person: Lee Gutkind
Address: 5501 Walnut St, Ste. 202
Pittsburgh, PA 15232-2329
Web Site Address: http://www.creativenonfiction.org
Publishes: essays and nonfiction
Editorial Focus: First journal devoted exclusively to literary nonfiction. Publishes personal essay, memoir, and literary journalism.

Representative Authors: Richard Rodriguez, Tracy Kidder, and Annie Dillard
Submissions Policy: Accepts hard copy only. SASE and cover letter required for reply. No queries. No reprints.
Simultaneous Submissions: yes
Reading Period: Year-round
Reporting Time: three to five months
Author Payment: cash, copies, and subscription
Contests: Has sponsored essay contests with awards of up to $10,000; see web site for contest guidelines.
Founded: 1993
Non Profit: yes
Paid Staff: six
Unpaid Staff: three
Distributors: Ingram, Media Solutions
ISSN Number/ISBN Number: ISSN 1070-0714
Number of Books Published per Year: 3
Titles in Print: 32
Average Print Run: 5,000
Average Percentage Printed: Paperback 100%
Average Price: $10

Organization: Creighton University Press

Type: press
CLMP member: yes
Primary Editor/Contact Person: Dr. David Gardiner
Address: Department of Fine and Performing Arts
2500 California Plaza
Omaha, NE 68178
Website Address:
http://www2.creighton.edu/cupress/
Publishes: essays, fiction, nonfiction, reviews, and art
Editorial Focus: We publish books and journals addressing contemporary Irish Studies, Jesuit Studies and Theology, welcoming both new and established scholars.
Representative Authors: Gerald Dawe, Sighle Bhreathnach-Lynch, and James Liddy
Submissions Policy: Submissions made in duplicate in academic standards. Contributor's name on separate cover sheet for blind review. Double space.
Simultaneous Submissions: yes
Reading Period: year-round
Reporting Time: up to 6 months
Author Payment: royalties
Founded: 1994
Non Profit: yes
Paid Staff: 2

Unpaid Staff: 0
Distributors: Fordham University Press
Wholesalers: Fordham University Press
ISSN Number/ISBN Number: 1554-8953/99781881871521
Number of Books Published per Year: 3
Titles in Print: 5
Average Print Run: 500
Average Percentage Printed: Paperback 100%
Average Price: $25.00

Organization: Creosote: A Journal of Poetry and Prose

Type: magazine
CLMP member: no
Primary Editor/Contact Person: Ken Raines
Address: Dept. of English, Mohave Community Coll.
1977 W. Acoma Blvd.
Lake Havasu City, AZ 86403
Publishes: essays, fiction, nonfiction, and poetry
Editorial Focus: We have a slight bias in favor of traditional forms and verse. However, all quality work is considered.
Representative Authors: Ruth Moose, Charles Springer, and Ryan G. Van Cleave
Submissions Policy: Up to five poems or 5,000 words of prose considered in each submission. No previously published material.
Simultaneous Submissions: yes
Reading Period: 8/1 to 3/1
Reporting Time: two to six months
Author Payment: copies
Founded: 1999
Non Profit: yes
Paid Staff: no
Unpaid Staff: yes
Total Circulation: 400
Paid Circulation: 45
Subscription Rate: Individual $4/Institution $4
Single Copy Price: $4
Current Volume/Issue: 4/1
Frequency per Year: annual
Backfile Available: yes
Unsolicited Ms. Received: yes
% of Unsolicited Ms. Published per Year: 3-5%
Format: stapled
Size: H 8.5" W 5.5"
Average Pages: 48
Ads: no

Organization: The Crier

Type: magazine
CLMP member: yes
Primary Editor/Contact Person: Doree Shafrir
Address: 220 DeKalb Avenue
Brooklyn, NY 11205
Website Address: www.thecriermag.com
Publishes: essays, nonfiction, reviews, and art
Editorial Focus: We publish non-fiction exclusively--
everything from long-form narrative journalism to critical essays.
Submissions Policy: Submit queries via email.
Simultaneous Submissions: yes
Reading Period: year-round
Reporting Time: 4 to 6 weeks
Author Payment: copies and subscription
Founded: 2006
Non Profit: no
Paid Staff: 0
Unpaid Staff: 6
Distributors: Ubiquity
ISSN Number/ISBN Number: ISSN: 1933-3927
Total Circulation: 1,000
Paid Circulation: 200
Average Print Run: 1,000
Subscription Rate: Individual $28/Institution $50
Single Copy Price: $9.00
Current Volume/Issue: Issue 4
Frequency per Year: 4
Backfile Available: yes
Unsolicited Ms. Received: yes
% of Unsolicited Ms. Published per Year: 10%
Format: perfect
Average Pages: 96
Ads: yes
Ad Rates: See website for details

Organization: Crossing Rivers Into Twilight: CRIT Journal

Type: online
CLMP member: no
Primary Editor/Contact Person: Elizabeth Kate Switaj
Address: 215 163rd Place SE
Bellevue, WA 98008
Web Site Address: www.critjournal.com
Publishes: essays, fiction, nonfiction, poetry, art and translation
Editorial Focus: CRIT Journal seeks work that deals with themes of transition,.liminality, and gray areas. Hybrid work is especially valued.
Representative Authors: Jade Sylvan, Francis Raven, and Bob Marcacci
Submissions Policy: We will consider previously published work. Longer texts must be of especially high quality.
Simultaneous Submissions: yes
Reading Period: year-round
Reporting Time: one to two months
Author Payment: none
Founded: 2006
Non Profit: yes
Paid Staff: zero
Unpaid Staff: one
Average Page Views Per Month: 150
Average Unique Visitors Per Month: 75
Frequency: 4
Publish Print Anthology: no
Average Percentage of Pages per Category: Fiction 9%, Poetry 70%, Essays 1%, Art 20%
Ads: no

Organization: CROWD

Type: magazine
CLMP member: yes
Primary Editor/Contact Person: Aimee Kelley
Address: P.O. Box 1373
New York, NY 10276
Web Site Address: http://www.crowdmagazine.com
Publishes: essays, fiction, nonfiction, poetry, and art
Editorial Focus: CROWD publishes visual art and writing from all genres.
Representative Authors: Shelley Jackson, Paul Muldoon, and Lyn Hejinian
Submissions Policy: Please include SASE for reply. We encourage purchasing a copy or submission prior to submitting work.
Simultaneous Submissions: yes
Reading Period: 9/15 to 5/15
Reporting Time: one to four months
Author Payment: copies
Founded: 2001
Non Profit: yes
Paid Staff: zero
Unpaid Staff: four
Distributors: DeBoer, Ingram, Ubiquity
Total Circulation: 1,000
Paid Circulation: 125
Average Print Run: 1,000

Subscription Rate: Individual $18/Institution $25
Single Copy Price: $10
Current Volume/Issue: Issue 5/6
Frequency per Year: biannual
Backfile Available: yes
Unsolicited Ms. Received: yes
% of Unsolicited Ms. Published per Year: 65%
Format: perfect
Size: H 9" W 6.75"
Average Pages: 130
Ads: yes
Ad Rates: $150 per full page

Organization: Crying Sky: Poetry and Conversation

Type: magazine
CLMP member: yes
Primary Editor/Contact Person: W.E. Butts and S. Stephanie
Address: 164 Maple St. Unit 1
Manchester, NH 03103
Publishes: essays and poetry
Editorial Focus: Features established and emerging poets, and interviews. Seeks well-crafted poetry reflecting the human condition.
Representative Authors: David Wojahn, Betsy Sholl, and Robert Wrigley
Submissions Policy: Submit three to five typed poems, bio and SASE.
Simultaneous Submissions: no
Reading Period: Year-round
Reporting Time: one to two months
Author Payment: copies
Contests: Occasionally sponsors judged contests.
Founded: 2004
Non Profit: no
Paid Staff: zero
Unpaid Staff: two
Distributors: DeBoer
ISSN Number/ISBN Number: ISSN 1551-9848
Total Circulation: 500
Paid Circulation: 60
Average Print Run: 500
Subscription Rate: Individual $16/Institution $12.80
Single Copy Price: $9
Current Volume/Issue: 2/3
Frequency per Year: biannual
Backfile Available: yes
Unsolicited Ms. Received: yes
% of Unsolicited Ms. Published per Year: 5%

Format: stapled
Size: H 8 1/2" W 5 1/2"
Average Pages: 84
Ads: no

Organization: Curbstone Press

Type: press
CLMP member: yes
Primary Editor/Contact Person: Alexander Taylor
Address: 321 Jackson St.
Willimantic, CT 06226
Web Site Address: http://www.curbstone.org
Publishes: essays, fiction, poetry, and translation
Editorial Focus: literature that reflects a commitment to human rights and intercultural understanding.
Representative Authors: Claribel Alegria, Marnie Mueller, and Luis J. Rodr,guez
Submissions Policy: Please make sure your ms. fits Curbstone's mission. Then send query letter, author info, publication history, and sample of ms.
Simultaneous Submissions: yes
Reading Period: Year-round
Reporting Time: one to three months
Author Payment: royalties
Contests: See web site for contest guidelines.
Founded: 1975
Non Profit: yes
Paid Staff: four
Unpaid Staff: two
Distributors: Consortium
Wholesalers: most of them
ISSN Number/ISBN Number: ISBN 1-880684/1-931896
Number of Books Published per Year: 9-12
Titles in Print: 162
Average Print Run: 2,000
Average Percentage Printed: Hardcover 7%, Paperback 93%
Average Price: $14

Organization: Cutbank

Type: magazine
CLMP member: no
Primary Editor/Contact Person: Jason McMackin
Address: Department of English
University of Montana
Missoula, MT 59812
Web Site Address:
http://www.umt.edu/cutbank/default.htm

Publishes: essays, fiction, nonfiction, and poetry
Editorial Focus: Quality poetry, fiction, and literary non-fiction by established writers and new voices. Global in scope with a regional bias.
Submissions Policy: up to 40 pp prose, five poems.
Simultaneous Submissions: yes
Reading Period: 8/15 to 4/15
Reporting Time: one to two months
Author Payment: copies
Contests: Patricia Goedicke Prize in poetry, CutBank Prize in Fiction, and CutBank Prize in Nonfiction. Each $500. Submit Dec.-Feb.; see website for guidelines.
Founded: 1973
Non Profit: yes
Paid Staff: zero
Unpaid Staff: six
Total Circulation: 500
Paid Circulation: 150
Average Print Run: 1000
Subscription Rate: Individual $6. per/Institution $6
Single Copy Price: $7.95
Current Volume/Issue: Issue 62
Frequency per Year: biannual
Backfile Available: yes
Unsolicited Ms. Received: yes
% of Unsolicited Ms. Published per Year: 1-2%
Format: perfect
Average Pages: 125
Ads: yes
Ad Rates: see website for details

Organization: CUZ Editions

Type: press
CLMP member: no
Primary Editor/Contact Person: Richard Meyers
Address: PO Box 1599
Stuyvesant Station
New York, NY 10009-1599
Web Site Address: www.richardhell.com/cuzlist.html
Publishes: essays, fiction, nonfiction, poetry, art, and translation
Editorial Focus: Primarily poetry.
Representative Authors: Ron Padgett, Maggie Dubris, and Rene Ricard
Submissions Policy: We do not look at unsolicited manuscripts at present.
Simultaneous Submissions: no
Author Payment: copies
Founded: 1998
Non Profit: no

Paid Staff: zero
Unpaid Staff: one
Number of Books Published per year: one
Titles in Print: seven
Average Print Run: 500
Average Percentage Printed: chapbook 100%
Average Price: $6.95

Organization: Dalkey Archive Press

Type: press
CLMP member: yes
Primary Editor/Contact Person: Martin Riker
Address: University of Illinois
605 E. Springfield Ave., MC-475
Champaign, IL 61820
Web Site Address: http://www.dalkeyarchive.com
Publishes: fiction and translation
Editorial Focus: Modern and contemporary works of innovative world literature.
Representative Authors: Flann O'Brien, Gilbert Sorrentino, and Ishmael Reed
Simultaneous Submissions: yes
Reading Period: Year-round
Reporting Time: two to six months
Author Payment: royalties, cash, and copies
Founded: 1984
Non Profit: yes
Paid Staff: 15
Unpaid Staff: two
Distributors: University of Nebraska Press
Wholesalers: Ingram, Baker & Taylor
ISSN Number/ISBN Number: ISBN 1-56478-, 0-916583-
Number of Books Published per Year: 25
Titles in Print: 360
Average Percentage Printed: Hardcover 10%, Paperback 90%
Average Price: $12.50

Organization: Dan River Press

Type: press
CLMP member: no
Primary Editor/Contact Person: Richard S. Danbury, III
Address: P.O. Box 298
Thomaston, ME 04861
Web Site Address: http://www.americanletters.org
Publishes: fiction and nonfiction
Editorial Focus: Fiction and biography only.

Representative Authors: Jim Ainsworth, Andrew Laszlo, and James R. Clifford
Submissions Policy: No electronic submissions, nothing previously published. Send personal marketing plan.
Simultaneous Submissions: yes
Reading Period: Year-round
Reporting Time: one to six weeks
Author Payment: royalties
Founded: 1976
Non Profit: yes
Paid Staff: one
Unpaid Staff: one
Distributors: Ingram, Baker & Taylor, Barnes & Noble, amazon.com
ISSN Number/ISBN Number: ISBN 0-89754-xxx-x
Titles in Print: 30
Average Percentage Printed: Hardcover 5%, Paperback 95%

Organization: dANDelion

Type: magazine
CLMP member: no
Primary Editor/Contact Person: Managing Editor
Address: Dept. of English, U. of C.
2500 University Drive NW
Calgary, AB T2N 1N4
Web Site Address: http://www.dandelionmagazine.ca
Publishes: essays, fiction, nonfiction, poetry, reviews, and art
Editorial Focus: dANDelion magazine showcases fiction and poetics, imagery and artwork by some of the most culturally innovative writers and artists in the world, be they interregional, transnational or or international in their audiences. Each issue of the magazine documents its own distinctive, fashionable attitude toward the modern milieu of literary activity and artistic practice. The magazine exemplifies a continued, dedicated commitment to support for new writing and new artwork by a diverse variety of cultural thinkers.
Recent Awards Received: Alberta Magzine Publishers Association (Cover Art), Western Magazine Awards (Nominee)
Representative Authors: George Bowering, Robert Kroetsch, and Nicole Brossard
Submissions Policy: Canadian/international writers/artists, unpublished works, challenge form, Apr. & Dec. Go to www.dandelionmagazine.ca for details.

Simultaneous Submissions: no
Reading Period: Year-round
Reporting Time: one month
Author Payment: cash and copies
Founded: 1974
Non Profit: yes
Paid Staff: two
Unpaid Staff: 30
Distributors: Magazines Canada, EBSCO, SWETS
ISSN Number/ISBN Number: ISSN 0383-9575
Total Circulation: 1,000
Paid Circulation: 300
Average Print Run: 500
Subscription Rate: Individual $18/Institution $25
Single Copy Price: $10
Current Volume/Issue: 32/1
Frequency: biannual
Backfile Available: yes
Unsolicited Ms. Received: yes
% of Unsolicited Ms. Published per Year: 90%
Format: perfect
Size: H 7" W 6"
Average Pages: 100
Ads: yes
Ad Rates: see website for details

Organization: David Paul Books

Type: press
CLMP member: no
Primary Editor/Contact Person: David Paul
Address: 25 Methuen Park
London
England, UK N10 2JR
Web Site Address: http://www.davidpaulbooks.com
Publishes: fiction, nonfiction, and translation
Editorial Focus: Good quality cutting edge fiction, translations, focus on themes of Jewish or intercultural interest
Recent Awards Received: International PEN Tucholsky Award to Palestinian writer Samir El Youssef for his novella in Gaza Blues.
Representative Authors: Etgar Keret, Esther Singer Kreitman, and Samir El Youssef
Submissions Policy: Will only take submissions from previously published authors
Simultaneous Submissions: no
Reading Period: Year-round
Reporting Time: two to six weeks
Author Payment: royalties and copies
Founded: 2001

Non Profit: no
Paid Staff: one
Unpaid Staff: one
Distributors: Central Books (not N America)
Wholesalers: Gardners, Bertrams
Number of Books Published per Year: three
Titles in Print: nine
Average Print Run: 1,500
Average Percentage Printed: Hardcover 25%, Paperback 75%
Average Price: $16

Organization: Davus Publishing

Type: press
CLMP member: no
Primary Editor/Contact Person: David Beasley
Address: 150 Norfolk St South
Simcoe, ON N3Y 2W2
Web Site Address: www.kwic.com/davus
Publishes: fiction, nonfiction, and art
Editorial Focus: specializes in works by David Beasley
Recent Awards Received: best novel award from Hamilton and Region arts council
Representative Authors: David Beasley and Major John Richardson
Submissions Policy: do not accept submissions
Simultaneous Submissions: no
Reading Period: year-round
Reporting Time: one to six weeks
Author Payment: none
Founded: 1983
Non Profit: no
Paid Staff: zero
Unpaid Staff: one
Distributors: none at moment
Wholesalers: Blitzprint, Calgary, AB
ISSN Number/ISBN Number: ISBN 0-95317
Number of Books Published per year: one
Titles in Print: 20
Average Print Run: 300
Average Percentage Printed: paperback 100%
Average Price: $15

Organization: DC Books

Type: press
CLMP member: no
Primary Editor/Contact Person: Steve Luxton
Address: Box 662

950 Decarie
Montreal, QC H4L4V9
Web Site Address: http://www.dcbooks.ca
Publishes: essays, fiction, nonfiction, poetry, and translation
Editorial Focus: Literary publisher of Canadian fiction, drama, and poetry. Some foreign English language work also considered.
Recent Awards Received: IPPY Award Best Fiction Eastern Canada, QWF Best First Novel, Frank Collymore Award
Representative Authors: Keith Henderson, Todd Swift, and Louis Dudek
Submissions Policy: Query first.
Simultaneous Submissions: yes
Reading Period: Year-round
Reporting Time: 6 to 12 months
Author Payment: royalties, cash, and copies
Founded: 1974
Non Profit: no
Paid Staff: zero
Unpaid Staff: three
Distributors: LitDistCo
ISSN Number/ISBN Number: ISBN 0919688, 1897190
Number of Books Published per Year: five
Titles in Print: 65
Average Print Run: 600
Average Percentage Printed: Hardcover 10%, Paperback 90%
Average Price: $17

Organization: Deep South

Type: online
CLMP member: no
Primary Editor/Contact Person: Cy Mathews
Address: English Dept. Otago University, PO Box 56, Dunedin, New Zealand
Web Site Address: www.otago.ac.nz/Deep South/
Publishes: essays, fiction, nonfiction, poetry, reviews, art, and translation
Editorial Focus: Showcases original poetry, fiction, and critical/academic articles on literature, media, culture and the arts.
Representative Authors: Iain Britton, Mary Cresswell, and Richard Reeve
Submissions Policy: Electronic submissions preferred. If sent by mail, please include a copy on disk.
Simultaneous Submissions: no
Reading Period: year-round

Reporting Time: one to two months
Author Payment: none
Founded: 1995
Non Profit: yes
Paid Staff: zero
Unpaid Staff: seven
Average Page Views per Month: 2,040
Average Unique Visitors per Month: 130
Frequency per year: annual
Publish Print Anthology: no
Average Percentage of Pages per Category: fiction 16%, nonfiction 4%, poetry 53%, reviews 3%, essays 24%
Ad Rates: see web site for details

Organization: Del Sol Press

Type: press
CLMP member: no
Primary Editor/Contact Person: Joan Houlihan
Address: 2020 Pennsylvania Ave.
Ste. 443
Washington, DC 20006
Web Site Address: http://webdelsol.com/DelSolPress
Publishes: fiction and poetry
Editorial Focus: DSP seeks to publish exceptional work by both new and recognized writers, as well as republish literary works that we consider extremely significant and that have gone out of print.
Representative Authors: Michael Brodksy, Kimberly Nichols, and Joan Houlihan
Submissions Policy: Currently, DSP is not taking unsolicited submissions, synopses, or outlines in any form, however, query letters and all other communications, including requests for review copies can be sent to dspress@webdelsol.com. In your query letter, please include a bio, publishing history for this project (if any), and other previous publications. Poetry queries should be sent to dsp-poetry@webdelsol.com.
Simultaneous Submissions: yes
Reading Period: Year-round
Reporting Time: two to six weeks
Author Payment: copies
Contests: Del Sol Press Poetry Prize: http://webdelsol.com/DelSolPress/contest.htm
Founded: 2003
Non Profit: yes
Paid Staff: zero
Unpaid Staff: three
Distributors: Ingram, Baker & Taylor
Number of Books Published per Year: four to five

Titles in Print: four
Average Percentage Printed: Paperback 100%

Organization: The Del Sol Review

Type: online
CLMP member: no
Primary Editor/Contact Person: Michael Neff
Address: 2020 Pennsylvania Ave., NW
Ste. 443
Washington, DC 20006
Web Site Address:
http://webdelsol.com/Del_Sol_Review
Publishes: essays, fiction, nonfiction, poetry, and reviews
Editorial Focus: Strong original fiction, experimental fiction, all types of poetry except for language poetry.
Representative Authors: Forrest Gander, Paul West, and Luisa Costa Gomes
Submissions Policy: See our site at: http://webdelsol.com/Del_Sol_Review. Theme issues upcoming.
Simultaneous Submissions: yes
Reading Period: Year-round
Reporting Time: one to six weeks
Author Payment: none
Founded: 1997
Non Profit: yes
Paid Staff: zero
Unpaid Staff: six
Average Page Views per Month: 8,000
Average Unique Visitors per Month: 2,000
Frequency per Year: triquarterly
Publish Print Anthology: no
Average Percentage of Pages per Category: Fiction 60%, Nonfiction 5%, Poetry 20%, Reviews 10%, Essays 5%
Ads: no

Organization: Denver Quarterly

Type: magazine
CLMP member: yes
Primary Editor/Contact Person: Danielle Dutton
Address: University of Denver
2000 E Asbury
Denver, CO 80208
Web Site Address: http://www.denverquarterly.com
Publishes: essays, fiction, poetry, reviews, art, and translation
Simultaneous Submissions: yes
Reading Period: 9/15 to 5/15

Reporting Time: three to four months
Author Payment: cash, copies, and subscription
Founded: 1964
Non Profit: yes
Paid Staff: two
Unpaid Staff: one
Total Circulation: 1,500
Paid Circulation: 1,000
Average Print Run: 1,500
Subscription Rate: Individual $22/Institution $25
Single Copy Price: $6
Current Volume/Issue: 40/1
Frequency per Year: quarterly
Backfile Available: yes
Unsolicited Ms. Received: yes
% of Unsolicited Ms. Published per Year: 85%
Format: perfect
Average Pages: 200
Ads: no

Organization: Descant

Type: magazine
CLMP member: yes
Primary Editor/Contact Person: Mary Newberry
Address: P.O. Box 314
Station P
Toronto, ON M5T1L4
Web Site Address: http://www.descant.ca
Publishes: essays, fiction, nonfiction, poetry, and art
Editorial Focus: We focus on poetry and short fiction from both emerging and established writers. We publish both themed and general issues.
Recent Awards Received: Four National Magazine Award nominations
Representative Authors: Jane Urquhart, P.K. Page, and Mark Kingwell
Submissions Policy: We consider unpublished poetry, short stories, nonfiction and art. Please send postage or IRC for reply.
Simultaneous Submissions: no
Reading Period: Year-round
Reporting Time: 9 to 12 months
Author Payment: cash
Founded: 1970
Non Profit: yes
Paid Staff: three
Unpaid Staff: five to six
Distributors: TTS Distribution
Wholesalers: Magazines Canada
Total Circulation: 1,200

Paid Circulation: 700
Average Print Run: 1,300
Subscription Rate: Individual $46/Institution $35
Single Copy Price: $15
Current Volume/Issue: 38/1
Frequency per Year: quarterly
Backfile Available: yes
Unsolicited Ms. Received: yes
% of Unsolicited Ms. Published per Year: 5%
Format: perfect
Size: H 9" W 6"
Average Pages: 220
Ads: yes
Ad Rates: full page $300, 1/2 page $180, 1/4 page $75; see website for details

Organization: Diagram

Type: online
CLMP member: yes
Primary Editor/Contact Person: Ander Monson
Address: 648 Crescent NE
Grand Rapids, MI 49503
Web Site Address: http://thediagram.com
Publishes: essays, fiction, nonfiction, poetry, reviews, art, translation, and audio
Editorial Focus: Schematic, literary fiction, poetry, short-shorts, and genre-bending or -transcending work. See web site for examples.
Representative Authors: Medbh McGuckian, Ben Marcus, and Miranda July
Submissions Policy: Read year-round, e-mail submissions much preferred. See web site for complete guidelines and mailing addresses.
Simultaneous Submissions: yes
Reading Period: Year-round
Reporting Time: one to three months
Author Payment: copies
Contests: See web site for contest guidelines.
Founded: 2000
Non Profit: no
Paid Staff: zero
Unpaid Staff: six
Distributors: Ingram (for periodic print edition)
ISSN Number/ISBN Number: ISSN 1543-5784
Average Page Views per Month: 200,000
Average Unique Visitors per Month: 25,000
Frequency per Year: six
Publish Print Anthology: yes
Price: $15
Average Percentage of Pages per Category: Fiction

20%, Nonfiction 5%, Poetry 35%, Reviews 15%, Essays 5%, Art 15%, Audio 5%
Ads: no

Organization: Dicey Brown

Type: magazine
CLMP member: no
Address: 80 St. Mark's Place (#2GN)
Staten Island, NY 10301
Web Site Address: http://www.diceybrown.com
Publishes: fiction, poetry, and art
Reading Period: Year-round
Reporting Time: one to two months
Author Payment: none
Founded: 2002
Non Profit: no
Backfile Available: yes

Organization: Dirt Press

Type: press
CLMP member: no
Primary Editor/Contact Person: Brian Lemond
Address: 15 N. Oxford St., 3rd Floor
Brooklyn, NY 11205
Web Site Address: http://www.dirtpress.com
Publishes: fiction, poetry, and art
Representative Authors: Derek Ableman, David J. Alworth, and Dewayne Washington
Submissions Policy: rolling, open call for submissions
Simultaneous Submissions: yes
Reading Period: Year-round
Reporting Time: one to two months
Author Payment: none
Contests: Hendrickson Memorial Prize in Short Fiction and Poetry-alternates annually between the disciplines. $300 1st prize, $100 2nd prize
See web site for contest guidelines.
Founded: 2002
Non Profit: no
Paid Staff: zero
Unpaid Staff: five
ISSN Number/ISBN Number: 1553-2135/0-97633368-0-4
Number of Books Published per Year: one
Titles in Print: one
Average Print Run: 2,000
Average Percentage Printed: Paperback 100%
Average Price: $20

Organization: The Dirty Goat

Type: magazine
CLMP member: no
Primary Editor/Contact Person: Joe Bratcher and Elzbieta Szoka
Address: 1000 E. 7th St.
Ste. 201
Austin, TX 78702
Web Site Address: http://www.thedirtygoat.com
Publishes: essays, fiction, poetry, art, and translation
Editorial Focus: Bringing the world to the US, The Dirty Goat focuses on little known US literature and great works from around the world.
Representative Authors: Goran Sonnevi, Avrom Sutzkever, Plinio Marcos
Submissions Policy: Send work with SASE.
Simultaneous Submissions: yes
Reading Period: Year-round
Reporting Time: 3 to 6 months
Author Payment: copies
Founded: 1989
Non Profit: no
Paid Staff: three
Unpaid Staff: zero
Distributors: Small Press Distribution
ISSN Number/ISBN Number: ISSN 1042-4768
Total Circulation: 500
Paid Circulation: 200
Average Print Run: 750
Subscription Rate: Individual $10/Institution $20
Single Copy Price: $10
Current Volume/Issue: Issue 16
Frequency per Year: biannual
Backfile Available: yes
Unsolicited Ms. Received: yes
% of Unsolicited Ms. Published per Year: 20%
Format: perfect
Size: H 10" W 8"
Average Pages: 175
Ads: no

Organization: Dislocate Literary Journal

Type: magazine
CLMP member: yes
Primary Editor/Contact Person: Alyson Sinclair
Address: 222 Lind Hall
207 Church St. SE

Minneapolis, MN 55455
Web Site Address: www.dislocate.org
Publishes: fiction, nonfiction, and poetry
Editorial Focus: Contemporary literary works, as well as interviews with authors
Representative Authors: Elizabeth Willis, Phillip Lopate, and Christopher Cokinos
Submissions Policy: Submit via mail only (no electronic submissions). Please specify genre on the envelope.
Simultaneous Submissions: Yes
Reading Period: September to Dec. 15th
Reporting Time: three to six months
Author Payment: copies
Founded: 2001
Non Profit: yes
Unpaid Staff: eight
Distributors: Bernhard DeBour and Don Olson, Inc.
ISSN Number/ISBN Number: ISBN 0-9768669-1-9
Total Circulation: 700
Average Print Run: 1,000
Subscription Rate: individual $7 institution $ 7
Single Copy Price: $7
Current Volume/Issue: issue #2
Frequency per year: annual (soon to be bi-annual)
Backfile Available: yes
Unsolicited MSS Received: yes
% of Unsolicited MSS Published per year: 1-3%
Format: perfect
Average Pages: 140
Ads: yes
Ad Rates: Full Page: $100

Organization: divide

Type: magazine
CLMP member: no
Primary Editor/Contact Person: Ginger Knowlton
Address: Program for Writing and Rhetoric
University of Colorado-Boulder
Boulder, CO 80309
Web Site Address: http://www.colorado.edu/journals/divide/
Publishes: essays, fiction, nonfiction, poetry, reviews, art, and translation
Editorial Focus: We are an annual literary journal of creative responses to contemporary social questions. See web site for issue themes.
Representative Authors: Richard Rodriguez, Naomi Shihab Nye, and Joanne Greenberg
Submissions Policy: Submissions of all kinds are

read during the academic year. We print all varieties of work and consider reprints if on theme.
Simultaneous Submissions: yes
Reading Period: 9/1 to 1/1
Reporting Time: three months
Author Payment: copies
Contests: We do not currently have contests, but hope to in the future.
Founded: 2002
Non Profit: yes
Paid Staff: three
Unpaid Staff: seven
Distributors: Kent News and other regional distributors TBD
ISSN Number/ISBN Number: ISSN 1542-6424
Total Circulation: 850
Paid Circulation: 150
Subscription Rate: Individual $8/issue/Institution $8/issue
Single Copy Price: $8
Current Volume/Issue: Issue 2
Frequency per Year: annual
Backfile Available: yes
Unsolicited Ms. Received: yes
% of Unsolicited Ms. Published per Year: 8%
Format: perfect
Size: H 11" W 8 1/2"
Average Pages: 96
Ads: no

Organization: Doorjamb Press

Type: press
CLMP member: yes
Primary Editor/Contact Person: Christine Monhollen
Address: P.O. Box 1296
Royal Oak, MI 48069
Web Site Address: http://www.doorjambpress.org
Publishes: essays, fiction, nonfiction, poetry, art, and translation
Editorial Focus: Small press publishes Dispatch Detroit journal, poetry/prose of national/local writers. Non-traditional writing featured.
Representative Authors: George Tysh, Ted Pearson, and Carla Harryman
Submissions Policy: For Dispatch Detroit (annually), editor looks for original use of language, form and continuing body of work.
Simultaneous Submissions: yes
Reading Period: Year-round
Reporting Time: 1 month

Author Payment: copies
Founded: 1998
Non Profit: yes
Paid Staff: zero
Unpaid Staff: one
Distributors: SPD
Wholesalers: books can be ordered through Paypal
ISSN Number/ISBN Number: 1-884118-09-7/1-884118-02-X
Number of Books Published per Year: one to two
Titles in Print: 10
Average Print Run: 500
Average Percentage Printed: Paperback 90%, Chapbook 10%
Average Price: $13

Organization: The Dos Passos Review

Type: magazine
CLMP member: yes
Primary Editor/Contact Person: Mary Carroll-Hackett
Address: Department of English, Longwood University
Farmville, VA 23909
Web Site Address: http://www.brierycreekpress.org
Publishes: fiction, nonfiction, and poetry
Editorial Focus: In the spirit of John Dos Passos, we seek innovative strong work in all genres written by emerging and established writers
Recent Awards Received: Pushcart Nominations from external sources
Representative Authors: Simon Perchik, Robert Bausch, and Sandra Kohler
Submissions Policy: Submit three to five poems, one story or essay no more than 3,000 words, disposable copies only, SASE for reply, no electronic submissions
Simultaneous Submissions: yes
Reading Period: 2/1 to 7/31
Reporting Time: one to three months
Author Payment: copies
Contests: Associated with Briery Creek Press and The Liam Rector First Book Prize for Poetry
Founded: 2003
Non Profit: yes
Paid Staff: zero
Unpaid Staff: 14
ISSN Number/ISBN Number: ISBN 0-9765110-1-0
Total Circulation: 300
Paid Circulation: 100+
Average Print Run: 500
Subscription Rate: Individual $20/Institution $26
Single Copy Price: $6

Current Volume/Issue: 4/1
Frequency per Year: biannual
Backfile Available: yes
Unsolicited Ms. Received: yes
% of Unsolicited Ms. Published per Year: 95%
Format: perfect
Average Pages: 115

Organization: Double Room

Type: online
CLMP member: no
Primary Editor/Contact Person: Peter Conners/Mark Tursi
Address: 2020 Pennsylvania Ave.
Ste. 443
Washington, DC 20006
Web Site Address:
http://webdelsol.com/Double_Room
Publishes: essays, fiction, poetry, reviews, art, and translation
Editorial Focus: Double Room focuses exclusively on prose poetry and flash fiction. New writing, mini-essays, reviews, and original artwork.
Representative Authors: Rosmarie Waldrop, Russell Edson, and Sean Thomas Dougherty
Submissions Policy: Our submission policies vary between solicit-only and open submission periods. Visit our web site for current policy.
Simultaneous Submissions: yes
Reading Period: Year-round
Reporting Time: one to six months
Author Payment: none
Founded: 2002
Non Profit: yes
Paid Staff: zero
Unpaid Staff: five
Distributors: Web del Sol
Average Page Views per Month: 5,000
Average Unique Visitors per Month: 1,000
Frequency per Year: biannual
Publish Print Anthology: no
Average Percentage of Pages per Category: Fiction 25%, Poetry 25%, Reviews 15%, Essays 25%, Art 10%
Ads: no

Organization: Drexel Online Journal

Type: online
CLMP member: no
Primary Editor/Contact Person: Albert DiBartolomeo

Address: 3210 Cherry St.
Philadelphia, PA 19104
Web Site Address: http://www.drexel.edu/doj
Publishes: essays, fiction, nonfiction, poetry, reviews, art, translation, and audio
Editorial Focus: The arts, culture, current events, personalities, photography, medicine, science, technology, travel
Representative Authors: Gerald Stern, Henry Petroski, and Paula Cohen
Submissions Policy: Submit to the site or, in hard copy, to the address. We reply only to accepted material, unless ms. is accompanied by SASE.
Simultaneous Submissions: yes
Reading Period: Year-round
Reporting Time: four to six weeks
Author Payment: cash
Contests: Successive Years: fiction-science/medicine-poetry-creative nonfiction
See web site for contest guidelines.
Founded: 1999
Non Profit: yes
Distributors: Drexel University
Average Page Views per Month: 2,500
Average Unique Visitors per Month: 1,200
Frequency per Year: biannual
Publish Print Anthology: no
Average Percentage of Pages per Category: Fiction 10%, Nonfiction 25%, Poetry 15%, Reviews 10%, Essays 20%, Art 10%, Translation 5%, Audio 5%
Ads: no

Organization: driftwood press

Type: magazine
CLMP member: yes
Primary Editor/Contact Person: Michael Colonna
Address: 4329 California St.
San Francisco, CA 94118
Web Site Address: http://driftwoodpress.com
Publishes: essays, fiction, nonfiction, poetry, and translation
Editorial Focus: We will consider short fiction (not exceeding 6,000 words), essays and photographic profiles.
Representative Authors: Harrison Solow, Sophie Powell, and Jacob M. Appel
Submissions Policy: Driftwood accepts unsolicited submissions. Absolutely no email submissions. Please keep all manuscripts no longer than 8,000 words.
Simultaneous Submissions: yes

Reading Period: year-round
Reporting Time: three to six months
Author Payment: copies and subscription
Contests: see web site for contest guidelines
Founded: 2006
Non Profit: no
Paid Staff: zero
Unpaid Staff: two
ISSN Number/ISBN Number: ISBN 0-9774596-1-6
Total Circulation: 500
Paid Circulation: 16
Average Print Run: 500
Subscription Rate: individual $30/institution $30
Single Copy Price: $13
Current Volume/Issue: I/II
Frequency per year: triquarterly
Backfile Available: yes
Unsolicited MSS Received: yes
% of Unsolicited MSS Published per Year: 50%
Format: perfect
Size: H 9" W 6"
Average Pages: 185
Ads: yes
Ad Rates: $300

Organization: Drunken Boat

Type: online
CLMP member: yes
Primary Editor/Contact Person: Ravi Shankar
Address: 119 Main St.
Chester, CT 06412
Web Site Address: http://www.drunkenboat.com
Publishes: essays, fiction, nonfiction, poetry, reviews, art, translation, and audio
Editorial Focus: Publishing the best of more traditional forms of representation alongside works of art endemic to the medium of the web.
Representative Authors: Alice Fulton, Mark Amerika, and Suji Kwock Kim
Submissions Policy: We accept unsolicited submissions year-round. Work should be sent as an attachment AND pasted into e-mail (URLs are fine).
Simultaneous Submissions: yes
Reading Period: Year-round
Reporting Time: four to six months
Author Payment: none
Contests: Drunken Boat plans to host a contest in 2005 for writers and new media artists. Details will appear on web site.
Founded: 1998

Non Profit: yes
Paid Staff: zero
Unpaid Staff: eight
ISSN Number/ISBN Number: ISSN 1537-2812
Backfile Available: yes
Average Page Views per Month: 10,000
Average Unique Visitors per Month: 6,000
Frequency per Year: annual
Publish Print Anthology: no
Average Percentage of Pages per Category: Fiction 15%, Nonfiction 10%, Poetry 25%, Reviews 10%, Essays 10%, Art 15%, Translation 5%, Audio 10%
Ads: yes
Ad Rates: $250 per banner ad; ads will also be considered for exchange

Organization: Ducky Magazine

Type: online
CLMP member: no
Primary Editor/Contact Person: Tom Hartman
Address: no snail mail!
Philadelphia, PA 19125
Web Site Address: http://www.duckymag.com
Publishes: essays, fiction, nonfiction, poetry, and translation
Editorial Focus: Contemporary poetry, fiction, interviews and essays in English
Representative Authors: Russell Edson, Joe Wenderoth, and Matthew Rohrer
Submissions Policy: Send three to five poems, one story. Attach sub to e-mail, MS Word, please. Send one doc. No snail mail! Follow guides on site!
Simultaneous Submissions: yes
Reading Period: Year-round
Reporting Time: six months
Author Payment: none
Founded: 2001
Non Profit: yes
Paid Staff: zero
Unpaid Staff: five
Average Page Views per Month: 6,000+
Average Unique Visitors per Month: 3,000
Frequency per Year: biannual
Publish Print Anthology: yes
Price: $TBD
Average Percentage of Pages per Category: Fiction 40%, Nonfiction 10%, Poetry 50%
Ads: no
Ad Rates: Happy to exchange with other journals -- e-mail us!

Organization: Ducts Webzine

Type: online
CLMP member: yes
Primary Editor/Contact Person: Jonathan Kravetz
Address: 158 Noble St., #2
Brooklyn, NY 10163
Web Site Address: http://ducts.org
Publishes: essays, fiction, nonfiction, poetry, reviews, art, and audio
Editorial Focus: Ducts was founded in 1999 with the intent of giving emerging writers a venue to regularly publish their work.
Representative Authors: Charles Salzberg, Tim Tomlinson, and Cindy Moore
Submissions Policy: Query via e-mail with attachment for works of fiction, art, poetry and nonfiction.
Simultaneous Submissions: yes
Reading Period: Year-round
Reporting Time: two to six weeks
Author Payment: none
Founded: 1999
Non Profit: yes
Paid Staff: zero
Unpaid Staff: eight
Backfile Available: yes
Average Page Views per Month: 10,000
Average Unique Visitors per Month: 500
Frequency per Year: biannual
Average Percentage of Pages per Category: Fiction 20%, Nonfiction 15%, Poetry 15%, Reviews 15%, Essays 15%, Art 15%, Audio 5%

Organization: Eclipse

Type: magazine
CLMP member: yes
Primary Editor/Contact Person: Bart Edelman
Address: 1500 N. Verdugo Rd.
Glendale, CA 91208
Publishes: fiction and poetry
Editorial Focus: Eclipse publishes quality fiction and poetry. It encourages all writers to contribute their work. We read year-round.
Representative Authors: William Heyen, Dana Gioia, and Wanda Coleman
Submissions Policy: Submissions are limited to five poems-any length. Contributors can also submit one story, 6,000 words maximum.
Simultaneous Submissions: yes
Reading Period: Year-round

Reporting Time: one to three months
Author Payment: copies
Founded: 1989
Non Profit: yes
Paid Staff: 1
Distributors: Ingram
ISSN Number/ISBN Number: 1530-5066/0-9701938-5-8
Total Circulation: 1,800
Paid Circulation: 100
Average Print Run: 2,000
Subscription Rate: Individual $8/Institution $10
Single Copy Price: $8
Current Volume/Issue: 16/one
Frequency per Year: annual
Backfile Available: yes
Unsolicited Ms. Received: yes
% of Unsolicited Ms. Published per Year: 90%
Format: perfect
Size: H 9" W 6"
Average Pages: 200
Ads: no
Ad Rates: none

Organization: Edgar Literary Magazine

Type: magazine
CLMP member: yes
Primary Editor/Contact Person: S.M. Geiger
Address: P.O. Box 5776
San Leon, TX 77539
Web Site Address: http://www.edgarliterary-magazine.com
Publishes: essays, fiction, and poetry
Editorial Focus: Well-crafted literary prose
Submissions Policy: Please see our web site:
http://www.edgarliterarymagazine.com
Simultaneous Submissions: yes
Reading Period: Year-round
Reporting Time: three to six months
Author Payment: copies
Founded: 2003
Non Profit: yes
Paid Staff: zero
Unpaid Staff: four
Total Circulation: 10,000
Average Print Run: 3,000
Current Volume/Issue: Issue 12
Frequency per Year: quarterly
Backfile Available: yes

Unsolicited Ms. Received: yes
Format: Saddle-stitched
Size: H 11" W 8.5"
Average Pages: 30

Organization: edifice WRECKED

Type: online
CLMP member: yes
Primary Editor/Contact Person: Leigh Hughes
Address: 3602 Melrose Ln.
Temple, TX 76502
Web Site Address: http://www.edificewrecked.com
Publishes: essays, fiction, nonfiction, poetry, reviews, and art
Editorial Focus: Our only requirement is that you fully express your creative vision in such a way that your reality becomes the only reality.
Submissions Policy: Submissions must be made via online submission form. Simultaneous submissions okay; multiple submissions not.
Simultaneous Submissions: yes
Reading Period: Year-round
Reporting Time: one to two months
Author Payment: copies and subscription
Contests: Flash Fiction Contest
See Web Site for Contest Guidelines.
Founded: 2004
Non Profit: yes
Paid Staff: zero
Unpaid Staff: six
ISSN Number/ISBN Number: ISSN 1552-2342
Average Page Views per Month: 45,000
Average Unique Visitors per Month: 2,500
Frequency per Year: bimonthly
Publish Print Anthology: yes
Price: $15
Average Percentage of Pages per Category: Fiction 45%, Nonfiction 5%, Poetry 15%, Reviews 5%, Essays 5%, Art 25%
Ad Rates: See web site for details.

Organization: The Eighth Mountain Press

Type: press
CLMP member: no
Primary Editor/Contact Person: Ruth Gundle
Address: 624 SE 29th Ave.
Portland, OR 97214
Publishes: essays, fiction, nonfiction, and poetry

Editorial Focus: literature, travel books and books for writers

Recent Awards Received: Lambda Book Award, finalist for PEN/Martha Albrand Award for the art of Memoir

Representative Authors: Judith Barrington, Ursula K. Le Guin, and Naomi Shihab Nye

Submissions Policy: Please send letter of inquiry by snail mail or email

Simultaneous Submissions: no

Reading Period: year-round

Reporting Time: one to two months

Author Payment: royalties

Contests: none

Founded: 1985

Non Profit: no

Paid Staff: one

Unpaid Staff: zero

Distributors: Consortium

Wholesalers: Ingram, Baker & Taylor

ISSN Number/ISBN Number: ISSN 0-933377

Number of Books Published per year: one

Titles in Print: 38

Average Print Run: 4,000

Average Percentage Printed: hardcover 2%, paperback 98%

Average Price: $15

Organization: Ekstasis Editions

Type: press

CLMP member: no

Primary Editor/Contact Person: Richard Olafson

Address: Box 8474, Main Postal Outlet

Victoria, BC V8W 3S1

Web Site Address: http://www.ekstasiseditions.com

Publishes: essays, fiction, nonfiction, poetry, reviews, art, translation, and audio

Editorial Focus: Literary texts: from neoformalism to language poetry

Representative Authors: Jim Christy, Ted Joans, and Ludwig Zeller

Submissions Policy: SASE, neatly typed, no e-mail or faxes, on hardcopy

Simultaneous Submissions: yes

Reading Period: Year-round

Reporting Time: two to eight months

Author Payment: royalties

Contests: Mocambo Prize

See web site for contest guidelines.

Founded: 1982

Non Profit: yes

Paid Staff: three

Distributors: Canadabooks Ltd.

ISSN Number/ISBN Number: 1896860/1894800

Number of Books Published per Year: 16

Titles in Print: 246

Average Print Run: 1,500

Average Percentage Printed: Hardcover 20%, Paperback 80%

Average Price: $16

Organization: The Electronic Book Review

Type: online

CLMP member: no

Primary Editor/Contact Person: Joseph Tabbi/Dave Ciccoricco

Address: 601 S. Morgan St.

UIC Dept of English

Chicago, IL 60607

Web Site Address: http://www.electronicbookreview.com

Publishes: essays, reviews, art, and audio

Editorial Focus: Cutting-edge lit crit, theory and philosophy re: literary, theoretical, and artistic innovations in digital environments.

Representative Authors: Joseph McElroy, Raymond Federman, and Michael Berube

Submissions Policy: Send proposals and submissions in a plain-text e-mail to the editors, ebr@altx.com. Freestanding hypertexts considered also.

Simultaneous Submissions: yes

Reading Period: Year-round

Reporting Time: one to six weeks

Author Payment: none

Founded: 1995

Non Profit: yes

Paid Staff: six

Unpaid Staff: four

Distributors: http://www.altx.com

Average Page Views per Month: 30,000

Average Unique Visitors per Month: 6,000

Frequency per Year: annual

Publish Print Anthology: no

Average Percentage of Pages per Category: Fiction 2%, Poetry 2%, Reviews 40%, Essays 50%, Art 5%, Audio 1%

Ads: no

Organization: Ellipsis...Literature and Art

Type: magazine
CLMP member: yes
Primary Editor/Contact Person: Natasha Saje
Address: 1840 South 1300 East
Salt Lake City, UT 84105
Web Site Address:
http://westminstercollege.edu/ellipsis
Publishes: essays, fiction, nonfiction, poetry, art, and translation
Editorial Focus: Newly discovered writers as well as published writers, with a focus on poetry and fiction.
Representative Authors: Crystal Williams, William Greenway, and Karen Garthe
Submissions Policy: poetry: send three to five poems. Prose: short fiction or literary non-fiction. Art: inside is b/w with one color piece for the cover.
Simultaneous Submissions: yes
Reading Period: 8/1 to 11/1
Reporting Time: 1 to 52 weeks
Author Payment: cash and copies
Contests: Ellipsis Poetry Prize and Academy of American Poets student prize.. See web site for contest guidelines
Founded: 1966
Non Profit: yes
Paid Staff: three to six
Unpaid Staff: 15
Distributors: Self-distributed
ISSN Number/ISBN Number: ISSN 1536-402X
Total Circulation: 1,000
Paid Circulation: 100
Average Print Run: 2,000
Subscription Rate: individual $7.50/institution $7.50
Single Copy Price: $7.50
Current Volume/Issue: issue 43
Frequency per year: annual
Backfile Available: yes
Unsolicited MSS Received: yes
% of Unsolicited MSS Published per Year: 3%
Format: perfect
Size: H 7" W 5"
Average Pages: 128
Ads: yes
Ad Rates: trades

Organization: Emergency Press/The Emergency Almanac

Type: press
CLMP member: yes
Primary Editor/Contact Person: Scott Zieher, Bryan Tomasovich
Address: 531 W. 25th St.
New York, NY 10001
Web Site Address: http://www.emergencypress.org
Publishes: essays, fiction, nonfiction, poetry, and art
Editorial Focus: Emergency Collective writers report on issues using a craft that highlights facts/research/utility.
Representative Authors: Scott Zieher, Molly McQuade, and Bryan Tomasovich
Submissions Policy: Send a short letter that introduces you to us, and tells why, and what you would like to write for the Emergency Almanac.
Simultaneous Submissions: no
Reading Period: Year-round
Reporting Time: one to two months
Author Payment: none
Contests: Emergency Press runs an annual book contest open to members who contribute to the Emergency Almanac the current year.
Founded: 2001
Non Profit: yes
Paid Staff: zero
Unpaid Staff: 40
Distributors: Ingram, Baker & Taylor
ISSN Number/ISBN Number: ISBN 0-9753623
Number of Books Published per Year: one to two
Titles in Print: three
Average Print Run: 300
Average Percentage Printed: Paperback 100%
Average Price: $15

Organization: Emrys Foundation

Type: press
CLMP member: yes
Primary Editor/Contact Person: Lydia Dishman
Address: P.O. Box 8813
Greenville, SC 29604
Web Site Address: http://www.emrys.org
Publishes: essays, fiction, nonfiction, and poetry
Editorial Focus: Engaging poetry and short stories, creative nonfiction and essays.
Representative Authors: Ron Rash, Jan Bailey, and Rosa Shand
Submissions Policy: Please enclose SASE. Send no more than 5 poems. Short fiction, essay and nonfiction should be no more than 7,500 words.
Simultaneous Submissions: yes
Reading Period: 8/15 to 12/1

Reporting Time: six to ten weeks
Author Payment: copies
Founded: 1983
Non Profit: yes
Paid Staff: five
Unpaid Staff: 10
ISSN Number/ISBN Number: ISBN 0960324674
Number of Books Published per Year: one
Titles in Print: three
Average Percentage Printed: Hardcover 45%, Paperback 45%, Other 10%

Organization: The Emrys Journal

Type: magazine
CLMP member: yes
Primary Editor/Contact Person: L.B. Dishman
Address: P.O. Box 8813
Greenville, SC 29604
Web Site Address: http://www.emrys.org
Publishes: essays, fiction, and poetry
Editorial Focus: literary fiction, creative nonfiction and memoir, contemporary poetry
Representative Authors: Rosa Shand, Elizabeth Swados, and Jessica Goodfellow
Submissions Policy: submit five poems or two essays or short stories, max 5,000 words. No genre fiction. Please SASE for reply.
Simultaneous Submissions: yes
Reading Period: 8/1 to 11/1
Reporting Time: one to two months
Author Payment: copies
Contests: One award for best of each category published in the annual Fiction, Creative Nonfiction, Poetry $250 prize for each winner. See web site for contest guidelines.
Founded: 1984
Non Profit: yes
Paid Staff: three
Unpaid Staff: six
Distributors: Emrys Foundation, Open Book, Barnes & Noble
Total Circulation: 400
Paid Circulation: 150
Average Print Run: 400
Subscription Rate: Individual $50/Institution $50
Single Copy Price: $12
Current Volume/Issue: 22/1
Frequency per Year: annual
Backfile Available: yes
Unsolicited Ms. Received: yes

% of Unsolicited Ms. Published per Year: 100%
Format: perfect
Average Pages: 120
Ad Rates: no ads

Organization: Epicenter: A Literary Magazine

Type: magazine
CLMP member: yes
Primary Editor/Contact Person: Jeff Green
Address: P.O. Box 367
Riverside, CA 92502
Web Site Address:
http://www.epicentermagazine.org
Publishes: essays, fiction, nonfiction, poetry, and art
Editorial Focus: We publish a variety of poetry, short stories, and nonfiction. We review submissions from any author, printing what we like.
Representative Authors: Ilya Kaminsky, Egon H.E. Lass, and Virgil Suarez
Submissions Policy: We review poetry, short stories, nonfiction, and artwork. We are open to a wide variety of styles, forms and subjects.
Simultaneous Submissions: yes
Reading Period: Year-round
Reporting Time: one to two months
Author Payment: copies
Founded: 1994
Non Profit: yes
Paid Staff: zero
Unpaid Staff: four
ISSN Number/ISBN Number: ISSN 1552-9169
Total Circulation: 500
Paid Circulation: 20
Average Print Run: 500
Subscription Rate: Individual $28/Institution $28
Single Copy Price: $9
Current Volume/Issue: 11/1
Frequency per Year: two
Backfile Available: yes
Unsolicited Ms. Received: yes
% of Unsolicited Ms. Published per Year: 5%
Format: perfect
Size: H 8.5" W 5.5"
Average Pages: 128
Ads: no

Organization: The Epiphany

Type: magazine
CLMP member: no

Primary Editor/Contact Person: Willard Cook, Editor
Address: 71 Bedford St.
New York, NY 10014
Web Site Address: http://www.epiphanyzine.com
Publishes: essays, fiction, nonfiction, poetry and art
Simultaneous Submissions: yes
Reading Period: 9/01 to 5/31
Reporting Time: five to six months
Author Payment: none
Founded: 2003
Non Profit: yes
Paid Staff: none
Unpaid Staff: four
Total Circulation: 800
Paid Circulation: 600
Average Print Run: 1,000
Subscription Rate: Individual $10/Institution $15
Single Copy Price: $10
Current Volume/Issue: 2/1
Frequency per Year: annual
Backfile Available: yes
Unsolicited Ms. Received: yes
% of Unsolicited Ms. Published per Year: 75%
Format: perfect
Average Pages: 200
Ads: yes
Ad rates: $300 per page, $150 for half-page, $75 per 1/4; see website for details

Organization: EPOCH

Type: magazine
CLMP member: yes
Primary Editor/Contact Person: Michael Koch
Address: 251 Goldwin Smith Hall
Cornell University
Ithaca, NY 14853-3201
Publishes: essays, fiction, nonfiction, poetry, and art
Editorial Focus: Literary fiction, poetry, essays, memoir. Graphic art.
Submissions Policy: SASE required. No electronic or e-mail submissions accepted.
Simultaneous Submissions: no
Reading Period: 9/15 to 4/15
Reporting Time: one to two months
Author Payment: cash and copies
Founded: 1947
Non Profit: yes
Paid Staff: nine
Unpaid Staff: 15
Distributors: Ubiquity Distributors

ISSN Number/ISBN Number: ISSN 0145-1391
Total Circulation: 1,000
Paid Circulation: 574
Subscription Rate: Individual $11/Institution $11
Single Copy Price: $5
Current Volume/Issue: 53/2
Frequency per Year: triquarterly
Backfile Available: yes
Unsolicited Ms. Received: yes
Format: perfect
Size: H 9" W 6"
Average Pages: 128
Ads: yes
Ad Rates: write for details

Organization: Esopus Foundation Ltd.

Type: magazine
CLMP member: yes
Primary Editor/Contact Person: Tod Lippy
Address: 532 LaGuardia Place, #486
New York, NY 10012
Web Site Address: www.esopusmag.com
Publishes: essays, fiction, nonfiction, poetry, art, audio
Editorial Focus: Providing an unmediated, noncommercial forum through which artists can reach a general public.
Recent Awards Received: Named "One of the 10 Best New Magazines" by Library Journal in 2003.
Representative Authors: Stephen Adly Guirgis, Suji Kwock Kim, and Heather Larson
Submissions Policy: Please submit Word documents, JPGs or PDFs via email, or direct us to a URL.
Simultaneous Submissions: no
Reading Period: year-round
Reporting Time: one to three months
Author Payment: cash
Founded: 2003
Non Profit: yes
Paid Staff: one
Unpaid Staff: zero
Distributors: DAP, Ingram, DeBoer, Ubiquity, Central Books
ISSN Number/ISBN Number: ISSN 1545-9306
Total Circulation: 8,000
Paid Circulation: 2,000
Average Print Run: 8,000
Subscription Rate: individual $18 (1 yr)/institution same
Single Copy Price: $10
Current Volume/Issue: issue six

Frequency per year: biannual
Backfile Available: yes
Unsolicited MSS Received: yes
% of Unsolicited MSS Published per Year: 5%
Format: perfect
Size: H 11.5" W 9"
Average Pages: 116
Ads: no

Organization: Essay Press

Type: press
CLMP member: yes
Primary Editor/Contact Person: Eula Biss
Address: 131 North Congress Street
Athens, OH 45701
Web Site Address: http://www.essaypress.org
Publishes: essays and nonfiction
Editorial Focus: Essay Press is dedicated to publishing innovative, explorative, and culturally relevant essays in book form.
Representative Authors: Albert Goldbarth, Kristin Prevallet, and Jenny Boully
Submissions Policy: Mail complete nonfiction manuscripts of about 40 to 80 pages. No proposals or excerpts, please.
Simultaneous Submissions: yes
Reading Period: 6/1 to 9/30
Reporting Time: two to four months
Author Payment: royalties and copies
Founded: 2005
Non Profit: yes
Paid Staff: zero
Unpaid Staff: five
Distributors: SPD
Number of Books Published per Year: two to four
Titles in Print: three
Average Percentage Printed: Paperback 100%
Average Price: $12.95

Organization: Essays on Canadian Writing

Type: magazine
CLMP member: no
Primary Editor/Contact Person: Kevin Flynn
Address: 2120 Queen St. East
Ste. 200
Toronto, ON M4E 1E2
Web Site Address: http://www.ecw.ca
Publishes: essays and reviews

Editorial Focus: ECW publishes scholarly essays on all aspects of Canadian literature, and from all theoretical perspectives.
Submissions Policy: Submissions must be made in triplicate, and must conform to the MLA Handbook, fifth edition. Please include SASE.
Simultaneous Submissions: no
Reading Period: Year-round
Reporting Time: 9 to 12 weeks
Author Payment: none
Contests: See web site for Contest Guidelines.
Founded: 1974
Non Profit: yes
Paid Staff: three
Unpaid Staff: six
ISSN Number/ISBN Number:
03130300/2527405002
Total Circulation: 1,400
Paid Circulation: 900
Subscription Rate: Individual $25/Institution $50
Single Copy Price: $9
Current Volume/Issue: Issue 82
Frequency per Year: three
Backfile Available: yes
Unsolicited Ms. Received: yes
Format: perfect
Average Pages: 230
Ads: no

Organization: Etruscan Press

Type: press
CLMP member: no
Primary Editor/Contact Person: Cathy Jewell
Address: P.O. Box 9685
Silver Spring, MD 20906
Web Site Address: http://www.etruscanpress.org
Publishes: essays, fiction, nonfiction, and poetry
Editorial Focus: Etruscan is a cooperative of poets producing books that nurture the dialogue among genres and achieve a distinctive voice.
Representative Authors: H.L. Hix, William Heyen, and Tom Bailey
Submissions Policy: Currently not accepting unsolicited submissions.
Simultaneous Submissions: yes
Reading Period: Year-round
Reporting Time: one to three months
Author Payment: royalties and copies
Founded: 2001
Non Profit: yes

Paid Staff: one
Unpaid Staff: four
Distributors: SPD, Mint Publishers Group
ISSN Number/ISBN Number: ISBN 0-9718228
Number of Books Published per Year: three
Titles in Print: five
Average Percentage Printed: Hardcover 15%,
Paperback 85%

Organization: Euphony

Type: magazine
CLMP member: yes
Primary Editor/Contact Person: Sarah Kull
Address: 5706 S. University Ave.
Chicago, IL 60637
Web Site Address: http://euphony.uchicago.edu
Publishes: essays, fiction, poetry, reviews, and translation
Editorial Focus: Euphony is dedicated to publishing the finest work currently being done by writers both accomplished and aspiring.
Representative Authors: Charles Wright, Mark Strand, and Adam Zagajewski
Submissions Policy: Unpublished work only. Mail manuscripts or e-mail in MS Word attachments to euphony@uchicago.edu.
Simultaneous Submissions: yes
Reading Period: 9/15 to 5/15
Reporting Time: two to three months
Author Payment: copies
Founded: 2000
Non Profit: yes
Paid Staff: zero
Unpaid Staff: 15
Distributors: Staff
Total Circulation: 3,500
Paid Circulation: N/A
Subscription Rate: Individual $12/Institution $24
Single Copy Price: free
Current Volume/Issue: 7/1
Frequency per Year: biannual
Backfile Available: no
Unsolicited Ms. Received: yes
% of Unsolicited Ms. Published per Year: 80%
Format: perfect
Size: H 8.5" W 5.5"
Average Pages: 100
Ads: yes
Ad Rates: $100 for half-page, $250 for full page
See web site for Details.

Organization: Exhibition

Type: magazine
CLMP member: no
Primary Editor/Contact Person: Victoria Josslin
Address: Bainbridge Island Arts and Humanities Council
Bainbridge Island, WA 98110
Web Site Address: http://www.artshum.org
Publishes: essays, fiction, nonfiction, poetry, and art
Editorial Focus: Exhibition publishes original art and writing by people who live in or are connected to Bainbridge Island. We value diversity
Representative Authors: John Willson, Richard M. West, and Margi Berger
Submissions Policy: Typed submissions, e-mail, or attached Word documents are welcome. 1,600 word limit.
Simultaneous Submissions: yes
Reading Period: 1/1 to 12/31
Reporting Time: three to six months
Author Payment: none
Founded: 1985
Non Profit: yes
Paid Staff: one
Unpaid Staff: two
Total Circulation: 1,000
Paid Circulation: zero
Single Copy Price: $7
Current Volume/Issue: Issue 2004
Frequency per Year: biannual
Backfile Available: no
Unsolicited Ms. Received: yes
Format: stapled
Size: H 11" W 8.5"
Average Pages: 36
Ads: yes
Ad Rates: See web site for details.

Organization: eye-rhyme

Type: magazine
CLMP member: no
Primary Editor/Contact Person: Laura Brian
Address: 1003 SE Grant St.
Portland, OR 97214
Web Site Address: http://www.eye-rhyme.com
Publishes: fiction, poetry, and art
Editorial Focus: eye-rhyme: journal of experimental literature publishes new poetry and short fiction in

beautiful biannual editions.

Representative Authors: Fiona Hile, Alan Catlin, and B.Z. Niditch

Submissions Policy: We consider previously unpublished poetry (six poems max), short fiction (10,000 words max), and B&W art. Send w/bio and SASE.

Simultaneous Submissions: yes

Reading Period: Year-round

Reporting Time: 4 to 16 weeks

Author Payment: copies

Founded: 1998

Non Profit: no

Paid Staff: zero

Unpaid Staff: three

Wholesalers: Baker & Taylor

ISSN Number/ISBN Number: ISSN 1540-6113

Total Circulation: 1,000

Paid Circulation: 100

Subscription Rate: Individual $8/Institution $10

Single Copy Price: $5

Current Volume/Issue: Issue 6

Frequency per Year: two

Backfile Available: no

Unsolicited Ms. Received: yes

% of Unsolicited Ms. Published per Year: 70%

Format: perfect

Size: H 6.5" W 4.5"

Average Pages: 104

Ads: no

Organization: Factorial Press

Type: press

CLMP member: no

Primary Editor/Contact Person: Sawako Nakayasu

Address: (please see web site)

San Francisco, CA 94118

Web Site Address: http://www.factorial.org

Publishes: essays, fiction, nonfiction, poetry, art, and translation

Editorial Focus: Factorial Press has a shifting editorial focus, including collaborations & translations. Please see web site for more details.

Representative Authors: Takashi Hiraide, Ayanne Kawata, and Ryoko Sekiguchi

Submissions Policy: Please query first by e-mail regarding all book and project proposals.

Simultaneous Submissions: no

Reading Period: Year-round

Reporting Time: one to six months

Author Payment: copies

Founded: 2001

Non Profit: yes

Paid Staff: zero

Unpaid Staff: four

Distributors: amazon.com

ISSN Number/ISBN Number: ISSN 1541-2660

Number of Books Published per Year: one

Titles in Print: four

Average Print Run: 500

Average Percentage Printed: Paperback 100%

Average Price: $8

Organization: failbetter

Type: online

CLMP member: yes

Primary Editor/Contact Person: Thom Didato

Address: 2022 Grove Avenue

Richmond, VA 23220

Web Site Address: http://www.failbetter.com

Publishes: fiction, poetry, and art

Editorial Focus: failbetter.com is a quarterly online magazine published in the spirit of a traditional literary journal.

Recent Awards Received: Honorable Mention in Pushcart Prize Collection; in 2006 Best American Poetry

Representative Authors: Jim Shepard, Lou Mathews, and Jill Allyn Rosser

Submissions Policy: Please read submission guidelines at: http://www.failbetter.com/Submit.html. Note: new online submissions database in 2007

Simultaneous Submissions: yes

Reading Period: Year-round

Reporting Time: three to five months

Author Payment: none

Founded: 2000

Non Profit: yes

Paid Staff: zero

Unpaid Staff: seven

Average Page Views per Month: 110,000

Average Unique Visitors per Month: 30,000

Frequency per Year: four

Publish Print Anthology: yes

Price: $TBD

Average Percentage of Pages per Category: Fiction 40%, Poetry 40%, Art 20%

Ad rates: online ad exchange program with print and online mags; see website for details

Organization: Faultline

Type: magazine
CLMP member: no
Primary Editor/Contact Person: Sarah Cohen/Sara J. Robinson
Address: Department of English
University of California, Irvine
Irvine, CA 92697-2650
Web Site Address: www.humanities.uci.edu/faultline
Publishes: essays, fiction, nonfiction, poetry, art, and translation
Editorial Focus: High quality poetry and prose that speaks with an original and compelling voice.
Recent Awards Received: Pushcart & O'Henry Prizes
Representative Authors: C. K. Williams, Larisa Szporluk, and Steve Almond
Submissions Policy: Up to 20 pages of prose and up to five pages of poetry. Note genre on envelope.
Simultaneous Submissions: yes
Reading Period: 9/15 to 2/15
Reporting Time: three to six months
Author Payment: copies
Founded: 1992
Non Profit: yes
Paid Staff: two
Unpaid Staff: 12
Distributors: Armadillo
ISSN Number/ISBN Number: ISSN 1076-0776
Total Circulation: 800
Paid Circulation: 200
Average Print Run: 900
Subscription Rate: individual $10/yr/institution $10/yr
Single Copy Price: $10-5
Current Volume/Issue: issue 15
Frequency per year: annual
Backfile Available: yes
Unsolicited MSS Received: yes
% of Unsolicited MSS Published per year: 1%
Format: perfect
Size: H 9" W 6"
Average Pages: 140-180
Ads: yes
Ad Rates: see web site for details

Organization: Faultline

Type: press
CLMP member: no
Primary Editor/Contact Person: Sarah Cohen/Sara J Robinson
Address: Dept. of English & Comp. Lit.
University of California, Irvine
Irvine, CA 92697-2650
Web Site Address:
http://www.humanities.uci.edu/faultline
Publishes: essays, fiction, nonfiction, poetry, art, and translation
Editorial Focus: High quality poetry and prose that speaks with an original and compelling voice.
Representative Authors: C.K. Williams, Larisa Szporluk, and Steve Almond
Submissions Policy: Up to 20 pages of prose and up to 5 pages of poetry. Note genre on envelope.
Simultaneous Submissions: yes
Reading Period: 9/1 to 3/1
Reporting Time: three to six months
Author Payment: copies
Founded: 1992
Non Profit: yes
Paid Staff: two
Unpaid Staff: 12
Distributors: Ingram, Armadillo
ISSN Number/ISBN Number: ISSN 1076-0776
Number of Books Published per Year: one
Titles in Print: 14
Average Print Run: 900
Average Percentage Printed: Paperback 100%
Average Price: $5-10

Organization: Faux Press

Type: press
CLMP member: no
Primary Editor/Contact Person: Jack Kimball
Address: 24 Dale
Newton, MA 02460-1902
Web Site Address: http://www.fauxpress.com
Publishes: poetry
Representative Authors: David Larsen, Tony Towle, and Alice Notley
Simultaneous Submissions: no
Reading Period: Year-round
Reporting Time: one to two months
Author Payment: copies
Founded: 2000
Non Profit: yes
Paid Staff: zero
Unpaid Staff: one
Distributors: SPD
Number of Books Published per Year: three to four
Titles in Print: 12
Average Print Run: 500

Average Percentage Printed: Paperback 100%
Average Price: $15

Organization: FC2 (Fiction Collective Two)

Type: press
CLMP member: yes
Primary Editor/Contact Person: Brenda L. Mills
Address: Department of English
Florida State University
Tallahassee, FL 32306-1580
Web Site Address: http://fc2.org
Publishes: fiction
Editorial Focus: FC2 is devoted to publishing fiction considered too challenging, innovative, or heterodox for the commercial milieu.
Representative Authors: Ronald Sukenick, Cris Mazza, and Brian Evenson
Submissions Policy: See submission guidelines at http://fc2.org.
Simultaneous Submissions: yes
Reading Period: year-round
Reporting Time: four to nine months
Author Payment: royalties and cash
Founded: 1973
Non Profit: yes
Paid Staff: two
Unpaid Staff: four
Distributors: University of Alabama Press
ISSN Number/ISBN Number: 157366 . . . ./091459 . . .
Number of Books Published per Year: five
Titles in Print: 150
Average Print Run: 1,800
Average Percentage Printed: Paperback 100%
Average Price: $16.95

Organization: Featherproof Books

Type: press
CLMP member: yes
Primary Editor/Contact Person: Jonathan Messinger
Address: 2754 N Artesian #2
Chicago, IL 60647
Web Site Address: http://www.featherproof.com
Publishes: fiction, nonfiction, and translation
Editorial Focus: We publish novels by up-and-coming authors and short stories designed as their own downloadable mini-books.
Representative Authors: Elizabeth Crane, Todd Dills, and Brian Costello

Submissions Policy: Email short stories and the first 50 pages of novels as attachments to submissions@featherproof.com.
Simultaneous Submissions: yes
Reading Period: Year-round
Reporting Time: one to three months
Author Payment: royalties, copies, and subscription
Founded: 2005
Non Profit: no
Paid Staff: zero
Unpaid Staff: four
Distributors: Biblio Distribution, NBN
Wholesalers: as above
ISSN Number/ISBN Number: ISBN 0-9771992
Number of Books Published per Year: 2-3
Titles in Print: 4
Average Percentage Printed: Paperback 100%
Average Price: $13.95

Organization: Feile-Festa

Type: magazine
CLMP Member: yes
Primary Editor/Contact Person: Frank Polizzi
Address: P.O. Box 436
Prince Street Station
New York, NY 10012
Web Site Address: www.medcelt.org/feile-festa/index.html
Publishes: essays, fiction, nonfiction, poetry, reviews, art, and translation
Editorial Focus: Writing related to Irish and Italian/Sicilian themes, but open to other Mediterranean and Celtic cultures, as well as life in New York City.
Recent Awards Received: Selected by Poets & Writers and NewPages.com as a linked literary magazine.
Representative Authors: Maureen Tolman Flannery, Maria Mazziotti Gillan, and Gil Fagiani
Submissions Policy: Send 1-3 poems or 1 prose piece (microfiction -- 500 words or less, an articles -- 1,000 words or less).
Simultaneous Submissions: yes
Reading Period: 10/07 to 1/08
Reporting Time: two to six weeks
Author Payment: copies
Contests: none; see website for guidelines
Founded: 2006
Non Profit: yes
Paid Staff: zero

Unpaid Staff: four
Distributors: Amazon.com
ISSN Number/ISBN Number: ISSN 1931-7263
Total Circulation: 500
Paid Circulation: 25
Average Print Run: 500
Subscription Rate: individual $7.00/institution $10.00
Single Copy Price: $5.00
Current Volume/Issue: issue 2007
Frequency per year: annual
Backfile Available: yes
Unsolicited MSS Received: yes
% of Unsolicited MSS Published per year: 70%
Format: perfect
Size: H 8.5" W 5.5"
Average Pages: 68
Ads: no

Organization: Feile-Festa

Type: online
CLMP member: yes
Primary Editor/Contact Person: Frank Polizzi
Address: P.O. Box 436
Prince Street Station
New York, NY 10012
Web Site Address: www.medcelt.org/feile-festa/index.html
Publishes: essays, fiction, nonfiction, poetry, reviews, art, and translation
Editorial Focus: Writing related to Irish and Italian/Sicilian themes, but open to other Mediterranean and Celtic cultures, as well as life in New York City.
Recent Awards Received: Selected by Poets & Writers and NewPages.com as a linked literary magazine.
Representative Authors: Maureen Tolman Flannery, Maria Mazziotti Gillan, and Gil Fagiani
Submissions Policy: Send 1-3 poems or 1 prose piece (microfiction -- 500 words or less, an articles -- 1,000 words or less).
Simultaneous Submissions: yes
Reading Period: 10/07 to 1/08
Reporting Time: two to six weeks
Author Payment: copies
Contests: none
Founded: 2006
Non Profit: yes
Paid Staff: one
Unpaid Staff: three

ISSN Number/ISBN Number: 1931-7271
Average Page Views per Month: 530
Average Unique Visitors per Month: 148
Frequency per Year: annual
Publish Print Anthology: no
Average Percentage of Pages per Category: Fiction 5%, Nonfiction 5%, Poetry 60%, Reviews 5%, Essays 5%, Art 15%, Translation 5%
Ads: no

Thom Didato
Editor and Publisher, failbetter

How did you arrive at your current position?

During *failbetter*'s early years, I was working for a big-time book publisher, where I saw editors who did little if any editing, and didn't have all that much say in what the house published. I wanted to be an editor too, but one who both edited and made my own publishing decisions. So the logical thing was to start a publishing operation—which is what *failbetter* is. When we set out, David McLendon and I thought about doing a print journal. But several of our friends had gone this route, only to run out of money and shut them down after an issue or two. So we decided to publish online, which is a lot cheaper—and, as a bonus, enables us to reach far more readers.

Of course we didn't really know what we were doing—we had our Beckett quote, our tastes, an agreement that we'd never publish our own work...and that was about it. But good things, I think, often come from diving right into something, prepared or not, and that's certainly been the case with *failbetter*.

What is the staff structure at your magazine?

At the start, *failbetter* was basically a two-man operation—David and I did pretty much everything ourselves. Andrew Day helped us get online, and built our site, and we had occasional tech and editorial help from other friends as well. Then in 2003, David left *failbetter* to pursue his own writing, and Andy, who used to be an acquisitions editor at Westview, began to play a more active role, as our managing editor. Today, Andy handles all the tech stuff, and we share the "big-picture" editorial decisions, working with four section editors and several readers.

What challenges do you face as a publisher?

The answer to this question has changed over the years. Back in 2000, many writers, readers, and editors were suspicious of online journals, thinking they weren't "serious." That's changed, in part because we, and editors of other online journals, have done a lot to sell ourselves—we take part in AWP, and regularly speak at writers' conferences, including Breadloaf, Squaw Valley, and Napa. But the main thing is that online journals have gotten better—*failbetter* included, as shown by the fact that last year, we had pieces featured in both the *Pushcart Prize* and *Best American Poetry* anthologies.

Now that we feel that we've won the battle for respectability, we're focused more on winning the battle for profitability. Fortunately, our costs are low enough that even if we never win that battle, we'll be able to keep going, and hopefully both improving our product, and diversifying our publication line.

Do you have any cover letter advice?

Let the work speak for itself. If you want to mention that you've been published in *The New Yorker*, great, but keep your introduction short and sweet. Don't tell us what the story means, or why it's so great—if it is, we'll figure that out for ourselves.

What do you look for in a submission?

Our "official aesthetic" is eclectic... How's that for a non-answer?

Truth be told, each of our editors has his or her own tastes, and generally if one of us really wants to publish a piece, and it doesn't horrify the rest of us, we'll run it. Though usually we find we're pretty much in consensus about what's good and what's not. I have a hard time figuring out why that is...but it is.

That being said, I think Andy sums up what we look for in fiction, when he says, "We look for stuff that doesn't drag its heels, gets right into the action, likes its characters and wants the reader to like them, too." Also—and on this one, you can check with Caitlin Johnson, our fiction editor—we frown on adverbs.

As to poetry, I don't want to speak for Mary Donnelly and Ben Gantcher, our poetry editors—if you want to know what we look for in a poem, read the ones on the site. I confine myself to insisting that we never publish a poem that includes mention of a leaf falling from a tree. Nor can a poem use the word "panty." Following these two rules helps us eliminate about 10 percent of our poetry slush.

How are submissions processed at your magazine?

All our submissions come by email, and we read every single one. Andy does an initial scan of the slush, looking for pieces that have promise, and flagging them for a closer look. Then I read the whole lot of it, and once I've skimmed the ten to twenty percent that's worth a second look, I pass it on to our section editors and readers. At the start, this process was quicker than it is now, as we got "only" about a thousand subs a year. Now we get about six thousand, so we're a bit slower to respond to submitters, and I'm starting to reevaluate the whole process. Technically, things run pretty smoothly, as Andy keeps everything in a database and we have great records about who submitted what, when, what our response was, and so forth. But the editorial side can be overwhelming. Going forward, we'll probably take on more readers, to speed things up.

One other thing: in the online world, a quick response is usually not a good thing. More often than not, the longer we keep a piece, the more likely we're considering it seriously. I hope our submitters take solace in this, when we take more than a couple of months to respond, which, unfortunately, we often do.

Do you have a favorite unsolicited submission discovery or anecdote?

In this business, success begets success. As our reputation grew, we started to get better and better submissions, including more pieces from writers we already knew and admired. Indeed, there have been one or two cases where one week we said, "Oh man, we should try to get a story from _____," and then, wouldn't you know it, a week or two later _____ sends us a story. A recent example is that of Jeffrey Lent—I've always loved his work, and earlier this year, his agent sent us an excerpt from his latest novel, which we published in our most recent issue.

Of course we also pride ourselves on having published writers who weren't "known" at the time, but later hit it big—Sam Lipsyte, Myla Goldberg, and the late Amanda Davis being three cases in point.

Then there's the real pleasure, as an editor, of going back and forth with a writer until you find something that works. I recall telling one writer, after we had rejected him a couple for times, that I really couldn't give him a concrete reason why we were rejecting him again. I told him something like, "_____, it's not that your story is bad. It's just that it's a lot like broccoli. I know it's good, and good for me, but I don't like it." Thankfully, that writer sent us another story and the third time was the charm.

What advice do you have for first-time submitters?

I think I'd say the same thing most editors would say: read what we publish before you submit, to see if your work would fit in with it.

What are your long-term plans for your magazine?

World domination…one reader at a time.

Seriously, we are in it for the long haul. We'll keep publishing online, and will shoot to reach more readers—we currently have about sixty thousand per issue. Also I can see us, at some point, doing select print projects as well, not necessarily a regular journal, but perhaps the occasional themed anthology, beautifully designed and a cool thing to both read and look at—something like what *McSweeney's* puts out. For us, print publications will be bused to market our online publication.

What's your evaluation of the current literary landscape?

If the pundits are right, fewer and fewer folks are reading these days.

Supposedly fewer than forty percent of Americans actually read a single literary work (a poem, novel, short story, etc.) in any given year. And yet there are more mag and book publishers appearing all the time, and someone must be reading the stuff they put out—which suggests that we in the publishing business should be optimistic about our future. And we are.

More and more readers feel comfortable reading "serious" stuff online, and more and more writers realize that online publication offers the chance to reach those readers. We think we're on the verge of an "online literature" boom, and having established ourselves as one of the preeminent online literary journal, we're well-positioned to take advantage of that boom.

Organization: The Feminist Press

Type: press
CLMP member: no
Primary Editor/Contact Person: Livia Tenzer
Address: at the City University of New York
365 Fifth Ave.
New York, NY 10016
Web Site Address: http://www.feministpress.org
Publishes: essays, fiction, nonfiction, and translation
Editorial Focus: The Feminist Press is a nonprofit literary and educational publisher dedicated to publishing work by and about women.
Representative Authors: Charlotte Perkins Gilman, Paule Marshall, and Dorothy Hughes
Submissions Policy: To submit a proposal or query, send an e-mail to jcasella@gc.cuny.edu with the word "Submission" in the subject line.
Simultaneous Submissions: no
Reading Period: Year-round
Reporting Time: 1 month
Author Payment: royalties
Founded: 1970
Non Profit: yes
Paid Staff: eight
Unpaid Staff: four
Distributors: Consortium
Wholesalers: Ingram, Baker & Taylor
ISSN Number/ISBN Number: 0732-/1-55861-
Number of Books Published per Year: 22
Titles in Print: 256
Average Percentage Printed: Hardcover 30%, Paperback 70%

Organization: Feminist Studies

Type: magazine
CLMP member: no
Primary Editor/Contact Person: Claire G. Moses
Address: 0103 Taliaferro
University of Maryland
College Park, MD 20742
Web Site Address: http://www.feministstudies.org
Publishes: essays, fiction, poetry, reviews, and art
Editorial Focus: Founded to encourage analytic responses to feminist issues and to open new areas of research, criticism, and speculation.
Representative Authors: Bernice L. Hausman, Leslie J. Reagan, and Susan K. Cahn
Submissions Policy: We will publish serious writing of a critical, scholarly, speculative, and political nature.

Simultaneous Submissions: no
Reading Period: Year-round
Reporting Time: three to four months
Author Payment: none
Founded: 1973
Non Profit: yes
Paid Staff: two
Unpaid Staff: nine
ISSN Number/ISBN Number: ISSN 0046-3663
Total Circulation: 5,000
Paid Circulation: 4,880
Average Print Run: 5,000
Subscription Rate: Individual $35/Institution $230
Single Copy Price: $17
Current Volume/Issue: 33/1
Frequency per Year: three
Backfile Available: yes
Unsolicited Ms. Received: yes
% of Unsolicited Ms. Published per Year: 7%
Format: perfect
Size: H 9" W 6"
Average Pages: 240
Ads: yes
Ad Rates: $360
See Web Site for Details.

Organization: Fence Books

Type: press
CLMP member: yes
Primary Editor/Contact Person: Rebecca Wolff
Address: 303 E. 8th St. #B1
New York, NY 10009
Web Site Address: http://www.fencebooks.com
Publishes: poetry
Editorial Focus: To provide expanded exposure to poets whose work is excellent, challenging, and truly original. (see web site)
Representative Authors: Joyelle McSweeney, Anthony McCann, and Catherine Wagner
Submissions Policy: Fence Books is a self-selecting publisher; manuscripts come to our attention through our contests. (see website)
Simultaneous Submissions: yes
Reading Period: 11/1 to 2/28
Reporting Time: six to seven months
Author Payment: royalties, cash, and copies
Contests: See web site for Contest Guidelines.
Founded: 2001
Non Profit: yes
Paid Staff: zero

Unpaid Staff: two
Distributors: UPNE (Univ. Press New England)
Wholesalers: SPD
Number of Books Published per Year: four
Titles in Print: 13
Average Percentage Printed: Paperback 100%
Average Price: $13

Organization: Fence

Type: magazine
CLMP member: yes
Primary Editor/Contact Person: Rebecca Wolff
Address: New Library 320
University at Albany
Albany, NY 12222
Web Site Address: http://www.fencemag.com
Publishes: fiction, nonfiction, poetry, art, and translation
Editorial Focus: Fence publishes poetry, fiction, art and criticism distinguished by idiosyncrasy and intelligence.
Representative Authors: Anne Carson, Lynne Tillman, and Joyelle McSweeney
Submissions Policy: see http://www.fencemag.com
Simultaneous Submissions: yes
Reading Period: year-round
Reporting Time: two to nine months
Author Payment: copies and subscription
Contests: See Web Site for Contest Guidelines.
Founded: 1998
Non Profit: yes
Paid Staff: one
Unpaid Staff: nine
Distributors: DeBoer, Ingram
Wholesalers: SPD
ISSN Number/ISBN Number: 1097-9980/0-9713189-9-9
Total Circulation: 3,000
Paid Circulation: 1,800
Average Print Run: 3,000
Subscription Rate: Individual $17/Institution $25
Single Copy Price: $10
Current Volume/Issue: 9.1/17
Frequency per Year: two
Backfile Available: yes
Unsolicited Ms. Received: yes
% of Unsolicited Ms. Published per Year: 5%
Format: perfect
Size: H 9" W 7"
Average Pages: 200

Ads: yes
Ad Rates: contact fence@albany.edu; see website for details.

Organization: Fiction

Type: magazine
CLMP member: yes
Primary Editor/Contact Person: Mark Jay Mirsky
Address: c/o English Department
138 St. and Convent Ave.
NY, NY 10031
Web Site Address: http://fictioninc.com
Publishes: fiction and translation
Editorial Focus: Fiction goes to terra incognita in the writing of the imagination and asks that modern fiction set itself serious questions.
Representative Authors: Joseph McElroy, Robert Musil, and Clarice Lispector
Submissions Policy: We take simultaneous submissions of Fiction. Manuscripts will not be returned without SASEs.
Simultaneous Submissions: yes
Reading Period: 9/15 to 4/15
Reporting Time: six to nine months
Author Payment: cash and copies
Contests: Check web site for contest announcements.
Founded: 1972
Non Profit: yes
Paid Staff: four
Unpaid Staff: 20
Distributors: DeBoer Distributors, Ingram
ISSN Number/ISBN Number: ISSN 7447080497
Total Circulation: 600
Paid Circulation: 550
Subscription Rate: Individual $38/Institution $30
Single Copy Price: $10
Current Volume/Issue: 18/1
Frequency per Year: biannual
Backfile Available: yes
Unsolicited Ms. Received: yes
% of Unsolicited Ms. Published per Year: 75%
Format: perfect
Size: H 9" W 5"
Average Pages: 200
Ads: yes
Ad Rates: See web site for details.

Organization: The Fiddlehead

Type: magazine
CLMP member: no
Primary Editor/Contact Person: Kathryn Taglia
Address: 11 Garland Ct. Campus House
PO Box 4400
Frederictron, NB E3B 5A3
Web Site Address:
www.lib.unb.ca/Texts/Fiddlehead
Publishes: fiction, poetry, and reviews
Editorial Focus: Literature of excellence, with an emphasis on freshness and surprise.
Recent Awards Received: Two stories selected for Journey Prize Anthology 19 (2007); another story cited in Best American Stories
Representative Authors: Patricia Young, Al Moritz, and Brian Bartlett
Submissions Policy: Typed, double-spaced. Stories not over 4,000 words; poems up to 10 per submission. Simultaneous acc.but not preferred
Simultaneous Submissions: yes
Reading Period: year-round
Reporting Time: one to six months
Author Payment: cash
Contests: Yes. Annual Contest, Two $1,000 prizes for best poem & best story, Four $500 prizes for honourary mentions
See web site for contest guidelines
Founded: 1945
Non Profit: yes
Paid Staff: three
Unpaid Staff: six
Distributors: Magazines Canada
ISSN Number/ISBN Number: ISSN 015-0639
Total Circulation: 1,300
Paid Circulation: 900
Average Print Run: 1,400
Subscription Rate: individual $30/institution $30
Single Copy Price: $10 to16
Current Volume/Issue: issue 232
Frequency per year: quarterly
Backfile Available: yes
Unsolicited MSS Received: yes
% of Unsolicited MSS Published per year: 3-6%
Format: perfect
Size: H 9" W 6.5"
Average Pages: 130
Ads: yes
Ad Rates: 200 per full page
See web site for details

Organization: FIELD: Contemporary Poetry and Poetics

Type: magazine
CLMP member: yes
Primary Editor/Contact Person: Linda Slocum, Managing Editor
Address: 50 N. Professor St.
Peters G 08
Oberlin, OH 44074-1091
Web Site Address: http://www.oberlin.edu/ocpress
Publishes: essays and poetry
Editorial Focus: FIELD is published twice a year; features established and emerging poets, symposia on famous poets and poetry book reviews
Representative Authors: Carol Moldaw, Franz Wright, and Venus Khoury-Ghata
Submissions Policy: Send three to five poems to Editors/FIELD, 50 N. Professor St. Oberlin, OH 44074. Enclose a SASE; allow six weeks for response.
Simultaneous Submissions: no
Reading Period: Year-round
Reporting Time: six to eight weeks
Author Payment: cash and copies
Contests: FIELD Poetry Prize held annually in May for manuscripts of 50 to 80 pages. $1,000 and publication.$22 reading fee.
See Web Site for Contest Guidelines.
Founded: 1969
Non Profit: yes
Paid Staff: .five
Unpaid Staff: six
Wholesalers: Ingram; Baker & Taylor
ISSN Number/ISBN Number: ISSN 0015-0657
Total Circulation: 1,400
Paid Circulation: 1,250
Average Print Run: 1,500
Subscription Rate: Individual $14/Institution $14
Single Copy Price: $7
Current Volume/Issue: Issue 74
Frequency per Year: two
Backfile Available: yes
Unsolicited Ms. Received: yes
% of Unsolicited Ms. Published per Year: .5%
Format: perfect
Size: H 8.5" W 5.25"
Average Pages: 100
Ads: no

Organization: Finishing Line Press

Type: press
CLMP member: no
Primary Editor/Contact Person: Leah Maines
Address: P.O. Box 1626
Georgetown, KY 40324
Web Site Address: http://www.finishinglinepress.com
Publishes: poetry
Editorial Focus: At this time we are publishing mostly poetry chapbooks. However, we are open to short story and creative nonfiction chaps.
Recent Awards Received: San Diego Book Award for a book of poetry, National Federation of Press Women's annual competition, in category 75-creative verse
Representative Authors: Tony Crunk, George Held, and Abigail Gramig
Submissions Policy: Up to 26 pages, bio, SASE, acknowledgements (including book publication): e-mail FinishingBooks@aol.com for current guidelines
Simultaneous Submissions: yes
Reading Period: Year-round
Reporting Time: three to six months
Author Payment: cash and copies
Contests: See web site for Contest Guidelines.
Founded: 1998
Non Profit: no
Paid Staff: two
Unpaid Staff: four
ISSN Number/ISBN Number: yes/yes
Number of BooksPublished per Year: 75
Titles in Print: 41
Average Print Run: 500
Average Percentage Printed: Paperback 1%, Chapbook 99%
Average Price: $12

Organization: Firewheel Editions

Type: press
CLMP member: yes
Primary Editor/Contact Person: Brian Clements, Editor
Address: P.O. Box 7, Western Conn. St. University
181 White St.
Danbury, CT 06810
Web Site Address: http://firewheel-editions.org
Publishes: poetry
Editorial Focus: Poetry and innovative work, such as hybrid or experimental texts, that might not see print if we didn't publish it.

Representative Authors: Denise Duhamel, Joe Ahearn, and Charles Kesler
Submissions Policy: Check the web site.
Simultaneous Submissions: yes
Reading Period: Year-round
Reporting Time: one to six months
Author Payment: royalties and copies
Contests: Check the web site
Founded: 2002
Non Profit: yes
Paid Staff: zero
Unpaid Staff: three
Wholesalers: DeBoer, Amazon
Number of Books Published per Year: two to-four
Titles in Print: six
Average Print Run: 1,000
Average Percentage Printed: Paperback 80%, Chapbook 20%
Average Price: $10

Organization: First Class

Type: magazine
CLMP member: no
Primary Editor/Contact Person: Christopher M.
Address: P.O. Box 86
Friendship, IN 47021
Web Site Address: http://www.four-sep.com
Publishes: fiction, poetry, and art
Editorial Focus: Belt out a graphic, uncommon, thought-provoking poem or short story that will leave the reader thinking
Representative Authors: spiel, John Bennett, and Gary Every
Submissions Policy: Please send disposable mss.with a cover letter and SASE. Expect a response within a month (to give it a good, careful read).
Simultaneous Submissions: yes
Reading Period: Year-round
Reporting Time: four to six weeks
Author Payment: copies
Contests: No
Founded: 1995
Non Profit: yes
Paid Staff: zero
Unpaid Staff: two
Distributors: Tower Magazines/Records
Total Circulation: 300ish
Paid Circulation: 50
Average Print Run: 300ish
Subscription Rate: Individual $11/Institution $11

Single Copy Price: $6
Current Volume/Issue: Issue 29
Frequency per Year: two
Backfile Available: yes
Unsolicited Ms. Received: yes
% of Unsolicited Ms. Published per Year: 10%
Format: stapled
Size: H 11" W 4.25"
Average Pages: 52
Ads: no

Organization: First Intensity

Type: magazine
CLMP member: no
Primary Editor/Contact Person: Lee Chapman
Address: P.O. Box 665
Lawrence, KS 66044
Web Site Address: http://www.FirstIntensity.com
Publishes: essays, fiction, nonfiction, poetry, reviews, and translation
Editorial Focus: To promote innovative writing through publishing the best in contemporary literature.
Representative Authors: Robert Kelly, Laura Moriarty, and Barry Gifford
Submissions Policy: Send up to 15 pp for fiction; up to five poems; no electronic submissions. Allow eight weeks for response.
Simultaneous Submissions: no
Reading Period: Year-round
Reporting Time: 8 to 10 weeks
Author Payment: copies
Founded: 1993
Non Profit: no
Paid Staff: zero
Unpaid Staff: one
Distributors: SPD
ISSN Number/ISBN Number: ISSN 1540-8019
Total Circulation: 175
Paid Circulation: 50-80
Average Print Run: 250
Subscription Rate: Individual $28/Institution $32
Single Copy Price: $14
Current Volume/Issue: 22/20
Frequency per Year: one
Backfile Available: yes
Unsolicited Ms. Received: yes
% of Unsolicited Ms. Published per Year: 10%
Format: perfect
Size: H 9" W 6"
Average Pages: 220

Ads: yes
Ad Rates: $150/full page; $75/half page

Organization: The First Line

Type: magazine
CLMP member: no
Primary Editor/Contact Person: David LaBounty
Address: P.O. Box 250382
Plano, TX 75025-0382
Web Site Address: http://www.thefirstline.com
Publishes: essays and fiction
Editorial Focus: We print stories that stem from the same first line.
Simultaneous Submissions: no
Reading Period: Year-round
Reporting Time: two to six weeks
Author Payment: cash and copies
Founded: 1999
Non Profit: no
Paid Staff: one
Unpaid Staff: one
ISSN Number/ISBN Number: ISSN 1525-9382
Total Circulation: 1,000
Paid Circulation: 725
Average Print Run: 1,200
Subscription Rate: Individual $2/Institution $12
Single Copy Price: $3.50
Current Volume/Issue: 9/2
Frequency per Year: four
Backfile Available: yes
Unsolicited Ms. Received: yes
% of Unsolicited Ms. Published per Year: 95%
Format: perfect
Size: H 8" W 5"
Average Pages: 72
Ads: no

Organization: Five Fingers Review

Type: magazine
CLMP member: yes
Primary Editor/Contact Person: Jaime Robles
Address: P.O. Box 4
San Leandro, CA 94577-0100
Web Site Address: http://www.fivefingersreview.org
Publishes: essays, fiction, poetry, reviews, art, and translation
Editorial Focus: We are interested in fresh, innovative writing and art that is not defined by aesthetic ideology. Each issue is theme based.

Representative Authors: Rosmarie Waldrop, Elizabeth Willis, and Rafael Campo
Submissions Policy: Include SASE.
Simultaneous Submissions: yes
Reading Period: 6/1 to 8/31
Reporting Time: three to four months
Author Payment: copies
Contests: See web site for contest guidelines.
Founded: 1984
Non Profit: yes
Paid Staff: zero
Unpaid Staff: eight
Distributors: Ingram, SPD
Total Circulation: 800
Paid Circulation: 50-100
Subscription Rate: Individual $20/Institution $22
Single Copy Price: $12
Current Volume/Issue: Issue 21
Frequency per Year: one
Backfile Available: yes
Unsolicited Ms. Received: yes
Format: perfect
Size: H 9" W 6"
Average Pages: 224
Ads: yes
Ad Rates: $500 full page; $300 half page; $150 quarter page

Organization: Five Points

Type: magazine
CLMP member: yes
Primary Editor/Contact Person: Megan Sexton
Address: Five Points, Georgia State University
P.O. Box 3999
Atlanta, GA 30302-3999
Web Site Address: http://webdelsol.com/Five_Points
Publishes: essays, fiction, poetry, art, and translation
Editorial Focus: Original poetry, fiction, essays, also translations, art, and interviews rich in the craft of language and imagination.
Representative Authors: Melanie Rae Thon, Alice Hoffman, and Mark Doty
Submissions Policy: Two submissions per genre per reading period.
Simultaneous Submissions: no
Reading Period: 9/1 to 4/30
Reporting Time: three to four months
Author Payment: cash and copies
Contests: James Dickey Poetry Prize; see website for guidelines

Founded: 1996
Non Profit: yes
Paid Staff: seven
Unpaid Staff: zero
Distributors: Ingram, Media Solutions
ISSN Number/ISBN Number: ISSN 1088-8500
Total Circulation: 2,000
Paid Circulation: 800
Average Print Run: 2,000
Subscription Rate: Individual $25/Institution $54
Single Copy Price: $8
Current Volume/Issue: 11/3
Frequency per Year: three
Backfile Available: yes
Unsolicited Ms. Received: yes
% of Unsolicited Ms. Published per Year: 5%
Format: perfect
Size: H 6.5" W 9"
Average Pages: 150
Ads: yes
Ad Rates: e-mail: info@langate.gsu.edu

Organization: Flash!Point Literary Journal

Type: magazine
CLMP member: no
Primary Editor/Contact Person: Frances LeMoine
Address: P.O. Box 540
Merrimack, NH 03054
Publishes: essays, fiction, poetry, reviews, translation
Editorial Focus: Largely poetry, but accept any and all writing considered excellent by editorial staff
Representative Authors: R.D. Armstrong, Cheryl Snell, and Corey Mesler
Submissions Policy: Up to five poems, 30 lines max. Fiction/essays up to 1,500 words max. No pornography. Send SASE for reply
Simultaneous Submissions: yes
Reading Period: Year-round
Reporting Time: one to six months
Author Payment: copies and subscription
Contests: Annual poetry and short fiction contests, usually announced in Poets & Writers Magazine
Founded: 1998
Non Profit: yes
Paid Staff: zero
Unpaid Staff: one
Distributors: Barnes & Noble, Nashua NH, Toadstool Books, Milford NH
Total Circulation: 300

Paid Circulation: 50
Subscription Rate: Individual $33/Institution $33
Single Copy Price: $11
Current Volume/Issue: 9/9
Frequency per Year: 3
Backfile Available: yes
Unsolicited Ms. Received: yes
% of Unsolicited Ms. Published per Year: 10%
Format: perfect
Size: H 8.5" W 5.5"
Average Pages: 90
Ads: no

Organization: FlashPoint

Type: online
CLMP member: no
Primary Editor/Contact Person: JR Foley
Address: 13906 Shippers Lane
Rockville, MD 20853
Web Site Address: www.flashpointmag.com
Publishes: essays, fiction, nonfiction, poetry, reviews, and art
Editorial Focus: art & politics. Poetry in Pound/Olson tradition of Modern Epic.
Representative Authors: Peter Dale Scott, Carlo Parcelli, and Joe Brennan
Submissions Policy: Unsolicited essays, fiction, art considered. No unsolicited poetry considered.
Simultaneous Submissions: yes
Reading Period: year-round
Reporting Time: one to two weeks
Author Payment: none
Founded: 1996
Non Profit: yes
Paid Staff: zero
Unpaid Staff: four
Average Page Views per Month: 980
Average Unique Visitors per Month: 484
Frequency per year: annual
Publish Print Anthology: no
Average Percentage of Pages per Category: fiction 2%, nonfiction 2%, poetry 60%, reviews 4%, essays 30%, art 2%
Ads: no

Organization: Flint Hills Review

Type: magazine
CLMP member: yes
Primary Editor/Contact Person: Kevin Rabas

Address: PO Box 4019, Dept. of English
Emporia, KS 66801
Web Site Address: www.emporia.edu/fhr
Publishes: fiction, nonfiction, poetry, reviews, and art
Editorial Focus: FHR publishes both established writers and new talents. We value work that focuses on region and place. Also, be an observer.
Representative Authors: Kim Stafford, Elizabeth Dodd, and Gary Lechliter
Submissions Policy: Send 2-6 poems, 1 short play, or 1 short story at a time. No previously published work. SASE required. Include a short cover letter.
Simultaneous Submissions: yes
Reading Period: 01/01 to 03/31
Reporting Time: one to four months
Author Payment: copies
Contests: FHR Non-fiction contest. $10 entry fee. Postmark deadline March 15 each year. Pays $200.
Founded: 1995
Non Profit: yes
Paid Staff: two
Unpaid Staff: one
Distributors: Flint Hills Review/Bluestem Press
ISSN Number/ISBN Number: n/a
Total Circulation: 500
Paid Circulation: 15
Average Print Run: 500
Subscription Rate: individual $7/institution $7
Single Copy Price: $7
Current Volume/Issue: issue 12
Frequency per year: annual
Backfile Available: yes
Unsolicited MSS Received: yes
% of Unsolicited MSS Published per Year: 95%
Format: perfect
Size: H 9" W 6"
Average Pages: 90
Ads: no

Organization: The Florida Review

Type: magazine
CLMP member: yes
Primary Editor/Contact Person: Jeanne M. Leiby
Address: The University of Central Florida
Department of English
Orlando, FL 32816-1346
Web Site Address: http://www.flreview.com
Publishes: essays, fiction, nonfiction, poetry, and reviews
Editorial Focus: Mainstream and experimental literary

fiction, poetry, and nonfiction
Representative Authors: Ron McFarland, Billy Collins, and Wendell Mayo
Submissions Policy: Poetry, max 5 poems. Literary fiction and nonfiction up to 7,500 words. Short shorts okay. Include SASE.
Simultaneous Submissions: yes
Reading Period: Year-round
Reporting Time: two to four months
Author Payment: copies
Contests: Annual Editors' award. $1,000 prize in fiction, nonfiction, and poetry. $15 reading fee. Deadline Spring; See Web Site for Contest Guidelines.
Founded: 1972
Non Profit: yes
Paid Staff: three
Unpaid Staff: 15
Distributors: amazon.com
Total Circulation: 1,750
Paid Circulation: 1,100
Average Print Run: 2,000
Subscription Rate: Individual $15/Institution $20
Single Copy Price: $8
Current Volume/Issue: 31/2
Frequency per Year: two
Backfile Available: yes
Unsolicited Ms. Received: yes
% of Unsolicited Ms. Published per Year: 90%
Format: perfect
Size: H 6" W 9"
Average Pages: 168
Ads: yes
Ad Rates: $200 page. Nonprofit discount and 1/2 and 1/4 pgs available

Organization: Flume Press
Type: press
CLMP member: yes
Primary Editor/Contact Person: Casey Huff
Address: California State University, Chico
400 W. 1st St.
Chico, CA 95929-0830
Web Site Address:
http://www.csuchico.edu/engl/flumepress/
Publishes: fiction and poetry
Editorial Focus: Flume Press aims to help newer writers get the sort of exposure that can help them achieve the recognition they deserve.
Representative Authors: John Brehm, Sherrie Flick, and Luis Aine Greaney

Submissions Policy: Our annual chapbook contest deadline is December 1. Send for guidelines or see our web site: http://www.csuchico.edu/engl/flume-press/
Simultaneous Submissions: yes
Reading Period: 06/07 to 12/07
Reporting Time: five to six months
Author Payment: cash
Contests: See Web Site for Contest Guidelines.
Founded: 1983
Non Profit: yes
Paid Staff: one
Unpaid Staff: 12
ISSN Number/ISBN Number: ISBN 1-886226
Number of Books Published per Year: one
Titles in Print: 22
Average Print Run: 500
Average Percentage Printed: Chapbook 100%
Average Price: $8

Organization: flying fish press
Type: press
CLMP member: no
Primary Editor/Contact Person: kimberly narenkivicius
Address: secret of salt: an indigenous journal
1118c white street
key west, fl 33040
Web Site Address: http://www.thesecretofsalt.com
Publishes: essays, fiction, nonfiction, poetry, reviews, and art
Editorial Focus: the secret of salt is a biannual collection of fiction. poetry, essays, interviews and images inspired by the unique environment of the florida keys and key west. The journal explores a new theme with each issue and encourages thoughtful artistic expression. We celebrate our diverse island community...artists, writers, healers...fishermen, sailors, dreamers...and are grateful for the opportunity to live in a place where we can really be ourselves.
Representative Authors: rosalind brackenbury, cricket desmarais, and matt dukes jordan
Submissions Policy: We look for quality submissions that resonate with the intention of "the secret of salt" and the current theme. Art & poetry, fiction & non-fiction, articles & essays...all are included in our pages. Writers: Please send your previously unpublished work to us either via email or snail-mail (provided your work is clearly typed and not your only copy). Send 3-5 poems, short stories, articles, essays and other works

of 2,500 words or less (though we are flexible if need be).

Simultaneous Submissions: yes
Reading Period: Year-round
Reporting Time: one to two months
Author Payment: copies
Founded: 2006
Non Profit: no
Paid Staff: two
Unpaid Staff: five
Number of Books Published per Year: 2
Titles in Print: 1
Average Percentage Printed: Paperback 100%
Average Price: $20

Organization: Flyway: A Literary Review

Type: magazine
CLMP member: no
Primary Editor/Contact Person: Steve Pett
Address: 206 Ross Hall
Iowa State University
Ames, IA 50011
Web Site Address: http://www.flyway.org
Publishes: essays, fiction, nonfiction, poetry, and art
Editorial Focus: We are looking for solid, quality writing regardless of an author's publishing history.
Representative Authors: Jane Smiley, Naomi Shihab Nye, and Gina Ochsner
Simultaneous Submissions: yes
Reading Period: 9/06 to 4/07
Reporting Time: three to eight weeks
Author Payment: copies
Contests: Sweet Corn Prize Contest
See web site for Contest Guidelines.
Founded: 1995
Non Profit: yes
Paid Staff: zero
Unpaid Staff: four
Total Circulation: 500
Paid Circulation: 500
Average Print Run: 600
Subscription Rate: Individual $18/Institution $18
Single Copy Price: $6
Current Volume/Issue: 10/1
Frequency per Year: three
Backfile Available: yes
Unsolicited Ms. Received: yes
% of Unsolicited Ms. Published per Year: 95%
Format: perfect

Size: H 9" W 6"
Average Pages: 120
Ads: yes
Ad Rates: Exchange Ads

Organization: Folio, A Literary Journal at American U.

Type: magazine
CLMP member: no
Primary Editor/Contact Person: Lauren Fanelli
Address: Department of Literature
American University
Washington, DC 20016
Web Site Address: http://www.foliojournal.org
Publishes: fiction, nonfiction, poetry, and art
Editorial Focus: We are looking for work that ignites and endures, is artful, natural, daring, and elegant.
Representative Authors: Denise Duhamel, Alice Fulton, and E. Ethelbert Miller
Submissions Policy: Submit four to soix poems; no more than 3,500 words for prose. SASE for response. Include cover letter with contact info. and bio.
Simultaneous Submissions: yes
Reading Period: 8/15 to 3/1
Reporting Time: one to three months
Author Payment: copies
Founded: 1984
Non Profit: yes
Paid Staff: nine
Unpaid Staff: zero
ISSN Number/ISBN Number: ISSN 1547-4151
Total Circulation: 150
Paid Circulation: 25
Average Print Run: 200
Subscription Rate: Individual $12/Institution $24
Single Copy Price: $6
Current Volume/Issue: 20/1
Frequency per Year: two
Backfile Available: yes
Unsolicited Ms. Received: yes
% of Unsolicited Ms. Published per Year: 20%
Format: perfect
Average Pages: 70
Ads: yes

Organization: Foreword

Type: magazine
CLMP member: no
Primary Editor/Contact Person: Alex Moore

Address: 129 1/2 E. Front St.
Traverse City, MI 49684
Web Site Address:
http://www.forewordmagazine.com/
Publishes: reviews
Editorial Focus: Reviews and feature stories focusing on great books from small presses.
Recent Awards Received: FOLIO Eddy Award for Editorial Excellence 2003/2004
Submissions Policy: please e-mail managing editor for details.
Simultaneous Submissions: yes
Reading Period: Year-round
Reporting Time: one to two months
Author Payment: cash
Contests: Book of the Year Awards program for titles published in current year
See web site for Contest Guidelines.
Founded: 1998
Non Profit: no
Paid Staff: five
Unpaid Staff: zero
Distributors: USPS
ISSN Number/ISBN Number: ISSN 1099-2642
Total Circulation: 8,500
Paid Circulation: 400
Average Print Run: 7,500
Subscription Rate: Individual $40/Institution $34
Single Copy Price: $10
Current Volume/Issue: 8/6
Frequency per Year: bimonthly
Backfile Available: yes
Unsolicited Ms. Received: no
Format: perfect
Average Pages: 72
Ad Rates: See web site for details.

Organization: Four Way Books

Type: press
CLMP member: yes
Primary Editor/Contact Person: Martha Rhodes
Address: POB 535 Village Station
NY, NY 10014
Web Site Address: http://www.fourwaybooks.com
Publishes: fiction and poetry
Editorial Focus: We are primarily a poetry press although we publish short story collections and novellas.
Representative Authors: Catherine Bowman, Sarah Manguso, and Jeffrey Harrison

Submissions Policy: For contest and open reading period, check our web site first as reading dates may change year-to-year.
Simultaneous Submissions: yes
Reading Period: 6/1 to 6/30
Reporting Time: one to five months.
Author Payment: royalties and cash
Contests: We read January 1-March 31 for contest. See web site for contest guidelines.
Founded: 1993
Non Profit: yes
Paid Staff: five
Unpaid Staff: two
Distributors: University Press of New England (UPNE)
ISSN Number/ISBN Number: ISBN 1884800
Number of Books Published per Year: six to eight
Titles in Print: 70
Average Print Run: 1,000
Average Percentage Printed: Paperback 100%
Average Price: $14.95

Organization: Fourteen Hills

Type: magazine
CLMP member: no
Primary Editor/Contact Person: Jason Snyder
Address: Creative Writing Dept.
1600 Holloway Ave.
San Francisco, CA 94132-1722
Web Site Address: http://www.14hills.net
Publishes: essays, fiction, nonfiction, poetry, art, and translation
Editorial Focus: Biannual journal committed to presenting experimental and progressive work by emerging, established, and cross-genre writers.
Simultaneous Submissions: yes
Reading Period: Year-round
Reporting Time: two to eight months
Author Payment: copies
Contests: Holmes Awards: $250 each; best poem, best prose published each year by emerging writers who have not yet published first book
Founded: 1994
Non Profit: yes
Paid Staff: one
Unpaid Staff: 20
Total Circulation: 600
Paid Circulation: 50
Subscription Rate: Individual $12/Institution $18
Single Copy Price: $7
Current Volume/Issue: 10/1

Frequency per Year: two
Backfile Available: yes
Unsolicited Ms. Received: yes
% of Unsolicited Ms. Published per Year: 2%
Format: perfect
Size: H 9" W 6"
Average Pages: 180
Ads: yes
Ad Rates: $50 half page; $80 full page

Organization: Freefall Magazine

Type: magazine
CLMP member: no
Primary Editor/Contact Person: Lynn Fraser
Address: 922-9 Ave. SE
Calgary, AB T2G 0S4
Web Site Address: http://www.freefallmagazine.ca
Publishes: essays, fiction, nonfiction, poetry, reviews, art, and translation
Editorial Focus: We publish primarily poetry, fiction, reviews, author interview, and artwork.
Recent Awards Received: Alberta Magazine Publishers Association 2007 Best Cover Award for Vol. XVI No. 1 'Experience' by Brian McFadden
Representative Authors: Karen Connelly, Tom Wayman, and Christopher Wiseman
Submissions Policy: See guidelines on website; 3,000 words for fiction/nonfiction. Poetry 3-5 poems electronic submissions accepted.
Simultaneous Submissions: no
Reading Period: Year-round
Reporting Time: six to eight months
Author Payment: cash
Contests: See Web Site for Contest Guidelines.
Founded: 1990
Non Profit: yes
Paid Staff: 1/2
Unpaid Staff: nine
Distributors: Magazines Canada
ISSN Number/ISBN Number: ISSN 1203-9586
Total Circulation: 500
Paid Circulation: 250
Average Print Run: 500
Subscription Rate: Individual $20/Institution $28
Single Copy Price: $10
Current Volume/Issue:XVII/1
Frequency per Year: biannual
Backfile Available: yes
Unsolicited Ms. Received: yes
% of Unsolicited Ms. Published per Year: 100%

Format: perfect
Size: H 5" W 8.5"
Average Pages: 80
Ads: yes
Ad Rates: See web site for details.

Organization: Frigate

Type: online
CLMP member: no
Primary Editor/Contact Person: Patricia Eakins
Address: 1200 Broadway
New York, NY 11021
Web Site Address: http://www.frigatezine.com
Publishes: essays, fiction, nonfiction, poetry, reviews, and art
Editorial Focus: We are multi-syncratic, with a spectrum of vivid voices. We like quirk and flavor. We read difficult writing for the sheer pleasure of its language. We are fond of all things experimental, innovative and playful. We loathe blandness, earnestness, and pious correctitude.
Representative Authors: Eric Darton, Elain Terranova, and Gerry Gomez Pearlberg
Submissions Policy: Solicited only.
Simultaneous Submissions: yes
Reading Period: Year-round
Reporting Time: two to four months
Author Payment: none
Founded: 2000
Non Profit: yes
Paid Staff: three
Unpaid Staff: 21
Average Page Views per Month: 10,000
Average Unique Visitors per Month: 3,000
Frequency per Year: annual
Publish Print Anthology: no
Average Percentage of Pages per Category: Fiction 5%, Nonfiction 10%, Poetry 5%, Reviews 35%, Essays 35%, Art 10%
Ads: no

Organization: FRiGG: A Magazine of Fiction and Poetry

Type: online
CLMP member: yes
Primary Editor/Contact Person: Ellen Parker
Address: 9036 Evanston Ave. N.
Seattle, WA 98103
Web Site Address: http://www.friggmagazine.com

Publishes: fiction, nonfiction, poetry, and art
Recent Awards Received: Top 100 online stories in Million Writers Awards
Simultaneous Submissions: yes
Reading Period: Year-round
Reporting Time: two to twelve weeks
Author Payment: none
Founded: 2003
Non Profit: yes
Paid Staff: zero
Unpaid Staff: five
Average Page Views per Month: varies
Average Unique Visitors per Month: varies
Frequency per Year: quarterly
Average Percentage of Pages per Category: Fiction 45%, Nonfiction 5%, Poetry 40%, Art 10%

Organization: From the Fishouse

Type: online
CLMP member: yes
Primary Editor/Contact Person: Matt O'Donnell
Address: 87 Stage Road
Pittston, ME 04345
Web Site Address: www.fishousepoems.org
Publishes: poetry
Editorial Focus: Audio, emerging poets (one book or fewer at submission) reading their poems, and audio Q&A w/poets about the craft.
Representative Authors: Geoffrey Brock, V. Penelope Pelizzon, and Ilya Kaminsky
Submissions Policy: Closed to unsolicited submissions.
Simultaneous Submissions: yes
Reading Period: year-round
Reporting Time: two to three weeks
Author Payment: none
Founded: 2004
Non Profit: yes
Paid Staff: zero
Unpaid Staff: two
Average Page Views per Month: 66,148
Average Unique Visitors per Month: 6,169
Frequency per year: bimonthly
Publish Print Anthology: no
Average Percentage of Pages per Category: Audio 100%
Ads: no

Organization: Fugue State Press

Type: press
CLMP member: no
Primary Editor/Contact Person: James Chapman
Address: P.O. Box 80, Cooper Station
New York, NY 10003
Web Site Address: http://www.fuguestatepress.com
Publishes: fiction
Editorial Focus: Experimental and advanced fiction: novels only
Representative Authors: Andre Malraux, Joshua Cohen, and Noah Cicero
Submissions Policy: We're looking for experimental novels that are ambitious, visionary, private, idiosyncratic, emotional.
Simultaneous Submissions: yes
Reading Period: Year-round
Reporting Time: one to ten weeks
Author Payment: royalties, cash, and copies
Founded: 1992
Non Profit: no
Paid Staff: zero
Unpaid Staff: one
Wholesalers: Baker & Taylor
ISSN Number/ISBN Number: ISBN 1879193
Number of Books Published per Year: three
Titles in Print: 18
Average Print Run: 1,000
Average Percentage Printed: Paperback 100%
Average Price: $15

Organization: Fugue

Type: magazine
CLMP member: no
Primary Editor/Contact Person: Sara Kaplan and Justin Jainchill
Address: University of Idaho, English Department
200 Brink Hall
Moscow, ID 83844-1102
Web Site Address:
http://www.uidaho.edu/fugue/home.htm

Publishes: fiction, nonfiction, and poetry
Editorial Focus: Fugue brings together diverse modes of expression and voices within each issue.
Representative Authors: W.S. Merwin, Dean Young, and Maura Stanton
Submissions Policy: Prose: 6,000 words. Poetry: three to five poems, not more than 10 pages. Address to appropriate editor.

Simultaneous Submissions: yes
Reading Period: 9/1 to 5/1
Reporting Time: three to six months
Author Payment: cash and copies
Contests: See web site for contest guidelines.
Founded: 1990
Non Profit: yes
Unpaid Staff: 21
Distributors: DeBoer, Ingram
ISSN Number/ISBN Number: ISSN 10546014
Total Circulation: 1,000
Paid Circulation: zero
Average Print Run: 800
Subscription Rate: Individual $14/Institution $22
Single Copy Price: $8
Current Volume/Issue: 1/27
Frequency per Year: biannual
Backfile Available: yes
Unsolicited Ms. Received: yes
% of Unsolicited Ms. Published per Year: 80%
Format: perfect
Size: H 9" W 6"
Average Pages: 175
Ads: yes
Ad Rates: Inquire

Organization: Full Circle Journal

Type: magazine
CLMP member: no
Primary Editor/Contact Person: Allegra Wong/Daniel Blasi
Address: P.O. Box 15554
Boston, MA 02215
Web Site Address: http://www.fullcirclejrnl.com
Publishes: essays, fiction, nonfiction, poetry, and translation
Editorial Focus: We seek outstanding literature.
Representative Authors: Robert Pinsky, Elizabeth Arnold, and Allan Peterson
Submissions Policy: We accept submissions via postal mail. Include a self-addressed stamped envelope and a brief bio.
Simultaneous Submissions: yes
Reading Period: Year-round
Reporting Time: three to five months
Author Payment: copies
Contests: varies
See Web Site for Contest Guidelines.
Founded: 2002
Non Profit: yes

Paid Staff: zero
Unpaid Staff: four
ISSN Number/ISBN Number: ISSN 1542-197X
Total Circulation: 1,000
Paid Circulation: 350
Subscription Rate: Individual $18/Institution $18
Single Copy Price: $10
Current Volume/Issue: one/two
Frequency per Year: biannual
Backfile Available: yes
Unsolicited Ms. Received: yes
% of Unsolicited Ms. Published per Year: 3%
Format: perfect
Size: H 8" W 5.5"
Average Pages: 225
Ads: yes
Ad Rates: query for rates

Organization: The Furnace Review

Type: online
CLMP member: yes
Primary Editor/Contact Person: Ciara LaVelle
Address: 905 Michigan Ave. #3
Miami Beach, FL 33139
Web Site Address: http://www.thefurnacereview.com
Publishes: fiction and poetry
Editorial Focus: contemporary works from up and coming writers
Representative Authors: Dominic Preziosi, Jona Colson, Teneice Delgado
Submissions Policy: No submissions via postal mail. Submit via email:
submissions@thefurnacereview.com. Fiction up to 7,000 words and up to five poems (75 lines maximum) will be considered. Include name, email address and a short bio with each submission.
Simultaneous Submissions: yes
Reading Period: year-round
Reporting Time: four months
Author Payment: none
Founded: 2004
Non Profit: yes
Paid Staff: one
Unpaid Staff: nine
Total Circulation: 5,000 visits per issue/64,000 hits per issue
Frequency per year: Four issues/year
Backfile Available: Archives available online
Unsolicited MSS Received: 200/issue
% of Unsolicited MSS Published per year: 35

Format: online
Ads: yes
Ad Rates: negotiable based on size and quantity. Average 120x90 pixel banner **ad:** $40

Organization: FuseBox

Type: online
CLMP member: no
Primary Editor/Contact Person: Ram Devineni
Address: 532 La Guardia Place
Ste. 353
New York, NY 10012
Web Site Address: http://www.rattapallax.com/fuse-box.htm
Publishes: essays, fiction, nonfiction, poetry, reviews, art, translation, and audio
Editorial Focus: Focus on international poetry and performance.
Representative Authors: Robert Creeley, Arnaldo Antunes, and AJA (Adisa Jelani Andwele)
Submissions Policy: Contact editor by e-mail.
Simultaneous Submissions: yes
Reading Period: Year-round
Reporting Time: one to two months
Author Payment: none
Founded: 2003
Non Profit: yes
Paid Staff: zero
Unpaid Staff: four
Distributors: online
Average Page Views per Month: 60
Average Unique Visitors per Month: 1,200
Publish Print Anthology: yes
Price: $24
Average Percentage of Pages per Category: Fiction 5%, Nonfiction 5%, Poetry 40%, Reviews 5%, Essays 5%, Art 5%, Translation 30%, Audio 5%
Ad Rates: See web site for details.

Organization: Future Tense Books

Type: press
CLMP member: no
Primary Editor/Contact Person: Kevin Sampsell
Address: P.O. Box 42416
Portland, OR 97242
Web Site Address: http://www.futuretensebooks.com
Editorial Focus: We publish chapbooks and paperbacks from emerging and established writers, often dealing with work that other presses ignore.

Representative Authors: Eric Spitznagel, Susannah Breslin, and Magdalen Powers
Submissions Policy: Please send a query and SASE or an e-mail describing the work before submitting. Mostly interested in fiction or memoir.
Simultaneous Submissions: yes
Reading Period: Year-round
Reporting Time: two to eight weeks
Author Payment: copies
Founded: 1990
Non Profit: no
Paid Staff: two
Unpaid Staff: two
Distributors: Last Gasp
Number of Books Published per Year: two to four
Titles in Print: 24
Average Print Run: 500
Average Percentage Printed: Paperback 25%, Chapbook 75%
Average Price: $5

Organization: Futurepoem books

Type: press
CLMP member: yes
Primary Editor/Contact Person: Dan Machlin
Address: c/o Dan Machlin, Editor, PO Box 7687
JAF Station
New York, NY 10116
Web Site Address: http://www.futurepoem.com
Publishes: fiction and poetry
Editorial Focus: Innovative poetry and prose. Works that blur the line between literary genres.
Recent Awards Received: 2006 Asian American Literary Award for Poetry. 2004-05 AIGA 50 Books/50 Covers Award.Books/50 Covers for best Covers of 2004
Representative Authors: Laura Mullen, Shanxing Wang, and Marcella Durand
Submissions Policy: Unsolicited manuscripts are accepted only during open reading period. Please join Email List at website for details.
Simultaneous Submissions: yes
Reading Period: 9/1 to 9/30
Reporting Time: five to six months
Author Payment: royalties and copies
Founded: 2001
Non Profit: yes
Paid Staff: zero
Unpaid Staff: five
Distributors: Amazon.com

Wholesalers: SPD Books
ISSN Number/ISBN Number: ISBN 0-9716800
Number of Books Published per Year: two
Titles in Print: seven
Average Print Run: 750
Average Percentage Printed: Paperback 100%
Average Price: $14

Organization: Gargoyle Magazine

Type: magazine
CLMP member: yes
Primary Editor/Contact Person: Richard Peabody
Address: 3819 N. 13th St.
Arlington, VA 22201
Web Site Address:
http://www.gargoylemagazine.com
Publishes: essays, fiction, nonfiction, poetry, art, translation, and audio
Editorial Focus: We tend to be edgy and bent. We collect books and mags, love to read and write, and actually believe lit matters. Silly us.
Representative Authors: Toby Olson, Elizabeth Swados, and Kit Reed
Submissions Policy: Prefer electronic submissions in the body of an e-mail. If we like something we'll ask for a Word attachment. Snail mail OK.
Simultaneous Submissions: yes
Reading Period: 5/30 to 9/4
Reporting Time: one to three months
Author Payment: copies
Founded: 1976
Non Profit: no
Paid Staff: zero
Unpaid Staff: three
Distributors: DeBoer
ISSN Number/ISBN Number: ISSN 0162-1149
Total Circulation: 1,500
Paid Circulation: 25
Average Print Run: 1,500
Subscription Rate: Individual $30/Institution $40
Single Copy Price: $15.95
Current Volume/Issue: Issue 52
Frequency per Year: annual
Backfile Available: yes
Unsolicited Ms. Received: yes
% of Unsolicited Ms. Published per Year: 35%
Format: perfect
Size: H 8.5" W 5.5"
Average Pages: 300+
Ads: yes

Ad Rates: $100 full-page; $60 half page

Organization: Geist Magazine

Type: magazine
CLMP member: yes
Primary Editor/Contact Person: Stephen Osborne
Address: 341 Water St., Ste. 200
Vancouver, BC V6B 1B8
Web Site Address: http://www.geist.com
Publishes: essays, fiction, nonfiction, poetry, and art
Editorial Focus: A literary magazine of Canadian Ideas and Culture.
Recent Awards Received: Magazine of the Year at the Western Magazine Awards 2001 and 2003.
Submissions Policy: Submissions should have a connection to Canada, either by content or author nationality.
Simultaneous Submissions: yes
Reading Period: Year-round
Reporting Time: one to five months
Author Payment: cash and copies
Contests: Annual Literal Literary Postcard Contest (December deadline)
See web site for contest guidelines.
Founded: 1990
Non Profit: yes
Paid Staff: two
Unpaid Staff: 12
Distributors: Magazines Canada, Disticor, Doormouse
ISSN Number/ISBN Number: ISSN 1181-6554
Total Circulation: 10,000
Paid Circulation: 4,691
Average Print Run: 12,000
Subscription Rate: Individual $20/Institution $25
Single Copy Price: $5.95
Current Volume/Issue: 15/61
Frequency per Year: quarterly
Backfile Available: yes
Unsolicited Ms. Received: yes
Format: stapled
Size: H 10.5" W 8"
Average Pages: 58
Ads: yes
Ad Rates: See web site for details.

Organization: Georgetown Review

Type: magazine
CLMP member: yes
Primary Editor/Contact Person: Steven Carter

Address: 400 E. College St.
P.O. Box 227
Georgetown, KY 40324
Web Site Address: http://georgetownreview.george-towncollege.edu
Publishes: essays, fiction, nonfiction, and poetry
Editorial Focus: We're simply looking to publish quality fiction, poetry, creative nonfiction, and essays.
Representative Authors: David Allan Evans, Ben Brooks, and David Romtvedt
Submissions Policy: No page length limit for fiction or essays; please limit poetry submissions to 10 pages.
Simultaneous Submissions: yes
Reading Period: 9/1 to 3/15
Reporting Time: one to three months
Author Payment: copies and submission
Contests: Held yearly, $1,000 first prize, runners-up considered for publication.
See Web Site for Contest Guidelines.
Founded: 1992
Non Profit: yes
Paid Staff: no
Unpaid Staff: yes
Distributors: DeBoer, Ubiquity
Total Circulation: 1,000
Paid Circulation: 75
Average Print Run: 1,200
Subscription Rate: Individual $5/1 year/Institution $9/1 year
Single Copy Price: $5
Current Volume/Issue: 7/1
Frequency per Year: annual
Backfile Available: yes
Unsolicited Ms. Received: yes
% of Unsolicited Ms. Published per Year: 15%
Format: perfect
Size: H 9" W 6"
Average Pages: 192
Ads: yes
Ad Rates: See web site for details.

Organization: The Georgia Review

Type: magazine
CLMP member: yes
Primary Editor/Contact Person: Stephen Corey
Address: 012 Gilbert Hall
The University of Georgia
Athens, GA 30602-9009
Web Site Address: http://www.uga.edu/garev

Publishes: essays, fiction, nonfiction, poetry, reviews, and art
Editorial Focus: A rich gathering of stories, essays, poems, book reviews and visual art orchestrated to invite and sustain repeated readings.
Representative Authors: Philip Levine, Barry Lopez, and Maary Hood
Submissions Policy: See web site or send SASE. No electronic submissions.
Simultaneous Submissions: no
Reading Period: 8/5 to 5/15
Reporting Time: two to four months
Author Payment: cash, copies, and subscription
Founded: 1947
Non Profit: yes
Paid Staff: seven
Unpaid Staff: zero to two
Distributors: DeBoer, Ingram, Media Solutions, Ubiquity
ISSN Number/ISBN Number: ISSN 0016-8386
Total Circulation: 4,000
Paid Circulation: 3,500
Average Print Run: 4,000
Subscription Rate: Individual $30/Institution $30
Single Copy Price: $10
Current Volume/Issue: LX/1
Frequency per Year: quarterly
Backfile Available: yes
Unsolicited Ms. Received: yes
% of Unsolicited Ms. Published per Year: 1%
Format: perfect
Size: H 10" W 6.75"
Average Pages: 210
Ads: yes
Ad Rates: $425 cover, $350 page, $225 half page, $600 2-pg. spread
See web site for details.

Organization: The Germ: A Journal of Poetic Research

Type: magazine
CLMP member: no
Primary Editor/Contact Person: Andrew Maxwell
Address: 1440 Allison Ave.
Los Angeles, CA 90026
Web Site Address: http://germspot.blogspot.com
Publishes: essays, fiction, poetry, and translation
Editorial Focus: Belles lettres. "The poem of the act of the mind." Translation, sidelong glances: "literalists of the imagination."

Recent Awards Received: The Arthur Symons Living Difficultly Inappropriate Endurance Award, 2005.
Representative Authors: Eugene Ostashevsky, Charles North, and Paul LaFarge
Submissions Policy: Check to see if we're reading first by e-mail. Warning: we're an occasional with sudden, unpredictable eruptions of activity.
Simultaneous Submissions: no
Reading Period: Year-round
Reporting Time: one to three months
Author Payment: copies
Contests: See web site for contest guidelines.
Founded: 1996
Non Profit: yes
Paid Staff: zero
Unpaid Staff: two
Distributors: SPD, Consortium, Armadillo
ISSN Number/ISBN Number: ISSN 1093-6610
Total Circulation: 400
Paid Circulation: 150
Average Print Run: 1,000
Subscription Rate: Individual $20/Institution $25
Single Copy Price: $10
Current Volume/Issue: Issue seven
Frequency per Year: annual
Backfile Available: yes
Unsolicited Ms. Received: yes
% of Unsolicited Ms. Published per Year: 40%
Format: perfect
Size: H 8.5" W 7"
Average Pages: 250
Ads: no

Organization: The Gettysburg Review

Type: magazine
CLMP member: yes
Primary Editor/Contact Person: Peter Stitt
Address: Gettysburg College
300 N. Washington St.
Gettysburg, PA 17325-1491
Web Site Address: http://www.gettysburgreview.com
Publishes: essays, fiction, nonfiction, poetry, reviews, and art
Editorial Focus: Our central criterion is high literary quality; we seek writers who can shape the language in unique and beautiful ways.
Recent Awards Received: Best New Design, CLMP
Representative Authors: Scott Schrader, Pattiann Rogers, and Bret Lott
Submissions Policy: Please visit our web site at

http://www.gettysburgreview.com for submission guidelines
Simultaneous Submissions: yes
Reading Period: 9/1 to 5/31
Reporting Time: three to six months
Author Payment: cash, copies, and subscription
Founded: 1988
Non Profit: yes
Paid Staff: four
Unpaid Staff: one
Distributors: Ingram; Ubiquity Distributors
ISSN Number/ISBN Number: ISSN 0898-4557
Total Circulation: 2,250
Paid Circulation: 1,800
Average Print Run: 2,500
Subscription Rate: Individual $24/Institution $24
Single Copy Price: $7
Current Volume/Issue: 19/2
Frequency per Year: quarterly
Backfile Available: yes
Unsolicited Ms. Received: yes
% of Unsolicited Ms. Published per Year: 2%
Format: perfect
Size: H 10" W 6.75"
Average Pages: 168
Ad Rates: E-mail kkupperm@gettysburg.edu for information

Organization: Ghost Road Press

Type: press
CLMP member: yes
Primary Editor/Contact Person: Sonya Unrein
Address: 5303 E. Evans. Ave. #309
Denver, CO 80222
Web Site Address: http://www.ghostroadpress.com
Publishes: fiction, nonfiction, and poetry
Editorial Focus: Social relevant fiction; poetry; memoir and nonfiction that presents a compelling story and historical relevance.
Recent Awards Received: Honorable Mention, Nonfiction Memoir, Foreword Magazine for Desert of the Heart; SPUR award, poetry: Across the High Divide
Representative Authors: Aaron Anstett, Clay Matthews, and Aaron Abeyta
Submissions Policy: reading period January to July; see website for submission procedures: ghostroadpress.com/submissions.htm
Simultaneous Submissions: yes
Reading Period: 01/01 to 7/31

Reporting Time: three to seven months
Author Payment: royalties
Contests: Open Windows Creative Writing contest; $500 for best story, poem, and nonfiction essay; see website for guidelines
Founded: 2004
Non Profit: yes
Paid Staff: one
Unpaid Staff: four
Distributors: Small Press Distributors
Wholesalers: Ingram
Number of Books Published per Year: 12
Titles in Print: 35
Average Print Run: 300
Average Percentage Printed: Paperback 100%
Average Price: $15

Organization: Gingko Tree Review

Type: magazine
CLMP member: no
Primary Editor/Contact Person: Randall Fuller
Address: Drury University
900 N. Benton Ave.
Springfield, MO 65802
Web Site Address: http://www.drury.edu/gingkotree/
Publishes: essays, fiction, nonfiction, and poetry
Editorial Focus: We strive to publish both new and established authors who captivate us with singular voices and exceptional language.
Representative Authors: Rick Moody, Ioanna Carlsen, and Roy Kesey
Submissions Policy: The Gingko Tree Review invites submissions of poetry, fiction and nonfiction. There are no length restrictions.
Simultaneous Submissions: yes
Reading Period: Year-round
Reporting Time: one to two months
Author Payment: copies
Contests: The Annual Bob Shacochis Short Story Contest awards $1,000 and publication. See web site for contest guidelines.
Founded: 2001
Non Profit: yes
Paid Staff: one
Unpaid Staff: seven
Total Circulation: 800
Paid Circulation: 500
Subscription Rate: Individual $14/Institution $14
Single Copy Price: $10
Current Volume/Issue: 2/1

Frequency per Year: biannual
Backfile Available: yes
Unsolicited Ms. Received: yes
% of Unsolicited Ms. Published per Year: 70%
Format: perfect
Size: H 8" W 5"
Average Pages: 200
Ads: no

Organization: Ginosko Literary Journal

Type: online
CLMP member: no
Primary Editor/Contact Person: Robert Paul Cesaretti
Address: PO Box 246
Fairfax, CA 94978
Website Address: www.GinoskoLiteraryJournal.com
Publishes: fiction and poetry
Editorial Focus: Literature with a transcendent aspect.
Recent Awards Received: n/a
Representative Authors: Lisa Harris, Grace Cavalieri, and Andrena Zawinski
Submissions Policy: Accepts reprints. Copyright reverts to author.
Simultaneous Submissions: yes
Reading Period: year-round
Reporting Time: 1 to 3 months
Author Payment: none
Contests: n/a
Founded: 2003
Non Profit: yes
Paid Staff: 1
Unpaid Staff: 0
ISSN Number/ISBN Number: ISSN none
Average Page Views per Month: 150
Average Unique Visitors per Month: 150
Frequency: 2
Price: free
Average Percentage of Pages per Category: Fiction 50%, Poetry 50%
Ads: no

Organization: Gival Press

Type: press
CLMP member: yes
Primary Editor/Contact Person: Robert L. Giron
Address: P.O. Box 3812
Arlington, VA 22203
Web Site Address: http://www.givalpress.com

Publishes: essays, fiction, nonfiction, poetry, and translation

Editorial Focus: We look for quality works that have a message, be it philosophical or social. Books are in English, Spanish, and French.

Recent Awards Received: 2005 DIY Book Festival Award, 2004 Lambda Literary Award for Poetry; ForeWord Magazine Book of the Year for Translation (Silver in 2003; Bronze in 2002)

Representative Authors: Charles Casillo, Beverly Burch, and Paula Goldman

Submissions Policy: Query 1st with info re: the project; say if simultaneous submission. MSS sent per contests must follow the specific guidelines.

Simultaneous Submissions: yes

Reading Period: 3/1 to 5/30

Reporting Time: three to four months

Author Payment: royalties, cash, and copies

Contests: See web site for contest guidelines.

Founded: 1998

Non Profit: no

Paid Staff: two

Unpaid Staff: two

Distributors: Ingram; Baker & Taylor; Whitaker

Wholesalers: BookMasters; Academic Book Center; Blackwell's

ISSN Number/ISBN Number: ISSN 1-928589

Number of Books Published per Year: five

Titles in Print: 29

Average Print Run: 500

Average Percentage Printed: Paperback 99%, Chapbook 1%

Average Price: $15

Organization: Glimmer Train Stories

Type: magazine

CLMP member: yes

Primary Editor/Contact Person: Susan Burmeister-Brown

Address: 1211 NW Glisan St., Ste. 207
Portland, OR 97209-3054

Web Site Address: http://www.glimmertrain.com

Publishes: fiction

Editorial Focus: Literary short stories by emerging and established fiction writers. Unsolicited work is welcomed.

Representative Authors: George Makana Clark, Karen Outen, and Daniel Wallace

Submissions Policy: Payment and response time vary by category. Check guidelines and submit online:

http://www.glimmertrain.com

Simultaneous Submissions: no

Reading Period: Year-round

Reporting Time: two to three months

Author Payment: cash

Contests: See web site for contest guidelines.

Founded: 1991

Non Profit: no

Paid Staff: zero

Unpaid Staff: two

Distributors: IPD, Ingram, Ubiquity

ISSN Number/ISBN Number: ISSN 1055-7520

Total Circulation: 12,000

Paid Circulation: 6,000

Average Print Run: 12,500

Subscription Rate: Individual $36/Institution $36

Single Copy Price: $12

Current Volume/Issue: Issue 63

Frequency per Year: quarterly

Backfile Available: yes

Unsolicited Ms. Received: yes

Format: perfect

Size: H 9-3/4" W 6-1/4"

Average Pages: 260

Ads: no

Organization: Golden Handcuffs Review

Type: magazine

CLMP member: no

Primary Editor/Contact Person: Lou Rowan

Address: Box 20158
Seattle, WA 98102

Web Site Address: http://goldenhandcuffsreview.com

Publishes: essays, fiction, nonfiction, poetry, reviews, art, and translation

Editorial Focus: Seek the new, fresh, experimental.

Representative Authors: Robert Coover, Toby Olson, and Jerome Rothenberg

Submissions Policy: Prefer submissions in mail with SASE.

Simultaneous Submissions: yes

Reading Period: Year-round

Reporting Time: 1 to 12 weeks

Author Payment: copies

Founded: 2002

Non Profit: no

Paid Staff: one

Unpaid Staff: two

Distributors: Ingram; DeBoer

ISSN Number/ISBN Number: ISSN 1541-2547
Total Circulation: 2,300
Paid Circulation: 100
Subscription Rate: Individual $14/Institution $14
Single Copy Price: $6.95
Current Volume/Issue: 1/2
Frequency per Year: biannual
Backfile Available: yes
Unsolicited Ms. Received: yes
% of Unsolicited Ms. Published per Year: 2%
Format: perfect
Size: H 9" W 5"
Average Pages: 120
Ads: yes
Ad Rates: $100/page
See web site for details.

Organization: Good Foot

Type: magazine
CLMP member: no
Primary Editor/Contact Person: Carmine Simmons, Co-editor
Address: P.O. Box 681
Murray Hill Station
New York, NY 10156
Web Site Address:
http://www.goodfootmagazine.com
Publishes: poetry
Editorial Focus: Compelling, readable work from across the poetry spectrum.
Representative Authors: Mike White, Simon Perchik, and Esther Lee
Submissions Policy: Submit no more than 3 poems with 50-word bio and cover letter. Responses by email only; no SASE required.
Simultaneous Submissions: yes
Reading Period: 2/1 to 10/31
Reporting Time: two to four months
Author Payment: copies
Contests: To be announced. Visit web site for details.
Founded: 2001
Non Profit: yes
Paid Staff: zero
Unpaid Staff: four
Distributors: DeBoer
ISSN Number/ISBN Number: ISSN 1540-9708
Total Circulation: 0
Paid Circulation: 0
Average Print Run: 0
Subscription Rate: Individual $14/Institution $28

Single Copy Price: $8
Current Volume/Issue: Issue seven
Frequency per Year: biannual
Backfile Available: yes
Unsolicited Ms. Received: yes
Format: perfect
Average Pages: 120
Ads: yes
Ad Rates: Full-page $150; half-page $85. Please inquire for details.

Organization: Grain Magazine

Type: magazine
CLMP member: no
Primary Editor/Contact Person: Kent Bruyneel
Address: P.O. Box 67
Saskatoon, SK S7K 3K1
Web Site Address: http://www.grainmagazine.ca
Publishes: fiction, nonfiction, and poetry
Editorial Focus: New and original poetry and fiction from across North America and the world. Some creative nonfiction.
Recent Awards Received: Journey Prize for Fiction, 2003; National Magazine Awards; Western Magazine Awards (Canada)
Representative Authors: Yann Martel, Tim Lilburn, and Tom Wayman
Submissions Policy: Maximum eight poems or two stories, paper copy only, SASE or e-mail response. No returns with insufficient Canadian postage or IRC.
Simultaneous Submissions: no
Reading Period: 9/1 to 5/31
Reporting Time: 12 to 16 months
Author Payment: cash and copies
Contests: Short Grain Contest-various categories, $500 cash prize, deadline January 31.
See web site for contest guidelines.
Founded: 1973
Non Profit: yes
Paid Staff: six
Unpaid Staff: zero
Distributors: Prairie Advertising, Magazines Canada
ISSN Number/ISBN Number: ISSN 1491-0497
Total Circulation: 1,400
Paid Circulation: 850
Average Print Run: 1,500
Subscription Rate: Individual $29.95/Institution $35
Single Copy Price: $9.95
Current Volume/Issue: 35/1
Frequency per Year: quarterly

Backfile Available: yes
Unsolicited Ms. Received: yes
% of Unsolicited Ms. Published per Year: 3%
Format: perfect
Size: H 9" W 6"
Average Pages: 125
Ads: yes
Ad Rates: $225 per full page; $150 per half page; $275 inside front

Organization: Graywolf Press

Type: press
CLMP member: yes
Primary Editor/Contact Person: Katie Dublinski
Address: 2402 University Ave, Ste. 203
St. Paul, MN 55114
Web Site Address: www.graywolfpress.org/
Publishes: essays, fiction, nonfiction, poetry, and translation
Editorial Focus: Graywolf publishes work that combines a distinct voice with a distinct vision.
Submissions Policy: Graywolf does not accept unsolicited manuscripts, we ask that you first send a query letter by regular mail.
Simultaneous Submissions: no
Reading Period: year-round
Reporting Time: three to four months
Author Payment: none, royalties, cash, and copies
Contests: S. Mariella Gable Prize for fiction and the Graywolf Press nonfiction Prize
See web site for contest guidelines
Founded: 1974
Non Profit: yes
Paid Staff: eight
Unpaid Staff: two
Distributors: Farrar, Straus & Giroux
Number of Books Published per year: 21-23
Titles in Print: 300
Average Percentage Printed: hardcover 10%, paperback 90%
Backfile Available: no

Organization: Great Marsh Press/The Reading Room

Type: magazine
CLMP member: yes
Address: P.O. Box 2144
Lenox Hill Station
New York, NY 10021

Web Site Address: http://www.greatmarshpress.com
Publishes: fiction, nonfiction, and translation
Simultaneous Submissions: yes
Reading Period: Year-round
Reporting Time: one to two months
Author Payment: none
Founded: 1999
Non Profit: yes
Unpaid Staff: five
Wholesalers: Ingram
Backfile Available: yes

Organization: Great River Review

Type: magazine
CLMP member: yes
Primary Editor/Contact Person: Robert Hedin
Address: 163 Tower View Dr.
Red Wing, MN 55066
Web Site Address: http://www.andersoncenter.org
Publishes: essays, fiction, nonfiction, poetry, and translation
Editorial Focus: To publish the best work.
Representative Authors: Ted Kooser, Linda Pastan, and Robert Bly
Submissions Policy: No e-mail submissions
Simultaneous Submissions: no
Reading Period: Year-round
Reporting Time: one to two months
Author Payment: copies
Contests: no
Founded: 1977
Non Profit: yes
Paid Staff: zero
Unpaid Staff: two
Total Circulation: 1,000
Paid Circulation: 750
Subscription Rate: Individual $14/Institution $30
Single Copy Price: $6
Current Volume/Issue: Issue 40
Frequency per Year: biannual
Backfile Available: yes
Unsolicited Ms. Received: yes
% of Unsolicited Ms. Published per Year: 10%
Format: perfect
Size: H 9" W 6"
Average Pages: 100
Ads: no

Organization: Greenboathouse Books

Type: press
CLMP member: no
Primary Editor/Contact Person: Jason Dewinetz
Address: 3303 - 25th Street
Vernon, BC V1T 4R4
Web Site Address: http://www.greenboathouse.com
Publishes: fiction and poetry
Editorial Focus: Greenboathouse Books is a small literary press focusing on poetry, fiction and mixed-form work by writers from across Canada.
Recent Awards Received: Recent publications have received four consecutive national book design awards.
Representative Authors: Shane Rhodes, Laisha Rosnau, and Matt Rader
Submissions Policy: Please visit our web site for submission guidelines. Please do not submit without first reading those guidelines.
Simultaneous Submissions: yes
Reading Period: 6/1 to 7/31
Reporting Time: three to six months
Author Payment: copies
Founded: 1999
Non Profit: no
Paid Staff: one
Unpaid Staff: one
ISSN Number/ISBN Number: ISBN 0-9685357 and 1-894744
Number of Books Published per Year: two to five
Titles in Print: four
Average Print Run: 120
Average Percentage Printed: Hardcover 10%, Chapbook 90%
Average Price: $15-35

Organization: Green Hills Literary Latern

Type: magazine
CLMP member: no
Primary Editor/Contact Person: Adam Davis
Address: Truman State University, Lang. & Lit.
Kirksville, MO 63501
Website Address: ll.truman.edu/ghllweb
Publishes: essays, fiction, poetry, reviews, and translation
Editorial Focus: We're open to new writers as well as more established writers. Work must reflect strong awareness of craft.
Representative Authors: Jim Thomas, Francine Tolf, and Ian MacMillan

Submissions Policy: Submit 3-7 poems, typed, one poem per page. Free or formal verse. We accept stories up to 7,000 words and short-shorts.
Simultaneous Submissions: yes
Reading Period: year-round
Reporting Time: 1 to 4 months
Author Payment: copies
Founded: 1990
Non Profit: yes
ISSN Number/ISBN Number: ISSN 1089-2060
Total Circulation: 300
Paid Circulation: 100
Subscription Rate: Individual $10/Institution $10
Single Copy Price: $10
Current Volume/Issue: Issue 15
Frequency: annual
Backfile Available: yes
Unsolicited Ms. Received: yes
% of Unsolicited Ms. Published per Year: 2%
Format: perfect
Size: H 9" W 6"
Average Pages: 300-400
Ads: yes

Organization: Green Hills Literary Lantern

Type: online
CLMP member: no
Primary Editor/Contact Person: Adam Brooke Davis
Address: McClain Hall
Truman State University
Kirksville, MO 63501
Web Site Address: ll.truman.edu/ghllweb/
Publishes: essays, fiction, nonfiction, poetry, reviews, art, and translation
Editorial Focus: We publish the best of contemporary fiction and poetry, with some bias towards the classically shaped and disciplined voice.
Representative Authors: Ian MacMillan, Karl Harshbarger, and Wendy Wisner
Submissions Policy: See web site; if submitting by snailmail, include SASE.
Simultaneous Submissions: yes
Reading Period: year-round
Reporting Time: two to four months
Author Payment: none
Contests: See web site; will be launching new prizes in fiction and poetry with volume xviii
Founded: 1990
Non Profit: yes

Paid Staff: zero
Unpaid Staff: three
ISSN Number/ISBN Number: ISSN 1089-2060
Average Page Views per Month: unknown
Average Unique Visitors per Month: unknown
Frequency per year: annual
Publish Print Anthology: no
Average Percentage of Pages per Category: fiction 40%, poetry 40%, reviews 10%, essays 10%
Ad Rates: exchange
See web site for details

Organization: The Greensboro Review

Type: magazine
CLMP member: yes
Primary Editor/Contact Person: Jim Clark
Address: 3302 Hall for Humanities and Research University of North Carolina Greensboro
Greensboro, NC 27402-6170
Web Site Address: http://www.uncg.edu/eng/mfa/
Publishes: fiction and poetry
Editorial Focus: We want to see the best being written, regardless of theme, subject, or style.
Representative Authors: George Singleton, Thomas Lux, and Daniel Wallace
Submissions Policy: No previously published works, works accepted for publication, or dual submissions. No e-mail or fax submissions.
Simultaneous Submissions: no
Reading Period: Year-round
Reporting Time: three to four months
Author Payment: copies
Contests: The Robert Watson Literary Prizes in poery and fiction. Yearly Deadline Sept. 15h.
See web site for contest guidelines.
Founded: 1966
Non Profit: yes
Paid Staff: three
Unpaid Staff: four
Distributors: DeBoer
Wholesalers: Total Circulation Services
ISSN Number/ISBN Number: ISSN 0017-4084
Total Circulation: 800
Paid Circulation: 400
Average Print Run: 800
Subscription Rate: Individual $10/Institution $10
Single Copy Price: $5
Current Volume/Issue: Issue 81
Frequency per Year: biannual
Backfile Available: yes

Unsolicited Ms. Received: yes
% of Unsolicited Ms. Published per Year: 90%
Size: H 9" W 6"
Average Pages: 144
Ads: yes
Ad Rates: Exchange

Organization: The Groundwater Press

Type: press
CLMP member: no
Primary Editor/Contact Person: Eugene Richie
Address: P.O. Box 704
Hudson, NY 12534
Web Site Address:
http://webpage.pace.edu/erichie/groundwater
Editorial Focus: A non-profit press, we publish literature and sponsor readings and other cultural events and activities.
Representative Authors: John Ashbery, Jaime Manrique, and Thomas Weatherly
Submissions Policy: We do not accept unsolicited material, except when we have a grant for an anthology. Material is not returned without a SASE.
Simultaneous Submissions: no
Reading Period: 10/1 to 3/31
Reporting Time: one to two months
Author Payment: copies
Founded: 1984
Non Profit: yes
Paid Staff: zero
Unpaid Staff: three
Distributors: SPD
Wholesalers: All
ISSN Number/ISBN Number: none/1-877593
Number of Books Published per Year: one
Titles in Print: 25
Average Print Run: 500
Average Percentage Printed: Paperback 100%
Average Price: $12.95

Organization: The Grove Review

Type: magazine
CLMP member: yes
Primary Editor/Contact Person: Matt Barry
Address: 1631 NE Broadway, PMB #137
Portland, OR 97232
Web Site Address: www.thegrovereview.org
Publishes: fiction, poetry, and art

Editorial Focus: Dedicated to serving writers and artists by offering a first-rate venue for publishing their craft.
Representative Authors: Michael Collier, Tess Gallagher, and Ursula K. LeGuin
Submissions Policy: Submissions by regular mail only. Accepts poetry, short fiction (5,000 words or less), photography & artwork. SASE required.
Simultaneous Submissions: no
Reading Period: year-round
Reporting Time: two to four months
Author Payment: cash and copies
Contests: A prize of $1,000 and publication in TGR is given annually for an unpublished poem. Deadline is November 1.
See web site for contest guidelines
Founded: 2004
Non Profit: yes
Paid Staff: 0
Unpaid Staff: 10
Distributors: Small Changes
ISSN Number/ISBN Number: ISSN 1551-983X
Total Circulation: 1,000
Paid Circulation: 150
Average Print Run: 1,500
Subscription Rate: individual $20/institution $20
Single Copy Price: $11
Current Volume/Issue: issue three
Frequency per year: biannual
Backfile Available: yes
Unsolicited MSS Received: yes
% of Unsolicited MSS Published per Year: 5%
Format: perfect
Size: H 9" W 6"
Average Pages: 150
Ads: yes
Ad Rates: see web site for details

Organization: The Grunge Papers

Type: press
CLMP member: no
Primary Editor/Contact Person: Grant Wilkins
Address: P.O. Box 20517
390 Rideau St.
Ottawa, ON K1N 1A3
Web Site Address: http://www.grungepapers.com
Publishes: essays, fiction, poetry, and translation
Editorial Focus: Mostly interested in reissuing old Canadian Lit and classic poetry, which we print as broadsheets by letterpress on handmade paper.

Representative Authors: Archibald Lampman, Isabella Valancy Crawford, and P.B. Shelley
Submissions Policy: Probably no point in submitting anything at the moment, unless you've been dead for a long while.
Simultaneous Submissions: no
Reading Period: Year-round
Reporting Time: one to three months
Author Payment: cash and copies
Founded: 2000
Non Profit: no
Paid Staff: zero
Unpaid Staff: one
Number of Books Published per Year: three to six
Titles in Print: fifteen
Average Print Run: 50
Average Percentage Printed: Chapbook 20%, Other 80%
Average Price: $3 to $6

Organization: Guernica: A Magazine of Art and Politics

Type: online
CLMP member: no
Primary Editor/Contact Person: Elizabeth Onusko
Address: Fordham University
New York, NY 10023
Web Site Address: http://www.guernicamag.com
Publishes: essays, fiction, nonfiction, poetry, art, translation, audio, and video
Editorial Focus: We believe that it's imperative for art and politics to be addressed as what they are areas that constantly collide and intersect instead of being regarded as autonomous subjects.
Representative Authors: Eamon Grennan, Elisabeth Frost, and Julian Rios
Submissions Policy: Please check the web site for our complete submissions policy.
Simultaneous Submissions: yes
Reading Period: Year-round
Reporting Time: one to three months
Author Payment: none
Contests: Coming soon.
See web site for contest guidelines.
Founded: 2004
Non Profit: yes
Paid Staff: zero
Unpaid Staff: 15
Average Page Views per Month: 100,000
Average Unique Visitors per Month: 25,000

Frequency per Year: Monthly
Publish Print Anthology: no
Average Percentage of Pages per Category: Audio
100%
Ads: no

Organization: Gulf Coast: A Journal of Literature and Fine Arts

Type: magazine
CLMP member: yes
Primary Editor/Contact Person: Darin Ciccote,
Managing Editor
Address: Department of English
University of Houston
Houston, TX 77204-3013
Web Site Address: http://www.gulfcoastmag.org
Publishes: fiction, nonfiction, poetry, reviews, art, and
translation
Recent Awards Received: Pushcart Prize, Best
American Poetry
Representative Authors: Terrance Hayes, Anne
Carson, and Karen An-Hwei Lee
Submissions Policy: Send three to five poems, one
story, or one essay w/ cover letter and SASE. No entire
manuscripts, novellas, or electronic submissions.
Simultaneous Submissions: yes
Reading Period: 8/15 to 4/15
Reporting Time: three to six months
Author Payment: cash, copies, and subscription
Contests: See web site for contest guidelines.
Founded: 1986
Non Profit: yes
Unpaid Staff: 37-47
Distributors: Ingram, DeBoer
ISSN Number/ISBN Number: ISSN 0896-2551
Total Circulation: 2,500
Paid Circulation: 1,000
Average Print Run: 2,500
Subscription Rate: Individual $14/Institution $20
Single Copy Price: $8
Current Volume/Issue: 19/2
Frequency per Year: biannual
Backfile Available: yes
Unsolicited Ms. Received: yes
% of Unsolicited Ms. Published per Year: 60%
Format: perfect
Size: H 9" W 7"
Average Pages: 300
Ads: no
Ad Rates: n/a

Fiona McCrae
Publisher, Graywolf Press

How did you arrive at your current position?
I was working as a senior editor at Faber and Faber, Ltd., in London when, in 1991, I was asked to join the Boston office of that company. That gave me the taste for independent small-press publishing in the States. After nearly four years I made the move to Graywolf, which was a natural next step at that time. I had followed Graywolf, even in my London days, so it was a big thrill and an honor for me to become Graywolf's publisher.

What is the staff structure at your press?
We have two main publishing departments—editorial and marketing, each with a separate director who works with two or three other members of staff. In addition, there is a managing director, responsible for development and the smooth running of all operations. I am director and publisher, responsible for the overall strategic and editorial direction of the press. We use freelance help for accounting, design, and production. In addition, we have just created a new position of editor-at-large in New York City, who we're hoping will help maintain a Graywolf presence in the city. We have about three interns at any one time.

What challenges do you face as a publisher?
Perhaps a main challenge for all publishers is that we do not sell (on the whole) direct to the customer. There is a built-in disconnect between the press and its audience. We don't know who has bought our books, and customers themselves do not always pay attention to who has published the book they are reading. However, the internet is a wonderful way to bridge this gap, and we are continually looking at creative new ways to connect with our readers. We recently created a MySpace page, and had an online launch for Percival Everett's new novel, *The Water Cure*. The internet is an incredible boon for smaller publishers.

Do you have any cover letter advice?
The most common failing we notice in the cover letters we receive is the authors' tendency to over-describe their work. Of course, we understand the impulse, but brevity really is best, because we will read the work itself. Our advice to them is to be concise, clear, and relevant. Tell us the genre of your book and a little about the work itself—resist the temptation to summarize the plot at great length. Demonstrate familiarity with the press to whom you're submitting, and have a good idea about where your book would fit in their list. Absolutely include a list of previous publications—but, again, a couple of lines giving us a general idea of the sorts of places in which you've published are quite good enough.

What do you look for in a submission?
We watch for writing that pushes established literary boundaries in some way, whether it pushes on the side of contemporary experimentation or highly traditional formalism. We also watch for writing that combines the two. We look for work that elicits a strong reaction from the reader—we aren't so interested in taking on work that is solid but not singular. We tend to value strong prose writing that features well-drawn characters with rich interior lives over stories that bank on a convoluted plot. We appreciate texts that engage on some level with the outside world, texts that visit contemporary issues, rather than insular domestic novels.

Rolph Bythe, marketing director; Fiona McCrae, publisher; and Katie Dublinski editorial director, standing by manuscripts submitted for Graywolf's nonfiction prize

How are submissions processed at your press?
Most of the work we publish comes from returning authors, contest winners, and solicited submissions. After those commitments are made, very few slots remain for other material. Additionally, we have ongoing relationships with several literary agents and agencies, whose judgment we respect and whose suggestions we consider pretty seriously. For a prose author, having an agent does make a difference in how the manuscript is considered. Therefore, for a prose author to get published out of the slush pile is really a remarkable occurrence. For poetry it's different, since very few poets have agents at all, and so in that case the top level of consideration goes to poets recommended to us by our current authors, and also to poets whose work we've been seeing in good journals and so on. However, all that said, it really is about the quality of your work. Everything that comes in gets read—if the work is good, someone will see that.

Do you have a favorite unsolicited submission discovery or anecdote?
One day, a few years ago, I passed Jeffrey Shotts, our senior editor, a copy of *Ploughshares*, with a poem by Nick Flynn circled. I had noticed it and thought perhaps we should follow up. Coincidentally, that very day Nick sent us his poems, and we subsequently published that manuscript, *Some Ether*, to great success.

What advice do you have for first-time submitters?
Do your homework. Particularly for independent presses like ourselves, it's a fact of life that we have to make strict decisions about what sorts of books we're going to publish. For example, someone might send us a manuscript written by the next John Grisham, and we're just not going to publish it because we just don't publish those sorts of books. At that point it's not really about the quality of your work anymore; it's a question of fit. The good part is that this is very easy work for an author to do, and it makes an enormous difference. Our other piece of advice is just to try publishing small pieces in magazines before you send out the whole book. This is particularly true for poets and short-story writers. Nonfiction writers can investigate our nonfiction prize by visiting our website, www.graywolfpress.org. All that said, remember not to lose hope. We're watching for you. We want you to write great work and we want to publish it. Where would Graywolf be without creative writers?

What are your long-term plans for your press?
Our strength has two main sources: our ability to find great new work, and our ability to then market it. So, I am always looking for ways to strengthen Graywolf in these two areas. We have recently raised $1,000,000, to enable us to offer authors higher advances at the acquisition stage, and to have more resources for promotion once the book is published. I think this will have a tremendous impact on Graywolf's future. We will continue to build on our strengths: publishing great poetry, literary fiction, and essays; seeking out important international authors; offering contemporary literature that shapes and engages with the new world. We have had inspirational models in presses like New Directions and Farrar, Straus and Giroux. The question now becomes, how do you take that example and transpose it into the 21st century? What will that look like?

What's your evaluation of the current literary landscape?
There are always obstacles to great writing reaching great readers, and yet it is happening all the time. The larger houses have their share of significant writers, but across the world, I see a real energy emerging from the dynamic independent houses and magazines. I'm excited to see Canongate's success in the UK, for example, and what Dave Eggers has created with his publishing activities here in the States is very encouraging for us all. The world is always changing, so we need contemporary authors to map the new terrain for us.

Organization: Gulf Stream

Type: magazine
CLMP member: yes
Primary Editor/Contact Person: Denise Sebesta Lanier
Address: English Dept, FIU
Biscayne Bay Campus, 3000 NE 151st St.
North Miami, FL 33181
Web Site Address: http://www.gulfstreamlitmag.com
Publishes: essays, fiction, nonfiction, and poetry
Editorial Focus: Gulf Stream seeks writing that is intelligent, distinct, and establishes a strong bond with the reader.
Representative Authors: Dennis Lehane, David Kirby, and Richard Blanco
Submissions Policy: We accept prose (5,000 words max) and up to 5 poems. Electronic submissions (only) through FormSite via our website.
Simultaneous Submissions: yes
Reading Period: 9/1 to 3/31
Reporting Time: two to three months
Author Payment: copies and subscription
Contests: See web site for contest guidelines.
Founded: 1989
Non Profit: yes
Paid Staff: two
Unpaid Staff: six
Total Circulation: 1,000
Paid Circulation: 550
Average Print Run: 1,000
Subscription Rate: Individual $15/Institution $15
Single Copy Price: $8
Current Volume/Issue: 28/28
Frequency per Year: biannual
Backfile Available: yes
Unsolicited Ms. Received: yes
% of Unsolicited Ms. Published per Year: 50%
Format: perfect
Size: H 8 1/2" W 5 1/2"
Average Pages: 120
Ads: yes
Ad Rates: $400 for full page

Organization: Haight Ashbury Literary Journal

Type: magazine
CLMP member: yes
Primary Editor/Contact Person: Alice E. Rogoff
Address: 558 Joost Ave.
San Francisco, CA 94127
Web Site Address: http://www.haightashbury.org/poetry.html
Publishes: fiction and poetry
Editorial Focus: Personal and social, urban and nature, diverse cultures, leans towards realism, national but encourages local writers
Representative Authors: Clara Hsu, Al Young, and A.D. Winans
Submissions Policy: Send six poems or less, per issue, (every six months) with SASE, prefer poems under two pages. Use only one or two stories.
Simultaneous Submissions: yes
Reading Period: Year-round
Reporting Time: four to six months
Author Payment: copies
Contests: None currently
Founded: 1980
Non Profit: yes
Paid Staff: zero
Unpaid Staff: four
Distributors: Readmore, Yankee Book Peddler
ISSN Number/ISBN Number: ISBN 0-926664-0402
Total Circulation: 2,000
Paid Circulation: 200
Subscription Rate: Individual $8, 16, 40/Institution $0--prison
Single Copy Price: $3
Current Volume/Issue: 25/1
Frequency per Year: biannual
Backfile Available: yes
Unsolicited Ms. Received: yes
% of Unsolicited Ms. Published per Year: 10%
Format: tabloid
Size: H 8.5" W 11"
Average Pages: 16
Ads: yes
Ad Rates: 30, 50, 75

Organization: Hamilton Stone Editions

Type: press
CLMP member: no
Primary Editor/Contact Person: Meredith Sue Willis
Address: PO Box 43
Maplewood, NJ 07040
Web Site Address: www.hamiltonstone.org
Publishes: essays, fiction, nonfiction, and poetry
Editorial Focus: literary
Representative Authors: Edith Konecky, Halvard

Johnson, and Lynda Schor
Submissions Policy: no unsolicited submissions
Simultaneous Submissions: no
Reading Period: year-round
Reporting Time: 3 to 12 months
Author Payment: copies
Founded: 1998
Non Profit: yes
Paid Staff: zero
Unpaid Staff: eight
Wholesalers: Ingram, Baker and Taylor, etc.
Number of Books Published per year: two to three
Titles in Print: 12
Average Print Run: 500
Average Percentage Printed: paperback 100%
Average Price: $14.95

Organization: Hamilton Stone Review

Type: online
CLMP member: no
Primary Editor/Contact Person: Halvard Johnson
Address: PO Box 43
Maplewood, NJ 07040
Publishes: essays, fiction, nonfiction, and poetry
Editorial Focus: literary
Representative Authors: Sheila E. Murphy, Jan
Clausen, and Richard Kostelanetz.
Submissions Policy: by email only. Poetry to Halvard
Johnson at halvard@earthlink.net and prose to Lynda
Schor at lynda.schor@gmail.com
Simultaneous Submissions: yes
Reading Period: year-round
Reporting Time: two to six months
Author Payment: none
Founded: 2003
Non Profit: yes
Paid Staff: zero
Unpaid Staff: eight
Average Page Views per Month: 1,600
Average Unique Visitors per Month: 500
Frequency per year: triquarterly
Publish Print Anthology: no
Average Percentage of Pages per Category: fiction
45%, poetry 50%, essays 5%
Ads: no

Organization: Hanging Loose

Type: magazine
CLMP member: yes

Primary Editor/Contact Person: Robert Hershon
Address: 231 Wyckoff St.
Brooklyn, NY 11217
Web Site Address:
http://www.hangingloosepress.com
Publishes: fiction and poetry
Editorial Focus: Lively, humorous and non-academic
poetry. We occasionally publish fiction, rarely nonfic-
tion, but there are exceptions.
Recent Awards Received: NY State Council on the Arts
Representative Authors: Sherman Alexie, Ha Jin, and
Hettie Jones
Submissions Policy: As a rule, send up to six poems
or one story at a time. Enclose an SASE. We also have
a section of work by high school writers
Simultaneous Submissions: no
Reading Period: Year-round
Reporting Time: one to five months
Author Payment: cash and copies
Contests: no
Founded: 1966
Non Profit: yes
Distributors: SPD, Ingram, DeBoer
Wholesalers: 0
ISSN Number/ISBN Number: ISSN 0440-2316
Total Circulation: 1.750
Paid Circulation: 1,000
Average Print Run: 2,000
Subscription Rate: Individual $22/Institution $27
Single Copy Price: $9
Current Volume/Issue: Issue 87
Frequency per Year: biannual
Backfile Available: yes
Unsolicited Ms. Received: yes
Format: perfect
Size: H 8.5" W 7"
Average Pages: 120
Ads: no

Organization: Hanging Loose Press

Type: press
CLMP member: yes
Primary Editor/Contact Person: Robert Hershon
Address: 231 Wyckoff St.
Brooklyn, NY 11217
Website Address: hangingloosepress.com
Publishes: fiction and poetry
Editorial Focus: Our emphasis is on the fresh,ener-
getic work of new and neglected writers.
Recent Awards Received: Paterson Poetry Prize,

Theodore Roethke Memorial Prize, PSA Norma Farber First Book Prize
Representative Authors: Sherman Alexie, Joan Larkin, and Keith Taylor
Submissions Policy: Book manuscripts are by invitation only because of our very small staff. Try the magazine first.
Simultaneous Submissions: no
Reading Period: year-round
Reporting Time: 1 to 4 months
Author Payment: royalties and copies
Contests: none
Founded: 1966
Non Profit: yes
Paid Staff: 2
Unpaid Staff: 3
Distributors: Small Press Distribution
Wholesalers: Baker & Taylor, Partners West, Brodart, Blackwell,
ISSN Number/ISBN Number: 978-1-931236
Number of Books Published per Year: 6-9
Titles in Print: 150
Average Print Run: 2,000
Average Percentage Printed: Hardcover 20%, Paperback 80%
Average Price: $25H, 15P

Organization: Harbour Publishing
Type: press
CLMP member: no
Primary Editor/Contact Person: Alicia Miller
Address: P.O. Box 219
4437 Rondeview Road
Madeira Park, BC V0N 2H0
Web Site Address:
http://www.harbourpublishing.com
Publishes: fiction, nonfiction, and poetry
Editorial Focus: Nonfiction, fiction and children's books with a focus on the Pacific Northwest and Pacific Northwest authors.
Representative Authors: Al Purdy, Stephen Hume, and Edith Iglauer
Submissions Policy: Accept unsolicited ms with SASE.
Simultaneous Submissions: yes
Reading Period: Year-round
Reporting Time: three to six months
Author Payment: royalties and copies
Founded: 1974
Non Profit: no

Paid Staff: 10
Unpaid Staff: zero
Distributors: Canada: Harbour Publishing. USA: GACPC.
ISSN Number/ISBN Number: ISBN 1-55017-, 0-920080
Number of Books Published per Year: 24
Titles in Print: 400
Average Percentage Printed: Hardcover 50%, Paperback 50%

Organization: Harpur Palate
Type: magazine
CLMP member: yes
Primary Editor/Contact Person: Kathryn Henion
Address: Dept. of English, Binghamton University
P.O. Box 6000
Binghamton, NY 13902-6000
Web Site Address:
http://harpurpalate.binghamton.edu
Editorial Focus: We have no restrictions on subject matter or form. We are mainly interested in the highest-quality writing.
Representative Authors: Lee K. Abbott, Sascha Feinstein, and Stephen Corey
Submissions Policy: fiction and creative non-fiction: 250-8,000 words; no more than one submission per author. Poetry: 3-5 poems; no more than 10 pages per author.
Simultaneous Submissions: yes
Reading Period: Year-round
Reporting Time: four to eight months
Author Payment: copies
Contests: John Gardner Memorial Prize for Fiction, $500 prize; Milton Kessler Memorial Prize for Poetry, $500 prize
See Web Site for Contest Guidelines.
Founded: 2000
Non Profit: yes
Paid Staff: zero
Unpaid Staff: 30
Distributors: Ingrams
ISSN Number/ISBN Number: ISSN 0-9749107-2-4
Total Circulation: 750
Paid Circulation: 100
Average Print Run: 1,000
Subscription Rate: Individual $16/Institution $20
Single Copy Price: $10
Current Volume/Issue: 7/1
Frequency per Year: biannual

Backfile Available: yes
Unsolicited Ms. Received: yes
% of Unsolicited Ms. Published per Year: 70%
Format: perfect
Size: H 8.5" W 6"
Average Pages: 180
Ads: yes
Ad Rates: See web site for details.

Organization: Harvard Review

Type: magazine
CLMP member: yes
Primary Editor/Contact Person: Christina Thompson, Editor
Address: Lamont Library
Harvard University
Cambridge, MA 02138
Web Site Address: http://hcl.harvard.edu/harvardreview
Publishes: essays, fiction, poetry, reviews, art, and translation
Recent Awards Received: Best American Short Stories, 2005, 2003; Best American Essays, 2004, 2003; Best American Poetry, 2006, 2002.
Simultaneous Submissions: yes
Reading Period: Year-round
Reporting Time: four to six months
Author Payment: none
Founded: 1992
Non Profit: yes
Paid Staff: two
Unpaid Staff: two
Distributors: Ingram, Ubiquity, Source Interlink
Total Circulation: 2,500
Paid Circulation: 500
Average Print Run: 2,500
Subscription Rate: Individual $16/Institution $24
Single Copy Price: $10
Current Volume/Issue: Issue 32
Frequency per Year: biannual
Backfile Available: yes
Unsolicited Ms. Received: yes
Format: perfect
Size: H 9" W 6"
Average Pages: 240
Ads: yes
Ad Rates: $500 full-page, $350 half page; see website for details

Organization: Hawai'i Pacific Review

Type: magazine
CLMP member: no
Primary Editor/Contact Person: Ms. Patrice Wilson
Address: 1060 Bishop St., LB 402
Honolulu, HI 96813
Web Site Address: http://www.hpu.edu
Publishes: essays, fiction, and poetry
Editorial Focus: Open theme, open form, would like more experimental work
Representative Authors: Wendell Mayo, Bob Hicok, and Wendy Bishop
Submissions Policy: Sept 1-Dec 31, five poems or 5,000 words, one submission per issue, no previously published work.
Simultaneous Submissions: yes
Reading Period: 9/1 to 12/31
Reporting Time: 12 to 15 weeks
Author Payment: copies
Contests: none
Founded: 1987
Non Profit: yes
Paid Staff: one
Unpaid Staff: tem
Distributors: Booklines Hawai'i
ISSN Number/ISBN Number: 1047-4331/0-9703239-3-X
Total Circulation: 500
Paid Circulation: 25
Average Print Run: 500
Subscription Rate: Individual $8.95/Institution $10
Single Copy Price: $5
Current Volume/Issue: 17/1
Frequency per Year: annual
Backfile Available: yes
Unsolicited Ms. Received: yes
% of Unsolicited Ms. Published per Year: 18%
Format: perfect
Size: H 9" W 6"
Average Pages: 100
Ads: yes
Ad Rates: Exchange

Organization: Hayden's Ferry Review

Type: magazine
CLMP member: yes
Primary Editor/Contact Person: Beth Staples
Address: Piper Center for Creative Writing
Box 875002, Arizona State University
Tempe, AZ 85287-5002

Web Site Address: http://www.asu.edu/piper/publications/haydensferryreview/
Publishes: essays, fiction, nonfiction, poetry, art, and translation
Editorial Focus: We publish the best quality poetry, creative nonfiction, fiction, and translations by emerging and established writers.
Representative Authors: David St. John, C.D. Wright, and Ron Carlson
Submissions Policy: Submit poetry and prose separately. Include SASE for response. Please, no email submissions.
Simultaneous Submissions: yes
Reading Period: Year-round
Reporting Time: four to five months
Author Payment: cash, copies and subscription
Founded: 1986
Non Profit: yes
Paid Staff: six
Unpaid Staff: 20
Distributors: Ingram
ISSN Number/ISBN Number: ISSN 0887-5170
Total Circulation: 1,200
Paid Circulation: 400
Average Print Run: 1,300
Subscription Rate: Individual $14/Institution $14
Single Copy Price: $6
Current Volume/Issue: 38
Frequency per Year: biannual
Backfile Available: yes
Unsolicited Ms. Received: yes
% of Unsolicited Ms. Published per Year: 80%
Format: perfect
Size: H 6 3/4" W 10"
Average Pages: 162
Ads: yes

Organization: HazMat Review

Type: magazine
CLMP member: no
Primary Editor/Contact Person: Norm Davis
Address: P.O. Box 30507
Rochester, NY 14603-0507
Web Site Address: http://www.hazmatlitreview.org
Publishes: essays, fiction, nonfiction, poetry, reviews, art, and translation
Editorial Focus: Social consciousness, women's consciousness a high priority, anti-imperialist, political writing welcome.
Representative Authors: Lyn Lifshin, Marc Olmsted, and Koon Woon
Submissions Policy: No prose over 2,500 words. Send three poems plus SASE. Incarcerated writers need not send SASE. No Hallmark verse.
Simultaneous Submissions: yes
Reading Period: Year-round
Reporting Time: one to three months
Author Payment: copies
Founded: 1996
Non Profit: yes
Paid Staff: zero
Unpaid Staff: 12
Distributors: Writers & Books, Rochester, New York
ISSN Number/ISBN Number: ISSN 1521-7639
Total Circulation: 150
Paid Circulation: 50
Subscription Rate: Individual $18/Institution $18
Single Copy Price: $12
Current Volume/Issue: 7/1
Frequency per Year: biannual
Backfile Available: yes
Unsolicited Ms. Received: yes
% of Unsolicited Ms. Published per Year: 15%
Format: perfect
Size: H 8 1/2" W 5 1/2"
Average Pages: 110
Ads: no

Organization: Heartlands

Type: magazine
CLMP member: no
Primary Editor/Contact Person: Larry Smith
Address: One University Road
Huron, OH 44839
Web Site Address: http://www.theheartlandstoday.net/
Publishes: essays, fiction, nonfiction, poetry, reviews, and art
Editorial Focus: Midwest themes for each issue, please inquire
Representative Authors: Stephen Ostrander, Gary Snyder, and Larry Smith
Simultaneous Submissions: yes
Reading Period: 1/1 to 6/6
Reporting Time: one to two months
Author Payment: cash and copies
Founded: 1990
Non Profit: yes
Paid Staff: one
Unpaid Staff: seven

Distributors: Bottom Dog Press, SPD
ISSN Number/ISBN Number: ISSN 01066-6176
Total Circulation: 600
Paid Circulation: 150
Average Print Run: 600
Subscription Rate: Individual $7.50/Institution $7.50
Single Copy Price: $7.50
Current Volume/Issue: Issue one
Frequency per Year: biannual
Backfile Available: no
Unsolicited Ms. Received: yes
% of Unsolicited Ms. Published per Year: 75%
Format: perfect
Size: H 11" W 8.5"
Average Pages: 90
Ads: yes
Ad Rates: apply
See web site for details.

Organization: Heat Press

Type: press
CLMP member: yes
Primary Editor/Contact Person: Christopher Natale Peditto
Address: P.O. Box 26218
Los Angeles, CA 90026
Publishes: poetry
Editorial Focus: Poets close to the Beat Generation in their coming of age and oral sensibilities. Jazz and poetry.
Representative Authors: Eric Priestley, Charles Bivins, and Elliott Levin
Submissions Policy: No unsolicited manuscripts
Simultaneous Submissions: no
Reading Period: Year-round
Reporting Time: one to three months
Author Payment: royalties
Founded: 1993
Non Profit: no
Paid Staff: zero
Unpaid Staff: three
Distributors: SPD
ISSN Number/ISBN Number: ISSN 1-884773
Number of Books Published per Year: one
Titles in Print: four
Average Print Run: 1,500
Average Percentage Printed: Paperback 100%
Average Price: $9.95

Organization: Heaven Bone Magazine

Type: magazine
CLMP member: no
Primary Editor/Contact Person: Steve Hirsch
Address: P.O. Box 486
Chester, NY 10918
Publishes: essays, fiction, nonfiction, poetry, reviews, art, and translation
Editorial Focus: Poetry, Fiction, Essays, Reviews and artwork with an emphasis on the experimental, surreal, "post-Beat" and Buddhist/Hindu.
Representative Authors: Anne Waldman, Stephen-Paul Martin, and Diane DiPrima
Submissions Policy: 10 Pages poetry max.; 7,500 words fiction max. Always include SASE. Simultaneous submissions OK if notified. Read a sample issue!!!
Simultaneous Submissions: yes
Reading Period: Year-round
Reporting Time: 3 months
Author Payment: copies
Contests: Bi-Annual Chapbook Contest welcomes manuscripts from all over the world. Watch Poets & Writers for announcements and deadlines.
Founded: 1986
Non Profit: yes
Paid Staff: zero
Unpaid Staff: six
Distributors: SPD; Amazon.com
ISSN Number/ISBN Number: ISSN 1042-5381
Total Circulation: 2,500
Paid Circulation: 160
Average Print Run: 2,500
Subscription Rate: Individual $10/Institution $10
Single Copy Price: $10
Current Volume/Issue: Issue 13
Frequency per Year: annual
Backfile Available: yes
Unsolicited Ms. Received: yes
% of Unsolicited Ms. Published per Year: 3%
Format: perfect
Size: H 11" W 8.5"
Average Pages: 128
Ads: yes
Ad Rates: Query by e-mail for current rates

Organization: The Heaven Bone Press

Type: press
CLMP member: no
Primary Editor/Contact Person: Steve Hirsch
Address: P.O. Box 486

Chester, NY 10918
Publishes: essays, fiction, nonfiction, poetry, reviews, art, and translation
Editorial Focus: Poetry and fiction with an emphasis on the surreal, experimental, "post-Beat" and Buddhist/Hindu. Chapbooks mostly.
Representative Authors: Anne Waldman, Stephen-Paul Martin, and Diane DiPrima
Submissions Policy: Query first with sample. Simultaneous submissions OK if notified. See a sample of our magazine, Heaven Bone.
Simultaneous Submissions: yes
Reading Period: Year-round
Reporting Time: 3 months
Author Payment: copies
Contests: Bi-Annual Chapbook contest awards cash prize $500. Query for guidelines or watch Poets & Writers for announcement of deadline
Founded: 1986
Non Profit: no
Paid Staff: zero
Unpaid Staff: six
Distributors: SPD; Amazon.com
Number of Books Published per Year: one
Titles in Print: 16
Average Percentage Printed: Paperback 20%, Chapbook 80%

Organization: Helen Marx Books
Type: press
CLMP member: yes
Primary Editor/Contact Person: Helen Marx or Heather Bartlett
Address: 23 E. 69th St., #BF
New York, NY 10021
Web Site Address: http://www.turtlepoint.com/
Publishes: fiction, nonfiction, and poetry
Editorial Focus: Forgotten literary fiction, contemporary fiction, biography
Recent Awards Received: Franco-American Foundation Translation Award (2006)
Representative Authors: Jaques de Lacretelle and Brian O'Doherty
Simultaneous Submission: yes
Reading Period: Year-round
Reporting Time: one to two months
Author Payment: royalties
Founded: 1997
Non Profit: no
Paid Staff: 1

Unpaid Staff: 0
Distributors: Consortium
Number of Books Published per Year: 2
Titles in Print: 20
Average Print Run: 3,500
Average Percentage Printed: Hardcover 50%, Paperback 50%
Average Price: $16.00

Organization: Helicon Nine Editions
Type: press
CLMP member: no
Primary Editor/Contact Person: Gloria Vando Hickok
Address: P.O. Box 22412
Kansas City, MO 64113
Web Site Address: http://www.heliconnine.com
Publishes: essays, fiction, and poetry
Representative Authors: Sheila Kohler and Philip Miller
Submissions Policy: We are not accepting unsolicited manuscripts at this time.
Simultaneous Submissions: no
Reading Period: Year-round
Reporting Time: 6 to 10 months
Author Payment: royalties and copies
Founded: 1977
Non Profit: yes
Paid Staff: one
Unpaid Staff: two
Distributors: Baker & Taylor, Brodart, Barnes & Noble
ISSN Number/ISBN Number: ISBN 1-884235-
Number of Books Published per Year: two to three
Titles in Print: 46
Average Percentage Printed: Paperback 100%

Organization: Heliotrope, a Journal of Poetry
Type: magazine
CLMP member: yes
Primary Editor/Contact Person: Susan Sindall, the Editors
Address: P.O. Box 456
Shady, NY 12409
Web Site Address: http://www.heliopoems.com
Publishes: poetry
Editorial Focus: High quality work by a broad range of poets. We encourage older women.
Representative Authors: Cortney Davis, David Dodd Lee, and Jean Monahan

Submissions Policy: Three to five pages, single-spaced, with author's name and address on each page. SASE required.
Simultaneous Submissions: yes
Reading Period: Year-round
Reporting Time: 8 months
Author Payment: copies
Founded: 2000
Non Profit: yes
Paid Staff: zero
Unpaid Staff: three
ISSN Number/ISBN Number: ISSN 1533-0052
Total Circulation: 250
Paid Circulation: 75
Subscription Rate: Individual $22/Institution $ 22
Single Copy Price: $8
Current Volume/Issue: Issue #4
Frequency per Year: annual
Backfile Available: no
Unsolicited Ms. Received: yes
% of Unsolicited Ms. Published per Year: 5%
Format: perfect
Average Pages: 75

Organization: High Desert Journal

Type: magazine
CLMP member: yes
Primary Editor/Contact Person: Elizabeth Quinn
Address: 2630 NE Daggett Lane
Bend, OR 97701
Web Site Address: http://www.highdesertjournal.com
Publishes: essays, fiction, nonfiction, poetry, and art
Editorial Focus: An ecology of story, memory and imaganiation from the high deserts of OR, WA, CA, ID, NV, UT, MT.
Representative Authors: David James Duncan, Robert Wrigley, and Kim Barnes
Submissions Policy: Accept fiction, non-fiction, poetry, essays, short plays, creative journalism. See web site for more details.
Simultaneous Submissions: yes
Reading Period: year-round
Reporting Time: one to four months
Author Payment: none
Contests: Call for Obsidian Prize will begin in August '06. Awarded July of '07.
See web site for contest guidelines
Founded: 2004
Non Profit: yes
Paid Staff: one

Unpaid Staff: zero
ISSN Number/ISBN Number: ISSN 1555-7251
Total Circulation: 3,000
Paid Circulation: 300
Average Print Run: 4,000
Subscription Rate: individual $14/institution $14
Single Copy Price: $10
Current Volume/Issue: issue three
Frequency per year: biannual
Backfile Available: yes
Unsolicited MSS Received: yes
% of Unsolicited MSS Published per year: 60%
Format: stapled
Size: H 12" W 9"
Average Pages: 48
Ads: yes
Ad Rates: see web site for details

Organization: Hobart

Type: magazine
CLMP member: yes
Address: 394 Waymarket
Ann Arbor, MI 48103
Web Site Address: http://www.hobartpulp.com
Publishes: essays and fiction
Reading Period: Year-round
Reporting Time: one to two months
Author Payment: none
Founded: 2001
Non Profit: yes
Backfile Available: yes

Organization: Hobblebush Books

Type: press
CLMP member: yes
Primary Editor/Contact Person: Sidney Hall Jr.
Address: 17A Old Milford Road
Brookline, NH 03033
Website: http://www.hobblebush.com
Publishes: nonfiction and poetry
Editorial Focus: Poetry and other literary, humor, regional
Recent Awards Received: PMA Benjamin Franklin Award for humor book
Representative Authors: Cora Schwartz, Lawrence Millman, and Rick Davis
Submission Policy: Please query publisher; no unsolicited mss
Simultaneous Submissions: yes

Reading Period: year-round
Reporting Time: one to two months
Author Payment: royalities and copies
Founded: 1993
Non Profit: no
Paid Staff: 3
Unpaid Staff: 1
Wholesalers: Baker & Taylor
ISSN Number/ISBN Number: ISBN 09760896
Number of Books Pulished per Year: 4
Titles in Print: 20
Average Print Run: 1,000
Average Percentage Printed: Hardcover 50%,
Paperback 50%
Average Price: $18

Organization: The Hollins Critic

Type: magazine
CLMP member: yes
Primary Editor/Contact Person: Amanda Cockrell
Address: P.O. Box 9538
Hollins University
Roanoke, VA 24020
Web Site Address:
http://www.hollins.edu/grad/eng_writing/critic/critic.htm
Publishes: essays, poetry, and reviews
Editorial Focus: Essays on the work of contemporary poets, fiction writers and dramatists; poetry; brief book reviews
Representative Authors: George Garrett, Kelly Cherry, and Henry Taylor
Submissions Policy: Submit up to five poems with SASE. No e-mail submissions. Unsolicited essays not accepted. Unsolicited reviews rarely accepted.
Simultaneous Submissions: yes
Reading Period: 9/1 to 12/15
Reporting Time: one to two months
Author Payment: cash and copies
Founded: 1964
Non Profit: yes
Paid Staff: three
Unpaid Staff: two
ISSN Number/ISBN Number: ISSN 0018-3644
Total Circulation: 500
Paid Circulation: 350
Average Print Run: 500
Subscription Rate: Individual $8/Institution $8
Single Copy Price: $2
Current Volume/Issue: XLIV/1

Frequency per Year: five
Backfile Available: yes
Unsolicited Ms. Received: yes
% of Unsolicited Ms. Published per Year: 5%
Format: stapled
Size: H 10" W 7"
Average Pages: 24
Ads: no

Organization: Home Planet News

Type: magazine
CLMP member: yes
Primary Editor/Contact Person: Donald Lev
Address: Home Planet Publications
P.O. Box 455
High Falls, NY 12440
Web Site Address: http://www.homeplanetnews.org
Publishes: essays, fiction, poetry, and reviews
Editorial Focus: Poetry
Representative Authors: Enid Dame, Andrew Glaze, and Hal Sirowitz
Submissions Policy: Three to five poems w/SASE-fiction up to 3,000 words. Reviews and articles, please query.
Simultaneous Submissions: no
Reading Period: Year-round
Reporting Time: one to three months
Author Payment: copies and subscription
Founded: 1979
Non Profit: yes
Paid Staff: zero
Unpaid Staff: 18
Distributors: Sunspot Distribution, Marina Penzner
ISSN Number/ISBN Number: ISSN 023-303x
Total Circulation: 1,000
Paid Circulation: 287
Average Print Run: 1,000
Subscription Rate: Individual $10/Institution $10
Single Copy Price: $4
Current Volume/Issue: 15/57
Frequency per Year: three
Backfile Available: yes
Unsolicited Ms. Received: yes
% of Unsolicited Ms. Published per Year: 2%
Format: tabloid
Size: H 14.5" W 10"
Average Pages: 24
Ads: yes
Ad Rates: $1 per square inch

Organization: Horse & Buggy Press

Type: press
CLMP member: no
Primary Editor/Contact Person: Dave Wofford
Address: 2016 Englewood Ave.
Durham, NC 27705
Web Site Address:
http://www.antfarmstudios.org/dwofford/
Publishes: essays, fiction, nonfiction, and poetry
Editorial Focus: Short-length books (36-64) pages.
Two editions are published, a trade edition, and a
hand-printed letterpress edition.
Representative Authors: Allan Gurganus, Stephen
Gibson, and John Lane
Submissions Policy: Manuscript accepted at all
times but are not returned.
Simultaneous Submissions: yes
Reading Period: Year-round
Reporting Time: one to two months
Author Payment: copies
Contests: Annual poetry chapbook contest. 36-page
book, printed letterpress and hand-bound. Winner
receives 50 of 200 books
Founded: 1996
Non Profit: no
Paid Staff: one
Unpaid Staff: one
Distributors: SPD
Number of Books Published per Year: two
Titles in Print: nine
Average Percentage Printed: Hardcover 10%,
Paperback 40%, Other 50%

Organization: Host Publications, Inc.

Type: press
CLMP member: yes
Primary Editor/Contact Person: Susan Lesak
Address: 100 E. 7th St.
Ste. 201
Austin, TX 78702
Web Site Address: http://www.hostpublications.com
Publishes: fiction, poetry, and translation
Editorial Focus: International in scope, Host
Publications brings literature from around the world to
US readers.
Representative Authors: Pablo Neruda, Dave
Oliphant, and Alfred Leslie
Submissions Policy: Send abstract of work with
author CV. We will respond as quickly as possible.
Simultaneous Submissions: yes

Reading Period: Year-round
Reporting Time: 6 months
Author Payment: cash and copies
Founded: 1988
Non Profit: no
Paid Staff: three
Unpaid Staff: zero
Distributors: Ingram Distribution, Baker & Taylor
ISSN Number/ISBN Number: ISBN 0-924047
Number of Books Published per Year: two
Titles in Print: 16
Average Print Run: 1,500
Average Percentage Printed: Hardcover 10%,
Paperback 90%
Average Price: $15

Organization: Hot Metal Bridge

Type: online
CLMP member: yes
Primary Editor/Contact Person: Carolyn Kellogg
Address: English Dept, 526 Cathedral of Learning
4200 Fifth Ave, University of Pittsburgh
Pittsburgh, PA 15260
Website Address; www.hotmetalbridge.org
Publishes: essays, fiction, nonfiction, poetry, and
reviews
Editorial Focus: The most fun you can have by your-
self is reading. HMB is dedicated to writing that
makes you go yowsa! or eek! or oof!
Representative Authors: Michael Martone, Alan
DeNiro, and Simone Poirer-Bures
Submission Policy: Submissions are reviewed twice
annually, for fall and spring publication. See our web-
site for our Calls for Entries.
Simultaneous Submissions: Yes
Reading Period: Year-Round
Reporting Time: 1 to 3 months
Author Payment:none
Contests: Contests are on the way; see website for
details
Founded: 2007
Non Profit: yes
Paid Staff: 0
Unpaid Staff: 8
Average Page Views per Month: 3,000
Average Unique Visitors per Month: 1,400
Frequency: 2
Publish Print Annthology: No
Average Percentage of Pages per Category: Fiction
25%, Nonfiction 25%, Poetry 25%, Reviews 15%,

Essays 10%
Ads: no

Organization: Hourglass Books

Type: press
CLMP member: yes
Primary Editor/Contact Person: W.C. Scheurer
Address: P.O. Box 132
Antioch, IL 60002-0132
Web Site Address: http://www.hourglassbooks.com
Publishes: fiction
Editorial Focus: Hourglass Books publishes themed anthologies of literary short stories for the general reading public.
Representative Authors: Pam Houston, Peter Ho Davies, and Aimee Bender
Submissions Policy: See http://www.hourglass-books.com for current theme. We accept previously published stories from literary magazines and collections.
Simultaneous Submissions: yes
Reading Period: Year-round
Reporting Time: two to six months
Author Payment: royalties
Founded: 2003
Non Profit: yes
Paid Staff: three
Unpaid Staff: thirteen
Wholesalers: Ingram; Baker & Taylor
ISSN Number/ISBN Number: ISBN 0972525424
Number of Books Published per Year: two
Titles in Print: two
Average Percentage Printed: Paperback 100%
Backfile Available: yes

Organization: HOW2 Magazine

Type: online
CLMP member: no
Primary Editor/Contact Person: Kate Fagan
Address: 26 Iredale St.
Newtown, Sydney, AUS, 2042
Web Site Address: http://how2journal.com
Publishes: essays, poetry, reviews, art, translation, audio, and video
Editorial Focus: Contemporary innovative and modernist writing by women; non-traditional directions in scholarship.
Representative Authors: Redell Olsen, Leslie Scalapino, and Lola Ridge

Submissions Policy: Submissions must be by or about women innovators, with an emphasis on poetry. International focus.
Simultaneous Submissions: yes
Reading Period: Year-round
Reporting Time: one to two months
Author Payment: none
Contests: none
Founded: 1999
Non Profit: yes
Paid Staff: zero
Unpaid Staff: three to nine
Distributors: Archives hosted by Arizona State University
Average Page Views per Month: 600
Average Unique Visitors per Month: 300
Frequency per Year: two
Publish Print Anthology: no
Average Percentage of Pages per Category: Fiction 15%, Nonfiction 15%, Poetry 25%, Reviews 10%, Essays 25%, Art 10%, Translation 10%, Audio 5%
Ads: no

Organization: Howling Dog Press

Type: press
CLMP member: yes
Primary Editor/Contact Person: Michael Annis, senior editor
Address: P.O. Box 853
Berthoud, CO 80513-0853
Website Address:
www.howlingdogpress.com/OMEGA
Publishes: essays, fiction, nonfiction, poetry, reviews, art, translation, and audio
Editorial Focus: Progressive political, peace, anti-war activism, visionary poetics, on-the-edge, surreal; NO academic back-patting, NO tepid.
Recent Awards Received: Kansas Arts Comission, Colorado Council on the Arts,
Representative Authors: William Burroughs, David Ray, and Oswald Le Winter
Submissions Policy: Read OMEGA (online) before submitting. Do not send more than 30 pages, either by email or hard copy (pref.). Contact first.
Simultaneous Submissions: yes
Reading Period: year-round
Reporting Time: one to twelve months
Author Payment: royalties and copies
Founded: 1981
Non Profit: no

Paid Staff: none
Unpaid Staff: one
Wholesalers: Baker & Taylor, YBP Library Services
ISSN Number/ISBN Number: ISBN 978-1-882863
Number of Books Published per Year: four
Titles in Print: 14
Average Print Run: 500
Average Percentage Printed: Hardcover 5%, Paperback 90%, Chapbook 5%
Average Price: $14.95

Organization: Hub City Writers Project

Type: press
CLMP member: no
Primary Editor/Contact Person: Betsy Teter
Address: P.O. Box 8421
Spartanburg, SC 29305
Web Site Address: http://www.hubcity.org
Publishes: essays, fiction, nonfiction, and poetry
Editorial Focus: Hub City publishes books with a strong sense of place and is primarily interested in books by authors from the Carolinas.
Representative Authors: Ron Rash, John Lane, and Rosa Shand
Submissions Policy: We take three-page book proposals with a sample chapter in March and September.
Simultaneous Submissions: yes
Reading Period: 4/1 to 5/1
Reporting Time: two to three months
Author Payment: none, royalties, cash, and copies
Founded: 1995
Non Profit: yes
Paid Staff: two
Unpaid Staff: zero
Wholesalers: Ingram, Baker & Taylor
ISSN Number/ISBN Number: ISBN 1891885
Number of Books Published per Year: two to four
Titles in Print: 18
Average Print Run: 1,000
Average Percentage Printed: Hardcover 20%, Paperback 80%
Average Price: $15

Organization: The Hudson Review

Type: magazine
CLMP member: yes
Primary Editor/Contact Person: Paula Deitz

Address: 684 Park Ave.
New York, NY 10021
Web Site Address: http://www.hudsonreview.com
Publishes: essays, fiction, nonfiction, poetry, reviews, and translation
Editorial Focus: A forum for the work of new writers and for exploration and development in literature and the arts.
Submissions Policy: Poetry: April 1 through June 30. Fiction: September 1 through November 30. Nonfiction: January 1 through March 31.
Simultaneous Submissions: no
Reading Period: Year-round
Reporting Time: four to seven months
Author Payment: cash
Founded: 1948
Non Profit: yes
Paid Staff: four
Unpaid Staff: two
Total Circulation: 4,500
Paid Circulation: 3,500
Subscription Rate: Individual $32/Institution $38
Single Copy Price: $9
Current Volume/Issue: LVII/2
Frequency per Year: four
Backfile Available: yes
Unsolicited Ms. Received: yes
Format: perfect
Ads: yes
Ad Rates: See web site for details.

Organization: The Hudson Valley Writers' Center

Type: press
CLMP member: yes
Primary Editor/Contact Person: Margo Stever
Address: Slapering Hol Press
300 Riverside Dr.
Sleepy Hollow, NY 10591
Web Site Address: http://www.writerscenter.org
Publishes: poetry
Editorial Focus: SHP publishes chapbooks by poets who have not previously published a book or chapbook; and occasionally, thematic anthologies
Representative Authors: David Tucker, Dina Ben-Lev, and Rachel Loden
Submissions Policy: see web site (www.writerscenter.org) for guidelines
Simultaneous Submissions: yes
Reading Period: 2/1 to 5/15

Reporting Time: two to three months
Author Payment: cash and copies
Contests: See web site for contest guidelines.
Founded: 1990
Non Profit: yes
Paid Staff: zero
Unpaid Staff: two
Distributors: SPD
ISSN Number/ISBN Number: ISBN 0-9700277
Number of Books Published per Year: one to two
Titles in Print: 17
Average Print Run: 500
Average Percentage Printed: Paperback 5%,
Chapbook 95%
Average Price: $12

Organization: Hunger Mountain

Type: magazine
CLMP member: yes
Primary Editor/Contact Person: Caroline Mercurio
Address: 36 College St.
36 College St.
Montpelier, VT 05602
Web Site Address: http://www.hungermtn.org
Publishes: essays, fiction, nonfiction, poetry, art, and
translation
Editorial Focus: The Vermont College Journal of Arts
& Letters accepts unpublished work by both estab-
lished and emerging writers and artists.
Representative Authors: Alice Hoffman, Maxine
Kumin, and James Tate
Submissions Policy: Refer to submission guidelines
on web site. No genre fiction, reviews, or multiple sub-
missions.
Simultaneous Submissions: yes
Reading Period: 4/1 to 1/31
Reporting Time: one to four months
Author Payment: cash and copies
Contests: See web site for contest guidelines.
Founded: 2002
Non Profit: yes
Paid Staff: three
Unpaid Staff: 25
ISSN Number/ISBN Number: ISSN 1539-9931
Total Circulation: 1,500
Paid Circulation: 700
Average Print Run: 1,600
Subscription Rate: Individual $17/Institution $17
Single Copy Price: $10
Current Volume/Issue: Issue seven

Frequency per Year: two
Backfile Available: yes
Unsolicited Ms. Received: yes
% of Unsolicited Ms. Published per Year: 5%
Format: perfect
Size: H 10" W 7"
Average Pages: 200
Ads: yes
Ad Rates: contact Managing Editor
(hungermtn@tui.edu) for info

Organization: Ibex Publishers, Inc.

Type: press
CLMP member: no
Primary Editor/Contact Person: Farhad Shirzad
Address: P.O. Box 30087
Bethesda, MD 20824
Web Site Address: http://www.ibexpublishers.com
Publishes: fiction, nonfiction, poetry, translation, and
audio
Editorial Focus: Ibex Publishers has beenpublishing
English and Persian language books about Iran and
the Middle East since 1979.
Representative Authors: Hafez of Shiraz, E.G.
Browne, and Wheeler M. Thackston
Submissions Policy: Please send outline, synopsis
and CV. Books should have some relevance to the
Middle East.
Simultaneous Submissions: no
Reading Period: Year-round
Reporting Time: two to three months
Author Payment: none, royalties, and copies
Founded: 1979
Non Profit: no
Paid Staff: three
Unpaid Staff: zero
Wholesalers: Ingram, Baker & Taylor
ISSN Number/ISBN Number: ISBN 0-936347 1-
58814-
Number of Books Published per Year: 12
Titles in Print: 150
Average Print Run: 1,500
Average Percentage Printed: Hardcover 50%,
Paperback 50%
Average Price: varies

Organization: Ibis Editions

Type: press
CLMP member: yes

Primary Editor/Contact Person: Peter Cole, Adina Hoffman
Address: P.O. Box 8074
Jerusalem, Israel
Web Site Address: http://www.ibiseditions.com
Publishes: essays, fiction, nonfiction, poetry, and translation
Editorial Focus: Literature of the Levant in Translation from Arabic, Hebrew, French, Ladino, Greek, German, and other languages.
Representative Authors: Muhyaddin Ibn al-Arabi, Gershom Scholem, and Taha Muhammad Ali
Submissions Policy: query letters only
Simultaneous Submissions: no
Reading Period: Year-round
Reporting Time: one to three months
Author Payment: copies
Contests: none
Founded: 1998
Non Profit: yes
Paid Staff: zero
Unpaid Staff: three
Distributors: SPD, Reuben Mass
Wholesalers: none
ISSN Number/ISBN Number: ISBN 965-901-2
Number of Books Published per Year: one to two
Titles in Print: 14
Average Percentage Printed: Paperback 100%
Average Price: $11

Organization: The Ice Cube Press

Type: press
CLMP member: no
Primary Editor/Contact Person: S.H. Semken
Address: 205 N Front
North Liberty, IA 52317
Web Site Address: http://www.icecubepress.com
Publishes: essays, fiction, and nonfiction
Editorial Focus: Regional and place-based writing on the environment and spirit of the Midwest. Stories, biography and essays.
Recent Awards Received: Iowa Arts Council Humanities Iowa (NEH), Rockwell Collins
Simultaneous Submissions: yes
Reading Period: Year-round
Reporting Time: two to three months
Author Payment: copies
Founded: 1993
Non Profit: no
Paid Staff: one

Unpaid Staff: zero
ISSN Number/ISBN Number: ISBN 1-888160
Number of Books Published per Year: five
Titles in Print: 35
Average Print Run: 500
Average Percentage Printed: Hardcover 5%, Paperback 90%, Other 5%
Average Price: $11.95

Organization: Iconoclast

Type: magazine
CLMP member: no
Primary Editor/Contact Person: Philip Wagner
Address: 1675 Amazon Road
Mohegan Lake, NY 10547-1804
Publishes: essays, fiction, nonfiction, poetry, reviews, art, and translation
Editorial Focus: original, creative work showing craft, intelligence, and more than a passing acquaintance with the world at large
Submissions Policy: send hard copy only, with SASE appropriate for reply and/or return of material
Simultaneous Submissions: no
Reading Period: Year-round
Reporting Time: three to eight weeks
Author Payment: cash and copies
Founded: 1992
Non Profit: no
Paid Staff: zero
Unpaid Staff: eight
Distributors: in house
Wholesalers: in house
ISSN Number/ISBN Number: ISSN 1064-1777
Total Circulation: 850
Paid Circulation: 425
Average Print Run: 3,000
Subscription Rate: Individual $16/8/Institution $16/8
Single Copy Price: $5
Current Volume/Issue: Issue 90
Frequency per Year: five
Backfile Available: yes
Unsolicited Ms. Received: yes
% of Unsolicited Ms. Published per Year: 5%
Format: stapled
Size: H 10.5" W 8"
Average Pages: 96
Ads: yes
Ad Rates: $100 full page/$60 half page

Organization: The Idaho Review

Type: magazine
CLMP member: yes
Primary Editor/Contact Person: Mitch Wieland, Editor
Address: Boise State University
1910 University Dr.
Boise, ID 83725
Website Address: english.boisestate.edu/idahoreview/
Publishes: essays, fiction, poetry, and reviews
Editorial Focus: High quality literary work.
Recent Awards Received: Reprints in Best American Short Stories, Prize Stories: The O. Henry Awards, Pushcart Prize, and New Stories from the South
Representative Authors: Joy Williams, Ann Beattie, and Richard Bausch
Submissions Policy: Fiction, no length requirement. One ms. per submission.
Simultaneous Submissions: yes
Reading Period: 8/1 to 5/1
Reporting Time: three to five months
Author Payment: cash and subscription
Contests: none at present
Founded: 1998
Non Profit: yes
Paid Staff: two
Unpaid Staff: seven
ISSN Number/ISBN Number: 1520-8389/0-9706392-4-4
Total Circulation: 1,000
Paid Circulation: 150
Subscription Rate: Individual $24/3 yr./Institution $30/3 yr.
Single Copy Price: $10
Current Volume/Issue: 2007/IV
Frequency per Year: one
Backfile Available: no
Unsolicited Ms. Received: yes
% of Unsolicited Ms. Published per Year: 30%
Format: perfect
Size: H 9 " W 6 "
Average Pages: 200
Ads: yes
Ad Rates: Exchange ads with literary journals

Organization: Ig

Type: press
CLMP member: no
Primary Editor/Contact Person: Robert Lasner
Address: 178 Clinton Ave.
Brooklyn, NY 11205
Web Site Address: http://www.igpub.com
Publishes: fiction, nonfiction, and translation
Editorial Focus: Ig Publishing publishes literary fiction with an alternative edge, and progressive political nonfiction
Representative Authors: Tom Hayden, Jim Derych, and Kirby Gann
Submissions Policy: Prefer e-mail submissions to igsubmissions@earthlink.net
Simultaneous Submissions: yes
Reading Period: Year-round
Reporting Time: three to six months
Author Payment: royalties
Founded: 2002
Non Profit: no
Paid Staff: two
Unpaid Staff: zero
Distributors: Consortium
ISSN Number/ISBN Number: ISBN 0-9703125
Number of Books Published per Year: 8-10
Titles in Print: 30
Average Print Run: 3,000
Average Percentage Printed: Hardcover 9%, Paperback 91%
Average Price: $12-$15

Organization: Image

Type: magazine
CLMP member: yes
Primary Editor/Contact Person: Gregory Wolfe
Address: 3307 Third Ave. W
Seattle, WA 98119
Web Site Address: http://www.imagejournal.org
Publishes: essays, fiction, nonfiction, poetry, reviews, art, and translation
Editorial Focus: Image is a unique forum for the best writing and artwork that are informed by-or grapple with-religious faith.
Recent Awards Received: Nominated by Utne Reader for Alternative Press Awards; work reprinted in Harper's, Utne, Pushcart, Best American, O. Henry, Poems.com.
Representative Authors: Mark Jarman, Julia Kasdorf, and Robert Olen Butler
Submissions Policy: We welcome unsolicited submissions. Include SASE for response. No e-mail submissions, please.
Simultaneous Submissions: yes
Reading Period: Year-round

Reporting Time: two to three months
Author Payment: cash and copies
Founded: 1989
Non Profit: yes
Paid Staff: three
Unpaid Staff: three to five
Distributors: Ingram
ISSN Number/ISBN Number: ISSN 1087-3503
Total Circulation: 4,500
Paid Circulation: 4,100
Average Print Run: 5,000
Subscription Rate: Individual $39.95/Institution $49.95
Single Copy Price: $12
Current Volume/Issue: Issue 50
Frequency per Year: four
Backfile Available: yes
Unsolicited Ms. Received: yes
% of Unsolicited Ms. Published per Year: 3%
Format: perfect
Size: H 10" W 7"
Average Pages: 128
Ads: yes
Ad Rates: See web site for details.

Organization: Images For Media, Yefief

Type: press
CLMP member: no
Primary Editor/Contact Person: Ann Racuya-Robbins
Address: P.O. Box 8505
Santa Fe, NM 87504
Web Site Address: http://www.ifm.com
Publishes: essays, fiction, nonfiction, poetry, art, translation, and audio
Editorial Focus: new forms, transcultural, quality work of all kinds
Representative Authors: Nicole Brossard, Xue Di, and Lucia Pavia Ticzon
Simultaneous Submissions: yes
Reading Period: Year-round
Reporting Time: one to three months
Author Payment: copies
Founded: 1993
Non Profit: no
Paid Staff: one
Unpaid Staff: one
Distributors: Amazon.com, ifm.com
ISSN Number/ISBN Number: 1074-5629/1-884432
Number of Books Published per Year: zero to six

Titles in Print: nine
Average Percentage Printed: Paperback 100%

Organization: Impetus Press

Type: online
CLMP member: no
Primary Editor/Contact Person: Cheryl A Townsend
Address: 4975 Comanche Trail
Stow, OH 44224-1217
Web Site Address: http://www.impetuspress.com
Publishes: essays, fiction, nonfiction, poetry, reviews, and art
Editorial Focus: Impetus wants poetry that screams. Poetry so real it hurts. No rhyme. No oatmeal. No taboos (other than -isms)
Representative Authors: Ron Androla, Lyn Lifshin, and Jim Chandler
Submissions Policy: It is highly suggested that you first read an issue of Impetus before submitting to get a better idea of what we are looking for. All written text must be sent within the e-mail. No attachments will be opened other than jpgs or gifs of artwork. Please write "Submission" in subject line of e-mail.
Simultaneous Submissions: yes
Reading Period: Year-round
Reporting Time: one to two months
Author Payment: none
Founded: 1984
Non Profit: yes
Paid Staff: zero
Unpaid Staff: three
Distributors: Past print issues/anthology through Waterrow Books
Wholesalers: Via publisher
ISSN Number/ISBN Number: ISSN 1044-7490
Frequency per Year: four
Publish Print Anthology: yes
Price: $10
Average Percentage of Pages per Category: Fiction 1%, Nonfiction 1%, Poetry 56%, Reviews 1%, Essays 1%, Art 40%
Ads: no

Organization: Impetus Press

Type: press
CLMP member: no
Primary Editor/Contact Person: J. Banash W. Blackmore
Address: P.O. Box 10025
Iowa City, IA 52240

Web Site Address: http://www.impetuspress.com
Publishes: fiction and nonfiction
Editorial Focus: Impetus Press publishes serious literary fiction with a pop edge **Representative Authors:** Nick Antosca, Christian TeBordo, and Kate Hunter
Submissions Policy: query via email only at submissions@iimpetuspress.com
Simultaneous Submissions: yes
Reading Period: year-round
Reporting Time: one to two months
Author Payment: royalties and copies
Founded: 2005
Non Profit: no
Paid Staff: three
Unpaid Staff: zero
Distributors: Biblio Book Distribution
Wholesalers: Ingram Baker & Taylor
Number of Books Published per Year: five
Titles in Print: five
Average Print Run: 2,000
Average Percentage Printed: Paperback 100%
Average Price: $16.95

Organization: Indian Bay Press

Type: press
CLMP member: yes
Primary Editor/Contact Person: Jay Ross, Editor
Address: One West Mountain Street
Fayetteville, AR 72701
Web Site Address: http://www.IndianBayPress.com
Publishes: essays, poetry and reviews
Editorial Focus: Poetry, particularly from Arkansas poets, unpublished poets, and foreign poets with translations.
Representative Authors: Jay Ross, J. Edwin Whitlaw, and Leonard Cirino
Submissions Policy: Please see updated submission requirements on our website www.IndianBayPress.com.
Simultaneous Submissions: no
Reading Period: Year-round
Reporting Time: one to two months
Author Payment: cash, and copies
Contests: Oliver W. Browning Poetry Content, Annually See web site for contest guidelines.
Founded: 2003
Non Profit: no
Paid Staff: zero
Unpaid Staff: four

ISSN Number/ISBN Number: ISSN 1547-448X
Number of Books Published per Year: 2,000
Titles in Print: Poesia
Average Print Run: 500
Average Percentage Printed: Paperback 100%
Average Price: $ 5.00

Organization: Indiana Review

Type: magazine
CLMP member: yes
Primary Editor/Contact Person: Abdel Shakur
Address: 465 Ballantine Hall
1020 E. Kirkwood Ave.
Bloomington, IN 47405-7103
Web Site Address: http://www.indiana.edu/~inreview
Publishes: essays, fiction, nonfiction, poetry, reviews, art, and translation
Editorial Focus: Showcasing talents of emerging and established writers, while offering the highest quality writing within a wide aesthetic.
Recent Awards Received: O'Henry Award 2006, O'Henry Award 2005, multiple Pushcart nominations
Representative Authors: Lucia Perillo, Denise Duhamel, and Michael Martone
Submissions Policy: See http://www.indiana.edu/~inreview/general/guidelines.html
Simultaneous Submissions: yes
Reading Period: 9/1 to 5/31
Reporting Time: two to four months
Author Payment: cash, copies, and subscription
Contests: See web site for contest guidelines.
Founded: 1976
Non Profit: yes
Paid Staff: four
Unpaid Staff: 15
Distributors: Ingram
ISSN Number/ISBN Number: ISSN 0738-386X
Total Circulation: 3,000
Paid Circulation: 2,000
Average Print Run: 5,000
Subscription Rate: Individual $17/Institution $20
Single Copy Price: $9
Current Volume/Issue: 27/2
Frequency per Year: two
Backfile Available: yes
Unsolicited Ms. Received: yes
% of Unsolicited Ms. Published per Year: 1%
Format: perfect
Size: H 9" W 6"

Average Pages: 180
Ads: yes
Ad Rates: $300 for full page

Organization: Inkwell Magazine

Type: magazine
CLMP member: yes
Primary Editor/Contact Person: Christine O. Adler
Address: Manhattanville College
2900 Purchase St.
Purchase, NY 10577
Web Site Address: http://www.inkwelljournal.org
Publishes: essays, fiction, nonfiction, poetry, and art
Editorial Focus: A platform for quality veteran and up-and-coming writers.
Representative Authors: Alice Elliott Dark, Mithran Somasundrum, and Benjamin Cheever
Submissions Policy: Guidelines available at our web site.
Simultaneous Submissions: yes
Reading Period: 8/1 to 11/30
Reporting Time: two to six months
Author Payment: cash and copies
Contests: See web site for contest guidelines.
Founded: 1995
Non Profit: yes
Paid Staff: two
Unpaid Staff: nine
Distributors: DeBoer, Ingram
ISSN Number/ISBN Number: ISSN 1085-0287
Total Circulation: 400
Paid Circulation: 20
Subscription Rate: Individual $15 /Institution $15
Single Copy Price: $8
Current Volume/Issue: 15/2004
Frequency per Year: biannual
Backfile Available: yes
Unsolicited Ms. Received: yes
% of Unsolicited Ms. Published per Year: 60%
Format: perfect
Size: H 8.5" W 5 3/8"
Average Pages: 150
Ads: yes
Ad Rates: Reciprocal available, or $200/full page, $100/half page

Organization: insolent rudder

Type: online
CLMP member: no

Primary Editor/Contact Person: Tim Ljunggren
Address: P.O. Box 433
Bristol, IN 46507
Web Site Address: http://www.insolentrudder.net/
Publishes: fiction and reviews
Editorial Focus: An electronic magazine dedicated to "furiously fresh flash fiction."
Representative Authors: Lisette Garcia, Paul A. Toth, and Susan Henderson
Submissions Policy: We accept stories of 500 words or less. For more information, please go to http://www.insolentrudder.org/submissions.
Simultaneous Submissions: yes
Reading Period: 10/1 to 6/30
Reporting Time: four to six weeks
Author Payment: none
Contests: See web site for contest guidelines.
Founded: 2001
Non Profit: yes
Paid Staff: zero
Unpaid Staff: five
Average Page Views per Month: 1,250
Average Unique Visitors per Month: 900
Publish Print Anthology: no
Average Percentage of Pages per Category: Fiction 95%, Reviews 5%
Ads: no

Organization: Insurance

Type: magazine
CLMP member: no
Primary Editor/Contact Person: C. Tokar/K. Anaglnopoulos
Address: 132 N. 1st St. #11
Brooklyn, NY 11211
Publishes: essays, fiction, nonfiction, and poetry
Editorial Focus: Contemporary previously unpublished work; we lean toward experimental but seek work from a variety of "schools."
Submissions Policy: We read poetry, short fiction, and prose. We prefer submissions of at least 6 pages of work (multiple pieces).
Simultaneous Submissions: yes
Reading Period: Year-round
Reporting Time: one to three months
Author Payment: cash and copies
Founded: 1999
Non Profit: yes
Paid Staff: zero
Unpaid Staff: two to four

Distributors: DeBoer
Total Circulation: 500
Paid Circulation: 75
Subscription Rate: Individual $18/Institution $18
Single Copy Price: $10
Current Volume/Issue: 3/3
Frequency per Year: one
Backfile Available: yes
Unsolicited Ms. Received: yes
% of Unsolicited Ms. Published per Year: 70%
Format: perfect
Average Pages: 90
Ads: no

Organization: Interim

Type: magazine
CLMP member: yes
Primary Editor/Contact Person: Claudia Keelan
Address: Department of English
University of Nevada Las Vegas
Las Vegas, NV 89154
Web Site Address:
www.unlv.edu/Colleges/Liberal_arts/Eng
Publishes: essays, nonfiction, poetry, reviews, and translation
Editorial Focus: New, exciting, and intelligent work. We have no prevailing aesthetic.
Submissions Policy: Submissions via mail only. Send no more than five poems or single prose piece.
Simultaneous Submissions: yes
Reading Period: year-round
Reporting Time: one to two months
Author Payment: copies
Founded: 1946
Non Profit: yes
Paid Staff: two
Unpaid Staff: zero
ISSN Number/ISBN Number: ISSN 0888-2452
Total Circulation: 300
Paid Circulation: 100
Average Print Run: 300
Subscription Rate: individual $12/institution $14
Single Copy Price: $12
Current Volume/Issue: 24/1
Frequency per year: annual
Backfile Available: yes
Unsolicited MSS Received: yes
% of Unsolicited MSS Published per Year: 50%
Format: perfect
Size: H 8" W 6.5"

Average Pages: 200
Ads: yes

Organization: Interlope Magazine

Type: magazine
CLMP member: no
Primary Editor/Contact Person: Summi Kaipa
Address: P.O. Box 423058
San Francisco, CA 94142-3058
Web Site Address: http://www.interlope.org
Publishes: essays, fiction, poetry, and art
Editorial Focus: Interlope publishes innovative writing by Asian Americans.
Representative Authors: Linh Dinh, Eileen Tabios, and Hoa Nguyen
Submissions Policy: 6 to 10 pages of unsolicited writing considered. Writers should familiarize themselves with Interlope before submitting.
Simultaneous Submissions: yes
Reading Period: Year-round
Reporting Time: 6 to 12 weeks
Author Payment: copies
Founded: 1998
Non Profit: yes
Paid Staff: zero
Unpaid Staff: one
Total Circulation: 50
Paid Circulation: 25
Subscription Rate: Individual $10/Institution $20
Single Copy Price: $5
Current Volume/Issue: Issue 9
Frequency per Year: 2
Backfile Available: yes
Unsolicited Ms. Received: yes
% of Unsolicited Ms. Published per Year: 30%
Format: stapled
Size: H 8.5" W 8.5"
Average Pages: 65
Ads: no

Organization: International Poetry Review

Type: magazine
CLMP member: no
Address: U. of North Carolina at Greensboro
Dept. of Romance Languages
Greensboro, NC 27412-5001
Website Address:
http://www.uncg.edu/rom/IPR/IPRcurrent.htm

Publishes: poetry and translation
Reading Period: Year-round
Reporting Time: one to two months
Author Payment: none
Non Profit: no

Organization: Into the Teeth of the Wind

Type: magazine
CLMP member: no
Primary Editor/Contact Person: Amber Wallace
Address: College of Creative Studies
UCSB
Santa Barbara, CA 93106
Web Site Address: http://www.ccs.ucsb.edu/windsteeth
Publishes: poetry
Editorial Focus: Into the Teeth of the Wind publishes a variety of poems from both well-known and previously unpublished poets.
Representative Authors: John Ridland and John Wilson
Submissions Policy: All manuscripts, up to eight pages of previously unpublished poetry, are considered. SASE required for response.
Simultaneous Submissions: yes
Reading Period: Year-round
Reporting Time: six to twelve weeks
Author Payment: copies
Contests: none
Founded: 1999
Non Profit: yes
Paid Staff: zero
Unpaid Staff: 10
Total Circulation: 200
Paid Circulation: 25
Subscription Rate: Individual $18/Institution $18
Single Copy Price: $5.50
Current Volume/Issue: 3/4
Frequency per Year: four
Backfile Available: yes
Unsolicited Ms. Received: yes
% of Unsolicited Ms. Published per Year: 20%
Format: perfect
Size: H 8.5" W 5.5"
Average Pages: 64
Ads: no

Organization: iota

Type: magazine
CLMP member: no
Primary Editor/Contact Person: Janet Murch
Address: 1 Lodge Farm
Snitterfield
Stratford-on-Avon, UK CV37 0LR
Web Site Address: http://www.iotapoetry.co.uk
Publishes: poetry and reviews
Editorial Focus: Contemporary poetry with something interesting to say.
Representative Authors: Michael Kriesel, Eric Paul Shaffer, and Jane Kinninmont
Submissions Policy: Up to six poems by post (with SASE/IRC) or in main body of e-mail. State if previously published and detail when and where.
Simultaneous Submissions: no
Reading Period: Year-round
Reporting Time: three to twelve weeks
Author Payment: copies
Contests: iota annual poetry competition. Deadline: April 15th.
See web site for Contest Guidelines.
Founded: 1987
Non Profit: yes
Paid Staff: zero
Unpaid Staff: two
ISSN Number/ISBN Number: ISSN 0266-2922
Total Circulation: 290
Paid Circulation: 175
Average Print Run: 300
Single Copy Price: UK £4.50
Current Volume/Issue: Issue 74
Frequency per Year: quarterly
Backfile Available: yes
Unsolicited Ms. Received: yes
% of Unsolicited Ms. Published per Year: 100%
Format: perfect
Size: H 210mm W 148mm
Average Pages: 60
Ads: no
Ad Rates: See web site for details.

Organization: The Iowa Review

Type: magazine
CLMP member: yes
Primary Editor/Contact Person: David Hamilton
Address: 308 English/Philosophy Bldg.
University of Iowa
Iowa City, IA 52242

Web Site Address: http://iowareview.org
Publishes: essays, fiction, nonfiction, poetry, and reviews
Editorial Focus: Contemporary writing, the best we can find.
Recent Awards Received: Work selected for 2007 Best American Essays and Best American Short Stories
Representative Authors: Robert Dana, Phong Nguyen, and Joanna Klink
Submissions Policy: Only in hard copy, with SASE, and through the fall semester.
Simultaneous Submissions: yes
Reading Period: 9/1 to 12/1
Reporting Time: one to three months
Author Payment: cash, copies, and subscription
Contests: See web site for contest guidelines.
Founded: 1970
Non Profit: yes
Paid Staff: four
Unpaid Staff: 12
Distributors: Ingram and DeBoer
ISSN Number/ISBN Number: ISSN 0021-065X
Total Circulation: 2,500
Paid Circulation: 1,000
Subscription Rate: Individual $24/Institution $24
Single Copy Price: $8.95
Current Volume/Issue: 37/1
Frequency per Year: three
Backfile Available: yes
Unsolicited Ms. Received: yes
% Unsolicited Ms. Published per Year: 3%
Format: perfect
Size: H 8.5" W 5.5"
Average Pages: 192
Ads: yes
Ad Rates: $200/page

Organization: iris

Type: magazine
CLMP member: no
Primary Editor/Contact Person: Annie Schutte
Address: The Women's Center
P.O. Box 800588-0588
Charlottesville, VA 22908
Web Site Address: http://iris.virginia.edu
Publishes: essays, fiction, nonfiction, poetry, and art
Simultaneous Submissions: yes
Reading Period: 8/3 to 5/4
Reporting Time: one to four months

Author Payment: none
Founded: 1980
Non Profit: yes
Paid Staff: three
Unpaid Staff: 13
Total Circulation: 2,500
Paid Circulation: yes, $9
Average Print Run: 2,500
Subscription Rate: Individual $9/Institution $40
Single Copy Price: $5
Current Volume/Issue: Issue 51
Frequency per Year: two
Backfile Available: yes
Unsolicited Ms. Received: yes
Format: stapled

Organization: Iron Horse Literary Review

Type: magazine
CLMP member: no
Primary Editor/Contact Person: Jill Patterson
Address: English Dept., Texas Tech University
MS 43091
Lubbock, TX 79409-3091
Web Site Address: http://english.ttu.edu/ih
Publishes: fiction, nonfiction, poetry, reviews, and art
Representative Authors: Melanie Rae Thon, Lee Martin, and Li-Young Lee
Submissions Policy: Please let us respond to one manuscript before submitting another. We do not publish previously published work.
Simultaneous Submissions: yes
Reading Period: 8/15 to 4/15
Reporting Time: one to three months
Author Payment: cash and copies
Founded: 1999
Non Profit: yes
Paid Staff: four
Unpaid Staff: 12
Total Circulation: 472
Paid Circulation: 433
Subscription Rate: Individual $12/Institution $12
Single Copy Price: $6
Current Volume/Issue: 8/2
Frequency per Year: two
Backfile Available: yes
Unsolicited Ms. Received: yes
% of Unsolicited Ms. Published per Year: 85%
Format: perfect
Size: H 6" W 9"

Average Pages: 200
Ads: yes
Ad Rates: ad swap program

Organization: Isotope

Type: magazine
CLMP member: yes
Primary Editor/Contact Person: Christopher Cokinos
Address: Dept. of English, Utah State University
3200 Old Main Hill
Logan, UT 84322-3200
Web Site Address: http://isotope.usu.edu/
Publishes: essays, fiction, nonfiction, poetry, and art
Editorial Focus: Literary nonfiction, fiction, poetry and artwork that engages the varied relationships between the human and nonhuman worlds.
Representative Authors: Pattiann Rogers, D.K. McCutchen, and R.T. Smith
Submissions Policy: See web site http://isotope.usu.edu/ for writer's guidelines.
Simultaneous Submissions: yes
Reading Period: 9/1 to 11/30
Reporting Time: four to six months
Author Payment: cash, copies, and subscription
Contests: Yearly Editors' Prizes in Nonfiction, Fiction and Poetry
See web site for Contest Guidelines.
Founded: 2003
Non Profit: yes
Paid Staff: three
Unpaid Staff: zero
Distributors: Kent News Agency, Ubiquity
ISSN Number/ISBN Number: ISSN 1544-8479
Total Circulation: 1,100
Paid Circulation: 750
Average Print Run: 1,400
Subscription Rate: Individual $10/Institution $10
Single Copy Price: $5
Current Volume/Issue: 6/1
Frequency per Year: two
Backfile Available: yes
Unsolicited Ms. Received: yes
% of Unsolicited Ms. Published per Year: 5%
Format: stapled
Size: H 11" W 8.5"
Average Pages: 52

Organization: Jane's Stories Press Foundation

Type: press
CLMP member: yes
Primary Editor/Contact Person: Linda Mowry
Address: 5500 N. 50 W
Fremont, IN 46737
Web Site Address: http://www.janesstories.org
Publishes: essays, fiction, nonfiction, and poetry
Editorial Focus: women's literature, multicultural literary traditions
Representative Authors: Cheryl Klein, Meta Commerse, and Marci Stillerman
Submissions Policy: Submissions by invitation or contest entry only at this time. Send contact information to join our mailing list.
Simultaneous Submissions: yes
Reading Period: Year-round
Reporting Time: two to four months
Author Payment: none
Contests: See web site for contest guidelines.
Founded: 2000
Non Profit: yes
Paid Staff: zero
Unpaid Staff: two to four
Distributors: Baker & Taylor
Number of Books Published per Year: one to three
Titles in Print: eight
Average Print Run: 750
Average Percentage Printed: Paperback 50%, Chapbook 50%
Average Price: $14

Organization: The Journal

Type: magazine
CLMP member: no
Primary Editor/Contact Person: Kathy Fagan
Address: Department of English
164 W. 17th Ave.
Columbus, OH 43210
Web Site Address:
http://english.osu.edu/journals/the_journal/
Publishes: essays, fiction, nonfiction, poetry, reviews, and art
Representative Authors: Bob Hicok, Mark Conway, and Lore Segal
Submissions Policy: Quality fiction, poetry, nonfiction and reviews of new books of poetry. No length restrictions. Submissions by mail only. Include e-mail address or SASE for response.
Simultaneous Submissions: yes
Reading Period: Year-round

Reporting Time: four to twelve weeks
Author Payment: cash and copies
Contests: See web site for contest guidelines.
Founded: 1972
Non Profit: yes
Paid Staff: four
Unpaid Staff: 10
Distributors: Ingram
ISSN Number/ISBN Number: ISSN 1045-084X
Total Circulation: 1,500
Paid Circulation: 800
Average Print Run: 1,200
Subscription Rate: Individual $12/Institution $14
Single Copy Price: $7
Current Volume/Issue: 28/2
Frequency per Year: two
Backfile Available: yes
Unsolicited Ms. Received: yes
Format: perfect
Size: H 9" W 6"
Average Pages: 140
Ads: yes
Ad Rates: negotiable

Organization: Journal of New Jersey Poets

Type: magazine
CLMP member: yes
Primary Editor/Contact Person: Sander Zulauf, Editor
Address: County College of Morris
214 Center Grove Road
Randolph, NJ 07869
Web Site Address: http://www.ccm.edu
Publishes: essays, poetry, and reviews
Editorial Focus: The Journal of New Jersey Poets is dedicated to publishing the best new poetry, essays and reviews by poets from New Jersey.
Recent Awards Received: Excellence in Print Award from The Poet and the Poem, WPFW-FM, Washington, DC and the Library of Congress
Representative Authors: Joe Weil, Tina Kelley, and Ruth Moon Kempher
Submissions Policy: Annual deadline Sept. 1. Send up to three poems and SASE for acceptance or return, or instructions to recycle manuscripts.
Simultaneous Submissions: yes
Reading Period: 9/1 to 10/15
Reporting Time: six months
Author Payment: copies and subscription

Contests: None.
Founded: 1976
Non Profit: yes
Paid Staff: zero
Unpaid Staff: four
Distributors: DeBoer
ISSN Number/ISBN Number: ISSN 0363-4205
Total Circulation: 900
Paid Circulation: 360
Average Print Run: 650
Subscription Rate: Individual $16/2/Institution $16/1
Single Copy Price: $10
Current Volume/Issue: 2006/43
Frequency per Year: one
Backfile Available: yes
Unsolicited Ms. Received: yes
% of Unsolicited Ms. Published per Year: 5-7%
Format: perfect
Size: H 8 1/2" W 5 1/2"
Average Pages: 90
Ads: yes
Ad Rates: Exchange.

Organization: Journal of Ordinary Thought

Type: magazine
CLMP member: no
Primary Editor/Contact Person: Annie Knepler
Address: Neighborhood Writing Alliance
1313 E. 60th St.
Chicago, IL 60637
Web Site Address: http://www.jot.org
Publishes: essays, fiction, and poetry
Editorial Focus: JOT publishes reflections people make on their personal histories and everyday experiences.
Representative Authors: Charlie Clements, Pennie Holmes Brinson, and Felicia Madlock
Submissions Policy: Only work produced in weekly workshops hosted by the Neighborhood Writing Alliance in Chicago neighborhoods are considered.
Simultaneous Submissions: yes
Reading Period: Year-round
Reporting Time: one to two months
Author Payment: none
Founded: 1991
Non Profit: yes
Paid Staff: three
Unpaid Staff: six
Distributors: Neighborhood Writing Alliance

ISSN Number/ISBN Number: ISSN 1535-0614
Total Circulation: 2,500+
Paid Circulation: 500
Average Print Run: 3,000
Subscription Rate: Individual $25/Institution $50
Single Copy Price: $10
Current Volume/Issue: 2006/Sprg
Frequency per Year: four
Backfile Available: yes
Unsolicited Ms. Received: no
Format: perfect
Size: H 9 1/2" W 6 1/2"
Average Pages: 75
Ads: no

Organization: jubilat

Type: magazine
CLMP member: yes
Primary Editor/Contact Person: Jessica Fjeld
Address: English Dept., Bartlett Hall
University of Massachusetts
Amherst, MA 01003-0515
Web Site Address: http://www.jubilat.org
Publishes: poetry, art, and translation
Editorial Focus: Contemporary poetry alongside art, translations, interviews, poetic prose, and found/forgotten pieces.
Recent Awards Received: Inclusion in multiple editions of Pushcart Prize and Best American Poetry anthologies
Representative Authors: Dean Young, C.D. Wright, and John Ashbery
Submissions Policy: Submit via website. Poetry and art, as well as other forms of writing on poetry, poetics, or other subjects. We do not consider short stories.
Simultaneous Submissions: yes
Reading Period: 9/1-5/1
Reporting Time: four to six months
Author Payment: cash, copies and subscription
Founded: 1999
Non Profit: yes
Paid Staff: one
Unpaid Staff: seven
Distributors: Ingram, DeBoer, SPD
ISSN Number/ISBN Number: ISSN 1529-0999
Total Circulation: 1,400
Paid Circulation: 700
Subscription Rate: Individual $14/Institution $28
Single Copy Price: $8

Current Volume/Issue: 4/1
Frequency per Year: biannual
Backfile Available: yes
Unsolicited Ms. Received: yes
% Unsolicited Ms. Published per Year: 1-2%
Format: perfect
Size: H 7.5" W 5.5"
Average Pages: 160
Ads: yes
Ad Rates: Full Page: $200

Organization: Juked

Type: online
CLMP member: no
Primary Editor/Contact Person: J.W. Wang
Address: 110 Westridge Drive
Tallahassee, FL 32304
Web Site Address: http://www.juked.com
Publishes: essays, fiction, nonfiction, and poetry
Editorial Focus: Fiction, poetry, photography
Recent Awards Received: Best of the Net 2006, The High Hat Top Ten Literary Websites 2006
Representative Authors: Stephen Graham Jones, Claudia Smith, and Kim Chinquee
Simultaneous Submissions: yes
Reading Period: Year-round
Reporting Time: one to three months
Author Payment: none
Contests: Yearly fiction and poetry prizes;
See web site for Contest Guidelines.
Founded: 1999
Non Profit: yes
Paid Staff: zero
Unpaid Staff: three
Average Page Views per Month: 40,000
Average Unique Visitors per Month: 6,500
Frequency per Year: 12
Publish Print Anthology: yes
Price: $10
Average Percentage of Pages per Category: Fiction 50%, Nonfiction 5%, Poetry 40%, Essays 5%
Ad Rates: See web site for details.

Organization: Junction Press

Type: press
CLMP member: yes
Primary Editor/Contact Person: Mark Weiss
Address: P.O. Box F
New York, NY 10034

Publishes: poetry
Editorial Focus: Modernist/Postmodernist US and Latin American poetry
Representative Authors: Rochelle Owens, Armand Schwerner, and Jose Kozer
Submissions Policy: 10 pages with SASE
Simultaneous Submissions: yes
Reading Period: Year-round
Reporting Time: one to twelve weeks
Author Payment: copies
Founded: 1992
Non Profit: yes
Paid Staff: zero
Unpaid Staff: one
Distributors: SPD, Latin American Book Service
Wholesalers: Baker & Taylor, Brodart, Ingram, Midwest, Coutts
ISSN Number/ISBN Number: ISBN 1-881523
Number of Books Published per Year: one
Titles in Print: 13
Average Print Run: 1,000
Average Percentage Printed: Paperback 100%
Average Price: $16

Organization: Kaleidoscope Magazine

Type: magazine
CLMP member: yes
Primary Editor/Contact Person: Gail Willmott
Address: United Disability Services
701 S. Main St.
Akron, OH 44311-1019
Web Site Address: http://www.udsakron.org
Publishes: essays, fiction, nonfiction, poetry, reviews, and art
Editorial Focus: Explores the experience of disability from the perspective of individuals, families, professionals and society as a whole.
Representative Authors: Laurence Becker, Sharon Wachsler, and Michele Free
Submissions Policy: Considers unsolicited material, accepts simultaneous submissions, publishes previously published work. Double-spaced, typed, and SASE.
Simultaneous Submissions: yes
Reading Period: Year-round
Reporting Time: six to nine months
Author Payment: cash and copies
Founded: 1979
Non Profit: yes
Paid Staff: four

Unpaid Staff: one
ISSN Number/ISBN Number: ISSN 0748-8742
Total Circulation: 1,000
Paid Circulation: 350
Average Print Run: 1,000
Subscription Rate: Individual $10/Institution $15
Single Copy Price: $6
Current Volume/Issue: Issue 55
Frequency per Year: two
Backfile Available: yes
Unsolicited Ms. Received: yes
% of Unsolicited Ms. Published per Year: 75%
Format: stapled
Size: H 11" W 8.5"
Average Pages: 64
Ads: no

Organization: Kalliope, a Journal of Women's Literature & Art

Type: magazine
CLMP member: yes
Primary Editor/Contact Person: Margaret L. Clark, Ph.D.
Address: 11901 Beach Blvd.
Jacksonville, FL 32246
Web Site Address:
http://opencampus.fccj.org/kalliope/index.html
Publishes: fiction, poetry, reviews, and art
Editorial Focus: Kalliope publishes poetry, short fiction, Q&A interviews, and fine B&W art by established and excellent new writers.
Representative Authors: Marge Piercy, Kim Bradley, and Ruth Moon Kempher
Submissions Policy: Send three-to five poems, one to two short fiction under 3,500 words, query Q&A interviews. Send B&W photos of fine art. SASE and bio.
Simultaneous Submissions: no
Reading Period: Year-round
Reporting Time: six to nine months
Author Payment: copies and subscription
Contests: See web site for contest guidelines.
Founded: 1978
Non Profit: yes
Paid Staff: one
Unpaid Staff: 20
Distributors: Ingram, Ubiquity
ISSN Number/ISBN Number: ISSN 0-74470-81705-5
Total Circulation: 1,600

Paid Circulation: 600
Average Print Run: 1,600
Subscription Rate: Individual $20/Institution $35
Single Copy Price: $12
Current Volume/Issue: 29/1
Frequency per Year: two
Backfile Available: yes
Unsolicited Ms. Received: yes
% of Unsolicited Ms. Published per Year: 99%
Format: perfect
Size: H 6" W 9"
Average Pages: 12
Ads: no

Organization: Karamu

Type: magazine
CLMP member: yes
Primary Editor/Contact Person: Olga Abella
Address: English Dept, Eastern Illinois Univ.
600 Lincoln Ave.
Charleston, IL 61920
Web Site Address: http://www.eiu.edu/~karamu/
Publishes: essays, fiction, nonfiction, poetry, and art
Editorial Focus: writing that builds around real experiences, real images, and real characters, avoiding overt philosophizing and preaching
Recent Awards Received: Illinois Arts Council Literary Award
Representative Authors: Jenifer Garfield, J.E. Robinson, and Joyce Goldenstern
Submissions Policy: poetry: five poems at a time. Prose: one piece not longer than 3,500 words. All submissions must include SASE.
Simultaneous Submissions: no
Reading Period: 9/1 to 2/15
Reporting Time: four to six months
Author Payment: copies
Founded: 1966
Non Profit: yes
Paid Staff: zero
Unpaid Staff: seven to eight
Distributors: Illini Bookstore, Canio's Books
ISSN Number/ISBN Number: ISBN 0022-8990
Total Circulation: 700
Paid Circulation: 150
Average Print Run: 500
Subscription Rate: Individual $8/Institution $8
Single Copy Price: $8
Current Volume/Issue: 20/2
Frequency per Year: one

Backfile Available: yes
Unsolicited Ms. Received: yes
% of Unsolicited Ms. Published per Year: 100%
Format: perfect
Size: H 8" W 5"
Average Pages: 150
Ads: no

Organization: Katabasis

Type: press
CLMP member: no
Primary Editor/Contact Person: Dinah Livingstone
Address: 10 St. Martin's Close
London, UK NW1 0HR
Web Site Address: http://www.katabasis.co.uk
Publishes: fiction, nonfiction, poetry, and translation
Editorial Focus: Katabasis publishes English and Latin American poetry and prose.
Representative Authors: Dinah Livingstone, Ernesto Cardenal, and Kathleen McPhilemy
Submissions Policy: No unsolicited manuscripts
Simultaneous Submissions: no
Reading Period: Year-round
Reporting Time: six to twelve weeks
Author Payment: none
Founded: 1967
Non Profit: yes
Paid Staff: zero
Unpaid Staff: one
Distributors: Central Books
ISSN Number/ISBN Number: ISBN 0904872
Number of Books Published per Year: one to two
Titles in Print: 28
Average Print Run: 500
Average Percentage Printed: Paperback 100%
Average Price: £6.95

Organization: Kaya Press

Type: press
CLMP member: no
Primary Editor/Contact Person: Julie Koo
Address: 116 Pinehurst Ave. #E51
New York, NY 10033
Web Site Address: http://www.kaya.com
Publishes: fiction, nonfiction, poetry, art, and translation
Editorial Focus: Publisher of Asian, Pacific Islander, and API diasporic fiction, poetry, critical essays, art, and culture

Representative Authors: R. Zamora Linmark, Sesshu Foster, and Ishle Park
Submissions Policy: See http://www.kaya.com/submit.html
Simultaneous Submissions: yes
Reading Period: 1/4 to 5/4
Reporting Time: 3 months
Author Payment: royalties and copies
Founded: 1994
Non Profit: yes
Paid Staff: zero
Unpaid Staff: two
Distributors: DAP
Wholesalers: SPD
ISSN Number/ISBN Number: ISBN 1-885030
Number of Books Published per Year: two
Titles in Print: 12
Average Percentage Printed: Hardcover 5%, Paperback 95%
Backfile Available: yes

Organization: Kegedonce Press

Type: press
CLMP member: no
Primary Editor/Contact Person: Renee Abram
Address: Cape Croker First Nation
RR#5
Wiarton, ON N0H 2T0
Web Site Address: http://www.kegedonce.com
Publishes: fiction, nonfiction, and poetry
Editorial Focus: Indigenous Literature
Recent Awards Received: WordCraft Circle of Writers-2002
Representative Authors: Daniel Heath Justice, Basil Johnston, and Al Hunter
Submissions Policy: Publishing history, sample chapter or max. 30 pages, SASE if require return of materials
Simultaneous Submissions: yes
Reading Period: Year-round
Reporting Time: two to three months
Author Payment: royalties and copies
Founded: 1993
Non Profit: no
Paid Staff: 1.5
Unpaid Staff: one
Distributors: LitDistCo (The Literary Press Group Canada)
ISSN Number/ISBN Number: ISBN 0-9731396/0-9697120

Number of Books Published per Year: two
Titles in Print: 12
Average Print Run: 1,500
Average Percentage Printed: Paperback 100%
Average Price: $15

Organization: The Kelsey Review

Type: magazine
CLMP member: no
Primary Editor/Contact Person: Robin Schore
Address: Mercer County College
Trenton, NJ 08690
Web Site Address: http://www.mccc.edu/community_kelsey-review.shtml
Publishes: essays, fiction, nonfiction, poetry, and art
Editorial Focus: Regional literary journal accepting contributions exclusively from people living and working in Mercer County, NJ
Representative Authors: Bruce Petronio, Janet Kirk, and Helen Gorenstein
Submissions Policy: Deadline: May 1; prose: max 2,000 words; poetry: max six poems. Previously unpublished
Simultaneous Submissions: no
Reading Period: 5/4 to 6/4
Reporting Time: six to eight weeks
Author Payment: copies
Contests: none
Founded: 1988
Non Profit: yes
Paid Staff: one
Unpaid Staff: three
Distributors: Mercer County Community College
ISSN Number/ISBN Number: ISSN 0451-6338
Total Circulation: 1,800
Paid Circulation: zero
Single Copy Price: free
Current Volume/Issue: 23/1
Frequency per Year: one
Backfile Available: no
Unsolicited Ms. Received: yes
% of Unsolicited Ms. Published per Year: 100%
Format: stapled
Size: H 11" W 7"
Average Pages: 88
Ads: no

Organization: Kelsey Street Press

Type: press

CLMP member: yes
Primary Editor/Contact Person: Rena Rosenwasser
Address: 50 Northgate Ave.
Berkeley, CA 94708
Web Site Address: http://www.kelseyst.com
Publishes: poetry and art
Editorial Focus: The Press publishes poetry by contemporary women writers that challenges traditional notions about form, content, and expression, as well as collaborations between poets and visual artists.
Recent Awards Received: 7th Annual Asian American Award for Poetry, for Mei-mei Berssenbrugge's Nest
Representative Authors: Barbara Guest, Mei-mei Berssenbrugge, and Renee Gladman
Submissions Policy: Currently we are not accepting any unsolicited manuscripts. Check our web site for any changes regarding submissions.
Simultaneous Submissions: yes
Reading Period: 6/1 to 8/30
Reporting Time: two to three months
Author Payment: royalties
Contests: See web site for contest guidelines.
Founded: 1974
Non Profit: yes
Paid Staff: zero
Unpaid Staff: six
Distributors: SPD
ISSN Number/ISBN Number: none/0-932716
Number of Books Published per Year: two
Titles in Print: 45
Average Print Run: 1,000
Average Price: $12

Organization: The Kent State University Press

Type: press
CLMP member: no
Primary Editor/Contact Person: Joanna Hildebrand Craig
Address: Box 5190
Kent, OH 44242-0001
Web Site Address:
http://kentstateuniversitypress.com
Publishes: essays, fiction, nonfiction, poetry, and translation
Editorial Focus: US history, US literature, regional (Ohio) studies, military history, fantasy, literary criticism
Representative Authors: Verlyn Flieger, George

Knepper, and Joe Harsh
Submissions Policy: letter of inquiry explaining or introducing proposal, outline or table of contents, two sample chapters, resume/CV
Simultaneous Submissions: yes
Reading Period: Year-round
Reporting Time: four to seven months
Author Payment: royalties
Founded: 1965
Non Profit: yes
Paid Staff: 9
Unpaid Staff: one
Distributors: Bookmasters
Wholesalers: all
ISSN Number/ISBN Number: ISBN 87338
Number of Books Published per Year: 35
Titles in Print: 400
Average Print Run: Varies
Average Percentage Printed: Hardcover 30%, Paperback 60%, Chapbook 10%
Average Price: varies

Organization: The Kenyon Review

Type: magazine
CLMP member: yes
Primary Editor/Contact Person: David Lynn, Editor
Address: Walton House
104 College Dr.
Gambier, OH 43022
Web Site Address: http://www.kenyonreview.org
Publishes: essays, fiction, nonfiction, poetry, reviews, and translation
Editorial Focus: International in scope, KR publishes innovative work from emerging and established writers.
Recent Awards Received: Works appearing in KR have won Best American Poetry, Pushcart Prizes, O. Henry, and more.
Representative Authors: Alice Hoffman, Philip Deaver, and Ellen Bryant Voigt
Submissions Policy: Please see submissions guidelines on our web site:
http://www.kenyonreview.org/writers/guidelines.php
Simultaneous Submissions: no
Reading Period: 9/1 to 1/31
Reporting Time: three to four months
Author Payment: cash and copies
Contests: Patricia Grodd Poetry Prize for Young Writers; see website for guidelines
Founded: 1939

Non Profit: yes
Paid Staff: six
Unpaid Staff: 18
Distributors: Ingram; Media Solutions
ISSN Number/ISBN Number: ISSN 0163-075X
Total Circulation: 5,700
Paid Circulation: 3,380
Average Print Run: 6,000
Subscription Rate: Individual $30/Institution $35
Single Copy Price: $10
Current Volume/Issue: 28/3
Frequency per Year: four
Backfile Available: yes
Unsolicited Ms. Received: yes
Format: perfect
Size: H 10" W 7"
Average Pages: 232
Ads: yes
Ad Rates: See web site for details.

Organization: KGB BAR LIT

Type: online
CLMP member: no
Primary Editor/Contact Person: Susan Y. Chi
Address: 85 East 4th St.
New york, NY 10003
Publishes: essays, fiction, nonfiction, poetry, reviews, art, translation, audio, and video
Simultaneous Submissions: yes
Reading Period: year-round
Reporting Time: one to two months
Author Payment: none
Founded: 2006
Non Profit: no
Paid Staff: three
Unpaid Staff: 10
Average Page Views per Month: 700,000
Average Unique Visitors per Month: 60,000
Frequency per year: biannual
Publish Print Anthology: yes
Average Percentage of Pages per Category: fiction 20%, nonfiction 15%, poetry 15%, reviews 25%, essays 17%, art 2%, Translation 2%, Audio 2%, Video 2%
Ads: yes

Organization: The King's English

Type: online
CLMP member: yes
Primary Editor/Contact Person: Benjamin Chambers
Address: 3114 NE 47th Ave.
Portland, OR 97213
Web Site Address: http://www.thekingsenglish.org
Publishes: essays, fiction, poetry, and reviews
Editorial Focus: Novellas(11,000-48,000 words) and long personal essays (3,000-48,000 words). Also poetry and offbeat book reviews.
Recent Awards Received: Winner of the 2004/2005 Million Writers Award for Best Publisher of Novella-Length Fiction
Submissions Policy: See guidelines at http://www.thekingsenglish.org. Electronic submission preferred.
Simultaneous Submissions: yes
Reading Period: Year-round
Reporting Time: one to two months
Author Payment: none
Contests: Blodgett Waxwing Literary Prize in Fiction. $500 first prize, $100 second prize, $50 third prize; See web site for contest guidelines.
Founded: 2003
Non Profit: yes
Paid Staff: zero
Unpaid Staff: four
Average Page Views per Month: 1,000
Average Unique Visitors per Month: 500
Frequency per Year: four
Publish Print Anthology: no
Average Percentage of Pages per Category: Fiction 70%, Poetry 5%, Reviews 5%, Essays 20%
Ads: no

Organization: Kitchen Press

Type: press
CLMP member: yes
Primary Editor/Contact Person: Justin Marks
Address: 746 10th Ave
Apt. 3s
New York, NY 10019
Web Site Address: www.kitchenpresschapbooks.blogspot.com/
Publishes: poetry
Editorial Focus: specializes in publishing handmade chapbooks by emerging poets
Recent Awards Received:
Representative Authors: Chris Tonelli, Mathias Svalina, and Elisa Gabbert
Submissions Policy: No open submissions; submissions are by solicitation only

Simultaneous Submissions: yes
Reading Period: n/a
Reporting Time: n/a
Author Payment: copies
Founded: 2005
Non Profit: no
Paid Staff: zero
Unpaid Staff: one
Distributors: self
Average Print Run: 150
Single Copy Price: $5 plus $1 shipping
Backfile Available: yes
Unsolicited MSS Received: no
Format: saddle staple
Average Pages: 25

Organization: KNOCK

Type: magazine
CLMP member: yes
Primary Editor/Contact Person: Bryan Tomasovich
Address: 2326 6th Ave.
Seattle, WA 98121
Web Site Address: http://www.knockjournal.org
Publishes: essays, fiction, nonfiction, poetry, and art
Editorial Focus: KNOCK publishes fiction, essays, poetry, plays, cartoons, and interviews.
Representative Authors: Jason Grote, Melanie Noel, and John Olson
Simultaneous Submissions: yes
Reading Period: 10/1 to 4/15
Reporting Time: one to five months
Author Payment: copies and subscription
Contests: Ecolit & Green Art annual contest. Deadline is May 1 each year; See website for guidelines.
Founded: 2003
Non Profit: yes
Paid Staff: two
Unpaid Staff: 10
ISSN Number/ISBN Number: ISSN 1551-5931
Total Circulation: 500
Paid Circulation: 45
Average Print Run: 500
Subscription Rate: Individual $16/Institution $20
Single copy Price: $9
Current Volume/Issue: 7
Frequency per Year: 2
Backfile Available: yes
Unsolicited Ms. Received: yes
% Unsolicited Ms. Published per Year: 10%
Format: perfect

Size: H 10" W 8.5"
Average Pages: 100
Ads: no

Organization: Konocti Books

Type: press
CLMP member: no
Primary Editor/Contact Person: Noel Peattie
Address: 23311 County Road 88
Winters, CA 95694
Publishes: poetry
Editorial Focus: Country poetry with depth.
Representative Authors: Doc Dachtler, Lynne Savitt, and Jane Blue
Submissions Policy: Presently inactive. Query with sample before sending.
Simultaneous Submissions: no
Reading Period: Year-round
Reporting Time: three to twelve weeks
Author Payment: copies
Founded: 1973
Non Profit: yes
Paid Staff: one
Unpaid Staff: zero
ISSN Number/ISBN Number: ISBN 0-914134
Number of Books Published per Year: one
Titles in Print: five
Average Percentage Printed: Paperback 100%

Organization: Konundrum Engine Literary Review

Type: online
CLMP member: no
Primary Editor/Contact Person: Pitchaya Sudbanthad
Address: 345 South End Ave, 6E
New York, NY 10280
Web Site Address: http://www.lit.konundrum.com
Publishes: essays, fiction, nonfiction, and poetry
Editorial Focus: Unique, kick-ass fiction and poetry by both new and established writers.
Representative Authors: Jim Shepard, Jonathan Lethem, and Oni Buchanan
Submissions Policy: Please visit our web site for guidelines.
Simultaneous Submissions: yes
Reading Period: Year-round
Reporting Time: one to four months
Author Payment: none

Founded: 2003
Non Profit: no
Paid Staff: zero
Unpaid Staff: four
Average Page Views per Month: 20,000
Average Unique Visitors per Month: 5,500
Frequency per Year: eight
Publish Print Anthology: no
Average Percentage of Pages per Category: Fiction 40%, Nonfiction 10%, Poetry 40%, Essays 10%

Organization: Kore Press

Type: press
CLMP member: yes
Primary Editor/Contact Person: Shannon Cain, Exec. Director
Address: P.O. Box 3044
Tucson, AZ 85702
Web Site Address: http://www.korepress.org
Publishes: fiction, nonfiction, and poetry
Editorial Focus: poetry, fiction and nonfiction by women, both emerging and established
Representative Authors: Alison Hawthorne Deming, Ofelia Zepeda, and Nancy Mairs
Simoltaneous Submissions: yes
Reading Period: Year-round
Reporting Time: two to four months
Author Payment: none
Contests: Annual Short Fiction chapbook Award: Annual First Book award in poetry (past judges: Sonia Sanchez, Carolyn Forche and others). See web site for Contest Guidelines
Founded: 1993
Non Profit: no
Paid Staff: three
Unpaid Staff: zero
Distributors: SPD
Number of Books Published per year: three to four
Titles in Print: 40
Average Print Run: 1,000
Average Percentage Printed: Paperback 50%, chapbook 25%, other 25%
Average price: $15

Organization: KRUPSKAYA

Type: press
CLMP member: no
Primary Editor/Contact Person: Jocelyn Saidenberg
Address: P.O. Box 420249
San Francisco, CA 94142-0249
Web Site Address: http://www.krupskayabooks.com
Publishes: fiction and poetry
Editorial Focus: Dedicated to publishing experimental poetry and prose. KRUPSKAYA is structured as a collective .
Representative Authors: Kevin Killian, Renee Gladman, and Stacy Doris
Submissions Policy: See web site for information.
Simultaneous Submissions: yes
Reading Period: Year-round
Reporting Time: four to six months
Author Payment: copies
Founded: 1998
Non Profit: yes
Paid Staff: zero
Unpaid Staff: three
Distributors: SPD
ISSN Number/ISBN Number: ISBN 1-928650-##-#
Number of Books Published per Year: two
Titles in Print: 26
Average Print Run: 750
Average Percentage Printed: Paperback 100%
Average Price: $14

Organization: La Alameda Press

Type: press
CLMP member: no
Primary Editor/Contact Person: J.B. Bryan
Address: 9636 Guadalupe Tr. NW
Albuquerque, NM 87114
Web Site Address: http://www.laalamedapress.com
Publishes: essays, fiction, nonfiction, and poetry
Editorial Focus: A micro-press. Beautiful books of artistic and cultural merit. Many, not all, titles are poetry-an essential art form.
Recent Awards Received: Anselm Hollo: Academy American Poet's 2004 Harold Morton Landon Translation Award, for Pentti Saarikoski's Trilogy (2003)
Representative Authors: Anselm Hollo, Kate Horsley, and Miriam Sagan
Submissions Policy: Sorry, we are not accepting manuscripts.
Simultaneous Submissions: no
Author Payment: copies
Founded: 1991
Non Profit: no
Paid Staff: two
Unpaid Staff: zero

Distributors: U of New Mexico Press, SPD
Wholesalers: Ingram's, Baker & Taylor, Blackwell's, etc
ISSN Number/ISBN Number: ISBN 0-9631909, 1-888809
Number of Books Published per Year: 2
Titles in Print: 48
Average Print Run: 1,000
Average Percentage Printed: Paperback 75%, Chapbook 25%
Average Price: $14

Organization: La Petite Zine

Type: online
CLMP member: yes
Primary Editor/Contact Person: Jeffrey Salane/Danielle Pafunda
Address: 270 5th St. #2E
Brooklyn, NY 11215
Web Site Address: http://lapetitezine.org
Publishes: essays, fiction, nonfiction, reviews, art, and translation
Editorial Focus: Established and new voices, which might be defined as "edgy," "rocking out," or "brilliant." To editors' subjective tastes.
Representative Authors: Heidi Lynn Staples, Joyelle McSweeney, and David Lehman
Submissions Policy: Submit via e-mail to lapetitezine@yahoo.com. For greater detail, see lapetitezine.org.
Simultaneous Submissions: yes
Reading Period: Year-round
Reporting Time: 6 to 10 weeks
Author Payment: none
Founded: 1998
Non Profit: yes
Paid Staff: no
Unpaid Staff: two
Backfile Available: yes
Average Page Views per Month: 100+
Average Unique Visitors per Month: 50+
Frequency per Year: triquarterly
Price: free
Average Percentage of Pages per Category: Fiction 20%, Nonfiction 5%, Poetry 60%, Reviews 5%, Art 10%
Ads: no

Organization: Lactuca

Type: magazine
CLMP member: no
Primary Editor/Contact Person: Mike Selender
Address: 159 Jewett Ave.
Jersey City, NJ 07304-2003
Publishes: fiction, poetry, reviews, art, and translation
Editorial Focus: Work with an sense of place or experience coming from an honest emotional depth.
Submissions Policy: Currently dormant. Query before sending work
Simultaneous Submissions: no
Reading Period: Year-round
Author Payment: copies
Founded: 1983
Non Profit: no
Paid Staff: zero
Unpaid Staff: one
ISSN Number/ISBN Number: ISSN 0896-8705
Frequency per Year: one
Backfile Available: yes
Unsolicited Ms. Received: yes
Format: stapled
Size: H 11 1/2" W 7"
Average Pages: 60
Ads: no

Organization: Lady Churchill's Rosebud Wristlet

Type: magazine
CLMP member: yes
Primary Editor/Contact Person: Gavin J. Grant
Address: 150 Pleasant St., Ste. 306
Easthampton, MA 01027
Website Address: http://www.lcrw.net/lcrw
Publishes: fiction, nonfiction, poetry, and translation
Recent Awards Received: Hugo Nomination
Representative Authors: Karen Joy Fowler, Marly Youmans, and Carol Emshwiller
Submissions Policy: We do not accept email, multiple, or simultaneous submissions. We tend toward speculative fiction but are not limited to it.
Simultaneous Submissions: no
Reading Period: Year-round
Reporting Time: three to four months
Author Payment: cash and copies
Founded: 1996
Non Profit: no
Paid Staff: three
Unpaid Staff: two
ISSN Number/ISBN Number: ISSN 1544-7782

Total Circulation: 750
Paid Circulation: 300
Average Print Run: 1,000
Subscription Rate: Individual $20/Institution $20
Single Copy Price: $5
Current Volume/Issue: 20
Frequency per Year: two
Backfile Available: yes
Unsolicited Ms. Received: yes
% Unsolicited Ms. Published per Year: 2%
Format: stapled
Size: H 8 1/2" W 7"
Average Pages: 60
Ads: yes
Ad Rates: http://lcrw.net/lcrw/rates.htm; see website for details

Organization: Lake Effect

Type: magazine
CLMP member: yes
Primary Editor/Contact Person: George Looney
Address: Penn State Erie
4951 College Drive
Erie, PA 16563-1501
Website Address: http://www.pserie.psu.edu/lakeeffect
Publishes: essays, fiction, nonfiction, and poetry
Editorial Focus: Writing that uses language with precision and a knowledge of craft to forge a genuine and rewarding experience.
Recent Awards Received: Edith Pearlman story reprinted in Best American Short Stories 2006.
Representative Authors: Edith Pearlman, T.R. Hummer, and David Kirby
Submissions Policy: Send three to five poems, one story (or several short shorts) or nonfiction piece to appropriate editor. Include SASE and cover letter.
Simultaneous Submissions: yes
Reading Period: Year-round
Reporting Time: one to four months
Author Payment: copies
Founded: 1978
Non Profit: yes
Paid Staff: zero
Unpaid Staff: 19
ISSN Number/ISBN Number: ISSN 1538-3105
Total Circulation: 800
Paid Circulation: 100
Average Print Run: 800
Subscription Rate: Individual $6/Institution $6

Single Copy Price: $6
Current Volume/Issue: 11
Frequency per Year: one
Backfile Available: yes
Unsolicited Ms. Received: yes
% of Unsolicited Ms. Published per Year: 7%
Format: perfect
Size: H 8 1/2" W 5 1/2"
Average Pages: 180
Ads: no

Organization: Lambda Book Report

Type: magazine
CLMP member: yes
Primary Editor/Contact Person: Charles Flowers
Address: P.O. Box 1957
Old Chelsea Station
New York, NY 10113
Website Address: http://www.lambdaliterary.org
Publishes: reviews
Editorial Focus: LBR is a review quarterly for LGBT books, featuring author interviews, calls for submissions, and more.
Representative Authors: Andrew Holleran, Michelle Tea, and Thomas Glave
Submissions Policy: Potential reviewers may approach LBR about review guidelines & ideas for articles.
Simultaneous Submissions: yes
Reading Period: year-round
Reporting Time: one to two months
Author Payment: copies and subscription
Founded: 1989
Non Profit: yes
Paid Staff: one
Unpaid Staff: six
ISSN Number/ISBN Number: ISSN 1048-9487
Total Circulation: 2,500
Paid Circulation: 1,800
Average Print Run: 2,500
Subscription Rate: Individual $30/Institution $39.95
Single Copy Price: $10
Current Volume/Issue: 15/2
Frequency per Year: four
Backfile Available: yes
Unsolicited Ms. Received: no
Format: stapled
Size: H 11" W 8 1/2"
Average Pages: 40-48
Ads: yes

Ad Rates: see website for details

Organization: The Land-Grant College Review

Type: magazine
CLMP member: no
Primary Editor/Contact Person: Dave Koch and Josh Melrod
Address: P.O. Box 1164
New York, NY 10159-1164
Web Site Address: http://www.lgcr.org
Publishes: fiction
Editorial Focus: The Land-Grant College Review publishes contemporary short stories.
Recent Awards Received: Utne Independent Press Award, Best American Non-Required Reading, O. Henry Awards
Representative Authors: Aimee Bender, Frederick Barthelme, and Padgett Powell
Submissions Policy: Send us only your very best work. Familiarize yourself with past issues to get an idea of the type of stories we like.
Simultaneous Submissions: yes
Reading Period: Year-round
Reporting Time: six to eight months
Author Payment: cash and copies
Contests: See web site for contest guidelines.
Founded: 2002
Non Profit: yes
Paid Staff: two
Unpaid Staff: eight
Distributors: DeBoer, Ingram
ISSN Number/ISBN Number: ISSN 0972867805
Total Circulation: 2,500
Paid Circulation: 750
Average Print Run: 2,500
Subscription Rate: Individual $18/Institution $45
Single Copy Price: $12
Current Volume/Issue: Issue three
Frequency per Year: one
Backfile Available: yes
Unsolicited Ms. Received: yes
% of Unsolicited Ms. Published per Year: 5%
Format: perfect
Size: H 9" W 6"
Average Pages: 200
Ads: no

Organization: Lapham's Quarterly

Type: magazine
CLMP member: yes
Primary Editor/Contact Person: Kira B. Don
Address: 33 Irving Place
8th Floor
New York, NY 10003
Web Site Address: http://www.LaphamsQuarterly.org
Publishes: essays, fiction, nonfiction, poetry, and art
Editorial Focus: LAPHAM'S QUARTERLY sets the story of the past in the frame of the present.
Representative Authors: Lewis H. Lapham, Mark Twain, and William Shakespeare
Submissions Policy: Lapham's Quarterly does not accept unsolicited original work.
Simultaneous Submissions: no
Reading Period: Year-round
Reporting Time: four to eight weeks
Author Payment: cash
Founded: 2007
Non Profit: yes
Paid Staff: 11
Unpaid Staff: two
Total Circulation: 18,000
Paid Circulation: n/a
Average Print Run: 18,000
Subscription Rate: Individual $60/Institution $60
Single Copy Price: $15
Current Volume/Issue: 1/1
Frequency per Year: four
Backfile Available: yes
Unsolicited Ms. Received: no
Format: perfect
Size: H 10" W 7"
Average Pages: 200
Ads: no

Organization: Latin American Literary Review Press

Type: press
CLMP member: no
Primary Editor/Contact Person: Yvette E. Miller
Address: P.O. Box 17660
Pittsburgh, PA 15235
Web Site Address: http://www.lalrp.org
Publishes: translation
Editorial Focus: Translations of Latin American Literature into English
Representative Authors: Pablo Neruda, Luisa Valenzuela, and Mempo Giardinelli
Submissions Policy: Translated Manuscripts Only.

Simultaneous Submissions: yes
Reading Period: Year-round
Reporting Time: up to 1 month
Author Payment: royalties and copies
Founded: 1980
Non Profit: yes
Paid Staff: three
Unpaid Staff: zero
Distributors: Bilingual Press
ISSN Number/ISBN Number: ISBN 1-891270
Number of Books Published per Year: 4
Titles in Print: 146
Average Print Run: 1,500
Average Percentage Printed: Hardcover 10%, Paperback 90%
Average Price: $15

Organization: Latin American Literary Review

Type: magazine
CLMP member: no
Primary Editor/Contact Person: Yvette E. Miller
Address: P.O. Box 17660
Pittsburgh, PA 15235
Web Site Address: http://www.lalrp.org
Publishes: essays and reviews
Editorial Focus: Critical journal for Latin American Literature
Submissions Policy: Please send subs on CD (not on 3.5 Mac diskette), saved in Word 5.0 or higher, Rich Text Format (.rtf, not .doc)
Simultaneous Submissions: no
Reading Period: Year-round
Reporting Time: four to seven months
Author Payment: none
Founded: 1980
Non Profit: yes
Paid Staff: three
Unpaid Staff: one
ISSN Number/ISBN Number: ISSN 0047
Total Circulation: 1,000
Paid Circulation: 750
Subscription Rate: Individual $27/Institution $49
Single Copy Price: $14
Current Volume/Issue: 35/69 and 70
Frequency per Year: two
Backfile Available: yes
Unsolicited Ms. Received: yes
% of Unsolicited Ms. Published per Year: 100%
Format: perfect

Size: H 9" W 6"
Average Pages: 150
Ads: yes
Ad Rates: Full Page, $260; Half Page, $150; Quarter Page, $80

Organization: The Laurel Review

Type: magazine
CLMP member: yes
Primary Editor/Contact Person: John Gallaher/Rebecca Aronson
Address: GreenTower Press
NW Missouri State U, Dept. of English
Maryville, MO 64468
Web Site Address: http://www.nwmissouri.edu/Dept/english/laurel.htm
Publishes: essays, fiction, nonfiction, poetry, reviews, and translation
Editorial Focus: Our focus is to present an eclectic mix of the best work.
Representative Authors: Angie Estes, Mary Ruefle, and Bin Ramke
Simultaneous Submissions: no
Reading Period: 9/1 to 5/1
Reporting Time: one to three months
Author Payment: copies and subscription
Contests: See web site for contest guidelines.
Founded: 1960
Non Profit: yes
Paid Staff: four
Unpaid Staff: four
Total Circulation: 600
Paid Circulation: 458
Average Print Run: 700
Subscription Rate: Individual $10/Institution $10
Single Copy Price: $7
Current Volume/Issue: 39/2
Frequency per Year: biannual
Backfile Available: yes
Unsolicited Ms. Received: yes
% of Unsolicited Ms. Published per Year: 3%
Format: perfect
Size: H 9" W 6"
Average Pages: 128
Ads: yes
Ad Rates: See web site for details.

Organization: Lazara Press

Type: press

CLMP member: no
Primary Editor/Contact Person: Penny Goldsmith
Address: Box 2269
VMPO
Vancouver, BC V5B 3W2
Web Site Address: http://www.lazarapress.ca
Publishes: essays, fiction, nonfiction, and poetry
Editorial Focus: Alternative, progressive literature and essays.
Representative Authors: Marusya Bociurkiw, Helen Potrebenko, and Elise Goldsmith
Simultaneous Submissions: yes
Reading Period: Year-round
Reporting Time: three to six months
Author Payment: royalties
Founded: 1982
Non Profit: yes
Paid Staff: zero
Unpaid Staff: one
ISSN Number/ISBN Number: ISBN 0-920999
Number of Books Published per Year: two
Titles in Print: 14
Average Print Run: 500
Average Percentage Printed: Paperback 20%, Chapbook 60%, Other 20%
Average Price: $12

Organization: The Left Curve Publications

Type: magazine
CLMP member: yes
Primary Editor/Contact Person: Csaba Polony
Address: P.O. Box 472
Oakland, CA 94604
Web Site Address: http://www.leftcurve.org
Publishes: essays, fiction, nonfiction, poetry, reviews, art, and translation
Editorial Focus: Artist-produced cultural journal that encourages non-institutional defetishized work (all forms) from a radical perspective.
Representative Authors: Amiri Baraka, Jack Hirschman, and devorah major
Simultaneous Submissions: no
Reading Period: Year-round
Reporting Time: one to six months
Author Payment: copies
Founded: 1974
Non Profit: yes
Paid Staff: zero
Unpaid Staff: 10

Distributors: Ingram, Source Interlink, DeBoer, Ubiquity
ISSN Number/ISBN Number: ISSN 0160-1857
Total Circulation: 1,900
Paid Circulation: 200
Subscription Rate: Individual $35/Institution $50
Single Copy Price: $12
Current Volume/Issue: Issue 31
Frequency per Year: one
Backfile Available: yes
Unsolicited Ms. Received: yes
% of Unsolicited Ms. Published per Year: 25%
Format: perfect
Size: H 11.5" W 8"
Average Pages: 144
Ads: yes
Ad Rates: full page $200, half-page $150, quarter-page $75

Organization: Leon Works

Type: press
CLMP member: no
Primary Editor/Contact Person: Renee Gladman
Address: Brown University
Box 1923
Providence, RI 02912
Web Site Address: www.leonworks.org
Publishes: essays, fiction and poetry
Editorial Focus: Leon Works focuses primarily on works of experimental prose and other thought projects based in the sentence.
Representative Authors: Mary Burger, Bhanu Kapil, and Melissa Buzzeo
Submissions Policy: Please inquire by email before submitting manuscripts.
Simultaneous Submissions: yes
Reading Period: year-round
Reporting Time: two to three months
Author Payment: copies
Founded: 2005
Non Profit: no
Distributors: Small Press Distribution
Number of Books Published per Year: one to two
Titles in Print: three
Average Print Run: 1,000
Average Percentage Printed: Paperback %100
Average Price: $14.95

Organization: Les Figues Press

Type: press

CLMP member: yes
Primary Editor/Contact Person: Teresa Carmody
Address: PO Box 35628
Los Angeles, CA 90035
Web Site Address: http://www.lesfigues.com
Publishes: fiction, poetry, art, and translation
Editorial Focus: Aesthetic-based annual series of experimental prose and poetry.
Representative Authors: Vanessa Place, Pam Ore, and Society for CUmln Linguistics
Submissions Policy: Check submissions' guidelines on our web site (under beauty tab). Aesthetic essay/poetics required.
Simultaneous Submissions: yes
Reading Period: year-round
Reporting Time: one to five months
Author Payment: royalties, copies, and subscription
Founded: 2005
Non Profit: yes
Paid Staff: zero
Unpaid Staff: two
Distributors: Small Press Distribution
ISSN Number/ISBN Number: ISBN 0-9766371
Number of Books Published per Year: five
Titles in Print: six
Average Print Run: 500
Average Percentage Printed: paperback 100%
Average Price: $15

Organization: Libellum

Type: press
CLMP member: yes
Primary Editor/Contact Person: Vincent Katz
Address: 211 West 19th Street, #5
New York, NY 10011
Web Site Address: http://www.vanitasmagazine.com
Publishes: essays and poetry
Editorial Focus: Libellum publishes poetry, essays, and criticism, as well as longer poems and hard-to-define texts.
Representative Authors: Michael Lally, Joanne Kyger, and Ed Sanders
Submissions Policy: Submissions are not accepted for Libellum.
Simultaneous Submissions: no
Reading Period: year-round
Reporting Time: two to six months
Author Payment: none
Founded: 2003

Non Profit: no
Paid Staff: two
Unpaid Staff: zero
Distributors: Small Press Distribution
Wholesalers: Fotofolio/Artpost
ISSN Number/ISBN Number: ISBN 0-9752993
Number of Books Published per Year: two
Titles in Print: two
Average Print Run: 500
Average Percentage Printed: Paperback 25%, Chapbook 75%
Average Price: $10

Organization: Lichen Arts & Letters Preview

Type: magazine
CLMP member: no
Primary Editor/Contact Person: The Editorial Board
Address: 234-701 Rossland Road East
Whitby, ON L1N 9K3
Web Site Address: http://www.lichenjournal.ca
Publishes: essays, fiction, nonfiction, poetry, reviews, and art
Editorial Focus: Each spring and fall, Lichen brings the best of new writing and artwork from Canada and abroad to readers, first.
Recent Awards Received: Grants from the Ontario Arts Council as well as The Ontario Trillium Foundation.
Representative Authors: George Elliott Clarke, Steven Heighton, and Robyn Sarah
Submissions Policy: Submit unpublished, original work in English:3-6 poems, or 1 short story (max. 3,000 words), or 1 essay (max. 1,500 words)
Simultaneous Submissions: no
Reading Period: Year-round
Reporting Time: four to six months
Author Payment: copies and subscription
Contests: "Tracking A Serial Poet" competition: Dec. 31 deadline. "Writing Between The Lines" fiction competition: July 31 deadline.
See web site for contest guidelines.
Founded: 1999
Non Profit: yes
Paid Staff: one
Unpaid Staff: 11
Distributors: Disticor Direct Inc.
ISSN Number/ISBN Number: ISSN 1488-1829
Total Circulation: 1,000
Paid Circulation: 400

Average Print Run: 1,000
Subscription Rate: Individual $19/Institution $19
Single Copy Price: $12
Current Volume/Issue: 7.2/Fall
Frequency per Year: two
Backfile Available: yes
Unsolicited Ms. Received: yes
% of Unsolicited Ms. Published per Year: 10%
Format: perfect
Size: H 8.25" W 5.25"
Average Pages: 144
Ads: yes
Ad Rates: Full: $200, 1/2: $110, 1/4: $60 (discounts available)
See web site for details.

Organization: The Licking River Review

Type: magazine
CLMP member: no
Primary Editor/Contact Person: P. Andrew Miller, Advisor
Address: Box 66 University Center
Northern Kentucky University
Highland Heights, KY 41099
Publishes: fiction and poetry
Editorial Focus: We take quality contemporary fiction and poetry. Seldom publish genre work like romance, SF/F.
Representative Authors: Mary Winters, Henryk Skwar, and Sam Vargo
Submissions Policy: Submit stories up to 25 pages and no more than five poems, 75 lines max, between 9/1-12/1 of each year.
Simultaneous Submissions: no
Reading Period: 9/1 to 12/1
Reporting Time: three to four months
Author Payment: copies
Founded: 1990
Non Profit: yes
Paid Staff: three
Unpaid Staff: six
Distributors: Northern Kentucky University
Total Circulation: 1,000
Paid Circulation: 20
Subscription Rate: Individual $5/Institution $5
Single Copy Price: $5
Frequency per Year: one
Backfile Available: yes
Unsolicited Ms. Received: yes

% of Unsolicited Ms. Published per Year: 5%
Format: perfect
Average Pages: 96

Organization: Light Quarterly

Type: magazine
CLMP member: yes
Primary Editor/Contact Person: John Mella
Address: P.O. Box 7500
Chicago, IL 60680
Web Site Address: http://www.lightquarterly.com
Publishes: essays, fiction, nonfiction, poetry, reviews, and art
Editorial Focus: Light Quarterly is the only publication in America to print Light Verse on an exclusive, regular basis.
Representative Authors: John Updike, X.J. Kennedy, and Tom Disch
Submissions Policy: one to six poems with SASE.
Simultaneous Submissions: no
Reading Period: Year-round
Reporting Time: one to six months
Author Payment: copies
Founded: 1992
Non Profit: no
Paid Staff: two
Unpaid Staff: zero
Distributors: DeBoer
ISSN Number/ISBN Number: ISSN 1064-8186
Total Circulation: 1,000
Paid Circulation: 650
Subscription Rate: Individual $20/Institution $20
Single Copy Price: $6
Current Volume/Issue: Issue 41
Frequency per Year: four
Unsolicited Ms. Received: yes
% of Unsolicited Ms. Published per Year: 8%
Format: perfect
Size: H 5-1/2" W 9"
Average Pages: 64
Ads: yes
Ad Rates: one page: $100, 1/2 page: $50

Organization: Lilies and Cannonballs Review

Type: magazine
CLMP member: yes
Primary Editor/Contact Person: Daniel Connor
Address: P.O. Box 702

Bowling Green Station
New York, NY 10274-0702
Web Site Address:
http://www.liliesandcannonballs.com
Publishes: essays, fiction, nonfiction, poetry, art, and translation
Editorial Focus: Aesthetically driven and socially conscious; traditional and experimental; crazy-man conservative and bleeding liberal
Representative Authors: John Bradley, James Doyle, and Lynn Crawford
Submissions Policy: Poetry: no more than four poems. Prose: 8,000 words max. Include SASE.
Simultaneous Submissions: yes
Reading Period: 5/1 to 7/1
Reporting Time: one to six months
Author Payment: copies
Founded: 2004
Non Profit: no
Paid Staff: zero
Unpaid Staff: five
Distributors: DeBoer
ISSN Number/ISBN Number: ISSN 1548-8365
Total Circulation: 475
Paid Circulation: 75
Average Print Run: 550
Subscription Rate: Individual $23/Institution $28
Single Copy Price: $12
Current Volume/Issue: 3/1
Frequency per Year: one
Backfile Available: yes
Unsolicited Ms. Received: yes
% of Unsolicited Ms. Published per Year: 10%
Format: perfect
Size: H 9" W 6"
Average Pages: 96
Ads: yes
Ad Rates: See web site for details.

Organization: Lilith Magazine

Type: magazine
CLMP member: yes
Primary Editor/Contact Person: Susan Weidman Schneider
Address: 250 W. 57th St., Ste. 2432
New York, NY 10107
Web Site Address: http://www.lilith.org
Publishes: essays, fiction, nonfiction, poetry, reviews, art, translation, and audio
Editorial Focus: Jewish women's issues from a feminist perspective; general women's issues through a Jewish lens.
Recent Awards Received: Indeppendent Press Associations Awards; Jewish Press Association Rockower Awards; Womens E-News 21st Century Leaders Award
Representative Authors: Dara Horn, Cynthia Ozick, and Myla Goldberg
Submissions Policy: Inform with ms if this is a simultaneous submission; further details for submitting are up on our website.
Simultaneous Submissions: yes
Reading Period: Year-round
Reporting Time: three to four months
Author Payment: cash
Contests: Poetry Contest for the anuual Charlotte Newberger Poetry Prize; Annual Lilith Fiction Contest; see website for guidelines.
Founded: 1976
Non Profit: yes
Paid Staff: six
Unpaid Staff: zero
Distributors: Ingram, Ubiquity, Don Olsen, Armadillo, Kent News
ISSN Number/ISBN Number: ISSN 0146-2334
Total Circulation: 10,000
Paid Circulation: 5,500
Average Print Run: 10,000
Subscription Rate: Individual $24.95/Institution $30.00
Single Copy Price: $4.95
Current Volume/Issue: 32/2
Frequency per Year: four
Backfile Available: yes
Unsolicited Ms. Received: yes
% of Unsolicited Ms. Published per Year: 50%
Format: stapled
Size: H 11" W 8 1/2"
Average Pages: 48
Ads: yes
Ad Rates: See website for details

Organization: Lips

Type: magazine
CLMP member: yes
Primary Editor/Contact Person: Laura Boss
Address: 7002 Blvd., #2-26G
Guttenberg, NJ 07093
Publishes: poetry
Editorial Focus: Strong poetry that is accessible and

has impact

Representative Authors: Allen Ginsberg, Ruth Stone, and Michael Benedikt

Submissions Policy: Send five poems, SASE

Simultaneous Submissions: no

Reading Period: 9/4 to 3/5

Reporting Time: three to six months

Author Payment: copies

Founded: 1981

Non Profit: no

Paid Staff: zero

Unpaid Staff: one

ISSN Number/ISBN Number: ISSN 0278-0933

Total Circulation: 2,000

Paid Circulation: 40

Average Print Run: 2,000

Subscription Rate: Individual $15/Institution $18

Single Copy Price: $10

Current Volume/Issue: Issue 29

Frequency per Year: two

Backfile Available: yes

Unsolicited Ms. Received: yes

% of Unsolicited Ms. Published per Year: 5%

Format: perfect

Size: H 8.5" W 5.5"

Average Pages: 154

Ads: yes

Ad Rates: $300

Organization: Lit Magazine

Type: magazine

CLMP member: yes

Primary Editor/Contact Person: Justin Marks

Address: New School Writing Program Rm. 514
66 W. 12th St.
New York, NY 10011

Web Site Address: lit-magazine.blogspot.com/

Publishes: essays, fiction, nonfiction, and poetry

Submissions Policy: We read from October to December and January to May. Submit five poems or 10 pages of poetry; up to 25 double-spaced pages of prose.

Simultaneous Submissions: yes

Reading Period: 10/12 to 1/5

Reporting Time: one to four months

Author Payment: copies

Founded: 1999

Non Profit: no

Paid Staff: zero

Unpaid Staff: 25

Distributors: Bernhard DeBoer

Total Circulation: 1,000

Paid Circulation: 15

Average Print Run: 1,000

Subscription Rate: individual $14/institution $8

Single Copy Price: $8

Current Volume/Issue: 6/11

Frequency per year: biannual

Backfile Available: yes

Unsolicited MSS Received: yes

% of Unsolicited MSS Published per year: 60%

Format: perfect

Average Pages: 250

Ads: no

Organization: Literal Latte

Type: press

CLMP member: no

Primary Editor/Contact Person: Jenine Gordon Bockman

Address: 61 E. 8th St., Ste. 240
New York, NY 10003

Web Site Address: http://www.literal-latte.com

Publishes: essays, fiction, nonfiction, poetry, reviews, and art

Editorial Focus: Mind stimulating words-all styles and subjects.

Submissions Policy: Stories/essays up to 6,000 words. Poems/plays up to 2,000 words. Send with SASE or e-mail for reply.

Simultaneous Submissions: yes

Reading Period: Year-round

Reporting Time: three to six months

Author Payment: copies and subscription

Contests: Fiction Awards; Poetry Awards; Essay Awards; Food Verse Contest; Short Shorts Contest See web site for contest guidelines.

Founded: 1994

Non Profit: no

Paid Staff: zero

Unpaid Staff: one

Average Percentage Printed: Other 100%

Backfile Available: yes

Organization: Literal, Latin American Voices

Type: magazine

CLMP member: yes

Primary Editor/Contact Person: Rose Mary Salum

Address: 770 S. Post Oak Ln., Ste. 530 Houston, TX 77056

Web Site Address: http://www.literalmagazine.com

Publishes: essays, fiction, nonfiction, poetry, reviews, art, and translation

Recent Awards Received: Two CELJ Awards for the best literary magazine in 2006, and a runner-up in 2005. Three Lone Star Awards.

Representative Authors: Mario Vargas Llosa, George Steiner, and Sandra Cisneros

Submissions Policy: Via regular mail. Only articles accepted will get notified.

Simultaneous Submissions: no

Reading Period: Year-round

Reporting Time: one to six months

Author Payment: copies and subscription

Founded: 2004

Non Profit: no

Paid Staff: two

Unpaid Staff: six

Distributors: Ingram and Ubiquity in the US and Alieri in Mexico

ISSN Number/ISBN Number: ISSN 1551-6962

Total Circulation: 10,000

Paid Circulation: 200

Average Print Run: 10,000

Subscription Rate: Individual $18/Institution $28

Single Copy Price: $4.50

Current Volume/Issue: 1/10

Frequency per Year: quarterly

Backfile Available: yes

Unsolicited Ms. Received: yes

% of Unsolicited Ms. Published per Year: 20%

Format: perfect

Average Pages: 54

Ad Rates: $500, $800 and $1,500; See web site for details.

Organization: Literary Imagination

Type: magazine

CLMP member: yes

Primary Editor/Contact Person: Sarah Spence, Editor

Address: Classics, 221 Park Hall University of Georgia Athens, GA 30602-6203

Web Site Address: http://www.bu.edu/literary

Publishes: essays, fiction, poetry, reviews, and translation

Editorial Focus: Works that explore and celebrate the literary imagination.

Recent Awards Received: 2005 Pushcart to Geoffrey Hill, contributor to 6.2 (Spring 2004) "On the Reality of the Symbol" (poem)

Representative Authors: Clare Cavanagh, Anne Ferry, and Karl Kirchwey

Submissions Policy: Cannot consider submissions sent by fax or e-mail.

Simultaneous Submissions: no

Reading Period: Year-round

Reporting Time: one to two months

Author Payment: none

Contests: none

Founded: 1999

Non Profit: yes

Paid Staff: three

Unpaid Staff: zero

Distributors: Ingram

ISSN Number/ISBN Number: 1523-9012

Total Circulation: 1,604

Paid Circulation: 121

Average Print Run: 2,133

Subscription Rate: Individual $25/Institution $60 in US

Single Copy Price: $8.95+

Current Volume/Issue: 7/2

Frequency per Year: triquarterly

Backfile Available: yes

Unsolicited Ms. Received: yes

% of Unsolicited Ms. Published per Year: 85%

Format: perfect

Size: H 10" W 7"

Average Pages: 160

Ads: yes

Ad Rates: Advertising available to members and their publishers. See web site for details.

Organization: Literary Mama

Type: online

CLMP member: no

Address: University of South Carolina Department of English Columbia, SC 29208

Web Site Address: http://www.literarymama.com

Publishes: essays, fiction, nonfiction, poetry, and reviews

Reading Period: Year-round

Reporting Time: one to two months

Author Payment: none

Founded: 2003
Non Profit: yes
Backfile Available: yes
Average Percentage of Pages per Category: Audio
100%

Organization: The Literary Review

Type: magazine
CLMP member: yes
Primary Editor/Contact Person: Walter Cummins
Address: 285 Madison Ave.
Madison, NJ 07940
Web Site Address: http://www.theliteraryreview.org/
Publishes: essays, fiction, nonfiction, poetry, reviews,
and translation
Editorial Focus: We publish writing from around the
world in translation, as well as new contemporary
American authors.
Representative Authors: Jeffery Allen, Thomas E.
Kennedy, and Douglas A. Martin
Submissions Policy: Poetry: submit up to six poems
at a time; Fiction: one story 10-20 pgs; contemporary
reviews and essays
Simultaneous Submissions: yes
Reading Period: 9/1 to 1/31
Reporting Time: three to four months
Author Payment: copies and subscription
Founded: 1957
Non Profit: yes
Paid Staff: four
Unpaid Staff: six
Distributors: Ingram; Media Solutions
Total Circulation: 2,000
Paid Circulation: 800
Average Print Run: 2,000
Subscription Rate: Individual $18/Institution $18
Single Copy Price: $7
Current Volume/Issue: 50/3
Frequency per Year: quarterly
Backfile Available: yes
Unsolicited Ms. Received: yes
% of Unsolicited Ms. Published per Year: 1.5%
Format: perfect
Size: H 9" W 6"
Average Pages: 175
Ads: no

Organization: Litmus Press

Type: press
CLMP member: yes
Primary Editor/Contact Person: E. Tracy Grinnell
Address: P.O. Box 25526
Brooklyn, NY 11202-5526
Web Site Address: http://www.litmuspress.org
Publishes: essays, fiction, nonfiction, and poetry
Editorial Focus: Established and emerging poets in
the experimental tradition and poetry/writing in trans-
lation.
Representative Authors: Keith Waldrop, Danielle
Collobert (in trans.), and Stacy Szymaszek
Submissions Policy: MS must be accompanied by
cover letter and current contact information. Please
query before submitting MS.
Simultaneous Submissions: yes
Reading Period: Year-round
Reporting Time: one to three months
Author Payment: copies
Founded: 2000
Non Profit: yes
Paid Staff: zero
Unpaid Staff: one
Distributors: SPD
Number of Books Published per Year: two
Titles in Print: 11
Average Print Run: 700
Average Percentage Printed: Paperback 100%
Average Price: $12

Organization: Little Pear Press

Type: press
CLMP member: no
Primary Editor/Contact Person: Martha Manno
Address: P.O. Box 343
Seekonk, MA 02771
Web Site Address: http://www.littlepearpress.com
Publishes: fiction, nonfiction, and poetry
Editorial Focus: Poetry and fiction. We also have one
title that is children's fiction.
Representative Authors: Mary E. Finger and Barbara
Schweitzer
Submissions Policy: Prefer submissions by regular
mail, will consider email. Please do not send newspa-
per clippings or promotional materials.
Simultaneous Submissions: yes
Reading Period: Year-round
Reporting Time: two to three months
Author Payment: royalties, cash, andcopies
Founded: 2003
Non Profit: no

Paid Staff: two
Unpaid Staff: zero
ISSN Number/ISBN Number: ISBN 0974
Number of Books Published per Year: one to two
Titles in Print: two
Average Print Run: 1,500
Average Percentage Printed: Paperback 100%
Average Price: $15

Organization: LiturgicalCredo.com

Type: online
CLMP member: yes
Primary Editor/Contact Person: Colin Burch
Address: 104 Holly Lane
Myrtle Beach, SC 29572
Web Site Address: http://www.liturgicalcredo.com
Publishes: essays, fiction, nonfiction, poetry, reviews, and art
Editorial Focus: Exploring ther intersections of liturgical religion with the arts, history, and ideas.
Representative Authors: D.S. Martin, Peter Reinhart, and Byron Harris
Submissions Policy: Essays, reviews, poetry, fiction, and photos with a relationship to liturgical faith. Submit to colin@liturgicalcredo.com
Simultaneous Submissions: no
Reading Period: Year-round
Reporting Time: four to six weeks
Author Payment: cash
Founded: 2006
Non Profit: no
Paid Staff: zero
Unpaid Staff: two
Average Page Views per Month: 69
Average Unique Visitors per Month: 25
Frequency per Year: 6
Publish Print Anthology: no
Average Percentage of Pages per Category:
Nonfiction 20%, Poetry 20%, Reviews 20%, Essays 20%, Art 20%

Organization: Living Forge

Type: magazine
CLMP member: yes
Primary Editor/Contact Person: Jerod J. Sikorskyj
Address: c/o Jerod J. Sikorskyj
43 Crescent Ave, Upper
Buffalo, NY 14214
Web Site Address: http://www.livingforge.com

Publishes: essays, fiction, nonfiction, poetry, reviews, art, audio, and video
Editorial Focus: Creative and critical work focusing on: Rustbelt, Rustbelt Diaspora, Great Lakes, industrial United States, developing world.
Representative Authors: Will Watson, Mark Nowak, and Carolyn Kraus
Submissions Policy: E-mail submissions (MS Word or Rich Text Document) to submissions@livingforge.com. Artwork = 300dpi min. Hardcopy accepted, SASE
Simultaneous Submissions: no
Reading Period: Year-round
Reporting Time: one to two months
Author Payment: copies
Founded: 2002
Non Profit: yes
Paid Staff: zero
Unpaid Staff: three
Distributors: Distributed privately to Rustbelt region
ISSN Number/ISBN Number: 1545-7176/1-932-583-(05/22)-x
Total Circulation: 500
Average Print Run: 500
Subscription Rate: Individual $10/Institution $15
Single Copy Price: $10
Current Volume/Issue: 3/1
Frequency per Year: annual
Backfile Available: yes
Unsolicited Ms. Received: yes
% of Unsolicited Ms. Published per Year: 50%
Format: perfect
Size: H 8.5" W 5.5"
Average Pages: 150
Ads: no

Organization: Living Forge

Type: press
CLMP member: yes
Primary Editor/Contact Person:
K.Ernst/J.Senchyne/J.Sikorskyj
Address: c/o Jerod J. Sikorskyj
43 Crescent Ave, Upper
Buffalo, NY 14214
Web Site Address: http://www.livingforge.com
Publishes: essays, fiction, nonfiction, poetry, reviews, art, audio, and video
Editorial Focus: Class studies (Creative/critical work): Rustbelt, Rustbelt Diaspora, Great Lakes, industrial United States, developing world
Recent Awards Received: N/A

Representative Authors: Will Watson, Mark Nowak, and Carolyn Kraus
Submissions Policy: E-mail submissions to submissions@livingforge.com(MS Word or Rich Text Document). Artwork = 300dpi min. Hardcopy accepted, SASE
Simultaneous Submissions: no
Reading Period: Year-round
Reporting Time: one to two months
Author Payment: copies
Founded: 2002
Non Profit: yes
Paid Staff: zero
Unpaid Staff: three
Distributors: Distributed privately to Rustbelt region
ISSN Number/ISBN Number: 1545-7176/1-932-583-(05/22)-x
Number of Books Published per Year: one
Titles in Print: two
Average Print Run: 500
Average Percentage Printed: Paperback 100%
Average Price: $10 w/CD

Organization: Livingston Press

Type: press
CLMP member: yes
Primary Editor/Contact Person: Joe Taylor
Address: Station 22
University of West Alabama
Livingston, AL 35470
Web Site Address:
http://www.livingstonpress.uwa.edu
Publishes: fiction
Editorial Focus: We are especially interested in form as it affects novels and story collections.
Representative Authors: Suzanne Hudson, Tom Abrams, and Corey Mesler
Submissions Policy: Send only in May, except for Tartt Award entries. If familiar with our line, send entire work; otherwise, send 30 pages.
Simultaneous Submissions: yes
Reading Period: 5/1 to 6/1
Reporting Time: three to five months
Author Payment: royalties and copies
Contests: Tartt First Fiction Award for story collections by an author who has yet to publish such. See Web Site for contest guidelines.
Founded: 1982
Non Profit: yes
Paid Staff: four

Unpaid Staff: five
Wholesalers: Ingram, Baker & Taylor, Brodart, Blackwell, Yankee
ISSN Number/ISBN Number: ISBN 1-931982
Number of Books Published per Year: 11
Titles in Print: 95
Average Print Run: 2,000
Average Percentage Printed: Hardcover 50%, Paperback 50%
Average Price: $20

Organization: The Long Story

Type: magazine
CLMP member: no
Primary Editor/Contact Person: R.P. Burnham
Address: 18 Eaton St.
Lawrence, MA 01843
Web Site Address:
http://web.mac.com/rpburnham/iWeb/Site/LongStory.html
Publishes: fiction and poetry
Editorial Focus: stories 8,000-20,000 words with thematic emphasis
Submissions Policy: include SASE, no electronic submissions; no unsolicited poetry
Simultaneous Submissions: yes
Reading Period: Year-round
Reporting Time: six to eight weeks
Author Payment: none
Founded: 1982
Non Profit: yes
Paid Staff: zero
Unpaid Staff: two
Distributors: Ingram
ISSN Number/ISBN Number: ISSN 0741-4242
Total Circulation: 800
Paid Circulation: 50
Average Print Run: 1,000
Subscription Rate: Individual $12/Institution $14
Single Copy Price: $7
Current Volume/Issue: Issue 25
Frequency per Year: annual
Backfile Available: yes
Unsolicited Ms. Received: yes
% of Unsolicited Ms. Published per Year: 2%
Format: perfect
Size: H 8.5" W 5.5"
Average Pages: 160
Ads: no

E. Tracy Grinnell
Founding Editor, Litmus Press and Aufgabe

How did you arrive at your current position?
I founded Litmus Press in 2001 with the publication of the first issue of *Aufgabe*, a journal of innovative poetry and translation. I worked on the first issue during graduate school, where I met Paul Foster Johnson, Mark Tardi and Rachel Bers who are now co-editors at Litmus. Over the past few years, we have acquired nonprofit status and created distinct editorial areas of focus.

What is the staff structure at your press/magazine?
At this time Litmus Press is run entirely by volunteers. Paul Foster Johnson is co-editor of *American Poetry* (both for the single author volumes and *Aufgabe*); Mark Tardi edits the review section of *Aufgabe* and Rachel Bers is art editor for the press. Julian T. Brolaski provides editorial and organizational assistance. We are also dependent on interns and other volunteers to keep things going.

What challenges do you face as a publisher?
Sustainability and distribution.

Do you have any cover letter advice?
Write one. Briefly introduce yourself and the work; keep it simple and straightforward. Tell us why you're sending it to Litmus Press rather than the next press on the list.

What do you look for in a submission?
A sense that the writer is acquainted with the press, our particular aesthetic and our aims. We read a range of work but we are interested in innovative and cross-genre work that is operating within an avant-garde tradition.

How are submissions processed at your press/magazine?
We accept only print submissions at this time. We read all submissions to *Aufgabe* within our annual January-February reading period. Each submission is discussed individually and in relation to the other work we receive. Essays and reviews are read separately and are often solicited by the reviews editor, though unsolicited work is welcome. For our full-length volumes, we hold open reading periods (roughly every other year) from which we select two or three manuscripts. Proposals for translated work are accepted on a rolling basis. We hold periodic editorial meetings to discuss specific manuscripts and projects as well as long-term goals/visions.

Do you have a favorite unsolicited submission discovery or anecdote?
All of the work we publish is the product of a certain amount of serendipity. Kate Colby's manuscript for *Fruitlands* was sent unsolicited and it won the 2007 Norma Farber First Book Award from the Poetry Society of America, which is of course very exciting for everyone concerned. But all of our publications have led to very rich and productive relationships with authors and other editors; we would not be where we are without the generous and proactive community of writers collected under the Litmus Press umbrella.

Staff of Litmus Press. From left to right: Rachel Bers, Paul Foster Johnson, E. Tracy Grinnell, Mark Tardi.

What advice do you have for first-time submitters?

In addition to my cover letter advice, I would add that part of our mission is to facilitate a poetic and critical dialogue on local, national and international levels, so that when sending work to Litmus Press or *Aufgabe* you demonstrate not only an awareness of but a sensitivity and commitment to that dialogue.

What are your long-term plans for your magazine/press?

To stay small and focused. To survive long-term.

What's your evaluation of the current literary landscape?

From my editorial standpoint, I can say that we are generally faced with the good problem of not being able to publish everything we would like to see published. The proliferation of small presses and publications is exciting because it means that even if we are not able to publish something, the work has a very good chance of making it into print with one of our small-press peers. The small-press community is very vibrant because it is (mostly) made up of writer-editors who are not only dedicated publishers but who also understand writing from the inside out and therefore understand the value of lively exchanges of ideas over financial rewards. We have recently begun collaborating and sharing ideas and resources with other small presses in ways that contribute to mutual sustainability, building a web-like structure that is based not on competition but on a shared vision of a diverse, dynamic and progressive literary culture.

Organization: Lost Horse Press

Type: press
CLMP member: yes
Primary Editor/Contact Person: Christine Holbert
Address: 105 Lost Horse Ln.
Sandpoint, ID 83864-8609
Web Site Address: http://www.losthorsepress.org
Publishes: poetry
Editorial Focus: LHP publishes poetry titles of high literary merit, and makes available other fine contemporary literature.
Recent Awards Received: Montana Book of the Year/Poetry, ForeWord Book of the Year/Poetry, IPPY Silver Award/Poetry
Representative Authors: Valerie Martin, Robert Pack, and Patricia Goedicke
Submissions Policy: Please check submissions policy at the LHP web site at http://www.losthorsepress.org.
Simultaneous Submissions: yes
Reading Period: Year-round
Reporting Time: 6 to 9 months
Author Payment: cash
Contests: The Idaho Prize for Poetry; See web site for contest guidelines.
Founded: 1998
Non Profit: yes
Paid Staff: zero
Unpaid Staff: two
Distributors: SPD
ISSN Number/ISBN Number: 0-9717265-/0-9668612-
Number of Books Published per Year: four
Titles in Print: 28
Average Print Run: 1,000
Average Percentage Printed: Hardcover 1%, Paperback 99%
Average Price: $16.95

Organization: Lotus Press, Inc.

Type: press
CLMP member: yes
Primary Editor/Contact Person: Naomi Madgett
Address: P.O. Box 21607
Detroit, MI 48221-0607
Web Site Address: http://www.lotuspress.org
Publishes: poetry
Editorial Focus: No preference in style or subject matter. Literary excellence and good taste are only criteria.

Recent Awards Received: 2007 Naomi Long Madgett Poetry Award received by Nagueyalti Warren for her manuscript, MARGARET.
Representative Authors: Remica L. Bingham, Carolyn Beard Whitlow, and Naomi Long Madgett.
Submissions Policy: No unsolicited manuscripts except award entries. Guidelines available on web site, by e-mail, or SASE
Simultaneous Submissions: no
Reading Period: 1/2 to 3/31
Reporting Time: two to three months
Author Payment: cash and copies
Contests: Naomi Long Madgett Poetry Awards open to African American poets. Judge varies annually. Winner receives $500 and publication. No fee.
Founded: 1972
Non Profit: yes
Paid Staff: zero
Unpaid Staff: three
Distributors: various
Wholesalers: various
ISSN Number/ISBN Number: 978-0-9797509/0-916418
Number of Books Published per Year: one to two
Titles in Print: 65
Average Print Run: 800
Average Percentage Printed: Hardcover 1%, Paperback 98%, Other 1%
Average Price: $17

Organization: Louisiana Literature

Type: magazine
CLMP member: yes
Primary Editor/Contact Person: Jack B. Bedell
Address: SLU Box 10792
Hammond, LA 70402-0792
Web Site Address: http://www.louisianaliterature.org
Publishes: fiction, poetry, and reviews
Editorial Focus: We strive to publish the highest quality creative work we receive. Our readers' focus is always on craft.
Representative Authors: Robert Olen Butler, Vivian Shipley, and Virgil Suarez
Submissions Policy: Submission guidelines are available on our web site.
Simultaneous Submissions: no
Reading Period: Year-round
Reporting Time: one to two months
Author Payment: copies and subscription
Contests: See web site for contest guidelines.

Founded: 1984
Non Profit: yes
Paid Staff: five
Unpaid Staff: two
ISSN Number/ISBN Number: ISSN 0890-0477
Total Circulation: 1,200
Paid Circulation: 400
Average Print Run: 1,500
Subscription Rate: Individual $12/Institution $18
Single Copy Price: $8
Current Volume/Issue: 20/1
Frequency per Year: biannual
Backfile Available: yes
Unsolicited Ms. Received: yes
% of Unsolicited Ms. Published per Year: 5%
Format: perfect
Size: H 9" W 6"
Average Pages: 146
Ads: yes
Ad Rates: By exchange only.

Organization: The Louisville Review/Fleur-de-Lis Press

Type: magazine
CLMP member: yes
Primary Editor/Contact Person: Kathleen Driskell
Address: Spalding University
851 S. Fourth St.
Louisville, KY 40203
Web Site Address: http://www.louisvillereview.org
Publishes: essays, fiction, nonfiction, and poetry
Submissions Policy: Unpublished manuscripts w/ self-addressed, stamped envelope for reply only. No electronic submissions. Guidelines on web site.
Simultaneous Submissions: yes
Reading Period: Year-round
Reporting Time: four to six months
Author Payment: none
Founded: 1976
Non Profit: yes
Paid Staff: zero
Unpaid Staff: five
Total Circulation: 1,000
Paid Circulation: 85%
Average Print Run: 700
Subscription Rate: Individual $14/Institution $14
Single Copy Price: $8
Current Volume/Issue: Issue 58
Frequency per Year: biannual
Backfile Available: yes

Unsolicited Ms. Received: yes
% of Unsolicited Ms. Published per Year: 95%
Format: perfect
Size: H 8.5" W 5.5"
Average Pages: 160+

Organization: Lullwater Review

Type: press
CLMP member: no
Primary Editor/Contact Person: Nina Wainwright
Address: P.O. Box 22036
Emory University
Atlanta, GA 30322
Publishes: essays, fiction, and poetry
Editorial Focus: none
Representative Authors: Lyn Lifshin, Arthur Gottlieb, and Julian Edney
Submissions Policy: No more than six poems, of any length or subject. No genre writing. Fiction must be limited to 5,000 words
Simultaneous Submissions: yes
Reading Period: 8/5 to 3/4
Reporting Time: three to five months
Author Payment: copies
Founded: 1990
Non Profit: yes
Paid Staff: zero
Unpaid Staff: 15
ISSN Number/ISBN Number: ISSN 1051-5968
Number of Books Published per Year: two
Titles in Print: 25
Average Percentage Printed: Paperback 100%

Organization: Lumen Books

Type: press
CLMP member: yes
Primary Editor/Contact Person: Ronald Christ
Address: 40 Camino Cielo
Santa Fe, NM 87506-2115
Publishes: essays, fiction, nonfiction, poetry, and translation
Editorial Focus: Literature in translation, especially from Spain and Latin America, as well as architecture and design, chiefly digital.
Recent Awards Received: Book of the Year Finalist, Kayden National Translation Award
Representative Authors: Diamela Eltit, Paul West, and Dennis Dollens
Submissions Policy: Inquiry previous to submission;

for translations: permission of copyright holder, original and sample (15 pages)
Simultaneous Submissions: no
Reading Period: year-round
Reporting Time: three to six months
Author Payment: royalties and cash
Founded: 1978
Non Profit: yes
Paid Staff: zero
Unpaid Staff: .5
Distributors: Consortium Book Sales and Distribution
ISSN Number/ISBN Number: ISBN 0978-0-930829
Number of Books Published per Year: two
Titles in Print: 45
Average Print Run: 1,500
Average Percentage Printed: Hardcover 10%, Paperback 90%
Average Price: $17

Organization: Luna Bisonte Prods

Type: press
CLMP member: no
Primary Editor/Contact Person: John M. Bennett
Address: 137 Leland Ave.
Columbus, OH 43214
Website Address: http://www.johnmbennett.net
Publishes: poetry, art, translation, and audio
Editorial Focus: Highly experimental and avant-garde poetry, visual poetry, new forms and processes
Representative Authors: Al Ackerman, Jim Leftwich, and John M. Bennett
Submissions Policy: Only by solicitation, but it doesn't hurt to send stuff. Include SASE.
Simultaneous Submissions: no
Reading Period: year-round
Reporting Time: 1 to 50 weeks
Author Payment: copies
Founded: 1974
Non Profit: yes
Paid Staff: zero
Unpaid Staff: 2
Distributors: Printed Matter, some bookstores
Number of Books Published per Year: ten
Titles in Print: 150
Average Print Run: 200
Average Percentage Printed: Paperback 25%, Chapbook 50%, Other 25%
Average Price: $9

Organization: LUNGFULL!magazine

Type: magazine
CLMP member: no
Primary Editor/Contact Person: Brendan Lorber
Address: 316 23rd St.
Brooklyn, NY 11215
Web Site Address: http://lungfull.org
Publishes: poetry and art
Editorial Focus: We print the rough draft of contributors' writing in addition to the final version so you can see the creative process.
Representative Authors: Alice Notley, Noelle Kocot, and Bill Kushner
Submissions Policy: Please read a copy before sending. Mentioning in your cover letter why you want to be in the journal is always nice.
Simultaneous Submissions: yes
Reading Period: Year-round
Reporting Time: 6 to 24 months
Author Payment: copies
Founded: 1994
Non Profit: no
Paid Staff: zero
Unpaid Staff: nine
Distributors: Ubiquity, DeBoer
Total Circulation: 1,200
Paid Circulation: 150
Average Print Run: 1,200
Subscription Rate: Individual $39.80/Institution $50
Single Copy Price: $11.50
Current Volume/Issue: Issue 15
Frequency per Year: annual
Backfile Available: yes
Unsolicited Ms. Received: yes
% of Unsolicited Ms. Published per Year: 2%
Format: perfect
Size: H 8.5" W 7"
Average Pages: 210
Ads: yes
Ad Rates: See web site for details.

Organization: Lyric Poetry Review

Type: magazine
CLMP member: yes
Primary Editor/Contact Person: Mira Rosenthal
Address: P.O. Box 2494
Bloomington, IN 47403
Web Site Address: http://www.lyricreview.org
Publishes: essays, fiction, nonfiction, poetry, reviews, and translation

Editorial Focus: Independent international journal of poetry and creative exchange.

Recent Awards Received: Best American Poetry 2004, Pushcart Prize 2004, Pushcart Prize 2006

Representative Authors: Mark Doty, Lucille Clifton, and Marilyn Hacker

Submissions Policy: We work hard to present newer writers along with more established figures. Unpublished work only.

Simultaneous Submissions: yes

Reading Period: Year-round

Reporting Time: one to four months

Author Payment: copies

Founded: 2000

Non Profit: yes

Paid Staff: zero

Unpaid Staff: five

Distributors: DeBoer

ISSN Number/ISBN Number: ISSN 1533-1776

Total Circulation: 600

Paid Circulation: 200

Average Print Run: 1,000

Subscription Rate: Individual $14/Institution $30

Single Copy Price: $8

Current Volume/Issue: 5/1

Frequency per Year: biannual

Backfile Available: yes

Unsolicited Ms. Received: yes

% of Unsolicited Ms. Published per Year: 5%

Format: perfect

Size: H 8.5" W 5"

Average Pages: 96

Ads: yes

Ad Rates: Swap with other Lit Mags; See web site for details.

Organization: The MacGuffin

Type: magazine

CLMP member: yes

Primary Editor/Contact Person: Steven A. Dolgin

Address: 18600 Haggerty Road
Livonia, MI 48152-2696

Web Site Address:
http://www.schoolcraft.edu/macguffin

Publishes: essays, fiction, nonfiction, poetry, and art

Editorial Focus: No religious, inspirations, juvenile, romance, horror, pornography

Representative Authors: Terry Blackhawk, Conrad Hilberry, and Laurence Lieberman

Submissions Policy: enclose a self-addressed, stamped envelope (SASE) or sufficient International Reply Coupons for reply only.

Simultaneous Submissions: yes

Reading Period: 8/15 to 6/1

Reporting Time: 12 to 16 weeks

Author Payment: copies

Founded: 1984

Non Profit: yes

Paid Staff: two

Unpaid Staff: 12

ISSN Number/ISBN Number: ISSN 1527-234 6

Total Circulation: 600

Paid Circulation: 150

Average Print Run: 500

Subscription Rate: Individual $22/Institution $22

Single Copy Price: $9

Current Volume/Issue: 21/3

Frequency per Year: triquarterly

Backfile Available: yes

Unsolicited Ms. Received: yes

% of Unsolicited Ms. Published per Year: 90%

Format: perfect

Size: H 9" W 6"

Average Pages: 200

Ads: no

Organization: Mad Hatters' Review

Type: online

CLMP member: yes

Primary Editor/Contact Person: Carol Novack

Address: http://www.madhattersreview.com
New York, NY 10011-7841

Web Site Address:
http://www.madhattersreview.com

Publishes: fiction, nonfiction, poetry, reviews, art, translation, audio, and video

Editorial Focus: Writings that address psychosocial issues, the pollution of minds, hearts, bodies and nature. Welcome aesthetic pieces, packed with surprising images and whimsical wordplays, "edgy," experimental, gutsy, thematically broad (i.e., saying something about the world and its creatures), psychologically and philosophically sophisticated writings. Black/dark humor, wise satire, erotica, irony, magic realism and surrealism. Traditional arc, resolution, story structure is far less important to us than originality, surprise, intellectual and emotional strength, lyricism and rhythm. Short dramas and collages are welcome. We love writers who stretch their imaginations to the limits and challenge pedestrian notions of reality; we're open to all styles and care little for categories. We also love collaborative ventures, between/among writers, writers and artists, and among writers, artists, and composers.

Recent Awards Received: Several awards listed on our website: www.madhattersreview.com/awards.shtml

Submissions Policy: http://www.madhattersreview.com/submit.shtml

Simultaneous Submissions: yes

Reading Period: Year-round

Reporting Time: one to six weeks

Author Payment: none

Contests: See web site for contest guidelines.

Founded: 2005

Non Profit: no

Paid Staff: one

Unpaid Staff: 23

ISSN Number/ISBN Number: ISSN 1556-147X

Average Page Views per Month: 14,204

Average Unique Visitors per Month: 4,794

Frequency per Year: 2

Average Percentage of Pages per Category: Fiction 15%, Nonfiction 5%, Poetry 15%, Reviews 5%, Art 25%, Translation 5%, Audio 25%, Video 5%

Ad Rates: http://www.madhattersreview.com/sponsorship.shtml

See web site for details.

Organization: Maelstrom

Type: magazine

CLMP member: no

Primary Editor/Contact Person: Christine L. Reed

Address: HC#1 Box 1624

Blakeslee, PA 18610

Web Site Address: http://www.geocities.com/~read-maelstrom

Publishes: essays, fiction, poetry, reviews, art, and translation

Editorial Focus: Tight, well-crafted poetry and gripping fiction.

Representative Authors: Mekeel McBride, Edgar Silex, and Grace Cavalieri

Submissions Policy: Send 4 poems or fiction 3,000 words or less. Art is held over for consideration in future issues unless otherwise requested.

Simultaneous Submissions: yes

Reading Period: Year-round

Reporting Time: one to four months

Author Payment: copies

Founded: 1997

Non Profit: yes

Paid Staff: zero

Unpaid Staff: four

ISSN Number/ISBN Number: ISSN 1096-3820

Total Circulation: 500

Paid Circulation: 50

Subscription Rate: Individual $20/Institution $20

Single Copy Price: $5

Current Volume/Issue: 4/3

Frequency per Year: quarterly

Backfile Available: yes

Unsolicited Ms. Received: yes

% of Unsolicited Ms. Published per Year: 2%

Format: stapled

Size: H 8 1/2" W 5 1/2"

Average Pages: 42

Ads: yes

Ad Rates: send query

Organization: Magick Mirror Communications

Type: press

CLMP member: yes

Primary Editor/Contact Person: Eugenia Macer-Story

Address: 511 Avenue of the Americas, PMB 173, New York, NY 10011

Web Site Address: magickmirror.com

Publishes: essays, fiction, nonfiction, poetry, reviews, art, and video

Editorial Focus: Quality literature on the supernatural, ufos, neo-physics and interdimensional consciousness, including poetry and play scripts

Representative Authors: Eugenia Macer-Story, Jack Sarfatti, and Steve Diamond

Submissions Policy: Format is not as important as quality content and style. Send one brief sample as entry submission.

Simultaneous Submissions: yes

Reading Period: Year-round

Reporting Time: 3 to 4 weeks

Author Payment: copies and subscription

Founded: 1990

Non Profit: no

Paid Staff: 3

Unpaid Staff: 8

Distributors: Amazon, New Leaf, Barnes & Noble online

ISSN Number/ISBN Number: 1-879980-/978-1-

879980-
Number of Books Published per Year: 2
Titles in Print: 23
Average Print Run: 500
Average Percentage Printed: Paperback 50%,
Chapbook 40%, Other 10%
Average Price: $12.00

Organization: Main Channel Voices, a Dam Fine Literary Mag

Type: magazine
CLMP member: yes
Primary Editor/Contact Person: N.K. Peterson & C.
Borzyskowski
Address: PO Box Box 492
Winona, MN 55987
Web Site Address: www.mainchannelvoices.com
Publishes: poetry
Editorial Focus: Fresh accessible poetry that triggers
an AHA! response in the reader.
Representative Authors: Sharon Chmielarz, Paul
Hostovsky, and Karla Linn Merrifield
Submissions Policy: Email submissions only via our
web site. Three to five poems in the body of an email,
no attachments will be opened.
Simultaneous Submissions: yes
Reading Period: year-round
Reporting Time: one to three months
Author Payment: copies
Contests: none
Founded: 2004
Non Profit: no
Pald Staff: zero
Unpaid Staff: two
ISSN Number/ISBN Number: ISSN 1551-0848
Total Circulation: 125
Paid Circulation: 100
Average Print Run: 200
Subscription Rate: individual $25/institution $25
Single Copy Price: $7.50
Current Volume/Issue: 2/3
Frequency per year: quarterly
Backfile Available: yes
Unsolicited MSS Received: yes
Format: stapled
Size: H 8.5" W 5.5"
Average Pages: 48
Ads: no

Organization: Main Street Rag

Type: magazine
CLMP member: no
Primary Editor/Contact Person: M. Scott Douglass
Address: 4416 Shea Ln.
Charlotte, NC 28227
Web Site Address: http://www.MainStreetRag.com
Publishes: essays, fiction, nonfiction, poetry, reviews,
and art
Editorial Focus: We like things that are alive with an
edge whether serious, humorous, political, satirical.
Not interested in garden poetry.
Representative Authors: David Chorlton, Joy Harjo,
and David Slavitt
Submissions Policy: Up to six pages of poetry, 6,000
words for short fiction, 2,000 words for essays. See
web site for reviews and/or interviews.
Simultaneous Submissions: no
Reading Period: Year-round
Reporting Time: three to twelve weeks
Author Payment: copies
Contests: Chapbook, full-length poetry, short fiction
See web site for contest guidelines.
Founded: 1996
Non Profit: no
Paid Staff: three
Unpaid Staff: zero
Distributors: Ingram
Total Circulation: 800
Paid Circulation: 200
Average Print Run: 800
Subscription Rate: Individual $20/Institution $20
Single Copy Price: $7
Current Volume/Issue: 10/3
Frequency per Year: quarterly
Backfile Available: yes
Unsolicited Ms. Received: yes
% of Unsolicited Ms. Published per Year: 10%
Format: perfect
Size: H 9" W 6"
Average Pages: 96
Ads: yes
Ad Rates: vary according to size, but cheap-mostly
swap ads

Organization: Maisonneuve

Type: magazine
CLMP member: no
Primary Editor/Contact Person: Derek Webster/Kena
Herod

Address: 400 de Maisonneuve Blvd.
Ste. 655
Montreal, QC H3A 1L4
Web Site Address: http://www.maisonneuve.org
Publishes: essays, fiction, nonfiction, poetry, reviews, art, translation, and audio
Editorial Focus: Eclectic Curiosity. The magazine balances diverse perspectives and topics, and aims to present it coherently and provocatively.
Recent Awards Received: Among many honors: the President's Medal and other awards from the National Magazine Awards and two Canadian Newsstand Awards.
Representative Authors: Jon Mooallem, Mona Awad, and Paul Winner
Submissions Policy: Anything else that demonstrates curiosity, energy or elegance across all fields of human endeavor. See web site for details.
Simultaneous Submissions: yes
Reading Period: Year-round
Reporting Time: one to four months
Author Payment: cash
Contests: See web site. for Contest Guidelines.
Founded: 2002
Non Profit: yes
Paid Staff: seven
Unpaid Staff: three
Distributors: LMPI
ISSN Number/ISBN Number: ISSN 1703-0056
Total Circulation: 14,000
Paid Circulation: 2,900
Average Print Run: 12,000
Subscription Rate: Individual $24/Institution $32
Single Copy Price: $6.95CAD
Current Volume/Issue: 2/4
Frequency per Year: bimonthly
Backfile Available: yes
Unsolicited Ms. Received: yes
% of Unsolicited Ms. Published per Year: 20%
Format: stapled
Size: H 11" W 8.5"
Average Pages: 96
Ads: yes
Ad Rates: See web site for details.

Organization: The Malahat Review
Type: magazine
CLMP member: no
Primary Editor/Contact Person: John Barton
Address: University of Victoria

Box 1700, Stn CSC
Victoria, BC V8V 2E6
Web Site Address: http://www.malahatreview.ca
Publishes: fiction, poetry, and reviews
Editorial Focus: Publish mainstream and experimental poetry and fiction by emerging and established writers from Canada and around the world.
Recent Awards Received: Journey Prize, 2004; O'Henry Award, 2001; National Magazine Award, 1995; Magazine of the Year, Western Magazine Awards, 1995
Representative Authors: Bill Gaston, Patricia Young, and Elisabeth Harvor
Submissions Policy: We invite submissions of previously unpublished one short story or five to eight poems for first world rights.
Simultaneous Submissions: no
Reading Period: Year-round
Reporting Time: one to three months
Author Payment: cash and subscription
Contests: Novella Contest; Long Poem Contest; Far Horizons Award (one Poetry, one for Short fiction; Creative Non-Fiction Prize; see website for guidelines.
Founded: 1967
Non Profit: yes
Paid Staff: four
Unpaid Staff: ten
Distributors: Magazines Canada
ISSN Number/ISBN Number: ISSN 0025-1216
Total Circulation: 1,000
Paid Circulation: 800
Average Print Run: 1,500
Subscription Rate: Individual $45/Institution $55
Single Copy Price: $11.95
Current Volume/Issue: Issue 159
Frequency per Year: quarterly
Backfile Available: yes
Unsolicited Ms. Received: yes
% of Unsolicited Ms. Published per Year: 2%
Format: perfect
Size: H 9" W 6"
Average Pages: 112
Ads: yes
Ad Rates: See Web Site for details.

Organization: MAMMOTH books
Type: press
CLMP member: yes
Primary Editor/Contact Person: Antonio Vallone
Address: MAMMOTH press Inc.

7 Juniata St.
DuBois, PA 15801
Publishes: essays, fiction, nonfiction, and poetry
Representative Authors: William Heyen, Liz Rosenberg, and Dinty W. Moore
Submissions Policy: We've ended our contests. No manuscripts are being accepted at this time.
Simultaneous Submissions: no
Reading Period: n/a
Reporting Time: n/a
Author Payment: copies
Contests: We've ended our contests.
Founded: 1997
Non Profit: yes
Paid Staff: one
Unpaid Staff: two
Distributors: SPD
Number of Books Published per Year: 4-5
Titles in Print: 25
Average Print Run: 300
Average Percentage Printed: Paperback 100%
Average Price: $11-20

Organization: Mandorla: New Writing from the Americas

Type: magazine
CLMP member: yes
Primary Editor/Contact Person: Kristin Dykstra
Address: Dept. of English, Illinois State University
Campus Box 4240
Normal, IL 61790-4240
Web Site Address: http://www.litline.org/Mandorla/
Publishes: essays, fiction, nonfiction, poetry, art, and translation
Editorial Focus: innovative writing in its original language-usually English or Spanish-and new translations; visual art; critical essays.
Recent Awards Received: Illinois Arts Council Literary Awards
Representative Authors: Jay Wright, Tamara Kamenszain, and Eduardo Miln
Simultaneous Submissions: no
Reading Period: 7/15 to 10/1
Reporting Time: two to four months
Author Payment: none
Founded: 1991
Non Profit: yes
Paid Staff: two
Unpaid Staff: three
ISSN Number/ISBN Number: ISSN 1550-7432

Total Circulation: 900
Paid Circulation: 400
Average Print Run: 1,000
Subscription Rate: Individual $12.50/Institution $18
Single Copy Price: $12.50
Current Volume/Issue: Issue 9
Frequency per Year: annual
Backfile Available: yes
Unsolicited Ms. Received: no
Format: perfect
Average Pages: 215
Ad Rates: full page $500. half page $250.

Organization: Mangrove

Type: magazine
CLMP member: no
Primary Editor/Contact Person: Neil de la Flor
Address: University of Miami, English Dept.
Box 248145
Miami, FL 33124-4632
Web Site Address: http://www.mangroveonline.org
Publishes: fiction, nonfiction, poetry, art, translation, audio, and video
Representative Authors: Terese Svoboda, Richard Grayson, and Denise Duhamel
Simultaneous Submissions: yes
Reading Period: 8/1 to 4/30
Reporting Time: one to two months
Author Payment: none
Contests: $500 Mangrove Literary Award alternates between fiction and poetry. Check mangroveonline.org for details.
See web site for contest guidelines.
Founded: 1994
Non Profit: yes
Paid Staff: zero
Unpaid Staff: eight
Total Circulation: 500
Paid Circulation: 50
Average Print Run: 50
Subscription Rate: Individual $28/Institution $20
Single Copy Price: $10
Current Volume/Issue: 1/15
Frequency per Year: biannual
Backfile Available: yes
Unsolicited Ms. Received: yes
% of Unsolicited Ms. Published per Year: 50%
Format: perfect
Ads: yes

Organization: The Manhattan Review

Type: magazine
CLMP member: yes
Primary Editor/Contact Person: Philip Fried
Address: 440 Riverside Dr. #38
New York, NY 10027
Web Site Address:
http://www.themanhattanreview.com
Publishes: essays, poetry, reviews, and translation
Editorial Focus: contemporary poetry in the US and abroad.
Representative Authors: D. Nurkse, Jeanne Marie Beaumont, and Baron Wormser
Submissions Policy: three to five poems. Brief bio. Notification if simultaneous.
Simultaneous Submissions: yes
Reading Period: Year-round
Reporting Time: three to five months
Author Payment: none
Founded: 1980
Non Profit: no
Paid Staff: no
Unpaid Staff: no
Distributors: DeBoer
ISSN Number/ISBN Number: ISSN 275-6889
Total Circulation: 500
Paid Circulation: 400
Average Print Run: 500
Subscription Rate: Individual $15/Institution $20
Single Copy Price: $7.50
Current Volume/Issue: 12/1
Frequency per Year: biannual
Backfile Available: yes
Unsolicited Ms. Received: yes
% of Unsolicited Ms. Published per Year: .5%
Format: perfect
Size: H 8-1/2" W 5-1/2"
Average Pages: 200
Ads: yes
Ad Rates: $50/page

Organization: Manic D Press

Type: press
CLMP member: no
Primary Editor/Contact Person: Jennifer Joseph
Address: P.O. Box 410804
San Francisco, CA 94141
Web Site Address: http://www.manicdpress.com
Publishes: essays, fiction, nonfiction, poetry, and art
Editorial Focus: Fiction, poetry, nonfiction, art.
Recent Awards Received: Publishing Triangle's Thom Gunn Award for Gay Poetry
Representative Authors: Justin Chin, Adrienne Su, and Myriam Gurba
Submissions Policy:
http://www.manicdpress.com/submissions.html
Simultaneous Submissions: yes
Reading Period: year-round
Reporting Time: one to six months
Author Payment: royalties
Founded: 1984
Non Profit: no
Paid Staff: two
Unpaid Staff: three
Distributors: Consortium, Publishers Group Canada, Turnaround UK
Wholesalers: SPD, Last Gasp, Ingram, Baker & Taylor, et al.
ISSN Number/ISBN Number: ISBN 0-916397, 1-933149
Number of Books Published per Year: 8
Titles in Print: 100
Average Print Run: 2,500
Average Percentage Printed: Hardcover 10%, Paperback 90%
Average Price: $14.95

Organization: Manifold Press

Type: press
CLMP member: yes
Primary Editor/Contact Person: Carol Frome
Address: 102 Bridge St.
Plattsburgh, NY 12901
Web Site Address: http://www.manifoldpress.com
Publishes: poetry
Editorial Focus: Well-crafted lyric poetry by known and unknown poets.
Representative Authors: N/A
Submissions Policy: We accept manuscripts year-round. Please include $20 reading fee and business-size SASE. Manuscripts will be recycled.
Simultaneous Submissions: yes
Reading Period: Year-round
Reporting Time: three to four months
Author Payment: royalties and cash
Contests: We are trying to avoid running contests.
Founded: 2003
Non Profit: no
Distributors: SPD Books

Number of Books Published per Year: one to four
Titles in Print: zero
Average Percentage Printed: Paperback 100%
Backfile Available: yes

Organization: Manoa

Type: magazine
CLMP member: yes
Primary Editor/Contact Person: Frank Stewart, Editor
Address: c/o UH English Dept.
1733 Donaghho Road
Honolulu, HI 96822
Web Site Address: http://manoajournal.hawaii.edu
Publishes: essays, fiction, nonfiction, poetry, reviews, art, and translation
Editorial Focus: New writing from Asia, the Pacific, and America
Recent Awards Received: Inclusion in O. Henry Prize Stories, Pushcart Prize, Best American Essays, Best American Short Stories, Best American Poetry.
Representative Authors: Arthur Sze, Tony Barnstone, and Leza Lowitz
Submissions Policy: we usually work with guest editors. Please see our web site for updates on our submissions policy
Simultaneous Submissions: yes
Reading Period: Year-round
Reporting Time: one to six months
Author Payment: cash and copies
Founded: 1988
Non Profit: yes
Paid Staff: four
Unpaid Staff: two
ISSN Number/ISBN Number: ISSN 1045-7909
Total Circulation: 3,000
Paid Circulation: 1,300
Average Print Run: 1,300
Subscription Rate: Individual $22/Institution $40
Single Copy Price: $20
Current Volume/Issue: 19/1
Frequency per Year: 2
Backfile Available: yes
Unsolicited Ms. Received: yes
% of Unsolicited Ms. Published per Year: 1%
Format: perfect
Size: H 7" W 10"
Average Pages: 220
Ads: yes

Organization: Mantis Journal

Type: magazine
CLMP member: yes
Primary Editor/Contact Person: Harris Feinsod/Bronwen Tate
Address: DLCL, Pigott Hall, Bld. 260
Stanford Unviersity
Stanford, CA 94305-2005
Website Address: http://mantisjournal.stanford.edu/
Publishes: essays, poetry, reviews, and translation
Editorial Focus: International poetry and poetics, translation, and collaborations between scholars and writers.
Representative Authors: Eleni Sikelianos, Raul Zurita, and Ko Un
Submissions Policy: Unsolicited poetry accepted August & September. Queries welcome for reviews, essays, & longer projects.
Simultaneous Submissions: yes
Reading Period: 08/01 to 09/31
Reporting Time: 4 to 6 weeks
Author Payment: copies
Founded: 2000
Non Profit: yes
Paid Staff: 3
Unpaid Staff: 5
ISSN Number/ISBN Number: ISSN 1540-4544
Total Circulation: 350
Paid Circulation: 100
Average Print Run: 500
Subscription Rate: Individual $20/Institution $35
Single Copy Price: $12
Current Volume/Issue: Issue 6
Frequency: 2
Backfile Available: yes
Unsolicited Ms. Received: no
Format: perfect
Size: H 9" W 6"
Average Pages: 200
Ads: no

Organization: Many Mountains Moving

Type: magazine
CLMP member: yes
Primary Editor/Contact Person: Jeffrey E. Lee/Jeffrey Bahr
Address: 549 Rider Ridge Drive
Longmont, CO 80501

Web Site Address: http://www.mmminc.org
Publishes: essays, fiction, nonfiction, poetry, reviews, art, and translation
Editorial Focus: Top-notch work from authors and artists from all walks of life.
Representative Authors: Isabel Allende, Sherman Alexie, and Ursula K. Le Guin
Submissions Policy: Please always visit the website for updates on the paper submission reading periods and the online submissions system.
Simultaneous Submissions: yes
Reading Period: year-round
Reporting Time: three to six months
Author Payment: copies
Contests: Poetry Book Contest in the spring (publication & cash). Poetry/flash fiction contest in the fall (cash prizes & publication).
Founded: 1994
Non Profit: yes
Paid Staff: zero
Unpaid Staff: eleven
Distributors: SPD
ISSN Number/ISBN Number: ISSN 1080-6474
TTotal Circulation: 400
Paid Circulation: 150
Average Print Run: 400
Subscription Rate: Individual $12/Institution $12
Single Copy Price: $13.95
Current Volume/Issue: 7/1
Frequency per Year: 1
Backfile Available: yes
Unsolicited Ms. Received: yes
% of Unsolicited Ms. Published per Year: 1%
Format: perfect
Size: H 9" W 6"
Average Pages: 248
Ads: yes
Ad Rates: See web site for details.

Organization: Many Names Press

Type: press
CLMP member: no
Primary Editor/Contact Person: Kate Hitt
Address: 1961 Main St. #244
Watsonville, CA 95076
Web Site Address:
http://www.manynamespress.com
Publishes: essays, fiction, nonfiction, poetry, and art
Editorial Focus: Poignant Creative Writing, Poetry, Environmental and Social Justice, Nonfiction, Quality,

Lasting Publications, Book Arts.
Recent Awards Received: Writers Almanac: Keillor read author on NPR. Western Books award for book design
Representative Authors: Andrea Rich, Amber Coverdale Sumrall, and Maude Meehan
Submissions Policy: Do not submit manuscripts. Grant fuel welcome for poets. Distinguished and liberal. Gay and Lesbian authors.
Simultaneous Submissions: no
Reading Period: June to September
Reporting Time: four to twelve weeks
Author Payment: copies
Founded: 1993
Non Profit: no
Paid Staff: zero
Unpaid Staff: one
Distributors: SPD, manynamespress.com
ISSN Number/ISBN Number: ISBN 09652575
Number of Books Published per Year: one to four
Titles in Print: 10
Average Print Run: 1,000
Average Percentage Printed: Paperback 75%, Chapbook 25%
Average Price: $15

Organization: Margin: Exploring Modern Magical Realism

Type: online
CLMP member: yes
Primary Editor/Contact Person: Tamara Kaye Sellman
Address: 321 High School Road NE
PMB 204
Bainbridge Island, WA 98110
Web Site Address: http://www.magical-realism.com
Publishes: essays, fiction, nonfiction, poetry, reviews, and translation
Editorial Focus: The world's only continuous survey of magical realism. Exists to answer the question, "What is literary magical realism?"
Recent Awards Received: Arete Wave of a Site
Representative Authors: Dr. Gregory Rabassa, Sondra Kelly-Green, and Michelle Cliff
Submissions Policy: Check website for details.
Simultaneous Submissions: yes
Reading Period: 9/4 to 4/5
Reporting Time: up to 6 months
Author Payment: cash and submission
Contests: See web site for contest guidelines or visit

Founded: 1999
Non Profit: yes
Paid Staff: zero
Unpaid Staff: five
Distributors: Web; we also offer Periphery, a print zine annual
Average Page Views per Month: 3,800
Average Unique Visitors per Month: 2,200
Frequency per Year: triquarterly
Publish Print Anthology: yes
Price: $6
Average Percentage of Pages per Category: Fiction 48%, Nonfiction 10%, Poetry 20%, Reviews 10%, Essays 10%, Art 1%, Translation 1%
Ad Rates: sponsorship rates online, trades discussed See web site for details.

Organization: Marick Press

Type: press
CLMP member: no
Primary Editor/Contact Person: Mariela Griffor
Address: P.O.Box 36253
Grosse Pointe Farms, MI 48236
Website Address: www.marickpress.com
Publishes: essays, fiction, nonfiction, poetry, and translation
Editorial Focus: Marick Press seeks and publishes the best new poetry from an eclectic range of aesthetics.
Recent Awards Received: Motor City Shine
Representative Authors: Franz Wright, Sean Thomas Dougherty, and Katie Ford
Submissions Policy: Marick Press publishes emerging and mid-career authors. Nearly all Marick authors have already had works published.
Simultaneous Submissions: yes
Reading Period: year-round
Reporting Time: 1 to 3 months
Author Payment: royalties and copies
Contests: see website for guidelines
Founded: 2005
Non Profit: yes
Paid Staff: 1
Unpaid Staff: 4
Distributors: Wayne State University Press, SPD Books
Wholesalers: Amazon.com and Barnes and Noble
ISSN Number/ISBN Number: ISBN 0-9712676
Number of Books Published per Year: 6
Titles in Print: 12

Average Print Run: 1,000
Average Percentage Printed: Hardcover 10%, Paperback 80%, Chapbook 10%
Average Price: $14.95

Organization: Marion Boyars Publishers

Type: press
CLMP member: no
Primary Editor/Contact Person: Catheryn Kilgarriff
Address: 24 Lacy Road
London, UK SW15 1NL
Web Site Address: http://www.marionboyars.co.uk
Publishes: fiction, nonfiction, and translation
Editorial Focus: Unusual fiction, written to arouse public interest and publicity. Nonfiction in the fields of cinema, drama and culture
Representative Authors: Hubert Selby Jr., Hong Ying, and Pauline Kael
Submissions Policy: Fiction via a literary agent. Nonfiction-synopsis and return postage.
Simultaneous Submissions: yes
Reading Period: Year-round
Reporting Time: six to twelve weeks
Author Payment: royalties and cash
Founded: 1975
Non Profit: no
Paid Staff: four
Unpaid Staff: zero
Distributors: Consortium
ISSN Number/ISBN Number: ISBN 0 7145
Number of Books Published per Year: 20
Titles in Print: 250
Average Print Run: 5,000
Average Percentage Printed: Hardcover 10%, Paperback 90%
Average Price: $14.95

Organization: mark(s)

Type: online
CLMP member: no
Primary Editor/Contact Person: Deb King
Address: 332 W. Woodland
Ferndale, MI 48220
Web Site Address: www.markszine.com
Publishes: essays, fiction, poetry, and art
Editorial Focus: mark(s) consistently presents new work across a wide variety of artistic practices.
Representative Authors: Nathaniel Mackey, Rachel

Blau DuPlessis, and Barrett Watten
Submissions Policy: At this time we can not accept unsolicited submissions.
Simultaneous Submissions: no
Reading Period: Year-round
Reporting Time: one to three months
Author Payment: none
Founded: 1999
Non Profit: yes
Paid Staff: zero
Unpaid Staff: three
Average Page Views per Month: 19,000
Average Unique Visitors per Month: 5,500
Frequency per Year: 2
Publish Print Anthology: no
Average Percentage of Pages per Category: Fiction 5%, Poetry 45%, Essays 5%, Art 45%
Ads: no

Organization: The Marlboro Review

Type: magazine
CLMP member: yes
Address: P.O. Box 243
Marlboro, VT 05344
Web Site Address: http://www.marlbororeview.com
Publishes: essays, fiction, poetry, and translation
Reading Period: Year-round
Reporting Time: one to two months
Author Payment: none
Founded: 1995
Non Profit: no
Unpaid Staff: five
Backfile Available: yes

Organization: Marsh Hawk Press

Type: press
CLMP member: yes
Primary Editor/Contact Person: Sandy McIntosh
Address: P.O. Box 206
East Rockaway, NY 11518
Web Site Address: http://www.marshhawkpress.org
Publishes: poetry
Editorial Focus: Poetry with affiliations to the visual arts.
Representative Authors: Eileen Tabios, Jane Augustine, and Edward Foster
Submissions Policy: Only through annual contest. Please see web site for details.
Simultaneous Submissions: no

Reading Period: 4/30 to 6/15
Reporting Time: one to two months
Author Payment: royalties
Contests: See Web Site for Contest Guidelines.
Founded: 2001
Non Profit: yes
Paid Staff: zero
Unpaid Staff: six
Distributors: Small Press Distributors
Wholesalers: Baker & Taylor
Number of Books Published per Year: five
Titles in Print: 42
Average Print Run: 1,000
Average Percentage Printed: Hardcover 1%, Paperback 99%
Average Price: $12.50

Organization: The Massachusetts Review

Type: magazine
CLMP member: yes
Primary Editor/Contact Person: Katherine Winger, Managing Ed.
Address: South College
University of Massachusetts
Amherst, MA 01003
Web Site Address: http://www.massreview.org
Publishes: essays, fiction, nonfiction, poetry, art, and translation
Editorial Focus: Ours is a generalist reader who cares deeply for both literature and the wider world.
Representative Authors: Bob Hicok, and Valerie Martin
Submissions Policy: SASE or see website for further guidelines. No queries are necessary.
Simultaneous Submissions: no
Reading Period: 10/1 to 5/31
Reporting Time: two to four months
Author Payment: cash and subscription
Founded: 1959
Non Profit: yes
Paid Staff: one
Unpaid Staff: 15
Distributors: Ubiquity, DeBoer
ISSN Number/ISBN Number: ISSN 0025-4878
Total Circulation: 1,500
Paid Circulation: 1,300
Average Print Run: 1,500
Subscription Rate: Individual $27/Institution $37
Single Copy Price: $9

Current Volume/Issue: 49/1
Frequency per Year: four
Backfile Available: yes
Unsolicited Ms. Received: yes
% of Unsolicited Ms. Published per Year: 5%
Format: perfect
Size: H 9" W 6"
Average Pages: 200
Ads: yes
Ad Rates: See web site for details.

Organization: Matter Magazine

Type: magazine
CLMP member: no
Primary Editor/Contact Person: Leigh Money/Emily Pedder
Address: 48 Beechwood Road
London, UK E8 3DY
Web Site Address: http://www.mattermagazine.co.uk
Publishes: fiction and poetry
Editorial Focus: Matter brings together the best of new writing, alongside the work of established guest authors
Representative Authors: Michel Faber, Ali Smith, and Toby Litt
Submissions Policy: No unsolicited submissions
Simultaneous Submissions: no
Reading Period: 3/30 to 5/30
Reporting Time: one to two months
Author Payment: copies
Founded: 2001
Non Profit: yes
Paid Staff: zero
Unpaid Staff: six
Distributors: INK Publishing
Wholesalers: Amazon.co.uk
ISSN Number/ISBN Number: ISBN 0954315014
Total Circulation: 1,000
Paid Circulation: 200
Single Copy Price: £4.99
Current Volume/Issue: 2003/3
Frequency per Year: annual
Backfile Available: yes
Unsolicited Ms. Received: no
Format: perfect
Size: H 6.5" W 4.75"
Average Pages: 170
Ads: yes
Ad Rates: £150 full page

Organization: McPherson & Company, Publishers

Type: press
CLMP member: yes
Primary Editor/Contact Person: Bruce McPherson
Address: P.O. Box 1126
Kingston, NY 12402
Web Site Address: http://www.mcphersonco.com
Publishes: fiction, nonfiction, and translation
Editorial Focus: American and British fiction; Italian, French and Spanish fiction in translation; art theory, filmmaking, cultural studies
Recent Awards Received: ForeWord Magazine, Book of the Year 2004: Historical Fiction, gold medal for John Shors's Beneath a Marble Sky
Representative Authors: Thomas McEvilley, Jaimy Gordon, and Robert Kelly
Submissions Policy: Query first. No unsolicited manuscripts.
Simultaneous Submissions: no
Reading Period: Year-round
Reporting Time: one to three months
Author Payment: royalties
Founded: 1974
Non Profit: yes
Paid Staff: one
Unpaid Staff: zero
Distributors: McPherson & Co.
Wholesalers: New Leaf, Central Books (London), Ingram
ISSN Number/ISBN Number: ISBN 0929701-, 0914232-
Titles in Print: 120
Average Print Run: 1,200
Average Percentage Printed: Hardcover 60%, Paperback 40%
Average Price: $18

Organization: McSweeney's Publishing

Type: press
CLMP member: yes
Primary Editor/Contact Person: Eli Horowitz/Andrew Leland
Address: 826 Valencia St.
San Francisco, CA 94110
Web Site Address: http://www.mcsweeneys.net
Publishes: fiction, nonfiction, reviews, and art
Editorial Focus: McSweeney's is committed to finding

Valerie Merians and Dennis Johnson
CEOs, Melville House Publishing

How did you arrive at your current position?

If you started your own company you'd get to be the CEO too.

What is the staff structure at your press?

It's like a band where we change instruments a lot. We all have some specialties (we're in charge of lunch) but basically whoever is the editor of the book is in charge of everything about that book—negotiating, editing, seeing it through production, then developing and overseeing the promotion and marketing. Acquiring titles in the first place, cover design and overall marketing concepts are group decisions, which Valerie and I sign off on.

What challenges do you face as a publisher?

Survival. This isn't a culture that's very friendly to intellectualism or art. And it's difficult to get American media, which is essentially geared for entertainment, to talk about serious books. Also, there's the general ignorance about the differences between conglomerate publishing and indie publishing. They're vastly different worlds that run on vastly different economic models. Writers working with small presses need to change their expectations of super-stardom and look at the experience as a real partnership with the actual people who are putting up money to support your work.

Do you have any cover letter advice?

Yes: Please read our submissions guidelines before you write to us and, for the love of God, keep it short and do not explain your writing at great length. If it needs 'splaining, it ain't any good. Also, be aware that knowing my mother won't do you any good either.

What do you look for in a submission?

Good writing and compelling content. If you consider our list so far—a wise thing to do—you'll see we publish a wide variety of books, but we have a consistent sensibility. Would your work play well with our others? We also look for work that is unagented. The small-press pie just isn't big enough, and we want to work in closer partnership with our writers than is typical at the big corporate houses (where you really do need an agent between writer and publisher).

How are submissions processed at your press?

We enter them in a databank so we can say yes it's here or no we never got it if you call. But in all honesty it takes a while for them to get read. Months usually. I mean, it's unasked-for work, and we're already pedal-to-the-metal on current titles. That said, we have published quite a few things that came to us first in the slush pile—for example *The Evasion-English Dictionary* and the novel *Our Nun*, to name just two. We're pretty flattered to get stuff like that and we try to respect it as best we can.

Do you have a favorite unsolicited submission discovery or anecdote?

We were pretty surprised to find a novel by a *Time Magazine* war correspondent in there one day. We were wondering what in the world a mainstream reporter would think was suitable for us, and it turned out to be a hilarious send-up of American foibles in the Iraq war. It turned out to be one of our bestselling novels to date, *Hocus Potus* by Malcolm MacPherson, a book we're extremely proud of.

What advice do you have for first-time submitters?

Study the books of the house you're submitting to—honor those you would have honor you. Beyond that, keep it simple and let the work speak for itself.

What are your long-term plans for your magazine?

We just want to stay in business.

What's your evaluation of the current literary landscape?

That requires a massive dissertation. The short answer is: While we dread the increasing dominance of the entertainment-military complex, there is some extremely interesting and exciting work going on in the small press and underground publisher world. Not just in terms of fiction, but in terms of non-fiction reportage as well. In terms of our list, we're excited not only by young writers we've discovered such as Tao Lin, A.C. Thompson and Benoit Duteurtre, but also by established writers who've come over from the dark side to write for Melville House—writers such as Paul Berman, Stephen Dixon and Lewis Lapham. Both things bode well for the future, we think.

new voices, printing gifted but underappreciated writers, and pushing form forward.

Representative Authors: Paul Collins, Lydia Davis, and Rick Moody

Submissions Policy: Please visit our web sites, http://www.mcsweeneys.net and http://www.believer-mag.com, for current submissions guidelines.

Simultaneous Submissions: yes

Reading Period: Year-round

Reporting Time: one to five months

Author Payment: cash and copies

Founded: 1998

Non Profit: no

Paid Staff: five

Unpaid Staff: zero

Number of Books Published per Year: 10 to 20

Titles in Print: 50

Average Print Run: varies

Average Percentage Printed: Hardcover 80%, Paperback 20%

Average Price: $22

Organization: Me Three Literary Journal

Type: magazine

CLMP member: no

Primary Editor/Contact Person: Sarah Stodola

Address: 101 Lafayette Ave.
Brooklyn, NY 11217

Web Site Address: www.methree.net

Publishes: essays, fiction, and nonfiction

Editorial Focus: Realistic fiction, along with criticism and the occasional journalistic essay.

Representative Authors: Steve Finbow, Tyler Gore, and Mark Grueter

Submissions Policy: We accept submissions via email. Response time can range from a couple of months to a year

Simultaneous Submissions: yes

Reading Period: year-round

Reporting Time: up to three months

Author Payment: copies

Contests: Satire Contest and Literary Criticism Contest. See web site for contest guidelines

Founded: 2003

Non Profit: no

Paid Staff: zero

Unpaid Staff: four

ISSN Number/ISBN Number: ISSN 1555-7111

Total Circulation: 400

Paid Circulation: zero

Average Print Run: 500

Subscription Rate: individual $15/institution $17

Single Copy Price: $9

Current Volume/Issue: issue two

Frequency per year: biannual

Backfile Available: yes

Unsolicited MSS Received: yes

% of Unsolicited MSS Published per year: 1%

Format: perfect

Size: H 9" W 6"

Average Pages: 96

Ads: yes

Ad Rates: see web site for details

Organization: The Melic Review

Type: online

CLMP member: no

Primary Editor/Contact Person: C.E. Chaffin

Address: c/o CE 220 N. Zapata Hwy #11A-179
Laredo, TX 78043

Web Site Address: http://www.melicreview.com

Publishes: essays, fiction, poetry, reviews, art, translation, and audio

Editorial Focus: After six years The Melic Review continues to publish the highest quality fiction, criticism, and poetry online.

Representative Authors: Scott Murphy, Alfred Corn, and C.E. Chaffin

Submissions Policy: Poetry under 50 lines, fiction approx. 1,000 words, exceptions made for longer works of merit and critical essays.

Simultaneous Submissions: no

Reading Period: Year-round

Reporting Time: one to three months

Author Payment: none

Founded: 1998

Non Profit: yes

Paid Staff: zero

Unpaid Staff: 10

ISSN Number/ISBN Number: ISSN pending

Average Page Views per Month: 15,000

Average Unique Visitors per Month: 1,500

Publish Print Anthology: yes

Average Percentage of Pages per Category: Fiction 25%, Poetry 50%, Essays 25%

Ads: no

Organization: Melville House Publishing

Type: press
CLMP member: yes
Primary Editor/Contact Person: Dennis Johnson
Address: 300 Observer Hwy, Third Floor, Hoboken, NJ 07030
Web Site Address: www.mhpbooks.com
Publishes: essays, fiction, nonfiction, poetry, and translation
Editorial Focus: Melville House eschews the concept of "niche" and simply describes itself as publishing literary fiction, nonfiction and poetry.
Recent Awards Received: 3 AIGA design awards; the Association of American Publishers'2007 Miriam Bass Award for Creativity in Independent Publishing
Representative Authors: Imre Kertesz, Bernard-Henri Levy, and Edith Wharton
Submissions Policy: No electronic submissions, full manuscripts only, SASE
Simultaneous Submissions: yes
Reading Period: Year-round
Reporting Time: three to six months
Author Payment: royalties
Founded: 2002
Non Profit: no
Paid Staff: 5
Unpaid Staff: 0
Distributors: Consortium Book Sales & Distribution
Wholesalers: Ingrams, Baker & Taylor, the usual suspects
Number of Books Published per Year: 20
Titles in Print: 100
Average Print Run: 3-5K
Average Percentage Printed: Hardcover 30%, Paperback 70%
Average Price: $10-25

Organization: Memorious: A Forum for New Verse and Poetics

Type: online
CLMP member: yes
Primary Editor/Contact Person: Robert Arnold
Address: 1 Stinson Ct. #3
Cambridge, MA 02139
Web Site Address: http://www.memorious.org
Publishes: essays, fiction, nonfiction, poetry, reviews, art, translation, and audio
Editorial Focus: Outstanding poetry and fiction by both established and emerging writers.
Representative Authors: Sean Singer, David Rivard,

and Maggie Dietz
Submissions Policy: Accepts e-mail submissions, simultaneous submissions if notified. Check web site for guidelines.
Simultaneous Submissions: yes
Reading Period: Year-round
Reporting Time: one to three months
Author Payment: none
Founded: 2003
Non Profit: yes
Paid Staff: zero
Unpaid Staff: four
Average Page Views per Month: 4,500
Average Unique Visitors per Month: 900
Frequency per Year: quarterly
Publish Print Anthology: no
Average Percentage of Pages per Category: Fiction 20%, Nonfiction 5%, Poetry 60%, Reviews 5%, Essays 5%, Art 1%, Translation 3%, Audio 1%
Ads: no

Organization: Mercury House

Type: press
CLMP member: no
Primary Editor/Contact Person: K. Janene-Nelson
Address: P.O. Box 192850
San Francisco, CA 94119-2850
Web Site Address: http://www.mercuryhouse.org
Publishes: essays, fiction, nonfiction, and translation
Editorial Focus: We are a nonprofit press guided by a dedication to literary values and works of social significance.
Representative Authors: Leonard Michaels, William Kittredge, and Bill Porter/Red Pine
Submissions Policy: We are not currently accepting submissions.
Reading Period: n/a
Reporting Time: n/a
Author Payment: royalties and cash
Founded: 1985
Non Profit: yes
Paid Staff: one
Unpaid Staff: five
Distributors: Consortium
Wholesalers: various
ISSN Number/ISBN Number: ISBN 1-56279-
Number of Books Published per Year: 1
Titles in Print: 85
Average Percentage Printed: Hardcover 10%, Paperback 90%

Organization: The Mercury Press

Type: press
CLMP member: no
Primary Editor/Contact Person: Beverley Daurio
Address: 22 Prince Rupert Ave.
Toronto, ON M6P 2A7
Web Site Address: http://www.themercurypress.ca
Publishes: fiction, nonfiction, poetry, and translation
Editorial Focus: The Mercury Press publishes poetry, fiction, murder mysteries, and culturally significant nonfiction by Canadian authors.
Representative Authors: Nicole Brossard, Sandra Shamas, and bp nichol
Submissions Policy: Manuscripts must be word typewritten on one side of page, double spaced. SASE. Only Canadian authors.
Simultaneous Submissions: yes
Reading Period: Year-round
Reporting Time: four to twelve weeks
Author Payment: royalties
Founded: 1978
Non Profit: no
Paid Staff: two
Unpaid Staff: zero
Distributors: LitDistCo
ISSN Number/ISBN Number: ISBN 1-55128
Number of Books Published per Year: nine
Titles in Print: 140
Average Percentage Printed: Paperback 100%

Organization: Meridian

Type: magazine
CLMP member: no
Primary Editor/Contact Person: James Livingood
Address: P.O. Box 400145
University of Virginia
Charlottesville, VA 22904-4145
Web Site Address: http://www.readmeridian.org
Publishes: essays, fiction, nonfiction, reviews, art, and translation
Editorial Focus: Ambitious, well-crafted literary fiction and poetry. We publish Nobel Prize-winners and first-time authors.
Representative Authors: Seamus Heaney, Ann Beattie, and Heather McHugh
Submissions Policy: Electronic submissions begin 10/1/05. If postal, include SASE. If simultaneous submission, mention in cover letter.
Simultaneous Submissions: yes
Reading Period: 9/1 to 5/1
Reporting Time: two to three months
Author Payment: cash and copies
Contests: Annual $1,000 prizes in poetry and fiction; Dec. due date. See web site.
Founded: 1998
Non Profit: yes
Paid Staff: three
Unpaid Staff: five
Distributors: Ingram
ISSN Number/ISBN Number: ISSN 1527-3555
Total Circulation: 1,000
Paid Circulation: 660
Average Print Run: 1,100
Subscription Rate: Individual $10/Institution $15
Single Copy Price: $7
Current Volume/Issue: Issue 14
Frequency per Year: biannual
Backfile Available: yes
Unsolicited Ms. Received: yes
% of Unsolicited Ms. Published per Year: 3%
Format: perfect
Size: H 9.25" W 6.5"
Average Pages: 150
Ads: yes
Ad Rates: $150/page

Organization: Michigan State University Press

Type: press
CLMP member: no
Primary Editor/Contact Person: Martha A. Bates
Address: 1405 S. Harrison Road, Ste. 25
East Lansing, MI 48823
Web Site Address: http://www.msupress. msu.edu
Publishes: essays, fiction, nonfiction, and poetry
Editorial Focus: Scholarly nonfiction, memoir, fiction, and poetry: Great Lakes, Environment, Rhetoric, Native American, Black American
Representative Authors: Valerie Miner, Martin J. Medhurst, and Gordon Henry
Submissions Policy: Query letter with sample chapters to Acquisitions Editor
Simultaneous Submissions: no
Reading Period: Year-round
Reporting Time: four to six months
Author Payment: royalties
Contests: Kohr-Campbell book award for Rhetoric and Public Affairs

See web site for Contest Guidelines.
Founded: 1948
Non Profit: yes
Paid Staff: 13
Unpaid Staff: five
Number of Books Published per Year: 35
Titles in Print: 468
Average Percentage Printed: Hardcover 35%, Paperback 65%

Organization: Mid-American Review

Type: magazine
CLMP member: yes
Primary Editor/Contact Person: Michael Czyzniejewski
Address: Department of English
Bowling Green State University
Bowling Green, OH 43403
Web Site Address: http://www.bgsu.edu/midamericanreview
Publishes: essays, fiction, nonfiction, poetry, reviews, and translation
Editorial Focus: Our goal is to put the best contemporary work in front of the largest audience, including both new and established writers.
Representative Authors: Steve Almond, Denise Duhamel, and Albert Goldbarth.
Submissions Policy: Send previously unpublished work and a cover letter, two to six poems or 6,000 words of prose. See web site for more information.
Simultaneous Submissions: yes
Reading Period: Year-round
Reporting Time: one to four months
Author Payment: copies and subscription
Contests: See web site for contest guidelines.
Founded: 1981
Non Profit: yes
Paid Staff: two
Unpaid Staff: 25
Distributors: DeBoer
Wholesalers: Swets
ISSN Number/ISBN Number: ISSN 0747-8895
Total Circulation: 2,200
Paid Circulation: 1,200
Average Print Run: 2,500
Subscription Rate: Individual $12/Institution $9.60
Single Copy Price: $9
Current Volume/Issue: XXVI/1
Frequency per Year: biannual
Backfile Available: yes

Unsolicited Ms. Received: yes
% of Unsolicited Ms. Published per Year: 85%
Format: perfect
Size: H 9" W 6"
Average Pages: 224
Ads: yes
Ad Rates: free exchange ads, or $250 per page
See Web site for details.

Midway

Type: online
CLMP member: yes
Primary Editor/Contact Person: Justin Maxwell/Rebecca Weaver
Address: PO Box 14499
St. Paul, MN 55114
Website Address: www.midwayjournal.com
Publishes: essays, fiction, nonfiction, poetry, audio, and video
Editorial Focus: Just off of I-94 and on the border between St. Paul and Minneapolis, the Midway, like any other state fairgrounds, is alive with a mix of energies and people. Its position as mid-way, as a place of boundary crossing, also reflects our vision for this journal. The work here complicates and questions the boundaries of genre, binary, and aesthetic. It offers surprises and ways of re-seeing, re-thinking, and re-feeling: a veritable banquet of literary fare. Which is why, in each new issue, we are honored to present work by both new and established writers alike. We are looking to act not only as a bridge between aesthetics (and maybe even coasts) but we are looking to create a sense of place as well.
Representative Authors: Chrales Bernstein, Mac Wellman, and kari edwards
Submissions Policy: Midway Journal accepts submissions of aesthetically ambitious work that occupies the realms between both the traditional and experimental.We accept submissions between December and June annually, only. We do not accept electronic submissions (exceptions can be made for international submissions). All manuscripts should be submitted with SASE and should be mailed to: The Editors, Midway Journal, PO Box 14499, St. Paul, MN 55114. All manuscripts should be double-spaced and single-sided (poetry may be single spaced or double spaced). Currently, since we publish electronically and do not incur traditional publication limitations, there are no page limits or word counts set for individual submissions. We do ask, however, that you please send no

more than 3-5 poems, or 1 piece of fiction, or 2 pieces of flash, or sudden, fiction, or 1 piece of creative non-fiction, mixed genre, or drama. Individuals may, however, submit in more than one genre simultaneously.Photocopies and computer printed copies are acceptable. Simultaneous submissions accepted. We will consider previously published work also if all rights are still retained by the author.

Simultaneous Submissions: yes
Reading Period: 12/1 to 5/31
Reporting Time: 1 to 6 months
Author Payment: none
Founded: 2006
Non Profit: no
Paid Staff: 0
Unpaid Staff: 5
Average Page Views per Month: 1,900
Average Unique Visitors per Month: 400
Frequency: 6
Publish Print Anthology: no
Average Percentage of Pages per Category: Fiction 30%, Nonfiction 10%, Poetry 30%, Essays 15%, Audio 5%, Video 10%
Ad Rates: see website for details

Organization: Milkweed Editions
Type: press
CLMP member: yes
Primary Editor/Contact Person: Daniel Slager
Address: 1011 Washington Ave. S., Ste. 300
Minneapolis, MN 55415-1246
Web Site Address: http://www.milkweed.org
Publishes: essays, fiction, nonfiction, and poetry
Editorial Focus: Milkweed Editions publishes literary writing with the intention of making a humane impact on society.
Representative Authors: Seth Kantner, Faith Sullivan, and Natasha Friend
Submissions Policy: Please visit our submission guidelines at http://www.milkweed.org.
Simultaneous Submissions: yes
Reading Period: Year-round
Reporting Time: one to six months
Author Payment: royalties
Contests: Milkweed National Fiction Prize and Milkweed Prize for Children's Literature
See web site for Contest Guidelines.
Founded: 1979
Non Profit: yes
Paid Staff: 11

Unpaid Staff: five
Distributors: Perseus Distribution
ISSN Number/ISBN Number: ISBN 1-57131
Number of Books Published per Year: 20
Titles in Print: 215
Average Print Run: 5,000
Average Percentage Printed: Hardcover 25%, Paperback 75%
Average Price: $14.00

Organization: the minnesota review
Type: magazine
CLMP member: yes
Primary Editor/Contact Person: Jeff Williams
Address: Carnegie Mellon University
Department of English
Pittsburgh, PA 15213-3890
Web Site Address: http://theminnesotareview.org
Publishes: essays, fiction, nonfiction, poetry, reviews, and translation
Editorial Focus: Cultural politics
Representative Authors: Bruce Robbins, Barbara Foley, and Jim Daniels
Simultaneous Submissions: yes
Reading Period: Year-round
Reporting Time: two to four months
Author Payment: copies
Founded: 1960
Non Profit: yes
Paid Staff: three
Unpaid Staff: three
Distributors: Ubiquity, DeBoer
Total Circulation: 1,500
Paid Circulation: 600
Subscription Rate: Individual $30/Institution $55
Single Copy Price: $15
Current Volume/Issue: Issue 63
Frequency per Year: biannual
Backfile Available: yes
Unsolicited Ms. Received: yes
% of Unsolicited Ms. Published per Year: 5%
Format: perfect
Size: H 8.5" W 5.5"
Ads: yes

Organization: MiPo Magazine
Type: online
CLMP member: no
Primary Editor/Contact Person: Didi Menendez

Address: 9240 SW 44 St.
Miami, FL 33165
Web Site Address: http://www.mipoesias.com
Publishes: essays, fiction, nonfiction, poetry, reviews, art, and audio
Editorial Focus: Our mission is to make digital publications the standard. We promote established and new writers via the Internet.
Representative Authors: David Trinidad, Denise Duhamel, and Lyn Lifshin
Submissions Policy: We accept submission via e-mail to editor@mipoesias.com. We do not accept previously published works.
Simultaneous Submissions: yes
Reading Period: Year-round
Reporting Time: one to three months
Author Payment: none
Contests: Bonsai Project. Our poetry board participates in the IBPC and PBL.
See web site for contest guidelines.
Founded: 2000
Non Profit: yes
Paid Staff: zero
Unpaid Staff: six
ISSN Number/ISBN Number: ISSN 1543-6063
Average Page Views per Month: 9,000
Average Unique Visitors per Month: 2,500
Frequency per Year: annual
Publish Print Anthology: no
Average Percentage of Pages per Category: Fiction 10%, Nonfiction 10%, Poetry 40%, Essays 5%, Art 30%, Audio 5%
Ads: no

Organization: Miranda Literary Magazine

Type: online
CLMP member: yes
Primary Editor/Contact Person: Ron Samul
Address: 27 Fowler Ct.
New London, CT 06320
Web Site Address: www.mirandamagazine.com
Publishes: essays, fiction, nonfiction, poetry, reviews, and art
Simultaneous Submissions: yes
Reading Period: year-round
Reporting Time: one to three months
Author Payment: none
Contests: Novella Contest fourth coming.
See web site for contest guidelines

Founded: 2006
Non Profit: no
Paid Staff: zero
Unpaid Staff: 20
Average Page Views per Month: 750
Average Unique Visitors per Month: 280-300
Frequency per year: quarterly
Publish Print Anthology: yes
Average Percentage of Pages per Category: fiction 25%, nonfiction 10%, poetry 25%, reviews 10%, essays 10%, art 20%
Ad Rates: see web site for details

Organization: Mississippi Review

Type: magazine
CLMP member: yes
Primary Editor/Contact Person: Frederick Barthelme
Address: 118 College Dr., #5144
Hattiesburg, MS 39406-5144
Web Site Address: http://www.mississippireview.com
Publishes: fiction and poetry
Editorial Focus: Contemporary fiction and poetry.
Representative Authors: Marlys West, Lisa Glatt, and Kate Braverman
Submissions Policy: Reading only for MR Prize competition. Not reading unsolicited work at this time.
Simultaneous Submissions: yes
Reading Period: 4/1 to 10/1
Reporting Time: two to three months
Author Payment: copies
Contests: See Web Site for Contest Guidelines.
Founded: 1971
Non Profit: yes
Paid Staff: three
Unpaid Staff: six
Distributors: DeBoer
ISSN Number/ISBN Number: ISSN 0047-7559
Total Circulation: 2,000
Paid Circulation: 200
Average Print Run: 2,000
Subscription Rate: Individual $15 one-year/$27 two-year/$40 three-year/Institution same
Single Copy Price: $12
Current Volume/Issue: 34/1
Frequency per Year: biannual
Backfile Available: yes
Unsolicited Ms. Received: no
Format: perfect
Size: H 8.5" W 5.5"
Average Pages: 170

Ads: yes
Ad Rates: $100/page

Organization: Mississippireview.com

Type: online
CLMP member: no
Primary Editor/Contact Person: Frederick Barthelme
Address: Box 5144
Hattiesburg, MS 39402
Web Site Address: http://mississippireview.com
Publishes: essays, fiction, nonfiction, poetry, reviews, art, and translation
Editorial Focus: Not reprints and not an ad for our print mag, we publish new literary work selected by our editors. See site for details.
Representative Authors: Stacey Richter, Rick Bass, and David Kirby
Submissions Policy: See web site. We have guest editors for each issue.
Simultaneous Submissions: yes
Reading Period: Year-round
Reporting Time: 1 to 12 weeks
Author Payment: none
Contests: See Mississippi Review Prize, annual contest associated with our print magazine. See web site for contest guidelines.
Founded: 1995
Non Profit: yes
Paid Staff: one
Unpaid Staff: 14
Distributors: online
Average Page Views per Month: 42,641
Average Unique Visitors per Month: 15,662
Frequency per Year: quarterly
Publish Print Anthology: no
Average Percentage of Pages per Category: Fiction 50%, Nonfiction 10%, Poetry 30%, Essays 10%
Ad Rates: See web site for details.

Organization: The Missouri Review

Type: magazine
CLMP member: yes
Primary Editor/Contact Person: Richard Sowienski
Address: 357 Hillcrest Hall, UMC
Columbia, MO 65211
Web Site Address: http://www.missourireview.com
Publishes: essays, fiction, nonfiction, poetry, reviews, and art
Editorial Focus: For over thirty years we've upheld a

reputation for discovering the very best writers. Established writers are also welcomed.
Recent Awards Received: We regularly have work anthologized in "Best of" series and Pushcart.
Representative Authors: Mimi Schwartz, Robert Olen Butler, and Talvikki Ansel
Simultaneous Submissions: yes
Reading Period: Year-round
Reporting Time: six to eight weeks
Author Payment: cash and copies
Contests: Editors' Prize in fiction, essay, and poetry. $3,000 and publication in each category. NEW: Audio Competition, $3500 in pr; see website for guidelines**Founded:** 1978
Non Profit: yes
Paid Staff: six
Unpaid Staff: 16
Distributors: Ingram
ISSN Number/ISBN Number: ISBN 7447081278
Total Circulation: 5000
Paid Circulation: 4,000
Average Print Run: 5,500
Subscription Rate: Individual $24/Institution $48
Single Copy Price: $8.95
Current Volume/Issue: 30/2
Frequency: 4
Backfile Available: yes
Unsolicited Ms. Received: yes
% of Unsolicited Ms. Published per Year: 90%
Format: perfect
Size: H 10" W 6 3/4"
Average Pages: 180
Ads: yes
Ad Rates: $500 per page; see website for details

Organization: The Mochila Review

Type: magazine
CLMP member: no
Primary Editor/Contact Person: Bill Church
Address: Missouri Western State College
4525 Downs Dr.
St. Joseph, MO 64507
Web Site Address: http://www.mwsc.edu/eflj/mochila/index.h
Publishes: essays, fiction, nonfiction, and poetry
Editorial Focus: Seeking quality writing in all genres. Fresh voices, fresh topics, fresh treatments.
Representative Authors: Ron McFarland, Murzban Shroff, and Sandra Kohler
Submissions Policy: Please specify genre on enve-

lope and submit genres separately.
Simultaneous Submissions: yes
Reading Period: 9/1 to 11/1
Reporting Time: two to three months
Author Payment: copies
Contests: John Gilgun Literary Awards annually in fiction and poetry.
See Web Site for contest guidelines.
Founded: 1998
Non Profit: yes
Paid Staff: two
Unpaid Staff: 10
Distributors: Missouri Western State College
Total Circulation: 300
Paid Circulation: 25
Subscription Rate: Individual $6/Institution $6
Single Copy Price: $6
Current Volume/Issue: 4/1
Frequency per Year: annual
Backfile Available: yes
Unsolicited Ms. Received: yes
% of Unsolicited Ms. Published per Year: 5%
Format: perfect
Size: H 9" W 6"
Average Pages: 152
Ads: no

The Modern Review

Type: magazine
CLMP member: no
Primary Editor/Contact Person: Simone dos Anjos & Pietro Aman
Address: RPO P.O. Box 32659
Richmond Hill, ON L4C 0A2
Website Address: www.modern-review.com
Publishes: essays, fiction, nonfiction, poetry, reviews, art, and translation
Editorial Focus: A relevant literature, one that refuses to oppose tradition to innovation, the personal to the objective.
Representative Authors: Robert Kelly, Jennifer Moxley, and Geoffrey G. O'Brien
Submissions Policy: Read the journal before submitting.
Simultaneous Submissions: no
Reading Period: year-round
Reporting Time: 1 to 8 weeks
Author Payment: subscription
Founded: 2005
Non Profit: yes

Paid Staff: 0
Unpaid Staff: 2
ISSN Number/ISBN Number: ISSN 1557-265X
Total Circulation: 250
Paid Circulation: 200
Average Print Run: 300
Subscription Rate: Individual $25/Institution $25
Single Copy Price: $7.95
Current Volume/Issue: III/1
Frequency: 4
Backfile Available: yes
Unsolicited Ms. Received: yes
% of Unsolicited Ms. Published per Year: 35%
Format: perfect
Average Pages: 150
Ads: yes
Ad Rates: All ads published free (books and journals we believe in).

Monkeybicycle Books

Type: press
CLMP member: yes
Primary Editor/Contact Person: Steven Seighman
Address: 824 Latimer St.
York, PA 17404
Website Address: www.monkeybicycle.net
Publishes: essays, fiction, nonfiction, and poetry
Editorial Focus: We focus primarily on short experimental fiction and humor, but will consider just about anything, really.
Recent Awards Received: Stories included in the 2005 and 2007 Best American Nonrequired Reading collections.
Submissions Policy: We'll read anything for our print editions. For the web, keep it under 1500 words please.
Simultaneous Submissions: yes
Reading Period: year-round
Reporting Time: 1 to 3 months
Author Payment: none
Contests: Sometimes?
Founded: 2002
Non Profit: yes
Paid Staff: 0
Unpaid Staff: 4
Number of Books Published per Year: 2
Titles in Print: 4
Average Print Run: 500
Average Percentage Printed: Paperback 100%
Average Price: $12.00

Organization: Montemayor Press

Type: press
CLMP member: yes
Primary Editor/Contact Person: Edward Myers
Address: P.O. Box 526
Millburn, NJ 07041
Web Site Address:
http://www.montemayorpress.com
Publishes: fiction and nonfiction
Editorial Focus: literary fiction, young-adult fiction, general nonfiction, books about the Latino experience in America
Recent Awards Received: Silver Award, Young-Adult Fiction category, 2004 ForeWord Magazine Book of the Year Awards (for ICE)
Representative Authors: Joanne Greenberg, Meredith Sue Willis, and Adrian Rodriguez
Submissions Policy: by invitation only; no unsolicited manuscripts accepted until further notice
Simultaneous Submissions: no
Reading Period: Year-round
Reporting Time: one to two months
Author Payment: royalties and copies
Founded: 1999
Non Profit: no
Paid Staff: one
Unpaid Staff: zero
Wholesalers: Ingram, Baker & Taylor, Quality Books Inc., Follett
ISSN Number/ISBN Number: ISBN 0-9674477-, 1-932727
Number of Books Published per Year: two to three
Titles in Print: 12
Average Print Run: 2,000
Average Percentage Printed: Paperback 100%
Average Price: $12.95

Organization: Moon City Review

Type: magazine
CLMP member: no
Address: English Dept., Southwest Missouri State University
901 S. National Ave.
Springfield, MO 65804
Web Site Address:
http://www.smsu.edu/English/moon_city_review.htm
Publishes: essays, fiction, nonfiction, poetry, and reviews
Reading Period: Year-round
Reporting Time: one to two months
Author Payment: none
Founded: 1905
Non Profit: yes
Backfile Available: yes

Organization: Mosaic Literary Magazine

Type: magazine
CLMP member: yes
Primary Editor/Contact Person: Ron Kavanaugh
Address: 314 W 231st St, Ste 470
Bronx, NY 10463
Web Site Address: http://www.mosaicbooks.com
Publishes: essays, fiction, nonfiction, poetry, and reviews
Editorial Focus: Mosaic Literary Magazine showcases and critiques Black and Latino literature.
Representative Authors: : Thomas Sayers Ellis, Gwendolyn Brooks, and Eisa Nefertari Ulen
Submissions Policy: Mosaic considers unsolicited essays and criticism. We do not consider unsolicited book reviews.
Simultaneous Submissions: yes
Reading Period: Year-round
Reporting Time: 8 to 12 weeks
Author Payment: cash and copies
Founded: 1997
Non Profit: yes
Paid Staff: four
Unpaid Staff:zero
ISSN Number/ISBN Number: ISSN 1531-0388
Total Circulation: 5000
Paid Circulation: 600
Average Print Run: 1,500
Subscription Rate: Individual $15/Institution $50
Single Copy Price: $6
Current Volume/Issue: Issue 19
Frequency per Year: quarterly
Backfile Available: yes
Unsolicited Ms. Received: no
Format: stapled
Size: H 10.5" W 8"
Average Pages: 50
Ads: yes
Ad Rates: $600/full page, See web site for details.

Organization: Mslexia

Type: magazine

CLMP member: no
Primary Editor/Contact Person: Daneet Steffens
Address: P.O. Box 656
Newcastle Upon Tyne, UK NE1 4XF
Web Site Address: http://www.mslexia.co.uk
Publishes: fiction, poetry, reviews, and art
Editorial Focus: The magazine for women who write. Advice and inspiration; news, reviews, interviews; competitions and grants.
Recent Awards Received: Winner of the Inc Writers Award for Outstanding Contribution to Literature
Representative Authors: Val McDermid (Guest Editor), Carol Ann Duffy (Guest Editor), and Wendy Cope (Guest Editor)
Submissions Policy: article proposal by email. Up to four poems of up to 40 lines; up to two stories of up to 3,000 words on our current themes.
Simultaneous Submissions: yes
Reading Period: year-round
Reporting Time: 2 to 3 months
Author Payment: cash and copies
Contests: Women's poetry Competition, Entry fee: Up to five poems for UK £5. Deadline each April. UK £1,000 first prize. UK £500 2nd, UK £250 3rd; see website for guidelines
Founded: 1999
Non Profit: yes
Paid Staff: 7
Unpaid Staff: 1
Distributors: Central Books
Total Circulation: 20,000
Paid Circulation: 11,000
Average Print Run: 300
Subscription Rate: Individual $30/Institution $30
Single Copy Price: £7.50
Current Volume/Issue: Issue 27
Frequency: quarterly
Backfile Available: yes
Unsolicited Ms. Received: yes
% of Unsolicited Ms. Published per Year: 10%
Format: stapled
Size: H 12" W 8.5"
Average Pages: 67
Ads: yes
Ad Rates: £330 half-page, £165 quarter-page; see website for details

Organization: Mudlark

Type: online
CLMP member: no

Primary Editor/Contact Person: William Slaughter
Address: Department of English
1 UNF Drive
Jacksonville, FL 32224-2645
Web Site Address: http://www.unf.edu/mudlark
Publishes: poetry
Editorial Focus: Accomplished work that locates itself anywhere on the spectrum of contemporary practice.
Representative Authors: Mike Smith, Christine Hartzler, and Timothy Bradford
Submissions Policy: To submit or not to submit? Have a look at Mudlark and then decide.
Simultaneous Submissions: yes
Reading Period: Year-round
Reporting Time: one to four weeks
Author Payment: none
Founded: 1995
Non Profit: yes
Paid Staff: zero
Unpaid Staff: one
ISSN Number/ISBN Number: ISSN 1081-3500
Average Page Views per Month: 75,000
Average Unique Visitors per Month: 5,000
Frequency per Year: 12
Publish Print Anthology: no
Average Percentage of Pages per Category: Poetry 100%
Ads: no

Muse & Stone

Type: magazine
CLMP member: yes
Primary Editor/Contact Person: Erik Murphy
Address: Waynesburg College
51 W. College St.
Waynesburg, pa 15370
Publishes: fiction, nonfiction, and poetry
Editorial Focus: Contemporary poetry, fiction, and creative nonfiction. All forms and styles considered.
Submissions Policy: Accepts only original, unpublished work. Submit up to 5 poems, fiction or creative nonfiction up to 6,000 words.
Simultaneous Submissions: yes
Reading Period: 8/1 to 11/15
Reporting Time: 2 to 4 months
Author Payment: copies
Founded: 2006
Non Profit: yes
Paid Staff: 0
Unpaid Staff: 20

Total Circulation: 100
Paid Circulation: 0
Average Print Run: 1000
Subscription Rate: Individual $0/Institution $0
Single Copy Price: $6
Current Volume/Issue: Issue 2
Frequency: 1
Backfile Available: yes
Unsolicited Ms. Received: yes
% of Unsolicited Ms. Published per Year: 40%
Format: perfect
Average Pages: 150
Ads: no

Organization: Mystery Scene Magazine

Type: magazine
CLMP member: yes
Primary Editor/Contact Person: Kate Stine
Address: 331 W. 57th St., Ste. 148
New York, NY 10019
Web Site Address:
http://www.mysteryscenemag.com
Publishes: essays, nonfiction, reviews. audio and video
Editorial Focus: Covers the entire crime and mystery genre-books, TV, films, audio, reference, adult and kids.
Recent Awards Received: 2004 Anthony Award "Best Mystery Magazine," 2006 Ellery Queen Award from Mystery Writers of America
Submissions Policy: See web site. Query first. No fiction.
Simultaneous Submissions: no
Reading Period: Year-round
Reporting Time: one to two months
Author Payment: cash and copies
Contests: no
Founded: 1985
Non Profit: no
Paid Staff: four
Unpaid Staff: zero
Distributors: Ingram, Ubiquity, Disticor, Small Changes, Kent
ISSN Number/ISBN Number: ISSN 1087-674X
Total Circulation: 12,000
Paid Circulation: 7,000
Average Print Run: 12,000
Subscription Rate: Individual $32/Institution $32
Single Copy Price: $7.50

Current Volume/Issue: 22/100
Frequency: five issues
Backfile Available: yes
Unsolicited Ms. Received: yes
% of Unsolicited Ms. Published per Year: 30%
Format: stapled
Size: H 10.5" W 8.25"
Average Pages: 80
Ads: yes
Ad Rates: see website for details

Organization: Nanny Fanny Poetry Magazine

Type: magazine
CLMP member: no
Primary Editor/Contact Person: Lou Hertz
Address: 2524 Stockbridge Dr #15
Indianapolis, IN 46268-2670
Publishes: poetry and reviews
Editorial Focus: "Nanny Fanny" publishes mostly character studies with a preference for accessible, upbeat poems.
Representative Authors: John Grey, Ellaraine Lockie, and Edward Michael Supranowicz
Submissions Policy: Prefer three to eight poems at a time, eight to 30 lines. A cover letter is preferred, SASE is a must.**Simultaneous Submissions:** no
Reading Period: Year-round
Reporting Time: 6 to 10 weeks
Author Payment: copies
Founded: 1998
Non Profit: no
Paid Staff: zero
Unpaid Staff: one
ISSN Number/ISBN Number: ISSN 1529-434X
Total Circulation: 150
Paid Circulation: 40
Subscription Rate: Individual $10/Institution $10
Single Copy Price: $4
Current Volume/Issue: Issue 20
Frequency per Year: triquarterly
Backfile Available: yes
Unsolicited Ms. Received: yes
% of Unsolicited Ms. Published per Year: 8%
Format: stapled
Size: H 8 1/2" W 5 1/2"
Average Pages: 40
Ads: Not using advertising currently but would consider it

Organization: Natural Bridge
Type: magazine
CLMP member: no
Primary Editor/Contact Person: Steven Schreiner
Address: University of Missouri-St. Louis
One University Blvd.
St. Louis, MO 63121
Web Site Address: http://www.umsl.edu/~natural
Publishes: essays, fiction, nonfiction, poetry, and translation
Editorial Focus: Eclectic mix of quality contemporary literature, no specific genre expectations.
Representative Authors: Beckian Fritz Goldberg, Timothy Liu, and Mark Jay Mirsky
Submissions Policy: Regular mail. Submit in one genre only. Enclose SASE. 2 reading periods: 11/1-12/31 and 7/1-8/31. Check web site for guidelines.
Simultaneous Submissions: yes
Reading Period: 11/1 to 12/31; 7/1-8/31
Reporting Time: three to five months
Author Payment: copies and subscription
Contests: no
Founded: 1998
Non Profit: yes
Paid Staff: zero
Unpaid Staff: 12
Distributors: Ubiquity
ISSN Number/ISBN Number: ISSN 1525-9897
Total Circulation: 900
Paid Circulation: 200
Average Print Run: 900
Subscription Rate: Individual $12/Institution $18
Single Copy Price: $8
Current Volume/Issue: Issue 16
Frequency per Year: biannual
Backfile Available: yes
Unsolicited Ms. Received: yes
% of Unsolicited Ms. Published per Year: 3%
Format: perfect
Size: H 8" W 6"
Average Pages: 225
Ads: no
Ad Rates: exchange only

Organization: Neshui
Type: press
CLMP member: no
Primary Editor/Contact Person: Bradley Hodge
Address: 8029 Forsyth Blvd. Ste. 204
St. Louis, MO 63105
Web Site Address:
homepage.mac.com/bbrigitte/neshui/index.html
Publishes: fiction, nonfiction, poetry, and translation
Editorial Focus: fiction and nonfiction books and 10 books of poetry and three books of translations
Representative Authors: Qiu Xiaolong, Michael Castro, and Ryan Jones
Submissions Policy: please send hard copy
Simultaneous Submissions: yes
Reading Period: Year-round
Reporting Time: six to twelve weeks
Author Payment: royalties
Founded: 1995
Non Profit: no
Paid Staff: three
Unpaid Staff: 40
Distributors: Baker & Taylor, Ingram
ISSN Number/ISBN Number: 1931190/1931190
Number of Books Published per Year: 25
Titles in Print: 50
Average Percentage Printed: Paperback 100%

Organization: New American Writing

Type: magazine
CLMP member: no
Primary Editor/Contact Person: Paul Hoover
Address: 369 Molino Ave.
Mill Valley, CA 94941
Web Site Address:
http://www.newamericanwriting.com
Publishes: essays, fiction, poetry, and translation
Editorial Focus: contemporary American poetry, with emphasis on the innovative, and poetry in translation
Representative Authors: Ann Lauterbach, Charles Bernstein, and Nathaniel Mackey
Submissions Policy: Send three to five poems and stories no longer than 15 pages, with accompanying SASE.
Simultaneous Submissions: yes
Reading Period: Year-round
Reporting Time: two to twelve weeks
Author Payment: copies
Founded: 1986
Non Profit: yes
Paid Staff: zero
Unpaid Staff: two
Distributors: Ingram
ISSN Number/ISBN Number: 0893-7842/none
Total Circulation: 3,500
Paid Circulation: 202
Average Print Run: 3,500
Subscription Rate: Individual $36/Institution $36
Single Copy Price: $15
Current Volume/Issue: Issue 24
Frequency per Year: annual
Backfile Available: yes
Unsolicited Ms. Received: yes
% of Unsolicited Ms. Published per Year: 5%
Format: perfect
Size: H 5.5" W 8.5"
Average Pages: 175
Ads: yes
Ad Rates: $250/page; $200/page for two or more ads.

Organization: The New Compass: A Critical Review

Type: online
CLMP member: no
Primary Editor/Contact Person: Michael John DiSanto
Address: 35 Flannery Ln.
Thorold, ON L2V 4V8
Web Site Address: http://www.thenewcompass.ca

Publishes: essays, fiction, nonfiction, poetry, reviews, and translation
Editorial Focus: We are interested in ethics and aesthetics and we invite critical essays on literature in English from a range of periods.
Submissions Policy: Electronic submissions are preferred. Use MS Word (.doc) attachment. Please include short abstract and biographical note.
Simultaneous Submissions: no
Reading Period: Year-round
Reporting Time: one to three months
Author Payment: none
Founded: 2002
Non Profit: yes
Paid Staff: zero
Unpaid Staff: five
ISSN Number/ISBN Number: ISSN 1708-3133
Average Page Views per Month: 250
Average Unique Visitors per Month: 100
Frequency per Year: biannual
Publish Print Anthology: no
Average Percentage of Pages per Category: Fiction 3%, Nonfiction 2%, Poetry 10%, Reviews 25%, Essays 60%
Ads: no

Organization: New Delta Review

Type: magazine
CLMP member: no
Address: Department of English
Louisiana State University
Baton Rouge, LA 70803-5001
Web Site Address: http://english.lsu.edu/journals/ndr
Publishes: essays, fiction, nonfiction, poetry, art, and translation
Reading Period: Year-round
Reporting Time: one to two months
Author Payment: none
Founded: 1984
Non Profit: no

Organization: New Directions Publishing

Type: press
CLMP member: no
Primary Editor/Contact Person: Peggy Fox
Address: 80 8th Ave, 19th Fl
NYC, NY 10011
Web Site Address: http://www.ndpublishing.com

Publishes: essays, fiction, poetry, and translation
Editorial Focus: Contemporary literary fiction and poetry.
Representative Authors: W.G. Sebald, Hilda Doolittle, and Ezra Pound
Simultaneous Submissions: no
Reading Period: Year-round
Reporting Time: three to four months
Author Payment: royalties, cash, and copies
Founded: 1934
Non Profit: no
Paid Staff: 10
Unpaid Staff: zero
Number of Books Published per Year: 30
Titles in Print: 900
Average Percentage Printed: Hardcover 15%, Paperback 85%

Organization: New England Review

Type: magazine
CLMP member: yes
Primary Editor/Contact Person: Carolyn Kuebler
Address: Middlebury College
Middlebury, VT 05753
Web Site Address: http://go.middlebury.edu/nereview
Publishes: essays, fiction, nonfiction, poetry, reviews, and translation
Editorial Focus: Committed to all forms of contemporary cultural expression in the US and abroad.
Recent Awards Received: Best American, Pushcart, O. Henry, New Stories from the South, Best American Nonrequired Reading
Representative Authors: Brigit Pegeen Kelly, Janet Kauffman, and Paul Muldoon
Submissions Policy: No simultaneous submissions in poetry (okay in prose). Submit during reading period only. SASE. No electronic. Thanks!
Simultaneous Submissions: yes
Reading Period: 9/1 to 5/31
Reporting Time: 10 to 12 weeks
Author Payment: cash and copies
Founded: 1978
Non Profit: yes
Paid Staff: three
Unpaid Staff: zero
Distributors: Ingram, Ubiquity, DeBoer
ISSN Number/ISBN Number: ISSN 1053-1297
Total Circulation: 1,800
Paid Circulation: 1,000
Average Print Run: 1,800

Subscription Rate: Individual $25/Institution $40
Single Copy Price: $8
Current Volume/Issue: 28/2
Frequency per Year: quarterly
Backfile Available: yes
Unsolicited Ms. Received: yes
% of Unsolicited Ms. Published per Year: 95%
Format: perfect
Size: H 10" W 7"
Average Pages: 216
Ads: yes
Ad Rates: $200 full page, $125 half page, some exchange ads available.

Organization: New Letters Magazine

Type: magazine
CLMP member: yes
Primary Editor/Contact Person: Robert Stewart, Editor
Address: University House
5101 Rockhill Road
Kansas City, MO 64110
Web Site Address: http://www.newletters.org
Publishes: essays, fiction, poetry, reviews, art, and translation
Editorial Focus: To continue the 75-year tradition of finding the best writing that is fresh and on the cutting edge in style and content.
Recent Awards Received: National Magazine Award finalist in 2007; Pushcart Prizes; Best New Poets three years in a row.
Representative Authors: Daniel Woodrell, Janet Burroway, and Naomi Shihab Nye
Submissions Policy: Please see our web site for complete writer's and artist's guidelines.
Simultaneous Submissions: yes
Reading Period: 10/1-5/1
Reporting Time: 8 to 16 weeks
Author Payment: cash and copies
Contests: See web site for contest guidelines.
Founded: 1934
Non Profit: yes
Paid Staff: three
Unpaid Staff: four
Distributors: Ingram and DeBoer
ISSN Number/ISBN Number: ISSN 0146-4930
Total Circulation: varies
Paid Circulation: 2,000
Average Print Run: 3,500
Subscription Rate: Individual $22/Institution $30

Single Copy Price: $10
Current Volume/Issue: 73/3
Frequency per Year: quarterly
Backfile Available: yes
Unsolicited Ms. Received: yes
% of Unsolicited Ms. Published per Year: 90%
Format: perfect
Size: H 9" W 6"
Average Pages: 150
Ads: yes
Ad Rates: exchange ads offered; paid ads start at $150.

Organizatioin: The New Madrid

Type: magazine
CLMP member: yes
Primary Editor/Contact Person: Ann Neelon
Address: 7C Faculty Hall, Dept of English & Phil.
Murray State University
Murray, KY 42071
Website Address: www.newmadridjournal.org
Publishes: essays, fiction, nonfiction, poetry, reviews, art, and translation
Editorial Focus: We focus primarily on quality work from the "flyover zone," but quality trumps everything.
Submissions Policy: Please see our website for submission details.
Simultaneous Submissions: yes
Reading Period: 08/15 to 12/01
Reporting Time: 3 to 6 months
Author Payment: copies
Founded: 2006
Non Profit: yes
Paid Staff: 2
Unpaid Staff: 0
Total Circulation: 1,500
Paid Circulation: 25
Average Print Run: 1500
Subscription Rate: Individual $15.00/Institution $15.00
Single Copy Price: $8.00
Current Volume/Issue: 2/2
Frequency: 2
Backfile Available: yes
Unsolicited Ms. Received: yes
% of Unsolicited Ms. Published per Year: 33%
Format: perfect
Average Pages: 150
Ads: no
Ad Rates: see website for details

Organization: New Michigan Press/DIAGRAM

Type: press
Primary Editor/Contact Person: Ander Monson
Address: 648 Crescent NE
Grand Rapids, MI 49503
Web Site Address:
http://newmichiganpress.com/nmp
Publishes: fiction, nonfiction, and poetry
Editorial Focus: Literary fiction, poetry, and especially genre-bending or -transcending work.
Representative Authors: Jason Bredle, Arielle Greenberg, and G C Waldrep
Submissions Policy: We read unsolicited submissions only through our yearly chapbook contest (guidelines on site), deadline in spring.
Simultaneous Submissions: yes
Reading Period: Year-round
Reporting Time: one to four months
Author Payment: cash and copies
Contests: See web site for contest guidelines.
Founded: 1999
Non Profit: no
Paid Staff: one
Unpaid Staff: eight
ISSN Number/ISBN Number: ISBN 0-9725095
Number of Books Published per Year: 4-6
Titles in Print: 10
Average Print Run: 500
Average Percentage Printed: Paperback 10%, Chapbook 90%
Average Price: $8

Organization: New Ohio Review--/nor

Type: magazine
CLMP member: yes
Primary Editor/Contact Person: John Bullock
Address: English Dept./360 Ellis Hall
Ohio University
Athens, OH 45701
Website Address: www.ohiou.edu/nor
Publishes: essays, fiction, nonfiction, poetry, art, translation, and video
Editorial Focus: Innovative work that blurs conventional boundaries and resists easy definition. We're not, however, deaf to convention.
Recent Awards Received: CLMP Mentorship Grant;Ohio Arts Council Arts Access Grant.

Representative Authors: Nathaniel Mackey, Thylias Moss, and David Shields
Submissions Policy: Please see website.
Simultaneous Submissions: yes
Reading Period: year-round
Reporting Time: 1 to 3 months
Author Payment: copies
Contests: Editors' Prize in poetry, non-fiction, and fiction. $750 prize per genre. Deadline November 1. $15 entry fee.
Founded: 2007
Non Profit: yes
Paid Staff: 1
Unpaid Staff: 2
Distributors: TBA
Wholesalers: TBA
ISSN Number/ISBN Number: 1935-357X/9 771935 357002
Total Circulation: 900
Paid Circulation: 200
Average Print Run: 1,000
Subscription Rate: Individual $20/Institution $26
Single Copy Price: $12
Current Volume/Issue: 1/2
Frequency: 2
Backfile Available: yes
Unsolicited Ms. Received: yes
% of Unsolicited Ms. Published per Year: 3%
Format: perfect
Size: H 8.5" W 6.5"
Average Pages: 175
Ads: yes
Ad Rates: Contact for details

Organization: The New Press

Type: press
CLMP member: yes
Primary Editor/Contact Person: Ellen Adler, Publisher
Address: 38 Greene St.
4th Floor
New York, NY 10013
Web Site Address: http://thenewpress.com
Publishes: essays, fiction, nonfiction, and translation
Editorial Focus: Contemporary social issues, immigration, human rights, labor and popular economics, education, law, international literature.
Representative Authors: Studs Terkel, Helen Caldicott, and David Cole
Submissions Policy: Unsolicited manuscripts and

proposals must be submitted with SASE.
Simultaneous Submissions: yes
Reading Period: Year-round
Reporting Time: four to six weeks
Author Payment: royalties, cash, and copies
Contests: Kenneth B. Clark Prize; see website for guidelines
Founded: 1992
Non Profit: yes
Paid Staff: 20
Unpaid Staff: three
Distributors: W.W. Norton (USA)
Wholesalers: Ingram, Baker & Taylor
ISSN Number/ISBN Number: ISBN 1-56584-
Number of Books Published per Year: 50
Titles in Print: 600
Average Print Run: 4,500
Average Percentage Printed: Hardcover 54%, Paperback 46%
Average Price: $21.95

Organization: New Rivers Press

Type: press
CLMP member: yes
Primary Editor/Contact Person: Donna Carlson, Managing Editor
Address: New Rivers Press, MSUM
1104 Seventh Ave. S.
Moorhead, MN 56563
Website Address: www.newriverspress.com
Publishes: essays, fiction, nonfiction, poetry, and translation
Editorial Focus: We consider work of every character from new and emerging writers, and are especially interested in upper Midwest writers.
Representative Authors: Cezarija Abartis, Ron Rindo, and Ronna Wineberg
Submissions Policy: We publish three books each year in our MVP contest. For information on it and other submissions, go to www.newriverspress.com
Simultaneous Submissions: yes
Reading Period: year-round
Reporting Time: 1 to 2 months
Author Payment: royalties, cash, and copies
Contests: see website for guidelines
Founded: 1968
Non Profit: yes
Paid Staff: 3
Unpaid Staff: 15+
Distributors: Consortium

ISSN Number/ISBN Number: ISBN 0-89823-
Number of Books Published per Year: 4-6
Titles in Print: 314
Average Print Run: 1,500
Average Percentage Printed: Paperback 100%
Average Price: $13.95

Organization: New Star Books

Type: press
CLMP member: no
Primary Editor/Contact Person: Carellin Brooks
Address: 107-3477 Commercial St.
Vancouver, BC V5K 1K8
Website Address: www.newstarbooks.com
Publishes: fiction, nonfiction, and poetry
Editorial Focus: Books on social issues, politics, British Columbia and the West, and literary works. Details on our website.
Representative Authors: Andrew Struthers, Brian Fawcett, and Noam Chomsky
Submissions Policy: Considers unsolicited fiction MS; does not consider unsolicited poetry. For nonfiction, send query first.
Simultaneous Submissions: yes
Reading Period: year-round
Reporting Time: 4 to 6 months
Author Payment: royalties and copies
Founded: 1969
Non Profit: no
Paid Staff: 3
Unpaid Staff: 0
Distributors: New Star Books
Number of Books Published per Year: 12
Titles in Print: 76
Average Print Run: 1,000
Average Percentage Printed: Paperback 100%
Average Price: $18

Organization: The New York Quarterly

Type: magazine
CLMP member: yes
Primary Editor/Contact Person: Raymond Hammond
Address: PO Box 693
Old Chelsea Station
New York, NY 10113
Website Address: www.nyquarterly.com
Publishes: essays and poetry
Editorial Focus: NYQ is devoted to excellence in the publication of the best cross-section of contemporary poetry.

Representative Authors: Charles Bukowski, W. D. Snodgrass, and X. J. Kennedy
Submissions Policy: Enclose a SASE and no more than 3-5 typewritten poems.
Simultaneous Submissions: yes
Reading Period: year-round
Reporting Time: 6 to 12 weeks
Author Payment: copies
Founded: 1969
Non Profit: yes
Paid Staff: 0
Unpaid Staff: 12
Distributors: DeBoer, Ubiquity
ISSN Number/ISBN Number: ISSN 0028-7482
Total Circulation: 1,000
Paid Circulation: 800
Average Print Run: 1,500
Subscription Rate: Individual $20/Institution $28
Single Copy Price: $8
Current Volume/Issue: Issue 60
Frequency: triquarterly
Backfile Available: yes
Unsolicited Ms. Received: yes
% of Unsolicited Ms. Published per Year: 5%
Format: perfect
Size: H 9" W 6"
Average Pages: 128
Ads: yes
Ad Rates: see website for details

Organization: The New York Theatre Experience, Inc

Type: press
CLMP member: no
Primary Editor/Contact Person: Martin Denton
Address: PO Box 1606
Murray Hill Station
New York, NY 10156
Website Address: www.nyte.org
Publishes: fiction
Editorial Focus: An annual anthology of plays by emerging playwrights recently produced.
Representative Authors: Paul Knox, Brian Sloan, and Joe Godfrey
Submissions Policy: Plays must be seen live by the editor and staff. No submissions
Simultaneous Submissions: no
Reading Period: year-round
Reporting Time: one to 10 months

Author Payment: copies
Founded: 1999
Non Profit: yes
Paid Staff: 1
Unpaid Staff: 1
Distributors: Amazon.com, Drama Bookshop, Barnes & Noble
Wholesalers: Baker & Taylor
ISSN Number/ISBN Number: 1546-1319/09670234xx
Number of Books Published per Year: 1-2
Titles in Print: 9
Average Print Run: 1,500
Average Percentage Printed: Paperback 100%
Average Price: $16

Organization: NeWest Press

Type: press
CLMP member: no
Primary Editor/Contact Person: Lou Morin
Address: 201-8540-109 St.
Edmonton, AB T6G 1E6
Website Address: www.newestpress.ccom
Publishes: essays, fiction, nonfiction, and poetry
Editorial Focus: The role of NeWest Press in Canadian publishing is to publish the voices of western Canada.
Recent Awards Received: 2005 Alberta Book Awards Trade fiction Book of the year for Displaced Persons by Margie Taylor
Submissions Policy: Full manuscripts only. Include appropriate SASE if you wish the manuscript returned. Currently not accepting poetry.
Simultaneous Submissions: yes
Reading Period: year-round
Reporting Time: six to nine months
Author Payment: royalties
Founded: 1977
Non Profit: yes
Paid Staff: 3
Unpaid Staff: 0
Distributors: LitDistCo, Gazelle Book Services
ISSN Number/ISBN Number: ISBN 1896300, 0920897,1897126
Number of Books Published per Year: 12
Titles in Print: 120
Average Print Run: 1,500
Average Percentage Printed: Paperback 100%
Average Price: $20

Organization: NewSouth Books

Type: press
CLMP member: no
Primary Editor/Contact Person: Suzanne La Rosa
Address: PO Box 1588
Montgomery, AL 36102
Website Address: www.newsouthbooks.com
Publishes: essays, fiction, nonfiction, and poetry
Editorial Focus: Literary fiction and non-fiction which examines our place in history and our cultural identities.
Recent Awards Received: Sydney Taylor Award, J. C. Coley Award, Silver Gavel Award
Representative Authors: Mark Ethridge, Anna Olswanger, and Paul Gaston
Submissions Policy: We prefer full manuscripts to be mailed with cover letter, synopsis, author bio. Follow-up by email okay.
Simultaneous Submissions: yes
Reading Period: year-round
Reporting Time: 3 to 6 months
Author Payment: royalties
Founded: 2000
Non Profit: yes
Paid Staff: six
Unpaid Staff: zero
Distributors: John F. Blair, Publisher
Wholesalers: Many, including Baker & Taylor, Ingram
ISSN Number/ISBN Number: ISSN 1-58838
Number of Books Published per Year: 20
Titles in Print: 120
Average Print Run: 3,500
Average Percentage Printed: Hardcover 75%, Paperback 25%
Average Price: $22.50

Organization: Newtopia Magazine

Type: online
CLMP member: no
Primary Editor/Contact Person: Charles Shaw
Address: 4410 N. Wolcott 2S
Chicago, IL 60640
Web Site Address: http://www.newtopiamagazine.net
Publishes: essays, fiction, nonfiction, poetry, reviews, art, and audio
Editorial Focus: a journal of countercultural thought covering alternative art, culture, economics, history, politics, and social movements.
Recent Awards Received: 2005 Democratic Media Award

Representative Authors: Charles Shaw, David Ray Griffin, and Kevin Zeese
Submissions Policy: Guidelines posted on the web site.
Simultaneous Submissions: yes
Reading Period: Year-round
Reporting Time: one to two months
Author Payment: none
Founded: 2002
Non Profit: yes
Paid Staff: zero
Unpaid Staff: 35
ISSN Number/ISBN Number: none/none
Average Page Views per Month: 813,000
Average Unique Visitors per Month: 200,000
Frequency per Year: biannual
Publish Print Anthology: yes
Average Percentage of Pages per Category: Fiction 10%, Nonfiction 10%, Poetry 10%, Reviews 10%, Essays 50%, Art 10%
Ad Rates: Usually our ads are free endorsements for friends and allies
See web site for details.

Organization: Night Train Publications/Night Train

Type: magazine
CLMP member: yes
Primary Editor/Contact Person: Rusty Barnes
Address: 212 Bellingham Ave.
#2
Revere, MA 02151-4106
Web Site Address:
http://www.nighttrainmagazine.com
Publishes: fiction and poetry
Editorial Focus: Night Train publishes flash fiction, fiction and poetry.
Representative Authors: Curtis Smith, Ed Falco, and Susann Cokal
Submissions Policy: Submit only through our website.
Simultaneous Submissions: yes
Reading Period: Year-round
Reporting Time: one to four weeks
Author Payment: none
Contests: See web site for contest guidelines.
Founded: 2002
Non Profit: yes
Paid Staff: zero
Unpaid Staff: four

ISSN Number/ISBN Number: ISSN 1540-5494
Single Copy Price: $14.95
Current Volume/Issue: Issue seven
Frequency per Year: annual
Backfile Available: yes
Unsolicited Ms. Received: yes
% of Unsolicited Ms. Published per Year: 98%
Format: perfect
Size: H 9" W 6"
Average Pages: 250
Ads: no

Organization: Nightboat Books, Inc

Type: press
CLMP member: yes
Primary Editor/Contact Person: Stephen Motika
Address: 7 Fishkill Ave
Cold Spring, NY 10516 **Web Site Address:**
http://www.nightboat.org
Publishes: essays, fiction, nonfiction, and poetry
Editorial Focus: Innovative poetry, prose, and mixed genre (or anti-genre!) work.
Representative Authors: Fanny Howe, Michael Burkard, and Nathalie Stephens
Submissions Policy: Poetry: please see web site for guidelines. Prose: no unsolicited mss. at this time. Please query with sample chapter.
Simultaneous Submissions: yes
Reading Period: 9/1 to 11/30
Reporting Time: one to two months
Author Payment: royalties, cash, and copies
Contests: See web site for contest guidelines.
Founded: 2003
Non Profit: yes
Paid Staff: zero
Unpaid Staff: six
Distributors: Small Press Distribution
Wholesalers: Baker & Taylor
ISSN Number/ISBN Number: ISBN 0-9767185
Number of Books Published per Year: two
Titles in Print: five
Average Print Run: 1,000
Average Percentage Printed: Paperback 100%
Average Price: $16

Organization: Nightshade Press

Type: press
CLMP member: yes
Primary Editor/Contact Person: Lynn Marie Petrillo

Address: Keystone College
One College Green
La Plume, PA 18440
Publishes: fiction, nonfiction, and poetry
Editorial Focus: Has been poetry; currently literary work relating to the "Keystone Culture"-education, diversity, nature, art, enlightenment
Representative Authors: Karen Blomain, Martha Silano, and David Watts
Submissions Policy: will accept open submissions from authors living in PA, NY, and other areas of the Northeastern US within reading period
Simultaneous Submissions: yes
Reading Period: 4/1 to 9/30
Reporting Time: up ro four months
Author Payment: copies
Founded: 1988
Non Profit: yes
Paid Staff: two
Unpaid Staff: ~six
Number of Books Published per Year: one
Titles in Print: 59
Average Percentage Printed: Paperback 100%
Backfile Available: yes

Organization: Nimrod International Journal

Type: magazine
CLMP member: yes
Primary Editor/Contact Person: Francine Ringold
Address: The University of Tulsa
600 S. College Ave.
Tulsa, OK 74104
Web Site Address: http://www.utulsa.edu/nimrod
Publishes: fiction, nonfiction, poetry, art, and translation
Editorial Focus: We are looking for writing of quality and vigor.
Representative Authors: Gina Ochsner, Don Welch, and Virgil Suarez
Submissions Policy: Open submissions all year. E-mails only from writers living overseas. Theme information for spring issue available in fall.
Simultaneous Submissions: yes
Reading Period: Year-round
Reporting Time: one to three months
Author Payment: copies
Contests: See web site for contest guidelines.
Founded: 1956
Non Profit: yes

Paid Staff: three
Unpaid Staff: 35
ISSN Number/ISBN Number: 0029-053X/changes
Total Circulation: 2,000
Paid Circulation: 1,400
Average Print Run: 2,500
Subscription Rate: Individual $17.50/Institution $30
Single Copy Price: $10
Current Volume/Issue: 50/2
Frequency per Year: biannual
Backfile Available: yes
Unsolicited Ms. Received: yes
% of Unsolicited Ms. Published per Year: 85%
Format: perfect
Size: H 9" W 6"
Average Pages: 200
Ads: yes
Ad Rates: exchange

Organization: Ninth Letter

Type: magazine
CLMP member: yes
Primary Editor/Contact Person: Jodee Stanley
Address: Dept. of English, Univ. of Illinois
608 S. Wright St.
Urbana, IL 61801
Web Site Address: http://www.ninthletter.com
Publishes: fiction, nonfiction, poetry, and translation
Editorial Focus: We are looking for a wide range of styles in all genres, from traditional forms to experimental.
Recent Awards Received: Best American Short Stories, Best New Poets, Pushcart, Best American Fantasy, Year's Best Fantasy/Horror, Best Creative Nonfiction
Representative Authors: Bob Hicok, Chris Abani, and Diane Comer
Submissions Policy: Please submit only one prose submission (max 30 pages) or up to six poems (max. 10 pages) at a time.
Simultaneous Submissions: no
Reading Period: 9/1 to 4/30
Reporting Time: eight to 10 weeks
Author Payment: cash and copies
Founded: 2003
Non Profit: yes
Paid Staff: six
Unpaid Staff: 10
Distributors: Ingram, Ubiquity
ISSN Number/ISBN Number: ISSN 1547-8440

Total Circulation: 2,500
Paid Circulation: 300
Average Print Run: 3,500
Subscription Rate: Individual $21.95/Institution $21.95
Single Copy Price: $14.95
Current Volume/Issue: 4/1
Frequency per Year: biannual
Backfile Available: yes
Unsolicited Ms. Received: yes
% of Unsolicited Ms. Published per Year: 75%
Format: perfect
Size: H 9" W 12"
Average Pages: 192
Ads: no

Organization: No: a journal of the arts

Type: magazine
CLMP member: yes
Primary Editor/Contact Person: Deb Klowden
Address: 208 President St., #3
Brooklyn, NY 11231
Web Site Address: http://www.nojournal.com
Publishes: essays, poetry, reviews, art, and translation
Submissions Policy: Submissions should be sent through post, SASE included. Electronic submissions are not accepted.
Simultaneous Submissions: yes
Reading Period: Year-round
Reporting Time: one to two months
Author Payment: none
Founded: 2003
Non Profit: yes
Paid Staff: yes
Unpaid Staff: yes
Distributors: SPD, DeBoer, Ingram
Total Circulation: 1,800
Paid Circulation: 350
Average {Print Run: 2,500
Subscription Rate: Individual $20/Institution $28
Single Copy Price: $12
Current Volume/Issue: Issue five
Frequency per Year: biannual
Backfile Available: yes
Unsolicited Ms. Received: yes
Format: perfect
Size: H 9" W 6"
Average Pages: 230
Ads: no

Organization: Non Serviam Press

Type: press
CLMP member: no
Primary Editor/Contact Person: Patrick Walsh
Address: 101 Stanton St, Apt 8
New York, NY 10009
Web Site Address: http://www.nonserviamnyc.com
Publishes: essays, fiction, and poetry
Editorial Focus: NSP seeks original styles and bold ideas.
Representative Authors: Alan Lockwood, Roger Ludwig, and Patrick Walsh
Submissions Policy: Send a sample of any kind of writing to the address above. Include SASE
Simultaneous Submissions: yes
Reading Period: Year-round
Reporting Time: four to twelve weeks
Author Payment: none
Contests: no contests
Founded: 2001
Non Profit: yes
Paid Staff: zero
Unpaid Staff: five
Number of Books Published per Year: two
Titles in Print: two
Average Percentage Printed: Paperback 90%, Chapbook 10%

Organization: NOON

Type: magazine
CLMP member: yes
Primary Editor/Contact Person: Diane Williams
Address: 1324 Lexington Ave.
PMB 298
New York, NY 10128
Publishes: essays, fiction, nonfiction, art, and translation
Recent Awards Received: two Pushcart Prizes, one O'Henry Prize
Representative Authors: Christine Schutt, Lydia Davis, and Gary Lutz
Submissions Policy: Include SASE and necessary postage.
Simultaneous Submissions: yes
Reading Period: Year-round
Reporting Time: one to three months
Author Payment: none
Founded: 2000

Non Profit: yes
Paid Staff: four
Unpaid Staff: eight
Distributors: DeBoer and Ingram
ISSN Number/ISBN Number: ISSN 15268055
Total Circulation: 5,000
Paid Circulation: 500
Average Print Run: 5,000
Subscription Rate: Individual $9/Institution $9
Single Copy Price: $9
Current Volume/Issue: 2006
Frequency per Year: annual
Backfile Available: yes
Unsolicited Ms. Received: yes
% of Unsolicited Ms. Published per Year: 85%
Format: perfect
Average Pages: 140
Ads: yes

Organization: North American Review

Type: magazine
CLMP member: yes
Primary Editor/Contact Person: Vince Gotera
Address: University of Northern Iowa
1222 W. 27th St.
Cedar Falls, IA 50614-0516
Web Site Address:
http://webdelsol.com/NorthAmReview/NARToday/htm
Publishes: essays, fiction, nonfiction, poetry, reviews,
art, and translation
Editorial Focus: We are interested in high-quality
poetry, fiction, nonfiction, and art on any subject.
Representative Authors: Gary Gildner, Maxine Hong
Kingston, and Marilyn Hacker
Submissions Policy: Address Submissions to: Fiction
Editor or Poetry Editor or Nonfiction Editor or Book
Review Editor
Simultaneous Submissions: no
Reading Period: Year-round
Reporting Time: three to six months
Author Payment: cash and copies
Contests: James Hearst Poetry Prize and Kurt
Vonnegut Fiction Prize; see website for guidelines
Founded: 1815
Non Profit: yes
Paid Staff: three
Unpaid Staff: 10
ISSN Number/ISBN Number: ISSN 0029-2397
Total Circulation: 2,500
Paid Circulation: 2,000

Average Print Run: 2900
Subscription Rate: Individual $22/Institution $22
Single Copy Price: $5
Current Volume/Issue: 289/5
Frequency per Year: five issues
Backfile Available: yes
Unsolicited Ms. Received: yes
% of Unsolicited Ms. Published per Year: 99%
Format: stapled
Size: H 10 7/8" W 8 1/8"
Average Pages: 54
Ads: yes
Ad Rates: Request from managing editor.
See web site for details.

Organization: The North Atlantic Review

Type: magazine
CLMP member: yes
Primary Editor/Contact Person: John Gill
Address: 15 Arbutus Ln.
Stony Brook, NY 11790-1408
Web Site Address: http://www.johnedwardgill.com
Publishes: essays, fiction, nonfiction, poetry, reviews,
and art
Editorial Focus: Looking for quality fiction, poetry and
or prose.
Representative Authors: Stephen Lewis, Margaret
Genovese, and Kim Tilbury
Submissions Policy: Manuscripts should be typed
and double-spaced. All correspondence must be
accompanied by a self-addressed, stamped envelope.
Simultaneous Submissions: yes
Reading Period: Year-round
Reporting Time: five to six months
Author Payment: copies
Founded: 1982
Non Profit: yes
Paid Staff: zero
Unpaid Staff: four
Distributors: http://www.johnedwardgill.com
ISSN Number/ISBN Number: ISSN 1040-7324
Total Circulation: 5,000
Paid Circulation: 100
Subscription Rate: Individual $18/Institution $18
Single Copy Price: $10
Current Volume/Issue: 16/2004
Frequency per Year: annual
Backfile Available: yes
Unsolicited Ms. Received: yes

% of Unsolicited Ms. Published per Year: 35%
Format: perfect
Size: H 9.75" W 6.75"
Average Pages: 300
Ads: yes
Ad Rates: complimentary

Organization: North Carolina Literary Review

Type: magazine
CLMP member: yes
Primary Editor/Contact Person: Margaret Bauer
Address: Dept. of English
East Carolina University
Greenville, NC 27858
Web Site Address: http://www.ecu.edu/nclr
Publishes: essays, fiction, nonfiction, poetry, reviews, and art
Editorial Focus: North Carolina literature and writers
Recent Awards Received: Council of Editors of Learned Journals Best Design Award (1999) and Best New Journal (1994); numerous design awards.
Representative Authors: Fred Chappell, James Applewhite, and Allan Gurganus
Submissions Policy: see our web site for submission guidelines
Simultaneous Submissions: no
Reading Period: 8/15 to 5/15
Reporting Time: one to six months
Author Payment: copies and subscription
Founded: 1991
Non Profit: yes
Paid Staff: one
Unpaid Staff: 10
Distributors: NC bookstores
Wholesalers: the NCLR office
ISSN Number/ISBN Number: ISSN 1063-00724
Total Circulation: 750
Paid Circulation: 325
Average Print Run: 1,000
Subscription Rate: Individual $20/2years/Institution $20/2years
Single Copy Price: $15
Current Volume/Issue: 16/2006
Frequency per Year: annual
Backfile Available: yes
Unsolicited Ms. Received: yes
% of Unsolicited Ms. Published per Year: 10%
Format: perfect
Size: H 10" W 7"

Average Pages: 200
Ads: yes
Ad Rates: $200 full-page, $125 half-page, $75 quarter-page.

Organization: North Dakota Quarterly

Type: magazine
CLMP member: yes
Primary Editor/Contact Person: Robert W. Lewis
Address: Merrifield Hall Room 110
276 Centennial Drive Stop 7209
Grand,Forks, ND 58202-7209
Web Site Address:
http://www.und.nodak.edu/org/ndq
Publishes: essays, fiction, nonfiction, poetry, reviews, and art
Editorial Focus: Ethnic/multicultural, historical, literary, especially interested in work by and about Native American writers.
Recent Awards Received: An essay in NDQ 73.3 selected for Pushcart Prize XXXII.
Representative Authors: Sandra Hunter, Peter Nabokov, and Robert Bagg
Submissions Policy: Hard copies only. No simultaneous poetry or essay submissions.
Simultaneous Submissions: yes
Reading Period: 09/01 to 05/31
Reporting Time: two to four months
Author Payment: copies
Founded: 1911
Non Profit: yes
Paid Staff: five
Unpaid Staff: two to three
Distributors: EBSCO, SWETS, North American Library Services
ISSN Number/ISBN Number: ISSN 0029-277X
Total Circulation: 500
Paid Circulation: 400
Average Print Run: 600
Subscription Rate: Individual $25/Institution $30
Single Copy Price: $10
Current Volume/Issue: 74/2
Frequency per Year: quarterly
Backfile Available: yes
Unsolicited Ms. Received: yes
% of Unsolicited Ms. Published per Year: 70%
Format: perfect
Size: H 9" W 6"
Average Pages: 200
Ads: yes

Ad Rates: Full page $150; half-page$100

Organization: Northeast African Studies

Type: magazine
CLMP member: no
Primary Editor/Contact Person: Carol Cole
Address: Michigan State University Press
1405 S. Harrison Rd., Ste. 25
East Lansing, MI 48823-5245
Web Site Address: http://msupress.msu.edu/journals/neas/
Publishes: essays and reviews
Editorial Focus: Interdisciplinary scholarly journal focusing on Ethiopia, Sudan, Eritrea, Somalia, and Djibouti
Representative Authors: Jon Abbink, Ludwien Kapteijns, and Donald Donham
Submissions Policy: Consult MSU Press before preparing manuscripts. Follow Chicago style 15th ed., endnote reference system or author-date system
Simultaneous Submissions: yes
Reading Period: Year-round
Reporting Time: three to six months
Author Payment: none
Founded: 1994
Non Profit: yes
Paid Staff: one
Unpaid Staff: two
Distributors: Michigan State University Press
ISSN Number/ISBN Number: ISSN 0740-9133
Total Circulation: 150
Paid Circulation: 120
Average Print Run: 350
Subscription Rate: Individual $40/Institution $55
Single Copy Price: $20
Current Volume/Issue: 8/2
Frequency per Year: triquarterly
Backfile Available: yes
Unsolicited Ms. Received: yes
Format: perfect
Size: H 9" W 6"
Average Pages: 125
Ads: yes
Ad Rates: See web site for details.

Organization: Northwest Review

Type: magazine
CLMP member: no
Primary Editor/Contact Person: John Witte
Address: 369 PLC
Eugene, OR 97403
Web Site Address:
http://www.uoregon.edu/~engl/deptinfo/NWR.html
Publishes: essays, fiction, nonfiction, poetry, reviews, art, and translation
Recent Awards Received: Our authors have recently been included in the Best American Poetry, Pushcart Prize, and Best American Essays anthologies.
Representative Authors: Ted Kooser, Lucia Perillo, and Charles Bukowski
Submissions Policy: Invites submissions of original poems, stories and essays.
Simultaneous Submissions: no
Reading Period: Year-round
Reporting Time: eight to 10 weeks
Author Payment: copies and subscription
Founded: 1957
Non Profit: yes
Paid Staff: three
Unpaid Staff: 15
Distributors: DeBoer
ISSN Number/ISBN Number: ISSN 0029 3423
Total Circulation: 1,400
Paid Circulation: 1,000
Average Print Run: 1,400
Subscription Rate: Individual $22/Institution $28
Single Copy Price: $8
Current Volume/Issue: 43/3
Frequency per Year: triquarterly
Backfile Available: yes
Unsolicited Ms. Received: yes
% of Unsolicited Ms. Published per Year: 100%
Format: perfect
Size: H 9" W 6"
Average Pages: 140
Ads: yes
Ad Rates: $165/full page
See Web site for details.

Organization: The Northwoods Journal, a mag for writers

Type: magazine
CLMP member: no
Primary Editor/Contact Person: Robert Olmsted
Address: PO BOX 298
Thomaston, ME 04861
Web Site Address: http://www.americanletters.org
Publishes: essays, fiction, nonfiction, poetry, and

reviews
Editorial Focus: Good stuff that might otherwise be lost. Real guidance to writers.
Representative Authors: J.F. Pytko, Richard Vaughn, and Mary Wallace
Submissions Policy: No electronic submission. Nothing previously published. Read guidelines before submitting. #10 SASE.
Simultaneous Submissions: no
Reading Period: Year-round
Reporting Time: one to three weeks
Author Payment: cash
Founded: 1974
Non Profit: yes
Paid Staff: one
Unpaid Staff: two
Total Circulation: 200
Paid Circulation: 200
Average Print Run: 225
Subscription Rate: Individual $18/Institution $18
Single Copy Price: $6.50
Current Volume/Issue: XI/1
Frequency per Year: quarterly
Backfile Available: yes
Unsolicited Ms. Received: yes
% of Unsolicited Ms. Published per Year: 50%
Format: stapled
Size: H 8.5" W 5.5"
Average Pages: 36-40
Ads: yes
Ad Rates: $70 page, $38 half-page $20 quarter-page. Almost none sold. See web site for details.

Organization: Northwoods Press

Type: press
CLMP member: no
Primary Editor/Contact Person: Robert W. Olmsted
Address: PO BOX 298
Thomaston, ME 04861
Web Site Address: http://www.americanletters.org
Publishes: nonfiction and poetry
Editorial Focus: Poetry and local/family history
Representative Authors: Robert Johnson, Diana Durham, and Paul Bellerive
Submissions Policy: Start with a personal marketing plan. Book must be 104 pages or more.
Simultaneous Submissions: yes
Reading Period: Year-round
Reporting Time: one to 12 weeks

Author Payment: royalties
Contests: See web site for contest guidelines.
Founded: 1972
Non Profit: yes
Paid Staff: one
Unpaid Staff: one
Distributors: Ingram, Baker & Taylor, Barnes & Noble, amazon.com
ISSN Number/ISBN Number: ISBN 0-89002-xxx-x
Number of Books Published per Year: five
Titles in Print: 20
Average Percentage Printed: Hardcover 5%, Paperback 90%, Other 5%

Organization: The Notre Dame Review

Type: magazine
CLMP member: yes
Primary Editor/Contact Person: Kathleen Canavan
Address: 840 Flanner Hall
University of Notre Dame
Notre Dame, IN 46556
Web Site Address:
http://www.nd.edu/~ndr/review.htm
Publishes: fiction, poetry, and reviews
Editorial Focus: an independent, non-commercial magazine of contemporary American and international fiction, poetry, criticism and art.
Representative Authors: Seamus Heaney, Czeslaw Milosz, and Emer Martin
Submissions Policy: Submit best fiction and poetry. All themes. We only read submissions from September through November and January through April.
Simultaneous Submissions: yes
Reading Period: 9/11 to 1/3
Reporting Time: two to four months
Author Payment: cash, copies, and subscription
Contests: See web site for contest guidelines.
Founded: 1994
Non Profit: yes
Paid Staff: yes
Unpaid Staff: 12
Distributors: Ingram, IPD, Media Solutions, Ubiquity
ISSN Number/ISBN Number: 1082-1864/1-892492-15-6
Total Circulation: 1,500
Paid Circulation: 220
Average Print Run: 1,500
Subscription Rate: Individual $15/Institution $20

Single Copy Price: $8
Current Volume/Issue: Issue 16
Frequency per Year: biannual
Backfile Available: yes
Unsolicited Ms. Received: yes
Format: perfect
Size: H 9" W 6"
Average Pages: 195
Ads: yes
Ad Rates: Exchange

Organization: Nuvein Magazine

Type: online
CLMP member: no
Primary Editor/Contact Person: Enrique Diaz
Address: 4522 N. Jerry Ave.
Baldwin Park, CA 91706
Web Site Address: http://www.nuvein.com
Publishes: essays, fiction, nonfiction, poetry, reviews, art, translation, and audio
Editorial Focus: Nuvein's editorial focus is on writing which is just off the mainstream path, publishing voices rarely heard.
Representative Authors: Tom Sheehan, Elaine Hatfield, and Paul A. Toth
Submissions Policy: Submit by e-mail or postal mail. There is no limit on the number of words per work or the number of works submitted.
Simultaneous Submissions: no
Reading Period: Year-round
Reporting Time: one to three months
Author Payment: subscription
Contests: See web site for contest guidelines.
Founded: 1982
Non Profit: yes
Paid Staff: zero
Unpaid Staff: six
ISSN Number/ISBN Number: ISSN 1523-7877
Average Page Views per Month: 8,000
Average Unique Visitors per Month: 3,500
Frequency per Year: quarterly
Publish Print Anthology: yes
Average Percentage of Pages per Category: Fiction 40%, Nonfiction 4%, Poetry 40%, Reviews 2%, Essays 10%, Art 1%, Translation 1%, Audio 2%
Ad Rates: See web site for details.

Organization: Oasis

Type: magazine

CLMP member: no
Primary Editor/Contact Person: Neal Storrs
Address: P.O. Box 626
Largo, FL 33779-0626
Publishes: essays, fiction, nonfiction, poetry, and translation
Editorial Focus: looking for work of literary distinction
Representative Authors: James Sallis, Caroline Stoloff, and Simon Perchik
Submissions Policy: Send complete work to POB 626 Largo FL 33779-0626. Include SASE. Or send to oasislit@aol.com
Simultaneous Submissions: yes
Reading Period: Year-round
Reporting Time: zero to six weeks
Author Payment: copies
Contests: no contests
Founded: 1992
Paid Staff: no
Unpaid Staff: no
Distributors: EBSCO Subscription Services
ISSN Number/ISBN Number: ISSN 1064-6299
Total Circulation: 300
Paid Circulation: 50
Subscription Rate: Individual $20/Institution $20
Single Copy Price: $6
Current Volume/Issue: XI/II
Frequency per Year: quarterly
Backfile Available: yes
Unsolicited Ms. Received: yes
% of Unsolicited Ms. Published per Year: 0.5%
Format: perfect
Average Pages: 70
Ads: no

Organization: Oberlin College Press

Type: press
CLMP member: no
Primary Editor/Contact Person: Linda Slocum, Managing Editor
Address: 50 N. Professor St.
Peters G23
Oberlin, OH 44074-1091
Web Site Address: http://www.oberlin.edu/ocpress
Publishes: essays, poetry, and translation
Editorial Focus: The FIELD Translation Series, FIELD Poetry Series, and FIELD Editions (anthologies) make world's best poetry available.
Representative Authors: Franz Wright, Marianne Boruch, and Eugenio Montale

Submissions Policy: Submit English manuscripts to FIELD Poetry Prize in May. Send translation inquiry/samples to Editor David Young any time.
Simultaneous Submissions: yes
Reading Period: 5/1 to 5/31
Reporting Time: two to three months
Author Payment: royalties, cash, and copies
Contests: See web site for contest guidelines.
Founded: 1969
Non Profit: yes
Paid Staff: .5
Unpaid Staff: three
Distributors: Orders filled by Cornell University Press Services
ISSN Number/ISBN Number: ISBN 0932440---
Number of Books Published per Year: three
Titles in Print: 49
Average Print Run: 1,000
Average Percentage Printed: Paperback 100%
Average Price: $16.95

Organization: Omnidawn Publishing

Type: press
CLMP member: yes
Primary Editor/Contact Person: Rusty Morrison
Address: 1632 Elm Ave.
Richmond, CA 94805-1614
Web Site Address: http://www.omnidawn.com
Publishes: fiction and poetry
Editorial Focus: Publishers of innovative poetry and new wave fabulist fiction.
Recent Awards Received: 2005 PEN USA Award in Poetry for Martha Ronk's poetry collection: In A Landscape of Having To Repeat
Representative Authors: Lyn Hejinian, Rosmarie Waldrop, and Elizabeth Robinson
Submissions Policy: varies. See our web site for full details.
Simultaneous Submissions: yes
Reading Period: see website for full details
Reporting Time: four to six months
Author Payment: royalties, cash, and copies
Founded: 1999
Non Profit: no
Paid Staff: one plus
Unpaid Staff: one
Wholesalers: SPD
ISSN Number/ISBN Number: ISBN 1-890650
Number of Books Published per Year: three
Titles in Print: 16

Average Print Run: varies
Average Percentage Printed: Paperback 100%
Average Price: varies

Organization: OnceWritten.com

Type: online
CLMP member: yes
Primary Editor/Contact Person: Monica Poling
Address: 1850 N. Whitley Ave. #404
Hollywood, CA 90028
Web Site Address: http://www.oncewritten.com
Publishes: essays, fiction, nonfiction, poetry, and reviews
Editorial Focus: Focuses on works by new authors including novels, fiction and poetry.
Recent Awards Received: Top 101 Websites for Writers, Writers Digest
Submissions Policy: Inquiries may be sent to monica@oncewritten.com
Simultaneous Submissions: yes
Reading Period: Year-round
Reporting Time: four to twelve weeks
Author Payment: cash
Contests: See web site for contest guidelines.
Founded: 2003
Non Profit: no
Paid Staff: zero
Unpaid Staff: zero
Average Page Views per Month: 420,000
Average Unique Visitors per Month: 14,000
Frequency per Year: monthly
Publish Print Anthology: no
Average Percentage of Pages per Category: Fiction 25%, Nonfiction 20%, Poetry 10%, Reviews 40%, Essays 5%
Ad Rates: Varies depending on size of ad
See web site for details.

Organization: One Story

Type: magazine
CLMP member: yes
Primary Editor/Contact Person: Hannah Tinti
Address: The Old American Can Factory
232 3rd Street, #A111
Brooklyn, NY 11215
Web Site Address: http://www.one-story.com
Publishes: fiction
Editorial Focus: Publishes one short story every three weeks. Seeks literary fiction of any style. Stories must be brave enough to stand alone.
Representative Authors: Kelly Link, Judy Budnitz,

and Karl Iagnemma

Submissions Policy: Stories must be between 3,000 and 8,000 words. We have an online submission tool and do not accept paper submissions.
Simultaneous Submissions: yes
Reading Period: 9/06 to 5/07
Reporting Time: two to six months
Author Payment: cash and copies
Contests: none.
Founded: 2001
Non Profit: yes
Paid Staff: zero
Unpaid Staff: seven
Distributors: Subscription Only
Wholesalers: Subscription Only
Total Circulation: 3,500
Paid Circulation: 3,200
Average Print Run: 3,800
Subscription Rate: Individual $21/Institution $21
Single Copy Price: $2
Current Volume/Issue: 5/8
Frequency per Year: 18
Backfile Available: yes
Unsolicited Ms. Received: yes
% of Unsolicited Ms. Published per Year: 2%
Format: stapled
Size: H 7" W 5"
Average Pages: 24
Ads: no

Organization: Ontario Review
Type: magazine
CLMP member: no
Address: 9 Honey Brook Dr.
Princeton, NJ 08540
Web Site Address:
http://www.ontarioreviewpress.com
Publishes: essays, fiction, nonfiction, poetry, and art
Reading Period: Year-round
Reporting Time: one to two months
Author Payment: none
Founded: 1974
Non Profit: no

Organization: Open City Books
Type: press
CLMP member: yes
Primary Editor/Contact Person: Thomas Beller and Joanna Yas

Address: 270 Lafayette St.
Ste. 1412
New York, NY 10012
Web Site Address: http://www.opencity.org
Publishes: essays, fiction, and poetry
Editorial Focus: Unusual voices and great story-telling-by new writers as well as undiscovered talents from the past.
Recent Awards Received: New York Times Notable Book, Booker Prize Finalist, New York Public Library Books to Remember
Representative Authors: David Berman, Edward St. Aubyn, and Rachel Sherman
Submissions Policy: No unsolicited manuscripts. We find books by reading submissions to Open City magazine; please follow those guidelines.
Simultaneous Submissions: no
Reading Period: year-round
Reporting Time: two to five months
Author Payment: royalties and cash
Founded: 1999
Non Profit: yes
Paid Staff: one
Unpaid Staff: four
Distributors: Publishers Group West
Wholesalers: Ingram, Koen, Baker & Taylor
ISSN Number/ISBN Number: ISBN 1890447
Number of Books Published per Year: three to four
Titles in Print: 15
Average Print Run: 6,000
Average Percentage Printed: Paperback 100%
Average Price: $14

Organization: Open City
Type: magazine
CLMP member: yes
Primary Editor/Contact Person: Joanna Yas and Thomas Beller
Address: 270 Lafayette St.
Ste. 1412
New York, NY 10012-3327
Web Site Address: http://www.opencity.org
Publishes: essays, fiction, poetry, art, and translation
Editorial Focus: Poetry and prose with a daring, youthful spirit.
Recent Awards Received: Best American Nonrequired Reading, Best American Poetry
Representative Authors: Sam Lipsyte, Maxine Swann, and Nick Tosches
Submissions Policy: One story, essay, or novel

excerpt at a time, up to 5,000 words; up to 5 poems; no unsolicited artwork.
Simultaneous Submissions: yes
Reading Period: 9/1 to 5/31
Reporting Time: three to six months
Author Payment: cash and copies
Contests: See web site for contest guidelines.
Founded: 1990
Non Profit: yes
Paid Staff: one
Unpaid Staff: four
Distributors: Publishers Group West, Ubiquity, DeBoer
Wholesalers: Ingram, Koen, Baker & Taylor
ISSN Number/ISBN Number: 10895523/1890447
Total Circulation: 5,000
Paid Circulation: 3,000
Average Print Run: 5,000
Subscription Rate: Individual $30/Institution $40
Single Copy Price: $10
Current Volume/Issue: Issue 25
Frequency per Year: biannual
Backfile Available: yes
Unsolicited Ms. Received: yes
% of Unsolicited Ms. Published per Year: 1%
Format: perfect
Size: H 9" W 6"
Average Pages: 250
Ads: yes
Ad Rates: $600/full page; discounts for writers and arts organizations.

Organization: Open Spaces Quarterly

Type: magazine
CLMP member: yes
Primary Editor/Contact Person: Ellen Teicher
Address: 6327-C SW Capitol Hwy.
Portland, OR 97239
Web Site Address: http://www.open-spaces.com
Publishes: essays, fiction, nonfiction, poetry, reviews, and art
Editorial Focus: Creative writing and nonfiction articles on science, history, politics, international relations, law, medicine and the arts.
Representative Authors: Robert Sullivan, Rick Bass, and Jane Lubchenco
Submissions Policy: On our web site at http://www.open-spaces.com
Simultaneous Submissions: yes
Reading Period: Year-round
Reporting Time: one to six months

Author Payment: cash, copies, and subscription
Founded: 1997
Non Profit: no
Paid Staff: five
Unpaid Staff: 22
Distributors: Small Changes, Ingram, Newsgroup, etc.
ISSN Number/ISBN Number: ISSN 1096-3901
Total Circulation: 6,500
Paid Circulation: 4,500
Average Print Run: 6,500
Subscription Rate: Individual $25/Institution $25.
Single Copy Price: $7.95
Current Volume/Issue: 9/3
Frequency per Year: quarterly
Backfile Available: yes
Unsolicited Ms. Received: yes
% of Unsolicited Ms. Published per Year: 25%
Format: perfect
Size: H 11" W 8 1/2"
Average Pages: 64
Ads: yes
Ad Rates: Call 1-503-227-5764 or 1-503-313-4361 See Web site for details.

Organization: Opium Magazine

Type: magazine
CLMP member: yes
Primary Editor/Contact Person: Todd Zuniga and Elizabeth Koch
Address: 166 Albion St.
San Francisco, CA 94110
Web Site Address: http://www.OpiumDen.org
Publishes: essays, fiction, nonfiction, poetry, reviews, art, and audio
Editorial Focus: We love hilarious, heartbreaking, innovative, engaging writing that dizzies our senses.
Recent Awards Received: Two stories were given Honorable Mentions for Best American Non-Required Reading 2008.
Representative Authors: Ben Greenman, Jack Handey, and Etgar Keret
Submissions Policy: There is a 4,000 word limit on submissions.
Simultaneous Submissions: yes
Reading Period: Year-round
Reporting Time: one to two months
Author Payment: none
Contests: We feature new, fun, high-paying contests in each issue; see website for guidelines.
Founded: 2001

Non Profit: no
Paid Staff: three
Unpaid Staff: 25
Distributors: Ingram, DeBoer, Ubiquity, Armadillo
Total Circulation: 2,200
Paid Circulation: 100
Average Print Run: 2,500
Subscription Rate: Individual $18/Institution $18
Single Copy Price: $10
Current Volume/Issue: 3/1
Frequency per Year: 2
Backfile Available: yes
Unsolicited Ms. Received: yes
% of Unsolicited Ms. Published per Year: 70%
Format: perfect
Size: H 7" W 10"
Average Pages: 144
Ads: yes
Ad Rates: Contact us for Ad Rates Sheet: todd@opi-ummagazine.com

Organization: Opium Magazine

Type: online
CLMP member: yes
Address: 586 Dean St.
Brooklyn, NY 11238
Web Site Address: http://www.opiummagazine.com
Publishes: essays, fiction, nonfiction, poetry, reviews, art, and audio
Reading Period: year-round
Reporting Time: one to two months
Author Payment: none
Founded: 2001
Non Profit: yes
Backfile Available: yes
Average Percentage of Pages per Category: Audio 100%

Organization: Orchid: A Literary Review

Type: magazine
CLMP member: yes
Primary Editor/Contact Person: Keith Hood
Address: P.O. Box 131457
Ann Arbor, MI 48113-1457
Web Site Address: http://www.orchidlit.org
Publishes: fiction and art
Editorial Focus: Orchid celebrates stories and the art of storytelling. We welcome submissions of fiction and

interviews on fiction craft.
Representative Authors: Sarah Gerkensmeyer, Keya Mitra, and Daniel Mueller
Submissions Policy: We consider fiction of all lengths: including novellas and novel excerpts. We do not consider unsolicited poetry.
Simultaneous Submissions: yes
Reading Period: Year-round
Reporting Time: up to six months
Author Payment: cash and copies
Contests: See Web Site for contest guidelines.
Founded: 2001
Non Profit: yes
Paid Staff: 0
Unpaid Staff: 11
ISSN Number/ISBN Number: ISSN 1537-0763
Total Circulation: 1,000
Paid Circulation: 350
Average Print Run: 2,000
Subscription Rate: Individual $16/Institution $16
Single Copy Price: $8
Current Volume/Issue: Issue six
Frequency per Year: biannual
Backfile Available: yes
Unsolicited Ms. Received: yes
% of Unsolicited Ms. Published per Year: 95%
Format: perfect
Size: H 9" W 6"
Average Pages: 200
Ads: yes
Ad Rates: Full Page Ad-$100, Half Page Ad-$50

Organization: Orchises Press

Type: press
CLMP member: yes
Primary Editor/Contact Person: Roger Lathbury
Address: P.O. Box 20602
Alexandria, VA 22320-1602
Web Site Address: http://mason.gmu.edu/~rlathbur
Publishes: fiction, nonfiction and poetry
Editorial Focus: A literary press, Orchises does four books yearly, including reprints. No fiction, children's books, or cookbooks.
Representative Authors: David Kirby, Stephen Akey, and L.S. Asekoff
Submissions Policy: Prefer not to receive unsolicited poetry.
Simultaneous Submissions: yes
Reading Period: Year-round
Reporting Time: four to twelve weeks

Author Payment: royalties
Founded: 1983
Non Profit: no
Paid Staff: one
Unpaid Staff: one
Distributors: Washington Book Distributors
ISSN Number/ISBN Number: ISBN 0914061, 1932535
Number of Books Published per Year: five
Titles in Print: 110
Average Print Run: 750
Average Percentage Printed: Hardcover 20%, Paperback 77%, Chapbook 3%
Average Price: $14.95

Organization: Osiris

Type: magazine
CLMP member: yes
Primary Editor/Contact Person: Andrea Moorhead
Address: P.O. Box 297
Deerfield, MA 01342
Publishes: poetry
Editorial Focus: Multi-lingual contemporary poetry journal.
Representative Authors: Prospero Saiz, Yves Broussard, and Madeleine Gagnon
Submissions Policy: Four to five poems, short biography and SASE
Simultaneous Submissions: no
Reading Period: year-round
Reporting Time: two to twelve weeks
Author Payment: copies and subscription
Founded: 1972
Non Profit: yes
Paid Staff: zero
Unpaid Staff: three
ISSN Number/ISBN Number: ISSN 0095-019X
Total Circulation: 500
Paid Circulation: 125
Average Print Run: 500
Subscription Rate: Individual $15/Institution $15
Single Copy Price: $7.50
Current Volume/Issue: 60/60
Frequency per Year: biannual
Backfile Available: yes
Unsolicited Ms. Received: yes
% of Unsolicited Ms. Published per Year: 10%
Format: perfect
Size: H 9" W 6"
Average Pages: 54

Ads: yes
Ad Rates: 150 full page

Organization: Other Press, LLC

Type: press
CLMP member: no
Primary Editor/Contact Person: Juliet Barnes, Marketing Dir.
Address: 2 Park Ave.
24th Fl.
New York, NY 10016
Web Site Address: http://www.otherpress.com
Publishes: fiction, nonfiction, poetry, reviews, and translation
Editorial Focus: Contemporary American literature, literature in translation, trade and academic nonfiction.
Recent Rewards Recieved: ForeWord Book of the Year, IPPY Award, Gradiva Award, Goethe Award
Representative Authors: Leslie Epstein, Amity Gaige, and Peter Fonagy
Submissions Policy: Authors are encouraged to submit work through an agent. Email inquiries may be sent to editor@otherpress.com
Simultaneous Submissions: no
Reading Period: Year-round
Reporting Time: two to six months
Author Payment: royalties
Founded: 1998
Non Profit: no
Paid Staff: 20
Unpaid Staff: 0
Distributors: W.W. Norton
Wholesalers: Baker & Taylor, Ingram
ISSN Number/ISBN Number: ISBN 159051, 1892746
Number of Books Published per Year: 25
Titles in Print: 200
Average Print Run: Varies
Average Percentage Printed: Hardcover 40%, Paperback 60%
Average Price: Varies

Organization: Other Voices

Type: magazine
CLMP member: yes
Primary Editor/Contact Person: Gina Frangello, Exec. Ed.
Address: University of IL-Chicago, English Dept.
601 S. Morgan
Chicago, IL 60607-7120

Web Site Address: http://www.othervoices-magazine.org
Publishes: fiction and reviews
Editorial Focus: diverse, original literary short fiction, novel excerpts, one-act plays, interviews, book reviews.
Recent Awards Received: Illinois Arts Council Literary Awards, Pushcart Prize nominations, inclusion in Best American Short Stories of the Century.
Representative Authors: Pam Houston, Aimee Liu, and Dan Chaon
Submissions Policy: Submit entire manuscript with brief cover letter. We read between Oct 1 and April 1 only. 6,500 word max.
Simultaneous Submissions: yes
Reading Period: 10/1 to 4/1
Reporting Time: four to sixteen weeks
Author Payment: cash and copies
Contests: See Web site for contest guidelines.
Founded: 1985
Non Profit: yes
Paid Staff: 0
Unpaid Staff: 35
Distributors: Ingram, DeBoer
ISSN Number/ISBN Number: 87564696/7447079831
Total Circulation: 2,000
Paid Circulation: 650
Average Print Run: 2,000
Subscription Rate: Individual $26/Institution $28
Single Copy Price: $9
Current Volume/Issue: Issue 43
Frequency per Year: biannual
Backfile Available: yes
Unsolicited Ms. Received: yes
% of Unsolicited Ms. Published per Year: 2%
Format: perfect
Size: H 9" W 6"
Average Pages: 200
Ads: yes
Ad Rates: primarily through exchange

Organization: Out of Line

Type: magazine
CLMP member: yes
Primary Editor/Contact Person: Sam Longmire
Address: 843 Ashley Ct.
Trenton, OH 45067
Web Site Address: http://www.readoutofline.com
Publishes: essays, fiction, nonfiction, poetry, and translation
Editorial Focus: Issues of Peace and Justice. Focus on tolerance, nonviolence, diversity, healthy relationships, human rights and peace.
Representative Authors: Maureen Tolman Flannery, Lyn Lifshin, and Leza Lowitz
Submissions Policy: Manuscripts should not exceed 4,000 words. SASE for return. Open to all writers. Publication one year after acceptance.
Simultaneous Submissions: yes
Reading Period: Year-round
Reporting Time: one to three months
Author Payment: copies
Founded: 1998
Non Profit: no
Paid Staff: 0
Unpaid Staff: six
Distributors: Out of Line staff promote and distribute.
Wholesalers: Selected bookstores.
ISSN Number/ISBN Number: ISSN 1526-6109
Total Circulation: 500
Paid Circulation: 140
Subscription Rate: Individual $12.50/Institution $12.50
Single Copy Price: $12.50
Current Volume/Issue: 2004
Frequency per Year: annual
Backfile Available: yes
Unsolicited Ms. Received: yes
% of Unsolicited Ms. Published per Year: 25%
Format: perfect
Size: H 8" W 5"
Average Pages: 130
Ads: no

Organization: Outlaw Editions

Type: press
CLMP member: no
Primary Editor/Contact Person: Jay Ruzesky
Address: 2829 Dysart Road
Victoria, BC V9A 2J7
Web Site Address: http://web.mala.bc.ca/ruzeskyj/Outlaw/outlawedi-tions.htm
Publishes: essays, fiction, nonfiction, poetry, translation, and audio
Editorial Focus: Top quality, innovative, excellent work written for the chapbook form by groovy cats.
Representative Authors: P.K. Page, John Harley, and Michael Ondaatje

Submissions Policy: Query first.
Simultaneous Submissions: no
Reading Period: 5/1 to 8/31
Reporting Time: one to three months
Author Payment: copies
Founded: 1993
Non Profit: yes
Paid Staff: 0
Unpaid Staff: two
Number of Books Published per Year: two
Titles in Print: 12
Average Print Run: 100
Average Percentage Printed: Chapbook 95%, Other 5%
Average Price: $7

Organization: Overtime

Type: magazine
CLMP member: no
Primary Editor/Contact Person: David LaBounty
Address: P.O. Box 250382
Plano, TX 75025-0382
Web Site Address:
www.workerswritejournal.com/overtime.htm
Publishes: Fiction
Editorial Focus: Publiish one-story chapbooks about the workplace (between 8,000 and 12,000 words).
Simultaneous Submissions: yes
Reading Period: year-round
Reporting Time: two to four months
Author Payment: cash and copies
Founded: 2006
Non Profit: no
Paid Staff: one
Unpaid Staff: zero
ISSN Number/ISBN Number: ISSN 1933-768X
Total Circulation: 2,000
Paid Circulation: 0
Average Print Run: 2,000
Subscription Rate: Individual $0/Institution $0
Single Copy Price: $2.50
Current Volume/Issue: Issue 3
Frequency per Year: three
Backfile Available: yes
Unsolicited Ms. Received: yes
% of Unsolicited Ms. Published per Year: 100%
Format: stapled
Size: H 7" W 5"
Average Pages: 28
Ads: no

Organization: The Owl Press

Type: press
CLMP member: yes
Primary Editor/Contact Person: Albert Flynn DeSilver
Address: P.O. Box 126
Woodacre, CA 94973
Web Site Address: http://www.theowlpress.com
Publishes: poetry
Editorial Focus: Innovative Poetry and Poetic Collaboration
Representative Authors: Frank O'Hara, Bernadette Mayer, and Edmund Berrigan
Submissions Policy: No unsolicited submissions at this time!
Simultaneous Submissions: no
Reading Period: Year-round
Reporting Time: two to twelve weeks
Author Payment: copies
Founded: 1997
Non Profit: yes
Paid Staff: 0
Unpaid Staff: one
Distributors: SPD, Baker & Taylor, Amazon
Number of Books Published per Year: two
Titles in Print: seven
Average Print Run: 750
Average Percentage Printed: Paperback 80%, Chapbook 20%
Average Price: $12

Organization: Oyez Review

Type: magazine
CLMP member: yes
Primary Editor/Contact Person: Janet Wondra
Address:
Department of Literature and Languages
Roosevelt University
430 S. Michigan Avenue
Chicago, IL 60605
Web Site Address:
www.roosevelt.edu/oyezreview/default.htm
Publishes: Poetry, fiction, creative nonfiction, art (black and white or reproducible as black and white)
Editorial Focus: The best of contemporary fiction, creative nonfiction, and poetry drawn from national and international submissions. Also features a portfolio of work by a single artist
Recent Awards Received: Illinois Arts Council Literary Award

Representative Authors: Gary Fincke, Rich Ives, Martha Modena Vertreace-Doody
Submissions Policy: For full details, see www.roosevelt.edu/oyezreview/guidelines.html. No previously published work. Submit up to 5 poems, not to exceed 10 pages total, or about 15-20 pages of fiction or creative nonfiction.
Simultaneous Submissions: NO
Reading Period: August 1 through October 1
Reporting Time: up to six months
Author Payment: copies
Founded: 1965
Non Profit: Yes
Paid Staff: 0
Unpaid Staff: 8-12
Distributors: Self-distributed
Total Circulation: 600
Paid Circulation: 50
Average Print Run: 600
Subscription Rate: individual $10 institution/ $20 (2 year sub)
Single Copy Price: $5
Frequency per year: Annual
Backfile Available: Yes
Unsolicited Ms. Received: 300
% of Unsolicited Ms. Published per year: 7%
Format: Perfect bound
Average Pages: 100
Ads: No

Organization: Oyster Boy Review

Type: magazine
CLMP member: no
Primary Editor/Contact Person: Damon Sauve
Address: Post Office Box 77842
San Francisco, CA 94107-0842
Web Site Address: http://www.oysterboyreview.com
Publishes: essays, fiction, nonfiction, poetry, reviews, and art
Editorial Focus: Fiction and poetry by new and upcoming authors.
Representative Authors: Kevin McGowin, C.A. Conrad, and Corvin Thomas
Submissions Policy: Submissions are open from January through September. Prior to sending work, read the guidelines available on the web site.
Simultaneous Submissions: no
Reading Period: 1/1 to 9/30
Reporting Time: three to six months
Author Payment: copies

Founded: 1994
Non Profit: no
Paid Staff: 0
Unpaid Staff: seven
ISSN Number/ISBN Number: ISSN 1085-2727
Total Circulation: 250
Paid Circulation: 50
Subscription Rate: Individual $20/Institution $20
Single Copy Price: $5
Current Volume/Issue: 10/1
Frequency per Year: quarterly
Unsolicited Ms. Received: yes
% of Unsolicited Ms. Published per Year: 100%
Format: stapled
Size: H 11" W 6"
Average Pages: 72
Ads: no

Organization: P.R.A. Publishing

Type: press
CLMP member: no
Primary Editor/Contact Person: Lucinda Clark
Address: P.O. Box 211701
Martinez, GA 30917
Web Site Address: http://www.prapublishing.com
Publishes: fiction and poetry
Representative Authors: Deanna Shapiro, Sheema Kalbasi, and Heyward Inabinett
Simultaneous Submissions: yes
Reading Period: year-round
Reporting Time: two to four months
Author Payment: royalties and copies
Contests: Annual Poetry Month tribute contest. Cash prizes awarded and public readings for the month of April; see website for guidelines.
Founded: 2002
Non Profit: no
Paid Staff: two
Unpaid Staff: two
Number of Books Published per Year: three to five
Titles in Print: seven
Average Print Run: 500
Average Percentage Printed: Paperback 100%
Average Price: $12.95

Organization: Paintbrush: A Journal of Poetry & Translation

Type: magazine
CLMP member: no

Primary Editor/Contact Person: Dr. Ben Bennani
Address: College of Humanities & Social Sciences
UAE University, P.O. Box 17771
Al Ain, AD U.A.E.
Web Site Address: http://www.paintbrush.org
Publishes: essays, poetry, reviews, and translation
Editorial Focus: Any theme is welcome, but work
must reflect a genuine commitment to, and expertise
in, new technique and style.
Representative Authors: Ruth Stone, Charles E.
Eaton, and Bruce Bennett
Submissions Policy: 3-5 poems in hard copy and/or
electronically. Include cover letter and short bio.
Simultaneous Submissions: no
Reading Period: 9/1 to 5/1
Reporting Time: four to twelve weeks
Author Payment: copies
Contests: Periodically announced.
See Web Site for contest guidelines.
Founded: 1974
Non Profit: yes
Paid Staff: 0
Unpaid Staff: one
Distributors: DeBoer
Total Circulation: 500
Paid Circulation: 100
Average Print Run: 1,000
Subscription Rate: Individual $15/Institution $20
Single Copy Price: $15
Frequency per Year: annual
Backfile Available: yes
Unsolicited Ms. Received: yes
% of Unsolicited Ms. Published per Year: 80%
Format: perfect
Size: H 8.5" W 5.5"
Average Pages: 200
Ads: yes
Ad Rates: $150/full page; $100/half page

Organization: The Painted Bride Quarterly

Type: online
CLMP member: yes
Primary Editor/Contact Person: Marion Wrenn/Kathy
Volk Miller
Address: Rutgers University-Camden
311 N. Fifth St.
Camden, NJ 08102
Web Site Address: http://pbq.rutgers.edu
Publishes: essays, fiction, nonfiction, poetry, reviews,

art, and translation
Editorial Focus: The writers PBQ has published over
the last three decades extend from the most tradition-
al to language school explorations
Representative Authors: Ruth Stone, Nick Flynn, and
Stephen Dunn
Submissions Policy: Accepts up to five poems, fiction
up to 5,000 words, essays and reviews up to 3,000
words, art also. No electronic submissions.
Simultaneous Submissions: yes
Reading Period: Year-round
Reporting Time: three to six months
Author Payment: copies
Contests: See website for contest guidelines.
Founded: 1973
Non Profit: yes
Paid Staff: 0
Unpaid Staff: 12
Distributors: Ingram and DeBoer
ISSN Number/ISBN Number: ISBN 0-9728565-0-1
Average Page Views per Month: 5,000
Average Unique Visitors per Month: 500
Frequency per Year: quarterly
Publish Print Anthology: yes
Price: $15
Average Percentage of Pages per Category: Fiction
20%, Nonfiction 10%, Poetry 35%, Reviews 10%,
Essays 10%, Art 10%, Translation 5%
Ad Rates: See Web site for details.

Organization: Pale House

Type: magazine
CLMP member: yes
Primary Editor/Contact Person: Brent Pearson
Address: 1494 Sunset Blvd.
Los Angeles, CA 90026
Web Site Address: http://www.palehouse.com
Publishes: essays, fiction, nonfiction, poetry, reviews,
and art
Editorial Focus: Literature, Art, Original Thought
Representative Authors: Larry Fondation, Billy
Collins, and Julian Lauren
Submissions Policy: 3,000 words max/anything goes
Simultaneous Submissions: yes
Reading Period: year-round
Reporting Time: four to six months
Author Payment: copies
Founded: 2006
Non Profit: no
Paid Staff: five

Unpaid Staff: two
Total Circulation: yes
Paid Circulation: yes
Average Print Run: 5,000
Subscription Rate: Individual $10/Institution $5
Single Copy Price: $10
Current Volume/Issue: 5/5
Frequency per Year: six
Backfile Available: yes
Unsolicited Ms. Received: yes
Format: perfect
Average Pages: 70-150
Ads: yes
Ad Rates: varies; see website for details

Organization: Paper Street

Type: magazine
CLMP member: yes
Primary Editor/Contact Person: Arlan Hess
Address: P.O. Box 14786
Pittsburgh, PA 15234-0786
Web Site Address: http://www.paperstreetpress.org
Publishes: fiction and poetry
Editorial Focus: Character driven fiction and lyric/narrative poetry
Recent Awards Received: Two stories given Honorable Mention for Pushcart Prizes
Representative Authors: Erin Malone, Lori Wilson, and Terry Dubow
Submissions Policy: See website.
Simultaneous Submissions: yes
Reading Period: 5/1 to 8/31
Reporting Time: three to nine months
Author Payment: copies and subscription
Contests: forthcoming
Founded: 2003
Non Profit: yes
Paid Staff: 0
Unpaid Staff: eight
ISSN Number/ISBN Number: ISSN 1547-2922
Total Circulation: 350+
Paid Circulation: 165
Average Print Run: 500
Subscription Rate: Individual $16/yr/Institution $16/yr
Single Copy Price: $9
Current Volume/Issue: 4/1
Frequency per Year: biannual
Backfile Available: yes
Unsolicited Ms. Received: yes

% of Unsolicited Ms. Published per Year: 100%
Format: perfect
Size: H 9" W 6"
Average Pages: 120
Ads: no

Organization: Paradiso-Parthas Press

Type: press
CLMP member: yes
Primary Editor/Contact Person: Robert Colvin
Address: 214 Mulberry Street
New York, NY 10012
Web Site Address: http://medcelt.org/paradiso-parthaspress/index.html
Publishes: fiction, nonfiction, poetry, and art
Editorial Focus: Independent press promoting accessible and literary writing that explores world cultures made richer by the nature of their shared qualities.
Submissions Policy: Looking for novels, poetry and memoirs with a Mediterranean and/or Celtic link. Do not accept unsolicited manuscripts—send an inquiry letter.
Simultaneous Submissions: yes
Reading Period: year-round
Reporting Time: one to two months
Author Payment: royalties and copies
Contests: none
Founded: 2006
Non Profit: no
Paid Staff: two
Unpaid Staff: three
Distributors: Amazon.com
ISSN Number/ISBN Number: ISBN 0-9787226
Number of Books Published per Year: one
Titles in Print: two
Average Print Run: 500
Average Percentage Printed: Paperback 100%
Average Price: $7.00

Organization: Parakeet

Type: magazine
CLMP member: yes
Primary Editor/Contact Person: Deb Olin Unferth
Address: 515 Indiana #A
Lawrence, KS 66044
Publishes: essays, fiction, nonfiction, and poetry
Editorial Focus: Innovative and experimental writing

Representative Authors: Diane Williams, Lydia Davis, and David Ohle
Simultaneous Submissions: yes
Reading Period: Year-round
Reporting Time: two to three months
Author Payment: none
Founded: 2004
Non Profit: yes
Paid Staff: zero
Unpaid Staff: two
Total Circulation: 750
Paid Circulation: 100
Average Print Run: 750
Subscription Rate: Individual $10/Institution $10
Single Copy Price: $10
Current Volume/Issue: issue two
Frequency per Year: annual
Backfile Available: yes
Unsolicited Ms. Received: yes
% of Unsolicited Ms. Published per Year: 30%
Format: perfect
Average Pages: 120

Organization: Paris Press

Type: press
CLMP member: yes
Primary Editor/Contact Person: Jan Freeman
Address: P.O. Box 487
1117 West Rd.
Ashfield, MA 01330
Web Site Address: http://www.parispress.org
Publishes: fiction, nonfiction, poetry, and audio
Editorial Focus: Paris Press publishes daring literature by women that has been neglected or misrepresented by the commercial publishing world
Representative Authors: Ruth Stone, Muriel Rukeyser, and Virginia Woolf
Submissions Policy: Submit a 10-20 page excerpt, along with a resume and an SASE, between November and February.
Simultaneous Submissions: yes
Reading Period: 11/3 to 2/4
Reporting Time: nine to twelve months
Author Payment: royalties
Founded: 1995
Non Profit: yes
Paid Staff: one
Unpaid Staff: zero
Distributors: Consortium

Wholesalers: Ingram, Baker & Taylor, etc.
ISSN Number/ISBN Number: ISBN 0-9638183 ; 1-930464
Number of Books Published per Year: 1-3
Titles in Print: 15
Average Print Run: 7,000
Average Percentage Printed: Hardcover 10%, Paperback 80%, Chapbook 5%, Other 5%
Average Price: $16.00

Organization: The Paris Review

Type: magazine
CLMP member: yes
Primary Editor/Contact Person: Editor (see below)
Address: 62 White St.
New York, NY 10013
Web Site Address: http://www.theparisreview.org
Publishes: essays, fiction, nonfiction, poetry, art, and translation
Editorial Focus: The Paris Review publishes the finest in original new fiction, poetry, interviews, essays, and art in its quarterly issues.
Submissions Policy: Fiction should be sent to the attention of the Fiction Editor, poetry to the Poetry Editor, at the address above.
Simultaneous Submissions: yes
Reading Period: Year-round
Reporting Time: two to three months
Author Payment: cash and copies
Contests: See Web site for contest guidelines.
Founded: 1953
Non Profit: yes
Paid Staff: seven
Unpaid Staff: four
Distributors: Ingram, DeBoer, Small Changes
Wholesalers: Total Circulation Services, Kent News
ISSN Number/ISBN Number: ISSN 0031-2037
Total Circulation: 6,000
Paid Circulation: 4,500
Subscription Rate: Individual $40/Institution $49
Single Copy Price: $12
Current Volume/Issue: 46/170
Frequency per Year: quarterly
Backfile Available: yes
Unsolicited Ms. Received: yes
Format: perfect
Size: H 8.5" W 5.50"
Average Pages: 300
Ads: yes
Ad Rates: Full Page, $1,000. 1/2 Page, $600.

See Web site for details.

Organization: Parnassus: Poetry in Review

Type: magazine
CLMP member: yes
Primary Editor/Contact Person: Herbert Leibowitz
Address: 205 W. 89th St., #8F
New York, NY 10024
Web Site Address: http://www.parnassuspoetry.com
Publishes: essays, fiction, nonfiction, poetry, reviews, art, and translation
Editorial Focus: Critical essays and reviews of poetry written in stylish prose. Poems that employ complex syntax, rhythm, and subject matter.
Recent Awards Received: Poets House 2002 Elizabeth Kray Award
Representative Authors: David Barber, Mary Karr, and Eric Ormsby
Submissions Policy: We read all unsolicited work. Authors should read Parnassus before submitting poems or prose for an idea of our taste.
Simultaneous Submissions: yes
Reading Period: Year-round
Reporting Time: one to three months
Author Payment: cash, copies, and subscription
Founded: 1972
Non Profit: yes
Paid Staff: five
Unpaid Staff: one to two
ISSN Number/ISBN Number: ISBN 0048-3028
Total Circulation: 2,500
Paid Circulation: 1,200
Average Print Run: 1,800
Subscription Rate: Individual $24/Institution $46
Single Copy Price: $12-15
Current Volume/Issue: 29/1
Frequency per Year: annual
Backfile Available: yes
Unsolicited Ms. Received: yes
% of Unsolicited Ms. Published per Year: 2-5%
Format: perfect
Average Pages: 435
Ads: yes
Ad Rates: See web site for details.

Organization: Parsifal Press

Type: press
CLMP member: no
Primary Editor/Contact Person: Simone dos Anjos and Pietro Aman
Address: RPO P.O. Box 32659
Richmond Hill, ON L4C 0A2
Web Site Address: http://www.parsifal-press.com
Publishes: essays, fiction, nonfiction, poetry, and translation
Editorial Focus: A relevant literature, one that refuses to oppose tradition to innovation, the personal to the objective
Submissions Policy: Query first
Simultaneous Submissions: yes
Reading Period: year-round
Reporting Time: one to three months
Author Payment: royalties and copies
Contests: none
Founded: 2005
Non Profit: yes
Paid Staff: zero
Unpaid Staff: two
Number of Books Published per Year: four
Titles in Print: four
Average Print Run: 100+
Average Percentage Printed: Paperback 100%
Average Price: $13.95

Organization: Parthenon West Review

Type: magazine
CLMP member: no
Primary Editor/Contact Person: David Holler, Chad Sweeney
Address: 15 Littlefield Terrace
San Francisco, CA 94107
Web Site Address:
http://www.ParthenonWestReview.com
Publishes: poetry
Simultaneous Submissions: yes
Reading Period: Year-round
Reporting Time: one to four months
Author Payment: none
Founded: 2004
Non Profit: yes
Paid Staff: zero
Unpaid Staff: two
Total Circulation: 300
Paid Circulation: 50
Average Print Run: 500
Subscription Rate: Individual $20/Institution $20
Single Copy Price: $12
Current Volume/Issue: Issue three

Frequency per Year: biannual
Backfile Available: yes
Unsolicited Ms. Received: yes
Format: perfect

Organization: Passager

Type: magazine
CLMP member: yes
Primary Editor/Contact Person: Kendra Kopelke
Address: University of Baltimore
1420 N. Charles St.
Baltimore, MD 21201
Web Site Address: http://www.passagerpress.com
Publishes: fiction, nonfiction, and poetry
Editorial Focus: Special focus on older writers.
Passager explores the imagination in later life.
Promotes new thinking about aging.
Simultaneous Submissions: yes
Reading Period: Year-round
Reporting Time: two to four months
Author Payment: copies
Contests: Poetry contest for writers over 50. Reading
period: Sept. 1-Feb.15. Reading fee: $20, includes 1-
year subcription.
See Web Site for contest guidelines.
Founded: 1990
Non Profit: yes
Paid Staff: one
Unpaid Staff: two
Total Circulation: 1,000
Paid Circulation: 850
Average Print Run: 1,500
Subscription Rate: Individual $20/Institution $20
Single Copy Price: $8
Current Volume/Issue: Issue 43
Frequency per Year: biannual
Backfile Available: yes
Unsolicited Ms. Received: yes
% of Unsolicited Ms. Published per Year: 100%
Format: perfect
Size: H 8 1/2" W 8 1/2"
Average Pages: 64
Ads: no

Organization: Paterson Literary Review

Type: magazine
CLMP member: yes
Primary Editor/Contact Person: Maria Mazziotti

Gillan
Address: Poetry Center at Passaic County Community
College
1 College Blvd.
Paterson, NJ 07505-1179
Web Site Address: http://www.pccc.edu/poetry
Publishes: essays, fiction, nonfiction, poetry, reviews,
art, and translation
Editorial Focus: High quality literary magazine; favors
clear narrative poetry. Work is not esoteric.
Recent Awards Received: NPR's The Poet and the
Poem's Special Recognition Award; Library Journal
Top 10 Literary Mag; Best American Poetry, Pushcart
Representative Authors: Diane di Prima, Phillip
Levine, and Galway Kinnell
Submissions Policy: Send five poems or one story,
essay, nonfiction piece. Reviews are assigned.
Simultaneous Submissions: yes
Reading Period: 11/06 to 3/07
Reporting Time: three to six months
Author Payment: copies
Contests: See Web site for contest guidelines.
Founded: 1977
Non Profit: yes
Paid Staff: one
Unpaid Staff: zero
Distributors: DeBoer, Ingram
ISSN Number/ISBN Number: ISSN 0743-2259
Total Circulation: 2,000
Paid Circulation: 872
Average Print Run: 1,000
Subscription Rate: Individual $15./Institution $20
Single Copy Price: $15
Current Volume/Issue: 39/35
Frequency per Year: annual
Backfile Available: yes
Unsolicited Ms. Received: yes
% of Unsolicited Ms. Published per Year: 10%
Format: perfect
Size: H 9" W 6"
Average Pages: 350
Ads: yes
Ad Rates: $300 full page; $150 half- page

Organization: Pathwise Press

Type: press
CLMP member: no
Primary Editor/Contact Person: Christopher Harter
Address: P.O. Box 178
Erie, PA 16512

Web Site Address: www.pathwisepress.com
Publishes: essays, fiction, and poetry
Editorial Focus: Strong emphasis on imagery. Nothing overly academic or Bukowski-esque
Representative Authors: Mark Terrill, Kell Robertson, and Mike James
Submissions Policy: Query first. Then send complete manuscript hardcopy if press is accepting manuscripts.
Simultaneous Submissions: yes
Reading Period: Year-round
Reporting Time: four to twelve weeks
Author Payment: royalties and copies
Founded: 1997
Non Profit: yes
Paid Staff: zero
Unpaid Staff: one
Distributors: via website and catalogs
Wholesalers: Baker & Taylor
ISSN Number/ISBN Number: ISBN 1-932840
Number of Books Published per Year: 2-3
Titles in Print: 11
Average Print Run: 300
Average Percentage Printed: Chapbook 100%
Average Price: $5.95

Organization: Paul Dry Books

Type: press
CLMP member: no
Primary Editor/Contact Person: Paul Dry
Address: 117 S. 17th St. (1102)
Philadelphia, PA 19103
Web Site Address: http://www.pauldrybooks.com
Publishes: essays, fiction, nonfiction, and translation
Editorial Focus: We publish new work, translations, and reprints. Our line includes the Nautilus Series for Young Adult readers.
Representative Authors: Eva Brann, James McConkey, and Peter Cashwell
Submissions Policy: Request submissions guidelines via our web site.
Simultaneous Submissions: yes
Reading Period: Year-round
Reporting Time: two to twelve weeks
Author Payment: royalties
Founded: 1998
Non Profit: no
Paid Staff: three
Unpaid Staff: zero
Distributors: Consortium

Wholesalers: All major wholesalers through our distributor
Number of Books Published per Year: five
Titles in Print: 46
Average Print Run: 2,500
Average Percentage Printed: Hardcover 20%, Paperback 80%
Average Price: $15

Organization: Pavement Saw Press

Type: press
CLMP member: no
Primary Editor/Contact Person: David Baratier
Address: P.O. Box 6291
Columbus, OH 43206
Web Site Address: http://pavementsaw.org
Publishes: poetry
Editorial Focus: A wide range of poetry, from collected poems of recognizable authors to experimental book length poems written in 7 languages
Representative Authors: Simon Perchik, Sofia Starnes, and Alan Catlin
Submissions Policy: We have a yearly first book contest and a open chapbook contest. Otherwise books are chosen through journal contributors.
Simultaneous Submissions: yes
Reading Period: 6/1 to 8/15
Reporting Time: two to four months
Author Payment: royalties and copies
Contests: See Web site for contest guidelines.
Founded: 1993
Non Profit: yes
Paid Staff: one
Unpaid Staff: eight
Distributors: Baker & Taylor, SPD, Brodart,
ISSN Number/ISBN Number: ISBN 978-1-886350
Number of Books Published per Year: seven
Titles in Print: 63
Average Print Run: 1,000
Average Percentage Printed: Paperback 58%, Chapbook 28%, Other 14%
Average Price: $12

Organization: Pavement Saw

Type: magazine
CLMP member: no
Primary Editor/Contact Person: David Baratier
Address: P.O. Box 6291
Columbus, OH 43206

Web Site Address: http://pavementsaw.org
Publishes: poetry
Editorial Focus: Each has a name and featured poet. #10 The Low Carb Issue, #9 VISPO Issue, #8 The All Male Unfinished Interview, etcetera.
Recent Awards Received: Since appearing in Pavement Saw our featured poets have won the Walt Whitman Award, Four Way Books Award, and the Ohio Lottery.
Representative Authors: There are no three authors useful, to understand our great, and wonderously variable taste
Submissions Policy: We only publish good poetry. If you write good poetry, please send some. Guidelines regularly change.
Simultaneous Submissions: no
Reading Period: 6/1 to 8/30
Reporting Time: three to eight weeks
Author Payment: copies
Founded: 1992
Non Profit: yes
Paid Staff: one
Unpaid Staff: eight
Distributors: Baker & Taylor, SPD, Brodart
ISSN Number/ISBN Number: ISBN 1-886350
Total Circulation: 551
Paid Circulation: 50
Average Print Run: 551
Subscription Rate: Individual $14/Institution $14
Single Copy Price: $7
Current Volume/Issue: 1/10
Frequency per Year: annual
Backfile Available: yes
Unsolicited Ms. Received: yes
% of Unsolicited Ms. Published per Year: 100%
Format: perfect
Size: H 7" W 10"
Average Pages: 88
Ads: no

Organization: Pearl Editions

Type: press
CLMP member: yes
Primary Editor/Contact Person: Marilyn Johnson
Address: 3030 E. Second St.
Long Beach, CA 90803
Web Site Address: http://www.pearlmag.com
Publishes: poetry
Editorial Focus: Specializes in books of reader-friendly poetry that are as readable, dramatic, and enter-

taining as a good novel or memoir.
Representative Authors: Lisa Glatt, Donna Hilbert, and Andrew Kaufman
Submissions Policy: Only accepts submissions to the annual Pearl Poetry Prize. All others are by invitation only.
Simultaneous Submissions: yes
Reading Period: 5/1 to 7/15
Reporting Time: five to six months
Author Payment: royalties and copies
Contests: See Web site for contest guidelines.
Founded: 1974
Non Profit: no
Paid Staff: zero
Unpaid Staff: three
Wholesalers: Baker & Taylor
ISSN Number/ISBN Number: ISBN 1888219
Number of Books Published per Year: three
Titles in Print: 25
Average Print Run: 1,000
Average Percentage Printed: Paperback 70%, Chapbook 30%
Average Price: $12

Organization: Pearl

Type: magazine
CLMP member: yes
Primary Editor/Contact Person: Marilyn Johnson
Address: 3030 E. 2nd St.
Long Beach, CA 90803
Web Site Address: http://www.pearlmag.com
Publishes: fiction, poetry, and art
Editorial Focus: Accessible, humanistic poetry and fiction that communicates and is related to real life. No taboos. Humor and wit welcome.
Representative Authors: Jim Daniels, Frank X. Gaspar, and Lisa Glatt
Submissions Policy: Submit three to five poems, up to 40 lines, and short-short stories, up to 1,200 words, with SASE. No e-mail submissions.
Simultaneous Submissions: yes
Reading Period: 9/1 to 5/31
Reporting Time: six to eight weeks
Author Payment: copies
Contests: See web site for contest guidelines.
Founded: 1974
Non Profit: no
Paid Staff: zero
Unpaid Staff: three
Total Circulation: 500

Paid Circulation: 150
Average Print Run: 600
Subscription Rate: Individual $21/Institution $25
Single Copy Price: $10
Current Volume/Issue: Issue 37
Frequency per Year: biannual
Backfile Available: yes
Unsolicited Ms. Received: yes
% of Unsolicited Ms. Published per Year: 5%
Format: perfect
Size: H 8.5" W 5.5"
Average Pages: 148
Ads: no

Organization: Pecan Grove Press

Type: press
CLMP member: yes
Primary Editor/Contact Person: H. Palmer Hall
Address: P.O. Box AL, St. Mary's University
1 Camino Santa Maria
San Antonio, TX 78228
Web Site Address:
http://library.stmarytx.edu/pgpress/
Publishes: poetry
Editorial Focus: Fresh, original poetry, with each poem acting as a kind of art exhibit: poems gaining strength through interrelationships.
Representative Authors: Edward Byrne, Patricia Fargnoli, and Trinidad Sanchez
Submissions Policy: Prefers complete manuscript of from 34 to 56 pages; inc. SASE, prefers recycling Mss.
Simultaneous Submissions: yes
Reading Period: Year-round
Reporting Time: two to four months
Author Payment: copies
Contests: See Web site for contest guidelines.
Founded: 1985
Non Profit: yes
Paid Staff: zero
Unpaid Staff: two
Distributors: Baker & Taylor, Amazon.com
ISSN Number/ISBN Number: ISBN 1-931247-
Number of Books Published per Year: six to nine
Titles in Print: 57
Average Print Run: 500
Average Percentage Printed: Paperback 67%, Chapbook 33%
Average Price: $9-$12

Organization: The Pedestal Magazine.com

Type: online
CLMP member: no
Primary Editor/Contact Person: John Amen
Address: 6815 Honors Ct.
Charlotte, NC 28211
Web Site Address:
http://www.ThePedestalMagazine.com
Publishes: fiction, poetry, reviews, and art
Editorial Focus: New and established writers and visual artists.
Representative Authors: Philip Levine, W.S. Merwin, and Maxine Kumin
Submissions Policy: Submissions via web site only.
Simultaneous Submissions: yes
Reading Period: Year-round
Reporting Time: six to eight weeks
Author Payment: cash
Founded: 2000
Non Profit: yes
Paid Staff: three
Unpaid Staff: two
Average Page Views per Month: 128,000
Average Unique Visitors per Month: 13,000
Frequency per Year: bimonthly
Publish Print Anthology: no
Average Percentage of Pages per Category: Fiction 7%, Poetry 60%, Reviews 10%, Art 23%
Ad Rates: See Web site for details.

Organization: Pedlar Press

Type: press
CLMP member: no
Primary Editor/Contact Person: Beth Follett
Address: PO Box 26 Station P
Toronto, ON M5S 2S6
Publishes: essays, fiction, nonfiction, and art
Editorial Focus: An independent literary press devoted to the publication of innovative novels, poems, and art essays by Canadian authors.
Recent Awards Received: Archibald Lampman Award 2006, CAA Emerging Author 2006, Trillium Award for poetry 2005, ReLit 2004, City of Toronto 2001
Representative Authors: Camilla Gibb, Stan Dragland, and Souvankham Thammavongsa
Submissions Policy: Query first. Submissions received 1 September to 31 December only.
Simultaneous Submissions: yes

Reading Period: 1/1 to 4/3
Reporting Time: six to eight months
Author Payment: royalties
Founded: 1996
Non Profit: no
Paid Staff: one
Unpaid Staff: zero
Distributors: LitDist Co
ISSN Number/ISBN Number: ISBN 0-9681884, 0-9686522, 1-897141
Number of Books Published per year: six to eight
Titles in Print: 44
Average Print Run: 700
Average Percentage Printed: Hardcover 20%, Paperback: 80%
Average Price: $20

Organization: Peepal Tree Press

Type: press
CLMP member: no
Primary Editor/Contact Person: J. Poynting/Hannah Bannister
Address: 17 King's Ave.
Leeds, UK LS6 1QS
Web Site Address: www.peepaltreepress.com
Publishes: essays, fiction, nonfiction, poetry, art, and translation
Editorial Focus: Peepal Tree Press aims to publish the very best in Caribbean & Black British writing.
Recent Awards Received: 2006 Commonwealth Writer's Prize Best Overall First Book-Mark McWatt's Suspended Sentences: Fictions of Atonement.
Representative Authors: Kwame Dawes, Lakshmi Persaud, and Kamau Brathwaite
Submissions Policy: Contact for submissions guidelines.+44 113 2451703 submissions@peepaltreepress.com
Simultaneous Submissions: yes
Reading Period: year-round
Reporting Time: up to four months
Author Payment: royalties and copies
Founded: 1986
Non Profit: no
Paid Staff: two
Unpaid Staff: one
Distributors: Independent Publishers Group
ISSN Number/ISBN Number: ISBN 184523, 1900715, 094833
Number of Books Published per year: 18
Titles in Print: 200

Average Print Run: 700
Average Percentage Printed: hardcover 1%, paperback 94%, chapbook 5%
Average Price: $16.99

Organization: PEN America: A Journal for Writers and Readers

Type: magazine
CLMP member: yes
Address: 568 Broadway, Ste. 401
New York, NY 10012-3225
Web Site Address:
http://www.pen.org/page.php/prmID/150
Publishes: essays, fiction, nonfiction, poetry, and translation
Simultaneous Submissions: no
Reading Period: Year-round
Reporting Time: one to two months
Author Payment: none
Founded: 2000
Non Profit: no
Unpaid Staff: six
Backfile Available: yes

Organization: Pennsylvania English

Type: magazine
CLMP member: no
Primary Editor/Contact Person: Antonio Vallone
Address: Penn State DuBois
College Place
DuBois, PA 15801
Publishes: essays, fiction, nonfiction, poetry, and translation
Editorial Focus: We look at all genres, all styles.
Representative Authors: Phil Terman, Henry Hughes, and William Heyen
Submissions Policy: We have no restrictions.
Simultaneous Submissions: yes
Reading Period: Year-round
Reporting Time: up to 6 months
Author Payment: copies
Contests: We do not have contests.
Founded: 1979
Non Profit: yes
Paid Staff: zero
Unpaid Staff: five
Wholesalers: EBSCO
ISSN Number/ISBN Number: ISSN 0741805
Total Circulation: 300

Paid Circulation: 200
Average Print Run: 350
Subscription Rate: Individual $10/Institution $10
Single Copy Price: $10
Current Volume/Issue: 28/1/2
Frequency per Year: annual
Backfile Available: yes
Unsolicited Ms. Received: yes
% of Unsolicited Ms. Published per Year: 20%
Format: perfect
Size: H 8.25" W 5.25"
Average Pages: 200
Ads: no

Organization: Perihelion

Type: online
CLMP member: no
Primary Editor/Contact Person: Joan Houlihan
Address: 2020 Pennsylvania Ave.
Ste. 443
Washington, DC 20006
Web Site Address: http://webdelsol.com/Perihelion
Publishes: poetry, reviews, and translation
Editorial Focus: To publish the best in contemporary poetry and poetry translations. To present articles, reviews and interviews that provide insights into the theory, style and content of contemporary poetry.
Representative Authors: Nick Flynn, Martha Zweig, and Larissa Szporluk
Simultaneous Submissions: yes
Reading Period: Year-round
Reporting Time: one to three months
Author Payment: none
Founded: 1996
Non Profit: yes
Paid Staff: zero
Unpaid Staff: four
Average Page Views per Month: 4,250
Average Unique Visitors per Month: 1,200
Publish Print Anthology: no
Average Percentage of Pages per Category: Poetry 50%, Reviews 25%, Translation 25%

Organization: Periphery: A Magical Realist Zine

Type: magazine
CLMP member: no
Primary Editor/Contact Person: Tamara Kaye Sellman

Address: 321 High School Road NE
PMB #204
Bainbridge Island, WA 98110
Web Site Address:
www.angelfire.com/wa2/margin/periphery.html
Publishes: fiction, poetry, and art
Editorial Focus: Annual print spinoff of MARGIN (www.magical-realism.com), which became an exclusively interactive community in 2006.
Representative Authors: Louis E. Bourgeois, Sheree Renee Thomas, and Dr. Lynn Veach Sadler
Submissions Policy: Will post call for submissions at web site
Simultaneous Submissions: yes
Reading Period: year-round
Reporting Time: up to six months
Author Payment: copies
Contests: Thematic. One winner earns cash prize. See site for theme, forms accepted, deadlines, fees. See web site for contest guidelines
Founded: 2002
Non Profit: yes
Paid Staff: zero
Unpaid Staff: three
Distributors: order through web site or buy via local booksellers
Total Circulation: 200
Average Print Run: 200
Single Copy Price: $8
Current Volume/Issue: 2006/4
Frequency per year: annual
Backfile Available: yes
Unsolicited MSS Received: yes
Format: stapled
Size: H 8.5" W 5.5"
Average Pages: varies
Ads: no

Organization: Perugia Press

Type: press
CLMP member: yes
Primary Editor/Contact Person: Susan Kan
Address: P.O. Box 60364
Florence, MA 01062
Web Site Address: http://www.perugiapress.com
Publishes: poetry
Editorial Focus: We publish one first or second book by a woman each year. Each book is the winner of our annual Perugia Press Prize.
Recent Awards Received: James Laughlin Award

Runner-Up; BookSense Top 10 Poetry Book, 2005; Ohioana Book of the Year; Pushcart Prize

Representative Authors: Diane Gilliam Fisher, Frannie Lindsay, and Lynne Thompson

Submissions Policy: Women can submit first or second book mss. to our annual Intro Award Contest. Guidelines are available online.

Simultaneous Submissions: yes

Reading Period: 8/1 to 11/15

Reporting Time: three to six months

Author Payment: royalties, cash, and copies

Contests: See web site for contest guidelines.

Founded: 1997

Non Profit: yes

Paid Staff: 1/2

Unpaid Staff: 1/2

Wholesalers: Baker & Taylor

ISSN Number/ISBN Number: ISBN 978-0-9660459, 978-0-9794582

Number of Books Published per Year: one

Titles in Print: 10

Average Print Run: 800

Average Percentage Printed: Paperback 100%

Average Price: $14

Organization: Phantasmagoria

Type: magazine

CLMP member: yes

Primary Editor/Contact Person: Abigail Allen

Address: English Dept, Century College

3300 Century Ave. N.

White Bear Lake, MN 55110

Publishes: essays, fiction, and poetry

Representative Authors: Thaddeus Rutkowski, Greg Mulcahy, and Paul Hostovsky

Submissions Policy: No previously published work. Include SASE for return/notification.

Simultaneous Submissions: no

Reading Period: Year-round

Reporting Time: two to four months

Author Payment: copies

Founded: 2000

Non Profit: yes

Paid Staff: three

Unpaid Staff: eight

Distributors: Ingram

ISSN Number/ISBN Number: ISSN 1534-6129

Total Circulation: 950

Paid Circulation: 53

Average Print Run: 1,000

Subscription Rate: Individual $15/Institution $20

Single Copy Price: $9

Current Volume/Issue: 7/1

Frequency per Year: biannual

Backfile Available: yes

Unsolicited Ms. Received: yes

% of Unsolicited Ms. Published per Year: 97%

Format: perfect

Average Pages: 160

Ad Rates: $100/pg

Organization: Philadelphia Stories

Type: magazine

CLMP member: yes

Primary Editor/Contact Person: Carla Spataro

Address: 2021 S. 11th St.

Philadelphia, PA 19148

Web Site Address: www.philadelphiastories.org

Publishes: essays, fiction, poetry, and art

Editorial Focus: Philadelphia Stories strives to publish the best work written by authors living in, or originally from, the Delaware Valley.

Representative Authors: Greg Downs, Aimee LaBrie, and Rachel Pastan

Submissions Policy: Submitters should either be from or currently living in Pennsylvania, New Jersey or Delaware.

Simultaneous Submissions: yes

Reading Period: year-round

Reporting Time: one to four months

Author Payment: copies

Founded: 2004

Non Profit: yes

Paid Staff: zero

Unpaid Staff: two

Total Circulation: 11,000

Paid Circulation: 100

Average Print Run: 12,000

Subscription Rate: individual $20-$1,000/Institution $1,000

Single Copy Price: free

Current Volume/Issue: 2/4

Frequency per year: quarterly

Backfile Available: yes

Unsolicited Ms. Received: yes

% of Unsolicited Ms. Published per year: 100%

Format: tabloid

Size: H 8.5" W 11"

Average Pages: 24

Ads: yes

Ad Rates: vary
See web site for details

Organization: Philos Press

Type: press
CLMP member: no
Primary Editor/Contact Person: Laura Beausoleil
Address: 8038A N. Bicentennial Loop S.E.
Lacey, WA 98503
Publishes: essays, fiction, poetry, and art
Editorial Focus: Publish primarily poetry.
Representative Authors: George Hitchcock, Dino
Siotis, and Gary Amdahl
Submissions Policy: No submissions accepted.
Simultaneous Submissions: no
Reading Period: Year-round
Reporting Time: up to six months
Author Payment: cash and copies
Contests: none
Founded: 1999
Non Profit: yes
Paid Staff: one
Unpaid Staff: two
Distributors: SPD, Amazon.com
Wholesalers: Blackwell's
Number of Books Published per Year: one
Titles in Print: five
Average Percentage Printed: Paperback 100%

Organization: The Pikestaff Press

Type: press
CLMP member: yes
Primary Editor/Contact Person: Robert D. Sutherland
Address: P.O. Box 127
Normal, IL 61761
Publishes: fiction and poetry
Representative Authors: Lucia C. Getsi, J.W. Rivers,
and Jeff Gundy
Submissions Policy: Send query letter first, with
SASE.
Simultaneous Submissions: yes
Reading Period: Year-round
Reporting Time: two to twelve weeks
Author Payment: copies
Founded: 1977
Non Profit: yes
Paid Staff: zero
Unpaid Staff: two
ISSN Number/ISBN Number: ISBN 0-936044

Number of Books Published per Year: one
Titles in Print: six
Average Print Run: varies
Average Percentage Printed: Hardcover 20%,
Paperback 80%
Average Price: varies

Organization: Pilgrimage

Type: magazine
CLMP member: no
Primary Editor/Contact Person: Peter Anderson
Address: Box 696
Crestone, CO 81131
Web Site Address: http://www.pilgrimagepress.org
Publishes: essays, nonfiction, and poetry
Editorial Focus: Reflective autobiographical writings;
place, spirit, peace and justice; in and beyond the
American Southwest.
Representative Authors: Kim Stafford, Parker Palmer,
and Nancy Mairs
Submissions Policy: Welcomes autobiographical
nonfiction and poetry
Simultaneous Submissions: yes
Reading Period: Year-round
Reporting Time: three to four months
Author Payment: cash and copies
Contests: See Web site for contest guidelines.
Founded: 1972
Non Profit: yes
Paid Staff: two
Unpaid Staff: zero
Distributors: Kent News
Wholesalers: EBSCO, Harrasowitz
Total Circulation: 600
Paid Circulation: 400
Average Print Run: 700
Subscription Rate: Individual $22/Institution $40
Single Copy Price: $8
Current Volume/Issue: 30/3
Frequency per Year: triquarterly
Backfile Available: yes
Unsolicited Ms. Received: yes
% of Unsolicited Ms. Published per Year: 20%
Format: perfect
Size: H 6" W 8"
Average Pages: 100

Organization: Pima Press

Type: press

CLMP member: yes
Primary Editor/Contact Person: Meg Files
Address: P.O. Box 85394
Tucson, AZ 85754
Publishes: fiction and poetry
Representative Authors: Dan Gilmore, Barrie Ryan, and Bernardo Taiz
Submissions Policy: by invitation only
Simultaneous Submissions: yes
Reading Period: Year-round
Reporting Time: one to two months
Author Payment: none
Founded: 1997
Non Profit: yes
Paid Staff: zero
Unpaid Staff: six
Distributors: Baker & Taylor, Ingram
Number of Books Published per Year: two
Titles in Print: 12
Average Print Run: 500
Average Percentage Printed: Paperback 100%
Average Price: $12

Organization: Pinball Publishing

Type: press
CLMP member: no
Primary Editor/Contact Person: Laura Brian
Address: 2621 SE Clinton St.
Portland, OR 97202
Web Site Address: http://www.pinballpublishing.com
Publishes: fiction, nonfiction, and poetry
Editorial Focus: We independently publish exceptional editions of contemporary poetry and fiction.
Representative Authors: Casey Kwang, David Harrison Horton, and Fiona Hile
Submissions Policy: We consider poetry, fiction, and creative nonfiction manuscripts. Send 30-page sample and bio w/query letter.
Simultaneous Submissions: yes
Reading Period: Year-round
Reporting Time: four to 16 weeks
Author Payment: royalties and copies
Founded: 2001
Non Profit: no
Paid Staff: two
Unpaid Staff: one
Wholesalers: Baker & Taylor
ISSN Number/ISBN Number: 1540-6113/0-9721926
Number of Books Published per Year: two
Titles in Print: six

Average Percentage Printed: Paperback 80%, Chapbook 20%
Backfile Available: yes

Organization: The Pinch (previously River City)

Type: magazine
CLMP member: yes
Primary Editor/Contact Person: Dr. Kristen Iversen
Address: 467 Patterson Hall
Memphis, TN 38152-3510
Web Site Address: www.thepinchjournal.com
Publishes: fiction, nonfiction, poetry, and art
Editorial Focus: We publish both seasoned writers and new work that we think has promise.
Representative Authors: Linda Gregorson, Scott Russell Sanders, and Beth Ann Fennelly
Submissions Policy: All typed manuscripts. Include brief cover letter and SASE. No email submissions. Maximum 7,000 words for fiction/nonfiction.
Simultaneous Submissions: yes
Reading Period: 8/25 to 3/15
Reporting Time: two to six months
Author Payment: copies
Contests: Entries must be postmarked by 3/15. Fee: $20 for first story or up to 3 poems; $10 for additional stories or sets of 3 poems;
See web site for contest guidelines
Founded: 1980
Non Profit: yes
Paid Staff: six
Unpaid Staff: 25
Distributors: Ingram
ISSN Number/ISBN Number: ISSN 1048-129X
Total Circulation: 1,500
Paid Circulation: 300
Average Print Run: 1,800
Subscription Rate: Individual $18/institution $18
Single Copy Price: $10
Current Volume/Issue: 27/2
Frequency per year: biannual
Backfile Available: yes
Unsolicited MSS Received: yes
% of Unsolicited MSS Published per Year: 8%
Format: perfect
Average Pages: 160
Ads: no

Organization: Pindeldyboz

Type: online
CLMP member: yes
Primary Editor/Contact Person: Whitney Pastorek
Address: 23-55 38th St.
Astoria, NY 11105
Web Site Address: http://www.pindeldyboz.com
Publishes: essays, fiction, nonfiction, poetry, and art
Editorial Focus: Write something that has to be told. Show us something familiar in a different light. Kick ass. Surprise us.
Recent Awards Received: some stuff here and there. hey, check out our web site for more specific info about us, no? yes!
Submissions Policy: We only accept shiny, unpublished work. Also, our website is always open for subs. More info @ www.pindledyboz.com/submit.
Simultaneous Submissions: yes
Reading Period: year-round
Reporting Time: two to four months
Author Payment: copies
Founded: 2000
Non Profit: no
Paid Staff: zero
Unpaid Staff: six
Distributors: DeBoer, Ubiquity
ISSN Number/ISBN Number: ISSN 1534-7869
Average Page Views per Month: 90,000
Average Unique Visitors per Month: 13,000
Frequency per Year: 40
Publish Print Anthology: yes
Price: $12
Average Percentage of Pages per Category: Fiction 85%, Nonfiction 5%, Essays 5%, Art 5%
Ads: no

Organization: Pleasure Boat Studio: A Literary Press

Type: press
CLMP member: yes
Primary Editor/Contact Person: Jack Estes
Address: 201 W. 89th St.
New York, NY 10024
Web Site Address: www.pleasureboatstudio.com
Publishes: essays, fiction, nonfiction, and poetry
Editorial Focus: New imprints Caravel Books (mysteries), Aequitas Books (nonfiction), Empty Bowl Books (ecological).
Recent Awards Received: Recent book nominated for an Edgar. Excellent reviews in key journals.
Representative Authors: Anne Argula, Inger

Frimansson, and Michael Blumenthal
Submissions Policy: Query first, via email. We take VERY FEW manuscripts. Include a brief description of your book.
Simultaneous Submissions: yes
Reading Period: year-round
Reporting Time: one to six months
Author Payment: royalties and copies
Founded: 1996
Non Profit: no
Paid Staff: two
Unpaid Staff: one
Distributors: SPD
Wholesalers: Ingram, Baker & Taylor, Partners/West
ISSN Number/ISBN Number: ISBN 978-1-929355
Number of Books Published per year: three to four
Titles in Print: 50
Average Print Run: 500
Average Percentage Printed: Paperback 75%, Chapbook 20%
Average Price: $15

Organization: Pleiades Press/LMWT Poetry Series

Type: press
CLMP member: yes
Primary Editor/Contact Person: Kevin Prufer and Susan Ludvigson
Address: Department of English
Central Missouri State University
Warrensburg, MO 64093
Web Site Address:
http://www.cmsu.edu/englphil/pleiades
Publishes: poetry
Editorial Focus: Poetry books by American authors.
Representative Authors: Nils Michals, Kathleen Jesme, and Julianna Baggott
Submissions Policy: Books are selected only through our annual competition.
Simultaneous Submissions: yes
Reading Period: 7/30 to 9/30
Reporting Time: three to six months
Author Payment: cash
Founded: 1998
Non Profit: yes
Paid Staff: two
Unpaid Staff: five
Distributors: Louisiana State University Press
Titles in Print: eight

Average Percentage Printed: Paperback 100%
Average Price: $15.95

Organization: Pleiades: A Journal of New Writing

Type: magazine
CLMP member: yes
Primary Editor/Contact Person: Kevin Prufer and Wayne Miller
Address: Dept. of English
The University of Central Missouri
Warrensburg, MO 64093
Web Site Address:
http://www.cmsu.edu/englphil/pleiades
Publishes: essays, fiction, nonfiction, poetry, reviews, and translation
Editorial Focus: We publish poetry, fiction, essays, and reviews of important small and university press books.
Recent Awards Received: Pushcart Prize 2002, 2004, 2005, 2007; Best American Poetry 2001, 2002, 2003, 2004, 2005, 2006.
Representative Authors: Chris Offutt, Wislawa Szymborska, and David Kirby.
Submissions Policy: Send submissions with SASE. We read all year, though are a little slower in the summer.
Simultaneous Submissions: yes
Reading Period: Year-round
Reporting Time: one to three months
Author Payment: none
Contests: See web site for contest guidelines.
Founded: 1991
Non Profit: yes
Paid Staff: five
Unpaid Staff: 12
Distributors: Ingram, DeBoer, Media Solutions
ISSN Number/ISBN Number: ISSN 1063-3391
Total Circulation: 3,000
Paid Circulation: 1,000
Average Print Run: 4,500
Subscription Rate: Individual $12/Institution $12
Single Copy Price: $6
Current Volume/Issue: 27/2
Frequency per Year: biannual
Backfile Available: yes
Unsolicited Ms. Received: yes
% of Unsolicited Ms. Published per Year: .5%
Format: perfect
Size: H 8.5" W 5"

Average Pages: 160
Ads: yes
Ad Rates: on request

Organization: Ploughshares

Type: magazine
CLMP member: yes
Primary Editor/Contact Person: Rob Arnold
Address: Emerson College
120 Boylston St.
Boston, MA 02116
Web Site Address: http://www.pshares.org
Publishes: fiction, nonfiction, and poetry
Editorial Focus: Guest-edited serially by prominent writers who explore different visions, aesthetics, and literary circles.
Representative Authors: Antonya Nelson, Toi Derricotte, and Jonah Winter
Submissions Policy: one story or one to three poems
Simultaneous Submissions: yes
Reading Period: 8/1 to 3/31
Reporting Time: three to five months
Author Payment: cash, copies, and subscription
Founded: 1971
Non Profit: yes
Paid Staff: four
Unpaid Staff: 20
Distributors: Ingram
ISSN Number/ISBN Number: ISSN 0048-4474
Total Circulation: 6,000
Paid Circulation: 3,600
Average Print Run: 7,500
Subscription Rate: Individual $24/Institution $27
Single Copy Price: $10.95
Current Volume/Issue: 30/2 and 3
Frequency per Year: triquarterly
Backfile Available: yes
Unsolicited Ms. Received: yes
% of Unsolicited Ms. Published per Year: 1%
Format: perfect
Size: H 8.5" W 5.375"
Average Pages: 220
Ads: yes
Ad Rates: full page $400, half-page $275
See web site for details.

Organization: PMS poemmemoirstory

Type: magazine
CLMP member: yes

Primary Editor/Contact Person: Linda Frost
Address: University of Alabama at Birmingham
HOH 1530 3rd Ave. South
Birmingham, AL 35294-4450
Web Site Address: http://www.pms-journal.org
Publishes: essays, fiction, and poetry
Editorial Focus: Top quality literary work by women; each issue includes one memoir by a woman who shares her historically significant experience.
Recent Awards Received: Best American Poetry 2003, 2004; New Stories from the South 2005; Best American Essays 2005
Representative Authors: Ruth Stone, Amy Gerstler, and Sonia Sanchez
Submissions Policy: five poems or 15 pages of prose with SASE.
Simultaneous Submissions: yes
Reading Period: 9/1 to 11/30
Reporting Time: four to twelve weeks
Author Payment: copies and subscription
Founded: 2001
Non Profit: yes
Paid Staff: zero
Unpaid Staff: 10
Distributors: Ingram Periodicals, Inc. and Bernard DeBoer, Inc.
ISSN Number/ISBN Number: 1535-1335/0-89732-578-8
Total Circulation: 1,000
Paid Circulation: 150
Average Print Run: 1,500
Subscription Rate: Individual $7/Institution $7
Single Copy Price: $5
Current Volume/Issue: Issue 6
Frequency per Year: annual
Backfile Available: yes
Unsolicited Ms. Received: yes
% of Unsolicited Ms. Published per Year: 75%
Format: perfect
Size: H 9" W 6"
Average Pages: 120
Ads: no

Organization: Poem

Type: magazine
CLMP member: yes
Primary Editor/Contact Person: Rebecca Harbor
Address: P.O. Box 2006
Huntsville, AL 35804
Web Site Address: http://www.hla-hsv.org

Publishes: poetry
Editorial Focus: mostly lyric poetry; traditional and free verse; compact language, precise diction, apt imagery
Representative Authors: Robert Cooperman, Kathryn Kirkpatrick, and Kim Bridgford
Submissions Policy: no translations, previously published works, or simultaneous submissions; three to five poems with cover letter and SASE
Simultaneous Submissions: no
Reading Period: Year-round
Reporting Time: one to two months
Author Payment: copies
Founded: 1967
Non Profit: yes
Paid Staff: zero
Unpaid Staff: three
Total Circulation: 475
Paid Circulation: 350
Average Print Run: 500
Subscription Rate: Individual $20/Institution $20
Single Copy Price: $10
Current Volume/Issue: Issue 98
Frequency per Year: biannual
Backfile Available: yes
Unsolicited Ms. Received: yes
% of Unsolicited Ms. Published per Year: 5-6%
Format: perfect
Size: H 7 1/4" W 4 3/8"
Average Pages: 90
Ads: no

Organization: Poemeleon: A Journal of Poetry

Type: online
CLMP member: yes
Primary Editor/Contact Person: Cati Porter
Address: no physical address at this time.
Web Site Address: http://www.poemeleon.org
Publishes: essays, poetry, and reviews
Editorial Focus: we are a poetry-only journal, with occasional publication of relevant essays, interviews, and reviews.
Recent Awards Received: Poems from the inaugural issue were chosen for Poetry Daily's web monthly feature and NewPages WordsMatter section.
Representative Authors: Bob Hicok, Katherine Varnes, and Tony Barnstone
Submissions Policy: published twice per year, each issue has a specific focus. Check the website for

guidelines before submitting.
Simultaneous Submissions: yes
Reading Period: Year-round
Reporting Time: one to four months
Author Payment: none
Contests: none at this time, but please check back as we may be adding something in the near future; see website for guidelines
Founded: 2005
Non Profit: yes
Paid Staff: zero
Unpaid Staff: three
ISSN Number/ISBN Number: ISSN 1933-6217
Average Page Views per Month: 8,414
Average Unique Visitors per Month: 1,250
Frequency per Year: biannual
Publish Print Anthology: no
Average Percentage of Pages per Category: Poetry 98%, Reviews 2%
Ads: no

Organization: Poems & Plays

Type: magazine
CLMP member: no
Primary Editor/Contact Person: Gaylord Brewer
Address: English Department
Middle Tennessee State University
Murfreesboro, TN 37132
Web Site Address: http://www.mtsu.edu/-english2/Journals/poemsandplays/
Publishes: poetry
Editorial Focus: Poems and short plays.
Representative Authors: Nancy Naomi Carlson, James Doyle, and Ron McFarland
Submissions Policy: We read submissions Oct.-Dec. for subsequent spring issue.
Simultaneous Submissions: yes
Reading Period: 10/1 to 11/30
Reporting Time: six to twelve weeks
Author Payment: copies
Contests: The Tennessee Chapbook Prize. 20-24 pages, published interiorly in issue. Submit Oct. -- Nov. with $10 and acknowledgments.
Founded: 1993
Non Profit: yes
Paid Staff: zero
Unpaid Staff: two to three
ISSN Number/ISBN Number: ISSN 1073-1172
Total Circulation: 900
Average Print Run: 900

Subscription Rate: Individual $10/Institution $20
Single Copy Price: $6
Current Volume/Issue: Issue 10
Frequency per Year: annual
Backfile Available: yes
Unsolicited Ms. Received: yes
% of Unsolicited Ms. Published per Year: 1%
Format: perfect
Size: H 9" W 6"
Average Pages: 88
Ads: no

Organization: Poesy Magazine

Type: magazine
CLMP member: yes
Primary Editor/Contact Person: Brian Morrisey
Address: P.O. Box 7823
Santa Cruz, CA 95061
Web Site Address: http://www.poesy.org
Publishes: poetry and art
Editorial Focus: Poesy is an anthology for poets across the country. Poesy's main concentration is Boston, MA and Santa Cruz, CA
Representative Authors: Diane di Prima, Jack Hirschman, and David Lerner
Submissions Policy: Requested but not limited to: 32 lines or less, five to seven poems may be considered for each issue.
Simultaneous Submissions: yes
Reading Period: Year-round
Reporting Time: seven to ten weeks
Author Payment: copies
Founded: 1990
Non Profit: yes
Paid Staff: zero
Unpaid Staff: three
Distributors: Ibbetson Street Press, City Lights, Quimby's
ISSN Number/ISBN Number: ISSN 1541-8162
Total Circulation: 1,000
Paid Circulation: 215
Average Print Run: 1,000
Subscription Rate: Individual $12/Institution $15
Single Copy Price: $2
Current Volume/Issue: Issue 32
Frequency per Year: quarterly
Backfile Available: yes
Unsolicited Ms. Received: yes
% of Unsolicited Ms. Published per Year: 10%
Format: stapled

Size: H 8.125" W 10.5"
Average Pages: 20
Ads: yes
Ad Rates: $20, $35, $50, $80
See Web site for details.

Organization: Poet Lore

Type: magazine
CLMP member: no
Primary Editor/Contact Person: Jason DeYoung
Address: The Writer's Center
4508 Walsh St.
Bethesda, MD 20815-8006
Web Site Address: http://www.writer.org/pubs/poet-lore.asp
Publishes: essays and poetry
Editorial Focus: Inviting all types of poetry, the editors look for a high level of craftsmanship, and imaginative use of language and image
Representative Authors: David Wagoner, Fleda Brown, and Linda Pastan
Submissions Policy: You may submit three to five poems. All poems must be typed with name and address on each poem. If a poem is more than one page, please indicate if the second page begins with a new stanza. Reviewers: Please query the editors with a sample of your writing. We ask you let us know in your cover letter if poems are simultaneously submitted, and notify us immediately if the work is accepted elsewhere.
Simultaneous Submissions: yes
Reading Period: Year-round
Reporting Time: one to three months
Author Payment: copies
Founded: 1889
Non Profit: yes
Paid Staff: one
Unpaid Staff: four
Distributors: EBSCO, Swets Blackwell, Harrassowitz
ISSN Number/ISBN Number: ISSN 0032-1966
Total Circulation: 800
Paid Circulation: 450
Average Print Run: 1,000
Subscription Rate: Individual $18/Institution $26.60
Single Copy Price: $9
Current Volume/Issue: 101/3/4
Frequency per Year: biannual
Backfile Available: yes
Unsolicited Ms. Received: yes
% of Unsolicited Ms. Published per Year: 5%

Format: perfect
Size: H 9" W 6"
Average Pages: 120
Ads: yes
Ad Rates: full page $100, half page $50

Organization: Poetic Matrix Press

Type: press
CLMP member: yes
Primary Editor/Contact Person: John Peterson
Address: P.O. Box 1223
Madera, CA 93639
Web Site Address: http://www.poeticmatrix.com
Publishes: poetry
Editorial Focus: Poetry that has something to say and is well-crafted. Poetry that does not tell but shows and is rich in the imaginal mind.
Recent Awards Received: Brandon Cesmat—San Diego Book Award for Poetry. Tomas Gayton—African American Writers Association Award.
Representative Authors: Brandon Cesmat, Gail Rudd Entrekin, and Tomas Gayton
Submissions Policy: Single poems for periodic online letter. Book length manuscripts primarily for Slim Volume Series. See website.
Simultaneous Submissions: yes
Reading Period: year-round
Reporting Time: two to four months
Author Payment: royalties, cash, and copies
Contests: Slim Volume Series—every two years; see website for guidelines
Founded: 1997
Non Profit: no
Paid Staff: one
Unpaid Staff: five
Distributors: Ingram Books, Baker & Taylor, Amazon
ISSN Number/ISBN Number: ISBN 978-0-9789597
Number of Books Published per Year: four
Titles in Print: 18
Average Percentage Printed: Hardcover 10%, Paperback 90%
Average Price: $15.00

Linda Frost
Editor, PMS poemmemoirstory

How did you arrive at your current position?

I am an associate professor of English at the University of Alabama at Birmingham with a specialty in nineteenth-century American literature and culture. Besides being an Americanist, I have also always written and published poetry and taught creative writing. (I've studied under some fine writers—June Jordan, David Ignatow, and Cornelius Eady, to name a few.) When the editor of a literary magazine at UAB retired and my friend Bob Collins, director of our creative writing program and editor of *Birmingham Poetry Review*, asked if I'd take it over, I said yes—without thinking, of course. The name of the journal then was *Astarte* for the goddess of that name; I told Bob that I would feel more comfortable with a name that better suited my temperament. And lo, *PMS poemmemoirstory* was born.

What is the staff structure at your magazine?

I have a wonderful voluntary crew of *PMS*ie girls (with a few *PMS*ie guys in there, to keep it interesting) who serve as my readers, assistant editors, literary scouts, my partners in crime and brownies and wine. I have had a number of splendid student interns, one of whom, Pam Williams, secured our first contracts for national distribution. My friend Heather serves as both assistant editor and business manager because she is too dependable for her own good. Another friend of *PMS*, Michael Alfano, has given generously of his time and talent to design our covers, and my diligent and absurdly supportive husband, Russell Helms of absnth.com, does our production work. I am the editor-in-chief, though, which means that all bucks stop with me—except in the case of *PMS* 8, our current issue, which is a special issue featuring all African-American women writers and guest-edited by Honoreé Fanonne Jeffers.

What challenges do you face as a publisher?

Like every other editor, we've had and have budget issues. Although we're now largely funded by our university, we'd like to be able to pay our writers. We struggle too like everyone else with distribution although we're now nationally distributed; still, we want more people to know about us because we're proud of the magazine and are well aware of the tangible benefits additional visibility brings. Aside from those issues, though, there is no doubt that my biggest

challenge personally is finding and making the time it takes to give the magazine its due and grow it as it should be and can be grown. I'm an active scholar in my area of research, associate director of our university honors program, and mom to two little girls. That's a hat or two too many, probably.

Do you have any cover letter advice?

Tell us something about yourself that we could include in your bio if we take your work but never hear from you again. I hate just saying, "Jill Poesy lives in West Virginia," when I *could* say, "Jill Poesy's work has appeared in *Nature, The Economist,* and *PMS poemmemoirstory*. She is an astronaut who relishes olives and lives in West Virginia." Don't forget your email address, etc., and always be brief but substantive. Economy rocks.

What do you look for in a submission?

Something fine. Something different. If I've just read ten memoirs about caring for an elderly parent, and even more so, if I've already taken one, it's unlikely that I'll accept another at that moment, despite whatever brilliance it may display. We publish between four and seven pieces of prose in each genre; that gives you an idea of the odds. We're not looking for work about the condition of PMS, but we'll publish it if it's fine and different. Like everyone else, we want work that's well written, but unlike almost everyone else, we'll only consider your work if you are a woman—or are up to masquerade as one on paper.

How are submissions processed at your magazine?

We have a set reading period—September 1 through November 30—each year and at least two members of our staff, including or additionally me, read every submission. Each reader rates each submission as either a "yes," a "no" or a "maybe," and then we get together as a whole staff once a month to go through the submissions, make our cases, and decide on our selections. I reserve the right to grab something without going through the ordinary channels of my readers if I feel a cosmic push to do so. I exercise this right about five times an issue. I write out the acceptances and usually a student intern writes out the rejections.

We do solicit a few pieces for each issue from well-established writers and also one essay from someone who is not a writer but who has experienced something of historic import for our featured memoir. We started this because my assistant editor, Margaret, brought in an essay from Emily Lyons for our first issue who was the nurse critically injured in the 1998 Eric Rudolph bombing of the Birmingham New Woman All Women clinic. As a staff, we brainstorm from whom this essay should come each year, in the very beginning of the fall, usually over Indian food.

Do you have a favorite unsolicited submission discovery or anecdote?

I've had the real privilege to read some great stuff over the last seven years and I love the rush you get as an editor when you pick something out of the pile and realize that it's truly excellent writing. My assistant editor, Delores, had that experience when she picked up Holly Welker's unsolicited essay "Satin Worship" about sewing and the joys of working with fabric. Delo and the rest of us at *PMS* weren't the only ones to love it, though; it also caught Susan Orlean's eye who included it in the issue of *Best American Essays* she was editing that year. And as I recently found out, someone else liked it enough to use a quote from it as the basis for a Sunday *New York Times* acrostic puzzle. How wacky a fame is that?

What advice do you have for first-time submitters?

Always send your best work and always send a reasonably small but solid sample of your writing. Keep your work in circulation. The writers that publish their work are the ones who routinely and stubbornly send it out. Also, make sure that your editors know if something you submitted was taken elsewhere. We do accept simultaneous submissions but it ruins everyone's credibility if writers simultaneously publish. We very much appreciate the updates our writers send us when their work has been taken elsewhere. To that end, keep good records of your submissions and stay in contact.

Also, meet your editors at the annual AWP conference and other book fairs. We're people too who really like nothing better than basking in your glory. My favorite part of doing *PMS* has been being a part of the communities it pulls together at every level— that of my staff, the writers in my city and my state, and the ones scattered across the nation who come together on our pages. It's virtual, but still satisfying.

What are your long-term plans for your magazine?

I am, have been, and remain thrilled by every anthology that reprints work from *PMS*. Of course, I'd like to see us in even more anthologies and more bookstores and more libraries and more, more, more bathroom magazine bins. I'd like to see us publish two issues a year; I'd like our look to get even sassier; I'd like to graduate to the world of the podcast. But all of that is frosting on this cake. What I *really* want to see is the good work *PMS* does continue. Like a number of wonderful artists and cultural activists I know here, we are changing people's minds about what can and does and will come out of Alabama. I'm very proud to be part of that.

What's your evaluation of the current literary landscape?

I hate to presume to describe what the world of literature is about now. I will say that I do not believe that print is dead or even dying. Yes, it is *much* cheaper to marry the web and avoid the printing press. Nevertheless, print is still the most sought-after technology for writers seeking to publish. Despite how the internet is changing how and what we know, the book isn't going anywhere yet. Nevertheless, since writers do really need and want these publications, writers have to support them. I'm afraid that a range of factors—lessening options for distribution, less money for the arts in general, etc.—will lead to a nasty drop in the overall number of literary magazines. Which means a nasty drop in the places where you can publish your stuff. We really need the support of the community our work supports. Just so you know.

I love the tone of much contemporary writing now; I love a broad sense of irony to my reading. Perhaps there is no other way to adequately respond to the insanity of the last eight years. Regardless, I'm happy to open the envelopes I get because I know there is bound to be gold in those hills.

Organization: The Poetry Church

Type: magazine
CLMP member: no
Primary Editor/Contact Person: Rev. John Waddington-Feather
Address: P.O. Box 438
Shrewsbury UK, Sa SY3 0WN
Web Site Address:
http://www.waddysweb.freeuk.com
Publishes: poetry and reviews
Editorial Focus: The current state of Christian art, music and writing. Often in the form of a sermonette.
Representative Authors: Walter Nash, Susan Glyn, and Laurie Bates
Submissions Policy: Poems must be 30 lines or less. Longer for our bi-annual Collections winter and summer. Typed and with SASE.
Simultaneous Submissions: yes
Reading Period: Year-round
Reporting Time: one to twelve weeks
Author Payment: none
Contests: None. But poetry contests are listed in our News section each quarter.
Founded: 1985
Non Profit: yes
Paid Staff: two
Unpaid Staff: five
Distributors: Feather Books, P.O. Box 438, Shrewsbury SY3 0WN
ISSN Number/ISBN Number: none/1 84175
Total Circulation: 1,000
Paid Circulation: 280
Subscription Rate: Individual $25/Institution $30
Single Copy Price: $6
Current Volume/Issue: 9/3
Frequency per Year: quarterly
Backfile Available: yes
Unsolicited Ms. Received: yes
% of Unsolicited Ms. Published per Year: 50%
Format: stapled
Size: H 8" W 6"
Average Pages: 40

Organization: Poetry Daily

Type: online
CLMP member: yes
Primary Editor/Contact Person: Don Selby
Address: P.O. Box 1306
Charlottesville, VA 22902-1306
Web Site Address: http://www.poems.com

Publishes: essays, poetry, and reviews
Editorial Focus: Poems, news, essays, reviews, and special editorial features selected from current books and journals; weekly e-mail newsletter
Representative Authors: Eavan Boland, Albert Goldbarth, and Susan Stewart
Submissions Policy: We do not take original submissions
Simultaneous Submissions: no
Author Payment: none
Founded: 1997
Non Profit: yes
Paid Staff: 2.5
Unpaid Staff: none
Backfile Available: no
Average Page Views per Month: 1.1 million
Average Unique Visitors per Month: 25,000
Frequency per Year: 52
Publish Print Anthology: yes
Price: $14.95
Average Percentage of Pages per Category: Poetry 98%, Reviews 1%, Essays 1%
Ad Rates: See web site for details.

Organization: Poetry Flash

Type: magazine
CLMP member: yes
Primary Editor/Contact Person: Joyce Jenkins
Address: 1450 Fourth St., #4
Berkeley, CA 94710
Web Site Address: http://www.poetryflash.org
Publishes: essays, poetry, reviews and translation
Editorial Focus: Book reviews, interviews, poems, submissions, fiction/nonfiction/poetry event calendar for California, Northwest, Southwest.
Recent Awards Received: American Book Award, Bay Area Book Reviewers Award in Publishing
Representative Authors: Richard Silberg, Stephen Kessler, and Mimi Albert
Simultaneous Submissions: yes
Reading Period: Year-round
Reporting Time: two to three months
Author Payment: copies and subscription
Contests: n/a
Founded: 1972
Non Profit: yes
Paid Staff: two
Distributors: self-distributed
Wholesalers: n/a
Total Circulation: 22,000
Paid Circulation: 2,500

Average Print Run: 22,000
Subscription Rate: Individual $12/Institution $12
Current Volume/Issue: Issue 298
Frequency per Year: quarterly
Backfile Available: yes
Unsolicited Ms. Received: yes
% of Unsolicited Ms. Published per Year: 10%
Format: tabloid
Size: H 15" W 11 1/2"
Average Pages: 60
Ads: yes
Ad Rates: full-page $630, half-page $315, quarter-page $165.37; See website for details

Organization: Poetry International

Type: magazine
CLMP member: yes
Primary Editor/Contact Person: Ilya Kaminsky
Address: Dept. of English
San Diego State University
San Diego, CA 92182
Web Site Address: http://poetryinternational.sdsu.edu
Publishes: essays, nonfiction, poetry, reviews, and art
Editorial Focus: Quality poetry and translations from throughout the world
Representative Authors: Billy Collins, Kim Addonizio, and Adrienne Rich
Submissions Policy: Send no more than five poems at a time.
Simultaneous Submissions: yes
Reading Period: 9/1 to 12/31
Reporting Time: three to four months
Author Payment: copies
Founded: 1997
Non Profit: yes
Paid Staff: four
Unpaid Staff: three
Distributors: Ingram Periodicals
ISSN Number/ISBN Number: 1093-054-X/varies
Total Circulation: 1,000
Paid Circulation: 400
Average Print Run: 1,500
Subscription Rate: Individual $45/Institution $54
Single Copy Price: $15
Current Volume/Issue: Issue 10
Frequency per Year: annual
Backfile Available: yes
Unsolicited Ms. Received: yes
% of Unsolicited Ms. Published per Year: 7%
Format: perfect

Average Pages: 200
Ad Rates: See web site for details.

Organization: Poetry Magazine

Type: magazine
CLMP member: yes
Primary Editor/Contact Person: Christian Wiman
Address: 444 North Michigan Avenue
Suite 1850
Chicago, IL 60611
Web Site Address: http://www.poetrymagazine.org
Publishes: essays, poetry, reviews, and translation
Editorial Focus: To print the best poetry written today, in whatever style, genre, or approach.
Submissions Policy: Submissions must be made by mail and accompanied by a SASE. We do not take e-mail submissions. Please refer to web site.
Simultaneous Submissions: no
Reading Period: Year-round
Reporting Time: four to six weeks
Author Payment: cash and copies
Contests: See Web Site for contest guidelines.
Founded: 1912
Non Profit: yes
Paid Staff: six
Unpaid Staff: zero
Distributors: DeBoer, Ingram, Ubiquity, Source Interlink
Total Circulation: 30,000
Paid Circulation: 27,000
Average Print Run: 35,000
Subscription Rate: Individual $35/Institution $38
Single Copy Price: $3.75
Current Volume/Issue: 186/5
Frequency per Year: monthly
Backfile Available: yes
Unsolicited Ms. Received: yes
% of Unsolicited Ms. Published per Year: 100%
Format: perfect
Size: H 9" W 5.5"
Average Pages: 72
Ads: yes
Ad Rates: $800 per page
See web site for details.

Organization: Poetry Midwest

Type: online
CLMP member: no
Primary Editor/Contact Person: Matthew W. Schmeer

Address: 5915 W. 100th Terrace
Overland Park, KS 66207
Web Site Address: http://www.poetrymidwest.org
Publishes: fiction, nonfiction, and poetry
Editorial Focus: We look for highly literary pieces that capture the essence of experience with vivid imagery while avoiding didacticism.
Representative Authors: Simon Perchik, Jack Stewart, and Kathryn Jacobs
Submissions Policy: E-mail submissions only. Send three poems or one piece of prose. No prose over 300 words. E-mail to submit@poetrymidwest.org.
Simultaneous Submissions: yes
Reading Period: Year-round
Reporting Time: one to six months
Author Payment: none
Founded: 2000
Non Profit: yes
Paid Staff: zero
Unpaid Staff: one
ISSN Number/ISBN Number: ISSN 1536-870X
Average Page Views per Month: 1,500
Average Unique Visitors per Month: 1,200
Frequency per Year: triquarterly
Publish Print Anthology: no
Average Percentage of Pages per Category: Fiction 10%, Nonfiction 10%, Poetry 80%
Ads: no

Organization: Poetry Miscellany

Type: magazine
CLMP member: no
Primary Editor/Contact Person: Richard Jackson
Address: English Dept. UT-Chattanooga
Chattanooga, TN 37411
Web Site Address:
http://www.utc.edu/~engldept/pm/pmhp.html
Publishes: essays, fiction, poetry, and reviews
Editorial Focus: Poetry from all schools and tastes; chapbook series of European writers in translation
Representative Authors: William Olsen, Maxine Kumin, and Marvin Bell
Submissions Policy: three to five poems; query for prose
Simultaneous Submissions: no
Reading Period: Year-round
Reporting Time: five to six months
Author Payment: none
Founded: 1970
Non Profit: yes

Paid Staff: one
Unpaid Staff: five
Total Circulation: 500
Paid Circulation: 100
Subscription Rate: Individual $5/Institution $5
Single Copy Price: $5
Current Volume/Issue: Issue 29
Frequency per Year: annual
Backfile Available: yes
Unsolicited Ms. Received: yes
% of Unsolicited Ms. Published per Year: 1%
Format: Saddle Stitched
Size: H 8" W 12"
Average Pages: 45
Ads: yes
Ad Rates: $100 (full page)

Organization: The Poetry Project Newsletter

Type: magazine
CLMP member: no
Primary Editor/Contact Person: Stacy Szymaszek/John Coletti
Address: The Poetry Project at St. Marks Church
131 E. 10th St.
New York, NY 10003
Web Site Address:
http://www.thepoetryproject.com/newsletter.php
Publishes: essays, poetry, and reviews
Editorial Focus: A bimonthly newsletter devoted to innovative poetry and poetics by way of essays, reviews, debate, and experimental writing.
Representative Authors: Brenda Coultas, Edwin Torres, and Ron Padgett
Submissions Policy: For potential book reviews, please send one copy of book and cover letter, attn: John Coletti.
Simultaneous Submissions: no
Reading Period: Year-round
Reporting Time: one to six months
Author Payment: none
Founded: 1973
Non Profit: yes
Paid Staff: six
Unpaid Staff: five+
Distributors: SPD
Total Circulation: 5,000
Paid Circulation: 2,000
Average Print Run: 5,000
Subscription Rate: Individual $25/Institution $25

Single Copy Price: $5
Current Volume/Issue: Issue 211
Frequency per Year: four issues
Backfile Available: yes
Unsolicited Ms. Received: no
Format: stapled
Size: H 8.5" W 11"
Average Pages: 32
Ads: yes
Ad Rates: Please contact info@poetryproject.com for ad inquiries.

Organization: Poetry Society of New Hampshire

Type: press
CLMP member: yes
Primary Editor/Contact Person: Patricia Frisella
Address: 31 Reservoir Road
Farmington, NH 03835
Publishes: poetry
Recent Awards Received: IPPY Bronze
Submissions Policy: We publish books, anthologies, rarely, but will solicit work broadly. So let us know you are out there.
Simultaneous Submissions: yes
Reading Period: Year-round
Reporting Time: three to four months
Author Payment: copies
Founded: 1964
Non Profit: yes
Paid Staff: zero
Unpaid Staff: one
Distributors: self
ISSN Number/ISBN Number: ISBN 98780972416719
Number of Books Published per Year: one
Titles in Print: two
Average Print Run: 2,000
Average Percentage Printed: Paperback 100%
Average Price: $16

Organization: The Poetz Group

Type: online
CLMP member: yes
Primary Editor/Contact Person: Jackie Sheeler
Address: P.O. Box 1401
New York, NY 10026
Web Site Address: http://www.poetz.com
Publishes: poetry
Editorial Focus: Crafted yet risky work that addresses the human, usually urban, experience.
Representative Authors: Martin Espada, Eileen McDermott, and Clara Sala
Submissions Policy: By invitation only. We hope to open submissions further. Check the web site for policy changes.
Simultaneous Submissions: yes
Reading Period: Year-round
Reporting Time: one to three months
Author Payment: none
Founded: 1999
Non Profit: yes
Paid Staff: zero
Unpaid Staff: one
Backfile Available: yes
Average Page Views per Month: 10,000
Average Unique Visitors per Month: unknown
Publish Print Anthology: no
Average Percentage of Pages per Category: Poetry 90%, Reviews 10%
Ads: no

Organization: Poltroon Press

Type: press
CLMP member: no
Primary Editor/Contact Person: Alastair Johnston
Address: P.O. Box 5476
Berkeley, CA 94705
Web Site Address: http://www.poltroonpress.com
Publishes: fiction, nonfiction, poetry, and translation
Representative Authors: Mark Coggins, Lucia Berlin, and Philip Whalen
Submissions Policy: Do not read unsolicited work
Simultaneous Submissions: yes
Reading Period: Year-round
Reporting Time: 12 to 24 months
Author Payment: royalties
Founded: 1975
Non Profit: yes
Paid Staff: zero
Unpaid Staff: two
Distributors: SPD
ISSN Number/ISBN Number: ISBN 0-918395-
Number of Books Published per Year: two
Titles in Print: 30
Average Percentage Printed: Hardcover 100%

Organization: POOL: A Journal of Poetry

Type: magazine

CLMP member: yes
Primary Editor/Contact Person: Judith Taylor
Address: P.O. Box 49738
Los Angeles,, CA 90049
Web Site Address: http://www.poolpoetry.com
Publishes: poetry and reviews
Editorial Focus: POOL is a national journal published in Los Angeles, featuring fresh and unexpected poetry.
Recent Awards Received: The Best American Poetry 2004, 2005 and 2006.
Representative Authors: Amy Gerstler, Jane Miller, and Michael Burkard
Submissions Policy: See web site for guidelines.
Simultaneous Submissions: yes
Reading Period: 12/1 to 2/28
Reporting Time: 2 to 3 months
Author Payment: copies
Founded: 2000
Non Profit: yes
Paid Staff: zero
Unpaid Staff: two
Distributors: DeBoer; Armadillo
ISSN Number/ISBN Number: ISBN 0-9721088-4-X
Total Circulation: 850
Paid Circulation: 80
Average Print Run: 900
Subscription Rate: Individual $10/18/24/Institution $12
Single Copy Price: $10
Current Volume/Issue: Issue 6
Frequency per Year: annual
Backfile Available: yes
Unsolicited Ms. Received: yes
% of Unsolicited Ms. Published per Year: 75%
Format: perfect
Size: H 9" W 6"
Average Pages: 120
Ads: yes
Ad Rates: Exchange ads only.

Organization: Portable Press at Yo-Yo Labs

Type: press
CLMP member: no
Primary Editor/Contact Person: Brenda Iijima
Address: 596 Bergen St.
Brooklyn, NY 11238
Publishes: poetry and art
Editorial Focus: experimental poetry, emergent hybridized writing, work that fuses the political, sociological, lingual and emotional realms.

Representative Authors: Peter Lamborn Wilson, Jill Magi, and Christina Strong
Submissions Policy: open submission policy, although most works are solicited.
Simultaneous Submissions: yes
Reading Period: Year-round
Reporting Time: one to two months
Author Payment: none
Founded: 2002
Non Profit: yes
Paid Staff: zero
Unpaid Staff: one
Number of Books Published per Year: five
Titles in Print: 25
Average Print Run: 150
Average Percentage Printed: Paperback 5%, Chapbook 90%, Other 5%
Average Price: $6

Organization: Portals Press

Type: press
CLMP member: no
Primary Editor/Contact Person: John P. Travis
Address: 4411 Fontainebleau Dr.
New Orleans, LA 70125
Web Site Address: http://www.portalspress.com
Publishes: fiction and poetry
Representative Authors: John Gery, Kay Murphy, and Grace Bauer
Submissions Policy: Query first.
Simultaneous Submissions: yes
Reading Period: Year-round
Reporting Time: one to six months
Author Payment: royalties and copies
Founded: 1993
Non Profit: no
Paid Staff: one
Unpaid Staff: 5
Distributors: Baker & Taylor; http://www.portals-press.com; Amazon
ISSN Number/ISBN Number: ISBN 0-916620-
Number of Books Published per Year: 2
Titles in Print: 20
Average Print Run: 750
Average Percentage Printed: Hardcover 10%, Paperback 90%
Average Price: $15

Organization: Post Road

Type: magazine
CLMP member: yes
Primary Editor/Contact Person: Mary Cotton, Publisher
Address: P.O. Box 600725
Newton, MA 02460
Web Site Address: http://www.postroadmag.com
Publishes: essays, fiction, nonfiction, poetry, art, and translation
Editorial Focus: Post Road seeks to publish new and original work by those writers and artists not represented in the mainstream.
Representative Authors: Nelly Reifler, Jonathan Ames, and Peter Rock.
Submissions Policy: Post Road accepts submissions in the following genres: fiction, nonfiction, poetry. See web site for submission guidelines.
Simultaneous Submissions: yes
Reading Period: Year-round
Reporting Time: two to three months
Author Payment: none
Contests: Yearly fiction and poetry contest; See website for contest guidelines.
Founded: 2000
Non Profit: yes
Paid Staff: zero
Unpaid Staff: 13
Distributors: Ingram; DeBoer
Total Circulation: 2,000
Paid Circulation: 100
Average Print Run: 2,000
Subscription Rate: Individual $18/Institution $34
Single Copy Price: $10.99
Current Volume/Issue: Issue 14
Frequency per Year: biannual
Backfile Available: yes
Unsolicited Ms. Received: yes
% of Unsolicited Ms. Published per Year: 70%
Format: perfect
Size: H 8.5" W 4.25"
Average Pages: 244
Ads: yes
Ad Rates: swap

Organization: The Post-Apollo Press

Type: press
CLMP member: no
Primary Editor/Contact Person: Simone Fattal
Address: 35 Marie St.
Sausalito, CA 94965
Publishes: essays, fiction, and poetry
Editorial Focus: Experimental poetry and prose, with an emphasis on international literature.
Representative Authors: Etel Adnan, Lyn Hejinian, and Jalal Toufic
Submissions Policy: TPAP generally solicits manuscripts, though unsolicited manuscripts are considered. We are not accepting fiction at this time.
Simultaneous Submissions: yes
Reading Period: Year-round
Reporting Time: four to eight months
Author Payment: copies
Founded: 1982
Non Profit: no
Paid Staff: one
Unpaid Staff: zero
Distributors: SPD, New Leaf
Number of Books Published per Year: three
Titles in Print: 41
Average Print Run: 1,000
Average Percentage Printed: Paperback 100%
Average Price: $12

Organization: Potomac Review

Type: magazine
CLMP member: yes
Primary Editor/Contact Person: Julie Wakeman-Linn, Editor
Address: Peck Humanities Inst., Montgomery Coll.
51 Mannakee St.
Rockville, MD 20850
Web Site Address:
http://www.montgomerycollege.edu/potomacreview
Publishes: essays, fiction, nonfiction, poetry, and translation
Editorial Focus: To explore the inner and outer terrain of the Mid-Atlantic region and beyond, via original prose, poetry, and nonfiction.
Representative Authors: Richard Peabody, David Housley, and Nancy Naomi Carlson
Submissions Policy: Poetry, up to three poems/five pages; Prose, up to 5,000 words. Photography, please inquire first.
Simultaneous Submissions: yes
Reading Period: 9/15 to 4/15
Reporting Time: two to six months
Author Payment: copies
Contests: Poetry contest forthcoming (Fall/Winter '07); See website for contest guidelines.

Founded: 1993
Non Profit: yes
Paid Staff: two
Unpaid Staff: 15
ISSN Number/ISBN Number: ISSN 10073-1989
Total Circulation: 800
Paid Circulation: 350
Subscription Rate: Individual $15/Institution $15
Single Copy Price: $10
Current Volume/Issue: Issue 42
Frequency per Year: biannual
Backfile Available: yes
Unsolicited Ms. Received: yes
% of Unsolicited Ms. Published per Year: 10%
Format: perfect
Size: H 8 1/2" W 5 3/8"
Average Pages: 248
Ads: yes
Ad Rates: Exchanges
See web site for details.

Organization: Prairie Schooner

Type: magazine
CLMP member: yes
Primary Editor/Contact Person: Hilda Raz/Erin Flanagan
Address: 201 Andrews Hall
The University of Nebraska
Lincoln, NE 68588-0334
Web Site Address:
http://www.unl.edu/schooner/psmain.htm
Publishes: essays, fiction, nonfiction, poetry, reviews, and translation
Editorial Focus: In our 77th year of continuous publication, we seek new work from established, mid-career, and beginning prose writers and poets.
Representative Authors: Judith Ortiz Cofer, Lee Martin, and Constance Merritt
Submissions Policy: SASE required. Eight poems or two stories/essays maximum per submission.
Simultaneous Submissions: no
Reading Period: 9/1 to 5/31
Reporting Time: two to three months
Author Payment: royalties and copies
Contests: $6,000+ in prizes for best prose and poetry published each year. Yearly Prize Book Series in fiction and poetry, two $300 prizes
Founded: 1926
Non Profit: yes
Paid Staff: two

Unpaid Staff: 13
Distributors: Ingram
Wholesalers: call direct: 1.800.715.2387
ISSN Number/ISBN Number: ISSN 0032-6682
Total Circulation: 2,000
Paid Circulation: 1,000
Subscription Rate: Individual $26/Institution $30
Single Copy Price: $9
Current Volume/Issue: 77/3
Frequency per Year: quarterly
Backfile Available: yes
Unsolicited Ms. Received: yes
% of Unsolicited Ms. Published per Year: 100%
Format: perfect
Size: H 9" W 6"
Average Pages: 200
Ads: yes
Ad Rates: $250 commercial publishers, discount to university presses

Organization: PREP Publishing

Type: press
CLMP member: yes
Primary Editor/Contact Person: Anne McKinney
Address: 1110 1/2 Hay St., Ste. C
Fayetteville, NC 28305
Web Site Address: http://www.prep-pub.com
Publishes: fiction and nonfiction
Editorial Focus: Primary emphasis is nonfiction and biographies, and some fiction.
Representative Authors: Gordon Beld, Anne McKinney, and Patty Sleem
Submissions Policy: Send self-addressed stamped envelope (.60 postage) for submissions info or visit web site at http://www.prep-pub.com
Simultaneous Submissions: yes
Reading Period: Year-round
Reporting Time: two to ten weeks
Author Payment: royalties
Founded: 1994
Non Profit: no
Paid Staff: five
Unpaid Staff: zero
Distributors: publisher
Wholesalers: Ingram, Baker & Taylor, Unique, Quality, others
ISSN Number/ISBN Number: ISBN 1-885288
Number of Books Published per Year: 12
Titles in Print: 45
Average Print Run: 3,000

Average Percentage Printed: Hardcover 5%,
Paperback 95%
Average Price: $20.00

Organization: Presa :S: Press

Type: press
CLMP member: no
Primary Editor/Contact Person: Roseanne Ritzema
Address: P.O. Box 792
Rockford, MI 49341
Web Site Address: http://www.presapress.com
Publishes: fiction, nonfiction, poetry, and translation
Editorial Focus: Prefers imagistic poetry where form
is an extension of content. Bias toward surrealism,
personal and experimental poetry.
Recent Awards Received: 2006 PEN Josephine
Miles Literary Achievement Award for This Land Is Not
My Land, by A.D. Winans.
Representative Authors: Hugh Fox, Eric Greinke, and
Lyn Lifshin
Submissions Policy: Send query letter and sample
of work. Include SASE.
Simultaneous Submissions: no
Reading Period: Year-round
Reporting Time: two to three months
Author Payment: copies
Founded: 2003
Non Profit: no
Paid Staff: zero
Unpaid Staff: three
Distributors: Gazelle Book Services, Ltd., United
Kingdom
Wholesalers: Baker & Taylor, Midwest Library
Services, Coutts
Number of Books Published per Year: six
Titles in Print: 24
Average Print Run: 500
Average Percentage Printed: Paperback 50%,
Chapbook 50%
Average Price: $15.00

Organization: PRESA

Type: magazine
CLMP member: yes
Primary Editor/Contact Person: Roseanne Ritzema
Address: P.O. Box 792
Rockford, MI 49341
Web Site Address: http://www.presapress.com
Publishes: essays, poetry, and reviews

Editorial Focus: Prefers imagistic poetry where form
is an extension of content. Bias toward surrealism,
personal and experimental poetry.
Representative Authors: Guy Beining, Harry Smith,
and A.D. Winans
Submissions Policy: Submit three to five poems. No
previously published poems or email submissions.
Cover letter is appreciated. First printing rights.
Simultaneous Submissions: no
Reading Period: Year-round
Reporting Time: two to three months
Author Payment: copies
Founded: 2005
Non Profit: no
Paid Staff: zero
Unpaid Staff: three
Total Circulation: 500
Paid Circulation: 25
Average Print Run: 500
Subscription Rate: Individual $20.00/Institution
$15.00
Single Copy Price: $8.50
Current Volume/Issue: Issue 6
Frequency per Year: biannual
Backfile available: yes
Unsolicited Ms. Received: no
Format: stapled
Size: H 8.5" W 5"
Average Pages: 56
Ads: yes
Ad Rates: half-page $35; full page $60; See website
for details.

Organization: Prick of the Spindle

Type: online
CLMP member: no
Primary Editor/Contact Person: Cynthia Reeser
Address: 305 Willow Bend Circle
Leesville, LA 71446
Web Site Address: http://www.prickofthespindle.com
Publishes: essays, fiction, nonfiction, poetry, and
reviews
Editorial Focus: High-caliber fiction, nonfiction, poet-
ry, drama, and literary reviews with a special bent
toward fresh, innovative voices.
Representative Authors: Joseph Murphy, Sandra
Maddux-Creech, and Scott Hartwich
Submissions Policy: See guidelines at website
Simultaneous Submissions: yes
Reading Period: Year-round

Reporting Time: one to three months
Author Payment: none
Founded: 2007
Non Profit: yes
Paid Staff: zero
Unpaid Staff: one
Average Page Views per Month: 100,000
Average Unique Visitors per Month: 20,000
Frequency per Year: four
Publish Print Anthology: no
Average Percentage of Pages per Category: Fiction 35%, Nonfiction 8%, Poetry 50%, Reviews 2%, Essays 5%
Ads: no

Organization: PRISM international

Type: magazine
CLMP member: no
Primary Editor/Contact Person: Editors
Address: Creative Writing Program, UBC
Buch E462-1866 Main Mall
Vancouver, BC V6T 1Z1
Web Site Address: http://www.prism.arts.ubc.ca
Publishes: fiction, nonfiction, poetry, art, and translation
Submissions Policy: See our web site for submissions guidelines.
Simultaneous Submissions: no
Reading Period: Year-round
Reporting Time: two to six months
Author Payment: cash, copies, and subscription
Contests: See Web site for contest guidelines.
Founded: 1959
Non Profit: yes
Paid Staff: four
Unpaid Staff: zero
Distributors: CMPA
ISSN Number/ISBN Number: ISSN 0032.8790
Total Circulation: 1,200
Paid Circulation: 700
Average Print Run: 1,250
Submission Rate: Individual $25/Institution $32
Single Copy Price: $9
Current Volume/Issue: 45/4
Frequency per Year: quarterly
Backfile Available: yes
Unsolicited Ms. Received: yes
% of Unsolicited Ms. Published per Year: 3%
Format: perfect
Size: H 9" W 6"

Average Pages: 80
Ads: yes
Ad Rates: See web site for details.

Organization: Pudding House Publications

Type: press
CLMP member: no
Primary Editor/Contact Person: Jennifer Bosveld
Address: 81 Shadymere Ln.
Columbus, OH 43213
Web Site Address: http://www.puddinghouse.com
Publishes: essays, fiction, poetry, and reviews
Editorial Focus: Poetry (some short short stories and essays), any style/subject. Make words dance together that haven't danced together before
Representative Authors: Roy Bentley, Charlene Fix, and David Chorlton
Submissions Policy: Standard professionalism, include SASE and e-mail, don't individually fold, no simultaneous, conserve by resending rejected work.
Simultaneous Submissions: no
Reading Period: Year-round
Reporting Time: one to twelve weeks
Author Payment: copies
Contests: See web site for contest guidelines.
Founded: 1979
Non Profit: yes
Paid Staff: two
Unpaid Staff: nine
Distributors: direct mail, web, phone directly to Pudding House
Wholesalers: We sell directly to bookstores, educational orgs
ISSN Number/ISBN Number: 0196-5913/many series
Number of Books Published per Year: 130
Titles in Print: 700
Average Print Run: 300
Average Percentage Printed: Paperback 2%, Chapbook 97%, Other 1%
Average Price: $8.95 chap

Organization: Puerto del Sol/Nightjar Press

Type: magazine
CLMP member: no
Address: New Mexico State University
Box 30001, Dept. 3E, English Bldg

Las Cruces, NM 88003-8001
Web Site Address:
http://www.nmsu.edu/~puerto/welcome.html
Publishes: essays, fiction, poetry, reviews, art, and translation
Reading Period: Year-round
Reporting Time: one to two months
Author Payment: none
Founded: 1960
Non Profit: no
Backfile Available: yes

Organization: PulpLit.com

Type: online
CLMP member: no
Primary Editor/Contact Person: Jason Clarke
Address: 411A Highland Ave. #376
Somerville, MA 02144
Web Site Address: http://www.pulplit.com
Publishes: essays, fiction, nonfiction, poetry, reviews, and art
Editorial Focus: We love genre fiction that transcends genre, literary analysis that goes beyond mundane formalism and exciting poetry.
Simultaneous Submissions: yes
Reading Period: Year-round
Reporting Time: one to six months
Author Payment: cash
Founded: 2002
Non Profit: no
Paid Staff: zero
Unpaid Staff: five
ISSN Number/ISBN Number: ISSN 1547-9374
Average Page Views per Month: 15,000
Average Unique Visitors per Month: 2,500
Frequency per Year: quarterly
Publish Print Anthology: yes
Price: free
Average Percentage of Pages per Category: Audio 100%
Ad Rates: $1 per thousand views; see website for details.

Organization: QRL

Type: press
CLMP member: no
Primary Editor/Contact Person: Renee Weiss
Address: 26 Haslet Ave.
Princeton, NJ 08540
Web Site Address: http://www.princeton.edu/~qrl
Publishes: essays, fiction, poetry, reviews, and translation
Editorial Focus: QRL is no longer publishing new work. But it will remain active to distribute its very large list of still available volumes.
Representative Authors: Ezra Pound, William Carlos Williams, and Wallace Stevens
Contests: see website
Founded: 1943
Non Profit: yes
Unpaid Staff: three
Distributors: QRL
Wholesalers: QRL
ISSN Number/ISBN Number: 1-888 545-43-7/1-888 545-44-5
Titles in Print: 70
Average Percentage Printed: Hardcover 60%, Paperback 40%

Organization: Quale Press

Type: press
CLMP member: yes
Primary Editor/Contact Person: Gian Lombardo
Address: 93 Main St.
Florence, MA 01062
Web Site Address: http://www.quale.com
Publishes: fiction, nonfiction, poetry, and translation
Editorial Focus: Prose poetry, political poetry (leftist), translations, experimental fiction, reissues.
Representative Authors: Sawako Nakayasu, Morton Marcus, and Joseph Torra
Submissions Policy: No unsolicited work. By invitation only.
Simultaneous Submissions: yes
Reading Period: Year-round
Reporting Time: two to six months
Author Payment: royalties
Founded: 1997
Non Profit: no
Paid Staff: two
Unpaid Staff: one
Distributors: SPD
ISSN Number/ISBN Number: ISBN 0-9700663, 0-9744503, 0-9792999
Number of Books Published per Year: two to five
Titles in Print: 26
Average Print Run: POD
Average Percentage Printed: Paperback 100%
Average Price: $14

Organization: Quarter After Eight

Type: magazine
CLMP member: yes
Primary Editor/Contact Person: Wendy Walker
Address: Ellis Hall
Ohio University
Athens, OH 45701
Web Site Address: http://www.quarteraftereight.org
Publishes: essays, fiction, nonfiction, poetry, reviews, art, and translation
Editorial Focus: QAE is an annual journal dedicated to exploring the prose form across distinctions of genre.
Representative Authors: David Lazar, Sean Thomas Dougherty, and Amy Locklin
Submissions Policy: Online only. Limit to three short or one long work. Must have innovative approach to prose form. No traditional, lineated poetry.
Simultaneous Submissions: yes
Reading Period: 10/15 to 4/15
Reporting Time: four to six months
Author Payment: copies
Contests: The Robert J. DeMott Short Prose Prize; see website for contest gidelines.
Founded: 1993
Non Profit: yes
Paid Staff: one
Unpaid Staff: 25
ISSN Number/ISBN Number: ISSN 1082-3697
Total Circulation: 400
Paid Circulation: 300
Average Print Run: 400
Submission Rate: Individual $10/Institution $10
Single Copy Price: $10
Current Volume/Issue: 14/1
Frequency per Year: annual
Backfile Available: yes
Unsolicited Ms. Received: yes
% of Unsolicited Ms. Published per Year: 98%
Format: perfect
Average Pages: 200
Ads: no

Organization: The Quarterly Conversation

Type: online
CLMP member: yes
Primary Editor/Contact Person: Scott Esposito
Address: 1719 Claridge Street
Arcadia, CA 91006
Web Site Address: http://www.quarterlyconversation.com
Publishes: essays, nonfiction, reviews, art, translation, and audio
Editorial Focus: Reviews and essays on books, new and old. Pieces should situate books within literature's larger context and go in-depth.
Representative Authors: Lance Olsen, Richard Grayson, and Dan Green
Submissions Policy: Submissions accepted year-round. No query necessary. Complete guidelines on our website.
Simultaneous Submissions: yes
Reading Period: Year-round
Reporting Time: eight to twelve weeks
Author Payment: none
Founded: 2005
Non Profit: yes
Paid Staff: zero
Unpaid Staff: 10
Average Page Views per Month: 5,000
Average Unique Visitors per Month: 3,500
Frequency per Year: quarterly
Publish Print Anthology: no
Average Percentage of Pages per Category: Nonfiction 5%, Reviews 60%, Essays 30%, Art 5%
Ads: no

Organization: Quarterly West

Type: magazine
CLMP member: no
Primary Editor/Contact Person: David C. Hawkins
Address: 255 S. Central Campus Dr.
Salt Lake City, UT 84112-9109
Web Site Address: http://www.utah.edu/quarterly-west
Publishes: essays, fiction, nonfiction, poetry, reviews, art, and translation
Editorial Focus: Quarterly West seeks original and accomplished literary verse, fiction, and creative nonfiction; also translations and reviews.
Representative Authors: Albert Goldbarth, George Saunders, and Eleanor Wilner
Submissions Policy: Submit three to five poems or short-shorts, or one story or essay. Translations should be accompanied by original.
Simultaneous Submissions: yes
Reading Period: 9/1 to 5/1
Reporting Time: four to six months
Author Payment: cash and copies

Contests: QW sponsors a biennial novella competition. Two winners receive a cash prize and publication. See web site for contest guidelines.
Founded: 1976
Non Profit: yes
Paid Staff: seven
Unpaid Staff: 22
Distributors: Ingram, DeBoer, Small Press Dist.
ISSN Number/ISBN Number: ISSN 0194-4231
Total Circulation: 1,400
Paid Circulation: 500
Submission Rate: Individual $14/Institution $15 (US)
Single Copy Price: $8.50
Current Volume/Issue: 56/1
Frequency per Year: biannual
Backfile Available: yes
Unsolicited Ms. Received: yes
% of Unsolicited Ms. Published per Year: 1%
Format: perfect
Size: H 10" W 7"
Average Pages: 176
Ads: yes
Ad Rates: Ad cards available upon request.

Organization: Quercus Review

Type: magazine
CLMP member: no
Primary Editor/Contact Person: Sam Pierstorff
Address: 435 College Ave.
Modesto Junior College
Modesto, CA 95350
Web Site Address: http://www.quercusreview.com
Publishes: fiction, poetry, and art
Editorial Focus: Poetry and fiction with a strong pulse.
Representative Authors: Amiri Baraka, Charles Harper Webb, and Dorianne Laux
Submissions Policy: We accept submissions year-round. Send three to five previously unpublished poems with cover letter, brief bio, and SASE.
Simultaneous Submissions: no
Reading Period: Year-round
Reporting Time: one to two months
Author Payment: copies
Contests: Quercus Review Poetry Series Annual Book Award
See web site for contest guidelines.
Founded: 1999
Non Profit: no
Paid Staff: one

Unpaid Staff: five
ISSN Number/ISBN Number: ISSN 1543-4532
Total Circulation: 250
Paid Circulation: 50
Average Print Run: 500
Submission Rate: Individual $20/Institution $20
Single Copy Price: $8
Current Volume/Issue: 1/5
Frequency per Year: biannual
Backfile Available: yes
Unsolicited Ms. Received: yes
% of Unsolicited Ms. Published per Year: 1%
Format: perfect
Average Pages: 112

Organization: Quick Fiction

Type: magazine
CLMP member: yes
Primary Editor/Contact Person: Jennifer Pieroni
Address: P.O. Box 4445
Salem, MA 01970
Web Site Address: http://www.quickfiction.org/
Publishes: fiction
Editorial Focus: stories and narrative prose poems under 500 words
Representative Authors: Mark Yakich, Wayne Sullins, and Dan Kaplan
Submissions Policy: 25-500 words. No more than five stories at a time. Send cover letter and SASE. No e-mail submissions and no certified mail.
Simultaneous Submissions: no
Reading Period: Year-round
Reporting Time: three to six months
Author Payment: copies
Contests: See Web site for contest guidelines.
Founded: 2001
Non Profit: no
Paid Staff: zero
Unpaid Staff: three
Distributors: DeBoer
ISSN Number/ISBN Number: 1543-8376/0-9724776
Total Circulation: 750
Paid Circulation: 500
Average Print Run: 1,800
Submission Rate: Individual $11/Institution $11
Single Copy Price: $6.50
Current Volume/Issue: Issue 10
Frequency per Year: biannual
Backfile Available: no
Unsolicited Ms. Received: yes

% of Unsolicited Ms. Published per Year: 3%
Format: perfect
Size: H 6" W 6"
Average Pages: 55
Ads: no

Organization: The Quillpen

Type: magazine
CLMP member: no
Primary Editor/Contact Person: Ron Seybold
Address: 11702 Buckingham Road
Austin, TX 78759
Web Site Address: http://www.workshopwriter.com
Publishes: essays, fiction, poetry, and audio
Editorial Focus: Character-driven stories and commentary with an eye toward the unexpected
Recent Awards Received: None
Representative Authors: Laurie Cosbey, Larisa Zlatic, and Mike Austin
Submissions Policy: By email only. Word files as attachments. No more than 2,000 words. No horror.
Simultaneous Submissions: yes
Reading Period: year-round
Reporting Time: two to four months
Author Payment: copies and subscription
Contests: see website for contest guidelines
Founded: 2006
Non Profit: yes
Paid Staff: one
Unpaid Staff: two
Distributors: None
Wholesalers: None
ISSN Number/ISBN Number: Pending
Total Circulation: 200
Paid Circulation: 15
Average Print Run: 200
Subscription Rate: individual $10/institution $8
Single Copy Price: $7
Current Volume/Issue: 1/1
Frequency per year: biannual
Backfile Available: no
Unsolicited MSS Received: yes
% of Unsolicited Ms. Published per Year: 50%
Format: stapled
Average Pages: 24
Ads: yes
Ad Rates: see web site for details

Organization: Radical Society

Type: magazine
CLMP member: no
Primary Editor/Contact Person: Kira Brunner
Address: P.O. Box 2329, Times Square Station
editors@radicalsociety.org
New York, NY 10108-2329
Publishes: essays, fiction, nonfiction, poetry, reviews, and art
Editorial Focus: is a forum for radical and progressive politics, cultural dissent, political economy and international relations to be debate
Representative Authors: Winifred Tate, William H. Thornton, and Tomaz Salamun
Simultaneous Submissions: no
Reading Period: Year-round
Reporting Time: one to two months
Author Payment: cash
Founded: 2001
Non Profit: yes
Paid Staff: five
Unpaid Staff: 15
Distributors: Routledge
ISSN Number/ISBN Number: ISSN 1476-0851
Total Circulation: 800
Paid Circulation: 400
Subscription Rate: Individual $39/Institution $180
Single Copy Price: $12
Current Volume/Issue: Issue four
Frequency per Year: quarterly
Backfile Available: yes
Unsolicited Ms. Received: yes
% of Unsolicited Ms. Published per Year: 30%
Format: perfect
Ads: yes

Organization: Ragged Raven Press

Type: press
CLMP member: no
Primary Editor/Contact Person: Janet Murch
Address: 1 Lodge Farm
Snitterfield
Stratford-on-Avon, UK CV37 0LR
Web Site Address: http://www.raggedraven.co.uk
Publishes: poetry
Editorial Focus: Contemporary poetry with something interesting to say.
Representative Authors: Chris Kinsey, Jane Kinninmont, and Christopher James
Submissions Policy: By post (with SASE/IRC) or in main body of e-mail. State if previously published and

detail when and where.
Simultaneous Submissions: no
Reading Period: Year-round
Reporting Time: four to eight weeks
Author Payment: royalties, cash, and copies
Contests: Ragged Raven Press annual poetry competition and anthology. Deadline: October 31st. See Web site for contest guidelines.
Founded: 1998
Non Profit: yes
Paid Staff: 0
Unpaid Staff: two
Number of Books Published per Year: two/three
Titles in Print: 14
Average Print Run: 300
Average Percentage Printed: Paperback 100%
Average Price: £6

Organization: Ragged Sky Press

Type: press
CLMP member: no
Primary Editor/Contact Person: Ellen Foos
Address: 270 Griggs Drive
Princeton, NJ 08540
Web Site Address: http://www.raggedsky.com
Publishes: fiction and poetry
Editorial Focus: literary fiction and poetry
Recent Awards Received: Isotope's Editors' Prize, MacDowell Colony Fellowship, Writer's Almanac selection
Representative Authors: Elizabeth Anne Socolow, Arlene Weiner, and Carlos Hernandez Pena
Submissions Policy: serious literary work only
Simultaneous Submissions: yes
Reading Period: Year-round
Reporting Time: one to two months
Author Payment: none
Founded: 1992
Non Profit: yes
Paid Staff: 0
Unpaid Staff: five
Distributors: Ingram, Bertrams, Lightening Source
ISSN Number/ISBN Number: ISBN 0-9633092
Number of Books Published per Year: 5
Titles in Print: 10
Average Print Run: 500
Average Percentage Printed: Paperback 100%
Average Price: $12

Organization: Rain Taxi Review of Books

Type: magazine
CLMP member: yes
Primary Editor/Contact Person: Eric Lorberer
Address: P.O. Box 3840
Minneapolis, MN 55403
Web Site Address: http://www.raintaxi.com
Publishes: essays and reviews
Editorial Focus: Reviews of fiction, poetry, art, photography, cultural studies, and other titles that might otherwise get overlooked.
Recent Awards Received: Utne Alternative Press Award
Representative Authors: Stephen Burt, Peter Gizzi, and Joyelle McSweeney
Submissions Policy: Visit http://www.raintaxi.com for complete submission guideline
Simultaneous Submissions: no
Reading Period: Year-round
Reporting Time: one to two months
Author Payment: none
Founded: 1995
Non Profit: yes
Paid Staff: two
Unpaid Staff: one
Total Circulation: 18,000
Paid Circulation: 900
Average Print Run: 18,000
Submission Rate: Individual $15/Institution $15
Single Copy Price: $5
Current Volume/Issue: 12/2
Frequency per Year: quarterly
Backfile Available: yes
Unsolicited Ms. Received: yes
% of Unsolicited Ms. Published per Year: 15%
Format: stapled
Size: H 10.25" W 8.25"
Average Pages: 56
Ads: yes
Ad Rates: 1/2: $400; 1/3: $300; 1/4: $250; 1/5: $200

Organization: Rainbow Curve

Type: magazine
CLMP member: yes
Primary Editor/Contact Person: Julianne Bonnet/Daphne Young
Address: P.O. Box 93206
Las Vegas, NV 89193-3206
Web Site Address: http://www.rainbowcurve.com

Publishes: fiction, poetry, and art
Editorial Focus: RC has been described as publishing work that is "hard hitting and somewhat uncomfortable to read."
Representative Authors: Catherine Ryan Hyde, Virgil Suárez, and Terry Ehret
Submissions Policy: For complete guidelines visit http://www.rainbowcurve.com
Simultaneous Submissions: yes
Reading Period: Year-round
Reporting Time: two to three months
Author Payment: copies
Founded: 2001
Non Profit: yes
Paid Staff: 0
Unpaid Staff: two
ISSN Number/ISBN Number: 1538-2826/0 74470 05514
Total Circulation: 350
Average Print Run: 500
Submission Rate: Individual $16/Institution $16
Single Copy Price: $8
Current Volume/Issue: Issue seven
Frequency per Year: biannual
Backfile Available: yes
Unsolicited Ms. Received: yes
% of Unsolicited Ms. Published per Year: 2%
Format: perfect
Ads: yes

Organization: Raritan

Type: magazine
CLMP member: no
Address: Rutgers/The State U. of New Jersey
31 Mine St.
New Brunswick, NJ 8903
Web Site: http://raritanquarterly.rtugers.edu/
Publishes: essays, fiction, poetry, and art
Reading Period: Year-round
Reporting Time: one to two months
Author Payment: none
Founded: 1981
Non Profit: no

Organization: Rattapallax Press

Type: press
CLMP member: yes
Primary Editor/Contact Person: Ram Devineni
Address: 532 La Guardia Place
Ste. 353
New York, NY 10012
Web Site Address: http://www.rattapallax.com
Publishes: fiction, poetry, translation, audio, and video
Editorial Focus: International poetry. and literary films.
Representative Authors: Willie Perdomo, Mark Nickels , and Suheir Hammad
Submissions Policy: Please contact editor before sending work.
Simultaneous Submissions: no
Reading Period: Year-round
Reporting Time: one to two months
Author Payment: royalties, cash, and copies
Founded: 1999
Non Profit: yes
Paid Staff: one
Unpaid Staff: three
Distributors: National Book Network
ISSN Number/ ISBN Number: ISBN 1-892494
Number of Books Publisher Per Year: five
Titles in Print: 30
Average Print Run: 2,000
Average Percentage Printed: hardcover 5%, paperback 90%, other 5%
Average Price: $12

Organization: Rattapallax

Type: magazine
CLMP member: yes
Primary Editor/Contact Person: Ram Devineni
Address: 532 La Guardia Place, Ste 353
Ste. 353
New York, NY 10012
Web Site Address: http://www.rattapallax.com
Publishes: essays, fiction, nonfiction, poetry, art, translation, and audio
Editorial Focus: Modern work that reflects the diversity of world cultures and is relevant to our society.
Representative Authors: MC Solaar, Glyn Maxwell, and Sonia Sanchez
Submissions Policy: Submit no more than five poems or two short stories. Translations are welcome.
Simultaneous Submissions: no
Reading Period: Year-round
Reporting Time: one to two months
Author Payment: copies
Founded: 1998
Non Profit: yes
Paid Staff: 0

Unpaid Staff: 15
Distributors: Ingram, Editora34 (Brazil), Plagio (Chile)
ISSN Number/ISBN Number: ISSN 1521-2483
Total Circulation: 2,500
Paid Circulation: 300
Submission Rate: Individual $14/Institution $14
Single Copy Price: $7.95
Current Volume/Issue: Issue 10
Frequency per Year: biannual
Backfile Available: yes
Unsolicited Ms. Received: yes
% of Unsolicited Ms. Published per Year: 5%
Format: perfect
Size: H 9.25" W 7.375"
Average Pages: 112
Ads: yes
Ad Rates: See Web site for details.

Organization: Rattle, Poetry for the 21st Century

Type: magazine
CLMP member: yes
Primary Editor/Contact Person: Stellasue Lee/Poetry Editor
Address: 12411 Ventura Blvd.
Studio City, CA 91604
Web Site Address: http://www.rattle.com
Publishes: essays, poetry, reviews, art, and translation
Editorial Focus: Quality work, accessible, image, moment. Please submit a cover letter, a short bio, along with all contact information.
Representative Authors: Robert Creeley, Gerald Stern, and Philip Levine
Submissions Policy: up to six poems, SASE, name and contact information in upper right-hand corner. Will consider e-mails submissions.
Simultaneous Submissions: no
Reading Period: Year-round
Reporting Time: six to twelve weeks
Author Payment: copies
Founded: 1995
Non Profit: yes
Paid Staff: yes
Unpaid Staff: no
Distributors: Ingram/SPD/DeBoer/Armadillo
ISSN Number/ISBN Number: ISBN 1-931307-07-5
Total Circulation: 4,000
Paid Circulation: 1,200
Submission Rate: Individual $3yr. 34/Institution $34

Single Copy Price: $8
Current Volume/Issue: 10/22
Frequency per Year: biannual
Backfile Available: yes
Unsolicited Ms. Received: yes
% of Unsolicited Ms. Published per Year: 1-2%
Format: perfect
Size: H 9" W 6"
Average Pages: 200
Ads: no

Eric Lorberer
Editor and Executive Director, Rain Taxi Review of Books

How did you arrive at your current position?
I heard from a friend that a new magazine was starting up and looking for reviews of poetry, so I submitted one. After it was published, I was impressed by the overall direction of the magazine—it seemed utterly unique to me—and I wanted to meet the people who had launched it, Randall Heath and Carolyn Kuebler. We met for coffee, and three hours later, I found myself enlisted on their board of directors; three months later, they asked me to play a staff role as co-editor. We three co-edited the magazine for about four years; but the struggles of growing a literary nonprofit eventually took their toll: Randall and Carolyn decided to find less stressful challenges in the publishing industry, while I decided, foolishly perhaps, to continue the quixotic quest to make it work.

What is the staff structure at your magazine?
We have two full-time people who each wear several different hats: myself (editor, publisher, event coordinator, executive director) and Kelly Everding (art director, business manager, webmaster). We also have a part-time editorial assistant who plays an absolutely key role in keeping things from becoming too overwhelming, and we're grateful to have noteworthy volunteers (and occasionally interns) who step up when needed.

What challenges do you face as a publisher?
It's unusual to publish a magazine devoted to critical rather than creative content, and it gives us a lot of prose to wade through, edit, and produce. Like every publisher, rising above the noisy herd is a constant battle, and can be demoralizing when you realize that just putting out quality work isn't

enough—you have to market it. It's challenging to interact with a hungry community of writers, all of whom want ink, and many of whom are less than kind when they don't get it. And raising money as a nonprofit is a giant challenge in a less-than-hospitable culture for the arts.

Do you have any cover letter advice?
Be clear, candid, and comprehensive, but most importantly, indicate that you've read our guidelines and are willing to abide by them. Publication is a collaboration, and it's a time-waster if someone is looking for a kind of process that you don't or can't offer.

What do you look for in a submission?
Because we view it as part of our mission to foster a dialogue about literature, we're open to a fairly wide range of submissions—but we are seeking a certain spark in the writing, an evident conciseness of approach, and a reasoned flow of ideas. We're also looking for people who join the conversation out of passion rather than the "what's in it for me" paradigm. We believe good criticism is more of a gift than a task.

How are submissions processed at your magazine?
Submissions are downloaded, vetted for appropriateness, then formatted and printed out by our editorial assistant; I read through this set and determine which I think are a good fit. Those pieces I then edit for publication, at which point we offer the writer a chance to view and respond to any changes. It's a labor-intensive process, but thankfully ninety-nine percent of the writers have

Ram Devineni
Publisher, Rattapallax

been complimentary, even gushing, about it. (The odd writer who responds "How dare you touch my golden prose!" is one we surely won't work with again.) On the other hand, time constraints mean we can't do quite as much education as we'd like, so sometimes things get rejected simply because we assess it may be too much work.

Do you have a favorite unsolicited submission discovery or anecdote?
"Discovery" is often about a kind of ownership . . . I want to foster a community of engaged writers, not a select group of the anointed "discovered." It's less sexy, but far truer to the chaotic stream of life.

What advice do you have for first-time submitters?
Read the guidelines. In the case of reviews, embrace the notion of serving the interests of others without personal gain other than your own intellectual development. Be brutally honest with yourself, and be interested in receiving constructive feedback—if you're not interested in revising your work, please stay far away!

What are your long-term plans for your magazine?
It's a plan just to survive in a hostile climate; that said, we hope to grow so that we may serve the community of innovative literature in more extensive ways. This doesn't necessarily mean more reviews, events, feedback; it might mean more reach for what already exists. This, I think, is a central paradox to the current state of literary publishing in our country.

What's your evaluation of the current literary landscape?
It's overflowing, which is both a boon and a problem; there are no doubt literary gems being written and published, but we also have tons more mediocre work and petty projects as well, and punishing competition for the same audiences and dollars. This is why our work is centered on trying to grow the audience for literature.

How did you arrive at your current position?
I discovered the best way to become president of a corporation is create your own corporation. Or in this case, I founded *Rattapallax* in 1999 and immediately became its publisher and president.

What is the staff structure at your magazine?
The editorial structure is pretty loose. We have multiple editors from around the world who are responsible for selecting work for each issue. Each editor tries to find innovative new work and translations. If possible, they try to solicit audio and video recordings for the DVDs that are included with each issue. Also, we have guest editors who work on specific sections in the issue dedicated to unique topics, such as "Indian Poets Respond to the Gujarat Riots" or "Endangered Languages and Poetry."

What challenges do you face as a publisher?
Keeping the magazine fresh and innovative, which is one of the reasons we switched from including CDs to DVDs.

Do you have any cover letter advice?
Make sure to include your email address. Email is indispensable when we begin to edit the magazine and need to reach the contributors. Also, I find it easier to send acceptance notifications by email. If you get an SASE in the mail from us, most likely it is a rejection slip.
Also, mentioning that you have read our magazine before is very important because it indicates that you know what kind of work we publish in the journal. Hopefully, that is the reason why you sent your work to *Rattapallax*.

What do you look for in a submission?
There are many elements that we are looking for when we read a submission. One critical thing is risk. Do the poets or writers take risks in their work? Will the reader be challenged and surprised?

How are submissions processed at your magazine?

My staff spends a few hours a month looking through a mountain of submissions. This really is not much time, and rarely do we find work that interests us. We rely heavily on our editors and contributing editors who recommend poets and writers that they discover.

Do you have a favorite unsolicited submission discovery or anecdote?

Although I do not have any "Charles Bukowskis" lurking in the background, there are a few poets first published in *Rattapallax* whose first collections of poems we eventually released. Mark Nickel's first and only book, *Cicada*, was one of the first books we published and remains one of our best.

What advice do you have for first-time submitters?

Try to read the magazine and know what the staff is looking for in your work. If they publish your work, then develop a relationship with the publication. If you can, attend events organized by the publication, and subscribing to the magazine is greatly appreciated. *Rattapallax* has published many of our poets in several issues because they continue to send us their "exceptional" work.

What are your long-term plans for your magazine?

Rattapallax is always exploring new avenues to present poetry and literature. We are producing literary short films and feature productions for theatrical release, podcasts, DVDs and online content. This is an exciting new approach and allows us to work with new artists and filmmakers in interpreting literary writing to film. Digital technology has made filmmaking relatively affordable and accessible to many people and we want Rattapallax to be on the forefront of this revolution.

What's your evaluation of the current literary landscape?

I think the literary landscape is wide and there is plenty of work being produced—probably more so than anytime in history. Go to blogger.com and you will see millions of pages of articles, poetry, fiction, diary entries, and endless amounts of clutter. Obviously, most of it is junk, but what is exciting

is that everyone (with online access) can publish his or her work. As a reader, the trick is filtering the barrage of content surrounding you. I guess they call this "narrowcasting"—selecting only what interests you. If you feel intimidated by the future and see a post-*Blade Runner* like existence, I suggest renting a cabin in Montana and watching reruns of *Gilligan's Island.* Or how about reading a good book?

Organization: The Raven Chronicles

Type: magazine
CLMP member: no
Primary Editor/Contact Person: Phoebe Bosch
Address: Richard Hugo House
1634-11th Ave.
Seattle, WA 98122-2419
Web Site Address: http://www.ravenchronicles.org
Publishes: essays, fiction, nonfiction, poetry, reviews, art, and translation
Editorial Focus: Raven publishes uncommon poetry, fiction, essays, reviews, black/white art, and interviews. In each issue we feature poetics, memorials, odes to places/things, beyond borders, The Pacific Northwest, food/culture, nature writing.
Representative Authors: Kathleen Alcalá, Haunani-Kay Trask, and John Olson
Submissions Policy: Emerging and established writers. three poems or 2-15 pgs fiction. Online guidelines, www.ravenchronicles.org/raven/rvsubm/html
Simultaneous Submissions: no
Reading Period: 1/1 to 9/15
Reporting Time: two to 12 weeks
Author Payment: copies
Founded: 1991
Non Profit: yes
Paid Staff: two **Unpaid Staff:** eight
ISSN Number/ISBN Number: ISSN 1066-1883
Total Circulation: 2,000
Paid Circulation: 200
Average Print Run: 2,000
Submission Rate: Individual $20/Institution $20
Single Copy Price: $6-7
Current Volume/Issue: 12/1
Frequency per Year: triquarterly
Backfile Available: yes
Unsolicited Ms. Received: yes
% of Unsolicited Ms. Published per Year: 35%
Format: stapled **Size:** H 8.5" W 11"
Average Pages: 96
Ads: yes
Ad Rates: See Web site for details.

Organization: Raving Dove

Type: online
CLMP member: yes
Primary Editor/Contact Person: Jo-Ann Moss
Address: PO Box 28
West Linn, OR 97068
Web Site Address: www.ravingdove.org
Publishes: essays, fiction, nonfiction, poetry, and art
Editorial Focus: Universal anti-war, anti-violence, humanitarian, peace-related themes
Representative Authors: Margarita Engle, Graham Fulton, and Diana Sher
Submissions Policy: Please go to: www.ravingdove.org/submissions
Simultaneous Submissions: yes
Reading Period: year-round
Reporting Time: two to three months
Author Payment: none
Founded: 2004
Non Profit: yes
Paid Staff: 0
Unpaid Staff: one
Average Page Views per Month: 1,000
Average Unique Visitors per Month: 1,000
Frequency per year: triquarterly
Publish Print Anthology: no
Average Percentage of Pages per Category: fiction 5%, nonfiction 25%, poetry 50%, essays 10%, art 10%
Ads: no

Organization: The Reading Room/Great Marsh Press

Type: magazine
CLMP member: yes
Primary Editor/Contact Person: Barbara Probst Solomon
Address: P.O. Box 2144
Lenox Hill Station
New York, NY 10021
Web Site Address: http://www.greatmarshpress.com
Publishes: essays, fiction, nonfiction, poetry, art, and translation
Editorial Focus: The best in contemporary writing.
Representative Authors: Saul Bellow, Alan Kaufman, and Daphne Merkin
Submissions Policy: No Web submissions.
Simultaneous Submissions: yes
Reading Period: Year-round
Reporting Time: three to five months
Author Payment: none
Founded: 2000
Non Profit: yes
Paid Staff: two
Unpaid Staff: four
Distributors: Ingram, Barnes & Noble, Amazon.com

Wholesalers: Ingram
ISSN Number/ISBN Number: 1535-6728/1-928863-09-4
Total Circulation: 8,000
Paid Circulation: 1,000
Average Print Run: 5,000
Submission Rate: Individual $65 for 4/Institution $65 for 4
Single Copy Price: $17.95
Current Volume/Issue: 1/4
Frequency per Year: biannual
Backfile Available: yes
Unsolicited Ms. Received: yes
% of Unsolicited Ms. Published per Year: 25%
Format: Book Form
Size: H 9" W 6"
Average Pages: 315
Ads: yes
Ad Rates: $1,000 for full page

Organization: Reconstruction Books Publishing LLC

Type: press
CLMP member: yes
Primary Editor/Contact Person: Susan Jenkins
Address: POB 1427
Mitchellville, MD 20717
Website Address: www.reconstructionbooks.com
Publishes: fiction, nonfiction, and poetry
Editorial Focus: Reconstruction Books is dedicated to the promotion of quality literature created by authors of works that have not previously found an outlet. While our primary goal is to provide an avenue by which authors of African descent can express their artistry, RB is exclusive only in regard to talent. Reconstruction Books has accepted an element of responsibility for exposing readers to poetry and prose that is determined to be not just unique, but decidedly enduring.
Representative Authors: Anthony B. Ashe and Malik Fleming
Submissions Policy: All manuscripts received will be given careful review. Unfortunately only a small number of the many manuscripts submitted will be selected for publication. Please send a SASE in order to insure return of your manuscript.
Simultaneous Submissions: yes
Reading Period: year-round
Reporting Time: 2 to 3 months
Author Payment: royalties and copies

Founded: 2006
Non Profit: no
Paid Staff: 3
Unpaid Staff: 0
Distributors: Baker and Taylor, African World Books
Wholesalers: Baker and Taylor, African World Books
ISSN Number/ISBN Number: ISBN 9789752
Number of Books Published per Year: 3
Titles in Print: 2
Average Print Run: 1,000
Average Percentage Printed: Hardcover 25%, Paperback 50%, Chapbook 25%
Average Price: $12.95

Organization: Red Hen Press

Type: press
CLMP member: no
Primary Editor/Contact Person: Mark E. Cull
Address: P.O. Box 3537
Granada Hills, CA 91344
Web Site Address: http://redhen.org
Publishes: fiction and poetry
Representative Authors: Chris Abani, Stephen Dixon, and Tom Hayden
Submissions Policy: No unsolicited material. Send query letters only.
Simultaneous Submissions: yes
Reading Period: 1/1 to 5/31
Reporting Time: one to two months
Author Payment: royalties
Contests: Benjamin Saltman Award, Short Fiction Award, Ruskin Poetry Award.
See Web site for contest guidelines.
Founded: 1994
Non Profit: yes
Paid Staff: four
Unpaid Staff: four
Distributors: SPD
Wholesalers: Baker & Taylor
ISSN Number/ISBN Number: 1543-3536/1888996, 159709
Number of Books Published per Year: 16
Titles in Print: 100
Average Print Run: 1,000
Average Percentage Printed: Hardcover 2%, Paperback 98%
Average Price: $14.95

Organization: Red Hills Review

Type: magazine
CLMP member: no
Primary Editor/Contact Person: Julia Park
Address: 3215J Encinal Ave
Alameda, CA 94501
Publishes: essays, fiction, nonfiction, poetry, reviews, art, and translation
Editorial Focus: A biannual literary magazine dedicated to publishing brilliant prose, luminous poetry, edgy fiction and scalding memoir.
Representative Authors: Joshilyn Jackson, Julia Park, and Gerry Cambridge
Submissions Policy: Email subs to redhillsreview@aol.com, up to three poems; short fiction to 2,000 words; nonfiction to 2,500 max. Query for info.
Simultaneous Submissions: yes
Reading Period: year-round
Reporting Time: three to six weeks
Author Payment: copies
Contests: Forthcoming
Founded: 2004
Non Profit: yes
Paid Staff: one
Unpaid Staff: two
Total Circulation: 400
Paid Circulation: 20
Average Print Run: 500
Subscription Rate: individual $10/institution $10
Single Copy Price: $5
Current Volume/Issue: 2/1
Frequency per year: biannual
Backfile Available: yes
Unsolicited MSS Received: yes
% of Unsolicited MSS Published per year: 10%
Format: stapled
Size: H 8.5" W 5.5"
Average Pages: 56
Ads: no

Organization: Red Moon Press

Type: press
CLMP member: no
Primary Editor/Contact Person: Jim Kacian
Address: PO Box 2461
winchester, va 22604-1661
Web Site Address:
http://www.haikuworld.org/books/redmoon/books.red-moon.html
Publishes: essays, fiction, nonfiction, poetry, and reviews
Editorial Focus: english-language haiku and related genres, plus reviews, criticism and theory
Recent Awards Received: Haiku Society of America Merit Book Awards for at least one volume produced for the past dozen years (highest award in genre).
Representative Authors: John Stevenson, Kai Falkman, and David Lanoue
Submissions Policy: we consider all submissions in our field, and nothing else
Simultaneous Submissions: no
Reading Period: year-round
Reporting Time: two to six weeks
Author Payment: cash, and copies
Contests: none
Founded: 1993
Non Profit: no
Paid Staff: one
Unpaid Staff: 15
Distributors: Ingram, Amazon, Baker & Taylor
ISSN Number/ISBN Number: ISBN 1893959
Number of Books Published per year: 6-8
Titles in Print: 40
Average Print Run: 500
Average Percentage Printed: hardcover 10%, paperback 80%, chapbook 10%
Average Price: $16.95

Organization: Red Morning Press

Type: press
CLMP member: no
Primary Editor/Contact Person: Andy Brown, Partner
Address: 1140 Connecticut Ave. Ste. 700
Washington, DC 20036
Web Site Address: www.redmorningpress.com
Publishes: poetry
Representative Authors: Sean Norton
Submissions Policy: Red Morning Press accepts unsolicited manuscripts year-round. There are no reading fees.
Simultaneous Submissions: yes
Reading Period: year-round
Reporting Time: one to two months
Author Payment: royalties
Contests: Red Morning Press does not sponsor a contest.
Founded: 2004
Non Profit: no
Paid Staff: 0

Unpaid Staff: three
Number of Books Published per year: 1-2
Titles in Print: one
Average Print Run: 1,000
Average Percentage Printed: paperback 100%
Average Price: $11.95

Organization: Red Mountain Review

Type: magazine
CLMP member: no
Primary Editor/Contact Person: T. J. Beitelman
Address: 1800 8th Ave. North
Birmingham, AL 35203
Web Site Address:
www.redmountainblog.blogspot.com
Publishes: essays, fiction, nonfiction, poetry, and
translation
Editorial Focus: RMR seeks poetry and prose that is
any combination of the following: wise, funny, crafted,
lyrical, empathic, true, human.
Representative Authors: Ander Monson, Bruce
Smith, and Katherine Soniat
Submissions Policy: Send your best work with a
SASE and an email address. Notify us if the work is
accepted elsewhere. Be patient if it isn't.
Simultaneous Submissions: yes
Reading Period: 10/1 to 4/30
Reporting Time: four to six months
Author Payment: copies
Contests: Red Mountain chapbook Contest-no entry
fee! $250 to the winner. 16-24 pages; submit 1/1 thru
4/15 each year.
See Web Site for contest guidelines
Founded: 2004
Non Profit: yes
Paid Staff: 0
Unpaid Staff: 15
Total Circulation: 750
Paid Circulation: 20
Average Print Run: 750
Subscription Rate: individual $10/institution $12
Single Copy Price: $6
Current Volume/Issue: issue two
Frequency per year: annual
Backfile Available: yes
Unsolicited MSS Received: yes
% of Unsolicited MSS Published per Year: 5%
Format: perfect
Size: H 9" W 6"
Average Pages: 150

Ads: yes
Ad Rates: Free swaps with other literary magazines

Organization: Red Rock Review

Type: magazine
CLMP member: yes
Primary Editor/Contact Person: Rich Logsdon, Sr.
Editor
Address: 3200 E. Cheyenne Ave.
N. Las Vegas, NV 89030
Web Site Address: http://www.ccsn.nevada.edu/eng-lish/
Publishes: essays, fiction, nonfiction, poetry, and
reviews
Editorial Focus: RRR seeks to publish the best in fic-tion and poetry. Essays, nonfiction, reviews welcome.
Emphasis on Southwestern writers.
Representative Authors: Marge Piercy, Charles
Harper Webb, and Adrian C. Louis
Submissions Policy: Stories: up to 7,500 words.
Essays: up to 5,000 words. Reviews: up to 1,500
words. Poetry: any length. Include SASE.
Simultaneous Submissions: no
Reading Period: 9/1 to 5/31
Reporting Time: four to five months
Author Payment: copies
Contests: See Web site for contest guidelines.
Founded: 1995
Non Profit: yes
Paid Staff: four
Unpaid Staff: five
Distributors: DeBoer
Wholesalers: Borders
Total Circulation: 750
Paid Circulation: 25
Average Print Run: 750
Submission Rate: Individual $9.50/Institution $9.50
Single Copy Price: $5.50
Current Volume/Issue: 500/17
Frequency per Year: biannual
Backfile Available: yes
Unsolicited Ms. Received: yes
% of Unsolicited Ms. Published per Year: 85%
Format: perfect
Size: H 9" W 6"
Average Pages: 140
Ads: yes
Ad Rates: inquire

Organization: Red Wheelbarrow Literary Magazine

Type: magazine
CLMP member: no
Primary Editor/Contact Person: Randolph Splitter
Address: De Anza College
21250 Stevens Creek Blvd.
Cupertino, CA 95014
Web Site Address: http://www.deanza.edu/redwheelbarrow
Publishes: essays, fiction, poetry, art, and translation
Editorial Focus: A diverse range of styles and voices from around the country and the world.
Representative Authors: Mark Brazaitis, Mario Susko, and J. Lorraine Brown
Submissions Policy: Poetry: max. five poems. Prose: max. 4,000 words. Art: max. five submissions.
Simultaneous Submissions: yes
Reading Period: 9/1 to 1/31
Reporting Time: two to four months
Author Payment: copies
Founded: 1976
Non Profit: yes
Paid Staff: one
Unpaid Staff: 12
ISSN Number/ISBN Number: 1543-1983/1-932133-79-8
Total Circulation: 300
Submission Rate: Individual $7.50/Institution $7.50
Single Copy Price: $7.50
Current Volume/Issue: 4/1
Frequency per Year: annual
Backfile Available: yes
Unsolicited Ms. Received: yes
% of Unsolicited Ms. Published per Year: 98%
Format: perfect
Size: H 9" W 6"
Average Pages: 140
Ads: yes
Ad Rates: inquire

Organization: RedBone Press

Type: press
CLMP member: yes
Primary Editor/Contact Person: Lisa C. Moore
Address: P.O. Box 15571
Washington, DC 20003
Web Site Address: http://www.redbonepress.com
Publishes: essays, fiction, and nonfiction
Editorial Focus: work that celebrates black lesbian culture, and that facilitates discussion between black gays/lesbians and black mainstream.
Recent Awards Received: Lambda Literary Awards, 1997, 1998
Representative Authors: Sharon Bridgforth, Marvin K. White, and Samiya Bashir
Submissions Policy: Send query letter with proposal first. Do not send your original manuscript.
Simultaneous Submissions: yes
Reading Period: Year-round
Reporting Time: two to six months
Author Payment: royalties, cash, and copies
Founded: 1997
Non Profit: no
Paid Staff: 0
Unpaid Staff: one
Distributors: SPD (Small Press Dist.), Marginal, Turnaround
ISSN Number/ISBN Number: ISBN 0-9656659, 0-9786251
Number of Books Published per Year: three
Titles in Print: nine
Average Print Run: 2,000
Average Percentage Printed: Paperback 100%
Average Price: $15

Organization: Redivider

Type: magazine
CLMP member: yes
Primary Editor/Contact Person: Chip Cheek
Address: Emerson College, Writing, Lit. & Publishing Dept.
120 Boylston St.
Boston, MA 2116
Web Site Address: http://pages.emerson.edu/publications/redivider/
Publishes: essays, fiction, nonfiction, poetry, art, and translation
Editorial Focus: Our content is eclectic and compulsively readable. We seek out the rough gems.
Representative Authors: Bob Hicok, Steve Almond, Pauls Toutonghi
Submissions Policy: Please see our web site for submissions guidelines.
Simultaneous Submissions: yes
Reading Period: Year-round
Reporting Time: one to five months
Author Payment: copies
Founded: 2004
Non Profit: yes

Paid Staff: 0
Unpaid Staff: all
ISSN Number/ISBN Number: ISSN 1551-9244
Total Circulation: 75
Paid Circulation: 50
Average Print Run: 1,000
Submission Rate: Individual $10/Institution $10
Single Copy Price: $6
Current Volume/Issue: 3/2
Frequency per Year: biannual
Backfile Available: yes
Unsolicited Ms. Received: yes
% of Unsolicited Ms. Published per Year: 75%
Format: perfect
Average Pages: 160

Organization: Regent Press

Type: press
CLMP member: no
Primary Editor/Contact Person: Mark Weiman
Address: 6020-A Adeline
Oakland, CA 94608
Web Site Address: http://regentpress.net
Publishes: essays, fiction, nonfiction, poetry, reviews, art, translation, and audio
Editorial Focus: We are a broad based Press doing everything from intense literary short stories to vegan cookbooks.
Representative Authors: Claire Burch, William Crossman, and Patricia Leslie
Submissions Policy: Query letter please
Simultaneous Submissions: yes
Reading Period: Year-round
Reporting Time: two to four weeks
Author Payment: royalties
Founded: 1978
Non Profit: no
Paid Staff: five
Wholesalers: Baker & Taylor; Ingram
Number of Books Published per Year: 25
Titles in Print: 120
Average Percentage Printed: Hardcover 2%, Paperback 90%, Chapbook 2%, Other 6%

Organization: The Rejected Quarterly

Type: magazine
CLMP member: no
Primary Editor/Contact Person: Daniel Weiss
Address: P.O. Box 1351

bplankton@juno.com
Cobb, CA 95426
Web Site Address: http://rejectedq.com
Publishes: essays, fiction, poetry, reviews, and art
Editorial Focus: We are looking for quality offbeat fiction. Only rejection-related poetry and essays. Always looking for cover art.
Representative Authors: Vera Searles, Jessica Anya Blau, and Lane Cohen
Submissions Policy: Five rejection slips must accompany each manuscript. Fiction to 8,000 words.
Simultaneous Submissions: yes
Reading Period: Year-round
Reporting Time: one to six months
Author Payment: cash and copies
Contests: to 8,000 words. 12/06-06/07. Up to two stories. Fee: $10 per story. Prizes: 1st: $200, 2nd: $1000, 3rd: $50. Five rejecions per story. See web site for contest guidelines.
Founded: 1998
Non Profit: no
Unpaid Staff: four
Distributors: EBSCO
ISSN Number/ISBN Number: ISSN 1525-2671
Total Circulation: 100
Paid Circulation: 60
Average Print Run: 180
Submission Rate: $20 per 4
Single Copy Price: $6
Current Volume/Issue: 4/15
Frequency per Year: biannual
Backfile Available: yes
Unsolicited Ms. Received: yes
% of Unsolicited Ms. Published per Year: 5%
Format: Saddle Stitched
Size: H 11" W 8 1/2"
Average Pages: 40
Ads: no

Organization: Review of Contemporary Fiction

Type: magazine
CLMP member: no
Primary Editor/Contact Person: Editor
Address: Center for Book Culture
ISU 8905
Normal, IL 61790-8905
Web Site Address:
http://www.centerforbookculture.org
Publishes: essays, nonfiction, and reviews

Editorial Focus: Discussion of modern and contemporary writers, particularly those whose work is of an innovative or challenging nature.
Representative Authors: Gilbert Sorrentino, Ishmael Reed, and Ann Quin
Submissions Policy: No unsolicited submissions.
Simultaneous Submissions: yes
Reading Period: Year-round
Reporting Time: two to six months
Author Payment: cash and copies
Contests: none
Founded: 1981
Non Profit: yes
Paid Staff: 15
Unpaid Staff: two
Distributors: Ingram, University of Nebraska Press
Wholesalers: SPD
ISSN Number/ISBN Number: 0276-0045/1-56478-
Total Circulation: 2,500
Paid Circulation: 1,750
Submission Rate: Individual $17/Institution $26
Single Copy Price: $8
Current Volume/Issue: 23/2
Frequency per Year: triquarterly
Backfile Available: yes
Unsolicited Ms. Received: no
Format: perfect
Size: H 9" W 6"
Average Pages: 200
Ads: yes
Ad Rates: $250 full page

Organization: Review: Literature and Arts of the Americas

Type: magazine
CLMP member: yes
Primary Editor/Contact Person: Daniel Shapiro
Address: The Americas Society
680 Park Ave.
New York, NY 10021
Website Address: www.americas-society.org
Publishes: essays, fiction, nonfiction, poetry, reviews, art, and translation
Editorial Focus: Contemporary literature in English/English translation by Caribbean, Latin American, and Canadian authors. Coverage of arts.
Representative Authors: Mario Vargas Llosa, Carmen Boullosa, and Gioconda Belli
Submissions Policy: We do not accept unsolicited submissions. Please send a query letter.

Simultaneous Submissions: no
Reading Period: year-round
Reporting Time: 2 to 3 months
Author Payment: cash and copies
Contests: no
Founded: 1968
Non Profit: yes
Paid Staff: 5
Unpaid Staff: 2
Distributors: Routledge, Taylor and Francis Ltd.
ISSN Number/ISBN Number: ISSN 0890-5762
Total Circulation: 2,000
Paid Circulation: 1,200
Average Print Run: 2,000
Subscription Rate: Individual $38/Institution $161
Single Copy Price: $26
Current Volume/Issue: SP/74
Frequency: 2
Backfile Available: yes
Unsolicited Ms. Received: no
Format: perfect
Size: H 11" W 8 1/2"
Average Pages: 100
Ads: yes
Ad Rates: see website for details

Organization: RFD Press

Type: magazine
CLMP member: no
Address:
P.O. Box 68
Liberty, TN 37095
Web Site Address: http://www.rfdmag.org/
Publishes: essays, fiction, nonfiction, poetry, and art
Reading Period: Year-round
Reporting Time: one to two months
Author Payment: none
Founded: 1974
Non Profit: no
Backfile Available: yes

Organization: Rhapsody Magazine

Type: online
CLMP member: no
Primary Editor/Contact Person: John Riddick
Address: P.O. Box 2443
Durham, NC 27715
Web Site Address:
http://www.rhapsodymagazine.com

Publishes: essays, fiction, poetry, reviews, and art
Editorial Focus: Creativity in all literary forms
Representative Authors: Linda Dominique Grosvenor and Monda Webb
Submissions Policy: please e-mail or send hard copy, be sure to include your contact information. Also include your "15 min. of Fame" info.
Simultaneous Submissions: yes
Reading Period: Year-round
Reporting Time: one to three months
Author Payment: copies
Contests: See Web site for contest guidelines.
Founded: 1997
Non Profit: yes
Paid Staff: two
Unpaid Staff: five
ISSN Number/ISBN Number: ISSN 1094-2041
Average Page Views per Month: 300
Average Unique Visitors per Month: 120
Frequency per Year: wuarterly
Publish Print Anthology: no
Average Percentage of Pages per Category: Fiction 15%, Poetry 50%, Reviews 15%, Essays 10%, Art 10%
Ad Rates: See Web site for details.

Organization: RHINO

Type: magazine
CLMP member: yes
Primary Editor/Contact Person: Kathleen Kirk, Jackie White
Address: P.O. Box 591
Evanston, IL 60204
Web Site Address: http://www.rhinopoetry.org/
Publishes: essays, fiction, poetry, and reviews
Editorial Focus: RHINO is a literary annual publishing compelling poetry, translations, and flash fiction by emerging and established writers.
Recent Awards Recieved: Illinois arts Council Literary Award for "Jezebel Remembering," a poem by Valerie Martt Wallace
Representative Authors: Michael Hettich, Lee Rossi, and Maureen Seaton
Simultaneous Submissions: yes
Reading Period: 4/1 to 10/1
Reporting Time: three to six months
Author Payment: copies
Founded: 1976
Non Profit: yes
Unpaid Staff: 10

ISSN Number/ISBN Number: ISSN 1521-8414
Total Circulation: 1,000
Paid Circulation: 100
Average Print Run: 1,000
Submission Rate: Individual $10/Institution $10
Single Copy Price: $10
Current Volume/Issue: Issue 2006
Frequency per Year: annual
Backfile Available: yes
Unsolicited Ms. Received: yes
Format: perfect
Average Pages: 175
Ad Rates: Exchange ads

Organization: Rivendell Journal

Type: magazine
CLMP member: no
Primary Editor/Contact Person: Sebastian Matthews
Address: P.O. Box 9594
Asheville, NC 28815
Web Site Address:
http://www.greenmanwalking.com
Publishes: essays, fiction, nonfiction, poetry, reviews, and art
Editorial Focus: Rivendell is a literary journal with an emphasis on place. Each issue focuses on a new locale, either geographic or thematic.
Representative Authors: David Budbill (New England), Peter J. Harris (Los Angeles), and Jean Pedrick (Workshop)
Submissions Policy: We accept submissions year-round. But we recommend you look at our web site for guidelines. We take work that fits our theme.
Simultaneous Submissions: yes
Reading Period: Year-round
Reporting Time: three to six weeks
Author Payment: copies
Contests: We are starting an Emerging Writers contest. More on this soon. (Check our web site for updated info.)
Founded: 1999
Non Profit: yes
Paid Staff: 0
Unpaid Staff: five
Distributors: we do it ourselves, working with ind. bookstores
ISSN Number/ISBN Number: ISSN different for each
Total Circulation: 500
Paid Circulation: 250
Submission Rate: Individual $14/Institution same

Single Copy Price: $10
Current Volume/Issue: 1/3
Frequency per Year: biannual
Backfile Available: yes
Unsolicited Ms. Received: yes
% of Unsolicited Ms. Published per Year: 5%
Format: perfect
Size: H 9" W 61/2"
Average Pages: 225
Ads: yes
Ad Rates: barter
See Web site for details.

Organization: River City Publishing

Type: press
CLMP member: yes
Primary Editor/Contact Person: Jim Gilbert
Address: 1719 Mulberry St.
Montgomery, AL 36106
Web Site Address:
http://www.rivercitypublishing.com
Publishes: fiction and nonfiction
Editorial Focus: novels, short stories, literary travel,
social history, and illustrated children's; works that
focus on the South
Recent Awards Received: 2006 IPPY winner, 2005
IPPY winner, 2004 IPPY finalist, 2004 ForeWord bronze,
BookSense 76 selection, SEBA Award nominees
Representative Authors: Carl T. Smith, Carolyn
Haines, William Hoffman, and Wayne Greenhaw
Submissions Policy: Unsolicited/unagented OK. No
electronic submissions. Include SASE for response,
short bio, at least first 5 chapters.
Simultaneous Submissions: yes
Reading Period: Year-round
Reporting Time: two to six months
Author Payment: royalties
Contests: Fred Bonnie Memorial Award-contest for
best first novel
See Web site for contest guidelines.
Founded: 1990
Non Profit: no
Paid Staff: seven
Unpaid Staff: 0
Number of Books Published per Year: 8-12
Titles in Print: 140
Average Print Run: 5,000
Average Percentage Printed: Hardcover 85%,
Paperback 15%
Average Price: $25

Organization: River Teeth

Type: magazine
CLMP member: no
Primary Editor/Contact Person: Joe Mackall and
Dan Lehman
Address: 401 College Ave.,
Ashland University
Ashland, OH 44805
Web Site Address: http://www.nebraskapress.unl.edu
Publishes: essays, fiction, and nonfiction
Editorial Focus: Creative nonfiction, including essays,
memoir, narrative journalism and critical essays about
creative nonfiction
Representative Authors: David James Duncan, Chris
Offutt, and Jon Franklin
Submissions Policy: We read year-round.
Submissions must be typed and double-spaced.
Include a brief bio with your submission.
Simultaneous Submissions: yes
Reading Period: Year-round
Reporting Time: one to three months
Author Payment: copies
Contests: See Web site for contest guidelines.
Founded: 1999
Non Profit: yes
Paid Staff: 0
Unpaid Staff: five
Distributors: University of Nebraska Press
ISSN Number/ISBN Number: 1544-1849/none
Total Circulation: 1,000
Paid Circulation: 750
Submission Rate: Individual $20/Institution $40
Single Copy Price: $12
Current Volume/Issue: 5/1
Frequency per Year: biannual
Backfile Available: yes
Unsolicited Ms. Received: yes
% of Unsolicited Ms. Published per Year: 2%
Format: perfect
Size: H 9" W 5"
Average Pages: 200
Ads: yes
Ad Rates: Contact University of Nebraska Press

Organization: Rock and Sling

Type: magazine
CLMP member: yes
Primary Editor/Contact Person: Susan Cowger
Address: PO Box 30865

Spokane, WA 99223
Website Address: www.rockandsling.org
Publishes: essays, fiction, nonfiction, poetry, reviews, art, and translation
Editorial Focus: Please visit our website.
Representative Authors: John Hodgen, Christopher Howell, and Rodney A. Nelsestuen
Submissions Policy: Please visit our website for submission guidelines.
Simultaneous Submissions: yes
Reading Period: year-round
Reporting Time: 1 to 4 months
Author Payment: copies
Contests: Virginia Brendemuehl Poetry Contest; see website for guidelines
Founded: 2004
Non Profit: yes
Paid Staff: 1
Unpaid Staff: 5
ISSN Number/ISBN Number: ISSN 1552-5929
Total Circulation: 400
Paid Circulation: 250
Average Print Run: 500
Subscription Rate: Individual $18/yr/Institution $18/yr
Single Copy Price: $10
Current Volume/Issue: 4/1
Frequency: 1
Backfile Available: yes
Unsolicited Ms. Received: yes
% of Unsolicited Ms. Published per Year: 75%
Format: perfect
Size: H 9" W 6"
Average Pages: 150
Ads: no

Organization: Ronsdale Press Ltd.

Type: press
CLMP member: no
Primary Editor/Contact Person: Ronald B. Hatch
Address: 3350 West 21st Ave.
Vancouver, BC V6S 1G7
Web Site Address: www.ronsdalepress.com
Publishes: essays, fiction, nonfiction, poetry, art, and translation
Editorial Focus: A literary press specializing in publishing Canadian writers of fiction, poetry, non-fiction, YA Canadian historical fiction
Recent Awards Received: Gerald LampertPat LowtherGolden OakRed Cedar

Representative Authors: Alan Twigg, Bill New, and Kevin Roberts
Submissions Policy: Submit the entire ms if it meets our web submission guidelines (with SASE) along with a brief bio and writing credits
Simultaneous Submissions: yes
Reading Period: year-round
Reporting Time: one to three months
Author Payment: royalties and copies
Founded: 1988
Non Profit: no
Paid Staff: three
Unpaid Staff: three
Distributors: LitDistCo
Wholesalers: Baker & Taylor, Ingram, Gazelle
ISSN Number/ISBN Number: ISBN 1-55380, 0-921870
Number of Books Published per year: 10
Titles in Print: 130
Average Print Run: 1,500
Average Percentage Printed: hardcover 10%, paperback 90%
Average Price: $21.95 CDN

Organization: Roof Books

Type: press
CLMP member: no
Primary Editor/Contact Person: James Sherry
Address: 300 Bowery
New York, NY 10012
Web Site Address: http://roofbooks.com
Publishes: essays and poetry
Editorial Focus: Since 1976 Roof Books has published innovative poetries and the writing around them.
Representative Authors: Ron Silliman, Charles Bernstein, and Nicole Brossard
Submissions Policy: Inquiries only, no mss., to geck044@earthlink.net.
Simultaneous Submissions: no
Reading Period: Year-round
Reporting Time: three to six months
Author Payment: royalties and copies
Founded: 1976
Non Profit: yes
Paid Staff: three
Unpaid Staff: one
Distributors: SPD
Wholesalers: SPD
ISSN Number/ISBN Number: ISBN 937804

Number of Books Published per Year: four
Titles in Print: 100
Average Percentage Printed: Paperback 100%

Organization: The Rose & Thorn Literary E-zine

Type: online
CLMP member: yes
Primary Editor/Contact Person: Barbara Quinn
Address: theroseandthornezine.com
Rockland, NY 10901
Web Site Address: http://www.therose-andthornezine.com
Publishes: essays, fiction, nonfiction, poetry, reviews, and art
Editorial Focus: Award-winning zine showcases fiction, nonfiction, poetry, art, interviews. Offers free newsletter w/ markets, contests and tips.
Recent Awards Received: Named an Internet Envy site by Writer's Digest. Listed as one of Writer's Digest's top 100 sites for writers.
Representative Authors: Janet Buck, Emily Hanlon, and Troy Morash
Submissions Policy: Guidelines posted at the site. 2,000 word maximum for stories and essays.
Simultaneous Submissions: yes
Reading Period: Year-round
Reporting Time: two to 14 weeks
Author Payment: none
Founded: 1997
Non Profit: yes
Paid Staff: 0
Unpaid Staff: 20
Average Page Views per Month: 300,000
Average Unique Visitors per Month: 9,000
Frequency per Year: quarterly
Publish Print Anthology: no
Average Percentage of Pages per Category: Fiction 50%, Nonfiction 20%, Poetry 15%, Essays 10%, Art 5%
Ad Rates: Start at $20
See Web site for details.

Organization: Round Magazine

Type: online
CLMP member: no
Primary Editor/Contact Person: Georg Pedersen and Beth Bayley
Address: 140 2nd St. Apt. C
Brooklyn, NY 11231
Web Site Address: http://www.roundonline.com
Publishes: essays, fiction, nonfiction, poetry, art, audio, and video
Representative Authors: Marcella Hammer and Nayiri Krikorian
Submissions Policy: Please see our web site: http://roundonline.com/submit.shtml
Simultaneous Submissions: yes
Reading Period: Year-round
Reporting Time: one to two months
Author Payment: none
Founded: 2002
Non Profit: yes
Paid Staff: 0
Unpaid Staff: three
Average Page Views per Month: 19,000
Average Unique Visitors per Month: 3,000
Frequency per Year: quarterly
Average Percentage of Pages per Category: Fiction 25%, Nonfiction 7%, Poetry 7%, Essays 25%, Art 35%, Video 1%

Organization: Ruminate Magazine

Type: magazine
CLMP member: yes
Primary Editor/Contact Person: Brianna Van Dyke
Address: 140 N Roosevelt Ave
Fort Collins, CO 80521
Website Address: www.ruminatemagazine.com
Publishes: essays, fiction, nonfiction, poetry, and art
Editorial Focus: Ruminate publishes work that both explicitly and implicitly explores the intersection of faith in literature and art.
Representative Authors: Susanna Childress, Paul Willis, and Tony Woodlief
Submissions Policy: see website. We accept previously unpublished work via email to submissions@ruminatemagazine.com.
Simultaneous Submissions: yes
Reading Period: year-round
Reporting Time: 2 to 3 months
Author Payment: copies and subscription
Contests: Janet B. McCabe Poetry Contest and Ruminate's Annual Fiction Contest; see website for guidelines
Founded: 2006
Non Profit: yes
Paid Staff: 2
Unpaid Staff: 5

Distributors: Kent News Company
ISSN Number/ISBN Number: ISSN 1923-6130
Total Circulation: 650
Paid Circulation: 300
Average Print Run: 700
Subscription Rate: Individual $28.00/Institution $32.00
Single Copy Price: $8.00
Current Volume/Issue: Issue 04
Frequency: 4
Backfile Available: yes
Unsolicited Ms. Received: yes
% of Unsolicited Ms. Published per Year: 95%
Format: stapled
Size: H 10" W 8"
Average Pages: 65
Ads: yes
Ad Rates: 100.00 dollars per page or exchange.

Organization: The Runaway Spoon Press

Type: press
CLMP member: no
Primary Editor/Contact Person: Bob Grumman
Address: Box 495597
Port Charlotte, FL 33949
Publishes: poetry
Editorial Focus: Xenovernacular Poetry, particularly litagraphy (i.e. "experimental" poetry, particularly "visual" poetry)
Recent Awards Received: 18 years in business and no awards, something I'm quite proud of.
Representative Authors: John M. Bennett, Geof Huth, and Gregory Vincent St. Thomasino
Submissions Policy: Standard-but presently over-loaded with titles to publish so not open for submissions
Simultaneous Submissions: yes
Reading Period: Year-round
Reporting Time: one to 50 months
Author Payment: copies
Contests: My press is not out to take poets.
Founded: 1987
Non Profit: no
Paid Staff: zero
Unpaid Staff: one
ISSN Number/ISBN Number: ISBN 1-57141
Number of Books Published per Year: four
Titles in Print: 150
Average Print Run: 100

Average Percentage Printed: Paperback 50%, Chapbook 50%
Average Price: $5

Organization: SABLE LitMag

Type: magazine
CLMP member: yes
Primary Editor/Contact Person: Kadija Sesay
Address: P.O. Box 33504
London, UK E97YE
Web Site Address: http://www.sablelitmag.org
Publishes: essays, fiction, nonfiction, poetry, reviews, translation, and audio
Editorial Focus: Showcasing creative writing by writers of color. Work by new authors and new work by established authors. Plus interview with major author.
Representative Authors: Ngugi wa Thiongo, Jhumpa Lahiri, and Marita Golden
Submissions Policy: All details are on the web site-http://www.sablelitmag.org/submissions/html. No e-mail submissions accepted except for micro fiction.
Simultaneous Submissions: yes
Reading Period: Year-round
Reporting Time: one to three months
Author Payment: none
Contests: Sable/Arvon creative writing residential course for writers of color at the Arvon Foundation in England.
Founded: 2000
Non Profit: yes
Paid Staff: no
Unpaid Staff: yes
Distributors: Ingram
ISSN Number/ISBN Number: ISSN TBA
Total Circulation: 750
Submission Rate: Individual $40/Institution $45
Single Copy Price: $12
Current Volume/Issue: Issue 5
Frequency per Year: quarterly
Backfile Available: yes
Unsolicited Ms. Received: yes
% of Unsolicited Ms. Published per Year: 85%
Format: perfect
Size: H A4" W A4"
Average Pages: 128
Ads: yes
Ad Rates: from $100 qtr; $175 half; $500 ROP; $750 cover
See Web site for details.

Organization: Sacramento Poetry Center

Type: magazine
CLMP member: no
Primary Editor/Contact Person: Heather Hutcheson/Luke Breit
Address: 1631 K St.
Sacramento, CA 95814
Web Site Address: http://www.sacramentopoetrycenter.org
Publishes: poetry
Representative Authors: Gary Snyder, Dennis Schmitz, and Sandra McPherson
Submissions Policy: Submissions of poems, artwork, literary criticism, and other work of interest to the Sacramento poetry community are welcome. Work must be accompanied by a SASE for return. B&W or high contrast color photos & brief bios of submitters are encouraged. Please note that submissions to any of the Sacramento Poetry Center's publications may appear on the Center's web site. Please submit to address above or e-mail poetrynow@sacramentopoetrycenter.org.
Simultaneous Submissions: yes
Reading Period: Year-round
Reporting Time: four to six weeks
Author Payment: copies
Contests: See Web site for contest guidelines.
Founded: 1979
Non Profit: yes
Paid Staff: one
Unpaid Staff: 22
Total Circulation: 1,000
Paid Circulation: 220
Submission Rate: Individual $25
Single Copy Price: $3
Current Volume/Issue: 9/10
Frequency per Year: 12
Backfile Available: yes
Unsolicited Ms. Received: yes
% of Unsolicited Ms. Published per Year: 20%
Format: 2 11x17 pages folded to 8.5x11
Size: H 8.5" W 11"
Average Pages: 8
Ads: yes
Ad Rates: See Web site for details.

Organization: The Sage of Consciousness

Type: online
CLMP member: yes
Primary Editor/Contact Person: Michelle Williams
Address: P.O. Box 1209
Ocala, FL 34478-1209
Web Site Address: http://www.sageofcon.com
Publishes: essays, fiction, nonfiction, poetry, and art
Editorial Focus: To publish a diverse magazine with many different genres of art, poetry, nonfiction, articles, and new media.
Recent Awards Received: Hot Point site of the Day. Webbie World top 10 People's Pick award. Webbie World Top 20 People's Pick award.
Representative Authors: Rob Rosen, Jennifer Thompson, and Janet Butler
Submissions Policy: Submissions accepted year-round. E-mail submissions in Word format. Through post, please include a disk in Word format.
Simultaneous Submissions: yes
Reading Period: Year-round
Reporting Time: one to two months
Author Payment: none
Founded: 2004
Non Profit: yes
Paid Staff: 0
Unpaid Staff: seven
ISSN Number/ISBN Number: 1555-192X/none
Average Page Views per Month: 55,000
Average Unique Visitors per Month: 5,000
Frequency per Year: quarterly
Publish Print Anthology: no
Average Percentage of Pages per Category: Fiction 30%, Nonfiction 5%, Poetry 35%, Essays 5%, Art 25%
Ad Rates: See Web site for details.

Organization: The Saint Ann's Review

Type: magazine
CLMP member: yes
Primary Editor/Contact Person: Beth Bosworth
Address: Saint Ann's School/129 Pierrepont St.
Brooklyn, NY 11201
Web Site Address: http://www.saintannsreview.com
Publishes: essays, fiction, nonfiction, poetry, reviews, art, and translation
Editorial Focus: Well-crafted work that stands out.
Representative Authors: Diane Greco, Jane Avrich, and Anthony Calypso

Submissions Policy: The longer it is, the better-crafted and more unusual it has to be. See an issue or our web site for details.
Simultaneous Submissions: yes
Reading Period: Year-round
Reporting Time: two to four months
Author Payment: cash and copies
Contests: For now, we prefer not to conduct contests.
Founded: 2000
Non Profit: yes
Paid Staff: five
Unpaid Staff: three
Distributors: Ingram, Ubiquity
ISSN Number/ISBN Number: ISSN 25274
Total Circulation: 1,500
Paid Circulation: 400
Submission Rate: Individual $18/Institution $18
Single Copy Price: $9
Current Volume/Issue: 4/1
Frequency per Year: biannual
Backfile Available: yes
Unsolicited Ms. Received: yes
% of Unsolicited Ms. Published per Year: 25%
Format: perfect
Size: H 9.5" W 7"
Average Pages: 160
Ads: yes
Ad Rates: Ad rates may vary.

Organization: Salamander

Type: magazine
CLMP member: yes
Primary Editor/Contact Person: Jennifer Barber
Address: Suffolk University/English Department
41 Temple St.
Boston, MA 02114-4280
Web Site Address: http://www.salamandermag.org
Publishes: essays, fiction, nonfiction, poetry, reviews, art, and translation
Editorial Focus: Salamander specializes in publishing highly accomplished work by writers who deserve a wider audience.
Representative Authors: Yiyun Li, Susan Rich, and Frannie Lindsay
Submissions Policy: Simultaneous submissions are accepted but we ask that you keep us informed
Simultaneous Submissions: yes
Reading Period: 9/1 to 5/30
Reporting Time: one to two months
Author Payment: cash, copies, and subscription

Founded: 1992
Non Profit: yes
Paid Staff: one
Unpaid Staff: six
Distributors: DeBoer
ISSN Number/ISBN Number: ISSN 1063-3359
Total Circulation: 1,000
Paid Circulation: 350
Average Print Run: 1,000
Submission Rate: Individual $23 (2 yr)/Institution $23
Single Copy Price: $7
Current Volume/Issue: 11/2
Frequency per Year: biannual
Backfile Available: yes
Unsolicited Ms. Received: yes
% of Unsolicited Ms. Published per Year: 5%
Format: perfect
Size: H 5 1/2" W 8 1/2"
Average Pages: 90
Ads: yes
Ad Rates: $150 (full page)

Organization: Salmagundi

Type: magazine
CLMP member: yes
Primary Editor/Contact Person: Peg Boyers/Robert Boyers
Address: Skidmore College
815 N. Broadway
Saratoga Springs, NY 12866
Web Site Address: www.skidmore.edu/salmagundi/
Publishes: essays, fiction, nonfiction, poetry, reviews, and translation
Editorial Focus: We seek to publish work of quality in a variety of genres. It's impossible to define the 'focus' beyond this general goal
Representative Authors: Mario Vargas Llosa, Marilynee Robinson, and Carolyn Forche
Submissions Policy: At this time we have suspended reading unsolicited mss. until Fall 2008, at least. Please phone if you have questions.
Simultaneous Submissions: yes
Reading Period: 10/15 to 5/1
Reporting Time: four to six months
Author Payment: copies and subscription
Founded: 1965
Non Profit: yes
Paid Staff: two
Unpaid Staff: one
Distributors: DeBoer, Ingram

Wholesalers: not applicable
ISSN Number/ISBN Number: ISSN 0036-3529
Total Circulation: 4,800
Paid Circulation: 3,500
Average Print Run: 5,000
Submission Rate: Individual $20/Institution $32
Single Copy Price: $8
Current Volume/Issue: 155
Frequency per Year: quarterly
Backfile Available: yes
Unsolicited Ms. Received: yes
% of Unsolicited Ms. Published per Year: 5%
Format: perfect
Size: H 8" W 5"
Average Pages: 200
Ads: yes
Ad Rates: $300 full page/no half pages accepted

Organization: Salt Hill

Type: magazine
CLMP member: yes
Primary Editor/Contact Person: Daniel Torday/ Tara Warman
Address: Salt Hill/Department of English
Syracuse University
Syracuse, NY 13244
Web Site Address: salthilljournal.com
Publishes: essays, fiction, nonfiction, poetry, reviews, art, and translation
Editorial Focus: We have an open aesthetic and revolving editorship. We are equally committed to publishing experimental and traditional work.
Representative Authors: Dean Young, Brian Evenson, and Steve Almond
Submissions Policy: Send manuscript, cover letter, and SASE with sufficient postage. We do not accept electronic submissions.
Simultaneous Submissions: yes
Reading Period: 8/1 to 4/1
Reporting Time: two to six months
Author Payment: copies
Contests: Poetry and short short fiction (1,500 words max) contests. Deadline-January 15. Reading fee-$10. Prizes: $500, $250, and $100
See Web site for contest guidelines.
Founded: 1995
Non Profit: yes
Unpaid Staff: 20
Distributors: Ingram
ISSN Number/ISBN Number: ISSN 1078-8689

Total Circulation: 1,000
Paid Circulation: 20
Average Print Run: 1,000
Submission Rate: Individual $15/Institution $20
Single Copy Price: $8
Current Volume/Issue: Issue 19
Frequency per Year: biannual
Backfile Available: yes
Unsolicited Ms. Received: yes
% of Unsolicited Ms. Published per Year: 80%
Format: perfect
Average Pages: 130
Ads: yes
Ad Rates: See Web site for details.

Organization: Sarabande Books

Type: press
CLMP member: yes
Primary Editor/Contact Person: Sarah Gorham
Address: 2234 Dundee Rd, Ste. 200
Louisville, KY 40205
Web Site Address: http://www.SarabandeBooks.org
Publishes: essays, fiction, nonfiction, and poetry
Editorial Focus: Sarabande publishes only the best literature, an eclectic mix of new and established writers both experimental and formal.
Recent Awards Received: National Jewish Book Award, Finalist Pulitzer Prize, Norma Farber First Book Award
Representative Authors: Cate Marvin, Ralph Angel, and Marjorie Sandor
Submissions Policy: Kathryn A. Morton Prize in Poetry, Mary McCarthy Prize in Short Fiction. Otherwise by invitation and recommendation.
Simultaneous Submissions: yes
Reading Period: 1/1 to 2/15
Reporting Time: 12 to 15 weeks
Author Payment: royalties, cash, and copies
Contests: See Web site for contest guidelines.
Founded: 1994
Non Profit: yes
Paid Staff: six
Unpaid Staff: two
Distributors: Consortium
Wholesalers: Baker & Taylor, Ingram
ISSN Number/ISBN Number: 889330/9641151
Number of Books Published per Year: 10-12
Titles in Print: 102
Average Print Run: 3,000
Average Percentage Printed: Hardcover 20%,

Paperback 70%, Chapbook 10%
Average Price: $14

Organization: The Saranac Review

Type: magazine
CLMP member: yes
Primary Editor/Contact Person: J.L. Torres
Address: Dept of English, CVH, SUNY Plattsburgh
101 Broad St
Plattsburgh, NY 12901
Website Address:
research.plattsburgh.edu/saranacreview
Publishes: fiction, nonfiction, poetry, reviews, and translation
Editorial Focus: The Saranac Review publishes the work of emerging and established writers from Canada, the US and beyond. Committed to dissolving boundaries of all kinds, the journal strives to be a textual clearing in which a space is opened for literary cross-pollination. We aim to publish diverse voices, a literal "cluster of stars," an illumination of the Iroquois roots of our namesake, the word, Saranac. We publish work that engages, provokes, and resonates. Our first two issues have included Jay Parini, Julia Alvarez, Donald Revell, Xu Xi, Jessica Grant, Gregory Pardlo, Frannie Lindsay, Ross Leckie, and Wesley Brown.
Recent Awards Received: Not yet.
Submissions Policy: Please check our website or www.newpages.com for detailed guidelines.
Simultaneous Submissions: yes
Reading Period: 09/01 to 02/15
Reporting Time: 4 to 6 months
Author Payment: copies and subscription
Contests: n/a
Founded: 2004
Non Profit: yes
Paid Staff: 1
Unpaid Staff: 10
Distributors: Ingram
ISSN Number/ISBN Number: ISSN 1556-1119
Total Circulation: 300
Paid Circulation: 50
Average Print Run: 500
Subscription Rate: Individual $15/2yrs/Institution $15/yr
Single Copy Price: $9.00
Current Volume/Issue: Issue 3
Frequency: 1
Backfile Available: yes
Unsolicited Ms. Received: yes

% of Unsolicited Ms. Published per Year: 90%
Format: perfect
Size: H 8 1/2" W 5 1/2"
Average Pages: 180
Ads: yes

Organization: Saturnalia Books

Type: press
CLMP member: Yes
Primary Editor/Contact Person: Henry Israeli
Address: 13 E. Highland Ave. 2nd Fl.
Philadelphia, PA 19118
Web Site Address: www.saturnaliabooks.com/
Publishes: poetry and art
Editorial Focus: Cutting edge poetry and poet/artist collaborations
Recent Awards Received: Small Press Traffic Book of the Year (Ing Grish by John Yau)
Representative authors: John Yau, Sabrina Orah Mark, Bill Knott
Submissions Policy: Contest only.
Simultaneous Submissions Accepted: Yes.
Reading Period: Contest only
Reporting Time: 2 to 4 months
Author Payment: cash and copies
Contests: Saturnalia Books Poetry Contest
Number of Unpaid Staff: four
Year Founded: 2001
Non Profit: UPNE
Paid Staff: 0
Unpaid Staff: 4
Distributors: SPD
ISBN Number: 0-9754990
Number of Books Published per year: five
Titles in Print: 11
Average Print Run: 1,200
Average Percentage Printed: paperback 100%
Average Price: $15

Organization: Seal Press

Type: press
CLMP member: no
Primary Editor/Contact Person: Brooke Warner
Address: 1400 65th Street, Suite 250
Emeryville, CA 94501
Web Site Address: http://www.sealpress.com
Publishes: fiction and nonfiction
Editorial Focus: Seal Press has a long, distinguished

reputation for publishing books by women of incredible variety and depth.

Representative Authors: Michelle Tea, Ayun Halliday, and Jessica Valenti

Submissions Policy: Please send either a query letter or proposal, with SASE, to our address. No e-mail or phone calls, please.

Simultaneous Submissions: yes

Reading Period: Year-round

Reporting Time: two to three months

Author Payment: royalties, cash, and copies

Founded: 1976

Non Profit: no

Paid Staff: three

Unpaid Staff: 0

Number of Books Published per Year: 20

Titles in Print: 125-50

Average Print Run: 5,000

Average Percentage Printed: Hardcover 5%, Paperback 95%

Average Price: $15.95

Organization: The Seattle Review

Type: magazine

CLMP member: yes

Primary Editor/Contact Person: Colleen J. McElroy

Address: University of Washington
Padelford Hall, P. O. Box 354330
Seattle, WA 98195-4330

Web Site Address: http://www.seattlereview.org

Publishes: fiction, nonfiction, and poetry

Editorial Focus: See Website

Representative Authors: Sharon Olds, Yusef Komunyakaa, and Daniel Orozco

Submissions Policy: See Website

Simultaneous Submissions: no

Reading Period: 10/1 to 5/31

Reporting Time: two to four months

Author Payment: none

Contests: Annual Poetry and Fiction Prize. Submissions accepted between January 1st and March 31st. Please visit web site for details. See Web site for contest guidelines.

Founded: 1978

Non Profit: yes

Paid Staff: two

Unpaid Staff: 15

Total Circulation: 800

Paid Circulation: 184

Average Print Run: 800

Submission Rate: Individual $20-32/Institution $20-32.

Single Copy Price: $8

Current Volume/Issue: 27/2

Frequency per Year: biannual

Backfile Available: yes

Unsolicited Ms. Received: yes

Format: perfect

Average Pages: 150

Ads: yes

Ad Rates: See Web Site for details.

Organization: Second Story Books

Type: press

CLMP member: no

Primary Editor/Contact Person: Mary Burger

Address: 591 63rd St.
Oakland, CA 94609

Web Site Address: http://www.2ndstorybooks.com

Publishes: fiction, nonfiction, and poetry

Editorial Focus: Cross-genre works of experimental narrative, using elements of fiction, poetry, memoir, philosophy, and other forms.

Representative Authors: Renee Gladman, Brenda Coultas, and Camille Roy

Submissions Policy: Second Story Books usually publishes solicited works. Requests for submissions will be posted on our web site.

Simultaneous Submissions: no

Reading Period: Year-round

Reporting Time: one to six months

Author Payment: copies

Contests: Future contests will be announced on our web site.

Founded: 1998

Non Profit: no

Paid Staff: 1/2

Unpaid Staff: one

Distributors: SPD

Number of Books Published per Year: one

Titles in Print: seven

Average Print Run: 500

Average Percentage Printed: Paperback 100%

Average Price: $12

Organization: Seneca Review

Type: magazine

CLMP member: yes

Primary Editor/Contact Person: Deborah Tall

Address: Hobart and William Smith Colleges Geneva, NY 14456

Web Site Address: http://www.hws.edu/SenecaReview

Publishes: essays, poetry, and translation

Editorial Focus: Seneca Review publishes a wide variety of ambitious poetry and lyric essays, and we have great interest in translations of modern poetry. We regularly publish both established figures and emerging writers.

Representative Authors: Fanny Howe, Carl Phillips, and Dionisio D. Martinez

Submissions Policy: Note that we do not publish fiction. Due to the great number of manuscripts we receive, we ask that you limit yourself to just one submission during our annual reading period. We do not accept manuscripts electronically. All submissions must be accompanied by a SASE.

Simultaneous Submissions: no

Reading Period: 9/1 to 5/1

Reporting Time: 10 to 12 weeks

Author Payment: copies and subscription

Founded: 1970

Non Profit: yes

Paid Staff: two

Unpaid Staff: two

ISSN Number/ISBN Number: ISSN 0037-2145

Total Circulation: 1,000

Paid Circulation: 400

Average Print Run: 1,200

Submission Rate: Individual $11/Institution $11

Single Copy Price: $7

Current Volume/Issue: 35/2

Frequency per Year: biannual

Backfile Available: yes

Unsolicited Ms. Received: yes

% of Unsolicited Ms. Published per Year: 1-2%

Format: perfect

Size: H 7.5" W 5.5"

Average Pages: 100

Ads: yes

Ad Rates: $75 full page

Organization: Sentence

Type: magazine

CLMP member: yes

Primary Editor/Contact Person: Brian Clements, Editor

Address: Box 7, Western Connecticut State University 181 White St.

Danbury, CT 06810

Web Site Address: http://firewheel-editions.org

Publishes: essays, poetry, reviews, and translation

Editorial Focus: Sentence publishes prose poems and work on the boundary of the prose poem, as well as reviews and essays on poetics

Recent Awards Received: Work selected for Best American Poetry 2005

Submissions Policy: Hard copy w/SASE or e-mail address. Electronic on CD, diskette, or in a SINGLE e-mail attachment (.doc, .pdf, .rtf, or .txt)

Simultaneous Submissions: yes

Reading Period: Year-round

Reporting Time:: one to three months

Author Payment: copies

Founded: 2002

Non Profit: yes

Unpaid Staff: three

Wholesalers: DeBoer, Amazon

ISSN Number/ISBN Number: ISSN 1545-5378

Total Circulation: 1,000

Paid Circulation: 350

Average Print Run: 1,000

Submission Rate: Individual $22/30/Institution $12/issue

Single Copy Price: $12

Current Volume/Issue: Issue three

Frequency per Year: biannual

Backfile Available: yes

Unsolicited Ms. Received: yes

Format: perfect

Size: H 7" W 5"

Average Pages: 200

Ads: yes

Ad Rates: $100 for full page or ad exchange See Web site for details.

Dan Simon
Publisher, Seven Stories Press

How did you arrive at your current position?

It's a funny question. In 1983 I came across a mass-market paperback edition of a short-story anthology edited by Robert Penn Warren and happened to read in it a short story by Nelson Algren called "A Bottle of Milk for Mother." That story took me by storm. I'd never read anything like it. Completely raw, and at the same time a masterly expression of writerly craft. Authentic realism that at the same time expressed heart-on-my-sleeve sentimentality. The lead character was an innocent teenager, a really charming boy, who in the story confesses to coldblooded murder. Algren's ability to embrace contradictions without breaking out in a sweat is magical and I'd never read him or heard of him before. So the impact of reading that short story—it's only about six or seven pages long—sent me reeling. I haven't recovered yet. I ended up reissuing just about all of Algren's books. Becoming a book publisher was just the aftereffect of that journey.

What is the staff structure at your press?

We're organized in three main divisions, editorial, production and promotion. Amy Scholder, our editor-in-chief, and I set out our editorial course. Jon Gilbert, our operations director, who's in our small Oakland, CA, office, drives the production side. Ruth Weiner, formerly head of publicity at Henry Holt, keeps us calm when a book starts to make waves, with help from Crystal Yakacki, who is also an editor. Anna Lui runs the foreign rights department. And Lars Reilly looks after all things Internet. Theresa Noll is our managing editor. Those last three run those accessory departments. Our college division, which presents our paperbacks to college professors and high school teachers, is run by Tara Parmiter, formerly of Norton. Beyond that our office is open, sort of like a newspaper, with almost no privacy. So we all have to like each other very much, and we do.

What challenges do you face as a publisher?

The greatest challenge we face is to be always getting stronger. You can only do that by drawing on internal strengths, so at Seven Stories we do talk a lot among ourselves and everyone's voice counts. There was a period when some of the younger staff were skeptical about that, but I think everyone here knows now that we're a chorus of voices and that we need every voice we have to do what we do.

Last night I happened to be at a poetry reading to hear the wonderful American poet Maxine Kumin, and between reading she was answering questions about her friendship with the poet Anne Sexton, that went back to the late 1950s. As the story goes, and Maxine confirmed this at the reading, she and Anne, who were both married with kids in the suburbs of Boston at the time, had a dedicated phone line installed and used to call each other first thing in the morning then leave the phone off the hook all day and whistle when they had something to tell one another. Along with that she described just how hard it was to be a poet, not to mention a woman poet, back in the '50s and early '60s, when they were both only allowed auxiliary membership in the local crummy poetry society. Nobody cared about how serious they were about poetry or how important they believed their work as poets was. So whatever strength they were going to find, they were going to have to look for within themselves. At least that was the message I walked away with. And it's a bit like that for book publishers today. We are carrying the torch. It's hard not to sound strident when I say that. But I say it anyway.

Do you have any cover letter advice?

Writers need to ask themselves the much harder questions about what it is they have to offer that's profoundly expressive of who they are. To ask and answer that question, they have to go deep. It's a sweat lodge ceremony between the writer and himself or herself. Very few writers can actually face that task. But I think it's the starting point. Do that and the cover letter will write itself.

What do you look for in a submission?

A familiarity with our list.

How are submissions processed at your press?

I don't think any publishing house has solved the problem of how to manage the first reading stage. Once something here gets to the second stage there are going to be several readers and intense discussion.

Do you have a favorite unsolicited submission discovery or anecdote?

Paul Krassner sent us an unsolicited manuscript. It made its way through the stages on its merits, since the first readers had no idea who he was. I always found that charming. He trusted in the gods, when he could easily have called and gotten a by into at least the quarter-finals. We did publish that book, and several others by Paul over the years.

What advice do you have for first-time submitters?

You only need to find one advocate. It isn't an election and you don't need to please a crowd.

What are your long-term plans for your press?

Survive if we can. Stay true to our mission regardless.

What's your evaluation of the current literary landscape?

It isn't bad now. We are about to go through a very, very difficult time though. And that has nothing to do with the vagaries of the business. It is just that so many of our best and freshest voices are coming to the end of their journeys. I'm speaking of writers and of publishers and of booksellers and editors and agents. There isn't a generation ready to step forward to take the place of those who are now ready to pass the torch. So first there'll be a dearth, and then people will step forward and fill the gap, but before they do will be the difficult time just ahead.

Organization: Sepulculture

Type: press
CLMP member: yes
Primary Editor/Contact Person: Scott DiPerna
Address: 623 Humboldt Street #1R
Brooklyn, NY 11222
Website Address: www.sepulculture.com
Publishes: essays, fiction, nonfiction, poetry, art, audio, and video
Editorial Focus: art that is literate, literature that is humorous, humor that is artful, and short of that, any old shit we think is cool.
Recent Awards Received: a few weeks back, on a Tuesday, we awarded ourselves an exclusive citation for looking pretty damn snazzy that day.
Representative Authors: Molly Crabapple, Jen Dziura, and John Leavitt
Submissions Policy: email project descriptions and/or manuscripts. anything delivered by carrier pigeon is likely to be published immediately.
Simultaneous Submissions: yes
Reading Period: year-round
Reporting Time: 1 to 2 months
Author Payment: royalties
Contests: are for losers. think about it.
Founded: 2006
Non Profit: yes
Paid Staff: 0
Unpaid Staff: 1
Distributors: Last Gasp
Wholesalers: Last Gasp
ISSN Number/ISBN Number: ISBN 9780978953409
Number of Books Published per Year: 1
Titles in Print: 1
Average Print Run: 1,500
Average Percentage Printed: Paperback 100%
Average Price: $20.00

Organization: Seven Stories Press

Type: press
CLMP member: yes
Primary Editor/Contact Person: Dan Simon
Address: 140 Watts St
New York, NY 10013
Web Site Address: www.sevenstoies.com
Publishes: literature, journalism, popular culture, human rights, social justice, graphic novels, women's interest, translation, young adult
Founded: 1995

Organization: The Sewanee Review

Type: magazine
CLMP member: yes
Primary Editor/Contact Person: Bob Jones
Address: 735 University Ave.
Sewanee, TN 37383-1000
Web Site Address: http://www.sewanee.edu/sewanee_review
Publishes: essays, fiction, nonfiction, poetry, and reviews
Editorial Focus: High quality fiction, poetry, essays, and book reviews. Literary criticism without jargon or particular critical theories.
Representative Authors: Wendell Berry, George Garrett, and Sam Pickering
Submissions Policy: Poetry: 40 lines or less, no more than 6. Fiction: 3,500-7,500 words, 1 per submission. Essays: 3,500-7,500, 1 per submission.
Simultaneous Submissions: no
Reading Period: 9/1 to 5/31
Reporting Time: five to twelve weeks
Author Payment: royalties, cash, and copies
Contests: Four annual awards: short story, poem(s), essay, book reviewing. Chosen by the board of editors; may not be applied for.
Founded: 1892
Non Profit: yes
Paid Staff: three
Unpaid Staff: 0
Distributors: Ingram
ISSN Number/ISBN Number: ISSN 0037-3052
Total Circulation: 3,070
Paid Circulation: 2,700
Submission Rate: Individual $24/Institution $30
Single Copy Price: $8.50
Current Volume/Issue: 112/1
Frequency per Year: quarterly
Backfile Available: yes
Unsolicited Ms. Received: yes
% of Unsolicited Ms. Published per Year: 1%
Format: perfect
Size: H 6" W 9"
Average Pages: 192
Ads: yes
Ad Rates: $250/page; $180/half-page
See Web site for details.

Organization: Shampoo

Type: online

CLMP member: no
Primary Editor/Contact Person: Del Ray Cross
Address: 903 Pine St., Apt. 35
San Francisco, CA 94108
Web Site Address: http://shampoopoetry.com
Publishes: poetry and art
Submissions Policy: always open. please attach .doc or .rtf files. previously unpublished. 3-10 pages of work is sufficient.
Simultaneous Submissions: yes
Reading Period: Year-round
Reporting Time: 0 to 4 months
Author Payment: none
Founded: 2000
Non Profit: yes
Paid Staff: 0
Unpaid Staff: one
Frequency per Year: quarterly
Publish Print Anthology: no
Average Percentage of Pages per Category: Poetry 99%, Art 1%
Ads: no

Organization: Shearsman Books Ltd

Type: press
CLMP member: no
Primary Editor/Contact Person: Tony Frazer
Address: 58 Velwell Road
Exeter, UK EX4 4LD
Web Site Address: www.shearsman.com
Publishes: poetry and translation
Editorial Focus: Contemporary poetry in the modernist tradition; translations of Hispanic and German authors.
Recent Awards Received: two Australian awards for MTC Cronin's <More or Less Than>1-100
Representative Authors: Lee Harwood, Gael Turnbull, and Cesar Vallejo
Submissions Policy: Send samples initially, not a full manuscript. Check out the Web site before submitting, see what else we publish.
Simultaneous Submissions: yes
Reading Period: year-round
Reporting Time: two to three months
Author Payment: royalties and copies
Founded: 1981
Non Profit: yes
Unpaid Staff: one
Distributors: Ingrams, Baker & Taylor, SPD
Wholesalers: SPD

ISSN Number/ISBN Number: ISBN 0-907562/1-905700
Number of Books Published per year: 20
Titles in Print: 80
Average Percentage Printed: paperback 100%
Average Price: $16

Organization: Shearsman

Type: magazine
CLMP member: no
Primary Editor/Contact Person: Tony Frazer
Address: 58 Velwell Road
Exeter, UK EX4 4LD
Web Site Address: www.shearsman.com
Publishes: essays, poetry, reviews, and translation
Editorial Focus: poetry in the modernist tradition.
Representative Authors: Lee Harwood, Gael Turnbull, and Cesar Vallejo
Submissions Policy: Email (email body text or PDF only) or mail submission. Minimum six poems.
Simultaneous Submissions: yes
Reading Period: year-round
Reporting Time: two to three months
Author Payment: copies
Founded: 1981
Non Profit: yes
Distributors: Ingrams, Baker & Taylor, SPD
ISSN Number/ISBN Number: ISBN 0-907562/1-905700
Total Circulation: 250
Paid Circulation: 75
Average Print Run: 250
Subscription Rate: individual UK£15/institution UK£15
Single Copy Price: $13.50
Current Volume/Issue: issue 70
Frequency per year: biannual
Backfile Available: yes
Unsolicited MSS Received: yes
% of Unsolicited MSS Published per year: 2%
Format: perfect
Size: H 8.5" W 5.5"
Average Pages: 108
Ads: no

Organization: Shearsman

Type: online
CLMP member: no
Primary Editor/Contact Person: Tony Frazer

Address: 58 Velwell Road
Exeter, UK EX4 4LD
Web Site Address: www.shearsman.com
Publishes: essays, poetry, reviews, and translation
Editorial Focus: poetry in the modernist tradition.
Representative Authors: Lee Harwood, Gael Turnbull, and Cesar Vallejo
Submissions Policy: Minimum six poems in the body of an email or as PDF attachment or by mail.
Simultaneous Submissions: yes
Reading Period: 9/1 to 9/30
Reporting Time: two to three months
Author Payment: copies
Founded: 1981
Non Profit: yes
Average Page Views per Month: 190,000
Average Unique Visitors per Month: 35,000
Frequency per year: biannual
Publish Print Anthology: yes
Price: $13.50
Average Percentage of Pages per Category: poetry 80%, reviews 10%, Translation 10%
Ads: no

Organization: The Sheep Meadow Press

Type: press
CLMP member: no
Primary Editor/Contact Person: Stanley Moss
Address: P.O. Box 1345
Riverdale, NY 10471
Publishes: fiction, nonfiction, poetry, art, and translation
Editorial Focus: Poetry, literary translations, cultural history, art history.
Representative Authors: Stanley Kunitz, Paul Celan, and Yehuda Amichai
Submissions Policy: We have a very small list and rarely accept unsolicited manuscripts.
Simultaneous Submissions: yes
Reading Period: Year-round
Reporting Time: four to six months
Author Payment: royalties
Contests: Multiple.
Founded: 1976
Non Profit: yes
Paid Staff: two
Unpaid Staff: 0
Distributors: University Presses of New England
Number of Books Published per Year: 10

Titles in Print: 150
Average Percentage Printed: Hardcover 5%, Paperback 95%

Organization: Shenandoah: The Washington & Lee University Review

Type: magazine
CLMP member: yes
Primary Editor/Contact Person: Lynn Leech, Man. Ed.
Address: Washington and Lee University
Mattingly House/ 2 Lee Ave.
Lexington, VA 24450-2116
Web Site Address: http://shenandoah.wlu.edu
Publishes: essays, fiction, nonfiction, poetry, reviews, and art
Editorial Focus: Work characterized by both formal and extemporaneous spirits.
Recent Awards Received: Pushcart Prize, 2007; New Stories from the South, 2006, 2007
Representative Authors: Mary Oliver, Pam Durban, and Rick Bass
Submissions Policy: Short stories and essays (One per submission), poems (Five per submission).
Simultaneous Submissions: yes
Reading Period: 9/1 to 5/15
Reporting Time: three to four weeks
Author Payment: cash, copies, and submission
Founded: 1950
Non Profit: yes
Paid Staff: 1.5
Unpaid Staff: one
Distributors: Ubiquity
ISSN Number/ISBN Number: ISSN 0037-3588
Total Circulation: 1,800
Paid Circulation: 1,450
Average Print Run: 2,100
Submission Rate: Individual $22/Institution $25
Single Copy Price: $10
Current Volume/Issue: 57/1-3
Frequency per Year: triquarterly
Backfile Available: yes
Unsolicited Ms. Received: yes
% of Unsolicited Ms. Published per Year: 2%
Format: perfect
Size: H 9" W 6"
Average Pages: 250
Ads: yes
Ad Rates: $300/full page; $150/half page
See web site for details.

Organization: Short Story

Type: magazine
CLMP member: yes
Primary Editor/Contact Person: Caroline Lord
Address: P.O. Box 50567
Columbia, SC 29250
Website Address: www.shortstoryreview.org
Publishes: fiction
Editorial Focus: short stories
Representative Authors: George Singleton, George Garrett, and Sayzie Koldys
Submissions Policy: Check website for guidelines.
Simultaneous Submissions: yes
Reading Period: 8/01 to 1/31
Reporting Time: 2 to 3 months
Author Payment: cash
Founded: 2006
Non Profit: yes
Paid Staff: 0
Unpaid Staff: 1
ISSN Number/ISBN Number: ISSN 1933-3137
Total Circulation: 450
Paid Circulation: 450
Average Print Run: 1000
Subscription Rate: Individual $12.00/Institution $12.00
Single Copy Price: $6.00
Current Volume/Issue: 2/2
Frequency: 2
Backfile Available: yes
Unsolicited Ms. Received: yes
Format: perfect

Organization: Silverfish Review Press

Type: press
CLMP member: yes
Primary Editor/Contact Person: Rodger Moody
Address: P.O. Box 3541
Eugene, OR 97403
Web Site Address:
http://www.silverfishreviewpress.com
Publishes: poetry
Editorial Focus: SRP publishes a book by winner of annual contest and other titles as well.
Recent Awards Received: Washington State Book Award for Breaking Ground by Paul Hunter
Representative Authors: Bruce Bond, Mark Conway, and Judith Skillman

Submissions Policy: We read manuscripts outside of the annual contest during the summer months only. Check web site for deadlines.
Simultaneous Submissions: yes
Reading Period: 6/15 to 10/15
Reporting Time: two to three months
Author Payment: cash and copies
Contests: Gerald Cable Book Award is given annually for a first book.
See Web Site for contest guidelines.
Founded: 1978
Non Profit: yes
Paid Staff: one
Unpaid Staff: three
Distributors: SPD and Spring Church Book Company.
ISSN Number/ISBN Number: ISBN 1-878851
Number of Books Published per Year: three
Titles in Print: 19
Average Print Run: 1,000
Average Percentage Printed: Paperback 100%
Average Price: $14.95

Organization: Sixteen Rivers Press

Type: press
CLMP member: yes
Primary Editor/Contact Person: Terry Ehret
Address: P.O. Box 640663
San Francisco, CA 94164-0663
Web Site Address: http://www.sixteenrivers.com
Publishes: poetry
Editorial Focus: Sixteen Rivers is a shared-work poetry publishing collective for the S.F. Bay Area. Members make a 3-year work commitment.
Representative Authors: Margaret Kaufman, Lynn Trombetta, and Diane Lutovich
Submissions Policy: Manuscript of 60-80 pgs. may be submitted. Two new members are selected from these manuscripts each year.
Simultaneous Submissions: yes
Reading Period: 1/1 to 3/1
Reporting Time: six to eight months
Author Payment: copies
Founded: 1999
Non Profit: yes
Paid Staff: zero
Unpaid Staff: seven
Distributors: SPD
Number of Books Published per Year: two
Titles in Print: six
Average Percentage Printed: Paperback 100%

Average Price: $15

Organization: Skidrow Penthouse
Type: magazine
CLMP member: yes
Primary Editor/Contact Person: Rob Cook/Stephanie Dickinson
Address: 44 Four Corners Road
Blairstown, NJ 07825
Web Site Address: http://skidrowpenthouse.com
Publishes: fiction, poetry, art, and translation
Editorial Focus: We're seeking work that is idiosyncratic, primitive, vulnerable, and that is both challenging and accessible
Representative Authors: Aase Berg, James Grinwis, and Karl Tierney
Submissions Policy: Three to five poems, one short story, any length. Include SASE and cover letter.
Simultaneous Submissions: yes
Reading Period: year-round
Reporting Time: two to three months
Author Payment: copies
Contests: Coming soon: the Ronald Wardall Prize (for a full-length poetry collection), also a novella contest. See web site for contest guidelines
Founded: 1997
Non Profit: no
Paid Staff: zero
Unpaid Staff: three
Total Circulation: 300
Paid Circulation: 300
Average Print Run: 500
Subscription Rate: individual $12/institution $10
Single Copy Price: $12
Current Volume/Issue: issue seven
Frequency per year: annual
Backfile Available: yes
Unsolicited MSS Received: yes
% of Unsolicited MSS Published per year: 2%
Format: perfect
Size: H 9" W 6"
Average Pages: 335
Ads: yes
Ad Rates: see web site for details

Organization: SLAB: Sound and Literary Art Book
Type: magazine
CLMP member: yes
Primary Editor/Contact Person: Mark O'Connor
Address: 312-I, SWC
Slippery Rock University
Slippery Rock, PA 16057
Web Site Address: http://www.slablitmag.com
Publishes: essays, fiction, nonfiction, poetry, and art
Editorial Focus: Contemporary fiction, poetry, nonfiction, and web-based art.
Representative Authors: Tom Whalen, Huang Xiang, Kelli Russell Agadon
Submissions Policy: Multiple, surface, and online submissions are accepted
Simultaneous Submissions: yes
Reading Period: Year-round
Reporting Time: two to three months
Author Payment: copies
Contests: Annual Poetry Contest. See web site for contest guidelines.
Founded: 1975
Non Profit: yes
Paid Staff: zero
Unpaid Staff: 30
ISSN Number/ISBN Number: ISSN 1559-288X
Total Circulation: 900
Paid Circulation: 100
Average Print Run: 1,000
Submission Rate: Individual $10-2 years/Institution $10-2 years
Single Copy Price: $7
Current Volume/Issue: 1/1
Frequency per Year: annual
Backfile Available: yes
Unsolicited Ms. Received: yes
% of Unsolicited Ms. Published per Year: 100%
Format: perfect
Size: H 8" W 6"
Average Pages: 154
Ads: yes
Ad Rates: Exchanges only w/ other literary magazines

Organization: Slapering Hol Press
Type: press
CLMP member: yes
Primary Editor/Contact Person: Margo Stever
Address: Hudson Valley Writers' Center
300 Riverside Dr.
Sleepy Hollow, NY 10591
Web Site Address: http://www.writerscenter.org
Publishes: poetry
Editorial Focus: SHP publishes chapbooks by poets

who have not previously published a book or chapbook; and occasionally, thematic anthologies

Representative Authors: David Tucker, Dina Ben-Lev, and Rachel Loden
Submissions Policy: see web site for guidelines
Simultaneous Submissions: yes
Reading Period: 2/1 to 5/15
Reporting Time: two to three months
Author Payment: cash and copies
Contests: See web site for contest guidelines.
Founded: 1990
Non Profit: yes
Paid Staff: zero
Unpaid Staff: two
Distributors: SP
ISSN Number/ISBN Number: ISBN 0-9700277
Number of Books Published per Year: 1-2
Titles in Print: 17
Average Print Run: 500
Average Percentage Printed: Paperback 5%, Chapbook 95%
Average Price: $12

Organization: Slidingpillar

Type: magazine
CLMP member: no
Primary Editor/Contact Person: Will Goodman
Address: 143 S. Waverly St.
Orange, CA 92866
Web Site Address: http://www.slidingpillar.com
Publishes: essays, fiction, nonfiction, and poetry
Editorial Focus: Original, intelligent, creative content.
Submissions Policy: Anything, so long as it is less then 10 pages.
Simultaneous Submissions: yes
Reading Period: Year-round
Reporting Time: one to three months
Author Payment: copies
Founded: 1999
Non Profit: no
Paid Staff: one
Unpaid Staff: zero
ISSN Number/ISBN Number: ISSN 1530-4124
Total Circulation: 1,000
Paid Circulation: three
Submission Rate: Individual $5/Institution $5
Single Copy Price: $1
Current Volume/Issue: 4/1
Frequency per Year: five issues
Backfile Available: yes
Unsolicited Ms. Received: yes

% of Unsolicited Ms. Published per Year: 50%
Format: stapled
Size: H 8.5" W 5.5"
Average Pages: 40
Ads: yes
Ad Rates: See web site for details.

Organization: Slipstream Publications

Type: press
CLMP member: no
Primary Editor/Contact Person: Dan Sicoli
Address: P.O. Box 2071
Niagara Falls, NY 14301
Web Site Address: http://www.slipstreampress.org
Publishes: poetry and art
Representative Authors: Gerald Locklin, David Chorlton, and Terry Godbey
Submissions Policy: Please refer to guidelines on web page.
Simultaneous Submissions: yes
Reading Period: Year-round
Reporting Time: one to three months
Author Payment: copies
Contests: Annual Poetry Chapbook Competition has a December 1st deadline. See web page for complete guidelines for submissions.
See web site for contest guidelines.
Founded: 1980
Non Profit: yes
Paid Staff: no
Unpaid Staff: yes
Number of Books Published per Year: one
Titles in Print: 18
Average Print Run: 700
Average Percentage Printed: Chapbook 100%
Average Price: $7

Organization: Slipstream

Type: magazine
CLMP member: no
Primary Editor/Contact Person: Dan Sicoli
Address: P.O. Box 2071
Niagara Falls, NY 14301
Web Site Address: http://www.slipstreampress.org
Publishes: poetry and art
Representative Authors: Terry Godbey, Jaso Irwin, and Alison Pelegrin
Submissions Policy: Please refer to guidelines on web page.

Simultaneous Submissions: yes
Reading Period: Year-round
Reporting Time: one to three months
Author Payment: copies
Contests: See web site for contest guidelines.
Founded: 1980
Non Profit: yes
Paid Staff: no
Unpaid Staff: yes
Total Circulation: 700
Paid Circulation: 450
Average Print Run: 700
Submission Rate: Individual $20/Institution $20
Single Copy Price: $7
Current Volume/Issue: Issue 25
Frequency per Year: annual
Backfile Available: yes
Unsolicited Ms. Received: yes
% of Unsolicited Ms. Published per Year: 7%
Format: perfect
Size: H 8.5" W 7"
Average Pages: 80-100
Ads: no

Organization: Slope Editions

Type: press
CLMP member: yes
Primary Editor/Contact Person: Ethan Paquin
Address: 340 Richmond Ave.
Buffalo, NY 14222
Web Site Address: http://www.slopeeditions.org
Publishes: poetry
Editorial Focus: Eclectic poetry
Representative Authors: Jenny Boully, Jonah Winter, and William Waltz
Submissions Policy: See web site for guidelines.
Simultaneous Submissions: no
Reading Period: Year-round
Reporting Time: 4 to 12 months
Author Payment: royalties and copies
Contests: See web site for contest guidelines.
Founded: 2001
Non Profit: yes
Paid Staff: zero
Unpaid Staff: eight
Distributors: Baker & Taylor, SPD
Number of Books Published per Year: three
Titles in Print: five
Average Percentage Printed: Paperback 100%

Organization: Slope

Type: online
CLMP member: yes
Primary Editor/Contact Person: Ethan Paquin
Address: 340 Richmond Ave.
Buffalo, NY 14222
Web Site Address: http://www.slope.org
Publishes: essays, poetry, reviews, translation, and audio
Editorial Focus: Eclectic
Representative Authors: Forrest Gander, James Tate, and Charles Bernstein
Submissions Policy: See web site for guidelines.
Simultaneous Submissions: no
Reading Period: Year-round
Reporting Time: one to six months
Author Payment: none
Founded: 1999
Non Profit: yes
Paid Staff: zero
Unpaid Staff: six
Average Page Views per Month: 10,0000s
Average Unique Visitors per Month: 10,000s
Frequency per Year: 4
Publish Print Anthology: no
Average Percentage of Pages per Category: Poetry 85%, Reviews 15%
Ads: no

Organization: Slovo/Word

Type: magazine
CLMP member: no
Address: Cultural Center for Soviet Refugees
139 E. 33rd St., Ste. 9M
New York, NY 10016
Publishes: essays and fiction
Reading Period: Year-round
Reporting Time: one to two months
Author Payment: none
Founded: 1986
Non Profit: no

Caroline Lord
Editor, Short Story

How did you arrive at your current position?

About two years ago, I got to know my across-the-street neighbor, Matthew Bruccoli, an F. Scott Fitzgerald scholar and English professor at the University of South Carolina. He'd been reading and critiquing my writing, and one day, while I was visiting, he said, "I think you should start a literary review." He went on to list the benefits of publishing and editing a review, such as meeting interesting people and helping would-be writers become published writers. His last words being, "And just think of the cost as an expensive trip around the world." I left his house and pondered the idea. I was tempted, but didn't know if I could commit to such an undertaking. Then one night, during a yoga class, the instructor read a quote, something about once one decides to commit to an idea, all sorts of wondrous consequences will flow from that decision. For some reason, I took that as a sign that I had to start the review. Six months later, *Short Story* came into existence, and I discovered that Dr. Bruccoli and the quote were right. I've loved every minute of starting and running a literary review, even if I could have traveled twice around the world by now.

What is the staff structure at your magazine?

I am the only staff member, but before each printing, I employ a typesetter and a copyeditor.

What challenges do you face as a publisher?

Everything from fundraising to having the binding too tight on the book covers and having to redo a printing.

Do you have any cover letter advice?

Keep it short and to the point.

What do you look for in a submission?

Stories that are forward driven, and stories where things happen. Stories with humor and wit are nice as well. I also look for stories with endings as strong as the beginnings, and lastly, I receive many stories with explicit sex scenes and gratuitous foul language, and I find that those two things don't add to a story, but only detract and distract from it. This is a bit off topic, but I recently read a Raymond Carver essay in which he wrote, "If the words are heavy with the writer's own unbridled emotions, or if they are imprecise and inaccurate for some other reason—if the words are in any way blurred—the reader's eyes will slide right over

them and nothing will be achieved. The reader's own artistic sense will simply not be engaged." His words resonated with me, because many times, when I am reading a story, that very thing happens. I lose my focus, and I begin to scan the story rather than become engaged by it. I don't have any magic bullets of advice on how to hold a reader's attention, except to say, try to make every sentence count.

How are submissions processed at your magazine?

I do all the reading.

Do you have a favorite unsolicited submission story?

I've only had one issue of unsolicited work, so no fun stories as of yet.

What advice do you have for first-time submitters?

Don't get discouraged by rejection letters. If you get one in the mail, just think of it as an opportunity to go back and look at your story with fresh eyes. I use the word "fresh" since you will have probably waited two to nine months for a response! (I send my work out, so I know.) Then decide what could be changed for the better, and send it out again.

What are your long-term plans for your magazine?

I'd like to increase the subscriber base, put on local literary events, and make the *Short Story* website more interactive, possibly with short shorts being read through podcasts.

How do you see the current literary landscape?

I often read reports stating that Americans are reading less and less, and my hunch is that the statistics are probably true. I think most people's lives are so harried that the thought of reading for pleasure doesn't even enter into their daily thought processes. But on the flipside, I'm heartened by the fact that so many

people are writing and submitting their work to journals. Despite all the odds of getting published, people feel driven to express themselves through stories.

Organization: Small Beer Press

Type: press
CLMP member: yes
Primary Editor/Contact Person: Gavin Grant
Address: 176 Prospect Ave.
Northampton, MA 01060
Web Site Address: http://www.lcrw.net
Publishes: fiction and non-ficton
Reading Period: Year-round
Reporting Time: one to two months
Author Payment: royalties and cash
Founded: 1996
Non Profit: no
Paid Staff: zero
Unpaid Staff: two
Distributors: SCB Distributors
Wholesalers: Ingram, Baker & Taylor, etc.
ISSN Number/ ISBN Number: 1544-7782/1931520
Titles in Print: 14
Avrage Print Run: 3,000
Average Percentage Printed: hardcover 48%, paperback 48%, chapbook 4%
Average Price: $16

Organization: Small Beer Press/ Lady Churchill's Rosebud Wristlet

Type: magazine
CLMP member: yes
Primary Editor/Contact Person: Gavin Grant
Address: 176 Prospect Ave.
Northampton, MA 01060
Web Site Address: http://www.lcrw.net
Publishes: fiction and nonfiction
Reading Period: Year-round
Reporting Time: one to two months
Author Payment: none
Founded: 1996
Non Profit: yes
Paid Staff: 2
Unpaid Staff: 2
Distributors: Consortium
Wholesalers: Ingram, Baker & Taylor, etc.
ISSN Number/ISBN Number: ISBN 1931520
Number of Books Published per Year: 4
Titles in Print: 22
Average Print Run: 3,000
Average Percentage Printed: Hardcover 48%, Paperback 48%, Chapbook 4%
Average Price: $16

Organization: Small Spiral Notebook

Type: magazine
CLMP member: yes
Primary Editor/Contact Person: Felicia C. Sullivan
Address: 172 5th Ave. #104
Brooklyn, NY 11217
Web Site Address: http://www.smallspiralnotebook.com
Publishes: fiction, nonfiction, poetry, and reviews
Editorial Focus: Small Spiral Notebook seeks the very best in literary fiction, nonfiction and poetry with a focus on emerging writers.
Representative Authors: Judy Budnitz, Lisa Glatt, and Ken Foster
Submissions Policy: Please view our submission guidelines at http://www.smallspiralnotebook.com/newsubmission.shtml
Simultaneous Submissions: yes
Reading Period: Year-round
Reporting Time: one to three months
Author Payment: copies
Founded: 2001
Non Profit: yes
Paid Staff: zero
Unpaid Staff: 10
Distributors: Ingram, DeBoer
ISSN Number/ISBN Number: ISSN 1557-1068
Total Circulation: 1,500
Paid Circulation: 200
Average Print Run: 1,500
Submission Rate: Individual $18/Institution $18
Single Copy Price: $10
Current Volume/Issue: 2/2
Frequency per Year: biannual
Backfile Available: yes
Unsolicited Ms. Received: yes
% of Unsolicited Ms. Published per Year: 60%
Format: perfect
Size: H 6" W 9"
Average Pages: 150
Ads: yes
Ad Rates: e-mail editor@smallspiralnotebook.com for details.

Organization: Small Spiral Notebook

Type: online
CLMP member: yes
Primary Editor/Contact Person: Felicia C. Sullivan

Address: 248 W. 17th St. Ste. 307
New York, NY 10011
Web Site Address:
http://www.smallspiralnotebook.com
Publishes: fiction, nonfiction, poetry, and reviews
Editorial Focus: Small Spiral Notebook seeks the very best in literary fiction, nonfiction and poetry. Submissions accepted year-round.
Representative Authors: Aimee Bender, Gary Lutz, and Jonathan Ames
Submissions Policy: Please view our submission guidelines at http://www.smallspiralnotebook.com/newsubmission.shtml
Simultaneous Submissions: yes
Reading Period: Year-round
Reporting Time: one to three months
Author Payment: none
Founded: 2001
Non Profit: yes
Unpaid Staff: seven
Backfile Available: yes
Average Page Views per Month: 16,000
Average Unique Visitors per Month: 8,500
Publish Print Anthology: yes
Price: $10
Average Percentage of Pages per Category: Fiction 40%, Nonfiction 10%, Poetry 40%, Reviews 10%
Ads: yes
Ad Rates: Ad swap. Contact Editor for details

Organization: The SNReview

Type: online
CLMP member: yes
Primary Editor/Contact Person: Joseph Conlin
Address: 197 Fairchild Ave.
Fairfield, CT 06825-4856
Web Site Address: http://www.snreview.org
Publishes: essays, fiction, nonfiction, and poetry
Editorial Focus: Quality writing conveying stimulating themes.
Representative Authors: Margaret Karmazin, Adrian Louis, and Jeanne Mackin
Submissions Policy: SNReview accepts only e-mailed submissions. Paste your work into the e-mail and send to editor@snreview.org. No attachments.
Simultaneous Submissions: yes
Reading Period: Year-round
Reporting Time: one to two months
Author Payment: none
Contests: No reading fees, no contests.

Founded: 1999
Non Profit: yes
Paid Staff: zero
Unpaid Staff: three
ISSN Number/ISBN Number: ISSN 1527-344X
Average Page Views per Month: 7,259
Average Unique Visitors per Month: 2,315
Frequency per Year: quarterly
Average Percentage of Pages per Category: :
Fiction 47%, Nonfiction 12%, Poetry 30%, Essays 11%
Ads: yes
Ad Rates: Won't turn down a reasonable offer.

Organization: So to Speak: A Feminist Journal of Language and Art

Type: magazine
CLMP member: no
Primary Editor/Contact Person: Sarah Anne Whiter
Address: George Mason University
4400 University Dr.
Fairfax, VA 22030
Web Site Address:
http://www.gmu.edu/org/sts/masthead.htm
Publishes: essays, fiction, nonfiction, poetry, and art
Editorial Focus: Publishes work that addresses issues of significance to women's lives and movements for women's equality.
Simultaneous Submissions: yes
Reading Period: 9/05 to 3/06
Reporting Time: four to five months
Author Payment: none
Contests: Poetry, Fiction, and Nonfiction Contests. See Web site for contest guidelines.
Founded: 1993
Non Profit: yes
Paid Staff: four
Total Circulation: 750
Paid Circulation: 50
Average Print Run: 1,000
Submission Rate: Individual $12/Institution $12
Single Copy Price: $7
Current Volume/Issue: 14/2
Frequency per Year: biannual
Backfile Available: yes
Unsolicited Ms. Received: yes
% of Unsolicited Ms. Published per Year: 80%
Format: perfect
Ads: yes

Organization: Soft Skull Press

Type: press
CLMP member: yes
Primary Editor/Contact Person: Richard Nash
Address: 19 W. 21 St.
Ste. 1101
New York, NY 10010
Web Site Address: http://www.softskull.com
Publishes: essays, fiction, nonfiction, poetry, and translation
Editorial Focus: Check out our catalog on our web site
Recent Awards Received: two PEN Award finalists, one Lambda winner, four Lambda shortlist, two Publishing triangle finalists, 2006 AAP Miriam Bass Award
Representative Authors: William Upski Wimsatt, Eileen Myles, and Matthew Sharpe
Submissions Policy: Check out our submissions guidelines on our web site
Simultaneous Submissions: yes
Reading Period: Year-round
Reporting Time: up to 2 months
Author Payment: royalties
Founded: 1993
Non Profit: no
Paid Staff: four
Unpaid Staff: six
Distributors: Publishers Group West
Wholesalers: All
ISSN Number/ISBN Number: ISBN 1-887128, 1-932360
Number of Books Published per Year: 40
Titles in Print: 200
Average Print Run: 3,500
Average Percentage Printed: Hardcover 8%, Paperback 90%, Other 2%
Average Price: $16

Organization: Soft Targets

Type: magazine
CLMP member: yes
Primary Editor/Contact Person: Front Office
Address: 114 Nassau Ave. #1
Brooklyn, NY 11222
Web Site Address: www.softtargetsjournal.com
Publishes: essays, fiction, nonfiction, poetry, reviews, art, translation, audio, and video
Editorial Focus: The flight from violence that drags violence along with it.
Representative Authors: Ben Lerner, Lara Glenum, and Wayne Koestenbaum
Submissions Policy: No unsolicited manuscripts
Simultaneous Submissions: no
Reading Period: 10/31 to 10/31
Reporting Time: one to three months
Author Payment: copies
Founded: 2006
Non Profit: yes
Paid Staff: zero
Unpaid Staff: six
ISSN Number/ISBN Number: 15579158/0977875105
Total Circulation: 1,000
Paid Circulation: 100
Average Print Run: 1,000
Subscription Rate: individual $10/institution $10
Single Copy Price: $10
Current Volume/Issue: 1/1
Frequency per year: annual
Backfile Available: yes
Unsolicited MSS Received: no
Format: perfect
Size: H 7.25" W 5.75"
Average Pages: 200
Ads: no

Organization: Soho Press

Type: press
CLMP member: no
Primary Editor/Contact Person: Laura M.C. Hruska
Address: 853 Broadway
New York, NY 10003
Web Site Address: http://www.sohopress.com
Publishes: fiction and nonfiction
Editorial Focus: We want to publish good books well. Gorgeous novels, mysteries, memoirs-whatever is interesting, moving, and well-written.
Representative Authors: Edwidge Danticat, Peter Lovesey, and Susan Richards
Submissions Policy: We prefer that a query letter precede any submission. We do consider unsolicited material.
Simultaneous Submissions: yes
Reading Period: Year-round
Reporting Time: one to two months
Author Payment: royalties and cash
Founded: 1986
Non Profit: no

Paid Staff: four
Unpaid Staff: one
Distributors: Consortium Book Sales and Distribution
ISSN Number/ISBN Number: ISBN 1-56947-
Number of Books Published per Year: 30-40
Titles in Print: 220+
Average Percentage Printed: Hardcover 60%, Paperback 40%
Average Price: $24.00

Organization: Sojourn, A Journal of the Arts

Type: magazine
CLMP member: yes
Primary Editor/Contact Person: Susan Rushing Adams
Address: School of Arts and Humanities, UT Dallas PO Box 830688, JO 31 Richardson, TX 75083
Website Address: www.sojournjournal.org
Publishes: essays, fiction, nonfiction, poetry, art, and translation
Editorial Focus: Interdisciplinary, fusing the literary and fine arts and exploring connections between various forms of artistic expression.
Representative Authors: Peter Cooley, Martha Crow, and Billy Collins
Submissions Policy: see website for updated guidelines. Deadline 12/1 each year; acceptances/rejections sent in February.
Simultaneous Submissions: yes
Reading Period: 10/1 to 12/1
Reporting Time: 8 to 12 weeks
Author Payment: copies
Contests: Editor's Choice Awards ($50) in Poetry, Fiction, Nonfiction, Visual Art, and Translation
Founded: 1987
Non Profit: yes
Paid Staff: 0
Unpaid Staff: 15
ISSN Number/ISBN Number: ISSN 1935-5238
Total Circulation: 800
Paid Circulation: 0
Average Print Run: 800
Subscription Rate: Individual $10.00/Institution $10.00
Single Copy Price: $10.00
Current Volume/Issue: 20/1
Frequency: 1
Backfile Available: yes

Unsolicited Ms. Received: yes
% of Unsolicited Ms. Published per Year: 16%
Format: perfect
Size: H 8.5" W 5.5"
Average Pages: 175
Ads: yes
Ad Rates: see website for details

Organization: SOLO CAFE: A Journal of Poetry

Type: magazine
CLMP member: yes
Primary Editor/Contact Person: Glenna Luschei
Address: 5146 Foothill Road Carpinteria, CA 93013-3017
Web Site Address: http://www.solopress.org
Publishes: poetry, reviews, and translation
Editorial Focus: SOLO celebrates great poetry, with a special interest in translations from Spanish and Portuguese.
Representative Authors: Al Young, Barry Spacks, and Perie Longo
Submissions Policy: Send up to four poems at a time. Translations must include permission by original poet.
Simultaneous Submissions: no
Reading Period: Year-round
Reporting Time: 8 to 12 weeks
Author Payment: copies
Contests: None right now. Visit website for changes
Founded: 1967
Non Profit: yes
Paid Staff: 0
Unpaid Staff: five
ISSN Number/ISBN Number: ISSN 1088-3495
Total Circulation: 500
Paid Circulation: 50
Submission Rate: Individual $20/Institution $60
Single Copy Price: $10
Current Volume/Issue: Issue three
Frequency per Year: annual
Backfile Available: yes
Unsolicited Ms. Received: yes
% of Unsolicited Ms. Published per Year: 10%
Format: perfect
Size: H 9" W 6"
Average Pages: 124
Ads: yes
Ad Rates: Exchange ads

Organization: Sona Books

Type: press
CLMP member: no
Primary Editor/Contact Person: Jill Magi
Address: 7825 Fourth Ave., F10
Brooklyn, NY 11209
Web Site Address: http://www.sonaweb.net
Publishes: essays, fiction, nonfiction, poetry, art, and audio
Editorial Focus: Risky and quiet works, project-based, inter-genre works, collaborations, audio and performance, art sized to fit the hands.
Representative Authors: Alicia Askenase, Jennifer Firestone, and Cecilia Vicuna
Submissions Policy: Unfortunately, no unsolicited submissions. Please query if you have a project in mind after seeing a Sona book or work.
Simultaneous Submissions: no
Reading Period: Year-round
Reporting Time: one to two months
Author Payment: none
Founded: 2002
Non Profit: yes
Distributors: by subscription, web-site.
Number of Books Published per Year: 2-4
Titles in Print: 10
Average Print Run: 150
Average Percentage Printed: Chapbook 70%, Other 30%
Average Price: $6

Organization: Sou'wester Magazine

Type: magazine
CLMP member: yes
Primary Editor/Contact Person: Allison Funk
Address: Campus Box 1438
Southern Illinois Univ. Edwardsville
Edwardsville, IL 62026
Web Site Address: www.siue.edu/ENGLISH
Publishes: essays, fiction, nonfiction, poetry, reviews, art, and translation
Editorial Focus: We publish the best poetry and prose we can find by new and established writers.
Representative Authors: Robert Wrigley, R.T. Smith, and Mary Troy
Submissions Policy: Limit of five poems or one piece of prose per submission
Simultaneous Submissions: yes
Reading Period: 8/51 to 4/15

Reporting Time: two to three months
Author Payment: copies and subscription
Founded: 1960
Non Profit: yes
Paid Staff: three
Unpaid Staff: ten
ISSN Number/ISBN Number: ISSN 0098499X/1-4243-0498-9
Total Circulation: 500
Paid Circulation: 250
Average Print Run: 500
Submission Rate: Individual $15/Institution $15
Single Copy Price: $8
Current Volume/Issue: 35/2
Frequency per Year: biannual
Backfile Available: yes
Unsolicited Ms. Received: yes
% of Unsolicited Ms. Published per Year: 90%
Format: perfect
Size: H 9" W 6"
Average Pages: 128
Ads: no

Organization: Soundings

Type: magazine
CLMP member: yes
Primary Editor/Contact Person: Marian Blue
Address: Whidbey Island Writers Association
PO Box 1289
Langley, WA 98260
Website Address: www.writeonwhidbey.org
Publishes: essays, fiction, and poetry
Editorial Focus: We seek accessible creative writing in any genre, style, voice; we want writers and readers to connect.
Representative Authors: Maurya Simon, Christopher Howell, and Susan Zwinger
Submissions Policy: SASE required. Double-space (except for poetry). Up to 8,000 words prose; poetry under 100 lines.
Simultaneous Submissions: yes
Reading Period: year-round
Reporting Time: 1 to 2 months
Author Payment: copies
Founded: 2004
Non Profit: yes
Paid Staff: 0
Unpaid Staff: 2
Distributors: Subscription
Total Circulation: 300

Paid Circulation: 0
Average Print Run: 300
Subscription Rate: Individual $9/Institution $9
Single Copy Price: $10
Current Volume/Issue: 1
Frequency: annual
Backfile Available: yes
Unsolicited Ms. Received: yes
% of Unsolicited Ms. Published per Year: 80%
Format: perfect
Size: H 9" W 6"
Average Pages: 200
Ads: yes
Ad Rates: see website for details

Organization: South Dakota Review

Type: magazine
CLMP member: yes
Primary Editor/Contact Person: Brian Bedard
Address: Dept of English/U of South Dakota
414 E. Clark St.
Vermillion, SD 57069
Website Address: www.usd.edu/sdreview
Publishes: essays, fiction, nonfiction, and poetry
Editorial Focus: A literary, scholarly journal for new and established writers. Primary interests: American West and Great Plains themes.
Representative Authors: Kent Meyers, Gary Fincke, and Debra Marquart
Submissions Policy: Manuscripts with SASE, MLA style. No previously published works. No electronic submissions.
Simultaneous Submissions: yes
Reading Period: year-round
Reporting Time: 2 to 4 months
Author Payment: copies and subscription
Founded: 1963
Non Profit: yes
Paid Staff: 2
Unpaid Staff: 6
ISSN Number/ISBN Number: ISBN 0038-3368
Total Circulation: 500
Paid Circulation: 350
Average Print Run: 550
Subscription Rate: Individual $30/Institution $30
Single Copy Price: $10
Current Volume/Issue: 44/1
Frequency: quarterly
Backfile Available: yes
Unsolicited Ms. Received: yes

% of Unsolicited Ms. Published per Year: 1%
Format: perfect
Size: H 9" W 6"
Average Pages: 125
Ads: no

Organization: South East Missouri State University Press

Type: press
CLMP member: yes
Primary Editor/Contact Person: Dr. Susan Swartwout
Address: MS 2650, One University Plaza
Cape Girardeau, MO 63701
Website Address: www6.semo.edu/universitypress/
Publishes: fiction, nonfiction, and poetry
Recent Awards Received: James Joyce First-novel Award, Langum Award, Pioneer America Award, 2 Governor's Book Awards
Representative Authors: Morley Swingle, Linda Busby Parker, and William Trowbridge
Submissions Policy: Query first.
Simultaneous Submissions: yes
Reading Period: year-round
Reporting Time: 4 to 6 months
Author Payment: royalties and copies
Contests: Copperdome Poetry Chapbook Award Wilda Hearne Flash Fiction Contest Mighty River Short-story Contest (all annual); see website for guidelines
Founded: 2001
Non Profit: yes
Paid Staff: 2
Unpaid Staff: 3
Distributors: Baker & Taylor, Partners, Brodart
ISSN Number/ISBN Number: 1532-9860/09760413-
Number of Books Published per Year: 4
Titles in Print: 14
Average Print Run: 3,000
Average Percentage Printed: Hardcover 25%, Paperback 70%, Chapbook 5%
Average Price: $20.00

Organization: The Southeast Review

Type: magazine
CLMP member: yes
Primary Editor/Contact Person: Michael Garriga, Editor
Address: Dept. of English
Florida State University
Tallahassee, FL 32306

Website Address: www.southeastreview.org
Publishes: essays, fiction, nonfiction, poetry, reviews, and art
Editorial Focus: We aim to discover exciting new writers of literary poetry and prose and to publish them alongside national award winners.
Representative Authors: Silas House, Aimee Nezhukumatathil, and David Gessner
Submissions Policy: Type all submissions. Send 3-5 poems. Fiction and nonfiction: up to 7,500 words. Include a brief cover letter and SASE.
Simultaneous Submissions: yes
Reading Period: year-round
Reporting Time: 1 to 2 months
Author Payment: copies
Contests: World's Best Short Short Story Contest and **The Southeast Review Poetry Contest. Prize:** $500 and publication. Deadline: Feb. 15; see website for guidelines
Founded: 1980
Non Profit: yes
Paid Staff: 1
Unpaid Staff: 35
ISSN Number/ISBN Number: ISSN 1543-1363
Total Circulation: 1,000
Paid Circulation: 500+
Average Print Run: 1,000
Subscription Rate: Individual $12/Institution $12
Single Copy Price: $6
Current Volume/Issue: 25/2
Frequency: biannual
Backfile Available: yes
Unsolicited Ms. Received: yes
% of Unsolicited Ms. Published per Year: 85%
Format: perfect
Size: H 9" W 6"
Average Pages: 180
Ads: yes

Organization: The Southern Humanities Review

Type: magazine
CLMP member: yes
Primary Editor/Contact Person: Dan Latimer
Address: 9088 Haley Center
Auburn University, AL 36849
Website Address:
www.auburn.edu/english/shr/home.htm
Publishes: essays, fiction, nonfiction, poetry, reviews, and translation

Editorial Focus: general humanities, scholarly
Representative Authors: Chris Arthur, Janette Turner Hospital, and Catharine Savage Brosman
Submissions Policy: SASE, one copy, double-space ms. 15,000 word max. for fiction and essays, 2-3 pages for poems. see website for further info.
Simultaneous Submissions: no
Reading Period: year-round
Reporting Time: 1 to 3 months
Author Payment: copies
Founded: 1967
Non Profit: yes
Paid Staff: 4
Unpaid Staff: 2
ISSN Number/ISBN Number: ISSN 0038-4186
Total Circulation: 650
Paid Circulation: 550
Average Print Run: 800
Subscription Rate: Individual $15/Institution $15
Single Copy Price: $5
Current Volume/Issue: 41/3
Frequency: quarterly
Backfile Available: yes
Unsolicited Ms. Received: yes
Format: perfect
Size: H 9" W 6"
Average Pages: 104
Ads: yes
Ad Rates: IBC full-page vertical only, with sufficient notice

Organization: The Southern Indiana Review

Type: magazine
CLMP member: yes
Primary Editor/Contact Person: Ron Mitchell
Address: University of Southern Indiana
8600 University Blvd.
Evansville, In 47712
Website Address: www.southernindianareview.org
Publishes: essays, fiction, nonfiction, poetry, reviews, art, and translation
Editorial Focus: New and established artists who strive for literary excellence, particularly when work conveys the character of the region.
Representative Authors: Robery Wrigley, Kevin McIlvoy, and Erin McGraw
Simultaneous Submissions: yes
Reading Period: 9/1 to 5/31
Reporting Time: 2 to 3 months

Author Payment: copies
Contests: Mary C. Mohr Award (genre rotates every year). First prize $1000, second prize $250, third prize $100 (and publication); see website for guidelines
Founded: 1992
Non Profit: yes
Paid Staff: 1
Unpaid Staff: 10
ISSN Number/ISBN Number: ISSN 1-903508-04-2
Total Circulation: 500
Paid Circulation: 225
Average Print Run: 750
Subscription Rate: Individual $16/Institution $16
Single Copy Price: $10
Current Volume/Issue: 13/1
Frequency: biannual
Backfile Available: yes
Unsolicited Ms. Received: yes
% of Unsolicited Ms. Published per Year: 5%
Format: perfect
Size: H 9" W 6"
Average Pages: 100
Ads: no

Organization: Southern Poetry Review

Type: magazine
CLMP member: yes
Primary Editor/Contact Person: Robert Parham
Address: Department of Lang., Lit., & Phil
Armstrong Atlantic State University
Savannah, GA 31419-1997
Web Site Address: http://www.spr.armstrong.edu
Publishes: poetry
Editorial Focus: The best contemporary poetry by established and new poets; editorially eclectic.
Recent Awards Received: Two 2005 Pushcart Prizes, one Honorable Mention
Submissions Policy: five to seven unpublished poems (10 pages max) with SASE; no electronic or disk submissions; indicate simultaneous submission.
Simultaneous Submissions: yes
Reading Period: Year-round
Reporting Time: two to three months
Author Payment: copies
Contests: See web site for contest guidelines.
Founded: 1958
Non Profit: yes
Paid Staff: two
Unpaid Staff: three

ISSN Number/ISBN Number: ISSN 0038-447X
Total Circulation: 800
Paid Circulation: 600
Average Print Run: 1,000
Submission Rate: Individual $12/Institution $15
Single Copy Price: $6
Current Volume/Issue: 43/2
Frequency per Year: biannual
Backfile Available: yes
Unsolicited Ms. Received: yes
% of Unsolicited Ms. Published per Year: 4%
Format: perfect
Size: H 6" W 9"
Average Pages: 80
Ads: yes
Ad Rates: Contact Associate Editor
See web site for details.

Organization: The Southern Quarterly

Type: magazine
CLMP member: no
Primary Editor/Contact Person: Douglas B. Chambers
Address: 118 College Dr. #5078
Hattiesburg, MS 39406
Publishes: essays, fiction, nonfiction, poetry, reviews, and art
Editorial Focus: Interdisciplinary study of southern culture through reasoned consideration of the arts to include literature, art & history.
Submissions Policy: Submit manuscript in M.S. Word with complete endnotes & bibliography for non-fiction works. Send files via email or USPS w/disk.
Simultaneous Submissions: no
Reading Period: year-round
Reporting Time: three to six months
Author Payment: copies and subscription
Founded: 1962
Non Profit: yes
Paid Staff: three
Unpaid Staff: three
ISSN Number/ISBN Number: ISSN 0038-4496
Total Circulation: 600
Paid Circulation: 450
Average Print Run: 750
Subscription Rate: individual $18/institution $35
Single Copy Price: varies
Current Volume/Issue: 43/3
Frequency per year: quarterly

Backfile Available: yes
Unsolicited MSS Received: yes
% of Unsolicited MSS Published per year: 20%
Format: perfect
Size: H 10" W 7"
Average Pages: 200
Ads: yes
Ad Rates: $100 full page
See web site for details.

Organization: The Southern Review

Type: magazine
CLMP member: yes
Primary Editor/Contact Person: Bret Lott
Address: Old President's House
Louisiana State University
Baton Rouge, LA 70803
Web Site Address: http://www.lsu.edu/thesouthern-review
Publishes: essays, fiction, nonfiction, poetry, and reviews
Editorial Focus: Contemporary literature in the US and abroad with special interest in Southern culture and history.
Recent Awards Received: Four works from 2004's volume were selected for Pushcart Prizes; two stories were selected for Best Stories from the South
Representative Authors: Mary Oliver, R.T. Smith, and Denis Donoghue
Submissions Policy: See web site or send SASE for guidelines
Simultaneous Submissions: yes
Reading Period: 9/1 to 5/31
Reporting Time: four to eight weeks
Author Payment: cash, copies, and submission
Contests: See Web Site for contest guidelines.
Founded: 1935
Non Profit: yes
Paid Staff: six
Unpaid Staff: zero
Distributors: Ingram Periodicals
ISSN Number/ISBN Number: ISSN 0038-4534
Total Circulation: 2,900
Paid Circulation: 2,000
Average Print Run: 2,900
Submission Rate: Individual $25/Institution $50
Single Copy Price: $8
Current Volume/Issue: 42/2
Frequency per Year: quarterly
Backfile Available: yes

Unsolicited Ms. Received: yes
% of Unsolicited Ms. Published per Year: 2%
Format: perfect
Size: H 10" W 6.75"
Average Pages: 232
Ads: yes
Ad Rates: 250/full page; 150/half page

Organization: Southwest Review

Type: magazine
CLMP member: yes
Primary Editor/Contact Person: Willard Spiegelman
Address: P.O. Box 750374
6404 Hilltop Ln., Rm. 307
Dallas, TX 75275-0374
Web Site Address: http://www.southwestreview.org
Publishes: essays, fiction, and poetry
Editorial Focus: Discover works by new writers and publish them beside those of more established authors.
Representative Authors: John Hollander, Rachel Hadas, and Sandra Cisneros
Submissions Policy: Please see web site for complete guidelines.
Simultaneous Submissions: no
Reading Period: 9/4 to 5/31
Reporting Time: one to two months
Author Payment: cash and copies
Contests: See web site for contest guidelines.
Founded: 1915
Non Profit: yes
Paid Staff: three
Unpaid Staff: zero
Distributors: DeBoer; Total Circulation
ISSN Number/ISBN Number: ISSN 0038-4712
Total Circulation: 1,500
Paid Circulation: 700
Average Print Run: 1300
Submission Rate: Individual $24/Institution $30
Single Copy Price: $6
Current Volume/Issue: 92/3
Frequency per Year: quarterly
Backfile Available: yes
Unsolicited Ms. Received: yes
% of Unsolicited Ms. Published per Year: 90%
Format: perfect
Size: H 9" W 6"
Average Pages: 175
Ads: yes
Ad Rates: Call for information.

Organization: Speakeasy

Type: magazine
CLMP member: no
Primary Editor/Contact Person: Bart Schneider
Address: The Loft Literary Center
1011 Washington Ave. South
Minneapolis, MN 55415
Web Site Address:
http://www.speakeasymagazine.org
Publishes: essays, fiction, nonfiction, poetry, and reviews
Editorial Focus: To offer a Literary Look at Life, presenting a wide range of voices on intriguing themes.
Representative Authors: Sven Birkerts, Naomi Shihab Nye, and Gerald Early
Submissions Policy: We only consider unsolicited manuscripts for fiction and poetry. Essays and book reviews are solicited by the editor.
Simultaneous Submissions: yes
Reading Period: Year-round
Reporting Time: one to three months
Author Payment: cash
Contests: See web site for contest guidelines.
Founded: 2002
Non Profit: yes
Paid Staff: two
Unpaid Staff: two
Distributors: Ingram and several independent distributors
ISSN Number/ISBN Number: ISSN 1540-9422
Total Circulation: 6,200
Paid Circulation: 3,500
Submission Rate: Individual $19.99/Institution $19.99
Single Copy Price: $5.95
Current Volume/Issue: 2/2
Frequency per Year: quarterly
Backfile Available: yes
Unsolicited Ms. Received: yes
Format: stapled
Size: H 8" W 10"
Average Pages: 56
Ads: yes
Ad Rates: $1,210 Full page, B&W
See web site for details.

Organization: Spillway

Type: magazine
CLMP member: yes
Primary Editor/Contact Person: Mifanwy Kaiser
Address: P.O. Box 7887
Huntington Beach, CA 92615-7887
Web Site Address: http://www.tebotbach.org
Publishes: essays and poetry
Representative Authors: Eleanor Wilner, Richard Jones, and Jeanette Clough
Submissions Policy: six poems, 10 pages max for poems, five to15 pages for essays and reviews. SASE with correct postage
Simultaneous Submissions: yes
Reading Period: Year-round
Reporting Time: one to four months
Author Payment: copies
Founded: 1993
Non Profit: yes
Paid Staff: zero
Unpaid Staff: three
Distributors: Ingram, Small Press, Armadillo, DeBoer
ISSN Number/ISBN Number: 1096-7389/1-893670-12-0
Total Circulation: 1,000
Paid Circulation: 100
Average Print Run: 1,000
Submission Rate: Individual $16/Institution $24
Single Copy Price: $9
Current Volume/Issue: Issue 11
Frequency per Year: biannual
Backfile Available: yes
Unsolicited Ms. Received: yes
Format: perfect
Size: H 6" W 9"
Average Pages: 176
Ads: yes
Ad Rates: $50 one half page, 100 full page, $25 quarter page

Organization: Spindrift

Type: magazine
CLMP member: no
Primary Editor/Contact Person: Deborah Handrich
Address: 16101 Greenwood Ave. N.
Shoreline, WA 98133
Web Site Address: http://www.shoreline.edu/spindrift/home.html
Publishes: fiction, poetry, and art
Submissions Policy: Check web site for details.
Simultaneous Submissions: no
Reading Period: 10/1 to 2/1
Reporting Time: one to two months

Author Payment: none
Founded: 1966
Non Profit: yes
Paid Staff: three
Unpaid Staff: 10
Total Circulation: Varies
Paid Circulation: Varies
Average Print Run: 500
Single Copy Price: $12
Current Volume/Issue: Issue 39
Frequency per Year: annual
Backfile Available: yes
Unsolicited Ms. Received: no
Format: perfect

Organization: Spinning Jenny

Type: magazine
CLMP member: yes
Primary Editor/Contact Person: C.E. Harrison
Address: P.O. Box 1373
New York, NY 10276
Web Site Address: http://www.blackdresspress.com
Publishes: fiction and poetry
Editorial Focus: Poetry, fiction, drama, experimental work.
Representative Authors: Tony Tost, Karla Kelsey, and John Colburn
Submissions Policy: By mail or e-mail. See full guidelines at http://www.blackdresspress.com.
Simultaneous Submissions: no
Reading Period: 9/15 to 5/15
Reporting Time: three to four months
Author Payment: copies
Founded: 1994
Non Profit: yes
Paid Staff: zero
Unpaid Staff: two
Distributors: DeBoer
ISSN Number/ISBN Number: 1082-1406/1-887872-07-9
Total Circulation: 1,000
Paid Circulation: 200
Average Print Run: 1,000
Submission Rate: Individual $15/Institution $15
Single Copy Price: $8
Current Volume/Issue: Issue 8
Frequency per Year: annual
Backfile Available: yes
Unsolicited Ms. Received: yes
% of Unsolicited Ms. Published per Year: 2%

Format: perfect
Size: H 9.5" W 5.5"
Average Pages: 96
Ads: no

Organization: Spire Press

Type: magazine
CLMP member: yes
Primary Editor/Contact Person: Shelly Reed
Address: 532 LaGuardia Place, Ste. 298
New York, NY 11217
Web Site Address: http://www.spirepress.org
Publishes: essays, fiction, nonfiction, poetry, and reviews
Representative Authors: Gayle Elen Harvey, Jennifer MacPherson, and Ann E. Michael
Simultaneous Submissions: yes
Reading Period: Year-round
Reporting Time: one to two months
Author Payment: copies
Contests: See web site for contest guidelines.
Founded: 2002
Non Profit: yes
Paid Staff: zero
Unpaid Staff: three
ISSN Number/ISBN Number: 1541-4582/0-9740701
Total Circulation: 1,200
Paid Circulation: 200
Submission Rate: Individual $24/Institution $12
Single Copy Price: $10
Current Volume/Issue: Issue five
Frequency per Year: biannual
Backfile Available: yes
Unsolicited Ms. Received: yes
% of Unsolicited Ms. Published per Year: 2-3%
Format: perfect
Size: H 11" W 8.5"
Average Pages: 60
Ads: yes
Ad Rates: The only ads are free or author's. Author's prices <$30

Organization: Spire Press

Type: press
CLMP member: yes
Primary Editor/Contact Person: Shelly Reed
Address: 532 LaGuardia Place, Ste. 298
New York, NY 10012
Web Site Address: http://www.spirepress.org

Publishes: essays, fiction, nonfiction, poetry, and reviews

Representative Authors: Gayle Elen Harvey, Jennifer MacPherson, and Ann E. Michael

Submissions Policy: We only accept book submissions through contests, but see the web site for journal guidelines.

Simultaneous Submissions: yes

Reading Period: Year-round

Reporting Time: two to three months

Author Payment: royalties, cash, and copies

Contests: Yearly poetry contest in the Fall. Please see the web site for details.

Founded: 2002

Non Profit: yes

Paid Staff: zero

Unpaid Staff: three

ISSN Number/ISBN Number: 1541-4582/0-9740701

Number of Books Published per Year: four to five

Titles in Print: five

Average Print Run: 500+

Average Percentage Printed: Paperback 50%, Chapbook 50%

Average Price: $14.95

Organization: The Spoon River Poetry Review

Type: magazine

CLMP member: yes

Primary Editor/Contact Person: Dr. Bruce Guernsey

Address: Department of English
Illinois State University, Box 4240
Normal, IL 61790-4241

Web Site Address: http://www.litline.org//spoon

Publishes: poetry, reviews, and translation

Editorial Focus: Contemporary poetry in English and English translation; review essays on poetry and poetics.

Representative Authors: Alicia Ostriker, Haki Madhubuti, and Karen An-Hwei Lee

Submissions Policy: Three to five unpublished poems, SASE. Translations, send poems in original language.

Simultaneous Submissions: yes

Reading Period: 9/15 to 4/15

Reporting Time: two to three months

Author Payment: copies and submission

Contests: Editors' Prize Contest, April 15, $1,000 for winner, $100 each for two runners-up. Fee, $16, includes submission.

See web site for contest guidelines.

Founded: 1974

Non Profit: yes

Paid Staff: two

Unpaid Staff: nine

Distributors: Ingram; Ubiquity

Wholesalers: EBSCO, Blackwells

ISSN Number/ISBN Number: ISSN 0738-8993

Total Circulation: 1,200

Paid Circulation: 750

Average Print Run: 2,000

Submission Rate: Individual $15/Institution $18

Single Copy Price: $10

Current Volume/Issue: 29/2

Frequency per Year: biannual

Backfile Available: no

Unsolicited Ms. Received: yes

% of Unsolicited Ms. Published per Year: 1%

Format: perfect

Size: H 5 1/2" W 8 1/2"

Average Pages: 128

Ads: yes

Ad Rates: $150 per page
See web site for details.

Organization: Spout Press

Type: press

CLMP member: yes

Primary Editor/Contact Person: Carrie Eidem

Address: PO Box 581067
Minneapolis, MN 55418-1067

Web Site Address: www.spoutpress.com

Publishes: essays, fiction, nonfiction, poetry, and art

Editorial Focus: We seek the best in contemporary fiction and poetry, emphasizing the work of new, experimental and emerging authors

Representative Authors: Joanna Fuhrman, Josie Rawson, and Jeffrey Little

Submissions Policy: Guidelines on site. Mail to PO Box, typed final drafts, include SASE and brief cover letter. five poems, or 15 page story max.

Simultaneous Submissions: yes

Reading Period: year-round

Reporting Time: three to six months

Author Payment: copies

Contests: Sponser annual Story of the Year Fiction Contest.
See web site for contest guidelines

Founded: 1989

Non Profit: no

Paid Staff: zero
Unpaid Staff: five
Distributors: SPD
Number of Books Published per year: one
Titles in Print: six
Average Print Run: 500
Average Percentage Printed: paperback 100%
Average Price: $10

Organization: Spout

Type: magazine
CLMP member: yes
Address: P.O. Box 581067
Minneapolis, MN 55458-1067
Web Site Address: http://www.spoutpress.com
Publishes: essays, fiction, nonfiction, poetry, and art
Reading Period: Year-round
Reporting Time: one to two months
Author Payment: none
Founded: 1989
Non Profit: yes
Backfile Available: yes

Organization: Spring, Journal of the E.E. Cummings Society

Type: magazine
CLMP member: no
Primary Editor/Contact Person: Michael Webster
Address: 129 Lake Huron Hall
Grand Valley State University
Allendale, MI 49401-9403
Web Site Address:
http://www.gvsu.edu/english/cummings/Index.html
Publishes: essays and poetry
Editorial Focus: E.E. Cummings and his contemporaries, along with visual poetry in the Cummings tradition.
Representative Authors: Norman Friedman, Michael Dylan Welch, and Bernard V. Stehle
Submissions Policy: Essay submissions should follow MLA Style Manual; send them in rtf format (PC).
Simultaneous Submissions: no
Reading Period: Year-round
Reporting Time: one to months
Author Payment: none
Founded: 1992
Non Profit: yes
Paid Staff: zero
Unpaid Staff: five
Distributors: DeBoer

ISSN Number/ISBN Number: ISSN 0735-6889
Total Circulation: 250
Paid Circulation: 200
Average Print Run: 500
Submission Rate: Individual $17.50/Institution $22.50
Single Copy Price: $17.50
Current Volume/Issue: 2003/12
Frequency per Year: annual
Backfile Available: yes
Unsolicited Ms. Received: yes
% of Unsolicited Ms. Published per Year: 30%
Format: perfect
Size: H 8 1/2" W 5 1/2"
Average Pages: 175-200
Ads: yes
Ad Rates: negotiable

Organization: The Square Table

Type: online
CLMP member: no
Primary Editor/Contact Person: Dina Di Maio
Address: 431 E. Central Blvd. #308
Orlando, FL 32801
Web Site Address: http://www.thesquaretable.com
Publishes: essays, fiction, nonfiction, poetry, reviews, and art
Editorial Focus: The Square Table showcases today's top talent in writing, art, photography, music, design and more. Take a seat.
Representative Authors: Bob Mustin, Lyn Strongin, and Tom Sheehan
Submissions Policy: Send all submissions to editor@thesquaretable.com with the section you are submitting to in the subject line.Do not mail.
Simultaneous Submissions: yes
Reading Period: Year-round
Reporting Time: two to twelve weeks
Author Payment: none
Founded: 2002
Non Profit: yes
Paid Staff: zero
Unpaid Staff: three
Average Page Views per Month: 15,000
Average Unique Visitors per Month: 2,000
Frequency per Year: biannual
Publish Print Anthology: no
Average Percentage of Pages per Category: Fiction 20%, Nonfiction 20%, Poetry 1%, Reviews 20%, Essays 20%, Art 19%

Ads: no

Organization: St. Andrews College Press

Type: press
CLMP member: no
Primary Editor/Contact Person: Pete Dulgar
Address: 1700 Dogwood Mile
Laurinburg, NC 28352
Web Site Address: http://www.sapc.edu/sapress
Publishes: fiction, nonfiction, and poetry
Editorial Focus: We offer book publication to authors selected from our literary magazine, Cairn, and our college reading series.
Representative Authors: Barry Gifford, Anthony Abbott, and Judy Goldman
Submissions Policy: No unsolicited manuscripts. Submit work to Cairn magazine and, if selected there, inquire about book publication.
Simultaneous Submissions: no
Reading Period: Year-round
Reporting Time: two to four months
Author Payment: copies and submission
Founded: 1969
Non Profit: yes
Paid Staff: two
Unpaid Staff: four
Number of Books Published per Year: three to four
Titles in Print: 80
Average Percentage Printed: Hardcover 2%, Paperback 73%, Chapbook 25%

Organization: Star Cloud Press

Type: press
CLMP member: yes
Primary Editor/Contact Person: Steven E. Swerdfeger, Ph.D.
Address: 6137 E. Mescal St.
Scottsdale, AZ 85254-5418
Web Site Address: http://StarCloudPress.com
Publishes: fiction, nonfiction, and poetry
Editorial Focus: We are a small, independent press committed to publishing poetry, fiction, and creative nonfiction of vision and enduring excellence.
Submissions Policy: Currently the submission of manuscripts is solely by invitation.
Simultaneous Submissions: no
Reading Period: Year-round
Reporting Time: three to six months

Author Payment: royalties and copies
Founded: 1995
Non Profit: no
Paid Staff: one
Unpaid Staff: zero
Distributors: Ingram
ISSN Number/ISBN Number: ISBN 9651835, 1-932842
Number of Books Published per Year: four to five
Titles in Print: four
Average Percentage Printed: Hardcover 50%, Paperback 50%
Backfile Available: yes

Organization: Starcherone Books

Type: press
CLMP member: yes
Primary Editor/Contact Person: Ted Pelton
Address: P.O. Box 303
Buffalo, NY 14201
Web Site Address: http://www.starcherone.com
Publishes: fiction
Editorial Focus: Innovative fiction.
Representative Authors: Raymond Federman, Aimee Parkison, and Nina Shope
Submissions Policy: Query first with CV and sample. Keep in mind that most manuscripts come to us through our contest.
Simultaneous Submissions: yes
Reading Period: 8/15 to 9/30
Reporting Time: three to nine months
Author Payment: royalties and copies
Contests: See web site for contest guidelines.
Founded: 2,000
Non Profit: yes
Paid Staff: zero
Unpaid Staff: six
Distributors: SPD
Wholesalers: Baker & Taylor
ISSN Number/ISBN Number: ISBN 09703165
Number of Books Published per Year: 4
Titles in Print: 10
Average Print Run: 750
Average Percentage Printed: Paperback 100%
Average Price: $17

Organization: Stone Buzzard Press

Type: press
CLMP member: yes

Primary Editor/Contact Person: Mike Selender
Address: 159 Jewett Ave.
Jersey City, NJ 07304-2003
Publishes: fiction and poetry
Editorial Focus: poetry and fiction.
Representative Authors: Joe Cardillo
Submissions Policy: Not looking for new material. Query before sending anything.
Simultaneous Submissions: no
Reading Period: year-round
Reporting Time: up to 6 months
Author Payment: copies
Contests: none
Founded: 1986
Non Profit: no
Paid Staff: 0
Unpaid Staff: 1
ISSN Number/ISBN Number: ISBN 0-9624082
Number of Books Published per Year: 0-1
Titles in Print: 2
Average Percentage Printed: Paperback 100%
Backfile Available: yes

Organization: Stone Canoe

Type: magazine
CLMP member: yes
Primary Editor/Contact Person: Robert Colley
Address: 700 University Avenue
Syracuse, NY 13244
Website Address: www.stonecanoejournal.org
Publishes: essays, fiction, nonfiction, poetry, reviews, art, and translation
Editorial Focus: A Syracuse University annual journal showcasing emerging and established writers and artists with ties to Upstate New York
Recent Awards Received: Bronze medal in anthology category, 2007 Independent Publisher's Awards competition
Representative Authors: George Saunders, Stephen Dunn, and Mary Gaitskill
Submissions Policy: unsolicited work welcome, by mail or email. Specifics in journal or on website
Simultaneous Submissions: yes
Reading Period: 3/1 to 9/1
Reporting Time: 2 to 4 weeks
Author Payment: copies and subscription
Contests: annual awards for emerging poet, fiction writer and visual artist; $500 and stone canoe sculpture; see website for guidelines
Founded: 2007

Non Profit: yes
Paid Staff: 2
Unpaid Staff: 8
Distributors: Syracuse University Press
Total Circulation: 2,500
Paid Circulation: 50
Average Print Run: 2500
Subscription Rate: Individual $18/Institution $12
Single Copy Price: $18
Current Volume/Issue: Issue 1
Frequency: 1
Backfile Available: yes
Unsolicited Ms. Received: yes
Format: perfect
Size: H 10" W 7"
Average Pages: 300
Ads: yes
Ad Rates: $500 full-page, $250 half page; see website for details

Organization: Stone Table Review

Type: online
CLMP member: yes
Primary Editor/Contact Person: Brad Stiles
Address: 1108 York Avenue
Lansdale, PA 19446
Website Address: stonetablereview.com
Publishes: essays, fiction, nonfiction, poetry, reviews, audio, and video
Editorial Focus: Publishes new works in traditional or new media formats by emerging and established writers. Published bi-annually.
Representative Authors: Bart Edelman, Ace Boggess, and Kathleen Flenniken
Submissions Policy: Publishes short stories, essays, poetry, and drama (traditional or new media). We only accept email submissions.
Simultaneous Submissions: no
Reading Period: year-round
Reporting Time: 2 to 4 months
Author Payment: none
Founded: 2006
Non Profit: yes
Paid Staff: 0
Unpaid Staff: 3
ISSN Number/ISBN Number: ISSN 1932-7935
Average Page Views per Month: 2,000
Average Unique Visitors per Month: unknown
Frequency: 2
Publish Print Anthology: no

Average Percentage of Pages per Category: Fiction 40%, Poetry 60%
Ads: no

Organization: StoryQuarterly

Type: magazine
CLMP member: yes
Primary Editor/Contact Person: M.M.M. Hayes
Address: 431 Sheridan Road
Kenilworth, IL 60043-1220
Web Site Address: http://www.storyquarterly.com
Publishes: fiction and translation
Editorial Focus: High quality literary fiction, no genre. Short-shorts, long stories, all styles and subjects. Look for new insights and ideas
Representative Authors: T.C. Boyle, Steve Almond, and Stephen Dixon
Submissions Policy: Accept manuscripts online only (except authors with no Internet). Go to http://www.storyquarterly.com and click Submissions link.
Simultaneous Submissions: yes
Reading Period: 10/1 to 3/31
Reporting Time: 6 to 12 weeks
Author Payment: copies and submission
Contests: Robie Macauley Award for Fiction; independently judged from fiction already accepted for magazine
See Web site for contest guidelines.
Founded: 1975
Non Profit: yes
Paid Staff: zero
Unpaid Staff: 45
Distributors: Ingram, DeBoer
ISSN Number/ISBN Number: 0361-0144/0-9722444-1-7
Total Circulation: 5,500
Paid Circulation: 2,000
Submission Rate: Individual $10/Institution $10
Single Copy Price: $10
Current Volume/Issue: Issue 39
Frequency per Year: 1
Backfile Available: yes
Unsolicited Ms. Received: yes
% of Unsolicited Ms. Published per Year: 95%
Format: perfect
Size: H 8.25" W 5.5"
Average Pages: 550
Ads: yes
Ad Rates: $300/pg. See web site for details.

Organization: the strange fruit

Type: magazine
CLMP member: yes
Primary Editor/Contact Person: Jessica Star Rockers, Editor
Address: 300 Lenora St., #250
Seattle, WA 98121
Web Site Address: http://www.thestrangefruit.com
Publishes: essays, fiction, nonfiction, and poetry
Editorial Focus: We aim to present poetry and prose that examine personal experiences for their commonly strange synchronicity.
Submissions Policy: Up to six poems or 6,000 words of prose. Include SASE.
Simultaneous Submissions: yes
Reading Period: Year-round
Reporting Time: one to three months
Author Payment: copies
Founded: 2005
Non Profit: no
Paid Staff: zero
Unpaid Staff: four
ISSN Number/ISBN Number: ISSN 1555-550X
Total Circulation: 400
Paid Circulation: 100
Average Print Run: 500
Submission Rate: Individual $11/Institution $10
Single Copy Price: $6
Current Volume/Issue: 2/2
Frequency per Year: biannual
Backfile Available: yes
Unsolicited Ms. Received: yes
% of Unsolicited Ms. Published per Year: 100%
Format: perfect
Size: H 8.5" W 5.5"
Average Pages: 100
Ads: yes
Ad Rates: See web site for details.

Organization: Studio: a Journal of Christians Writing

Type: magazine
CLMP member: no
Primary Editor/Contact Person: Paul Grover
Address: 727 Peel St.
Albury NSW Australia
Albury, NS 2640
Publishes: essays, fiction, nonfiction, poetry, and reviews

Editorial Focus: Studio publishes prose and poetry of literary merit: a venue for previously published, new and aspiring writers.
Representative Authors: Andrew Lansdown, Les Murray, and Warren Breninger
Submissions Policy: Via e-mail or postal service-A4 one side double-spaced. Address and name on each submission. International Reply Coupons.
Simultaneous Submissions: yes
Reading Period: Year-round
Reporting Time: one to three weeks
Author Payment: copies
Contests: Bi-annual Studio Award for poetry and prose. Special Contests for specific themes or events. details in Studio journals.
Founded: 1980
Non Profit: yes
Paid Staff: 0
Unpaid Staff: three
ISSN Number/ISBN Number: ISSN 0729-4042
Total Circulation: 300
Paid Circulation: 250
Average Print Run: 300
Submission Rate: Individual $60 (AUD)/Institution $60 (AUD)
Single Copy Price: $10(AUD)
Current Volume/Issue: Issue 105
Frequency per Year: quarterly
Backfile Available: yes
Unsolicited Ms. Received: yes
% of Unsolicited Ms. Published per Year: 95%
Format: stapled
Size: H 8" W 5"
Average Pages: 36
Ads: yes
Ad Rates: $50 (AUD) half page; $100 (AUD) full page; $50 (AUD) insert

Organization: subTerrain magazine

Type: magazine
CLMP member: no
Primary Editor/Contact Person: Brian Kaufman
Address: P.O. Box 3008, Main Post Office Vancouver, BC V6B3X5
Web Site Address: http://www.subterrain.ca
Publishes: essays, fiction, nonfiction, poetry, reviews, and art
Editorial Focus: "Strong words for a Polite Nation." subTerrain publishes fiction, commentary, poetry, and art from Canada and abroad.
Submissions Policy: No unsolicited poetry. Enclose

reply SASE or postage for ms return. No e-mail submissions. Read mag. first. Sample copy- $5.
Simultaneous Submissions: yes
Reading Period: Year-round
Reporting Time: two to four months
Author Payment: cash and copies
Contests: See web site for contest guidelines.
Founded: 1988
Non Profit: yes
Paid Staff: three
Unpaid Staff: five
ISSN Number/ISBN Number: ISSN 0840-7533
Total Circulation: 3,000
Paid Circulation: 880
Average Print Run: 1,200
Submission Rate: Individual $15/Institution $18
Single Copy Price: $5.95
Current Volume/Issue: 5/43
Frequency per Year: triquarterly
Backfile Available: yes
Unsolicited Ms. Received: yes
% of Unsolicited Ms. Published per Year: 10%
Format: stapled
Size: H 11" W 8.5"
Average Pages: 56
Ads: yes
Ad Rates: $200-$900; b/w and color; see website for details

Organization: Subtropics

Type: magazine
CLMP member: yes
Primary Editor/Contact Person: Mark Mitchell, David Leavitt
Address: P.O. Box 112075 University of Florida Gainesville, FL 32611-2075
Web Site Address: http://www.english.ufl.edu/subtropics
Publishes: essays, fiction, nonfiction, poetry, and translation
Editorial Focus: Some longer pieces, excerpts from longer works, works in translation, important works that are out of print, short shorts.
Recent Awards Received: Stories in BEST AMERICAN STORIES and O. HENRY PRIZE STORIES. Poems in BEST AMERICAN POETRY.
Representative Authors: John Barth, Anne Carson, and Joanna Scott
Submissions Policy: Submit in hard copy to address

above. Submissions accepted August through May. Submissions cannot be returned.

Simultaneous Submissions: of prose only, not poetry
Reading Period: 8/15 to 5/15
Reporting Time: four to six weeks
Author Payment: cash
Founded: 2005
Non Profit: yes
Paid Staff: five
Unpaid Staff: four
Distributors: Ingram, DeBoer, Ubiquity, Media Solutions
ISSN Number/ISBN Number: ISSN 1559-0704
Total Circulation: 3,000
Paid Circulation: 300
Average Print Run: 3,500
Current Volume/Issue: 1/2
Frequency per Year: triquarterly
Backfile Available: yes
Unsolicited Ms. Received: yes
% of Unsolicited Ms. Published per Year: 5%
Format: perfect
Size: H 9" W 6"
Average Pages: 160
Ads: yes
Ad Rates: Contact for trades.

Organization: Sugar Mule

Type: online
CLMP member: no
Primary Editor/Contact Person: M.L. Weber
Address: 2 N. 24th St.
Colorado Springs, CO 80904
Web Site Address: http://www.sugarmule.com
Publishes: essays, fiction, nonfiction, poetry, reviews, art, and translation
Editorial Focus: A literary magazine with eccentric Buddhist leanings, we accept all forms of prose and poetry.
Representative Authors: Andrei Codrescu, Paul Hoover, and Pierre Joris
Submissions Policy: Please check the schedule of upcoming issues (on the second page of the web site) before sending work.
Simultaneous Submissions: yes
Reading Period: Year-round
Reporting Time: one to two weeks
Author Payment: none
Founded: 1990
Non Profit: yes

Paid Staff: zero
Unpaid Staff: two
Average Page Views per Month: 600
Average Unique Visitors per Month: 300
Frequency per Year: triquarterly
Publish Print Anthology: no
Average Percentage of Pages per Category: Fiction 60%, Nonfiction 5%, Poetry 30%, Reviews 2%, Essays 1%, Art 1%, Translation 1%
Ad Rates: negotiable
See web site for details.

Organization: The Summerset Review

Type: online
CLMP member: yes
Primary Editor/Contact Person: Joseph Levens
Address: 25 Summerset Dr.
Smithtown, NY 11787
Web Site Address: http://www.summersetreview.org
Publishes: essays, fiction, nonfiction, and art
Editorial Focus: Contemporary literary fiction and nonfiction
Recent Awards Received: New York Public Library reading series, storySouth Best Online fiction of the Year, recipient of grants from NYSCA.
Submissions Policy: Guidelines are on the site at: http://www.summersetreview.org
Simultaneous Submissions: yes
Reading Period: Year-round
Reporting Time: four to eight weeks
Author Payment: cash
Founded: 2002
Non Profit: yes
Paid Staff: zero
Unpaid Staff: three
Average Page Views per Month: 14,000
Average Unique Visitors per Month: 8000
Frequency per Year: quarterly
Publish Print Anthology: yes
Price: $8
Average Percentage of Pages per Category: Fiction 60%, Nonfiction 10%, Essays 20%, Art 10%
Ads: no

Organization: The Sun

Type: magazine
CLMP member: no
Primary Editor/Contact Person: Sy Safransky, Editor
Address: 107 N. Roberson St.

Chapel Hill, NC 27516
Web Site Address: http://www.thesunmagazine.org
Publishes: essays, fiction, nonfiction, and poetry
Editorial Focus: We tend to favor personal writing, but we're also looking for thoughtful, well-written essays on political, cultural, and philosophical themes. Please, no journalistic features, academic works, or opinion pieces.
Representative Authors: Alison Luterman, Poe Ballantine, and Genie Zeiger
Submissions Policy: Submissions should be typed, double-spaced, and accompanied by a self-addressed, stamped envelope. Your work will not be returned without sufficient postage. Do not send your only copy. Please do not e-mail your submissions to us.
Simultaneous Submissions: yes
Reading Period: Year-round
Reporting Time: four to six months
Author Payment: cash, copies, and submission
Contests: None.
Founded: 1974
Non Profit: yes
Paid Staff: 15
Unpaid Staff: zero
Distributors: Armadillo, Bear Family, Desert Moon, Don Olson
ISSN Number/ISBN Number: ISSN 0744-9666
Total Circulation: 65,000
Paid Circulation: 59,000
Submission Rate: Individual $34/Institution $34
Single Copy Price: $3.95
Current Volume/Issue: Issue 333
Frequency per Year: biannual
Backfile Available: yes
Unsolicited Ms. Received: yes
% of Unsolicited Ms. Published per Year: 1%
Format: stapled
Size: H 11" W 8.5"
Average Pages: 48
Ads: no

Organization: The Sundry: A Journal of the Arts

Type: magazine
CLMP member: no
Primary Editor/Contact Person: Peter L. Riesbeck, Director
Address: 109 Jepson Ave.
St. Clairsville, OH 43950
Web Site Address: http://www.sundryjournal.com

Publishes: essays, fiction, nonfiction, poetry, reviews, and art
Editorial Focus: Open to all genres, especially experimental. Eager to work with new and unpublished writers.
Representative Authors: Donna Vitucci, Nora Beck, and Josh Wallaert
Submissions Policy: Send complete manuscripts to attn: Fiction Editor. Send poetry to attn: Poetry. All other submissions send to attn: Director
Simultaneous Submissions: yes
Reading Period: Year-round
Reporting Time: one to three months
Author Payment: copies
Contests: None Currently
See Web site for contest guidelines.
Founded: 1993
Non Profit: yes
Paid Staff: zero
Unpaid Staff: four
Total Circulation: 500
Paid Circulation: 50
Submission Rate: Individual $11.99/6 mo/Institution same
Single Copy Price: $3.50
Current Volume/Issue: 500/3
Frequency per Year: biannual
Backfile Available: no
Unsolicited Ms. Received: yes
% of Unsolicited Ms. Published per Year: 90%
Format: stapled
Size: H 8.5" W 5.5"
Average Pages: 50
Ads: yes
Ad Rates: See web site for details.

Organization: Suspect Thoughts Press

Type: press
CLMP member: no
Primary Editor/Contact Person: Ian Philips
Address: 2215-R Market St. #544
San Francisco, CA 94114
Web Site Address: www.suspectthoughtspress.com
Publishes: essays, fiction, nonfiction, and poetry
Editorial Focus: Contemporary authors and poets exploring provocativesocial, political, spiritual, queer, and sexual themes.
Recent Awards Received: Four Lambda Literary Award Winners, four Lambda Finalists, an Ashe Book

Award Finalist, a Stonewall Book Award Honor Book. Representative Authors: Kevin Killian, Dodie Bellamy, and Stephen Beachy
Submissions Policy: Email queries should contain a detailed synopsis, a short excerpt, and an author biography, all within the body of an email.
Simultaneous Submissions: yes
Reading Period: year-round
Reporting Time: two to six months
Author Payment: royalties, cash, and copies
Contests: The Project: QueerLit contest celebrates and brings media attention to unpublished authors of queer writing.
See web site for contest guidelines
Founded: 2001
Non Profit: no
Paid Staff: three
Unpaid Staff: one to three
Distributors: SCB Distributors
Wholesalers: Ingram, Baker & Taylor, etc.
ISSN Number/ISBN Number: ISBN 0-9771582
Number of Books Published per year: 10
Titles in Print: 28
Average Print Run: 3,000
Average Percentage Printed: paperback 100%
Average Price: $16.95

Organization: Swan Scythe Press

Type: press
CLMP member: no
Primary Editor/Contact Person: Sandra McPherson
Address: 2052 Calaveras Ave.
Davis, CA 95616-3021
Web Site Address: http://www.swanscythe.com
Publishes: poetry
Editorial Focus: Poetry chapbooks; multi-ethnic; primarily emerging authors.
Representative Authors: Emmy Perez, John Olivares Espinoza, and Pos Moua
Submissions Policy: We are "resting" and no longer have our annual contest. We cannot read submissions now or in the foreseeable future.
Simultaneous Submissions: yes
Author Payment: cash and copies
Contests: See web site for contest guidelines.
Founded: 1999
Non Profit: no
Paid Staff: zero
Unpaid Staff: three
Distributors: ourselves and Small Press Distribution

Wholesalers: ourselves
ISSN Number/ISBN Number: ISBN 1-930454-
Number of Books Published per Year: four
Titles in Print: 25
Average Print Run: 500
Average Percentage Printed: Paperback 100%
Average Price: $10-14

Organization: Swerve

Type: magazine
CLMP member: no
Primary Editor/Contact Person: Fred Schmalz
Address: 1405 8th Ave. #4D
Brooklyn, NY 11215
Web Site Address: http://www.swervemag.com
Publishes: poetry
Editorial Focus: swerve is a little magazine of contemporary poetry and art. Issues are hand-made in small editions (125-150 copies).
Representative Authors: Samantha Hunt, G.E. Patterson, and Ted Mathys
Submissions Policy: Swerve does not accept submissions. writing and artwork are solicited. See web site.
Simultaneous Submissions: no
Reading Period: Year-round
Reporting Time: 1 to 4 months
Author Payment: copies
Founded: 1999
Non Profit: yes
Paid Staff: zero
Unpaid Staff: two
Total Circulation: 145
Paid Circulation: 100
Average Print Run: 150
Submission Rate: Individual $30/Institution $30
Current Volume/Issue: Issue 15
Frequency per Year: biannual
Backfile Available: no
Unsolicited Ms. Received: no
Format: hand-bound, each issue different
Average Pages: 40
Ads: no

Organization: Swink

Type: magazine
CLMP member: yes
Primary Editor/Contact Person: Leelila Strogov
Address: 244 5th Ave. #2722

New York, NY 10001
Web Site Address: http://www.swinkmag.com
Publishes: essays, fiction, nonfiction, poetry, art, and translation
Editorial Focus: Swink publishes the highest caliber fiction, essays and poetry from established and emerging writers.
Submissions Policy: Prose should be mailed to the address above. Poetry should be sent to 5042 Wilshire Blvd. #628, Los Angeles, CA 90036.
Simultaneous Submissions: yes
Reading Period: Year-round
Reporting Time: one to four months
Author Payment: cash and copies
Contests: See web site for contest guidelines.
Founded: 2003
Non Profit: yes
Paid Staff: zero
Unpaid Staff: 14
Distributors: Ingram, DeBoer, Armadillo, Doormouse
Total Circulation: 4,000
Paid Circulation: 1,500
Average Print Run: 4,500
Submission Rate: Individual $16/Institution $16
Single Copy Price: $10
Current Volume/Issue: Issue 3
Frequency per Year: 2
Backfile Available: yes
Unsolicited Ms. Received: yes
% of Unsolicited Ms. Published per Year: .5%
Format: perfect
Size: H 9" W 7"
Average Pages: 224
Ads: yes
Ad Rates: Full page: $400

Organization: Switchback Books

Type: press
CLMP member: yes
Primary Editor/Contact Person: Brandi Homan
Address: PO Box 478868
Chicago, IL 60647
Website Address: www.switchbackbooks.com
Publishes: poetry
Editorial Focus: Switchback Books is a feminist press publishing poetry by women. Editorial preference varies, but tends toward experimental.
Representative Authors: Monica de la Torre, Caroline Noble Whitbeck, and Peggy Munson
Submissions Policy: Switchback Books does not cur-

rently accept unsolicited manuscripts outside of our annual contest, The Gatewood Prize.
Simultaneous Submissions: yes
Reading Period: year-round
Reporting Time: 0 to 4 months
Author Payment: royalties, cash, and copies
Contests: The Gatewood Prize for first full-length collection of poems by a woman writing in English between the ages of 18 and 39.
Founded: 2006
Non Profit: no
Paid Staff: 0
Unpaid Staff: 8
Distributors: Small Press Distribution
Number of Books Published per Year: 2
Titles in Print: 1
Average Print Run: 1,000
Average Percentage Printed: Paperback 100%
Average Price: $14.00

Organization: Sycamore Review

Type: magazine
CLMP member: yes
Primary Editor/Contact Person: Mehdi Okasi
Address: Purdue University, Dept. of English
500 Oval Dr.
West Lafayette, IN 47907
Web Site Address: http://www.sycamorereview.com
Publishes: fiction, nonfiction, poetry, reviews, art, and translation
Editorial Focus: The highest quality work.
Representative Authors: Lucia Perillo, Susannah Breslin, and Denise Duhamel
Submissions Policy: No electronic submissions.
Simultaneous Submissions: yes
Reading Period: 8/1 to 3/31
Reporting Time: two to three months
Author Payment: copies
Contests: Wabash Prize for Poetry. Please visit web site for more information.
Founded: 1988
Non Profit: yes
Paid Staff: two
Unpaid Staff: seven
Distributors: Ingram
ISSN Number/ISBN Number: ISSN 1043-1497
Total Circulation: 1000
Paid Circulation: 50
Average Print Run: 1000
Submission Rate: Individual $12/Institution $12

Single Copy Price: $7
Current Volume/Issue: 19/2
Frequency per Year: biannual
Backfile Available: yes
Unsolicited Ms. Received: yes
% of Unsolicited Ms. Published per Year: 5%
Format: perfect
Size: H 9" W 5.5"
Average Pages: 100
Ads: yes
Ad Rates: See web site for details.

Organization: Tacenda

Type: magazine
CLMP member: yes
Primary Editor/Contact Person: Penny Lynn Dunn, Editor
Address: P.O. Box 1205
Port Angeles, WA 98362
Publishes: essays, fiction, nonfiction, poetry, reviews, art, and translation
Editorial Focus: Special interest in environmental and political themes. "Arts for the Environment! Environment for the Arts!"
Representative Authors: Robert Cooperman, Simon Perchik, and Leonard J. Cirino
Submissions Policy: SASE Required. Snail-mail submissions preferred. No gratuitous profanity, please. Name/address on each page. Three to five poems.
Simultaneous Submissions: yes
Reading Period: 9/1 to 5/31
Reporting Time: two to four months
Author Payment: copies and submission
Founded: 1989
Non Profit: no
Paid Staff: zero
Unpaid Staff: four to six
Distributors: Pending
Wholesalers: Pending (Member IPA)
ISSN Number/ISBN Number: ISSN 1059-8553
Total Circulation: 1,000
Paid Circulation: 25
Submission Rate: Individual $20/Institution $22
Single Copy Price: $7
Current Volume/Issue: VII/II
Frequency per Year: quarterly
Backfile Available: yes
Unsolicited Ms. Received: yes
% of Unsolicited Ms. Published per Year: 80%
Format: Stapled and perfect-depends

Size: H 11" W 8"
Average Pages: 64
Ads: yes
Ad Rates: E-mail for rates.

Organization: Talon Books Ltd.

Type: press
CLMP member: no
Primary Editor/Contact Person: Sarah Warren
Address: P.O. Box 2076
Vancouver, BC V6B 3S3
Web Site Address: http://www.talonbooks.com
Publishes: fiction, nonfiction, poetry, drama, and translation
Editorial Focus: Talonbooks is dedicated to the publication of premier Canadian literature that engages in key social and political issues.
Recent Awards Received: The George Ryga Award for Social Awareness in BC Literature for In Plain Sight
Representative Authors: Michel Tremblay, Bill Bissett, and Morris Panych
Submissions Policy: No unsolicited poetry. Drama must first be professionally produced. Literary fiction and nonfiction. See talonbooks.com.
Simultaneous Submissions: no
Reading Period: Year-round
Reporting Time: six to twelve months
Author Payment: royalties
Founded: 1967
Non Profit: no
Paid Staff: four
Unpaid Staff: one
Distributors: PGC in Canada, Northwestern University Press in US
ISSN Number/ISBN Number: ISSN 0-88922-
Number of Books Published per Year: 20
Titles in Print: 368
Average Print Run: N/A
Average Percentage Printed: Hardcover 1%, Paperback 99%

Organization: Tameme Chapbooks -- Cuadernos

Type: press
CLMP member: yes
Primary Editor/Contact Person: C.M. Mayo
Address: 300 Third Street
Suite 9
Los Altos, CA 94022

Website Address: www.tameme.org
Publishes: essays, fiction, poetry, and translation
Editorial Focus: Bilingual (English/Spanish) chapbooks featuring new writing and translation from North America--Canada, the US and Mexico.
Representative Authors: Agustin Cadena, Jorge Fernandez Granados, and John Oliver Simon
Submissions Policy: Please see submissions guidelines on www.tameme.org We do not accept manuscripts except during specified reading periods.
Simultaneous Submissions: yes
Reporting Time: 1 to 25 weeks
Author Payment: cash and copies
Founded: 1998
Non Profit: yes
Paid Staff: 0
Unpaid Staff: 3
Distributors: Tameme, Inc.
ISSN Number/ISBN Number: ISBN 9780967049351
Number of Books Published per Year: 1
Titles in Print: 5
Average Print Run: 1,000
Average Percentage Printed: Paperback 20%, Chapbook 80%
Average Price: $7

Organization: Tampa Review

Type: magazine
CLMP member: yes
Primary Editor/Contact Person: Richard Mathews, Editor
Address: University of Tampa Press
401 W. Kennedy Blvd.
Tampa, FL 33606-1490
Web Site Address: http://tampareview.ut.edu
Publishes: essays, fiction, nonfiction, poetry, art, and translation
Editorial Focus: Dedicated to the integration of contemporary literature and visual arts featuring work from Florida and the world.
Representative Authors: Peter Meinke, Samrat Upadhyah, and Derek Walcott
Submissions Policy: Please send previously unpublished work accompanied by SASE. No e-mail submissions at this time. See guidelines on the web site
Simultaneous Submissions: no
Reading Period: 9/1 to 12/31
Reporting Time: two to six months
Author Payment: cash and copies
Contests: See Web site for contest guidelines.

Founded: 1988
Non Profit: yes
Paid Staff: one
Unpaid Staff: five
ISSN Number/ISBN Number: 0896-064X/1-879852-
Total Circulation: 700
Paid Circulation: 225
Average Print Run: 800
Submission Rate: Individual $15/Institution $15
Single Copy Price: $9.95
Current Volume/Issue: Issue 28
Frequency per Year: biannual
Backfile Available: yes
Unsolicited Ms. Received: yes
Format: Hardcover with color dust jacket
Size: H 10 1/2" W 7 1/2"
Average Pages: 80
Ads: no

Organization: TamTam Books

Type: press
CLMP member: no
Primary Editor/Contact Person: Tosh Berman
Address: 2601 Waverly Dr.
Los Angeles, CA 90039-2724
Web Site Address: http://www.tamtambooks.com
Publishes: essays, fiction, nonfiction, and translation
Editorial Focus: Focus on French literature from 1946 to 1980s. Specifically the works of Boris Vian.
Representative Authors: Boris Vian, Serge Gainsbourg, and Guy Debord
Submissions Policy: If you are a translator interested in the above three authors, you may write to me.
Simultaneous Submissions: yes
Reading Period: Year-round
Reporting Time: two to six months
Author Payment: cash and copies
Founded: 1998
Non Profit: no
Paid Staff: no
Unpaid Staff: yes
Distributors: SPD, AK Distribution, Marginal
Wholesalers: Ingram
Number of Books Published per Year: two
Titles in Print: four
Average Percentage Printed: Paperback 100%

Organization: Tantalum

Type: magazine

CLMP member: yes
Primary Editor/Contact Person: Yasmine Alwan
Address: 452 Park Place, 3F
Brooklyn, NY 11238
Website Address: www.tantalumjournal.org
Publishes: fiction
Editorial Focus: We publish prose that redefines the fictive--hybrid work that does not take its identity for granted.
Representative Authors: Carla Harryman, Camille Roy, and Leslie Scalapino
Submissions Policy: Please send by mail. Please include a SASE or email address.
Simultaneous Submissions: yes
Reading Period: year-round
Reporting Time: 3 to 4 months
Author Payment: copies
Founded: 2006
Non Profit: yes
Paid Staff: 0
Unpaid Staff: 3
ISSN Number/ISBN Number: ISSN 1938-6001
Total Circulation: 400
Paid Circulation: n/a
Average Print Run: varies
Subscription Rate: Individual $5/Institution $5
Single Copy Price: $6
Current Volume/Issue: Issue 2
Frequency: 1
Backfile Available: yes
Unsolicited Ms. Received: yes
Format: stapled
Average Pages: 72
Ads: no

Organization: Tar River Poetry

Type: magazine
CLMP member: yes
Primary Editor/Contact Person: Peter Mackuk
Address: Department of English
East Carolina University
Greenville, NC 27834
Web Site Address: http://www.ecu.edu/english.journals
Publishes: poetry and reviews
Editorial Focus: No haiku. Narrative and short image poems, open or closed forms. We publish both newcomers and established poets.
Representative Authors: Gary Jacobik, Louis Simpson, and Henry Taylor

Submissions Policy: four to five poems per submission.
Simultaneous Submissions: no
Reading Period: 9/1 to 4/30
Reporting Time: four to seven weeks
Author Payment: copies
Contests: no
Founded: 1965
Non Profit: yes
Paid Staff: two
Unpaid Staff: two
Wholesalers: Sold in a number of North Carolina stores.
ISSN Number/ISBN Number: ISSN 0740-9141
Total Circulation: 650
Paid Circulation: 240
Submission Rate: Individual $12/Institution $8
Single Copy Price: $6
Current Volume/Issue: 43/2
Frequency per Year: biannual
Backfile Available: yes
Unsolicited Ms. Received: yes
Format: stapled
Size: H 9" W 6"
Average Pages: 64
Ads: yes
Ad Rates: exchange

Organization: Tarpaulin Sky Press

Type: press
CLMP member: yes
Primary Editor/Contact Person: Christian Peet
Address: PO Box 155
Townshend, VT 05353
Website Address: www.tarpaulinsky.com
Publishes: essays, fiction, nonfiction, poetry, and translation
Editorial Focus: Cross-/trans-genre work and innovative poetry and prose; full-length books and chapbooks; handbound and perfectbound editons.
Representative Authors: Jenny Boully, Danielle Dutton, and Joyelle McSweeney
Submissions Policy: We read manuscripts from contributors to our journal and also have open readings.
Simultaneous Submissions: yes
Reading Period: year-round
Reporting Time: 1 to 4 months
Author Payment: royalties and copies
Contests: In the works; see website for guidelines
Founded: 2006

Non Profit: no
Paid Staff: 0
Unpaid Staff: 9
Distributors: Small Press Distribution
Wholesalers: Ingram, Baker & Taylor, et al
Number of Books Published per Year: 6
Titles in Print: 8
Average Print Run: 600
Average Percentage Printed: Hardcover 10%, Paperback 60%, Chapbook 30%
Average Price: $12

Organization: Tarpaulin Sky

Type: online
CLMP member: yes
Primary Editor/Contact Person: Various Editors.
Address: PO Box 155
Townshend, VT 05353
Website Address: www.tarpaulinsky.com
Publishes: fiction, poetry, reviews, art, and translation
Editorial Focus: Cross-/trans-genre work (hybrid forms) as well as innovative poetry and prose.
Representative Authors: Jenny Boully, Danielle Dutton, and Joyelle McSweeney
Submissions Policy: Please see guidelines on the website. Contributors are invited to submit book-length manuscripts to Tarpaulin Sky Press.
Simultaneous Submissions: yes
Reading Period: year-round
Reporting Time: 1 to 4 months
Author Payment: none
Founded: 2002
Non Profit: no
Paid Staff: 0
Unpaid Staff: 9
Average Page Views per Month: 60,000
Average Unique Visitors per Month: 12,000
Frequency: 3
Publish Print Anthology: no
Average Percentage of Pages per Category: Fiction 30%, Poetry 40%, Reviews 10%, Art 15%, Translation 5%
Ads: no

Organization: Tarragon Books

Type: press
CLMP member: yes
Primary Editor/Contact Person: Sara Stamey
Address: 1424 E. Maplewood Ave.

Bellingham, WA 98225
Website Address: www.tarragonbooks.com
Publishes: fiction
Editorial Focus: We support Pacific Northwest writers of "fusion fiction" challenging boundaries of genre & delineations of reality.
Recent Awards Received: AWP panelist for "6 New Northwest Presses" & featured in "Poets & Writers" Magazine.
Representative Authors: Richard Widerkehr and Sara Stamey
Submissions Policy: Northwest novelists please see our website and query by email or mail with intro letter & brief novel description/synopsis.
Simultaneous Submissions: yes
Reading Period: year-round
Reporting Time: 1 to 2 months
Author Payment: royalties
Founded: 2003
Non Profit: no
Paid Staff: 1
Unpaid Staff: 1
Wholesalers: Baker & Taylor
ISSN Number/ISBN Number: ISBN 0-9724986
Number of Books Published per Year: 0-1
Titles in Print: 2
Average Print Run: 2,000
Average Percentage Printed: Paperback 100%
Average Price: $13.95

Organization: TCG Books

Type: press
CLMP member: yes
Primary Editor/Contact Person: Terry Nemeth, Publisher
Address: Theatre Communications Group
520 Eighth Ave. 24th Floor
New York, NY 10018-4156
Web Site Address: http://www.tcg.org/
Publishes: essays and fiction
Editorial Focus: Plays, translations, theatre resource books
Recent Awards Received: Recent publication "Doubt" by John Patrick Shanley received 2005 Pulitzer Prize for Drama
Representative Authors: Tony Kushner, Suzan-Lori Parks, and Eric Bogosian
Simultaneous Submissions: yes
Reading Period: Year-round
Reporting Time: one to two months

Author Payment: royalties
Founded: 1961
Non Profit: yes
Paid Staff: 50
Unpaid Staff: zero
Distributors: Consortium Books Sales and Distribution
Number of Books Published per Year: 16
Titles in Print: 200
Average Print Run: 4,000
Average Percentage Printed: Paperback 100%
Average Price: $14.95

Organization: The Teacher's Voice

Type: online
CLMP member: yes
Primary Editor/Contact Person: Andres Castro
Address: P.O. Box 150384
Kew Gardens
New York, NY 1115
Website Address: www.the-teachers-voice.org
Publishes: fiction, nonfiction, poetry, and translation
Editorial Focus: We seek to establish a progressive dialogue within the pages of our little literary journal that reckons with a broad range of aesthetics and also demands serious consideration from any thinking person that cares about education, the human condition, and the power of language; this means our first priority is to create a new space for teachers, but we are not exclusionary: teachers or administrators, students or parents, radicals or conservatives, if you care about the development of American education and are willing to step up--now is the time to write it all down and gain an audience--please give us a try.
Representative Authors: Sapphire, Hal Horowitz, and Edward Francisco
Submissions Policy: We consider unpublished and previously published poems, short short stories, and creative nonfiction--including simultaneous submissions. Send up to 5 pages of poetry or prose pieces under 2000 words. A cover letter is not necessary, but appreciated. Are you a teacher, administrator, parent, student, librarian, custodian, coach, security officer, etc? We do not accept responsibility for submissions or queries not accompanied by a SASE with adequate postage.
Simultaneous Submissions: yes
Reading Period: year-round
Reporting Time: 6 to 12 months
Author Payment: copies
Founded: 2004

Non Profit: yes
Paid Staff: 0
Unpaid Staff: 3
ISSN Number/ISBN Number: ISSN 1556-6161
Average Page Views per Month: 5,800
Average Unique Visitors per Month: 420
Frequency: 2
Publish Print Anthology: yes
Price: to be announced
Average Percentage of Pages per Category: Fiction 15%, Poetry 70%, Essays 15%
Ads: no

Organization: Tebot Bach, Inc

Type: press
CLMP member: yes
Primary Editor/Contact Person: Mifanwy Kaiser
Address: Box 7887
Huntington Beach, CA 92615-7887
Web Site Address: http://www.tebotbach.org
Publishes: poetry
Editorial Focus: to provide national and international poets a venue to publish their poetry
Representative Authors: Robin S. Chapman, Richard Jones, and M. L. Liebler
Submissions Policy: Query first for full length books See Spillway for submission policy for the magazine
Simultaneous Submissions: yes
Reading Period: Year-round
Reporting Time: one to four months
Author Payment: copies
Founded: 1993
Non Profit: yes
Paid Staff: zero
Unpaid Staff: three
Distributors: Ingram, Small Press, Armadillo, DeBoer
Number of Books Published per Year: 3
Titles in Print: twelve
Average Print Run: 1,000
Average Percentage Printed: Paperback 100%
Average Price: $13

Organization: Templar Poetry

Type: press
CLMP member: no
Primary Editor/Contact Person: Alex McMillen
Address: Fenelon House
Matlock, De de4 3nb
Website Address: www.templarpoetry.co.uk

Publishes: poetry and audio
Editorial Focus: New contemporary poetry and emerging New poets
Representative Authors: Jane Weir
Submissions Policy: No unsolicited manuscripts. Annual Open Pamhlet Competition, winners invited to submit collections.
Simultaneous Submissions: no
Reading Period: year-round
Reporting Time: 1 to 3 months
Author Payment: royalties, cash, and copies
Contests: Annual Open Pamphlet & Collection Competition; see website for guidelines
Founded: 2005
Non Profit: no
Paid Staff: 3
Unpaid Staff: 3
Distributors: Own, Inpress Books
Wholesalers: Gardners & Central
ISSN Number/ISBN Number: ISBN 0-9550023
Number of Books Published per Year: 6-9
Titles in Print: 2
Average Print Run: 2,500
Average Percentage Printed: Hardcover 50%, Paperback 50%
Average Price: $14

Organization: Ten Penny Players

Type: press
CLMP member: yes
Primary Editor/Contact Person: Richard Spiegel/Barbara Fisher
Address: 393 Saint Pauls Ave.
Staten Island, NY 10304-2127
Web Site Address: http://www.tenpennyplayers.org
Publishes: essays, fiction, nonfiction, poetry, and art
Editorial Focus: Ten Penny Players publishes child, young adult and adult artists in print and online at our web site.
Recent Awards Received: For Arts in Ed work: NYS Council on the Arts & NYC Dept. of Cultural Affairs funding support
Representative Authors: Ida Fasel, James Penha, and Robert Cooperman
Submissions Policy: TPP, the press, only accepts submissions from students; adults are by invitation only. Adults submit to Waterways magazine.
Simultaneous Submissions: yes
Reading Period: Year-round
Reporting Time: one to four weeks

Author Payment: none and copies
Founded: 1967
Non Profit: yes
Paid Staff: three
Unpaid Staff: zero
ISSN Number/ISBN Number: 0197-4777/0-934830
Number of Books Published per Year: 70
Titles in Print: 500
Average Percentage Printed: Paperback 2%, Chapbook 98%

Organization: Tender Buttons press

Type: press
CLMP member: no
Primary Editor/Contact Person: Lee Ann Brown
Address: P.O. Box 13, Cooper Station
New York, NY 10276
Publishes: poetry
Editorial Focus: Experimental poetry by women under the vast sign of Stein
Representative Authors: Bernadette Mayer, Harryette Mullen, and Jennifer Moxley
Submissions Policy: we usually don't take unsolicited manuscripts-send letter of inquiry with short sample.
Simultaneous Submissions: yes
Reading Period: 6/1 to 9/1
Reporting Time: one to three months
Author Payment: copies
Contests: none
Founded: 1989
Non Profit: yes
Paid Staff: zero
Unpaid Staff: three
Distributors: SPD
Number of Books Published per Year: one to two
Titles in Print: five
Average Percentage Printed: Paperback 90%, Chapbook 10%

Organization: Terminus: A Magazine of the Arts

Type: magazine
CLMP member: no
Primary Editor/Contact Person: Travis Denton or Katie Chaple
Address: 1034 Hill St.
Atlanta, GA 30315
Web Site Address:

http://www.terminusmagazine.com
Publishes: essays, fiction, nonfiction, poetry, reviews, art, translation, and audio
Editorial Focus: Writing that pushes boundaries but endures-not trendy for its own sake. Accessible. Metaphoric over metonymic.
Representative Authors: Denise Duhamel, Louis Jenkins, and Christopher Buckley
Submissions Policy: Short and sweet is better than long and self-congratulatory for cover letters. Need more great fiction and nonfiction.
Simultaneous Submissions: yes
Reading Period: 8/1 to 4/30
Reporting Time: one to four months
Author Payment: copies
Contests: See web site for contest guidelines.
Founded: 2001
Non Profit: yes
Paid Staff: no
Unpaid Staff: yes
Distributors: Desert Moon Periodicals and DeBoer
ISSN Number/ISBN Number: ISSN 1540-1871
Total Circulation: 1,000
Paid Circulation: 100
Submission Rate: Individual $18/Institution $28
Single Copy Price: $9
Current Volume/Issue: Issue 4/5
Frequency per Year: biannual
Backfile Available: yes
Unsolicited Ms. Received: yes
% of Unsolicited Ms. Published per Year: 70%
Format: perfect
Size: H 6.75" W 9.75"
Average Pages: 200
Ads: yes
Ad Rates: $50/half page, $100/full page, negotiates ad-exchanges
See web site for details.

Organization: Terra Incognita

Type: magazine
CLMP member: yes
Primary Editor/Contact Person: Alexandra van de Kamp
Address: P.O. Box 150585
Brooklyn, NY 11215-0585
Web Site Address: http://www.terra-incognita.com
Publishes: essays, fiction, nonfiction, poetry, art, translation, and audio
Editorial Focus: Terra Incognita is an international lit-erary and cultural journal published in English and Spanish.
Representative Authors: Jose Saramago, Billy Collins, and Ray Gonzalez
Submissions Policy: Fiction to 5,000 words. Nonfiction to 3,000 words. No poetry in English. Poetry in Spanish okay. See web site for more info.
Simultaneous Submissions: yes
Reading Period: 9/1 to 5/1
Reporting Time: two to three months
Author Payment: copies
Founded: 1998
Non Profit: yes
Paid Staff: zero
Unpaid Staff: 10
Total Circulation: 900
Paid Circulation: 100
Average Print Run: 1,000
Submission Rate: Individual $9/$17/Institution $9/$17
Single Copy Price: $7.5
Current Volume/Issue: Issue six
Frequency per Year: annual
Backfile Available: yes
Unsolicited Ms. Received: yes
% of Unsolicited Ms. Published per Year: 2%
Format: perfect
Size: H 11.69" W 8.27"
Average Pages: 84
Ads: yes
Ad Rates: See web site for details.

Organization: Terra Nova

Type: press
CLMP member: no
Primary Editor/Contact Person: Wandee Pryor/Managing Editor
Address: New Jersey Institute of Technology Humanities Dept. NJIT
Newark, NY 07102
Web Site Address: http://www.terranovabooks.org
Publishes: essays, fiction, nonfiction, poetry, and art
Editorial Focus: Terra Nova anthologies encourage innovative writing and art on nature and culture, pre-sented in a serious and engaging way.
Representative Authors: Ellen Dissanayake, Edie Meidav, and John O'Grady
Submissions Policy: Visit Terra Nova's web-site for current information on submission deadlines and themes.

Simultaneous Submissions: no
Reading Period: Year-round
Reporting Time: up to 6 months
Author Payment: copies
Founded: 1996
Non Profit: yes
Paid Staff: two
Unpaid Staff: zero
Distributors: MIT Press
ISSN Number/ISBN Number: 0-262-18230-0/0-262-68136-6
Number of Books Published per Year: 1
Titles in Print: 6
Average Percentage Printed: Hardcover 60%, Paperback 40%

Organization: THEMA Literary Society

Type: magazine
CLMP member: yes
Primary Editor/Contact Person: Virginia Howard
Address: Box 8747
Metairie, LA 70011-8747
Web Site Address: http://members.cox.net/thema
Publishes: essays, fiction, nonfiction, poetry, and art
Editorial Focus: Each issue revolves around an unusual theme We're looking for the most original, clever interpretations of the theme.
Representative Authors: Linda Berry, Lolette Kuby, and Dan Stryk .
Submissions Policy: We do not accept electronic submissions. Submission for which no THEMA theme has been indicated will not be considered.
Simultaneous Submissions: yes
Reading Period: Year-round
Reporting Time: three to four months
Author Payment: cash and copies
Founded: 1988
Non Profit: yes
Paid Staff: zero
Unpaid Staff: 12
Distributors: EBSCO
ISSN Number/ISBN Number: ISSN 1041-4851
Total Circulation: 350
Paid Circulation: 220
Average Print Run: 500
Submission Rate: Individual $20/Institution $20
Single Copy Price: $10
Current Volume/Issue: 19/2
Frequency per Year: triquarterly
Backfile Available: yes

Unsolicited Ms. Received: yes
% of Unsolicited Ms. Published per Year: 100%
Format: perfect
Size: H 8.5" W 5.5"
Average Pages: 150
Ads: no

Organization: Theytus Books Ltd.

Type: press
CLMP member: no
Primary Editor/Contact Person: Anita Large-Publisher
Address: Green Mountain Rd. Lot 45
Penticton, BC V2A 6J7
Web Site Address: www.theytusbooks.ca
Publishes: fiction, nonfiction, poetry, and art
Editorial Focus: Canadian Aboriginal Authors
Representative Authors: Jeannette Armstrong, Larry Loyie, and Lee Maracle
Submissions Policy: Please view web site at www.theytusbooks.ca/sguide.asp
Simultaneous Submissions: no
Reading Period: year-round
Reporting Time: six to eight months
Author Payment: royalties
Contests: Not Yet
Founded: 1980
Non Profit: no
Paid Staff: two
Unpaid Staff: zero
Distributors: Sandhill, UTP and Orca Books
Wholesalers: None
Number of Books Published per year: four
Titles in Print: 61
Average Print Run: 1,000
Average Percentage Printed: paperback 100%
Average Price: $20

Organization: Third Coast

Type: magazine
CLMP member: yes
Primary Editor/Contact Person: Peter Geye
Address: Dept. of English, Western Michigan Univ.
Sprau Tower
Kalamazoo, MI 49008
Web Site Address: http://www.wmich.edu/thirdcoast
Publishes: essays, fiction, nonfiction, poetry, reviews, and translation
Editorial Focus: Established and emerging writers'

superior work. Recent anthologization: Best American Poetry, Pushcart fiction, elsewhere

Representative Authors: Trudy Lewis, John McNally, and Marvin Bell

Submissions Policy: Prose: We accept up to 9,000 words/30 pgs. For more info regarding all genres, please see our web site.

Simultaneous Submissions: yes

Reading Period: Year-round

Reporting Time: one to six months

Author Payment: copies and submission

Contests: 1st place: $1,000.
See web site for contest guidelines.

Founded: 1995

Non Profit: yes

Paid Staff: one

Unpaid Staff: 15

Distributors: Ingram

ISSN Number/ISBN Number: ISSN 1520-8206

Total Circulation: 2,775

Paid Circulation: 1,000

Average Print Run: 3,500

Submission Rate: Individual $14/Institution $14

Single Copy Price: $8

Current Volume/Issue: Issue 21

Frequency per Year: biannual

Backfile Available: yes

Unsolicited Ms. Received: yes

% of Unsolicited Ms. Published per Year: 1%

Format: perfect

Size: H 9" W 6"

Average Pages: 192

Ads: no

Organization: This Magazine

Type: magazine

CLMP member: no

Primary Editor/Contact Person: Lisa Whittington-Hill

Address: 396-401 Richmond St. W
Toronto, ON M5V 3A8

Web Site Address: http://www.thismagazine.ca

Publishes: essays, fiction, nonfiction, poetry, reviews, and art

Editorial Focus: This Magazine is Canada's leading independent magazine of politics, pop culture, and the arts.

Representative Authors: Clive Thompson, Gordon Laird, and Alex Roslin

Submissions Policy: Submissions by query only. We do not accept unsolicited fiction or poetry. Guidelines

are available at http://www.thismagazine.ca

Simultaneous Submissions: no

Reading Period: Year-round

Reporting Time: 8 to 12 weeks

Author Payment: cash and copies

Contests: See web site for contest guidelines.

Founded: 1966

Non Profit: yes

Paid Staff: two

Unpaid Staff: 10

Distributors: CMPA, Disticor

ISSN Number/ISBN Number: ISSN 1491-2678

Total Circulation: 5,000

Paid Circulation: 3,500

Average Print Run: 7,500

Submission Rate: Individual $25/Institution $37

Single Copy Price: $5

Current Volume/Issue: 39/2

Frequency per Year: bimonthly

Backfile Available: yes

Unsolicited Ms. Received: no

Format: stapled

Size: H 8.5" W 11"

Average Pages: 48

Ads: yes

Ad Rates: See web site for details.

Organization: Three Candles Press

Type: press

CLMP member: no

Primary Editor/Contact Person: Steve Mueske

Address: PO Box 1817
Burnsville, MN 55378

Website Address: threecandlespress.com

Publishes: poetry

Editorial Focus: Fine contemporary American poetry.

Representative Authors: Tony Trigilio and RJ McCaffery

Submissions Policy: For contests, read submission details on "contests" link. Non-contest reading periods are posted during downtimes.

Simultaneous Submissions: yes

Reading Period: year-round

Reporting Time: 3 to 6 months

Author Payment: royalties and cash

Contests: Alternate years with a First Book Contest and Open Book Contest, each judged by a national poet.

Founded: 2005

Non Profit: no

Paid Staff: 1
Unpaid Staff: 0
Distributors: Ingram
Number of Books Published per Year: 2-3
Titles in Print: 3
Average Print Run: POD
Average Percentage Printed: Paperback 100%
Average Price: $12.95

Organization: The Threepenny Review

Type: magazine
CLMP member: no
Primary Editor/Contact Person: Wendy Lesser
Address: P.O. Box 9131
Berkeley, CA 94709
Web Site Address: http://www.threepennyreview.com
Publishes: essays, fiction, nonfiction, poetry, reviews, art, and translation
Editorial Focus: Essays on literature, theater, film, television, music, dance, and visual arts as well as new poetry and original fiction.
Representative Authors: Anne Carson, David Mamet, and Javier Marias
Submissions Policy: Please check submissions guidelines and sample articles on our web site before sending work. Always include SASE.
Simultaneous Submissions: no
Reading Period: 1/1 to 8/31
Reporting Time: three to twelve weeks
Author Payment: cash and subscription
Founded: 1980
Non Profit: yes
Paid Staff: three
Unpaid Staff: zero
Distributors: Ingram; Ubiquity
ISSN Number/ISBN Number: ISSN 0275-1410
Total Circulation: 10,000
Average Print Run: 10,000
Submission Rate: Individual $25/Institution $22
Single Copy Price: $12
Current Volume/Issue: XXVI/3
Frequency per Year: quarterly
Backfile Available: yes
Unsolicited Ms. Received: yes
% of Unsolicited Ms. Published per Year: 1%
Format: tabloid
Average Pages: 32
Ads: yes
Ad Rates: See web site for details.

Organization: Tia Chucha Press

Type: press
CLMP member: yes
Primary Editor/Contact Person: Luis Rodriguez
Address: 12737 Glenoaks Blvd.
No. 20
Sylmar, CA 91342
Web Site Address: http://www.tiachucha.com
Publishes: poetry
Editorial Focus: Exclusively poetry, first books, writers of color, women writers
Representative Authors: A. Van Jordan, Angela Shannon, and Elizabeth Alexander
Submissions Policy: Please submit three to five poems that are the best examples of your work along with a letter of introduction.
Simultaneous Submissions: yes
Reading Period: Year-round
Reporting Time: four to 12 months
Author Payment: royalties
Founded: 1989
Non Profit: yes
Paid Staff: zero
Unpaid Staff: zero
Distributors: Northwestern University Press
ISSN Number/ISBN Number: ISBN 1-882688
Number of Books Published per Year: two to four
Titles in Print: 40
Average Percentage Printed: Paperback 90%, Chapbook 10%

Organization: Tiferet: A Journal of Spiritual Literature

Type: magazine
CLMP member: yes
Primary Editor/Contact Person: Cynthia Brown, Managing Editor
Address: P.O. Box 659
Peapack, NJ 07977
Web Site Address: http://www.tiferetjournal.com
Publishes: essays, fiction, nonfiction, poetry, art, and translation
Editorial Focus: Tiferet Journal publishes poetry, prose, and commentary that reveal Spirit in the human experience.
Representative Authors: Robert Bly, Mary Hays, and Ray Bradbury
Submissions Policy: Submit hardcopies or electronically through our web site. Include the genre and

author's name and contact info on each submission.
Simultaneous Submissions: yes
Reading Period: Year-round
Reporting Time: three to four months
Author Payment: copies
Contests: See web site for contest guidelines.
Founded: 2003
Non Profit: yes
Paid Staff: two
Unpaid Staff: three
Distributors: Ingram, New Leaf
ISSN Number/ISBN Number: ISSN 1547-2906
Total Circulation: 1,000
Paid Circulation: 400
Average Print Run: 1,000
Submission Rate: Individual $22/Institution $22
Single Copy Price: $14.95
Current Volume/Issue: 1/2
Frequency per Year: biannual
Backfile Available: yes
Unsolicited Ms. Received: yes
% of Unsolicited Ms. Published per Year: 85%
Format: perfect
Size: H 10" W 7"
Averag Pages: 176
Ads: yes
Ad Rates: $100-$300
See web site for details.

Organization: Tilbury House, Publishers

Type: press
CLMP member: no
Primary Editor/Contact Person: Jennifer Bunting
Address: 2 Mechanic St., Ste. 3
Gardiner, ME 04345
Web Site Address: http://www.tilburyhouse.com
Publishes: nonfiction
Editorial Focus: Maine, maritime, and New England
books, children's picture books, and teacher's guides.
Representative Authors: Neil Rolde, Mary Cerullo,
and Pegi Deitz Shea
Submissions Policy: Please read our guidelines on
our web site. Do not send e-mail attachments. Please
enclose SASE with submission.
Simultaneous Submissions: yes
Reading Period: Year-round
Reporting Time: four to six weeks
Author Payment: royalties
Founded: 1970

Non Profit: no
Paid Staff: six
Unpaid Staff: zero
Wholesalers: Ingram, Baker & Taylor, etc.
ISSN Number/ISBN Number: ISSN 0-88448
Number of Books Published per Year: 8
Titles in Print: 90
Average Print Run: 6,000
Average Percentage Printed: Hardcover 50%,
Paperback 50%
Average Price: $25

Organization: Time Being Books

Type: press
CLMP member: no
Primary Editor/Contact Person: Trilogy Mattson,
Office Manger
Address: 10411 Clayton Rd.
Ste.s 201-203
Frontenac, MO 63131
Web Site Address: http://www.timebeing.com
Publishes: poetry
Editorial Focus: We specialize in adult contemporary
poetry and short fiction.
Representative Authors: William Heyen, Albert
Goldbarth, and Rodger Kamenetz
Submissions Policy: We do not accept unsolicited
submissions.
Simultaneous Submissions: no
Reporting Time: 1 to 52 weeks
Author Payment: royalties
Founded: 1988
Non Profit: yes
Paid Staff: three
Unpaid Staff: zero
Distributors: Baker & Taylor, Blackwell's, Follett,
Amazon
Wholesalers: Baker & Taylor
ISSN Number/ISBN Number: ISBN 187777, 156809
Number of Books Published per Year: 6
Titles in Print: 91
Average Print Run: 500
Average Percentage Printed: Hardcover 2%,
Paperback 98%
Average Price: $15.95

Organization: Tin House

Type: magazine
CLMP member: yes

Primary Editor/Contact Person: Rob Spillman
Address: 2601 NW Thurman St.
Portland, OR 97210
Web Site Address: http://www.tinhouse.com
Publishes: essays, fiction, nonfiction, poetry, reviews, and translation
Representative Authors: Stacey Richter, James Salter, and Ron Carlson
Simultaneous Submissions: yes
Reading Period: 9/4 to 6/20
Reporting Time: one to two months
Author Payment: none
Founded: 1998
Non Profit: no
Paid Staff: seven
Unpaid Staff: four
Distributors: Ingram, Eastern News, Desert Moon, Small Changes.
Total Circulation: 10,500
Paid Circulation: 3,800
Submission Rate: Individual $29.90/Institution $29.90
Single Copy Price: $12.95
Current Volume/Issue: 5/4
Frequency per Year: quarterly
Backfile Available: yes
Unsolicited Ms. Received: yes
Format: perfect
Average Pages: 224
Ads: yes
Ad Rates: $400 for a full page

Organization: Tiny Lights: A Journal of Personal Narrative

Type: magazine
CLMP member: yes
Primary Editor/Contact Person: Susan Bono
Address: P.O. Box 928
Petaluma, CA 94953
Website Address: www.tiny-lights.com
Publishes: essays
Editorial Focus: Well-crafted autobiographical essays of less than 2,000 words that feature a shift of the narrator's perspective.
Representative Authors: Sheila Bender, Pat Schneider, and Jean Hegland
Submissions Policy: Currently, the summer issue is devoted to contest winners, the fall issue by invitation only
Simultaneous Submissions: yes

Reading Period: 9/15 to 2/15
Reporting Time: 1 to 3 months
Author Payment: cash, copies, and subscription
Contests: 1st Prize: $400; 2nd: $250; 3rd: $150; 2 Hon. Mention: $100; Flash winners: $300, $200. All receive contest issue; see website for guidelines
Founded: 1995
Non Profit: no
Paid Staff: 1
Unpaid Staff: 0
Distributors: subscription only
Total Circulation: 500
Paid Circulation: 375
Average Print Run: 600
Subscription Rate: Individual $10/Institution $10
Single Copy Price: $5
Current Volume/Issue: 13/1
Frequency: biannual
Backfile Available: yes
Unsolicited Ms. Received: yes
% of Unsolicited Ms. Published per Year: 7%
Format: stapled
Size: H 11" W 8.5"
Average Pages: 16
Ads: yes
Ad Rates: see website for details

Organization: Toad Press

Type: press
CLMP member: no
Primary Editor/Contact Person: Genevieve Kaplan
Address: 660 W. Bonita Ave #29B
Claremont, CA 91711
Web Site Address: www.toadpress.blogspot.com
Publishes: fiction, poetry, and translation
Editorial Focus: we publish chapbook-length contemporary translations of poetry and fiction
Submissions Policy: Annual reading period, no reading fee. See web site for details.
Simultaneous Submissions: yes
Reading Period: 10/1 to 12/31
Reporting Time: two to four months
Author Payment: copies
Founded: 2003
Non Profit: yes
Paid Staff: zero
Unpaid Staff: two
Number of Books Published per year: one
Titles in Print: five
Average Print Run: 150

Average Percentage Printed: chapbook 100%
Average Price: $5

Organization: Toadlily Press

Type: press
CLMP member: yes
Primary Editor/Contact Person: Myrna Goodman
Address: PO Box 2
Chappaqua, NY 10514
Web Site Address: www.toadlilypress.com
Publishes: poetry
Editorial Focus: The Quartet Series is committed to the chapbook, juxtaposing multiple voices in an imaginatively designed book.
Representative Authors: Maxine Silverman, Meredith Trede, and Jennifer Wallace
Submissions Policy: see our web site for guidelines
Simultaneous Submissions: yes
Reading Period: 01/01 to 01/31
Reporting Time: two to three months
Author Payment: cash and copies
Founded: 2005
Non Profit: no
Paid Staff: zero
Unpaid Staff: four
Distributors: bookstores (see web site) considering SPD & Amazon
ISSN Number/ISBN Number: ISBN 0-9766405
Number of Books Published per year: one
Titles in Print: 3
Average Print Run: 1,000
Average Percentage Printed: paperback 100%
Average Price: $14

Organization: Tool: A Magazine

Type: online
CLMP member: no
Primary Editor/Contact Person: Erik Sweet
Web Site Address: http://toolamagazine.com
Publishes: essays, fiction, nonfiction, poetry, reviews, art, translation, and audio
Editorial Focus: We publish a range of things, from poetry and prose to book and reading reviews. Our main goal is to support what we like.
Representative Authors: Brenda Coultas, Eileen Myles, and Eleni Sikelianos
Submissions Policy: Send submission queries via e-mail to esweet01@nycap.rr.com Thanks!
Simultaneous Submissions: yes

Reading Period: Year-round
Reporting Time: one to two months
Author Payment: none
Founded: 1998
Non Profit: yes
Paid Staff: zero
Unpaid Staff: one
Distributors: us
Wholesalers: us
Average Page Views per Month: unknown
Average Unique Visitors per Month: unknown
Frequency per Year: annual
Average Percentage of Pages per Category: Fiction 10%, Poetry 80%, Reviews 10%
Ads: no

Organization: Topic Magazine

Type: magazine
CLMP member: no
Primary Editor/Contact Person: David Haskell
Address: P.O. Box 502
New York, NY 10014
Web Site Address: http://www.topicmag.com
Publishes: essays and nonfiction
Editorial Focus: First-person, nonfiction essays that explore each chosen topic.
Recent Awards Received: Nominated for Best New Title, Best Design: Independent Press Awards. Regional Design Annual: Print Magazine
Representative Authors: Amy Bloom, Lee Aaron Blair, and Kenneth Hartman
Submissions Policy: Must be first-person, nonfiction and on topic at hand. Contact submissions@topic-mag.com for information on future topics.
Simultaneous Submissions: yes
Reading Period: Year-round
Reporting Time: two to twelve weeks
Author Payment: none
Founded: 2001
Non Profit: yes
Paid Staff: zero
Unpaid Staff: 40
Distributors: Ingram, Source Interlink, Comag, Ubiquity
ISSN Number/ISBN Number: ISSN 1477-5762
Total Circulation: 20,000
Paid Circulation: 8,000
Average Print Run: 20,000
Submission Rate: Individual $30/Institution $30
Single Copy Price: $8

Current Volume/Issue: Issue 9
Frequency per Year: quarterly
Backfile Available: yes
Unsolicited Ms. Received: yes
% of Unsolicited Ms. Published per Year: 15%
Format: perfect
Size: H 10" W 8"
Average Pages: 96
Ads: yes
Ad Rates: varies
See web site for details.

Organization: The Transcendental Friend

Type: online
CLMP member: no
Primary Editor/Contact Person: Garrett Kalleberg
Address: 80 Skillman Ave., 2nd fl.
Brooklyn, NY 11211
Web Site Address:
http://www.morningred.com/friend
Publishes: essays, fiction, poetry, reviews, art, and translation
Editorial Focus: Contemporary poetry and poetics, art and criticism.
Representative Authors: Laird Hunt, Heather Ramsdell, and Eleni Sikelianos
Submissions Policy: Section-specific: "Physiology," "Schizmatics," "Critical Dictionary," etc. See site for details.
Simultaneous Submissions: no
Reading Period: Year-round
Reporting Time: two to twelve weeks
Author Payment: none
Founded: 1998
Non Profit: yes
Paid Staff: zero
Unpaid Staff: one
ISSN Number/ISBN Number: ISSN 1526-6559
Average Page Views per Month: 6,793
Average Unique Visitors per Month: 1,267
Frequency per Year: quarterly
Average Percentage of Pages per Category: Fiction 15%, Poetry 50%, Reviews 5%, Essays 10%, Art 5%, Translation 15%
Ads: no

Organization: Transfer Magazine

Type: magazine

CLMP member: no
Primary Editor/Contact Person: Editor-in-chief
Address: Creative Writing Department, HUM 380
1600 Holloway Ave.
San Francisco, CA 94132
Web Site Address:
http://www.transfermagazine.sfsu.edu
Publishes: fiction, nonfiction, and poetry
Editorial Focus: Fiction, drama, poetry, and creative nonfiction of San Francisco State University students
Representative Authors: Anne Rice and Ernest J. Gaines
Submissions Policy: Writers of submissions must be enrolled in San Francisco State University
Simultaneous Submissions: yes
Reading Period: Year-round
Reporting Time: one to six months
Author Payment: none
Founded: 1956
Non Profit: yes
Paid Staff: zero
Unpaid Staff: four
ISSN Number/ISBN Number: ISSN 1533-3043
Total Circulation: 700
Paid Circulation: five to 25
Submission Rate: Individual $7/issue/Institution $7/issue
Single Copy Price: $6
Current Volume/Issue: Issue 87
Frequency per Year: biannual
Backfile Available: yes
Unsolicited Ms. Received: yes
% of Unsolicited Ms. Published per Year: 95%
Format: perfect
Size: H 8.5" W 5.5"
Average Pages: 130
Ads: no

Organization: Translation Review

Type: magazine
CLMP member: yes
Primary Editor/Contact Person: Rainer Schulte
Address: American Literary Translators Association
Richardson, TX 75083-0688
Web Site Address: http://www.literarytranslators.org
Publishes: essays
Editorial Focus: Essays, articles, and interviews on the art, theory, and practice of literary translation.
Simultaneous Submissions: no
Reading Period: Year-round

Reporting Time: one to two months
Author Payment: none
Founded: 1978
Non Profit: yes
Paid Staff: zero
Unpaid Staff: one
ISSN Number/ISBN Number: ISSN 0737-4836
Total Circulation: 1,300
Paid Circulation: 600
Submission Rate: Individual $60/Institution $90
Current Volume/Issue: Issue 67
Frequency per Year: twice yearly with membership to ALTA
Backfile Available: yes
Unsolicited Ms. Received: yes
% of Unsolicited Ms. Published per Year: 80%
Format: perfect
Size: H 11" W 8"
Average Pages: 80
Ads: yes
Ad Rates: See web site for details.

Organization: Trinity University Press

Type: press
CLMP member: yes
Primary Editor/Contact Person: Nancy Elliott
Address: One Trinity Place
San Antonio, TX 78212
Web Site Address: http://www.trinity.edu/tupress
Publishes: nonfiction
Editorial Focus: landscape; regional books; the art and craft of writing, including the series the Writer's World, edited by Edward Hirsch
Recent Awards Received: Book of the Year, American Horticultural Society; EDRA Research Award; AHS Book Award; ASLA Award of Excellence
Representative Authors: Barry Lopez, Rebecca Solnit, and Peter Turchi
Submissions Policy: Send proposal, sample chapter, with CV, by US mail with a SASE for return of materials
Simultaneous Submissions: yes
Reading Period: Year-round
Reporting Time: three to four months
Author Payment: none
Founded: 2002
Non Profit: yes
Paid Staff: four
Unpaid Staff: zero
Distributors: Publishers Group West
ISSN Number/ISBN Number: ISBN 1-59534

Number of Books Published per Year: six to eight
Titles in Print: 25
Average Print Run: 2,500
Average Percentage Printed: Hardcover 50%, Paperback 50%
Average Price: $28

Organization: TriQuarterly

Type: magazine
CLMP member: yes
Primary Editor/Contact Person: Susan Firestone Hahn
Address: 629 Noyes St.
Evanston, IL 60208
Web Site Address: http://www.triquarterly.org
Publishes: essays, fiction, nonfiction, poetry, and art
Editorial Focus: TriQuarterly publishes fiction and poetry, including longer works, contemporary and classical translation.
Recent Awards Received: Reprints in: Best American Poetry, Short Stories, and Mystery Stories; The Pushcart Prizes; and Stories of the New South.
Representative Authors: Stuart Dybek, David Ferry, and Susan Stewart
Submissions Policy: TriQuarterly accepts unsolicited work of all genres with SASE.
Simultaneous Submissions: no
Reading Period: 10/1 to 3/31
Reporting Time: two to four months
Author Payment: cash and copies
Founded: 1957
Non Profit: yes
Paid Staff: two
Unpaid Staff: two
Distributors: Ingram, Armadillo, Ubiquity
ISSN Number/ISBN Number: ISSN 0041 3097
Total Circulation: 2,000
Paid Circulation: 1,500
Average Print Run: 2,500
Submission Rate: Individual $24/Institution $36
Single Copy Price: $11.95
Current Volume/Issue: Issue 127
Frequency per Year: triquarterly
Backfile Available: yes
Unsolicited Ms. Received: yes
% of Unsolicited Ms. Published per Year: 30%
Format: perfect
Size: H 9 1/4" W 6"
Average Pages: 256
Ads: yes
Ad Rates: $250/page, $150/half page

Organization: Truman State Univ. Press

Type: press
CLMP member: no
Primary Editor/Contact Person: Nancy Rediger
Address: 100 E. Normal St.
Kirksville, MO 63501
Web Site Address: http://tsup.truman.edu
Publishes: nonfiction and poetry
Editorial Focus: Regional studies, early modern studies, poetry
Representative Authors: Michael Frome, Jason Offutt, and Rebecca Dunham
Submissions Policy: Proposal letter, table of contents, and sample chapters.
Simultaneous Submissions: no
Reading Period: Year-round
Reporting Time: three to six months
Author Payment: royalties and copies
Contests: See web site for contest guidelines.
Founded: 1986
Non Profit: yes
Paid Staff: three and 1/2
Unpaid Staff: zero
Distributors: Gazelle Book Services (Europe)
Wholesalers: Ingram, Baker & Taylor, Midwest Library Service
ISSN Number/ISBN Number: ISBN 1931112
Number of Books Published per Year: 10
Titles in Print: 100
Average Print Run: 1,000
Average Percentage Printed: Hardcover 40%, Paperback 60%
Average Price: $25-$30

Organization: Tuesday; An Art Project

Type: magazine
CLMP member: yes
Primary Editor/Contact Person: Jennifer S. Flescher
Address: P.O. Box 1074
Arlington, MA 02474
Website Address: www.tuesdayjournal.org
Publishes: poetry and art
Editorial Focus: Contemporary poetry, photographs and prints.
Representative Authors: David Rivard, Major Jackson, and Noel Sloboda
Submissions Policy: Up to 5 poems snail or email. Artists, please send disk or email link. No art attachments please. Check website.
Simultaneous Submissions: yes
Reading Period: year-round
Reporting Time: 1 to 3 months
Author Payment: copies
Founded: 2007
Non Profit: no
Paid Staff: 0
Unpaid Staff: 5
ISSN Number/ISBN Number: ISSN 1935-2417
Total Circulation: 400
Paid Circulation: n/a
Average Print Run: 1000
Subscription Rate: Individual $25/Institution $25
Single Copy Price: $13
Current Volume/Issue: 1/2
Frequency: 2
Backfile Available: yes
Unsolicited Ms. Received: yes
% of Unsolicited Ms. Published per Year: 50%
Format: unbound, hand-made
Size: H 7" W 5"
Average Pages: 19
Ads: no

Organization: Tupelo Press

Type: press
CLMP member: yes
Primary Editor/Contact Person: Jeffery Levine
Address: P.O. Box 539
Dorset, VT 05251
Web Site Address: http://tupelopress.org
Publishes: essays, fiction, nonfiction, and poetry
Editorial Focus: To publish stimulating works of poetry, literary fiction, and creative nonfiction by emerging and established writers.
Representative Authors: Ilya Kaminsky, Dan Beachy-Quick, Jennifer Michael Hecht.
Submissions Policy: Two annual competitions for poetry and a biennial competition for prose, in addition to general submissions.
Simultaneous Submissions: yes
Reading Period: Other than contests, July.
Reporting Time: one to three months
Author Payment: royalties
Contests: Annual first book prize for poetry, annual open poetry competition (Dorset Prize), biennial chapbook and prose competitions
See web site for contest guidelines.
Founded: 1999

Non Profit: yes
Paid Staff: four
Unpaid Staff: two
Distributors: Consortium
Wholesalers: Baker & Taylor, Ingram, SPD
Number of Books Published per Year: eight to twelve
Titles in Print: 61
Average Percentage Printed: Hardcover 15%, Paperback 85%
Backfile Available: yes

Organization: Turtle Point Press

Type: press
CLMP member: yes
Address: 233 Broadway Rm. 946
New York, NY 10279
Web Site Address: http://www.TurtlePoint.com
Publishes: essays, fiction, and poetry
Recent Awards Received: Lambda, Robert Frost Medal, Bay Area Booksellers Award
Representative Authors: Richard Howard, George Stade, and Joe Ashby Porter
Submissions Policy: Full mss. only, SASE
Reading Period: Year-round
Reporting Time: one to two months
Founded: 1991
Non Profit: yes
Distributors: Consortium
Wholesalers: Ingram, Baker & Taylor, SPD
Titles in Print: 60 plus
Average Print Run: 2,500
Average Percentage Printed: Paperback 90%, Chapbook 10%

Organization: Two Lines: A Journal of Translation

Type: magazine
CLMP member: yes
Primary Editor/Contact Person: Zack Rogow
Address: Center for the Art of Translation
35 Stillman St., Ste. 201
San Francisco, CA 94107
Web Site Address: http://www.catranslation.org
Publishes: essays and translation
Editorial Focus: Publishes translations into English from every language and literary genre. Each issue has a theme. See web for details.
Representative Authors: Marilyn Hacker, Tess

Gallagher, and Bill Zavatsky
Submissions Policy: Publishes previously unpublished translations only. Translator cannot be the author. Include original language and intro.
Simultaneous Submissions: no
Reading Period: 8/1 to 10/12
Reporting Time: two to four months
Author Payment: cash
Founded: 1994
Non Profit: yes
Paid Staff: two
Unpaid Staff: two
Distributors: SPD, Partners West, Kent News Co. Amazon.com
ISSN Number/ISBN Number: ISBN 1-931883
Total Circulation: 1,500
Average Print Run: 1,500
Submission Rate: Individual $13.45/Institution $13.45
Single Copy Price: $10.95
Current Volume/Issue: 13/1
Frequency per Year: annual
Backfile Available: yes
Unsolicited Ms. Received: yes
% of Unsolicited Ms. Published per Year: 10%
Format: perfect
Size: H 5.5" W 8.5"
Average Pages: 240
Ad Rates: By exchange with other journals
See web site for details.

Organization: Two Rivers Review

Type: magazine
CLMP member: yes
Primary Editor/Contact Person: Philip Memmer
Address: 2209 Gridley Paige Rd.
Deansboro, NY 13328
Web Site Address: http://trrpoetry.tripod.com
Publishes: fiction and poetry
Editorial Focus: Two Rivers Review prints contemporary poetry and short fiction, along with occasional works in translation.
Representative Authors: Baron Wormser, Reginald Shepherd, and Deena Linett
Submissions Policy: TRR will be on hiatus through 2008, and is not reviewing manuscripts. Please watch the website for updates in 2009.
Simultaneous Submissions: no
Reading Period: Year-round
Reporting Time: two to eight weeks

Author Payment: copies
Contests: See web site for contest guidelines.
Founded: 1997
Non Profit: yes
Paid Staff: zero
Unpaid Staff: two
ISSN Number/ISBN Number: ISSN 1524-2749
Total Circulation: 400
Paid Circulation: 200
Average Print Run: 400
Submission Rate: Individual $10/Institution $10
Single Copy Price: $6
Current Volume/Issue: 5/2
Frequency per Year: biannual
Backfile Available: yes
Unsolicited Ms. Received: yes
% of Unsolicited Ms. Published per Year: 1%
Format: stapled
Size: H 8.5" W 5.5"
Average Pages: 44
Ads: no

Organization: Uccelli Press

Type: press
CLMP member: no
Primary Editor/Contact Person: Toni Bennett
Address: P.O. Box 85394
Seattle, WA 98145-1394
Web Site Address: http://www.uccellipress.com
Publishes: essays, fiction, nonfiction, poetry, art, translation, and audio
Editorial Focus: Sophisticated fiction, poetry, art, photography, chapbooks, anthologies.
Representative Authors: John Amen and Nathan Leslie
Submissions Policy: Query via e-mail (preferred) or mail with sample of work.
Simultaneous Submissions: yes
Reading Period: Year-round
Reporting Time: three to six months
Author Payment: royalties, cash, and copies
Contests: See Web site for contest guidelines.
Founded: 2001
Non Profit: no
Paid Staff: zero
Unpaid Staff: one
Distributors: Baker & Taylor
ISSN Number/ISBN Number: ISBN 0-9723231-1-2
Number of Books Published per Year: 1-2
Titles in Print: 4

Average Percentage Printed: Paperback 90%, Chapbook 10%

Organization: Ugly Duckling Presse

Type: press
CLMP member: yes
Primary Editor/Contact Person: Anna Moschovakis
Address: The Old American Can Factory
232 Third Street, #E002
Brooklyn, NY 11215
Web Site Address:
http://www.uglyducklingpresse.org
Publishes: essays, fiction, poetry, art, translation, and audio
Editorial Focus: A non-profit arts and publishing collective, focused on non-commercial work, collaboration, and innovative book forms.
Representative Authors: Michael Ford, Jen Bervin, and Ivan Blatny
Submissions Policy: Not accepting submissions, except for our periodical, 6x6.
Simultaneous Submissions: yes
Reading Period: Year-round
Reporting Time: two to six months
Author Payment: copies
Founded: 2000
Non Profit: yes
Paid Staff:zero
Unpaid Staff: 10
Distributors: SPD
ISSN Number/ISBN Number: ISBN 1-933254-
Number of Books Published per Year: 10
Titles in Print: 30
Average Print Run: 500
Average Percentage Printed: Paperback 40%, Chapbook 50%, Other 10%
Average Price: $9

Organization: The Ugly Tree

Type: magazine
CLMP member: no
Primary Editor/Contact Person: Paul Neads
Address: Mucusart Publications, 6 Chiffon Way
Trinity Riverside
Gtr Manchester UK, UK M36AB
Web Site Address: www.mucusart.co.uk/theuglytree.htm
Publishes: poetry
Editorial Focus: Poetry magazine with emphasis on

relationship of performance to the page
Representative Authors: Duane Locke, Todd Swift, and Jim Bennett
Submissions Policy: email & postal accepted up to 100 lines. All forms & genres considered
Simultaneous Submissions: no
Reading Period: year-round
Reporting Time: two to six weeks
Author Payment: none and copies
Contests: Open Poetry Competition every 2 years; see website for guidelines
Founded: 2002
Non Profit: yes
Paid Staff: 0
Unpaid Staff: two
ISSN Number/ISBN Number: ISSN 1478-8349
Total Circulation: 100
Paid Circulation: 40
Average Print Run: 100
Subscription Rate: individual $16/institution $16
Single Copy Price: $5.50
Current Volume/Issue: 5/3/15
Frequency per year: triquarterly
Backfile Available: yes
Unsolicited MSS Received: yes
% of Unsolicited MSS Published per Year: 90%
Format: stapled
Size: H 8" W 5.5"
Average Pages: 40
Ads: yes
Ad Rates: see Web site for details.

Organization: United Artists Books

Type: press
CLMP member: no
Primary Editor/Contact Person: Lewis Warsh
Address: 114 W. 16th St., 5C
New York, NY 10011
Web Site Address:
http://www.mindspring.com/~lwarsh/uab/
Publishes: fiction and poetry
Editorial Focus: Experimental writing
Recent Awards Received: none
Representative Authors: Reed Bye, Bernadette Mayer, and Chris Tysh
Submissions Policy: Unsolicited mss. discouraged
Simultaneous Submissions: yes
Reading Period: Year-round
Reporting Time: two to twelve weeks
Author Payment: copies

Contests: none
Founded: 1977
Non Profit: yes
Paid Staff: 0
Unpaid Staff: one
Distributors: SPD
ISSN Number/ISBN Number: none//0-935992
Number of Books Published per Year: two
Titles in Print: 25
Average Print Run: 1,000
Average Percentage Printed: Paperback 100%
Average Price: $14

Organization: The University of Alabama Press

Type: press
CLMP member: yes
Primary Editor/Contact Person: Daniel J.J. Ross
Address: Box 870380
Tuscaloosa, AL 35487-0380
Website Address: uapress.ua.edu
Publishes: fiction and nonfiction
Editorial Focus: Publishes 80 to 90 books in the areas of American Literature, History, Civil War, Archeology and Anthropology.
Recent Awards Received: Diamond Anniversary Award, Religious Communication Association Outstanding Book of the Year, Lillian Smith
Representative Authors: William Christenberry, Mike Shannon, and Michael Joyce
Submissions Policy: Send a cover letter, a prospectus, curriculum vitae. If possible, send a sample chapter, introduction, and a table contents.
Simultaneous Submissions: yes
Reading Period: year-round
Reporting Time: 6 to 8 weeks
Author Payment: royalties
Founded: 1945
Non Profit: yes
Paid Staff: 15
Unpaid Staff: 4
Distributors: Chicago Distribution Center
Wholesalers: Ingram, American Wholesale
ISSN Number/ISBN Number: ISBN 978-0-8173
Number of Books Published per Year: 80
Titles in Print: 1,000
Average Print Run: 1,000
Average Percentage Printed: Hardcover 65%, Paperback 35%
Average Price: $24.95

Organization: The University of Georgia Press

Type: press
CLMP member: no
Primary Editor/Contact Person: Andrew Berzanskis
Address: 330 Research Dr.
Athens, GA 30602-4901
Web Site Address: http://www.ugapress.uga.edu
Publishes: fiction, nonfiction, and poetry
Editorial Focus: Scholarly nonfiction; poetry, short fiction, regional studies, environmental studies, American studies
Representative Authors: Roy Hoffman, Ted Levin, and James C. Cobb
Submissions Policy: Please visit our Web site for our submissions policy
Simultaneous Submissions: yes
Reading Period: Year-round
Reporting Time: three to four weeks
Author Payment: royalties
Contests: Flannery O'Connor Award for Short Fiction; Contemporary Poetry Series
See web site for contest guidelines.
Founded: 1938
Non Profit: yes
Paid Staff: 30
Unpaid Staff: five
ISSN Number/ISBN Number: ISBN 0-8203
Number of Books Published per Year: 70
Titles in Print: 915
Average Percentage Printed: Hardcover 60%, Paperback 40%

Organization: University of Massachusetts Press

Type: press
CLMP member: no
Primary Editor/Contact Person: Bruce Wilcox
Address: Box 429
Amherst, MA 01004
Web Site Address: http://www.umass.edu/umpress
Publishes: essays, fiction, nonfiction, and poetry
Editorial Focus: Scholarly books and serious nonfiction, with an emphasis on American studies, broadly construed.
Recent Awards Received: 2007 Book Award of National Council on Public History; 2007 Davenport Award; 2007 Communal Studies Association Book Award

Representative Authors: Ethan Carr, Marla Miller, and Carole O'Malley Gaunt
Submissions Policy: For nonfiction, submit letter, table of contents, and introduction. Send poetry and fiction to Juniper Prize competitions.
Simultaneous Submissions: yes
Reading Period: Year-round
Reporting Time: one to four weeks
Author Payment: royalties and copies
Contests: See web site for contest guidelines.
Founded: 1963
Non Profit: yes
Paid Staff: seven
Unpaid Staff: four
Distributors: Hopkins Fulfillment Services
Wholesalers: all major wholesalers
ISSN Number/ISBN Number: ISBN 1-55849-000-0
Number of Books Published per Year: 30-40
Titles in Print: 900
Average Print Run: 1,500
Average Percentage Printed: Hardcover 50%, Paperback 50%
Average Price: $19.95 paperback

Organization: University of Tampa Press

Type: press
CLMP member: yes
Primary Editor/Contact Person: Richard Mathews, Director
Address: 401 W. Kennedy Blvd.
Tampa, FL 33606
Web Site Address: http://utpress.ut.edu
Publishes: nonfiction and poetry
Editorial Focus: Contemporary literature, with an emphasis on poetry and drama. We also publish regional history and some academic titles.
Representative Authors: Richard Chess, Jordan Smith, and Julia B. Levine
Submissions Policy: Unsolicited book manuscripts are accepted only through Tampa Review Prize or Pinter Review Prize competitions.
Simultaneous Submissions: no
Reading Period: Year-round
Reporting Time: 8 to 16 weeks
Author Payment: royalties and copies
Contests: Tampa Review Prize for Poetry-http://tampareview.ut.edu/tr_prize.html and Pinter Review Prize for Drama (http://pinter.edu)
See Web site for contest guidelines.

Founded: 1952
Non Profit: yes
Paid Staff: one
Unpaid Staff: 14
ISSN Number/ISBN Number: 0896-064X/1-879852-
Number of Books Published per Year: 5-10
Titles in Print: 39
Average Print Run: 1,000
Average Percentage Printed: Hardcover 80%, Paperback 20%
Average Price: $25

Organization: University of Wisconsin Press

Type: press
CLMP member: no
Primary Editor/Contact Person: Raphael Kadushin, Editor
Address: 1930 Monroe St., 3rd floor
Madison, WI 53711
Web Site Address: http://www.wisc.edu/wisconsin-press
Publishes: fiction, nonfiction, and poetry
Editorial Focus: Scholarly, regional, and literary works of enduring value. Biography, memoir, selected fiction, Latino, GLBT, Wisconsin.
Recent Awards Received: 2004 Society of Midland Authors Book Award for Adult Nonfiction, 2004 Winner of the Triangle Award for Gay Poetry from the Publishing Triangle
Representative Authors: Will Fellows, Sara Rath, and Marilyn Ann Moss
Submissions Policy: see web site for instructions on submitting prospectus
Simultaneous Submissions: yes
Reading Period: Year-round
Reporting Time: one to three months
Author Payment: royalties and copies
Contests: The annual Brittingham and Felix Pollak prizes for poetry http://www.wisc.edu/wisconsin-press/poetryguide.html
See web site for contest guidelines.
Founded: 1937
Non Profit: yes
Paid Staff: 25
Unpaid Staff: 15
Distributors: Chicago Distribution Center
Wholesalers: Ingram, Baker & Taylor, NACS, Partners, others
ISSN Number/ISBN Number: ISBN 0-229

Number of Books Published per Year: 65
Titles in Print: 2,800
Average Print Run: 1,000
Average Percentage Printed: Hardcover 40%, Paperback 55%, Other 5%
Average Price: $30

Organization: Unpleasant Event Schedule

Type: online
CLMP member: yes
Primary Editor/Contact Person: Daniel Nester
Address: 49 Dove Street
Albany, NY 11210
Web Site Address: http://www.unpleasanteventschedule.com
Publishes: essays, fiction, nonfiction, poetry, art, translation, and audio
Editorial Focus: Unpleasant Event Schedule is for artists of modern life and against Rococo Romanticism, as was Baudelaire.
Representative Authors: Reamy Jansen, Betsy Boyd, and Peter Conners
Submissions Policy: Use our Submission Manager at http://unpleasanteventschedule.com/submissions. Send unpublished work. No reprints.
Simultaneous Submissions: yes
Reading Period: Year-round
Reporting Time: one to three months
Author Payment: none
Founded: 2003
Non Profit: yes
Paid Staff: zero
Unpaid Staff: three
Average Page Views per Month: 3,000
Average Unique Visitors per Month: 700
Frequency per Year: 48
Publish Print Anthology: no
Average Percentage of Pages per Category: Fiction 5%, Nonfiction 25%, Poetry 25%, Essays 25%, Art 20%
Ads: no
Ad Rates: Name your price.

Organization: Unsplendid

Type: online
CLMP member: yes
Primary Editor/Contact Person: Douglas Basford
Address: 410 George Street

Baltimore, MD 21201
Website Address: www.unsplendid.com
Publishes: essays, poetry, reviews, art, translation, audio, and video
Editorial Focus: Online journal of poetry in received and nonce forms, publishing sonnets, villanelles, blank verse, fibs, and more, made new.
Representative Authors: Greg Williamson, A. E. Stallings, and Mark Jarman
Submissions Policy: Email up to 5 poems (translators include originals) or 1 piece of prose to editor@unsplendid.com. No previously published work.
Simultaneous Submissions: yes
Reading Period: year-round
Reporting Time: 6 to 8 weeks
Author Payment: none
Founded: 2007
Non Profit: yes
Paid Staff: 0
Unpaid Staff: 4
Average Page Views per Month: 11,000
Average Unique Visitors per Month: 800
Frequency: 4
Publish Print Anthology: no
Average Percentage of Pages per Category: Poetry 77%, Reviews 10%, Essays 7%, Translation 6%
Ads: no

Organization: UpSet Press

Type: press
CLMP member: no
Primary Editor/Contact Person: Robert Booras
Address: 7214 6th Ave., Apt. 2
P.O. Box 200340, Brooklyn, NY 11220
Brooklyn, NY 11209
Web Site Address: http://www.upsetpress.org
Publishes: fiction and poetry
Representative Authors: Nicholas Powers
Simultaneous Submissions: yes
Reading Period: Year-round
Reporting Time: two to four months
Author Payment: none
Contests: none
Founded: 2000
Non Profit: yes
Paid Staff: zero
Unpaid Staff: three
ISSN Number/ISBN Number: ISBN 0-9760142-0-3
Number of Books Published per Year: one

Titles in Print: one
Average Print Run: 1,000
Average Percentage Printed: Paperback 100%
Average Price: $10.95

Organization: upstreet

Type: magazine
CLMP member: yes
Primary Editor/Contact Person: Vivian Dorsel
Address: P.O. Box 105
Richmond, MA 01254-0105
Website Address: www.upstreet-mag.org/
Publishes: essays, fiction, nonfiction, and poetry
Editorial Focus: Quality fiction, cnf, poetry, with edge; author interview assigned by editor.
Representative Authors: Margarita Cardenas, Frank Tempone, and Bill Zavatsky
Submissions Policy: Email submissions only; 5,000 words max for fiction or CNF; 3 poems max; name, contact info on cover, not on ms.
Simultaneous Submissions: yes
Reading Period: 7/1 to 3/1
Reporting Time: 1 to 9 months
Author Payment: copies
Founded: 2005
Non Profit: no
Paid Staff: 0
Unpaid Staff: 3
Distributors: Ubiquity
ISSN Number/ISBN Number: ISBN 978-0-9762371
Total Circulation: 325
Paid Circulation: n/a
Average Print Run: 750
Subscription Rate: Individual $14.50/Institution $14.50
Single Copy Price: $12.00
Current Volume/Issue: Issue 3
Frequency: 1
Backfile Available: yes
Unsolicited Ms. Received: yes
% of Unsolicited Ms. Published per Year: 4%
Format: perfect
Size: H 8.5" W 7"
Average Pages: 224
Ads: no

Organization: Vallum: contemporary poetry

Type: magazine

CLMP member: yes
Primary Editor/Contact Person: Joshua Auerbach, Eleni Auerbach
Address: P.O. Box 48003
Montreal, QC H2V 4S8
Web Site Address: http://www.vallummag.com
Publishes: essays, poetry, reviews, art, and translation
Editorial Focus: Vallum's focus is on the edgy and avant-garde, as well as on the best mainstream poetry. Publishes new and established poets.
Representative Authors: Paul Muldoon, Stephen Dunn, and Charles Bernstein
Submissions Policy: Send by regular mail, with SASE/IRC. Four to seven poems at a time. See web site for theme guidelines.
Simultaneous Submissions: no
Reading Period: 10/1 to 03/31
Reporting Time: 9 to 12 months
Author Payment: cash and copies
Contests: The Vallum Award for Poetry, an annual international competition. Two prizes of cash and publication.
See web site for contest guidelines.
Founded: 2001
Non Profit: yes
Paid Staff: five
Unpaid Staff: three
Distributors: Ingram, DeBoer, Disticor, Gordon and Gotch
ISSN Number/ISBN Number: ISSN 1496-5178
Total Circulation: 9,000
Paid Circulation: 200
Average Print Run: 3,000
Submission Rate: Individual $14 in USA/Institution $20 in USA
Single Copy Price: $5.95
Current Volume/Issue: 3/2
Frequency per Year: biannual
Backfile Available: yes
Unsolicited Ms. Received: yes
% of Unsolicited Ms. Published per Year: 1%
Format: perfect
Size: H 8.5" W 6.75"
Average Pages: 100
Ads: yes
Ad Rates: See web site for details.

Organization: Vanitas
Type: magazine

CLMP member: yes
Primary Editor/Contact Person: Vincent Katz
Address: 211 West 19th St. #5
New York, NY 10011
Web Site Address: www.vanitasmagazine.com
Publishes: essays, poetry, reviews, art, and translation
Editorial Focus: poetry, writings by artists, critical texts, and writing that deals with current political and social problems.
Recent Awards Received: Alvin Curran's texts on his music were nominated for a Pushcart Prize, Ange Mlinko's poems for Gertrude Stein prize.
Representative Authors: Judith Malina, Anne Waldman, and Elaine Equi
Submissions Policy: see Web site for guidelines. Send submissions to vanitas@el.net
Simultaneous Submissions: no
Reading Period: 01/10 to 30/03
Reporting Time: two to six months
Author Payment: none
Founded: 2003
Non Profit: yes
Paid Staff: two
Unpaid Staff: zero
Distributors: Small Press Distribution
Wholesalers: Ingram Periodicals, Fotofolio/Artpost
ISSN Number/ISBN Number: ISSN 1933-8988
Total Circulation: 500
Paid Circulation: 50
Average Print Run: 750
Subscription Rate: individual $10/ institution $10
Single Copy Price: $10
Current Volume/Issue: issue one
Frequency per year: annual
Backfile Available: yes
Unsolicited MSS Received: yes
% of Unsolicited MSS Published per Year: 5%
Format: perfect
Size: H 11" W 8"
Average Pages: 100
Ads: yes
Ad Rates: see web site for details

Organization: Véhicule Press
Type: press
CLMP member: no
Primary Editor/Contact Person: Simon Dardick
Address: P.O.B. 125
Place du Parc Station

Montreal, QC H2X 4A3
Web Site Address: http://www.vehiculepress.com
Publishes: essays, fiction, nonfiction, poetry, and translation
Editorial Focus: Prize-winning publications within the context of social history.
Recent Awards Received: Governor Generalâs Award for Translation, EJ Pratt Poetry Award, Quebec Writersâ Federation McAuslan First Book Prize
Representative Authors: Mary Dalton, Art Corriveau, and Mary Soderstrom
Submissions Policy: Send a profile, list of publications, SASE, and excerpt (25-30 pages double spaced). We mostly publish Canadian authors.
Simultaneous Submissions: yes
Reading Period: Year-round
Reporting Time: two to three months
Author Payment: royalties
Founded: 1973
Non Profit: no
Paid Staff: three
Unpaid Staff: zero
Distributors: Independent Publishers Group
ISSN Number/ISBN Number: ISBN 1-55065
Number of Books Published per Year: 14
Titles in Print: 260
Average Print Run: 1,200
Average Percentage Printed: Paperback 100%
Average Price: $16.95

Organization: VERBATIM: The Language Quarterly

Type: magazine
CLMP member: yes
Primary Editor/Contact Person: Erin McKean
Address: PO Box 597302
Chicago, IL 60659-7302
Web Site Address: www.verbatimmag.com
Publishes: essays, fiction, nonfiction, poetry, and reviews
Editorial Focus: VERBATIM: The Language Quarterly is the only magazine of language and linguistics for the layperson.
Representative Authors: Nick Humez, Richard Lederer, and Mark Peters
Submissions Policy: Please email queries first, and check out our web site. No poetry other than language-related light verse! No fiction!
Simultaneous Submissions: yes
Reading Period: year-round
Reporting Time: two to three months
Author Payment: cash and copies
Founded: 1974
Non Profit: yes
Paid Staff: two
Unpaid Staff: five
Distributors: DeBoer
ISSN Number/ISBN Number: ISSN 0162-0932
Total Circulation: 2,000
Paid Circulation: 1,600
Average Print Run: 2,250
Subscription Rate: individual $25/institution $25
Single Copy Price: $6.50
Current Volume/Issue: 31/1
Frequency per year: quarterly
Backfile Available: yes
Unsolicited MSS Received: yes
% of Unsolicited MSS Published per year: 25%
Format: stapled
Size: H 11" W 8.5"
Average Pages: 32
Ads: yes
Ad Rates: please email for details

Organization: Verb

Type: magazine
CLMP member: yes
Primary Editor/Contact Person: Daren Wang
Address: P.O. Box 2684
Decatur, GA 30031
Web Site Address: http://www.verb.org
Publishes: fiction, poetry, and audio
Editorial Focus: New fiction, poetry, and music exclusively in audio
Representative Authors: Robert Olen Butler, Ha Jin, and Thomas Lux
Submissions Policy: No unsolicited manuscripts-contact before submitting
Simultaneous Submissions: no
Reading Period: Year-round
Reporting Time: one to two months
Author Payment: cash, copies, and submission
Founded: 2004
Non Profit: no
Paid Staff: two
Unpaid Staff: three
Distributors: University of Georgia Press, Audible.com
Total Circulation: 10,000
Paid Circulation: 1,500
Average Print Run: 5,000

Submission Rate: Individual $50/Institution $50
Single Copy Price: $19.95
Current Volume/Issue: 1/1
Frequency per Year: quarterly
Backfile Available: yes
Unsolicited Ms. Received: no
Format: compact disc, download

Organization: Versal

Type: magazine
CLMP member: yes
Primary Editor/Contact Person: Megan M. Garr
Address: Eerste Helmersstraat 142-III
Amsterdam, NA 1054EJ
Website Address: versal.wordsinhere.com
Publishes: fiction, poetry, art, and translation
Editorial Focus: Versal carries on Holland's merchant tradition by collecting fiction, poetry and art from around the world.
Representative Authors: Marilyn Hacker, Julie Marie Wade, and Myronn Hardy
Submissions Policy: Send us your best. Electronic submissions only. Please check the website for complete details.
Simultaneous Submissions: yes
Reading Period: 09/15 to 01/15
Reporting Time: 1 to 4 months
Author Payment: copies
Founded: 2002
Non Profit: yes
Paid Staff: 0
Unpaid Staff: 10
Distributors: Independent bookstores--check website for listing
ISSN Number/ISBN Number: ISSN 1573-2207
Total Circulation: 500
Paid Circulation: 35
Average Print Run: 750
Subscription Rate: Individual $34/2yr/Institution $34/2yr
Single Copy Price: $15
Current Volume/Issue: Issue 5
Frequency: 1
Backfile Available: yes
Unsolicited Ms. Received: yes
% of Unsolicited Ms. Published per Year: 95%
Format: perfect
Size: H 8" W 8"
Average Pages: 100
Ads: no

Organization: Verse

Type: magazine
CLMP member: yes
Primary Editor/Contact Person: Brian Henry
Address: English Department
University of Richmond
Richmond, VA 23173
Web Site Address: http://versemag.blogspot.com
Publishes: essays, fiction, poetry, and reviews
Representative Authors: John Ashbery, Medbh McGuckian, and John Kinsella
Simultaneous Submissions: yes
Reading Period: 9/1 to 5/1
Reporting Time: two to twelve weeks
Author Payment: copies and subscription
Founded: 1984
Non Profit: yes
Paid Staff: zero
Unpaid Staff: four
Distributors: DeBoer
ISSN Number/ISBN Number: ISSN 0268-3830
Total Circulation: 1,000
Paid Circulation: 800
Average Print Run: 1,000
Submission Rate: Individual $18/Institution $36
Single Copy Price: $8-12
Current Volume/Issue: 22/1
Frequency per Year: triquarterly
Backfile Available: yes
Unsolicited Ms. Received: yes
Format: perfect
Size: H 6" W 9"
Ads: no

Organization: The Vincent Brothers Company

Type: press
CLMP member: no
Primary Editor/Contact Person: Kimberly Willardson
Address: 4566 Northern Circle
Riverside, OH 45424
Web Site Address: http://www.thevincentbrothersreview.org
Publishes: fiction, poetry, and art
Editorial Focus: Quality, collectible chapbooks for artists, and fiction and poetry writers.
Representative Authors: David Lee Garrison, Deanna Pickard, and Jud Yalkut
Submissions Policy: Not open to unsolicited submis-

sions of manuscripts as of now.
Author Payment: royalties and copies
Contests: We plan contests for the near future, but none as of yet. Check our web site.
See web site for contest guidelines.
Founded: 1988
Non Profit: yes
Paid Staff: two
Unpaid Staff: five
Number of Books Published per Year: one
Titles in Print: one
Average Percentage Printed: Chapbook 100%

Organization: The Vincent Brothers Review

Type: magazine
CLMP member: no
Primary Editor/Contact Person: Kimberly A. Willardson
Address: 4566 Northern Circle
Riverside, OH 45424
Web Site Address: http://www.thevincentbrothersreview.org
Publishes: essays, fiction, nonfiction, poetry, reviews, art, and translation
Editorial Focus: We seek original, creative work that excites us so much that we feel it imperative to pass the work along to our submissionscribers.
Representative Authors: Gordon Wilson, Deanna Pickard, and Jared Carter
Submissions Policy: See our web site for guidelines, or send us a SASE.
Simultaneous Submissions: yes
Reading Period: Year-round
Reporting Time: four to nine months
Author Payment: cash and copies
Contests: Annual Fiction and Poetry Contests-see guidelines for specific themes.
See web site for contest guidelines.
Founded: 1988
Non Profit: yes
Paid Staff: two
Unpaid Staff: five
ISSN Number/ISBN Number: ISSN 1044-615X
Total Circulation: 450
Paid Circulation: 250
Subscription Rate: Individual $20/Institution $24
Single Copy Price: $11.50
Current Volume/Issue: IX/1
Frequency per Year: biannual

Backfile Available: yes
Unsolicited Ms. Received: yes
% of Unsolicited Ms. Published per Year: 3%
Format: perfect
Size: H 8 and 1/2" W 5"
Average Pages: 164
Ads: no

Organization: Virginia Quarterly Review

Type: magazine
CLMP member: yes
Primary Editor/Contact Person: Ted Genoways
Address: One West Range
P.O. Box 400223
Charlottesville, VA 22904-4223
Web Site Address: http://www.vqronline.org
Publishes: essays, fiction, nonfiction, poetry, reviews, art, and translation
Editorial Focus: A journal of literature and contemporary affairs.
Recent Awards Received: Two National Magazine Awards in 2006 (General Excellence & Fictin), 2006 CELJ Phoenix Award.
Representative Authors: Tom Bissel, Brock Clarke, and Natasha Trethewey
Submissions Policy: Five poems at a time, or 2 stories at once. Not in summer months. SASE for reply
Simultaneous Submissions: no
Reading Period: 9/1 to 5/31
Reporting Time:three to four months
Author Payment: cash and copies
Contests: N/A
Founded: 1925
Non Profit: yes
Paid Staff: four
Unpaid Staff: 25
Distributors: Ingram, DeBoer, Ubiquity
ISSN Number/ISBN Number: ISSN 0042-675X
Total Circulation: 6,000
Paid Circulation: 4,000
Average Print Run: 6,500
Submission Rate: Individual $25/Institution $28
Single Copy Price: $11
Current Volume/Issue: 82/3
Frequency per Year: quarterly
Backfile Available: yes
Unsolicited Ms. Received: yes
% of Unsolicited Ms. Published per Year: 80%
Format: perfect

Size: H 6.75" W 10"
Average Pages: 288
Ads: yes
Ad Rates: full page: $300 B&W, $400 4C; 1/2 page: $180 B&W, $240 4C

Organization: Void Magazine

Type: online
CLMP member: yes
Primary Editor/Contact Person: Chris Steib
Address: 410 E. 13th St., 5E
c/o Void Media, LLC
New York, NY 10009
Web Site Address: http://www.voidmagazine.com
Publishes: essays, fiction, nonfiction, poetry, and reviews
Editorial Focus: Impressive, creative, original and readable fiction, poetry, reviews and essays.
Representative Authors: Aimmee Bender, Scott Snyder, and Thomas Sayers Ellis
Submissions Policy: Submissions accepted on a rolling basis. See web site for details.
Simultaneous Submissions: yes
Reading Period: Year-round
Reporting Time: one to two months
Author Payment: none
Contests: Free contests-prizes and giveaways. See web site for contest guidelines.
Founded: 2005
Non Profit: no
Paid Staff: four
Unpaid Staff: two
Average Page Views per Month: 65,000
Average Unique Visitors per Month: 10,000
Frequency per Year: biannual
Average Percentage of Pages per Category: Fiction 35%, Poetry 30%, Reviews 25%, Essays 10%
Ad Rates: $40-$350/month
See web site for details

Organization: War, Literature & the Arts

Type: magazine
CLMP member: yes
Primary Editor/Contact Person: Donald Anderson
Address: Dept. of English, US Air Force Academy
USAF Academy, CO 80840-6242
Web Site Address: http://www.WLAjournal.com
Publishes: essays, fiction, nonfiction, poetry, reviews, art, and translation
Editorial Focus: From time immemorial, war and art have reflected one another, and it is this intersection that WLA seeks to illuminate.
Representative Authors: Philip Caputo, Carolyn Forche, and Paul West
Submissions Policy: See the web site
Simultaneous Submissions: no
Reading Period: Year-round
Reporting Time: three to six months
Author Payment: copies
Founded: 1989
Non Profit: yes
Paid Staff: five
Unpaid Staff: 20
ISSN Number/ISBN Number: ISSN 1046-6967
Total Circulation: 500
Paid Circulation: 500
Average Print Run: 700
Current Volume/Issue: 18/1-2
Frequency per Year: biannual
Backfile Available: yes
Unsolicited Ms. Received: yes
% of Unsolicited Ms. Published per Year: 10%
Format: perfect
Size: H 9" W 6"
Average Pages: 300+
Ads: no

Organization: Washington Square

Type: magazine
CLMP member: no
Primary Editor/Contact Person: Adam Wiedewitsch
Address: 58 W 10th St
New York, NY 10011
Web Site Address:
http://www.cwp.fas.nyu.edu/page/wsr
Publishes: fiction, nonfiction, poetry, and art
Editorial Focus: our tastes are diverse; well-written and of literary merit
Representative Authors: Stephen Dunn, Kimiko Hahn, and Breyten Breytenbach
Submissions Policy: short fiction or creative nonfiction twenty pages or less; up to three poems; submit no more than twice annually
Simultaneous Submissions: yes
Reading Period: Year-round
Reporting Time: one to three months
Author Payment: none
Contests: See Web site for contest guidelines.

Founded: 1996
Non Profit: yes
Paid Staff: zero
Unpaid Staff: 18
Total Circulation: 2,000
Paid Circulation: 200
Average Print Run: 2,000
Subscription Rate: Individual $10/Institution $12
Single Copy Price: $6
Current Volume/Issue: Issue 14
Frequency per Year: biannual
Backfile Available: yes
Unsolicited Ms. Received: yes
% of Unsolicited Ms. Published per Year: 70%
Format: perfect
Average Pages: 132
Ads: yes

Organization: Washington Writers' Publishing House

Type: press
CLMP member: yes
Primary Editor/Contact Person: Piotr Gwiazda
Address: P O Box 15271
Washington, DC 20003
Web Site Address: http://www.wwph.org
Publishes: fiction and poetry
Editorial Focus: Open to writers living in the Baltimore/Washington area.
Representative Authors: Moira Egan, Jane Satterfield, and Ned Balbo
Submissions Policy: We accept manuscripts from Washington and Baltimore area writers for our annual competition.
Simultaneous Submissions: yes
Reading Period: 7/1 to 12/1
Reporting Time: two to three months
Author Payment: royalties and copies
Contests: See web site for contest guidelines.
Founded: 1973
Non Profit: yes
Paid Staff: zero
Unpaid Staff: five
Distributors: Baker & Taylor
Number of Books Published per Year: two
Titles in Print: two
Average Print Run: 1,000
Average Percentage Printed: Hardcover 10%, Paperback 90%
Average Price: $12

Organization: Watchword Press

Type: magazine
CLMP member: yes
Primary Editor/Contact Person: Liz Lisle
Address: P.O. Box 5755
Berkeley, CA 94705
Web Site Address: http://www.watchwordpress.org
Publishes: essays, fiction, nonfiction, poetry, art, and translation
Editorial Focus: We're interested in work that offers a unique perspective, approach, or style. We also publish modern translations.
Submissions Policy: We only read a few times a year. The best thing to do is check our web site for an update:.
Simultaneous Submissions: yes
Reading Period: Year-round
Reporting Time: two to four months
Author Payment: copies
Founded: 2,000
Non Profit: yes
Paid Staff: zero
Unpaid Staff: four
Total Circulation: 700
Paid Circulation: 400
Average Print Run: 1,000
Submission Rate: Individual $40/Institution $40
Single Copy Price: $10
Current Volume/Issue: six
Frequency per Year: biannual
Backfile Available: yes
Unsolicited Ms. Received: yes
% of Unsolicited Ms. Published per Year: 90%
Format: perfect
Size: H 8.5" W 5.5"
Average Pages: 100
Ads: no

Organization: Water~Stone Review:

Type: magazine
CLMP member: yes
Primary Editor/Contact Person: Mary F. Rockcastle
Address: GLS, Hamline University, MS-A1730
1536 Hewitt Ave.
St. Paul, MN 55104-1284
Website Address: www.waterstonereview.com
Publishes: essays, fiction, nonfiction, poetry, reviews, and translation
Editorial Focus: High-quality fiction, poetry, creative

nonfiction by new and established authors. Interested in a range of style and voice.

Recent Awards Received: Pushcart Prize, Best American poetry, bronze prize for design excellence from the MN. Magazine Publishers Association. Representative Authors: Elizabeth Alexander, Eavan Boland, and Naomi Shihab Nye

Submissions Policy: Submit, with SASE, up to five poems, 20 pages total, or up to 5,000 words of prose.

Simultaneous Submissions: yes

Reading Period: 10/15 to 12/15

Reporting Time: 1 to 4 months

Author Payment: copies and subscription

Contests: Jane Kenyon Poetry Prize, Brenda Ueland Prose Prize (alternate years); see website for guidelines

Founded: 1998

Non Profit: yes

Paid Staff: 3

Unpaid Staff: 10

Distributors: DeBoer, Don Olsen

ISSN Number/ISBN Number: 1520-457x/0-9723721-8-0

Total Circulation: 1,500

Paid Circulation: 700

Average Print Run: 1,500

Subscription Rate: Individual $15/Institution $16

Single Copy Price: $15

Current Volume/Issue: 9/1

Frequency: annual

Backfile Available: yes

Unsolicited Ms. Received: yes

% of Unsolicited Ms. Published per Year: 60%

Format: perfect

Size: H 9" W 6"

Average Pages: 250

Ads: yes

Ad Rates: full-page $250, half-page $150; 10% discount nonprofits; see website for details

Organization: Waterways: Poetry in the Mainstream

Type: magazine

CLMP member: yes

Primary Editor/Contact Person: Richard Spiegel/Barbara Fisher

Address: 393 Saint Pauls Ave.
Staten Island, NY 10304-2127

Web Site Address: http://www.tenpennyplayers.org

Publishes: poetry

Editorial Focus: Contemporary poets and theme issues

Representative Authors: Ida Fasel, Robert Cooperman, and Donald Lev

Submissions Policy: Themes are posted at our web site. Returns with SASE only. Rarely publish rhyme or haiku.

Simultaneous Submissions: yes

Reading Period: Year-round

Reporting Time: one to three weeks

Author Payment: copies

Founded: 1977

Non Profit: yes

Paid Staff: three

Unpaid Staff: 0

ISSN Number/ISBN Number: 0197-4777/0-934830

Total Circulation: 100

Paid Circulation: 50

Average Print Run: 100

Subcription Rate: Individual $33/Institution $33

Single Copy Price: $4

Current Volume/Issue: 28/2

Frequency per Year: 11

Backfile Available: yes

Unsolicited Ms. Received: yes

% of Unsolicited Ms. Published per Year: 60%

Format: stapled

Size: H 4 1/4" W 7"

Average Pages: 32

Ads: no

Organization: Wave Books

Type: press

CLMP member: yes

Primary Editor/Contact Person: Joshua Beckman

Address: 1938 Fairview Ave. E
Seattle, WA 98102

Web Site Address: http://www.wavepoetry.com

Publishes: poetry and translation

Representative Authors: Eileen Myles, Christian Hawkey, Dara Wier

Submissions Policy: Varies. See web site for guidelines.

Simultaneous Submissions: yes

Reading Period: 3/1 to 3/31

Reporting Time: two to six months

Author Payment: royalties

Founded: 2000

Non Profit: no

Paid Staff: four

Unpaid Staff: six
Distributors: SPD, Consortium
Number of Books Published per Year: five to eight
Titles in Print: 43
Average Print Run: Varies
Average Percentage Printed: Paperback 100%
Average Price: $14

Organization: The Waywiser Press

Type: press
CLMP member: no
Primary Editor/Contact Person: Philip Hoy
Address: 9 Woodstock Road
London, UK N4 3ET
Website Address: www.waywiser-press.com
Publishes: fiction, nonfiction, and poetry
Editorial Focus: Literary writing of high quality.
Recent Awards Received: Kate Tufts Discovery
Award for Eric McHenry's Potscrubber Lullabies
Representative Authors: Richard Wilbur, Anthony
Hecht, and Mark Strand
Submissions Policy: Send hard copy of entire poetry
manuscripts, and two chapters of any prose work.
Simultaneous Submissions: yes
Reading Period: 1/4 to 9/30
Reporting Time: 6 to 8 weeks
Author Payment: royalties
Contests: Anthony Hecht Poetry Prize, an annual
award for the best first or second collection submit-
ted. $3000 purse + publication; see website for
guidelines
Founded: 2001
Non Profit: no
Paid Staff: 0
Unpaid Staff: 4
Distributors: Dufours Editions Inc
ISSN Number/ISBN Number: ISBN 978-1-904130
Number of Books Published per Year: 5-7
Titles in Print: 30
Average Print Run: 1,000
Average Percentage Printed: Hardcover 20%,
Paperback 80%
Average Price: $18

Organization: Weber Studies

Type: magazine
CLMP member: yes
Primary Editor/Contact Person: Brad L. Roghaar
Address: Weber State University

1214 University Circle
Ogden, UT 84408-1214
Web Site Address: http://weberstudies.weber.edu/
Publishes: essays, fiction, nonfiction, poetry, and art
Editorial Focus: We seek quality work that provides
insight into the environment and culture (both broadly
defined) of the contemporary West.
Representative Authors: Robert Pinsky, Robert Dana,
and David James Duncan
Submissions Policy: Submit cover letter and two
copies of each manuscript÷3-6 poems, essays and
fiction should not exceed 5,000 words, include SASE.
Simultaneous Submissions: yes
Reading Period: Year-round
Reporting Time: three to four months
Author Payment: cash, copies, and subscription
Contests: O. Marvin Lewis Essay Award; Sherwin W.
Howard Poetry Award; Neila C. Seshachari Fiction
Award each ($500) awarded annually.
See web site for contest guidelines.
Founded: 1984
Non Profit: yes
Paid Staff: two
Unpaid Staff: three
ISSN Number/ISBN Number: ISSN 0891-8899
Total Circulation: 1,000
Paid Circulation: 800
Average Print Run: 1,100
Submission Rate: Individual $20/Institution $30
Single Copy Price: $8
Current Volume/Issue: 22/3
Frequency per Year: triquarterly
Backfile Available: yes
Unsolicited Ms. Received: yes
% of Unsolicited Ms. Published per Year: 10%
Format: perfect
Size: H 10" W 7 1/2"
Average Pages: 144
Ads: no

Organization: Wesleyan University Press

Type: press
CLMP member: no
Primary Editor/Contact Person: Suzanna Tamminen,
Editor-in-Chief
Address: 215 Long Ln.
Middletown, CT 06459
Web Site Address:
http://www.wesleyan.edu/wespress

Publishes: nonfiction, poetry, and translation
Editorial Focus: Scholarly books in the areas of music, dance, science fiction studies, film/TV/media, and poetry.
Representative Authors: Heather McHugh, Ann Cooper Albright, and Christopher Small
Submissions Policy: Poetry and all academic areas: submit proposal (see specific guidelines on web site).
Simultaneous Submissions: yes
Reading Period: Year-round
Reporting Time: two to six months
Author Payment: royalties
Founded: 1959
Non Profit: yes
Paid Staff: five
Unpaid Staff: zero
Distributors: University Press of New England
Wholesalers: Ingram, Koen, Baker & Taylor
ISSN Number/ISBN Number: ISBN 0-8195-
Number of Books Published per Year: 25-30
Titles in Print: 412
Average Percentage Printed: Hardcover 10%, Paperback 90%

Organization: West Branch

Type: magazine
CLMP member: yes
Primary Editor/Contact Person: Andrew Ciotola
Address: Bucknell Hall, Bucknell University
Lewisburg, PA 17837
Web Site Address: http://www.bucknell.edu/west-branch
Publishes: essays, fiction, nonfiction, poetry, reviews, and translation
Editorial Focus: Eclectic mix of traditional and innovative with preference for work displaying a strong attention to craft.
Recent Awards Received: Pushcart, 2006
Representative Authors: Mary Ruefle, Terrance Hayes, and Annie Finch
Submissions Policy: All manuscripts must be accompanied by appropriate retrn postage. Please see our web site for exceptions.
Simultaneous Submissions: yes
Reading Period: 8/15 to 4/15
Reporting Time: four to twelve weeks
Author Payment: cash and copies
Founded: 1977
Non Profit: yes
Paid Staff: three

Unpaid Staff: two
ISSN Number/ISBN Number: ISSN 0149-6441
Total Circulation: 1,100
Paid Circulation: 700
Average Print Run: 1,300
Submission Rate: Individual $10/Institution $16
Single Copy Price: $6
Current Volume/Issue: Issue 59
Frequency per Year: biannual
Backfile Available: yes
Unsolicited Ms. Received: yes
% of Unsolicited Ms. Published per Year: 1%
Format: perfect
Size: H 9" W 6"
Average Pages: 160
Ads: yes
Ad Rates: Exchange Only

Organization: West End Press

Type: press
CLMP member: yes
Primary Editor/Contact Person: John Crawford
Address: P.O. Box 27334
Albuquerque, NM 87125
Publishes: fiction, nonfiction, poetry, art, and translation
Editorial Focus: Progressive literature emphasizing "the political is personal" and asserting art can help transform reality. Includes drama.
Representative Authors: Meridel Le Sueur, Cherrie Moraga, and Sharon Doubiago
Submissions Policy: Send brief letter, samples of work, SASE.
Simultaneous Submissions: no
Reading Period: Year-round
Reporting Time: one to three months
Author Payment: royalties and copies
Founded: 1976
Non Profit: no
Paid Staff: two
Unpaid Staff: one
Distributors: University of New Mexico Press, Small Press Dist.
Wholesalers: Ingram, Baker & Taylor, etc.
ISSN Number/ISBN Number: ISBN 0-931122, 0-9705344, 0-9753486
Number of Books Published per Year: four
Titles in Print: 40
Average Print Run: 1,200
Average Percentage Printed: Paperback 90%, chap-

book 10%
Average Price: $13.95

Organization: Westchester Review

Type: magazine
CLMP member: yes
Primary Editor/Contact Person: JoAnn Terdiman
Address: P.O. Box 246H
Scarsdale, NY 10583
Website Address: www.westchesterreview.com
Publishes: essays, fiction, and poetry
Editorial Focus: Prose and poetry by established and emerging writers living or working in New York's Westchester County.
Submissions Policy: Previously unpublished, paper submissions only. Send up to 5 poems or stories up to 5,000 words with SASE.
Simultaneous Submissions: yes
Reading Period: year-round
Reporting Time: 1 to 4 months
Author Payment: copies
Founded: 2006
Non Profit: no
Paid Staff: 0
Unpaid Staff: 8
ISSN Number/ISBN Number: ISBN 0-615-13387-8
Total Circulation: 2,000
Paid Circulation: 0
Average Print Run: 3,000
Subscription Rate: Individual $8/Institution $8
Single Copy Price: $8
Current Volume/Issue: Issue 2
Frequency: 1
Backfile Available: yes
Unsolicited Ms. Received: yes
Format: perfect
Size: H 8.5" W 5.5"
Average Pages: 188
Ads: no

Organization: Western Humanities Review

Type: magazine
CLMP member: yes
Primary Editor/Contact Person: Managing Editor
Address: 255. S. Central Campus Dr., RM 3500
University of Utah
Salt Lake City, UT 84112-0494
Web Site Address: http://www.hum.utah.edu
Publishes: essays, fiction, nonfiction, poetry, and translation
Editorial Focus: Literary fiction, nonfiction, and poetry; critical articles of impressive humanistic scholarship.
Recent Awards Received: Best Spiritual Writing, 2005 Pushcart Prize, 2005 Best American Essays 2004
Representative Authors: Billy Collins, Alyson Hagy, and Richard Howard
Submissions Policy: See web site
Simultaneous Submissions: yes
Reading Period: 9/1 to 5/1
Reporting Time: one to six months
Author Payment: cash and copies
Contests: Annual Utah Writers' Contest, for Utah residents.
See web site for contest guidelines.
Founded: 1947
Non Profit: yes
Paid Staff: one
Unpaid Staff: six
ISSN Number/ISBN Number: ISSN 0043-3845
Total Circulation: 1,000
Paid Circulation: 900
Average Print Run: 1,100
Submission Rate: Individual $16/Institution $24
Single Copy Price: $10
Current Volume/Issue: 61/2
Frequency per Year: 3
Backfile Available: yes
Unsolicited Ms. Received: yes
% of Unsolicited Ms. Published per Year: 5%
Format: perfect
Size: H 9" W 6"
Average Pages: 170
Ads: yes
Ad Rates: Exchange: we run very few.

Organization: Whereabouts Press

Type: press
CLMP member: no
Primary Editor/Contact Person: David Peattie
Address: 1111 8th St.
Berkeley, CA 94710
Web Site Address:
http://www.whereaboutspress.com
Publishes: fiction
Editorial Focus: Literature in translation through our Traveler's Literary Companion Series

Submissions Policy: Not currently accepting submissions.
Simultaneous Submissions: yes
Reading Period: Year-round
Reporting Time: three to twelve weeks
Author Payment: royalties, cash, and copies
Founded: 1993
Non Profit: no
Paid Staff: zero
Unpaid Staff: one
Distributors: Consortium
Wholesalers: Ingram
Number of Books Published per Year: two
Titles in Print: 12
Average Percentage Printed: Paperback 100%
Backfile Available: yes

Organization: Whit Press

Type: press
CLMP member: yes
Primary Editor/Contact Person: Claudia Mauro
Address: 1634 Eleventh Ave.
1634 Eleventh Ave.
Seattle, WA 98122
Web Site Address: http://www.whitpress.org
Publishes: fiction, nonfiction, poetry, translation, and audio
Editorial Focus: Women, Writers of Color, Emerging Writers, Literary projects focusing on environmental and social justice
Submissions Policy: Please read the Whit Press Mission. If your project fits our mission, send a brief outline and four to ten sample pages.
Simultaneous Submissions: no
Reading Period: Year-round
Reporting Time: one to two months
Author Payment: royalties and copies
Founded: 2001
Non Profit: yes
Paid Staff: one
Unpaid Staff: one
Wholesalers: Partners West, SPD, Baker & Taylor
ISSN Number/ISBN Number: ISBN 0-9720205
Number of Books Published per Year: four
Titles in Print: eight
Average Print Run: 5,000
Average Percentage Printed: Paperback 90%, Other 10%
Average Price: $17

Organization: White Pine Press

Type: press
CLMP member: yes
Primary Editor/Contact Person: Dennis Maloney
Address: P.O. Box 236
Buffalo, NY 14201
Web Site Address: http://www.whitepine.org
Publishes: essays, fiction, nonfiction, poetry, and translation
Editorial Focus: We are a not-for-profit literary publisher.
Representative Authors: Pablo Neruda, Marjorie Agosin, and Rene Char
Submissions Policy: American poetry only as part of our annual competition. Others, send query letter.
Simultaneous Submissions: yes
Reading Period: Year-round
Reporting Time: one to three months
Author Payment: copies
Contests: See web site for contest guidelines.
Founded: 1973
Non Profit: yes
Paid Staff: three
Unpaid Staff: one
Distributors: Consortium
ISSN Number/ISBN Number: ISBN 1-893996
Number of Books Published per Year: 12
Titles in Print: 150
Average Print Run: 1,200
Average Percentage Printed: Hardcover 1%, Paperback 99%
Average Price: $15

Organization: Wild Berries Press

Type: press
CLMP member: yes
Primary Editor/Contact Person: Utahna Faith
Address: 1000 Bourbon St., #219
New Orleans, LA 70116
Web Site Address: http://www.wildstrawberries.org
Publishes: fiction, poetry, and art
Editorial Focus: Literary flash fiction and prose poetry
Representative Authors: Andrei Codrescu, Olympia Vernon, and Tom Bradley
Submissions Policy: Submissions considered for Wild Strawberries: a journal of flash fiction and prose poetry; see wildstrawberries.org
Simultaneous Submissions: yes
Reading Period: Year-round

Reporting Time: one to four months
Author Payment: cash, copies, and subscription
Founded: 2003
Non Profit: no
Paid Staff: zero
Unpaid Staff: one
ISSN Number/ISBN Number: ISSN 1552-4493
Number of Books Published per Year: two
Titles in Print: three
Average Percentage Printed: Chapbook 100%

Organization: Wild Strawberries

Type: magazine
CLMP member: yes
Primary Editor/Contact Person: Utahna Faith
Address: 1000 Bourbon St., #219
New Orleans, LA 70116
Web Site Address: http://www.wildstrawberries.org
Publishes: fiction and poetry
Reading Period: Year-round
Reporting Time: one to two months
Author Payment: none
Founded: 2003
Non Profit: yes
Backfile Available: yes

Organization: Willow Springs

Type: magazine
CLMP member: yes
Primary Editor/Contact Person: Sam Ligon
Address: 705 W. First Ave.
Spokane, WA 99201
Web Site Address: http://willowsprings.ewu.edu/
Publishes: essays, fiction, nonfiction, poetry, reviews, art, and translation
Editorial Focus: We publish poetry, short fiction, and nonfiction of literary merit.
Representative Authors: Alison Stine, Robert Gregory, and Gary Fincke
Submissions Policy: See web site for full submissions policy.
Simultaneous Submissions: yes
Reading Period: 9/15 to 5/15
Reporting Time: three to six months
Author Payment: none
Contests: Fiction and poetry contests opens in February. Send $10 per submission, up to six poems per entry.
See web site for contest guidelines.

Founded: 1977
Non Profit: yes
Paid Staff: five
Unpaid Staff: 30
Distributors: Ingram, DeBoer
ISSN Number/ISBN Number: 0739-1277/7477086570
Total Circulation: 1,100
Paid Circulation: 70
Subcription Rate: Individual $11.50/Institution $11.50
Single Copy Price: $6
Current Volume/Issue: Issue 54
Frequency per Year: biannual
Backfile Available: yes
Unsolicited Ms. Received: yes
% of Unsolicited Ms. Published per Year: 3%
Format: perfect
Size: H 8 3/4" W 6"
Average Pages: 144
Ads: yes
Ad Rates: Exchange only

Organization: Wind: A Journal of Writing & Community

Type: magazine
CLMP member: no
Primary Editor/Contact Person: Rebecca Howell
Address: P.O. Box 24548
Lexington, KY 40524
Publishes: essays, fiction, nonfiction, poetry, reviews, and art
Editorial Focus: We operate on the metaphor of neighborly conversation between writers about the differing worlds in which they live.
Representative Authors: Wendell Berry, Yael Flusberg, and Ann Fisher-Wirth
Submissions Policy: Unsolicited and simultaneous submissions are accepted year-round. For guidelines, write or visit web site: wind.wind.org
Simultaneous Submissions: yes
Reading Period: Year-round
Reporting Time: three to six months
Author Payment: cash, and copies
Contests: The Joy Bale Boone Poetry Prize; The James Still Fiction Prize; The Quentin R. Howard Poetry Chapbook Prize
See Web site for contest guidelines.
Founded: 1971
Non Profit: yes

Paid Staff: no
Unpaid Staff: yes
ISSN Number/ISBN Number: ISSN 0361-2481
Total Circulation: 1,000
Paid Circulation: 500
Submission Rate: Individual $21/Institution $25
Single Copy Price: $9
Current Volume/Issue: Issue 91
Frequency per Year: triquarterly
Backfile Available: yes
Unsolicited Ms. Received: yes
% of Unsolicited Ms. Published per Year: 1-2%
Format: perfect
Size: H 9" W 6"
Average Pages: 120
Ads: yes
Ad Rates: $100 for full page; 1/2 page $50

Organization: Windhover: A Journal of Christian Literature

Type: magazine
CLMP member: no
Primary Editor/Contact Person: Audell Shelburne
Address: UMHB Box 8008
900 College St.
Belton, TX 76513
Publishes: essays, fiction, nonfiction, poetry, reviews, and art
Editorial Focus: Windhover is devoted to promoting good writers and quality literary efforts with a Christian perspective.
Representative Authors: Larry Thomas, Cleatus Rattan, and Walt McDonald
Submissions Policy: Subs regular mail only (not email), max 3,500 words or four poems. June 1st deadline for next issue.
Simultaneous Submissions: yes
Reading Period: 6/08 to 8/08
Reporting Time: three to four months
Author Payment: copies
Founded: 1996
Non Profit: yes
Paid Staff: one
Unpaid Staff: six
Distributors: University of Mary Hardin-Baylor
Total Circulation: 450
Paid Circulation: 350
Average Print Run: 600
Submission Rate: Individual $15/Institution $15
Single Copy Price: $15

Current Volume/Issue: 12/1
Frequency per Year: anuual
Backfile Available: yes
Unsolicited Ms. Received: yes
% of Unsolicited Ms. Published per Year: 10%
Format: perfect
Size: H 9" W 6"
Average Pages: 220
Ads: no

Organization: Wings Press

Type: press
CLMP member: yes
Primary Editor/Contact Person: Bryce Milligan
Address: 627 E. Guenther
San Antonio, TX 78210
Web Site Address: http://www.wingspress.com
Publishes: fiction, nonfiction, and poetry
Editorial Focus: Well crafted, intelligent, liberal-minded multicultural fiction and poetry.
Recent Awards Received: Latino Book Awards (2), Feature on Wings in Poets & Writers (Sept 2007), Cover story in Bloomsbury Review (2), Balcones Prize
Representative Authors: John Howard Griffin, Cecile Pineda, and Lorna Dee Cervantes
Submissions Policy: We seldom accept open subs. Send a bio and a short sample by email and we will consider asking for a ms.
Simultaneous Submissions: yes
Reading Period: Year-round
Reporting Time: one to three months
Author Payment: royalties
Contests: See Web site for contest guidelines.
Founded: 1975
Non Profit: no
Paid Staff: one
Unpaid Staff: two
Distributors: Independent Publishers Group IPG
Wholesalers: Ingram, Baker & Taylor, Brodart, et al.
ISSN Number/ISBN Number: ISBN 0-930324- and 0-916727
Number of Books Published per Year: 12-15
Titles in Print: 124
Average Print Run: 2,500
Average Percentage Printed: Hardcover 20%, Paperback 70%, Chapbook 5%, Other 5%
Average Price: $18

Organization: Witness

Type: magazine
CLMP member: no
Primary Editor/Contact Person: Peter Stine
Address: Oakland Community College
27055 Orchard Lake Road
Farmington Hills, MI 48334
Web Site Address: http://www.oaklandcc/witness
Publishes: essays, fiction, nonfiction, and poetry
Editorial Focus: Witness will now publish one special issue per year on an announced theme.
Representative Authors: Joyce Carol Oates, Ron Carlson, and Bob Hicok
Submissions Policy: send for guidelines
Simultaneous Submissions: yes
Reading Period: Year-round
Reporting Time: one to three months
Author Payment: cash, and copies
Founded: 1987
Non Profit: yes
Paid Staff: one
Unpaid Staff: one
Distributors: Ingram, Ubiquity, DeBoer, Armadillo
ISSN Number/ISBN Number: 0891-1371/0891-1371
Total Circulation: 3,000
Paid Circulation: 800
Submission Rate: Individual $10/Institution $18
Single Copy Price: $12
Current Volume/Issue: 19/11
Frequency per Year: annual
Backfile Available: yes
Unsolicited Ms. Received: yes
% of Unsolicited Ms. Published per Year: 5%
Format: perfect
Size: H 9" W 6"
Average Pages: 212
Ads: yes
Ad Rates: $100 pages

Organization: Woman Poet

Type: magazine
CLMP member: yes
Primary Editor/Contact Person: Elaine Dallman
Address: 601 Van Ness Ave., Nr. 6
San Francisco, CA 94102
Publishes: poetry
Editorial Focus: Contemporary Poetry
Simultaneous Submissions: yes
Reading Period: Year-round
Reporting Time: one to two months

Author Payment: none
Founded: 1978
Non Profit: yes
Paid Staff: 0
Unpaid Staff: two
Total Circulation: 800
Paid Circulation: 60
Average Print Run: 500
Submission Rate: Individual $16/Institution $16
Single Copy Price: $16
Current Volume/Issue: Issue 28
Frequency per Year: annual
Backfile Available: yes
Unsolicited Ms. Received: no
Format: perfect
Average Pages: 60
Ad Rates: none

Organization: Women-in Literature Inc.

Type: press
CLMP member: yes
Primary Editor/Contact Person: Elaine Dallman, Ph.D.
Address: 601 Vanness Ave. #6
San Francisco, CA 94102
Publishes: poetry
Editorial Focus: poetry that is fine literature, from established or new-to-the-field poets.
Representative Authors: Marilyn Hacker, Lisel Mueller, and Marie Ponsot
Submissions Policy: Check with Poets and Writers. When we are collecting we list there.
Simultaneous Submissions: yes
Reading Period: year-round
Reporting Time: one to twelve weeks
Author Payment: copies
Founded: 1970
Non Profit: yes
Paid Staff: zero
Unpaid Staff: three
ISSN Number/ISBN Number: ISBN 0-910221
Number of Books Published per year: one
Titles in Print: four
Average Percentage Printed: hardcover 25%, paperback 75%

Organization: Women's Review of Books

Type: magazine
CLMP member: yes
Primary Editor/Contact Person: Amy Hoffman
Address: Wellesley Centers for Women CHE
Wellesley College, 106 Central St.
Wellesley, MA 02481
Web Site Address: www.wcwonline.org/womensreview
Publishes: essays, poetry, and reviews
Editorial Focus: women's studies books and fiction and poetry by women.
Representative Authors: Linda Gordon, Ann Snitow, and Tricia Rose
Submissions Policy: No unsolicited articles. Mail resume and published clips to be considered for assignments.
Simultaneous Submissions: no
Reading Period: year-round
Reporting Time: three to six months
Author Payment: cash, copies, and subscription
Founded: 1983
Non Profit: yes
Paid Staff: one
Unpaid Staff: zero
ISSN Number/ISBN Number: ISSN 0738-1433
Total Circulation: 3,500
Paid Circulation: 3,000
Average Print Run: 6,000
Subscription Rate: individual $33/institution $58
Single Copy Price: $5
Current Volume/Issue: 23/5
Frequency per year: bimonthly
Backfile Available: yes
Unsolicited MSS Received: no
Format: tabloid
Size: H 14" W 10.5"
Average Pages: 32
Ads: yes
Ad Rates: see web site for details

Organization: The Worcester Review

Type: magazine
CLMP member: yes
Primary Editor/Contact Person: Rodger Martin
Address: 6 Chatham St.
Worcester, MA 01609
Web Site Address:
http://www.geocities.com/Paris/LeftBank/6433
Publishes: essays, fiction, poetry, art, and translation
Editorial Focus: Essays and features with a Central New England (particularly Worcester literary history) focus, poetry and fiction open
Representative Authors: Marge Piercy, Yusef Komunyakaa, and Jim Daniels
Submissions Policy: three poems, one short story or critical essay with a New England connection,
Simultaneous Submissions: yes
Reading Period: Year-round
Reporting Time: six to nine months
Author Payment: copies and subscription
Contests: Annual Worcester County Poetry Assoc. contest, see http://www.wcpa.homestead.org for guidelines
Founded: 1973
Non Profit: yes
Paid Staff: zero
Unpaid Staff: 12
ISSN Number/ISBN Number: ISSN 11607681
Total Circulation: 750-1000
Paid Circulation: 225
Submission Rate: Individual $25/Institution $25
Single Copy Price: $12
Current Volume/Issue: XXII/2
Frequency per Year: anuual
Backfile Available: yes
Unsolicited Ms. Received: yes
% of Unsolicited Ms. Published per Year: 3%
Format: perfect
Size: H 9" W 69"
Average Pages: 128
Ads: yes
Ad Rates: generally only inside front and back covers, $375
See web site for details.

Organization: Word Riot Press

Type: press
CLMP member: yes
Primary Editor/Contact Person: Jackie Corley
Address: P.O. Box 414
Middletown, NJ 07748
Web Site Address: http://www.wordriot.org/press
Publishes: fiction, nonfiction, and poetry
Editorial Focus: We are dedicated to the forceful voices of up-and-coming writers and poets.
Representative Authors: David Barringer, Stephen Oliver, and Ryan Robert Mullen
Submissions Policy: See our web site: http://www.wordriot.org/press
Simultaneous Submissions: yes

Reading Period: Year-round
Reporting Time: two to three months
Author Payment: royalties and copies
Founded: 2003
Non Profit: yes
Paid Staff: one
Unpaid Staff: one
Number of Books Published per Year: five
Titles in Print: eight
Average Percentage Printed: Paperback 50%, Chapbook 50%

Organization: Word Riot

Type: online
CLMP member: no
Primary Editor/Contact Person: Jackie Corley
Address: 114 Four Winds Dr.
Middletown, NJ 07748
Web Site Address: http://www.wordriot.org
Publishes: essays, fiction, nonfiction, poetry, and reviews
Editorial Focus: We encourage the forceful voices of up-and-coming writers and poets.
Representative Authors: Steve Almond, David Barringer, and Pia Z. Ehrhardt
Submissions Policy: see our website
Simultaneous Submissions: yes
Reading Period: Year-round
Reporting Time: four to twelve weeks
Author Payment: none
Contests: See Web site for contest guidelines.
Founded: 2002
Non Profit: yes
Paid Staff: zero
Unpaid Staff: eight
Backfile Available: yes
Average Page Views per Month: 2,700
Average Unique Visitors per Month: 1,800
Frequency per Year: annual
Publish Print Anthology: yes
Price: $10 (for anthology)
Average Percentage of Pages per Category: Fiction 60%, Nonfiction 15%, Poetry 20%, Reviews 5%
Ad Rates: See web site for details.

Organization: Word Smitten

Type: online
CLMP member: no
Primary Editor/Contact Person: Kate Sullivan
Address: 3115 Beach Blvd., Editorial Office

P.O. Box 5067
St. Petersburg, FL 33737-5067
Web Site Address: http://www.wordsmitten.com
Publishes: fiction, nonfiction, reviews, and art
Editorial Focus: Word Smitten's award-winning online and print publications seek to inform writers about the business of book publishing.
Representative Authors: Noy Holland, Louise Domaratius, and John Ravenscroft
Submissions Policy: E-mail first with one-page query. Accepting flash fiction (fewer than 500 words) and short fiction (fewer than 4,000 words).
Simultaneous Submissions: no
Reading Period: Year-round
Reporting Time: two to four months
Author Payment: cash
Contests: Word Smitten sponsors two fiction contests (invited judges), Storycove Flash Fiction (May 1) and the Ten-Ten Award (July 1).
See web site for contest guidelines.
Founded: 1999
Non Profit: no
Paid Staff: seven
Unpaid Staff: five
Average Page Views per Month: 38,000
Average Unique Visitors per Month: 30,000
Frequency per Year: biannual
Publish Print Anthology: yes
Price: $11
Average Percentage of Pages per Category: Fiction 25%, Nonfiction 25%, Reviews 25%, Essays 10%, Art 15%
Ad Rates: See Web site for details.

Organization: Word: Toronto's Literary Calendar

Type: magazine
CLMP member: no
Primary Editor/Contact Person: Beverley Daurio
Address: 22 Prince Rupert Ave.
Toronto, ON M6P 2A7
Web Site Address:
http://www.themercurypress.ca/word
Publishes: essays, fiction, nonfiction, poetry, reviews, and art
Editorial Focus: Word is a monthly literary newspaper that features reviews, columns, and Toronto event listings.
Representative Authors: Stuart Ross, Maggie Helwig, and Bill Kennedy

Submissions Policy: Reviews? Letters? Contact our editor about possible publication at wordeditor@the-mercurypress.ca.
Simultaneous Submissions: yes
Reading Period: Year-round
Reporting Time: four to twelve weeks
Author Payment: copies
Founded: 1995
Non Profit: yes
Paid Staff: one
Unpaid Staff: three
Distributors: The Mercury Press
Total Circulation: 5,000
Paid Circulation: 200
Submission Rate: Individual $18/Institution $18
Single Copy Price: free
Current Volume/Issue: 10/9
Frequency per Year: nine issues
Backfile Available: yes
Unsolicited Ms. Received: no
Format: Newspaper
Size: H 17" W 11"
Average Pages: 8
Ads: yes
Ad Rates: See Web site for details.

Organization: Wordcraft of Oregon, LLC

Type: press
CLMP member: yes
Primary Editor/Contact Person: David Memmott
Address: P.O. Box 3235
La Grande, OR 97850
Website Address: www.wordcraftoforegon.com
Publishes: fiction and poetry
Editorial Focus: Primary interests are literary novels, poetry books and occasionally a story collection, preference for Northwest writers.
Recent Awards Received: 2007 finalist for Spur Award, 2006 Oregon Literary Fellowship for Publishing, 2005 Willa Award for Poetry.
Representative Authors: Thomas E. Kennedy, Duff Brenna, and George Venn
Submissions Policy: Please check our website as we are currently closed to submissions until Summer 2008.
Simultaneous Submissions: yes
Reading Period: year-round
Reporting Time: 2 to 3 months
Author Payment: royalties

Founded: 1988
Non Profit: no
Paid Staff: 0
Unpaid Staff: 2
Wholesalers: Amazon.com
ISSN Number/ISBN Number: ISBN 1-877655
Number of Books Published per Year: 4-6
Titles in Print: 38
Average Print Run: 500
Average Percentage Printed: Paperback 100%
Average Price: $12-$15

Organization: WordFarm

Type: press
CLMP member: yes
Primary Editor/Contact Person: Sally Sampson Craft
Address: 2010 Michigan Ave.
La Porte, IN 46350
Web Site Address: www.wordfarm.net
Publishes: essays, fiction, nonfiction, poetry, and audio
Editorial Focus: WordFarm publishes in three areas: fiction, literary nonfiction and poetry.
Recent Awards Received: WordFarm won ForeWord magazine's Book of the Year Award (essays category) for the title Bright Shoots of Everlastingness.
Representative Authors: John Leax, Paul J. Willis, and Luci Shaw
Simultaneous Submissions: yes
Reading Period: year-round
Reporting Time: three to six months
Author Payment: royalties
Founded: 2003
Non Profit: no
Paid Staff: one
Unpaid Staff: four
Distributors: Midpoint Trade Books, Ingram, Baker & Taylor
Number of Books Published per year: three
Titles in Print: seven
Average Print Run: 2,500
Average Percentage Printed: paperback 98%, chapbook 2%
Average Price: $12

Organization: Words and Pictures Magazine

Type: magazine
CLMP member: no

Primary Editor/Contact Person: Wendy Borrou
Address: 9805 NE 116th St.
Box A-139
Kirkland, WA 98034
Website Address: www.wordsandpicturesmag.com
Publishes: essays, fiction, nonfiction, poetry, reviews, art, and translation
Editorial Focus: Literature and Art with a focus on cultural connections
Representative Authors: Ron Carlson, Christianne Balk, and Tayeb Salih
Submissions Policy: We prefer online submissions for both written and visual. Please see website for guidelines.
Simultaneous Submissions: yes
Reading Period: year-round
Reporting Time: 2 to 3 months
Author Payment: cash and copies
Contests: Occasional poetry and fiction prizes, please visit website for postings.
Founded: 2004
Non Profit: no
Paid Staff: 2
Unpaid Staff: n/a
Distributors: Private
Total Circulation: 5,000
Paid Circulation: n/a
Average Print Run: 5000
Subscription Rate: Individual $19.00/Institution $19.00
Single Copy Price: $4.95
Current Volume/Issue: Issue 5
Frequency: 2
Backfile Available: yes
Unsolicited Ms. Received: yes
% of Unsolicited Ms. Published per Year: 80%
Format: stapled
Size: H 11" W 8.5"
Average Pages: 48
Ads: no

Organization: Words Without Borders

Type: online
CLMP member: yes
Primary Editor/Contact Person: Blake Radcliffe
Address: c/o Center for Literary Translation
Columbia Univ., 415 Dodge Hall
New York, NY 10027
Web Site Address: http://www.wordswithoutborders.org

Publishes: essays, fiction, poetry, translation, and audio
Editorial Focus: A sampling of the world's best contemporary writing translated into English.
Representative Authors: MuXin, Najem Wali, and Witold Gombrowicz
Submissions Policy: Stories, excerpts of novels, poetry and literary nonfiction rooted in a sense of place; submission of translation preferred
Simultaneous Submissions: yes
Reading Period: Year-round
Reporting Time: five to six months
Author Payment: cash
Founded: 2002
Non Profit: yes
Paid Staff: three
Unpaid Staff: four
Average Page Views per Month: 200,000
Average Unique Visitors Per Month: 5,000
Frequency per Year: biannual
Publish Print Anthology: yes
Price: $0
Average Percentage of Pages per Category:
Translation 100%
Ad Rates: upon request
See web site for details.

Organization: WordWrights Magazine

Type: magazine
CLMP member: no
Primary Editor/Contact Person: R.D. Baker
Address: 1620 Argonne Place NW
Washington, DC 20009
Web Site Address: http://www.wordwrights.com
Publishes: fiction and poetry
Editorial Focus: New and established poets and writers.
Representative Authors: David Franks, Rose Solari, and Grace Cavalieri
Submissions Policy: Open.
Simultaneous Submissions: yes
Reading Period: Year-round
Reporting Time: three to six months
Author Payment: cash
Founded: 1995
Non Profit: no
Paid Staff: zero
Unpaid Staff: 25
Distributors: Argonne House Press
Wholesalers: Argonne House Press

Total Circulation: 1,000
Paid Circulation: 500
Submission Rate: Individual $25/Institution $50
Single Copy Price: $5.95
Current Volume/Issue: Issue 30
Frequency per Year: quarterly
Backfile Available: yes
Unsolicited Ms. Received: yes
% of Unsolicited Ms. Published per Year: 10%
Format: stapled
Size: H 11" W 8.5"
Average Pages: 40
Ads: no

Organization: Workers Write!

Type: magazine
CLMP member: no
Primary Editor/Contact Person: David LaBounty
Address: PO Box 250382
Plano, TX 75025-0382
Web Site Address: www.workerswritejournal.com
Publishes: fiction and poetry
Editorial Focus: Each issue will be devoted to tales from a particular work environment.
Submissions Policy: Accepts simultaneous and previously published work. See web site for information about upcoming issues.
Simultaneous Submissions: yes
Reading Period: year-round
Reporting Time: six to twelve weeks
Author Payment: cash and copies
Founded: 2005
Non Profit: no
Paid Staff: one
Unpaid Staff: zero
Total Circulation: 500
Average Print Run: 750
Single Copy Price: varies
Current Volume/Issue: issue two
Frequency per year: annual
Backfile Available: yes
Unsolicited MSS Received: yes
% of Unsolicited MSS Published per Year: 95%
Format: perfect
Average Pages: 120
Ads: no

Organization: Writecorner Press

Type: press

CLMP member: yes
Primary Editor/Contact Person: Mary Sue Koeppel
Address: P.O. Box 16369
Jacksonville, FL 32245
Web Site Address: http://www.writecorner.com
Publishes: essays, fiction, nonfiction, poetry and reviews
Editorial Focus: Writecorner Press is a companion to http://www.writecorner.com Publishes winning contest fiction and notable fiction and nonfiction
Representative Authors: Andrea R. Kahn, Elaine Neil Orr, and Lones Seiber
Submissions Policy: Interested in short fiction, memoirs, and essays under 3,000 words. Send fiction and nonfiction books to be reviewed.
Simultaneous Submissions: yes
Reading Period: Year-round
Reporting Time: one to two months
Author Payment: cash
Contests: $1,100 E.M. Koeppel Short Fiction Annual Award; $100 Editors' Choice Award; $500 Scholarship. Annual $500 poetry Award; $100 Ed. Choice.
See web site for contest guidelines.
Founded: 2002
Non Profit: yes
Paid Staff: zero
Unpaid Staff: two
Number of Books Published per Year:
Titles in Print: 3
Average Print Run: 100
Average Percentage Printed: Other 100%
Average Price: $7

Organization: Xavier Review Press

Type: magazine
CLMP member: no
Primary Editor/Contact Person: Robert Skinner
Address: 1 Drexel Drive
New Orleans, LA 70125
Web Site Address: www.xula.edu/review/
Publishes: essays, fiction, nonfiction, poetry, reviews, and translation
Editorial Focus: African-American, postmodern
Representative Authors: Keith Cartwright, Naton Leslie, and James Doyle
Submissions Policy: MSS prepared according to MLA Handbook for Writers w/parenthetical notes. MSS accepted will be requested as electronic files.
Simultaneous Submissions: no

Reading Period: 01/09 to 15/05
Reporting Time: four to twelve weeks
Author Payment: copies
Founded: 1980
Non Profit: yes
Paid Staff: zero
Unpaid Staff: three
Distributors: Amazon, Baker & Taylor, Midwest, Book House
ISSN Number/ISBN Number: 0887-6681/1883275
Total Circulation: 200
Paid Circulation: 50
Average Print Run: 300
Subscription Rate: individual $10/institution $15
Single Copy Price: $5
Current Volume/Issue: 26/1
Frequency per year: biannual
Backfile Available: yes
Unsolicited MSS Received: yes
Format: perfect
Size: H 6" W 9"
Average Pages: 80
Ads: yes
Ad Rates: see web site for details

Organization: The Xavier Review

Type: magazine
CLMP member: no
Primary Editor/Contact Person: Dr. Nicole Greene
Address: P. O. Box 110, Xavier University of LA
1 Drexel Dr.
New Orleans, LA 70125-1098
Publishes: essays, fiction, nonfiction, poetry, and reviews
Editorial Focus: Creative writing from diverse cultures, including African-American, US South, Gulf/Caribbean basin
Representative Authors: Andre Codrescu, Catherine Savage Brosman, and Nachita Danilov
Submissions Policy: Print ms. using MLA style manual, accomp. diskette in ASCII, MS-DOS, or Mac, SASE. Fiction 8-12 pages, nonfiction 12-18 pages.
Simultaneous Submissions: no
Reading Period: 9/1 to 6/30
Reporting Time: four to eight weeks
Author Payment: copies
Founded: 1980
Non Profit: yes
Paid Staff: one
Unpaid Staff: 3

Distributors: EBSCO
Wholesalers: Baker & Taylor, Midwest Library Service
ISSN Number/ ISBN Number: 0887-6681
Totall Circulation: 100
Paid Circulation: 50
Submission Rate: Individual $10/Institution $15
Single Copy Price: $5
Current Volume/Issue: 27/2
Frequency per Year: biannual
Backfile Available: yes
Unsolicited Ms. Received: yes
% of Unsolicited Ms. Published per Year: 100%
Format: perfect
Size: H 9" W 6"
Average Pages: 95
Ads: yes
Ad Rates: $75/page, $35/half page

Organization: Xconnect Print Volumes & Web Issues

Type: magazine
CLMP member: no
Primary Editor/Contact Person: David E. Deifer
Address: PO Box 2317
Philadelphia, Pa 19103
Web Site Address: http://xconnect.org
Publishes: essays, fiction, nonfiction, poetry, reviews, art, and translation
Editorial Focus: Publishes a vast expanse of disciplines, from experimental to works well rooted in academia, tendency toward new writers . . .
Representative Authors: Gregory Djanikian, Tom Devaney, and Nicholas Montemarano
Submissions Policy: Send up to 10 poems or two stories including SASE and bio including address, phone number and email if available.
Simultaneous Submissions: no
Reading Period: year-round
Reporting Time: two to twelve weeks
Author Payment: cash and copies
Founded: 1995
Non Profit: yes
Paid Staff: two
Unpaid Staff: six
Distributors: Ingram , DeBoer, SPD
ISSN Number/ISBN Number: ISSN 1087-0474/0-9651450-6-9
Total Circulation: 900
Paid Circulation: none
Average Print Run: 1,100

Single Copy Price: $12
Current Volume/Issue: VIII/23
Frequency per year: biannual
Backfile Available: yes
Unsolicited MSS Received: yes
% of Unsolicited MSS Published per year: 3%
Format: perfect
Size: H 8.5" W 5.5"
Average Pages: 200
Ads: no

Organization: The Yalobusha Review

Type: magazine
CLMP member: yes
Primary Editor/Contact Person: Neal Walsh
Address: English Dept., University of Mississippi
P.O. Box 1848
University, MS 38677-1848
Web Site Address:
http://www.olemiss.edu/yalobusha
Publishes: essays, fiction, nonfiction, poetry, art, and translation
Editorial Focus: We seek quality work from any and all genres.
Representative Authors: Dan Chaon, George Singleton, and Charles Wright
Submissions Policy: Send disposable copy of manuscript w/cover letter and SASE for response to above address. See web site for full guidelines.
Simultaneous Submissions: no
Reading Period: 7/15 to 11/15
Reporting Time: one to three months
Author Payment: cash and copies
Contests: See web site for contest guidelines.
Founded: 1995
Non Profit: no
Paid Staff: one
Unpaid Staff: four
Total Circulation: 1,000
Average Print Run: 500
Submission Rate: Individual $8/Institution $8
Single Copy Price: $10
Current Volume/Issue: X/2005
Frequency per Year: annual
Backfile Available: yes
Unsolicited Ms. Received: yes
% of Unsolicited Ms. Published per Year: 5%
Format: perfect
Size: H 10" W 7"
Average Pages: 125

Ads: yes
Ad Rates: Free Exchange
See web site for details.

Organization: The Yemassee

Type: magazine
CLMP member: yes
Primary Editor/Contact Person: D. Cavanaugh or J. Maricle
Address: English Dept., University of South Carolina
P.O. Box 1848
Columbia, SC 29204
Web Site Address: http://yemasseejournal.org
Publishes: essays, fiction, nonfiction, poetry, reviews, and translation
Editorial Focus: To publish the best contemporary writing. We will consider high-quality genre stories
Representative Authors: James Dickey, Nikky Finney, and Chris Offutt.
Submissions Policy: No email submissions. Up to five poems or prose pieces at a time. All submissions should be under 7,500 words total. SASE.
Simultaneous Submissions: yes
Reading Period: year-round
Reporting Time: two to three months
Author Payment: copies
Contests: The William Richey Short Story Contest (fall) and The Pocataligo Poetry Contest (spring) pay $500 each; see website for guidelines.
Founded: 1993
Non Profit: yes
Paid Staff: two
Unpaid Staff: two
Total Circulation: 700
Paid Circulation: 50
Average Print Run: 750
Submission Rate: Individual $12/Institution $15
Single Copy Price: $6
Current Volume/Issue: 15/2
Frequency per Year: 2
Backfile Available: yes
Unsolicited Ms. Received: yes
Format: perfect
Size: H 8" W 5"
Average Pages: 100
Ads: yes
Ad Rates: Contact editors; See web site for details.

Organization: Zahir

Type: magazine

CLMP member: yes
Primary Editor/Contact Person: Sheryl Tempchin, editor
Address: 315 S. Coast Hwy. 101
Ste. U8
Encinitas, CA 92024
Web Site Address: www.zahirtales.com
Publishes: fiction
Editorial Focus: Zahir is a journal of short speculative fiction. We publish literary fantasy, science fiction and magical realism.
Representative Authors: Sonya Taaffe, William Alexander, and Davin Ireland
Submissions Policy: Stories up to 6,000 words accompanied by SASE. First serial rights required.
Simultaneous Submissions: no
Reading Period: year-round
Reporting Time: eight to 10 weeks
Author Payment: cash and copies
Founded: 2003
Non Profit: no
Paid Staff: zero
Unpaid Staff: one
ISSN Number/ISBN Number: ISSN 1544-5259
Total Circulation: 200
Paid Circulation: 60
Average Print Run: 200
Subscription Rate: individual $15/institution $15
Single Copy Price: $5
Current Volume/Issue: issue 13
Frequency per year: triquarterly
Backfile Available: yes
Unsolicited MSS Received: yes
% of Unsolicited MSS Published per year: 2%
Format: perfect
Size: H 8.25" W 5.25"
Average Pages: 80
Ads: no

Organization: Zeek: A Jewish Journal of Thought and Culture

Type: online
CLMP member: yes
Primary Editor/Contact Person: Bob Goldfarb
Address: 330 Seventh Avenue
21st Floor
New York, NY 10001
Web Site Address: www.zeek.net
Publishes: essays, fiction, poetry, reviews, art, translation, audio, and video
Editorial Focus: Zeek is an independent, intelligent, innovative Jewish journal of thought and culture.
Recent Awards: Rockower Jewish Press Award 2006 best Arts & Criticism
Representative Authors: Adam Mansbach, Jay Michaelson, and Douglas Rushkoff
Submissions Policy: Email only to zeek@zeek.net
Simultaneous Submissions: yes
Reading Period: year-round
Reporting Time: one to three months
Author Payment: copies
Founded: 2002
Non Profit: yes
Paid Staff: nine
Unpaid Staff: nine
Distributors: Ubiquity, DeBoer
ISSN Number/ISBN Number: ISSN 1548-2111
Average Page Views per Month: 250,000
Average Unique Visitors per Month: 100,000
Frequency per year: 12
Publish Print Anthology: yes
Price: $7
Average Percentage of Pages per Category: fiction 15%, nonfiction 20%, poetry 15%, reviews 5%, essays 20%, art 5%, Translation 10%, Audio 5%, Video 5%
Ad Rates: see web site for details

Organization: Zephyr Press/Adventures in Poetry

Type: press
CLMP member: no
Primary Editor/Contact Person: Christopher Mattison
Address: 50 Kenwood St.
Brookline, MA 02446
Web Site Address: http://www.zephyrpress.org
Publishes: essays, fiction, nonfiction, poetry, and translation
Representative Authors: Charles North, Hsia Yu, and Anatoly Naiman
Simultaneous Submissions: yes
Reading Period: Year-round
Reporting Time: one to three months
Author Payment: royalties, cash, and copies
Founded: 1980
Non Profit: yes
Paid Staff: two
Unpaid Staff: two
Distributors: Consortium and SPD
ISSN Number/ISBN Number: ISBN 0939010
Number of Books Published per Year: five

Titles in Print: 50
Average Print Run: 1,500
Average Percentage Printed: Paperback 100%
Average Price: $14

Organization: zingmagazine

Type: magazine
CLMP member: yes
Address: 83 Grand St.
New York, NY 10013
web site Address: http://www.zingmagazine.com/
Publishes: essays, fiction, nonfiction, poetry, and audio
Reading Period: Year-round
Reporting Time: one to two months
Author Payment: none
Founded: 1995
Non Profit: no

Organization: Zoetrope: All-Story

Type: magazine
CLMP member: no
Primary Editor/Contact Person: Tamara Straus,
Editor in Chief
Address: 916 Kearny St.
San Francisco, CA 94133
Web Site Address: all-story.com/
Publishes: essays, fiction, art, and translation
Editorial Focus: Classic short fiction with purpose,
compelling ideas, and intelligent prose.
Representative Authors: Susan Straight, A.M.
Homes, and Adam Haslett
Submissions Policy: Stories and one-act plays under
7,000 words accompanied by SASE. First serial
rights required.
Simultaneous Submissions: yes
Reading Period: Year-round
Reporting Time: one to five months
Author Payment: cash, copies, and subscription
Contests: See web Site for contest guidelines.
Founded: 1997
Non Profit: no
Paid Staff: four
Unpaid Staff: 25
Distributors: Ingram, Small Changes, OneSource, IPD,
Kent, Total
ISSN Number/ISBN Number: ISSN 1091-2495
Total Circulation: 20,000
Paid Circulation: 10,000
Submission Rate: Individual $19.95/Institution

$19.95
Single Copy Price: $6.95
Current Volume/Issue: 8/3
Frequency per Year: quarterly
Backfile Available: yes
Unsolicited Ms. Received: yes
% of Unsolicited Ms. Published per Year: 50%
Format: perfect
Size: H 10.75" W 8.25"
Average Pages: 128
Ads: yes
Ad Rates: See web site for details.

Organization: Zone 3

Type: magazine
CLMP member: yes
Primary Editor/Contact Person: Susan Wallace,
Managing Editor
Address: P. O. Box 4265
APSU
Clarkesville, TN 37044
Web Site Address: http://www.apsu.edu/zone3
Publishes: essays, fiction, nonfiction, poetry, and
reviews
Reading Period: Year-round
Reporting Time: one to three months
Author Payment: copies
Contest: see website for guidelines
Founded: 1986
Non Profit: yes
Paid Staff: 3
Unpaid Staff: 0
Distributors: Ingram, DeBoer, EBSCO
ISSN Number/ISBN Number: ISSN 088099X
Total Circulation: 1,200
Paid Circulation: 350
Average Print Run: 1, 200
Subscription Rate: Individual $10/Institution $12
Single Copy Price: $5
Current Volume/Issue: 22/2
Frequency: 2
Backfile Available: yes
% of Unsolicited Ms. Published per Year: 2%
Format: perfect
Size: H 9" W 6"
Average Pages: 135
Ads: yes
Ad Rates: exchange

Organization: Zora Magazine

Type: magazine
CLMP member: yes
Address: P.O. Box 588
Raleigh, NC 27606
Web Site Address: http://www.zoramagazine.com
Publishes: essays, fiction, nonfiction, poetry, audio and art
Reading Period: Year-round
Reporting Time: one to two months
Author Payment: none
Non Profit: yes
Backfile Available: yes

Organization: ZYZZYVA

Type: magazine
CLMP member: yes
Primary Editor/Contact Person: Howard Junker
Address: P.O. Box 590069
San Francisco, CA 94159-0069
Web Site Address: http://www.zyzzyva.org
Publishes: essays, fiction, nonfiction, and poetry
Editorial Focus: West Coast writers
Representative Authors: Kristin Soares, Ramon Arjona, and Jee Young Lee
Submissions Policy: We publish writers who are currently living on the West Coast (CA, OR, WA, AK, HI).
Simultaneous Submissions: no
Reading Period: Year-round
Reporting Time: three to four weeks
Author Payment: cash and copies
Founded: 1985
Non Profit: yes
Paid Staff: two
Unpaid Staff: one
Distributors: Armadillo, Ingram, Small Changes, Ubiquity
ISSN Number/ISBN Number: ISSN 8756-5633
Total Circulation: 2,500
Paid Circulation: 1,600
Average Print Run: 3,500
Submission Rate: Individual $24/Institution $44
Single Copy Price: $11
Current Volume/Issue: XXII/2
Frequency per Year: triquarterly
Backfile Available: yes
Unsolicited Ms. Received: yes
% of Unsolicited Ms. Published per Year: 1%
Format: perfect
Size: H 9" W 6"

Average Pages: 176
Ads: yes
Ad Rates: See web site for details.

Howard Junker
Editor, ZYZZYVA

How did you arrive at your current position?
I started *ZYZZYVA* when I was working in the PR department of a big engineering/construction company. I had once been an ambitious young journalist/critic and I was ashamed and depressed by where I had ended up. The proof reader in my department told me at lunch one day, in the depressing corporate cafeteria, that he had once had a lit mag in Cleveland in the early fifties and had published Olson and Creeley and Ferlinghetti and Carlos Williams. I thought we could do the same. It took me three years of talking and rounding up supporters...and getting laid off, before I actually launched in 1985.

What is the staff structure at your magazine?
Me, full time; the managing editor, half time; one or two volunteers, half a day a week.

What challenges do you face as a publisher?
Paying the bills is the big challenge. I'm helped in that area by acting as a traditional magazine publisher who sells advertising. It's very hard to do, and it takes a lot of time, but it's like my day job. Over the years, I've built up a strong relationship with local bookstores, galleries, publishers, writing programs, restaurants...

Do you have any cover letter advice?
I don't read cover letters, because I do read all the manuscripts that are submitted, and I want to spend my time reading them, not cover letters.

What do you look for in a submission?
I don't look for anything. I try to respond to what the writer has shown me. My taste is wide-ranging, and I sometimes buy work that I don't particularly like, but which I admire or for some reason or other feel should be included in the magazine.

How are submissions processed at your magazine?
A volunteer logs in each manuscript, then I "screen" it. About ten percent make it into a "careful read" bin. About one percent make it into the magazine. Although I make the decisions, the volunteers get to read the manuscripts in the "careful read" bin and are encouraged to express their opinions.

Do you have a favorite unsolicited submission discovery or anecdote?
Of course: I discovered F.X. Toole when he was sixty-nine. He had been submitting stories for thirty years before I gave him his first time in print. Nat Sobel, who subscribes to a zillion lit mags, saw the story, signed Toole up, and sold his collection to Ecco Press. Unfortunately, Toole died just before Clint Eastwood bought the film rights to his story "Million Dollar Baby." I was delighted when Toole came by one day and brought me a gooseberry pie he'd made himself.

What advice do you have for first-time submitters?
Keep the faith.

What are your long-term plans for your magazine?
I'm getting ready to retire in a couple of years, if all goes well, and I'm hoping that ZYZZYVA will be able to continue its independent existence after my tenure is up. The board is eager to keep it going; we think there is still a need for an on-paper journal devoted to West Coast writers and devoted to new voices, not the usual suspects.

What's your evaluation of the current literary landscape?
The landscape is always bleak, but it only takes two or three writers to illuminate an era. I think we are graced with many more than two or three writers who are thrilling to read.

Indices

Alphabetical

Geographical

CLMP Membership

Publisher Type

Magazine

Online

Press

Publisher Content

Fiction

Non-Fiction

Poetry

Reviews

Art

Translation

Audio

Accepting Unsolicited Manuscripts

Accepting Simultaneous Submissions